THE REPRESSED ECONOMY

ECONOMISTS OF THE TWENTIETH CENTURY

General Editors: Mark Perlman, *University Professor of Economics, University of Pittsburgh* and Mark Blaug, *Professor Emeritus, University of London; Professor Emeritus, University of Buckingham; and Visiting Professor, University of Exeter*

This innovative series comprises specially invited collections of articles and papers by economists whose work has made an important contribution to economics in the late twentieth century.

The proliferation of new journals and the ever-increasing number of new articles make it difficult for even the most assiduous economist to keep track of all the important recent advances. By focusing on those economists whose work is generally recognized to be at the forefront of the discipline, the series will be an essential reference point for the different specialisms included.

A list of published and future titles in this series is printed at the end of this volume.

The Repressed Economy

Causes, Consequences, Reform

Deepak Lal

James S. Coleman Professor of International Development Studies
University of California, Los Angeles
and
Emeritus Professor of Political Economy
University College London

Edward Elgar

Published by
Edward Elgar Publishing Limited
Gower House
Croft Road
Aldershot
Hants GU11 3HR
England

Edward Elgar Publishing Company
Old Post Road
Brookfield
Vermont 05036
USA

British Library Cataloguing in Publication Data
Lal, Deepak
Repressed Economy: Causes, Consequences, Reform. – (Economists of the Twentieth Century Series)
I. Title II. Series
330.1

Library of Congress Cataloguing in Publication Data
Lal, Deepak.
The repressed economy: causes, consequences, reform/Deepak Lal.
p. cm. — (Economists of the twentieth century)
Includes bibliographical references.
1. Economic policy. 2. Economic development. I. Title.
II. Series.
HD87.L35 1993
338.9—dc20 93–13953
CIP

Printed and bound in Great Britain by
Hartnolls Limited, Bodmin, Cornwall

ISBN 1 85278 888 7

For Barbara

Contents

Acknowledgements

The author and publishers wish to thank the following who have kindly given permission for the use of copyright material.

Basil Blackwell Ltd. for articles: (1989), ‘After the Debt Crisis: Modes of Development for the Longer Run in Latin America’ in Sebastian Edwards and Felipe Larraín (eds), *Debt, Adjustment and Recovery*, pp. 100–120; (with Sylvia Maxfield) (1993), ‘The Political Economy of Stabilization in Brazil’ in Robert H. Bates and Anne O. Krueger (eds), *Political and Economic Interactions in Economic Policy Reform*, pp. 27–40, 54–69, 74–7.

Frank Cass and Co. Ltd. for article: (1989), ‘A Simple Framework for Analysing Various Real Aspects of Stabilisation and Structural Adjustment Policies’, *Journal of Development Studies*, **25**(3) April, pp. 291–313.

Elsevier Science Publishing Co. Ltd. for articles: (1986), ‘Stolper–Samuelson–Rybczynski in the Pacific: Real Wages and Real Exchange Rates in the Philippines, 1956–1978’, *Journal of Development Economics*, **21**, pp. 181–204; (with Sweder van Wijnbergen) (1985), ‘Government Deficits, the Real Interest Rate and LDC Debt: On Global Crowding Out’, *European Economic Review*, **29**, pp. 157–91; (1990), ‘The Fable of the Three Envelopes: The Analytics and Political Economy of the Reform of Chinese State Owned Enterprises’, *European Economic Review*, **34**, pp. 1213–31.

Institute of Contemporary Studies for: (1988), ‘Economic Growth in India’, Country Studies No. 3, International Center for Economic Growth, pp. 1–51; (1990), ‘Political Economy and Public Policy’, Occasional Paper No. 19, International Center for Economic Growth, pp. 7–32.

Institute of Developing Economies for article: (1992), ‘Industrialization Strategies and Long-Term Resource Allocation’ in Teruyuki Iwasaki, Takeshi Mori and Hiroichi Yamaguchi (eds), *Development Strategies for the 21st Century*, pp. 480–507.

Kiel Institute of World Economics for article: (1985), ‘The Real Exchange Rate, Capital Inflows and Inflation: Sri Lanka 1970–82’, *Weltwirtschaftliches Archiv*, **121**(4), pp. 682–701.

Korea Development Institute for article: (1992), ‘Why Growth Rates Differ: The Political Economy of Social Capability in 21 Developing Countries’, KDI 20th Anniversary symposium on *Economic Growth and Social Capability*.

Macmillan Press Ltd. and St. Martins Press for articles: (1990), 'World Savings and Growth in Developing Countries', *Rivista di Politica Economica*, **LXXX**(XII) December, pp. 101–24, reprinted in Baladassari, Paganetto and Phelps (eds), *World Saving, Prosperity and Growth*; (1989), 'The Political Economy of Industrialisation in Primary Product Exporting Economies: Some Cautionary Tales' in Nurul Islam (ed.), *The Balance Between Industry and Agriculture in Economic Development*, Vol. 5: *Factors Influencing Change*, pp. 279–314.

Oxford University Press Inc. for articles: (1980), 'Public Enterprises' in John Cody, Helen Hughes and David Wall (eds), *Policies for Industrial Progress in Developing Countries*, International Bank for Reconstruction and Development/The World Bank, pp. 211–34; (1987), 'Shadow Prices and Political Economy (Comment on Harberger)' in Gerald M. Meier (ed.), *Pioneers in Development*, Second Series, International Bank for Reconstruction and Development/The World Bank, pp. 193–202; (1990), 'International Capital Flows and Economic Development' in Maurice Scott and Deepak Lal (eds), *Public Policy and Economic Development*, pp. 231–73.

Pergamon Press Ltd. for articles: (1976), 'Distribution and Development: A Review Article', *World Development*, **4**(9), pp. 725–38; (with Paul Collier) (1984), 'Why Poor People Get Rich: Kenya 1960–79', *World Development*, **12**(10), pp. 1007–18; (1985), 'Nationalism, Socialism and Planning: Influential Ideas in the South', *World Development*, **13**(6), pp. 749–59.

Princeton University, International Finance Section, Dept. of Economics for: (1980), 'A Liberal International Economic Order: The International Monetary System and Economic Development', Princeton Essays in International Finance No. 139, pp. 1–42.

The World Bank for articles: (1987), 'The Political Economy of Economic Liberalization', *World Bank Economic Review*, **1**(2), pp. 273–99; (with Sarath Rajapatirana) (1987), 'Foreign Trade Regimes and Economic Growth in Developing Countries', *World Bank Research Observer*, **2**(2), pp. 189–217.

Every effort has been made to trace all the copyright holders, but if any have inadvertently been overlooked, the publishers will be pleased to make the necessary arrangement at the first opportunity.

Introduction

Reprinting one's past essays in a book always requires some justification, even in a series entitled 'Economists of the Twentieth Century'. For an applied economist there is a double jeopardy in such an enterprise.

First, unlike theorists who can claim some permanence for their deductive theorems, an applied economist's work is of necessity ephemeral, though one hopes not like cut flowers. However, the continual importance of the subject matter – economic repression and liberalization – should calm some of these doubts.

Second, I have always maintained that a connected body of applied work on a particular theme should be reworked into a proper book, with a beginning, a middle and an end. In the past I have followed this prescription. My work on project evaluation of the 1960s and 1970s was consolidated into two books (Lal (1974), (1980)); that on the Indian economy into Lal (1988), and on labour markets in developing countries into Collier and Lal (1986) and Lal (1989a). As explained in the intellectual autobiography (reprinted as Chapter 1), since the late 1970s I have also been working and writing on the broad topic summarized by the title of this collection of essays – the Repressed Economy.

This term describes an economy which is within its technological and feasibility frontiers (to be discussed below) because of so-called 'policy induced' distortions in its working. My early work on shadow pricing attempted to provide estimates of the size of these distortions and their effects on economic welfare (consequences). The essays collected in this volume go a step further in attempting to explain both why governments create these distortions, and when (if at all) they are likely to heed the technocratic advice of the economist to eliminate or reduce them. What can broadly be termed 'political economy', then, becomes an important part of explaining two of the components of the subtitle of this collection – causes and reform.

I had hoped to consolidate this work into a proper book, with the present title. But time marches on. Given the life expectancy of an Indian of my sex in 1940 (when I was born), I should now have been dead for 20 years! Though thankful for the forbearance shown by the Grim Reaper, one cannot count on his indulgence forever and there are newer pastures I want to cultivate. Hence this second best – a collection of essays which are unavoidably repetitive in parts, particularly as no fresh editing was permissible given the facsimile method of reproduction adopted in reprinting them.

The next section explains the structure of the volume and how the various essays relate to each other. It also refers to how the literature on the particular topics has evolved since the essay at issue was written.

I. The essays

The essays in this book were written over the last 15 years. They are all studies in one way or another of repressed economies. Such an economy needs to be defined.

One must first identify the standard production possibility frontier (PPF) of an economy which, assuming perfect competition and complete markets, describes the maximum combination of various goods an economy can produce with given resources and available technology. Because most economies are imperfect due to institutional and structural constraints, and because in an uncertain world there are also many missing markets, this PPF will only be of notional value. One must then distinguish the production *feasibility* frontier which is likely to lie within the PPF. A repressed economy is one which, due to irrational dirigisme, is not operating even on its constrained feasibility frontier, but within it. As this inefficiency is caused by what are termed 'policy induced' distortions in the workings of the price mechanism, it is natural to ask why governments create these distortions, what are the consequences of their creation, and when (if ever) are they likely to be reduced or eliminated? As the subtitle of this volume states, it is thus the causes, consequences and reforms of repressed economies which constitute our subject matter.

The essays fall into five groups. The first set in Part I is primarily concerned with the question of why governments have repressed their economies, and why (and when) they are likely to liberalize them. Besides providing an intellectual biography of how – despite my upbringing – I came to adopt a position favouring markets over mandarins, Chapter 1 also sets out why I no longer find the technocratic public economics approach to public policy particularly useful. A recent cogent statement of the public economics viewpoint of the economic role of the state is contained in a book by Stiglitz et al. (1989) with that title. But as two of the commentators (Perlman and North) in that volume note, this view is ahistorical, suffers from amnesia concerning the history of economic thought, is ideological insofar as it sets up egalitarianism as a self-evident objective of public policy, is institutionally impoverished and, most seriously, makes assumptions about the character of most governments which – to put it mildly – are not universally valid!

I find the alternative public choice viewpoint more instructive, but have found that it cannot be applied as it stands to developing countries. First, because it has been developed to deal with the political economy of a specific polity (the US) and, secondly, because it does not take account of extra-economic motives (such as nationalism) which have moved rulers in many countries, at least since the Renaissance. The last half of the first essay, and the second essay, outline how rulers in all three worlds have at some time been moved by the desire to create 'nations' out of a myriad of groups within their territory. I have found the work of Heckscher (1955) particularly resonant in explaining how this motive had led to dirigiste policies in the present Third World, much as it did in the mercantilist states of Europe, and how mercantilism's internal contradictions led to economic liberalization (albeit for a brief period). Chapter 5 in this part takes up this theme, as does Chapter 14 in Part IV.

The positive political economy models I have found most useful in understanding developing countries are based on a model of Leviathan developed by Findlay and Wilson (1987) and those which marry the so-called Ricardo–Viner model of trade theory (see Jones (1971)) with those of pressure group type political behaviour (see Findlay and Wellisz (1982); Mayer (1984)). Chapter 3 applies these models to explain the industrialization policies of a number of Third World countries. The model of the predatory state was put forward in a paper (Lal, 1984) which later formed part of my book *The Hindu Equilibrium* (Ch. 13.2). Combining the Findlay–Wilson model with the theory of contestable markets of industrial organization (see Baumol et al. (1982)), this was initially used to explain the rise and fall of successive revenue states in India over the millennia (Lal (1988)).

Chapter 5 takes up another theme common to many of the subsequent essays: the incorporation of land and natural resources in the standard Heckscher–Ohlin (HO) model of an open economy. Krueger (1977) and Leamer (1987) pioneered this extension, Leamer's geometrical depiction of the model being a heuristic device I have found very useful, as can be seen in Chapters 14 and 20. Ever since my work on the Philippines (see below), I have felt that the standard HO model (with just two factors of production – labour and capital) was probably not the best way of understanding the behaviour and outcomes in land-abundant countries such as those in Latin America and parts of Africa. Chapter 4 shows how the three-factor, multi-commodity open economy Krueger–Leamer model can be used to explain the political economy as well as the seemingly peculiar outcomes in Latin American countries. This was written in the context of a multi-country comparative study I co-directed with Hal Myint for the World Bank (see below), and it helped in generating a typology of the economies and polities of developing countries for that study. Chapter 14 in Part IV provides a summary of some of the findings of that comparative study based on the resulting typology.

Chapter 5 in Part I provides an outline of what I have come to call the 'crisis' theory of economic liberalization – namely that it is only when the state seems to be withering away under the twin burdens of a fiscal and balance of payments crisis that it seeks economic liberalization. It also provides a discussion of the sequencing of the resulting reforms, assuming that a simultaneous scrapping of all controls is not possible. Though the proposed sequencing has been contested, in particular by Edwards (1984) and McKinnon (1991), some (see especially Sell (1988)) have expressed support for my position. (Also see Edwards (1992) and Funke (1992) for the most recent summaries of where the debate stands.)

While the essays in Part I set out general principles for the analysis of economic repression and liberalization, those in Part II provide broad surveys of the theories and evidence which have underpinned dirigiste policies, their consequences, as well as possible avenues for reform in several major areas of policy: the monetary system and exchange rates; the role and effects of various forms of foreign capital flows (including a discussion of the debt crisis); foreign trade policy and industrial policy. For completeness and to take account of the literature appearing since these essays were written, something more needs to be added here about exchange rate policy and foreign trade policy.

Chapter 6 on the international monetary system is one of the earliest of my essays reprinted here. It uses the so-called Australian model of balance of payments adjustment (see Salter (1959)) to argue for an international monetary system based on floating exchange rates. Since it was written there has been a flurry of interest in both the theory and practice of establishing some semi-fixed (adjustable peg) exchange rate system, the most notable example of this being the European Monetary System (EMS). On 'Black Wednesday' in September 1992, Britain had to leave the

EMS because of the one-way gamble speculators faced with the increasingly overvalued and 'incredible' parity of the pound. Until then, it appeared that the 'quasi-fixers' had once again won the day. But the arguments against the adjustable peg system outlined in Chapter 6 have gained further strength with these tribulations of the EMS. During the 1980s attempts were also made to manage exchange rates among the Group of Seven, through informal agreements such as the Louvre and Plaza accords. My Wincott Lecture (Lal (1990)) dealt in part with the arguments made in support of this international dirigisme, and found them wanting.

A major concern in the past decade about the 'non-system' based on floating rates (which I commend in Chapter 6) is that it is prone to speculative bubbles which lead to sustained divergences of exchange rates from their economic 'fundamentals'. The best discussion of the ensuing literature on rational speculative bubbles, together with a critique, is in Mussa (1990). As he concludes: 'A rational speculative bubble implies not only that people are sometimes crazy, but that they are systematically, calculatingly, and fanatically insane. ... I conclude, therefore, that rational speculative bubbles are empirically irrelevant and theoretically absurd' (pp. 13–14).

There have been two other complaints about the free floating system. First, that changes in exchange rates have been largely random and unpredictable. This reflects the fact that, in a free float, the exchange rate behaves like a stock market price – a forward-looking asset price. Not surprisingly, both will approximate a random walk.

More worrying is the observation that 'real' exchange rates (defined as the nominal exchange rate corrected for changes in the prices of goods in the foreign country relative to goods in the home country) also appear to follow the random walk of the nominal exchange rates. Over the long run, however, the 'real' exchange rate thus defined does appear to be bounded and to be related to economic fundamentals (see Huizinga (1987)). To counter this worry, note that the 'real' exchange in this literature is what is termed the purchasing power parity (PPP) exchange rate in Chapter 17. As that essay shows (in Appendix 1), movements in this 'real' exchange rate will not usually be the same as in the 'Australian' real exchange rate (the relative price of non-traded to traded goods). As it is the latter which is relevant for resource allocation and internal and external balance, we need to know whether this rate also follows a random walk. As few estimates exist for this rate for all the major 'free floating' countries in the world, it is not possible to judge whether it has been 'excessively' volatile. But even if such estimates were available, the excessiveness of the volatility would have to be judged against some norm. In an excellent theoretical and empirical discussion of the determinants of this 'correct' real exchange rate for developing countries, Edwards (1989) shows that both real and monetary factors will determine the 'equilibrium' real exchange rate; moreover, while changes in the equilibrium value will result from changes in real variables, 'monetary disturbances will normally generate departures of the actual from the equilibrium real exchange rate, or exchange rate misalignment' (Edwards, p. 353). Any volatility in real exchange rates is therefore likely to be due to real and monetary shocks. Though there is evidence from a number of countries, both developed and developing, that real exchange rate volatility has increased since the breakdown of the Bretton Woods system (see Edwards, op. cit., Table 1.1), it is moot whether this has been excessive.

Since 1973 the world has been subjected to major real shocks – two oil price shocks, the breakdown and subsequent incorporation of the former Communist countries in Eastern Europe into the world economy, German reunification, as well as the yo-yoing of capital flows to developing countries in the build-up and dénouement of the 'debt crisis'. Add to these the monetary shocks administered by the authorities in the major economies and it is not surprising that real exchange rates have been more volatile in the more volatile world since 1973. To blame the exchange rate regime would be to shoot the messenger for his message!

Two other points need to be made about the analytical framework now commonly employed in international macroeconomics. The first follows from the use of the inappropriate PPP effective exchange rate as the 'real' exchange rate. This has led to a belief that deviations from PPP necessarily measure some misalignment from economic fundamentals. But since Keynes' *Tract on Monetary Reform* it has been known that, whereas in the very long run there may be a relationship between movements in nominal exchange rates and in the ratio of national price levels, in the more relevant short to medium run it is the real exchange rate defined as in the Australian model which is relevant for analysing problems of internal-cum-external balance in a small open economy. Moreover, as Edwards' work on exchange rates in developing countries confirms, movements in the PPP effective exchange rates cannot be taken as surrogates for the correct real exchange rate: 'Using a large cross-country data set, it was found that real exchange rates ... did not behave according to the ... PPP theory' (Edwards (1989), p. 353). It is therefore time to stop using the PPP rate in analysing policy questions.

The second common analytical practice is to use the so-called Mundell–Fleming model as the standard workhorse of international macroeconomics. In this model there are only two goods: the home country's goods and the foreign country's goods. Apart from linking the nominal exchange rate directly to PPP, this model also implies that the only form of balance of trade adjustment is through changes in a country's international terms of trade. This can be highly misleading, particularly for developing countries, many of whom in effect face given terms of trade; for them, balance of payments adjustment necessitates a change in the relative price of non-traded to traded goods – the real exchange rate.

For all the above reasons and despite the vast expansion in the literature on exchange rates in the last decade (see Frenkel and Mussa (1985) and Mussa (1990) for valuable surveys), I still find that the Australian model retains a robustness that many of its new-fangled cousins lack.

Finally, as regards the appropriate international monetary system, I have not changed my mind from the position taken in Chapter 6. This is despite the large intellectual effort to recreate some formal or informal quasi-fixed exchange rate system, as well as the practical attempts to impose one – either globally (as in the Louvre and Plaza accords) or regionally (as with the European Monetary System). Here, oddly, classical liberals such as McKinnon (1988) have joined forces with dirigistes such as Williamson (1985). But I stand by the arguments against both given in Chapter 6: (1) that the dirigiste view is based on ignoring the Hayekian worry that in a truly uncertain world, 'experts' cannot obtain the necessary information to devise their 'ideal' plans; and (2) that the hope of restoring the Gold Standard, however desirable, is not feasible because of the politics of the modern-day world. (My Wincott lecture (Lal 1990)), reprinted in *Against Dirigisme* (Lal (forthcoming)), contains references to this continuing debate, as well as a discussion.)

This last point provides a useful juncture to state briefly why I have not found a type of political economy recently proliferating in the journals to be particularly useful. This uses game theoretic models to build on the 'political business cycle' theories of Lindbeck (1976) and Nordhaus (1975), and hence to tackle the problems of credibility associated with the so-called problem of time inconsistency of many public policies. A very cogent and concise account of this branch of political economy is contained in Persson and Tabellini (1990), while Rodrik (1993) surveys the use of this analysis for developing countries. The trouble with this theory, as with most applications of game theory, is the multiplicity of equilibria. As Persson and Tabellini write: 'from a practical point of view, a theory based on Nash equilibria has very low predictive power because it allows such a plethora of equilibria' (p. 54). Thus I have not found this branch of theory very helpful in considering the political economy problems of developing countries. (Also see Binmore (1990) and Kreps (1990) for insightful discussions concerning the limitations of game theory in dealing with many practical problems.)

The remaining essays in Part II are more up-to-date. Chapter 7 surveys the debate about inward versus outward orientation as it stood in the mid-1980s. Aspects of the 'new' trade theory, as it has been called, are discussed in Chapter 9. One of the essay's conjectures is that the 'new' trade theory argument for an industrial-cum-trade policy (which shifts profits from foreign oligopolists to domestic ones) is a variant of the classical optimum tariff argument. This has since been confirmed in an elegant and important paper by Baldwin (1992). He incorporates most of this new theory into the framework of the famous Baldwin envelope he invented, showing how it fits into the modern theory of trade and welfare developed in the 1950s and 1960s; its empirical validation by a number of comparative historical studies (beginning with Little–Scitovsky–Scott (1970)) provides a most persuasive case for an outward-oriented development policy.

More recently, however, a so-called 'market-governance' school on industrial and trade policy has made its voice heard. Starting with Chalmers–Johnson (1982) on Japan, Amsden (1989) on Korea and Wade (1990) on Taiwan, it has argued that, far from being cases validating 'neoclassical' beliefs about appropriate policy, these countries provide support for those who would want enlightened dirigisme to promote strategic sectors by 'getting the prices wrong'! I have dealt with these arguments in detail in Lal (1993) where I have tried to provide an alternative explanation of the undoubted industrial dirigisme in these countries in terms of the problems of agency emphasized in the industrial organization literature, most cogently by Demsetz (1988).

The essays in Part III are concerned with the social aspects of development. Egalitarianism has been a potent motive behind the advocacy and practice of many forms of economic repression. The totalitarian planned economies of the Communist world marked the culmination of this trend towards repression in the name of equality. In the 1970s many international institutions took up the cause, regretting that past growth in developing countries had not improved the distribution of income or alleviated poverty. Chapter 10 surveys the ensuing literature and pinpoints the ethical issues which must underpin distributional concerns. I have subsequently returned to this issue, first in an essay in honour of Peter Bauer (Lal (1987)) and most recently in an essay looking at social policy after socialism (Lal (1992)). These are being reprinted in *Against Dirigisme* and provide references to the subsequent debate which has continued to swirl around these controversial issues.

One of the instruments favoured by socialists to legislate their Utopia has been the public ownership of the means of production. Chapter 11 was written at a time when the case against public enterprises and in favour of privatization had not become self-evident, and when such enterprises were still ubiquitous in all three worlds. It takes a cool look at the ways in which the investment and pricing decisions of such enterprises could ideally be made in the context of the Little–Mirrlees shadow pricing framework, but also why in practice, because of incentive problems and the lack of an effective bankruptcy constraint, such enterprises were unlikely to be efficient.

This essay along with the next one (Chapter 12) provides a link with my earlier work in the 1960s and 1970s on shadow pricing. Chapter 12, which was my comment on Harberger's lecture in the World Bank's second series, *Pioneers on Development*, is my last word – I hope – on the debates on alternative methods of project evaluation which raged so passionately in the 1970s. Even though with the spread of privatization, the need for shadow pricing in the public sector has declined, the method remains essential in appraising and designing a whole host of public policies which form part of rational government intervention.

The final essay in Part III integrates the Australian model of balance of payments adjustment, the Ricardo–Viner model of trade theory and a simple dynamic monetary model to provide a heuristic diagrammatic apparatus for analysing the various social effects of adjustment packages designed to reform repressed economies. It deals with the issues rhetorically identified with the slogan 'adjustment with a human face'.

The essays in the final two parts of the volume are empirical studies. Those in Part IV are either global or multi-country; those in Part V deal with particular countries. Both demonstrate how the models and modes of analysis commended in previous parts can be practically applied – the bread and butter of applied economics.

Chapter 14 summarizes some of the results of the synthesis volume emerging from the multi-country comparative study Hal Myint and I have conducted for the World Bank on the political economy of poverty, equity and growth. This study used the Krueger–Leamer three-factor model together with a typology of the polities of the 21 countries studied to explain the differing growth and poverty alleviation outcomes in terms of deeper causes (stemming from differing endowments and polities) than the usual proximate causes – summarized for instance in standard neoclassical growth accounting. The essay also takes a brief but detached look at the 'new' growth theory. This is the work of mathematical economists who have sought to repair the purported lacunae – the exogeneity of the determinants of long-run growth – in the standard Solow–Swan model. The aim is laudable but the results are not, depending essentially upon arbitrary assumptions (see Stern (1991) for a judicious review). In various extensions, this tribe had added mathematical flesh and rediscovered various notions which were part of the old 'development economics' – like the need for a 'big push' in investment, low level 'development traps' and so on – in its search for new avenues of dirigisme. As these 'old' theories of development have been thoroughly scrutinized and found wanting – not least because of the experience of developing countries which have tried to implement them in the past (see Little (1982) for a survey) – their current popularity with the young can only be ascribed to that amnesia about the past (both theories and facts) which seems to have become a notable feature of training in American graduate schools. I have found an 'endogenous' growth model due to Scott (1989) much more useful in providing a more plausible account of the proximate sources of growth – the level and efficiency of investment (also see Riedel (forthcoming)). This model is outlined and applied in Chapter 16 to a question raised by one of the 'new' growth theorists: why savings do not flow massively from developed countries with high stocks of capital per head to those with low ones, such as India. The answer of course is that, largely because of economic repression, the rate of return on investment is much lower in India than in the US!

Chapter 15 (with Sweder van Wijnbergen) was written when I worked on the World Bank's World Development Report of 1984, that is at the height of the debt crisis. It provides a novel link between the actions of public sectors in developed countries – with welfare state expenditures rising inexorably as universal entitlements rise with demographic pressures – and the world capital market. The actions of public agents in the West are shown to crowd out other investment globally and hence to damage the prospects of developing countries because of the higher real rates of interest that result!

The essays in Part V all stand on their own. They deal with various specific issues concerning the causes, consequences and reform of economic repression in each respective country. Two of these, Chapter 19 on Kenya and Chapter 21 on India, are based on parts of larger book-length studies (Collier and Lal (1986) and Lal (1988)).

It might be useful to take note of various events which have taken place since the essays on India and China were written. By 1990 India was suffering from the twin fiscal and balance of payments crisis which is identified in Chapter 5 as leading to the withering away of the state, which in turn prompts economic liberalization. India fitted this pattern. A minority government installed a technocrat, Dr Manmohan Singh, as Minister of Finance. He began the dismantling of the mercantilist system of controls which had shackled the Indian economy. He also launched a fiscal programme seeking to overturn the many entitlements which had been created by past dirigisme and were the cause of the fiscal crisis. While there has been some success in the former area, the rescinding of the major entitlements – secure jobs in loss-making public sector enterprises – was not tackled in the early stages of the reform process. The government subsequently became embroiled in the passions aroused by the controversy surrounding the demolition of the mosque at Ayodhya and its replacement by a Hindu temple on the purported birth-place of the mythological Hindu 'god' Rama. The reform effort then stalled, and at the time of writing it is difficult to predict whether the promised wholesale liberalization of trade and exchange controls, together with the dismembering of the inefficient and loss-making public sector, will in fact occur.

In China the major event since Chapter 22 was written was Tiananmen Square and the government response. Since then, partly under the pressure of the demise of socialism in eastern Europe, the Chinese government seems to have decided to let capitalism rip in parts of the country: aside from the rural countryside, the areas around Guangdong and more recently Shanghai have been allowed to tread the capitalist road. But at the same time the Communist party has sought to maintain its political control over the people. The stupendous growth in those parts of the Chinese economy which have been freed from the dead hand of mandarins has meant that the share of the state industrial enterprises (whose reform is discussed in Chapter 22) in the national economy is shrinking; *mutatis mutandis*, the reform programme outlined in the essay is much less relevant now.

Needless to say it is my practical experience in working in and on these and other developing countries which has led me to the views I now hold. It may seem that since the 1980s' world-wide Age of Reform, the study of repressed economies may no longer be relevant. For as *The Economist* (14 March 1992) noted:

> During the past ten years a great change has swept through the developing world: governments everywhere are turning against economic interventionism and putting their trust in market forces. ... This bloodless revolution is a triumph for the relatively small group of economic thinkers who for years withstood the contempt of the development-economics establishment. ... In the 1990s Lord Bauer and economists such as Anne Krueger, Bela Balassa, Deepak Lal and Ian Little are regarded – above all in the third world itself as largely vindicated (p. 103).

I sincerely hope this is so. But, unfortunately, there are numerous straws in the wind, not least the change in the political climate in the US and the UK with both Mr Reagan and Mrs Thatcher being replaced by more 'interventionist' successors. This suggests that the pendulum might once again begin to swing towards dirigisme. If and when that happens, I hope these essays will help other 'neo-liberals' – in all three worlds – to keep the flame of classical liberalism alight.

All that remains is to provide a brief biographical sketch, as is required for volumes in this series. As I have straddled a number of different worlds which have all gone into making me what I am, I have tried in what follows to give some flavour of both the formative events and people in my life.

II. A life

I was born in Lahore in 1940 into a 'zamindar' family whose fortunes had been made at the turn of the century by my great-grandfather, Shankar Lal – one of the early practitioners of the 'new' English law in Hissar (Haryana). He used his new-found wealth to buy a number of villages and to marry the sister of Sir Ganga Ram, an engineer knighted for his work in irrigating the Punjab. The family lived off the rents from these villages for the next two generations. He built a magnificent house (to accommodate his innumerable sons and grandchildren) which he named after himself – 'Shankerniwas'. Surprisingly I have never visited Hissar. But my wife did in 1973, with my father, and was amazed at the feudal obeisance still shown members of the family.

As a collaborator and defender of the Raj, my great-grandfather was very keen on providing an English education for his children, and two of his sons (my great uncles) went to England and were called to the Bar. Neither practised. This tradition of briefless lawyers was continued by my father. As the eldest and favourite grandchild, my great-grandfather made him an offer he couldn't refuse. He would send my father to England to take the Bar exams if he gave up his desire to become an architect. My father regretted this 'deal' forever afterwards. But he indulged his undoubted talent for architecture by designing and constructing a large and beautiful joint family home (for my grandfather's sons and families) in Lahore in the late 1930s. This is where I was born. Later he built a large house in New Delhi. My great-grandfather was also an inveterate gambler and lost and made a number of small fortunes speculating in commodities and stock markets. The stock market has subsequently played a major part in the family's fortunes.

My mother came from a very old Delhi family who had lived in the old city (near the Red Fort) for nearly four to five hundred years. Like my father's family, hers were also 'Banias'. Her father owned a printing press, and her eldest brother (Sham Nath) was a nationalist Congressman who took part in Gandhi's non-cooperation movement against the Raj. Later after Independence, he was Mayor of Delhi, a member of Parliament and a Deputy Minister in the Central Cabinet. He lost his supposedly safe Old Delhi seat to the Jana Sangh on the issue of cow slaughter. He died at an early age thereafter – supposedly of jaundice, but many of us thought from the devastation of political defeat. He was one of my earliest supporters, took a keen interest in my progress and helped me in my earlier career.

The seemingly luxurious, idle and uncomplicated life of my parents till 1947 – with summers being spent in a house in the hill station Mussooriee, and winters in Lahore – was shattered by Independence and the partition of the country that followed. Until the bitter end, most of my family believed that Lahore would fall on the Indian side of the border. When it didn't, my family became refugees, losing all their property in the new state of Pakistan. Some of my earliest memories are of us wandering from one relative's house to another, and of various plans which came to nought to retrieve our moveable property from Lahore. One event in this context bears remembering. One of my father's closest friends in England when they were both studying for the Bar later became a very senior civil servant in the 'new' state of Pakistan, stationed near Lahore. My father wrote to him to ask if he would help us retrieve the moveable property we had left behind. He received no answer. He and my mother – whose family had always lived in close harmony with Muslims, as was the custom in the old city of Delhi – thereafter harboured a grudge against Muslims. But this story had an ironic twist. Towards the end of his life (he died in 1984), my father's Pakistani friend, having prospered, came to Delhi as his country's High Commissioner. In his first few weeks he sought out my father and explained to him why he had not answered his letter of so many years ago: it would have been too dangerous either for my father to have gone across the bloody border, or for him to have helped him. They then picked up the threads of an old friendship, though the friend died a few months after coming to Delhi.

The point of relating this story is both the complexity of relationships when nationalities and ethnic groups are at war, and the long memories that are generated by perceived hurts. Even though I do not suffer from any anti-Muslim prejudice,

I can at a visceral level still understand the appeal of these atavistic impulses. The essay on nationalism (Chapter 2) is an attempt to come to terms with these darker forces which have undoubtedly shaped our world and continue to influence it.

More importantly for my family, however, Independence meant the abolition of 'zamindari' and hence the economic security it had taken for granted for two generations. A complicated system of compensation (both for what we had lost as a result of the formation of Pakistan, and the land reforms of the new nationalist government) meant that suddenly the family faced a severe problem of liquidity. Even after the depredations resulting from the shocks of 1947, their wealth on paper was considerable, but most of it was illiquid. Much of the rest of my father's life was spent trying to convert this illiquid wealth into more liquid forms. In the process we were constantly strapped for income. He tried to become a diplomat, but nothing came of it, and after all those years living as a member of the idle rich fraternity, there was no obvious job he could turn to – as he was already close to 40! His one ambition was to finance a decent education for me and my two sisters. Scrimping and saving, he succeeded in doing so.

I was packed off to the Doon School, Dehra Dun, at the age of 11. This was a boarding school supposedly modelled on Winchester, but which ostensibly placed more weight – when I was there – on brawn rather than brains. I did well in my studies and was reasonably happy, partly because a number of exceptional teachers opened up the rich world of drama, poetry and the arts to me. These have been lifelong passions ever since. Having won all the prizes in a whole range of academic subjects, the question was what subject I should specialize in at University.

My father had decided that my great-grandfather had made an error in putting his wealth in land rather than industry. In post-Independence India, many of our poorer relations who had put their meagre savings into setting up small industries had suddenly become industrial tycoons. The examples of two of his cousins – one had married into a leading industrial family and another (her brother) went into setting up his own tractor factory – were much on his mind. He decided that I should become an engineer, as that would provide the necessary background for setting up industries on my own. After completing my Cambridge School Certificate examination, I therefore went on to sit the intermediate examination in science as a prelude to joining one of the national engineering colleges. Though I did well in the intermediate examination, I baulked at becoming an engineer. With the help of my maternal uncle Sham Nath, I persuaded my father to let me go to St Stephen's College in Delhi instead, to study mathematics. He agreed, but within two weeks I was bored stiff by mathematics. I wanted to understand the world. I decided to study history instead.

Also once I had turned my back on an engineering career, it was agreed that I should attempt to do what other initially 'poorer' members of the larger family had done – with great enhancement to their social status and relative incomes after Independence – to join the Mandarinate, the Indian Administrative Service, the successor to the fabled ICS (Indian Civil Service). History was considered to be an ideal subject to specialize in for the exams to get into the Services, and St Stephen's was then held to be the ideal training school for these exams. I therefore switched to history, completing the three-year course in two years, with some distinction.

But I was still too young to sit for the administrative service exams. I had dreamt of going on to study at Oxford, as many of my contemporaries from the Doon School and St Stephen's had done or were planning to do. But given the financial straits the family had slipped into, there was no way in which I could expect my father to provide the finance. However, a friend of mine had obtained a loan scholarship to finance his studies from the J.N. Tata Endowment. Having obtained the top first in my BA exam, I thought I might stand a good chance of getting this scholarship – even though only a handful were given for the whole of India. So I applied to Christ Church and Jesus College, Oxford. Both accepted me, but the Tata Scholarship competition was some months away. Jesus agreed to hold my place to the next year; Christ Church didn't. I got the scholarship and went to Jesus.

I loved Oxford. I read PPE with senior status; that is, I took the three-year degree in two. This was hard and cost me the first expected of me, which I missed by a whisker after a viva.

I had also discovered Economics. I knew, now, that I would need to go on to do graduate work to become a professional economist. With no money and no hope of getting a studentship at the only graduate college for economists at Oxford at the time – Nuffield – this seemed an impossibility. I owe an immense debt both to Francis Seton, who was one of my PPE examiners and thought I should have got my first, and to Christopher Foster, my Economics tutor at Jesus. They succeeded in getting me money to study for the B.Phil. at Jesus.

But meanwhile there was the thorny question of my parents' ambition for me to join the Indian mandarinate. I was set to take the examination for the central services in October 1962. I could see no way of avoiding this. But the thought of being imprisoned in a bureaucratic post in an Indian district frightened me. I opted to become a diplomat. My parents concurred. The only problem was that, by the early 1960s, the Indian Foreign Service was the first choice of most people who sat the administrative services examination; this meant that only those ranked within the first 15 out of the over 20,000 odd candidates who took the all-India examination could get in. Fortunately I got in, but (despite rather than because of my economics) I was judged by the examiners to have failed the elementary economics paper, even though I passed the more advanced paper with distinction!

Having finished one year (out of the two) required for the B.Phil. at Oxford, I now found myself back in India being trained for the Indian Foreign Service (IFS). This was a very instructive and by and large enjoyable year. The first six months were spent at the National Academy of Administration in Mussooriee, based on France's Ecole National d'Administration. I formed many lifelong friendships and also a network in the higher Indian bureaucracy which lasts to this day. But even then I was not a model civil servant. One of the requirements for recruits to the higher civil services was a hangover from the 19th century, when district officers had to know how to ride to be able to traverse their districts. As I do not get on well with horses, I baulked at the compulsory riding that was part of the curriculum. Things were not helped by the fact that riding along with PT took place at an unearthly hour when – having given in to my natural metabolism since my days at St Stephen's – I was usually asleep. So I slept while others rode or did calisthenics. Naturally the authorities challenged me, but had no response to the obvious retort that they would find it difficult to explain to Parliament why an IFS officer had been fired for refusing to take part in an unnecessary Imperialist practice such as horseriding.

The most interesting part of this year was what was termed 'district training' when we were sent off to work with a district commissioner in some state or other for about three months. I was sent to the Dharwar district in Mysore state. I learned a great deal about village India, as well as the trials and tribulations of administration in a highly politicized economy. As an illustration, I was asked towards the end of my term in the district to adjudicate in a land dispute which involved a powerful local politician. Being naive, I adjudicated to the best of my lights and against him. The result was that a few days afterwards, when my term ended, I had to be provided with an armed escort to see me out of the district.

But I still had another year of the B.Phil. at Oxford to complete. The Foreign Service very generously gave me leave to return to complete the degree, which I did with flying colours. I was supervised successively by Sir John Hicks, John Black and for the most part by Maurice Scott. I learned whatever Economics I know from them, and Maurice Scott has been a mentor and friend ever since. But I now had to take up my first Foreign Service post, which was as Third Secretary in Tokyo, with the requirement that I learn Japanese.

I set sail from Marseilles in July 1965 on a French boat in the luxury of a first-class cabin. It was a memorable journey, the last I took by sea. It was heightened by the penchant of the French sailors to make unscheduled stops of variable length en route, as their fancy and the local girls dictated. I visited most of the ports en route to Yokohama, including Saigon. The American build-up in the Vietnam War was just beginning, and in the week we spent there it was in clear evidence. As was the Vietcong terror. While walking in one of the most beautiful cities in the world, I suddenly found myself as the only pedestrian on my side of the street. When a terrifying explosion blew up a post office down the road, the reason became obvious!

Japan in the mid-1960s was still a Third World country but, to me, extremely exotic and romantic. I enrolled in Waseda University and to my surprise found that I became proficient in speaking Japanese fairly quickly, its structure being close to that of my mother tongue, Hindi. The problem was the writing – because of the Chinese characters. While performing my lowly duties as a Third Secretary, my direct contact with the Japanese, without an insurmountable language barrier, removed any feeling that I had stepped through some bamboo curtain. I have been baffled ever since by the perception of many people that the Japanese are inscrutable.

But within a few months it was clear to me that I would not be happy being a diplomat. I wanted to be an economist, preferably working for the Indian government. Sir John Hicks had kindly written to Professor R. Komiya at Tokyo University, when he heard I was going to Japan. This was to allow me to keep in touch with economics in the diplomatic wilderness. But then 'fortuna' again played a new card.

My old tutor at Jesus, Christopher Foster, was appointed to some high advisory post in the new Labour government. The College needed someone to do his teaching for a year while he was away (and making up his mind about resigning his Fellowship). Knowing of my desire to become an economist, he got the College to offer me a year's lectureship. With his help and that of my ambassador (Badruddin Tyabji), I was granted leave of absence for five years from the Foreign Service.

I returned to Oxford, jubilant for temporarily extricating myself from the diplomatic desert. But there was still the problem of getting a more permanent post as an economist. I was too raw to be able to get anything decent in the Indian government, while the state of Indian universities did not commend themselves as a suitable haven. I needed time to think, write and build up some reputation. I tried unsuccessfully to get my B.Phil. thesis on export promotion in India published. Sir Roy Harrod, who was one of my examiners (and later a colleague and friend – see below), thought very highly of it, but there was no market for it then.

Chance again played its part. My B.Phil. supervisor, Maurice Scott, had taken leave from his Christ Church studentship to work on the famous Little–Scitovsky–Scott project at the OECD Development Center. He and Roy Harrod persuaded Christ Church to offer me a two-year lectureship. The following two years at the House were among my happiest. It had an extraordinary collection of dons whom I got to know. Apart from Roy Harrod, the others I remember with great affection are Hugh Lloyd Jones (now Sir Hugh) and Hugh Trevor Roper (now Lord Dacre). Conversations at High Table and in the senior common room at that time did live up to their hoary reputation – witty, urbane, wide-ranging and iconoclastic. I have been a convert to the evening salon ever since. Good food, good wine and worldly conversation form an essential part of the good life!

Hugh Lloyd Jones shared my passion for modern novels and was also a friend and great admirer of Robert Graves. One of the great joys of this period were group holidays which I took with various friends. On one to Majorca organized by my old Jesus friend, Robert Skidelsky, we lived in a house found for us by Robert Graves. But he was keener on the girls in our party than on fraternizing with the boys, so I did not get to know him too well. But I do remember how he had us riveted describing his search for a hallucogenic mushroom which he thought was the source of the drug 'soma' used by the ancient Brahmins in India. He believed that these mushrooms were to be found in the dung of the *Bos Indicus*, which explained why Indian cows were sacred! Unconvinced by this, many years later I was to produce my own explanation for the sacred cow in *The Hindu Equilibrium*.

With my two years at Christ Church coming to an end, I needed another job. Fortunately (as described in Chapter 1), I had become involved in the shadow pricing exercises that Ian Little and Maurice Scott had set up around the Little–Mirrlees (1969) *Manual*, as it came to be called. I was elected to a Research Fellowship at Nuffield College, Oxford, where I wrote my first book *Wells and Welfare*. I have a special affection for this book. Research on it took me back to the adjoining district in Western India where I had done my district training during my first year in the Indian Foreign Service. Also, I learned about agronomy, hydrology, geology and meteorology!

Nuffield was altogether a greyer place than Christ Church. But once Maurice Scott and Max Corden took up Fellowships there, it was intellectually lively – with Ian Little the leader of a band of followers who were to be part of the neoclassical resurgence in development economics. In my last year at Nuffield, Wilfred Beckerman had moved (as Professor and Head of Department) to University College London (UCL) from Balliol. He asked me to give a course of lectures on economic development at UCL. Later in the year he offered me a Lectureship in his department, from October 1970, and I accepted – with relief, having been turned down in the previous months for a couple of Oxford tutorial fellowships I had put in for. One of these was at my old College Jesus, where I met Partha Dasgupta (another candidate for the fellowship) for the first time, and who has been a good friend since. We were both turned down, but in retrospect this probably did both of us much good as the life of an Oxford tutor can be stifling. I was happy to move on as the provincialism of Oxford had become more oppressive during my last years there. A season in my life had come to an end.

The Lectureship at UCL, which offered tenure till retirement age, finally allowed me to cast off the Indian Foreign Service, from which I resigned. But I was still not planning to be an academic. I hoped that, after a few years teaching and publishing and building a reputation, I would return to India to work as an economist for the government. This happened in 1973 when Lovraj Kumar, who had been appointed to set up a project evaluation division in the Indian Planning Commission, asked me to come and work for him as a full-time consultant. This was a turning point in many ways in my life. The intellectual reappraisal it led to is described in the first essay of this collection. But the personal one was equally important.

Soon after moving to London, I met an American sociologist on a Ford Foundation fellowship at the London School of Economics; Barbara Ballis, as she was then known, came from a modest Jewish background in New York. Her father was of Polish origin while her mother was a first generation immigrant from Russia. She had studied at Brandeis, St Louis and Berkeley and, like others of our generation, was a radical. When we got married in December 1971, her mother was on her way to visit various members of her family in the Soviet Union whom she had not seen since the 1930s. She sent us a card from Moscow, in early January, saying that while she had seen one brother, she was sorry to have missed the other one as he was holidaying in Siberia!

Soon after we got married, my wife got a lectureship at Goldsmith's College in the University of London. Then came the offer from the Planning Commission. We took leave from our respective colleges and went off to India for a year. She to finish a dissertation on a Chicago sociologist called Robert E. Park – me to save India!

We arrived at the beginning of the major inflation which resulted from the first oil price rise in late 1973. I was still a socialist (see Chapter 1) and believed that inherited wealth was immoral. I decided that we must live on my Planning Commission salary, which was near the top of the civil service scale. Even though we lived in the house my father had built in New Delhi, we soon found that my civil service salary was inadequate, first to meet the relative luxuries of life and then, as salaries remained frozen but prices rose, to meet even basic requirements such as petrol for the car, meat and vegetables. Pride took a fall before penury, when I finally decided to give up my principles and sell some shares to supplement my salary.

But despite this enforced simple living, we had a very happy time, making lots of new friends and catching up with old ones. The most notable were Dharma and Lovraj Kumar who have provided a second home for us in Delhi, besides running the best salon in India! But the impossibility of our living on an Indian civil servant's salary, together with the clouds on the political horizon – which led in 1975 to the imposition of the Emergency by Mrs Gandhi – convinced me that our future no longer lay in India. We returned to London and the academic life.

Since 1967 when Esra Bennathan asked me to come and write a report for the United Nations Economic Commission on Asia and the Far East (see Chapter 1), I have had a string of consultancies with international agencies. Besides allowing me to travel to nearly every developing country over the last 20 years, these have provided an opportunity to learn about development problems at first hand.

Esra had got in touch with me through Nicholas Kaldor, whose youngest daughter was a pupil of mine at Oxford and a close friend. I got to know the Kaldors fairly well and through them met the remaining Cambridge greats – Joan Robinson and Richard Kahn; I even caught a glimpse of Piero Sraffa. But even in my earlier professional incarnation, I found the Cambridge group unappealing, and the only impression I made on at least one of them was unfavourable. At one seminar being attended by Joan Robinson, I made some innocuous statement about rates of return to capital. Whereupon there was a hiss and Mrs Robinson screeched, 'You make my blood boil'. Much to his credit Amartya Sen (whom we had got to know when he took up a chair at the London School of Economics in the early 1970s) immediately shot up and said, 'but, Joan, it's all in *The Accumulation of Capital*', and proceeded to cite chapter and verse. He later explained to me that he was probably the only one who had read *The Accumulation of Capital* thoroughly, as he had been made to proofread it as a graduate student of Mrs Robinson's!

As part of the 'shadow pricing' circus at Nuffield, we had many visitors, the most notable being Al Harberger. He had the clearest and toughest mind of anyone I had hitherto met. We got on very well and spent many hours arguing late into the night. He has been a friend and mentor ever since and, in a marvellous turn in the wheel of fortune, we find ourselves as colleagues at UCLA after all these years. Chapter 12 in this collection is an attempt to sort out the arguments on shadow pricing that I have had with him intermittently since his Nuffield visit.

As the World Bank was (and probably still is) the largest potential user of 'shadow pricing', I became (through the good offices of David Henderson and Shlomo Reutlinger) one of the earliest salesmen of the Little–Mirrlees (L–M) method to the Bank. It is difficult in retrospect to understand the passions that alternative methods of project appraisal aroused. I wrote a small book, *Methods of Project Appraisal*, which tried to sort out the differences and also to relate the various methods to standard trade theory. This book seemed timely and brought me some modicum of fame.

During my last year in Oxford, the battle lines between the 'old' and 'new' development economics were drawn between two institutions – Nuffield (with Ian Little as its head) and Queen Elizabeth House (QEH), where Paul Streeten reigned. I admired both and both became friends. But increasingly (see Chapter 1), though my heart still remained with the QEH brigade, my head was siding with the Nuffield troops. To maintain some link with Oxford after I had left for London, Paul Streeten agreed to house a research project funded by the Overseas Development Administration at QEH. This applied the L–M methods to foreign investments in Kenya and India. A book called *Appraising Foreign Investment in Developing Countries* was the outcome.

In the late 1960s and early 1970s the International Labour Organization (ILO) had begun a series of country missions which surveyed a particular country and put together a report detailing a programme to tackle issues related to poverty and employment. Gus Ranis from Yale led the ILO mission to the Philippines. Ajit Bhalla at the ILO was simultaneously organizing a study of capital–labour substitution in road construction. He got me to join the Ranis mission to estimate shadow prices for the Philippines. I found the Philippines fascinating; though in Asia, it did not seem to be of Asia. I later went back (see below) on a study of its labour markets (see Chapter 18) and got the first inkling of its difference from, say, Korea. It was really a Latin American economy masquerading as an Asian one! This difference in typology, based in part upon differing resource endowments and in polity, is an important leitmotiv running through many of the essays collected in this volume.

As the ILO mission reported directly to the President, we were invited to a reception with President Marcos and First Lady Imelda. This was after the first of many referenda that Marcos held to justify his rule after suppressing democracy. They had won about a 98 per cent affirmative vote. One of the mission members standing next to me congratulated Mrs Marcos on this stupendous victory. Without batting an eyelid she replied, 'We are investigating the No's'!

The cost-benefit study of capital–labour substitution I did in collaboration with ILO engineers was published as a book called *Men or Machines*. This study was noteworthy in that the engineers actually built the road with alternative technologies. The study nicely complemented my earlier one of small-scale irrigation in India – in marrying engineering with economics. But from both I learnt that the engineering mind was very rigid and thought implicitly in terms of given standards and fixed input–output coefficients. This 'kinky' mind set is inexorably at odds with the economist's way of looking at the world, which is in terms of tradeoffs. I was glad I had not become an engineer.

After returning from India, I spent nearly a year turning the papers I had written on estimating shadow prices for the Indian Planning Commission into a book called *Prices for Planning*. This marked the end of one particular phase of my professional life. During it I had also produced estimates of shadow prices for Korea, Jamaica and Sri Lanka. This provided excellent training both in understanding an economy and in utilizing data. Whether the actual estimates were of much use to anyone is doubtful.

But by 1976 it was clear that it was time to get off this bandwagon. Chance again ruled. At a dinner at Nuffield I met Angus Maddison (who was then at the OECD); he asked me to spend the summer in Paris writing a report on macroeconomic policy in developed countries. This was a marvellous opportunity to learn about an area which, due to my obsession with shadow prices, I had neglected. The slim book that resulted, *Unemployment and Wage Inflation in Industrial Economies*, is not one I am now proud of. It is much too Keynesian! I returned to its themes in a paper I find much more acceptable now, again written at the instigation of Angus Maddison (see Lal (1982)). But it was not till Shankar Acharya, who had joined the Indian Institute of Public Finance in Delhi from the World Bank, asked me to give some lectures on macroeconomics that I finally caught up with the rational expectations revolution and all that! But by then (see Chapter 1), my world view had also changed.

One consequence of the OECD work was that it sparked my interest in labour markets. When Mark Leiserson suggested in 1978 that I join his employment and rural development division at the World Bank to set up a research project on wage and employment trends and structures in developing countries, I agreed with alacrity. I was also getting a bit restless in London, and the gypsy in me welcomed a change of scene.

We went to Washington via Canberra! Max Corden had asked me to come as a visiting fellow to the Australian National University. Apart from writing my piece on the international monetary system (Chapter 6), I also wrote another on the International Economic Order (Lal (1978b)) and made many new friends in Australia, notably Heinz Arndt.

The two years at the World Bank proved a very productive period. Besides the study of the Philippines (Chapter 18), they also generated two books: *Labor and Poverty in Kenya*, with Paul Collier, and Volume 2 of *The Hindu Equilibrium*, called *Aspects of Indian Labor*. These formed part of the general questioning by the 'neoclassical resurgents' of the assumptions of surplus labour and segmented labour markets which underlay much of the 'old' development economics. The study on India also led me to crystallize various ideas about the causes of Indian stagnation which had been germinating in my mind for a long time.

The first draft of Volume 1 of *The Hindu Equilibrium*, *Cultural Stability and Economic Stagnation*, was written in white heat over a period of three months in 1981. Polishing it into its final form took another five years! But among all my books, this was the most fun to write.

From the start of my academic career I had also indulged in pamphleteering. This allowed me to keep in touch with those who sell ideas to politicians and the public. An important forum was provided in the 1970s by the Trade Policy Research Centre (TPRC), set up by Harry Johnson and Hugh Corbett. I became involved with the TPRC in the mid-1970s, becoming a research associate after Martin Wolf left the World Bank to succeed the late Harry Johnson as the TPRC's Research Director. The TPRC was a unique forum for promoting the case for free trade; my writings for them, as well as participation in their numerous conferences (which brought politicians, bureaucrats, journalists and academics together), were important in keeping me in the real world. I first met Peter Bauer at one of these conferences. He has since become a close friend and an important intellectual influence.

By the early 1980s my views were much more congruent with those of the Institute of Economic Affairs than with the Fabian Society, for whom in the 1970s I had written two pamphlets. When Martin Wassell, the editorial manager of the IEA, suggested in 1982 that I write a Hobart paperback for them on development issues, I agreed. For before leaving for the World Bank in 1978, David Henderson – who greatly to my benefit had taken up a chair at University College in London in the mid-1970s – and I had decided to do a book on the political economy of the world economy. I considered that putting together my thoughts on the debates on development, in which willy-nilly I had been at least a witness and often a participant over the previous decade and a half, would be a help in writing the bigger book. This became *The Poverty of Development Economics*. Much to my surprise, it became an instant success – both reviled and applauded!

Nothing came of the bigger book as in 1983, at Anne Krueger's invitation, I returned to the World Bank, first as an economic adviser and then the research administrator in her Vice-Presidency. David Henderson meanwhile left UCL to become head of the economics directorate at the OECD. But he did put down some of what would have gone into our joint book in his excellent Reith lectures published as *Innocence and Design*.

I spent four years (1983–87) at the World Bank trying to help Anne Krueger restructure its research programme. I hope we had some success. But the World Bank is a strange animal with its own culture which does not take kindly to the alteration of its ways. Moreover, it resembles a mediaeval court, with barons constantly battling each other for the monarch's favour. It requires an essay of its own. Suffice to say that by the end of four years, I was ready to leave. The major success of this period was the establishment of two journals – the *World Bank Economic Review* and the *World Bank Research Observer* – as well as four large multi-country comparative studies on topics of importance to developing countries. The output from these is now entering the public domain and hopefully will be judged favourably by our professional peers. During this period we also tried to widen the Bank's intellectual horizons. To my surprise, many well-known economists had never been associated with the Bank's research endeavours. These included old friends like Jagdish Bhagwati, and those who became new ones, notably Assar Lindbeck, Ron Findlay and Stan Wellisz. Washington also contained many notable economists, some of whom (like Gottfried Haberler) I had got to know during my 1978 stint at the Bank, and others (like Alan Walters) whom I had first met in London but who became a close friend during this period. Other new friends included Gordon Tullock and Jim Buchanan.

During this period I travelled widely and got to know Latin America and many Latin American economists as well. The Latin American 'syndrome', whose first manifestations I had seen in the Philippines, was now transparent. Chapter 4 tries to delineate this, while the work I have recently done with Sylvia Maxfield on Brazil (Chapter 20) provides a more detailed study.

These differing typologies of developing countries, which had been emphasized in a different way by Chenery and Syrquin (1975) for instance, formed an important building block on the 21-country comparative study of the political economy of poverty, equity and growth that Hal Myint and I co-directed for nearly seven years for the World Bank. The synthesis volume is now in press, with Chapter 14 presenting some of its conclusions.

My experience at the World Bank had finally cured me of my desire to serve as an economic bureaucrat. Returning to London in 1987, I was finally reconciled to the fact that my vocation was that of an academic – albeit a worldly one! During the years I had been (intermittently) at UCL, I had been promoted first to a Readership (1979) and then to a personal chair (in 1984) in the University of London. We had acquired two children and a beautiful Lutyens house in the early 1980s; we had built up a large circle of friends including many outside the academy and were, I thought, set for the tranquil and civilized life of academics. Moreover, the Institute of Economic Affairs (IEA), the TPRC (until it collapsed) and the Centre for Policy Studies provided forums where ideas could be harnessed to public debates, listened to by politicians.

But I had not kept in touch with the depredations wrought on the universities, surprisingly by Conservative governments – culminating in Kenneth Baker's *de facto* nationalization in 1989. I wrote a pamphlet against this wanton destruction of one of the best university systems in the world (Lal (1989b)) and suggested its privatization. Even more eloquent was the late Eli Kedourie (1988). To no avail. It was clear that another season in our lives was ending.

When the University of California at Los Angeles offered me the newly established James Coleman Chair in International Development Studies in 1990, it was an offer I could not refuse. But baulking at educating our children (born in 1980 and 1981) in Los Angeles, we have kept them in boarding schools in England. So now my children usually live on a different continent and my mother and sister on another. I continue to wander the world. A gypsy at heart, I do not find this intolerable. Neither do my children. After all they have known nothing else. My wife, by contrast, though still hankering after rootedness, bears all this wandering with a wan smile. For her forbearance over the years this book is dedicated to her.

Finally, given the ever-changing hand dealt to me by 'fortuna', I cannot help but think of my great-grandfather – gambler, bon vivant, dynast, gypsy and collaborator of the British Raj. Wherever he has been reincarnated, I cannot help but feel that he would chuckle at what has become of his great-grandson.

References

Amsden, A. (1989), *Asia's New Giant: South Korea and Late Industrialization*, New York: Oxford University Press.

Baldwin, R. (1992), 'Are Economists' Traditional Trade Policy Views Still Valid?', *Journal of Economic Literature*, **30** (2).

Baumol, W., J. Panzar and R. Willig (1982), *Contestable Markets and the Theory of Industry Structure*, San Diego: Harcourt, Brace, Jovanovich.

Binmore, K. (1990), *Essays on the Foundations of Game Theory*, Oxford: Blackwell.

Chenery, H. and M. Syrquin (1975), *Patterns of Developments, 1950–1970*, New York: Oxford University Press.

Collier, P. and D. Lal (1986), *Labour and Poverty in Kenya 1900–1980*, Oxford, Clarendon Press.

Demsetz, H. (1988), 'The Control Function of Private Wealth' in his *Ownership, Control and the Firm*, Oxford: Blackwell, pp. 229–47.

Edwards, S. (1984), 'The Order of Liberalization of the External Sector in Developing Countries', *Essays in International Finance*, no. 156, Princeton: Princeton University Press.

Edwards, S. (1989), *Real Exchange Rates, Devaluation and Adjustment*, Cambridge, MA: MIT Press.

Edwards, S. (1992), *The Sequencing of Structural Adjustment and Stabilization*, Occasional Paper No. 34, International Center for Economic Growth, San Francisco: ICS Press.

Findlay, R. and S. Wellisz (1982), 'Endogenous Tariffs, the Political Economy of Trade Restrictions and Welfare' in J. Bhagwati (ed.), *Import Competition and Response*, Chicago: University of Chicago Press.

Findlay, R. and J. Wilson (1987), 'The Political Economy of Leviathan' in A. Razin and E. Sadka (eds), *Economic Policy in Theory and Practice*, New York: St Martins Press.

Frenkel, J. and M. Mussa (1985), 'Asset Markets, Exchange Rates and the Balance of Payments' in R. Jones and P. Kenen (eds), *The Handbook of International Economics*, Vol. 2, Amsterdam: North-Holland, pp. 679–747.

Funke, N. (1992), 'Timing and Sequencing of Reforms: Competing Views', Kiel Working Paper No. 552, Kiel, Germany: Kiel Institute of World Economics.

Heckscher, E. (1955), *Mercantilism*, 2 vols, revised 2nd edition, London: Allen & Unwin.

Henderson, P.D. (1986), *Innocence and Design – The Influence of Economic Ideas on Policy*, Oxford: Blackwell.

Huizinga, J. (1987), 'An Empirical Investigation of the Long-Run Behavior of Real Exchange Rates', *Carnegie-Rochester Conference Series on Public Policy*, no. 27, Amsterdam: North Holland.

Johnson, C. (1982), *MITI and the Japanese Miracle: The Growth of Industrial Policy, 1925–1975*, Stanford: Stanford University Press.

Jones, R. (1971), 'A Three Factor Model in Theory, Trade and History' in J. Bhagwati et al. (eds), *The Balance of Payments and Growth*, Amsterdam: North-Holland.
Kedourie, E. (1988), *Diamonds Into Glass – Universities and the Government*, London: Centre for Policy Studies.
Kreps, D.M. (1990), *Game Theory and Economic Modelling*, Oxford: Clarendon Press.
Krueger, A. (1977), 'Growth, Distortions, and Patterns of Trade Among Many Countries', *Princeton Studies in International Finance*, no. 40, Princeton, NJ: International Finance Section, Dept. of Economics, Princeton University.
Lal, D. (1972), *Wells and Welfare*, Paris: OECD Development Center.
Lal, D. (1974), *Methods of Project Analysis: A Review*, World Bank staff Occasional Paper No. 16, Baltimore: Johns Hopkins.
Lal, D. and associates (1975), *Appraising Foreign Investment in Developing Countries*, London: Heinemann Educational Books.
Lal, D. (1977), *Unemployment and Wage Inflation in Industrial Economies*, Paris: OECD.
Lal, D. (1978a), *Men or Machines*, Geneva: ILO.
Lal, D. (1978b), *Poverty, Power and Prejudice – The North–South Confrontation*, Fabian Research Series 340, London: Fabian Society.
Lal, D. (1980), *Prices for Planning: Towards the Reform of Indian Planning*, London: Heinemann Educational Books.
Lal, D. (1982), 'Do Keynesian Diagnoses and Remedies Need Revision?' in A. Maddison and B.S. Wilpstra (eds), *Unemployment – the European Perspective*, London: Croom Helm.
Lal, D. (1983, 1985), *The Poverty of Development Economics*, Hobart Paperback 16, London: Institute of Economic Affairs; American edition (1985), Cambridge, MA: Harvard University Press.
Lal, D. (1984), 'The Political Economy of the Predatory State', Development Research Dept. Discussion Paper No. 105, Washington, DC: World Bank; revised April 1988, London: University College.
Lal, D. (1987), 'Markets, Mandarins and Mathematicians', *Cato Journal*, **7** (1), pp. 43–70.
Lal, D. (1988), *The Hindu Equilibrium*, Vol. 1: *Cultural Stability and Economic Stagnation, India c 1500 AD–1980 AD*, Oxford: Clarendon Press.
Lal, D. (1989a), *The Hindu Equilibrium*, Vol. 2: *Aspects of Indian Labour*, Oxford: Clarendon Press.
Lal, D. (1989b), *Nationalized Universities – Paradox of the Privatization Age*, Policy Study No. 103, London: Centre for Policy Studies.
Lal, D. (1990), *The Limits of International Cooperation*, 20th Wincott Memorial Lecture, Occasional Paper No. 83, London: Institute of Economic Affairs.
Lal, D. (1992), 'Social Policy After Socialism' in H. Siebert (ed.), *The Transformation of Socialist Economies*, Tubingen: J.C.B. Mohr.
Lal, D. (1993), 'Does Openness Matter? How to Appraise the Evidence' in H. Siebert (ed.), *Economic Growth in the World Economy*, Tubingen: J.C.B. Mohr.
Lal, D. (forthcoming), *Against Dirigisme – Essays on the World Economy*, San Francisco: ICS Press.
Leamer, E. (1987), 'Paths of Development in the Three factor, n-Good General Equilibrium Model', *Journal of Political Economy*, **95** (5), pp. 961–99.
Lindbeck, A. (1976), 'Stabilization Policy in Open Economies with Endogenous Politicians', *American Economic Review*, **66** (2), pp. 1–19.
Little, I.M.D. (1982), *Economic Development*, New York: Basic Books.
Little, I.M.D. and J.A. Mirrlees (1969), *Manual of Industrial Project Analysis*, Vol. II: *Social Cost-Benefit Analysis*, Paris: OECD Development Center.
Little, I.M.D. and J.A. Mirrlees (1974), *Project Appraisal and Planning for Developing Countries*, London: Heinemann Educational Books.
Little, I.M.D., T. Scitovsky and M. Fg. Scott (1970), *Industry and Trade in Some Developing Countries*, London: Oxford University Press.
Mayer, W. (1984), 'Endogenous Tariff Formation', *American Economic Review*, **74** (5), December, pp. 970–85.
McKinnon, R. (1988), 'Monetary and Exchange Rate Policies for Financial Stability: A Proposal', *Journal of Economic Perspectives*, **2** (1).
McKinnon, R. (1991), *The Order of Economic Liberalization*, Baltimore: Johns Hopkins.
Mussa, M. (1990), 'Exchange Rates in Theory and in Reality', *Essays In International Finance*, no. 179, Princeton, NJ: International Finance Section, Dept. of Economics, Princeton University.
Nordhaus, W. (1975), 'The Political Business Cycle', *Review of Economic Studies*, **42**, pp. 169–90.
Persson, T. and G. Tabellini (1990), *Macroeconomic Policy, Credibility and Politics*, New York: Harwood Academic Publishers.
Riedel, J. (forthcoming), 'Strategies of Economic Development', mimeo, SAIS, Johns Hopkins University; in E. Grilli and D. Salvatore (eds), *Handbook of Economic Development*, Oxford: Blackwell.

Rodrik, D. (1993), 'The Positive Economics of Policy Reform', *Amercian Economic Review*, **83** (2).

Salter, W.E. (1959), 'Internal and External Balance: The Role of Price and Expenditure Effects', *Economic Record*, **35**, August, pp. 226–38.

Scott, M.Fg. (1989), *A New View of Growth*, Oxford: Clarendon Press.

Sell, F. (1988), 'True Exposure: The Analysis of Trade Liberalization in a General Equilibrium Framework', *Weltwirtschaftliches Archiv*, **124** (4).

Stern, N. (1991), 'The Determinants of Growth', *Economic Journal*, **101**, January, pp. 122–33.

Stiglitz, J. et al. (1989), *The Economic Role of the State*, Oxford: Blackwell.

Wade, R. (1990), *Governing the Market: Economic Theory and the Role of Government in East Asian Industrialization*, Princeton: Princeton University Press.

Williamson, J. (1985), *The Exchange Rate System*, revised edition, Washington, DC: Institute for International Economics.

PART I

[1]

DEEPAK LAL

Political Economy and Public Policy

As I understand it, one purpose of this series of Occasional Papers is to give authors an opportunity to describe their intellectual development. I am particularly pleased to present a brief intellectual autobiography, because it provides a useful introduction to the central subject of this paper: the evolution of thought on public policy in the past 100 years and a defense of economic liberalism as a framework to replace the neomercantilism that has characterized public policy in much of the third world since the end of the Second World War.

The Making of a Political Economist

I first studied economics at Oxford, in the school of Philosophy-Politics-Economics (PPE), after obtaining an honors degree in history at Delhi; but I did not become an economist until I had done graduate work at Oxford, after a brief stint in the Indian foreign service. At that time (in the mid-1960s), Ian Little had just moved to the Development Centre of the Organization for Economic Cooperation and Development (OECD) in Paris and was setting up his comparative study of trade and industry and writing the now-famous Little-Mirrlees manual on project analysis. Through the good offices of my old Oxford tutor

Maurice Scott, who was a collaborator on these studies, I became involved at an early stage (as "an attendant lord") in what has since been called the "neoclassical resurgence" in development economics, based on the application of the second-best economics of public policy for imperfect economies.[1]

I spent a good part of the next decade helping to clarify and apply this "new economics"—particularly the Little-Mirrlees shadow prices—to many developing countries. The travel this work entailed, along with the comparative study of the price structure of particular economies, constituted the best apprenticeship that a development economist could have. During this period, I was a child of my background and education—a social democrat, a Keynesian, and a believer in planning (albeit increasingly through the price mechanism).

Naturally, because I am an Indian, I was constantly drawn to the economic problems of India, where, by the late 1960s, the national planning and economic policy (which I had been brought up to believe was benevolent and wise) was in the midst of a crisis. In 1968, Esra Bennathan, who was then at the Economic Commission for Asia and the Far East (ECAFE), commissioned me to do a report on controls and liberalization in India and Pakistan. This work was an eye-opener for me. But I was still wedded to the ideology of Indian planning. Hence, my report, although correct in pointing out the irrationalities and inefficiencies of direct controls, was much too concerned with making marginal improvements in the existing system of Indian planning rather than questioning the concepts behind it.[2] My remarks were much more favorable to dirigisme than the famous Little-Scitovsky-Scott book[3] had been, and I was shaken when Ian Little told me after reading my report that he no longer believed in planning.

Nonetheless, it seemed that two of the main lessons I had learned from the new economics could provide some intellectual coherence to—if I may so call them—my Indian biases in favor of planning. The first lesson came from the then-new theory of trade and welfare expounded by Max Corden in his *Trade Policy and Economic Welfare*,[4] which he was writing when I was a research fellow at Nuffield College, Oxford, in the late 1960s, and which was empirically substantiated in the book by Little, Scitovsky, and Scott. This lesson was that the case for free trade was separable from that for laissez-faire, and, except for the optimum tariff argument, most arguments for protection were second or third or fourth best. Other domestic taxes or subsidies could deal with market distortions far better than tariff protection could. This lesson, which has not been controverted by either logic or experience since, has left me a staunch free trader.[5]

The second lesson was that the new second-best economics embodied in the Little-Mirrlees shadow pricing rules and its natural extension—the theory of optimum taxation—provided the grammar for arguments about all public policy. Armed with this new economics, an economist had only to explain its logic and demonstrate its applicability in order to convince the countries of the third world that they should adopt rational planning (taken to mean government intervention that supplements rather than supplants the price mechanism). It seemed self-evident that the assumption behind this technocracy—namely, that the so-called policy makers were truly benevolent public servants moved solely by logic, evidence, and the public interest—was applicable to most governments, and certainly to the government of India (or at least its bureaucrats, those guardians of the public interest installed by the British).

An opportunity to apply this new wisdom arose during 1973–1974 when I spent a year as a consultant to the Indian Planning Commission, helping Lovraj Kumar set up the new Project Appraisal Division (PAD). This turned into a formative experience that forced me to question not only all the assumptions I had previously held about the benevolence, or public spiritedness, of bureaucrats and politicians, but the very intellectual basis for planning and government intervention. A few examples must suffice to give the flavor of this traumatic, but enlightening, experience.

One of my first tasks on joining the commission was to edit the draft of the Fifth Five-Year Plan. Although this task turned out to be impossible to do (the original authors of the various parts of the plan took great umbrage at any tampering with what they considered to be their perfect English!), it allowed me to see firsthand how the plan was put together. What quickly became obvious was that this was a purely political process, as underlined by the acrimonious debate that erupted between the two economists on the commission over what should be considered a feasible rate of growth for the next five years. The politicians settled what I had naively thought was a technical question by choosing the higher of the two growth rates being advocated, even though the technical arguments supported the lower rate—whereupon the proponent of the latter rate duly resigned from the commission. Meanwhile one minister was heard to remark that he could not understand all the fuss about having a realistic plan when unrealistic plans had always been acceptable in the past.

As I began the task of estimating shadow prices for the Indian economy,[6] I became increasingly aware that the country's planners were experiencing serious information problems. The data used to derive the various targets in the plan were, on the whole, inadequate, and in some cases even fraudulent. This state of affairs was most surprising, since India possessed one of the best statistical and survey infrastructures in the third world.

To make matters worse, the politicians clearly believed that the function of the new Project Appraisal Division was not to ensure that public investment projects were sound (i.e., socially profitable), but merely to make adjustments that would give the appearance of serving the social weal. The PAD was allowed to make some small, marginal decisions; but where political or "rent-seeking" interests were concerned, its economists were invariably overruled—usually with disastrous results. On one occasion, I was asked to evaluate a large public project that on the simplest analysis could not possibly break even, let alone have a positive rate of return, unless its output was purchased at some huge price far beyond the world price. The ministry concerned informed me that some foreign dictator had indeed agreed to purchase this output at this break-even price. I was still unconvinced of the project's viability, particularly because implementation was going to take a long time. Also, who could rely on the promises of a dictator, whose regime might be overthrown? PAD's advice was overruled on political grounds. The project went ahead. A number of years later, after very large investments had been made and the output began appearing, the dictator fell, and India was left with yet another large white elephant!

This experience, and others like it, pointed to a systemic problem. Mere tinkering was not going to help India escape from the economic irrationalities introduced by public policy. Economic growth would continue to be throttled as long as the country tolerated the unholy combination of ideas and interests that had turned its civil servants—most of them decent and intelligent people—into mere instruments of predatory politicians and their clients. Although my colleagues were deeply concerned about the situation, they attributed it to a lack of political will, rather than to India's policies, which were based on ideas they themselves espoused.

When it was suggested that India needed to liberalize its economic controls, a highly intelligent and idealistic senior civil servant responded that my whole case was based on the erroneous assumption that the businessmen on whose decisions the economy's investment and production outcomes would then depend were honest—whereas the Indian businessmen we knew were not. Nothing I said would convince him that market forces took little notice of honesty or benevolence, or that the current alliance of dishonest businessmen and the politicians who granted them monopolistic favors would do more harm to the country's economy than if they were forced to compete with other dishonest businessmen!

Toward the end of my stay, Prime Minister Indira Gandhi announced that it had become necessary to detain so-called economic offenders without habeas corpus to stem their illegal activities. I remarked to a distinguished economist who was also a civil servant that this measure was the thin edge of a big wedge, since what were deemed their economic offenses had been prompted by the country's indefensible controls, and that the arbitrageurs had actually served a useful economic purpose. I also pointed out that, given the pervasiveness of the controls, anyone could be put in prison, particularly many middle-class Indians who were driven by the controls to engage in some economic offense, however small. My friend dismissed this view as economic liberalism gone mad. But I felt vindicated when a few months later Mrs. Gandhi used the same laws during her emergency regime to harass anyone opposed to the government, and even innocent bystanders.

This Indian experience made me question the relevance of the new economics of public policy in countries where its central assumption about the benevolence of governments did not hold. I was becoming a political economist. Subsequently, I found myself moving in two directions. First, I wanted to understand why nonbenevolent states act the way they do. Second, on a more personal level, I wanted to find the true cause of the deep-seated malaise that was troubling India's political economy. My conclusions in the latter case are presented in a two-volume work called *The Hindu Equilibrium.*[7] In the former case, I have been trying to devise models that best represent the types of polities actually found in the third world.[8] This effort has culminated in a study for the World Bank, written with Hla Myint, of the political economy of poverty, equity, and growth in twenty-one countries.[9] This is not the place to summarize the results of that study, or the political economy models we found most useful. Instead I wish to pick up one of the themes that emerged from that endeavor.

This recently completed study, as well as my frequent travels in numerous developing countries, has convinced me that the disjunction between reality and theory that I observed in India is actually a worldwide phenomenon that has its roots in what I call the dirigiste dogma.[10] In the rest of this essay, I outline what I now think were its causes and consequences.

The modern-day dirigiste dogma has had a strong hold on economists and intellectuals in two important respects. First, it has led most of them (except, until recently, those in the public-choice school) to neglect the polity completely in their economic policy prescriptions, which have otherwise been based on rigorous analysis. Second, it has led them to believe that questions of the efficiency of production and of the distribution of income can be separated in designing public policy. Their idea has been to strive for the optimal combination of the two (which, of course, may only be a second-best optimum when there is a trade-off between efficiency and equity). These views can be traced to J. S. Mill, whose *Principles of Political Economy* stands Janus-like looking back toward the concerns of the classical thinkers and forward to those of the later neoclassicists. The problem is that in designing public policy we can no more separate politics and economics than we can separate production and distribution. Why so many professional economists have come to accept almost unthinkingly these assumptions is an important question to examine.

The Evolution of Thought on Economic Policy

Broadly speaking, there have been only three cogent systems of thought on public policy—mercantilism, economic liberalism (of the nineteenth-century variety), and what can be called the neoclassical policy consensus. I am ruling out various more controversial systems such as Marxism and structuralism, which, despite their numerous adherents, have failed to build a following among mainstream economists over the past 200 years.

Historians of economic thought tend to agree that mercantilism provided the first coherent and systematic set of economic policy prescriptions to be adopted by states.[11] Interestingly, the policies of many third world countries—with their industrial regulations, state-created monopolies, import and export restrictions, price controls, and so on—are similar to the mercantilist policies adopted by the absolutist states of Europe after the Renaissance.[12] Furthermore, the goals of modern-day third world governments are also similar to those of their seventeenth- and eighteenth-century European predecessors. They can be described broadly as nation building.

In the mid-1970s, with my belief in the usefulness of technocratic economics greatly shaken, I turned back to two subjects that I had hitherto neglected—politics and philosophy. I needed to broaden my education beyond the narrow welfarist ken of my early years. The works of Hayek, Buchanan, Tullock, Olson, and later Bauer, on political economy, which my peers (and teachers) had ignored but which I now read avidly, stimulated me to reconsider what policy makers in most developing countries were up to.[13] This move seemed essential if I was to explain the motivations underlying that concoction of economic illiteracy, the "new international economic order." I wrote a pamphlet, published, surprisingly, by the Fabian Society, in which I tried to identify and explain these motivations.[14] In a later paper, I tried to explain the links between nationalism, socialism, and planning and the appeal of these three ideas for third world elites.[15]

The view that I came to can be put as follows. Whether it is because of memories of colonialism (in much of Africa and Asia) or a feeling of inferiority (in much of Latin America) with respect to the Western metropolitan powers, most third world governments think they lack power in their dealings with the West because they have a weak industrial base. They see industrialization as a means of restoring their self-respect and of waging modern wars. They think that by promoting industrialization they can overcome the inherent military weakness responsible for their subjugation by superior Western arms in the past. Consequently, they have found the dirigiste example of the Soviet Union (though not necessarily its communism) particularly attractive, since it was deemed to show how a weak and poor underdeveloped country, industrialized through planning, had become a great power within one generation.

The fact that these countries are suspicious of free trade and of foreign capital is another reflection of their desire for a national identity and economic independence. Third world rulers fear that their hold over the ruled may be subverted or weakened (through direct or indirect pressure) if they become dependent on foreign transactions. They also see this threat of direct or indirect subversion as a means of putting pressure on the medium-size or small powers to change a policy course "which the national interest—or the interest of its leaders—would appear to require."[16]

The dirigisme that has evolved in developing countries in the interest of nation building was given a fillip by their baleful experience during the Great Depression. Particularly hard hit were the countries of Latin America, which until then had been integrated into the world economy for nearly seven decades and had seen considerable economic expansion. In the early part of the twentieth century, many Latin American countries (notably Argentina) were considered part of the economically vigorous North. But the havoc caused by the Great Depression and Latin America's subsequent repudiation of outward-looking policies after the Second World War left them part of the economically pressed South.

Economic development under dirigiste regimes since the late 1940s has thus been guided by a desire for national integration and self-respect, which the elites believed would flow from the mounting national power that economic growth would foster. But the dirigiste policies have fallen far short of this goal. If anything, they have made it even more difficult to promote the economic progress required to provide the material basis for the desired national autonomy. In fact, many third world countries are now beginning to liberalize their repressed economies, as experience has taught them that the old dirigisme does not serve the twin purposes of economic development and national integration.

This pattern of economic repression followed by reform in the name of nation building is reminiscent of the course many European states followed during their evolution. As Heckshher has noted, mercantilist policies arose to consolidate the power of the relatively weak states built "on the ruins of the universal Roman Empire. . . . [T]he state was both the subject and the object of mercantilist economic policy." Its purpose was to achieve "unification and power," making the "State's purposes decisive in a uniform economic sphere and to make all economic activity subservient to considerations corresponding to the requirements of the State." Mercantilism sought to control economic forces "not directly in the interests of the subject but to strengthen the state authority itself; it concentrated on the *power* of the state . . . primarily [on] the state's external power, in relation to other states."[17]

This view that nation building should be served by mercantilist practice is similar to that espoused by most third world political leaders and elites.

One of the main objectives of the various mercantilist regulations of the sixteenth and seventeenth centuries was to exchange royal favors (by granting trade privileges) for revenue to meet the chronic fiscal crisis of the state—a problem shared by many countries of the modern-day third world. But the system collapsed under the administrative burden it created. As Keynes pointed out,

> Above all, the ineptitude of public administration strongly prejudiced the practical man in favour of laissez-faire—a sentiment which has by no means disappeared. Almost everything which the state did in the eighteenth century in excess of its minimum functions was it seemed, injurious or unsuccessful.[18]

The consequences of the regulations, particularly in internal trade and industry, were similar to those observed in many developing countries—corruption, rent seeking, tax evasion, and the growth of illegal activities in underground economies.[19] The French Revolution was in part a reaction to this mercantilist ancien régime. The processes that caused mercantilism to be replaced by economic liberalism for a brief period in the mid-nineteenth century are beyond the scope of this discussion. The important point here concerns the consequences of the new policy prescriptions that it generated. I do want to emphasize, however, that this (what I have elsewhere called) "unMarxian withering away of the State"[20] also helped to bring about the change in the policy regime in nonrevolutionary countries such as England.

Paradoxically, the new economic liberalism (although short-lived) achieved the goal sought by mercantilism:

> Great power for the state, the perpetual and fruitless goal of mercantilist endeavour, was translated into fact in the nineteenth century. In many respects this was the work of laissez-faire, even though the conscious efforts of the latter tended in an entirely different direction.
>
> The result was attained primarily by limiting the functions of the state, which task laissez-faire carried through radically. The maladjustment between ends and means was one of the typical features of mercantilism, but it disappeared once the aims were considerably limited. Disobedience and arbitrariness, unpunished infringements of the law, smuggling and embezzlement flourish particularly under a very extensive state administration and in periods of continually changing ordinances and interference with the course of economic life. It was because the *regime de l'ordre* bore this impress that disorder was one of its characteristic features.[21]

The resulting framework for economic policy can be described as economic liberalism in the original sense of the term, and not in the sense of social democracy used in the mid-twentieth century, at least in the United States.[22]

Mill defined explicitly the policy prescriptions of classical economic liberalism. Thus, it is useful to look at the justifiable government interventions listed in his *Principles*. He begins his chapter "Of the Grounds and Limits of the Laissez-faire or Non-interference Principle,"[23] by distinguishing two types of intervention. The first he calls *authoritative* interference (p. 305), by which he means legal prohibitions on private actions. Mill argues on moral grounds that such prohibitions should be limited to actions that affect the interests of others.

But, even here, "the onus of making out a case always lies on the defenders of legal prohibitions. Scarcely any degree of utility, short of absolute necessity, will justify a prohibitory regulation, unless it can also be made to recommend itself to the general conscience" (pp. 306–7).

The second form of intervention he calls *government agency*, which exists "when a government, instead of issuing a command and enforcing it by penalties, [gives] advice and promulgates information . . . or side by side with their [private agents] arrangements an agency of its own for like purpose" (p. 305). Thus the government can provide various public goods (the examples Mill gives are banking, education, public works, and medicine) without prohibiting private supply.

Most of the government interventions Mill allows belong to this second category. But he warns against their costs: They have large fiscal consequences; they increase the power of the government;[24] "every additional function undertaken by government, is a fresh occupation imposed upon a body already charged with duties," so that "most things are ill done; much not done at all" (p.. 309); and the results of government agency are likely to be counterproductive. In a passage that seems prophetic for many public enterprises in developing countries, he writes:

> The inferiority of government agency, for example, in any of the common operations of industry or commerce, is proved by the fact, that it is hardly ever able to maintain itself in equal competition with individual agency, where the individuals possess the requisite degree of industrial enterprise, and can command the necessary assemblage of means. All the facilities which a government enjoys of access to information; all the means which it possesses of remunerating, and therefore of commanding the best available talent in the market—are not an equivalent for the one great disadvantage of an inferior interest in the result. (P. 311)

On these grounds he concludes:

> Few will dispute the more than sufficiency of these reasons, to throw, in every instance, the burden of making out a strong case, not on those who resist, but on those who recommend, government interference. Laissez-faire, in short, should be the general practice: every

departure from it, unless required by some great good, is a certain evil. (P. 314)

But Mill also provides a bridge to the ideas that were later to undermine economic liberalism. The most important of these was the socialist ideal of equality, which was later used to develop a powerful antidote to the liberal tradition through Marxism and was implemented as state socialism by the Bolsheviks. Thus Mill allows various forms of government agency, many of which echo what later came to be recognized as causes of market failure that could seem to justify appropriate government intervention. Such causes might be externalities in the provision of basic education and public services like lighthouses and the need to supervise financial institutions against fraud, or to resolve various forms of what today would be called Prisoner's Dilemmas. Mill also cited the relief of poverty as another possible reason for government intervention:

> The question arises whether it is better that they should receive this help exclusively from individuals, and therefore uncertainly and casually, or by systematic arrangements in which society acts through its organ, the state. . . . The claim to help, . . . created by destitution, is one of the strongest which can exist; and there is *prima facie* the amplest reason for making the relief of so extreme an exigency as certain to those who require it, as by any arrangements in society it can be made. On the other hand, in all cases of helping, there are two sets of consequences to be considered; the consequences of the assistance, and the consequences of relying on the assistance. The former are generally beneficial, but the latter, for the most, part, injurious; so much so, in many cases, as greatly to outweigh the value of the benefit. And this is never more likely to happen than in the very cases where the need of help is the most intense. There are few things for which it is more mischievous that people should rely on the habitual aid of others, than for the means of subsistence, and unhappily there is no lesson which they more easily learn. The problem to be solved is therefore one of peculiar nicety as well as importance; how to give the greatest amount of needful help, with the smallest encouragement to undue reliance on it. (Pp. 333–34)

This is a prescient summary of both the attractions and pitfalls of welfare programs, which have since been validated empirically in many developed and developing countries alike.[25]

Indeed, nowhere in Mill's authoritative text on nineteenth-century economic liberalism do we find any hint that its principles worked against the state, or the poor, as has been charged by modern thinkers.[26] It is important to recognize, however, that although liberalism granted these important exceptions to Mill's "*practical maxim*, that the business of society can be best performed by private and voluntary agency" (p. 345), what Keynes called the "laissez-faire dogma" had become entrenched among the political classes.[27] But this "dogma" was not completely without its uses. As Hecksher notes,

> Free competition, individualism and the limitation of state encroachment often became pure dogmas among practical men of affairs and politicians . . . without any conscious rational foundations. That such a normative outlook existed is, in itself, by no means a criticism of laissez-faire. *Some norm or other is always behind conscious action, for every action presupposes such a conception of the norm as, in itself, is not demonstrable.* Here it was a question, in fact, not of science, but of economic policy, that is not of thought but action.[28] (Emphasis added)

This liberal "disposition toward public affairs," to use Keynes's phrase did not, however, outlast the economic nationalism and socialism that arose in Europe toward the end of the nineteenth century, and, more important, after the First World War.[29]

Diverse social and intellectual trends, including important advances in scientific economics, led to the subsequent development in the post-1930s world of what I have labeled the dirigiste dogma.[30] The various forms of discretionary government intervention, most cogently justified on grounds of market failure within the so-called Arrow-Debreu paradigm, provided the intellectual ballast for a new form of mercantilism, particularly in the third world. Can anyone doubt that the ensuing mercantilist view of social causation also underlies our modern-day optimal tax theory, planning in its various forms, and the discretionary use of public action to correct the perceived ills of private agency? In the modern variant of mercantilism, of course, the objective of economic policy is no longer the welfare of the state but the welfare of the citizens, as summarized in a social welfare function *laid down by the state*. Hecksher writes:

> The underlying idea of mercantilism may be expressed as follows: people should be taken as they are and should be guided by wise measures in the direction which will enhance the well being of the state. No one was more explicit in this view than Mandeville (1723). "Private vices," he observed, "*by the dexterous management of a skilful politician* maybe turned into public benefits."[31]

The consequences of the neomercantilist practices that the dirigiste dogma has engendered in the third world (and in its macroeconomic aspects in the first world), not to mention in the wholly centralized socialist states of the communist world, are very similar to those that helped undermine the mercantilist states of seventeenth- and eighteenth-century Europe.[32] The contemporary reaction (as in the past) has been to move toward economic liberalism, in large part to gain state control over unmanageable economies. This recent worldwide movement toward economic liberalism, embracing governments of all political complexions, has been labeled a new age of reform by OECD observer David Henderson. But it is still progessing half-heartedly, in part because the dirigiste dogma continues to have a hold on the minds of the thinking (or as Prime Minister Thatcher calls them, the "chattering") classes. There are a number of reasons for this state of affairs.

The first reason is self-interest. Enlightened government intervention (the neomercantilist objective) requires experts. The rise of the professional classes is well documented in Britain.[33] "It is professionals, whose power lies in expertise and in the rent they are able to extract for that, who have come to run the country . . . Its natural base was the state; its preferred model, what was later called corporatism."[34] These mandarins are, for self-interested reasons, supporters of the dirigiste dogma.

As we have seen, however, two other currents flow through the dirigiste dogma. The first is the belief initially propounded by Mill that questions of allocation can be separated from those concerning the distribution of income:

> The laws and conditions of the production of wealth, partake of the characters of physical truth. There is nothing optional, or arbitrary in them . . . It is not so with the distribution of wealth. That is a matter of human institution solely. The things once there, mankind, individually or collectively, can do with them as they like. They can place

> them at the disposal of whomsover they please and on whatever terms.[35]

This view, with its implicit support for what is technocratically called the social welfare maximization of an objective function encompassing both efficiency and equity, has since become the staple of every modern textbook on public policy. But it is at odds with the view of the classical thinkers, including Marx.[36] Economic history—not merely of the sample of developing countries Myint and I recently examined,[37] but also that of many Western economies and (as is increasingly apparent to their own rulers) also of commmunist countries—has shown that the efficiency-equity trade-off is a chimera, because it creates enormous information and incentive problems.

The second current, another legacy of Mill, is the neglect of the polity. This neglect has reached its apotheosis in contemporary technocratic economics, which assumes that the two fundamental theorems of welfare economics derived within the Arrow-Debreu framework are to be *applicable in practice* to any polity when it comes to policy analysis. The same framework, however, provides an antidote to this problem that is gaining increasing attention. According to Partha Dasgupta, one of the more distinguished theorists of this technocratic mold,

> The operational appeal of the Fundamental Theorem of Welfare Economics is of course minimal. The informational requirements for the state are awesome. It is required to know the preferences, endowments and the (personalised) production set of all individuals. These observations alone suggest that individual rights to certain private decisions may not only be a moral imperative, but may at once be a necessity prompted by the fact that the state possesses incomplete information.[38]

With support from the recent mathematical economic literature on "incentive compatibility," Dasgupta illustrates the problems this approach raises for a command economy run by mandarins, as Hayek and Mises pointed out at the start of the "planning debate" in the 1930s.[39] The only feasible incentive-compatible mechanism for allocating resources in this framework is not a command economy but one that achieves a full optimum by working through the price mechanism supplemented by optimal taxes and subsidies.

The question is, what sort of mandarins would be needed to design and administer optimal taxes? To achieve the desired outcomes, the mandarins would have to be "economic eunuchs" (in Professor James Buchanan's apt phrase), as Dasgupta has also pointed out:

> It has been an abiding shortcoming of applied welfare economics that it has for the overwhelming part supposed a perfect government—one that faithfully goes about its tasks. But if one addresses oneself to the question of what incentives there must be to ensure that governments undertake their tasks faithfully one is, at a minimum faced with the principal-agent problem with all its attendant difficulties.[40]

Both events (experience) and ideas have therefore undermined the postwar dirigiste dogma. Above all, particularly in the third and second worlds, the undesirable consequences of post–World War II neomercantilism—*not least for the state*—have made a return to economic liberalism possible, as did the consequences of seventeenth- and eighteenth-century mercantilism.

Toward an Economic Liberal Framework for Policy

A succinct restatement of the case for economic liberalism and what it does and does not entail has recently been provided by David Henderson:

> The objections to economic liberalism and the market economy centre round the role of governments and states, both nationally and internationally. For many people liberalism goes with laissez-faire, which in turn is viewed as outdated, negative, unconcerned with what happens to weaker members of society and de facto favouring the stronger, and uncompromisingly negative in its attitude to the state. This rests on a double misconception. First, it distorts the message of laissez-faire. Second, it wrongly identifies belief in a market economy with an extreme interpretation of the laissez-faire principle.
>
> As to the first point, laissez-faire gets an undeservedly bad press. The message it conveys is not that governments should be inert or indifferent. Its emphasis is a positive one. It is concerned with economic freedom, including the freedom of individuals and enterprises to enter industries or occupations, to choose their place of

> residence or operation within a country, and to decide their own products, processes and markets. There is nothing outdated about these principles, nor do they operate against the weak. To the contrary, they enable opportunities to be opened up more widely, and thus operate against special privileges within an economic system. It is no accident that outside the communist world the economy which most conspicuously departs from laissez-faire is that of the Republic of South Africa.
>
> In any case, liberalism is not to be identified with hostility to the state, nor with a doctrinaire presumption that governments have only a minor role in economic life. On the contrary, the liberal view of the role of the state, both internal and external, is strongly positive.[41]

What is even more important, however, the widespread acceptance of economic liberalism as a *practical maxim* would in all likelihood put a stop to the activities of the ubiquitous rent-seeking predatoriness of many third world states, as it did briefly in the liberal phase in Europe. It would provide some internalized commitments against those neomercantilist interventions of the state that have impaired growth performance and thus reduced the chances for alleviating poverty in many countries.

One of the main conclusions of the Lal-Myint study is that the mainsprings of growth (entrepreneurship, productivity, and thrift) can best be fostered within an economic framework that maintains relatively stable property rights. Various forms of dirigiste interventions upset the stability of these rights and hence increase the fog in which economic agents undertake their actions. The ignorance-based, externality-creating form of investment that Scott has recently emphasized as a source of growth, is considerably more difficult to undertake in such an environment.[42]

Many economic historians have argued that the European growth miracle of the eighteenth and nineteenth centuries is directly related to the creation of property rights that are broadly associated with a market economy.[43] These property rights made it possible to curb the inherent predatory power of the state through various forms of taxation based on representation. The resulting liberal economic framework gave freer rein to the entrepreneurial talents and instincts of private agents. The classical thinkers and their modern-day successors, the neo-Austrians, have always emphasized that the entrepreneur plays an important role in an economic environment characterized by ignorance, which, *faute de mieux*, is characteristic of the kinds of forward-looking investment decisions that typically fuel the growth process.[44] Investment efficiency depends just as much on free entry by potential competitors as it does on departure by unviable firms. This freedom of entry and exit by entrepreneurs must not be impaired, as it often is by dirigiste interventions.

These classical and neo-Austrian insights are not available to the technocratic tradition that now dominates public policy, since the entrepreneur is redundant in neoclassical economics, which assumes an environment of purely actuarial Knightian uncertainty.[45] But he is at the center of the neo-Austrian stage, creating and searching out investment opportunities and gambling on the future. The liberal economic framework allows this entrepreneurial function (which, even though unquantifiable, is undeniably at the heart of the growth process) its fullest play. The neomercantilist policies of most third world countries divert these entrepreneurial talents and resources away from productive activities into the zero-sum redistributive games involved in wasteful lobbying and rent seeking.[46] By contrast, the liberal economic framework provides the necessary incentives for entrepreneurship, productivity, and thrift. These qualities (and their determinants) are only dimly understood by economists in a formal sense. But at bottom they are the mainsprings of sustained and sustainable economic growth.

The two most important features of the liberal economic framework are its emphasis on Gladstonian finance and on sound money. The requirements of the latter are self-evident. The nature of the former is less well known and has stirred more debate. Schumpeter lists three basic principles of Gladstonian finance: (1) *Retrenchment* means that "the most important thing [is] to remove fiscal obstructions to private activity. And for this, it [is] necessary to keep public expenditure low." (2) *Neutrality* implies "rais[ing] the revenue that would still have to be raised in such a way as to deflect economic behaviour as little as possible from what it would have been in the absence of all taxation." (3) *Balance* refers to the principle of the balanced budget, or rather, since debt is to be reduced, "the principle that Robert Lowe . . . embodied in his definition of a minister of finance: 'an animal that ought to have a surplus.'"[47]

A recent OECD study concludes that the present-day concerns and objectives of most OECD countries, irrespective of their political complexion, seem to revolve around reinstituting the principles of Gladstonian finance in their economies.[48] Nevertheless, many mainstream economists, who are increasingly seen as irrelevant by governments and their populace in most of these countries, remain wedded to the highly sophisticated and interventionist optimal tax theory of F. P. Ramsey and his followers.

This theory assumes that "the government has coherent, unified and largely benevolent objectives, captured in the social welfare function, and we search for ways in which the tools available to it can be used to improve the measure of welfare."[49] That the theory does not apply to most developing countries is patently obvious, since their polities do not even come close to these assumptions about their character.

Once a predatory state or rent-seeking society is accepted as the norm, however, the pattern of optimal taxes envisioned by Ramsey—even from the point of view of a *neutral outside observer*—is no longer desirable. Thus,

> the well known inverse elasticity rule which calls for concentrating excise taxation on inelastically demanded commodities in order to minimise the social cost for acquiring a given amount of tax revenue is altered by the existence of rent-seeking. Rent-seeking increases the marginal social cost of excise taxation across commodities in such a way as to confound the traditional result. It can easily follow that the correct pattern of excises is to tax relatively more elastic demand curves first.[50]

An important distinction to make concerning the neutrality of taxation is that in the optimal tax tradition this means minimizing the deadweight costs of taxation, whereas in Gladstonian finance the term refers to the generality or uniformity of a tax.[51] A number of arguments (apart from rent seeking) can be made against the former and in favor of the latter, classical prescription of neutrality.

First, Ramsey's optimal taxation is based on the assumuption that even though nonuniform taxation tends to encourage individuals to shift their demands and supplies from taxed to nontaxed goods and activities, such leakages will be small. Only if tastes are given, as optimal tax theorists assume, will such counterproductive behavior, from their viewpoint, not arise. Second, as Harberger has argued,

> Economic theory assumes that the dominant source is substitution. . . . There is thus a very strong presumption that broadening the coverage and lowering the rate of a uniform tax will reduce the deadweight loss. . . . One can build policy on this basis without having any detailed knowledge of the parameters of supply and demand, without any particular hope of gaining anything more than a very patchy knowledge about them in the future, and indeed *with* an almost absolute assurance that wherever the relevant parameters might be now, they will undergo substantial changes in the future. If one believes that these conditions come close to describing our present and likely future state of knowledge about the relevant parameters he will likely be predisposed toward uniform as against Ramsey-rule taxation.[52]

Finally, as Harberger notes, "to tax salt more heavily than sugar" on Ramsey-optimal lines "simply and solely because it has a lower elasticity of demand is at least as capricious (from the standpoint of equity) as taxing people differently according to the colour of their eyes." The main difference between the two approaches to neutrality in taxation, according to Harberger, is their different philosophies of government, one of which corresponds to the classical liberal view, the other to the neomercantilist social-engineering view.[53] I have drawn attention in this essay to the importance of using the former and the perils of relying on the latter as a framework for public policy geared toward poverty-alleviating growth in the third world.

Concluding Remarks

To understand the differing wealth of nations, we need to return to the concerns and perspectives of the classical thinkers, but without abandoning our powerful theoretical and statistical tools. Mercantilism, in its various guises, remains the dominant impediment to the attainment of that poverty-redressing growth that many developing countries have shown to be feasible for all the countries of the third world. In fighting mercantilism—old or new—these countries should make it their top priority to establish a policy framework that emphasizes economic freedom (misleadingly called laissez-faire), in the classical sense.

NOTES

The research on which this paper is based is part of a comparative study funded by the World Bank, "The Political Economy of Poverty, Equity and Growth." Parts of the discussion are based on Chapters 8 and 11 of the draft synthesis, which I cowrote with Hla Myint. The final version, D. Lal & H. Myint, *The Political Economy of Poverty, Equity and Growth*, will be published for the World Bank by Oxford University Press.

1. See I. M. D. Little, *Economic Development* (New York: Basic Books, 1982).

2. This was published in the *ECAFE Survey 1969* and subsequently issued as *The Implications of Economic Controls and of Liberalisation*, ECAFE Growth Studies Series, no.6 (Bangkok: United Nations, 1969).

3. I. M. D. Little, T. Scitovsky, and M. Fg. Scott, *Industry and Trade in Some Developing Countries* (Oxford: Oxford University Press, 1970).

4. W. M. Corden, *Trade Policy and Economic Welfare* (Oxford: Clarendon Press, 1974).

5. The debate about protection in the United Kingdom in the mid-1970s clearly demonstrated that this lesson had yet to be learned by developed as well as developing countries. See my exchange with Edmund Dell, then secretary of trade and industry in the United Kingdom, in D. Lal, "The Wistful Mercantilism of Mr. Dell," *The World Economy*, June 1978; E. Dell, "The Wistful Liberalism of Deepak Lal," ibid., May 1979; Lal, "Politicians, Economists and Protection—the Deaf Meet the Blind," ibid., September 1980. For critiques of two other proponents of protection in the United Kingdom, see Lal, "Mr. John Biffen M.P. at the Pearly Gates," ibid., March 1982; and Lal, "Comment" [on R. Nield], in R. Major, ed., *Britain's Trade and Exchange Rate Policies* (London: Heinemann, 1979).

6. This work was published as part of a general book on Indian planning, *Prices for Planning—Towards the Reform of Indian Planning* (London: Heinemann, 1981).

7. D. Lal, *The Hindu Equilibrium*, vol. 1, *Cultural Stability and Economic Stagnation, India c1500BC–1980AD*; vol. 2, *Aspects of Indian Labour* (Oxford: Clarendon Press, 1988, 1989).

8. D. Lal, "The Political Economy of the Predatory State," Development Research Department Discussion Paper no. 105 (Washington, D.C.: World Bank, 1984), published as Chapter 13.2 of *The Hindu Equilibrium*, vol. 1; Lal, "The Political Economy of Industrialisation in Primary Product Export Economies: Some Cautionary Tales," in N. Islam, ed., *The Balance Between Industry and Agriculture*, vol. 5, *Factors Influencing Change* (London: International Economic Association and Macmillan, 1989); Lal, "After the Debt Crisis: Modes of Development for the Longer Run in Latin America," in S. Edwards and F. Larraine, eds., *The Aftermath of the Debt Crisis* (Oxford: Blackwell, in press).

9. D. Lal and H. Myint, *The Political Economy of Poverty, Equity and Growth* (London: University College, January 1990), photocopy. A revised version is to be published for the World Bank by Oxford University Press.

10. In *The Poverty of Development Economics* (London: International Economic Association, 1983; Cambridge, Mass.: Harvard University Press, 1985).

11. See, for instance, J. Schumpeter, *A History of Economic Analysis* (New York: Oxford University Press, 1954).

12. I noted this explicitly in *The Poverty of Development Economics*. This is also a major theme in H. De Soto, *The Other Path* (New York: Harper & Row, 1989).

13. This was also the period in which the philosophical scene was alight with the controversies surrounding the great books by J. Rawls and R. Nozick. I examined the growing distributivist literature emerging from many international organizations in the 1970s, in the context of these philosophical debates, in "Distribution and Development: A Review Article," *World Development* 4 (September 1976).

14. D. Lal, *Poverty, Power and Prejudice: The North-South Confrontation*, Fabian Research Series 340 (London: Fabian Society, December 1978).

15. D. Lal, "Nationalism, Socialism and Planning: Influential Ideas in the South," *World Development* 13 (June 1985).

16. D. Vital, *The Inequality of States* (Oxford: Clarendon Press, 1967): 5. Also see D. Lal, *Appraising Foreign Investment* (London: Heineman Educational Books, 1975).

17. E. Hecksher, *Mercantilism*, 2 vols., rev. 2d ed., (London: Allen & Unwin, 1955): 21, 22. The original Palgrave has the following entry on mercantilism. It notes that the various mercantilist measures undertaken in the sixteenth and seventeenth centuries were

> the result of the efforts of statesmen so to direct the economic forces of their time as to create a strong and independent state. The object of the mercantile system was the creation of an industrial and commercial state in which by encouragement or restraint imposed by the sovereign authority, private and

> sectional interests should be made to promote national strength and independence. . . . There are many points of resemblance between the mercantile system and state socialism. An organised industrial and commercial state is an ideal common to both, and many of the measures adopted under the former would no doubt reappear if any considerable approach to the latter took place.

"Mercantile System" in *Dictionary of Political Economy*, vol. 2, ed. by R. H. Inglis Palgrave (London: Macmillan, 1896): 727. The author of the entry was W. A. S. Hewins, then director of the London School of Economics.

18. J. M. Keynes, *The End of Laissez-Faire* (London: Hogarth Press, 1928): 12.

19. For a fuller elaboration and references, see De Soto, *The Other Path*.

20. See D. Lal, "The Political Economy of Economic Liberalization," *World Bank Economic Review*, January 1987.

21. Hecksher, *Mercantilism*, 325.

22. Schumpeter noted "the term has acquired a different—in fact almost, the opposite meaning—since about 1900 and especially since 1930 . . . as a supreme, if unintended compliment, the enemies of the system of private enterprise have thought it wise to appropriate its label," *History*, 394.

23. J. S. Mill, *Principles of Political Economy*, ed. Donald Winch (London: Pelican Classics, 1970). This is Chapter 11 of Book 5. Page numbers cited are from the Pelican edition.

24. Mill is not sanguine with the consequence that "the public collectivity is abundantly ready to impose, not only its generally narrow views of its interests, but its abstract opinions, and even its tastes, as laws binding individuals" (p. 308).

25. See Lal and Myint, *The Political Economy of Poverty, Equity and Growth*.

26. The refurbished modern text on economic liberalization remains F. Hayek, *The Constitution of Liberty* (London: Routledge and Kegan Paul, 1960). This point is argued more fully in T. Sowell, *Classical Economics Reconsidered* (Princeton, N.J.: Princeton University Press, 1977).

27. Keynes, *The End of Laissez-Faire*.

28. Hecksher, *Mercantilism*, vol. 2, 331.

29. Keynes, *The End of Laissez-Faire*, 5. Keynes cites Cairnes's introductory lecture "Political Economy and Laissez Faire," delivered at University College, London, in 1870, as the first by an orthodox economist to launch a frontal attack upon laissez-faire in general. That the socialist ends had grudgingly come to be accepted, however, is noted by Keynes, who quotes Cannan: "Scarcely a single English economist of repute, as Professor Cannan has expressed it, 'will join in a frontal attack upon socialism in general,'" although, as he adds, "nearly every economist, whether of repute or not, is

always ready to pick holes in most socialistic proposals." Keynes, *The End of Laissez-Faire*, 26. Of course Keynes himself explicitly claimed that his views were descended directly from the mercantilists in his *General Theory*. For a scathing critique of Keynes's support of mercantilism, see Hecksher, *Mercantilism*, vol. 2, Appendix, "Keynes and Mercantilism." As Keynes noted,

> experience in the organisation of socialised production has left some near observers optimistically anxious to repeat it in peace conditions. War socialism unquestionably achieved a production of wealth on a scale far greater than we ever knew in peace for though the goods and services delivered were destined for immediate and fruitless extinction, none the less they were wealth. (P. 35)

30. Lal, *The Poverty of Development Economics*, 25. Two books by A. O. Hirschman are important in exploring the changing fortunes of economic liberalism: *The Passions and the Interests—Political Arguments for Capitalism before Its Triumph* (Princeton, N.J.: Princeton University Press, 1977); and *Shifting Involvements—Private Interest and Public Action* (Princeton, N.J.: Princeton University Press, 1982).

31. Hecksher, *Mercantilism*, vol. 2, 293.

32. Although in this section I am emphasizing the evolution of ideas and relating them to changing policy regimes, this does not imply that I necessarily subscribe to the view most celebratedly propounded by Keynes, that ideas (often defunct) determine policies. On the lines of the new political economy, it is as likely that interests determine events, including changes in policy regime, and if these are far reaching, a new set of ideas may emerge (or reemerge) to rationalize them. That ideas lag behind events moved by interest seems to me as valid a position to take on the interaction of ideas and interests as the self-serving view of Keynes and many economists that ideas necessarily determine policy. For an interesting discussion of the issues, see the recent collection of essays from a Liberty Fund Conference published by the Institute of Economic Affairs, *Ideas, Interests and Consequences* (London, 1989).

An interest-based explanation for the rise and demise of mercantilism is provided by R. E. Ekelund and R. J. Tollison, *Mercantilism as a Rent-Seeking Society* (College Station: Texas A & M University Press, 1985).

33. See, for instance, the recent book by Harold Perkin, *The Rise of Professional Society: England since 1880* (London: Routledge and Kegan Paul, 1988); and the excellent review of this by Geoffrey Hawthorn, "A Triumph of Self-Interest," *Times Literary Supplement*, July 14–20, 1989, 266. In *The End of Laissez-Faire* Keynes explicitly recommended corporatism as his preferred form of economic organization.

34. Hawthorn, "A Triumph," 266.

35. Mill, *Principles*, Book 2, Chap. 1, 349–50.

36. John Gray, *Hayek on Liberty* (Oxford: Blackwell, 1984), 102, notes that Hayek has always recognized that Mill began the

> "manna from heaven" presumption of contemporary distributist theories. It may be said that what distinguishes Mill from Hayek—and, for that matter, from Marx—is Mill's lack of any clear view of production and distribution as inseparable parts of a single economic system. We may have a choice between economic systems (though it is the burden of the Mises-Hayek-Polanyi argument about resource allocation under socialism that our freedom is far more restricted than we suppose); we do not have the freedom to mix the productive arrangements of one system with the distributive arrangements of another. This is a truth understood by all classical economists, including Marx, which Mill's influence has helped to obscure.

37. In Lal and Myint, *The Political Economy of Poverty*.
38. P. Dasgupta, "Decentralisation and Rights," *Economica* 47 (May 1980): 112.
39. See F. Hayek, ed., *Collectivist Economic Planning* (London: Routledge, 1935).
40. Dasgupta, "Decentralisation," 119.
41. D. Henderson, *Innocence and Design—The Influence of Economic Ideas on Policy* (Oxford, Blackwell, 1986): 98–99.
42. M. Fg. Scott, *A New View of Economic Growth* (Oxford: Clarendon Press, 1989).
43. For instance, Hicks, North, and Braudel.
44. The early neoclassicists like Alfred Marshall were conscious of the importance of entrepreneurship. See, for instance, Marshall's "The Social Possibilities of Economic Chivalry," in A. C. Pigou, ed., *Memorials of Alfred Marshall*, especially 331–32. Keynes, of course, apart from attacking thrift also denigrated businessmen (see his comments on Marshall in this context in *The End of Laissez-Faire*, 36–38), picking up on a common sentiment among the educated bourgeoisie of which he was a self-confessed member. See his "Am I Liberal?" in his *Essays in Persuasion* (New York: W. W. Norton, 1963): 324. For the rise and growth of antibusiness sentiment among the English chattering classes, see M. Wiener, *English Culture and the Decline of the Industrial Spirit* (Cambridge: Cambridge University Press, 1981).
45. For a fuller discussion, see Lal, "Markets, Mandarins and Mathematicians," *Cato Journal* 7, no. 1 (1987). For the importance of entrepreneurship, see the detailed analysis in Alwyn Young's chapter on Hong Kong in R. Findlay and S. Wellisz, *Five Small Island Economies* (Oxford: Oxford University Press, in press). For a study that questions the usual pessimistic view about entrepreneurship in Africa, see W. Elkan, "Entrepreneurs and Entrepreneurship in Africa," *World Bank Research Observer* 3, no. 2 (July 1988): 171–88.

46. The seminal contributions on this phenomenon are by G. Tullock and A. Krueger, which are collected with various others in J. M. Buchanan, R. D. Tollison, and G. Tullock, eds., *Toward a Theory of the Rent-Seeking Society* (College Station: Texas A & M University Press, 1980).

47. Schumpeter, *History of Economic Analysis*, 403–5. Also see Henderson's lecture to the Institute of Fiscal Studies, "A New Age of Reform?" (1989), in which he notes the increasing acceptance of these principles in the fiscal policies of developed countries.

48. Organization for Economic Cooperation and Devlopment, *Economies in Transition* (Paris, 1989), cited in D. Henderson, "A New Age of Reform?"

49. A technically sophisticated and comprehensive application of these principles to developing countries is to be found in N. Stern and D. Newbery, *The Theory of Taxation for Developing Countries* (New York: Oxford University Press, 1987): 653. But they themselves acknowledge,

> The book is silent on the positive theory of public finance. The reason is not that we regard the study of ways in which policies are actually determined as uninteresting. . . . Rather we think it is important to discover what would be desirable even when it may be currently politically infeasible or when prudence cautions against creating an institutional framework to administer proposed taxes. (P. 14)

50. D. R. Lee and R. D. Tollison, "Optimal Taxation in a Rent-Seeking Environment," in C. K. Rowley, R. D. Tollison, and G. Tullock, eds., *The Political Economy of Rent-Seeking* (Boston: Kluwer Academic Publishers, 1988): 349.

51. See A. C. Harberger, "Neutral Taxation," in *The New Palgrave*, ed. J. Eatwell, M. Milgate, and P. Newman (London: Macmillan, 1987) 3: 645–47, for a lucid and important discussion of these traditions of "neutrality" in public finance, one classical, the other neoclassical, if we may so term them. The following discussion draws heavily on this source.

52. Harberger, "Neutral Taxation."

53. Thus Harberger writes:

> Consider the philosophy of government that assigns to governments the role of creating a framework of laws and regulations within which the private sector then is encouraged to operate freely. Under this philosophy a positive value is placed on the authorities not caring what private agents do. . . . It is a positive desideratum to create a tax system that is robust against changes in risks and technology. . . . On the other side of the coin we have a philosophy of social engineering in which the detailed tastes and technology of the society enter as data into a process by which the polity makers choose parameters such as tax rates and coverages so as to maximise some social measure of social benefit. (P. 646)

World Development, Vol. 13, No. 6, pp. 749–759, 1985.
Printed in Great Britain.

0305–750X/85 $3.00 + 0.00
Pergamon Press Ltd.

Nationalism, Socialism and Planning: Influential Ideas in the South*

DEEPAK LAL†
University College London
and
The World Bank, Washington, D.C.

Summary. — The paper discusses the origin of three influential ideas in the South, the reasons why they are found persuasive by Southern elites, and finally whether they are helpful in promoting modernization. It argues that all three ideas are Janus-faced, combining the 'modern' aspects of the rationalist Enlightenment with the partly 'pre-modern' rural nostalgia of the Romantic movement. But the ideas are dysfunctional in terms of the desired aims of 'nation-building' and attaining material progress. Nationalism, far from being an adhesive can become a disintegrative force in pluralistic societies. Planning becomes a means of suppressing the agents of the economic modernization that is desired. The waving of the Enlightenment and socialist banner of equality in suppressing the merchant, financier and entrepreneur is a smokescreen. The suppression reflects more atavistic impulses, which amount to a denial of the irreducible uncertainty that unavoidably attends commercialization, monetization and industrialization.

This paper is concerned with a set of ideas commonly associated with at least the official rhetoric of those countries that, though far from forming a homogenous category, are nevertheless collectively identified nowadays as the South.[1] I shall be concerned with the origins of these ideas; the reasons why they are found to be persuasive by Southern elites and their literate populace; and finally, whether (even though persuasive) they are likely to help in the attainment of that modernization envisaged (at least in part) to promote 'economic strength' and a lack of dependence on the West which all these elites wish to foster.

However, these ideas of 'nationalism,' 'socialism' and 'planning' are ambiguous. Nor is their frequent acclamation in the official rhetoric of the South shorn of paradox. For the South contains states that claim to be nations, but where sub-national loyalties and differences based on religion, region or race are rife and the source of deadly conflicts; states that claim to be socialist but in which economic inequalities are often more pronounced and may have been exacerbated by the 'socialist' policies of their rulers even by comparison with that bastion of capitalism — the United States; states that claim to be planned but where planning is little more than an epiphenomenal device for obtaining foreign aid.

At the same time, for many in the West, it is not this acclamation of basically Western ideas that distinguishes the South, but the values of spirituality, community and those primordial ties embodied in small-scale and more human forms of economic organization that characterize pre-modern cultural traditions — themselves assertively advertised by the cultural nationalists of these states.

The roots of this modern 'rural nostalgia,'[2] as I shall term it, do provide the key to understanding both the origins and nature of the three seemingly 'modern' ideas of nationalism, socialism and planning, as well as in explaining their persuasive power and in judging their usefulness in promoting modernization in the South.

---

*This paper was prepared for the Fourth Annual Sewanee Economics Symposium on 'The West, Communism, and the Third World,' 3–5 March 1983. The views expressed herein are those of the author and should not be attributed to the World Bank or to its affiliated organizations.

†Professor of Political Economy, University College London (on leave) and Research Administrator, The World Bank, Washington, D.C.

I

Broadly speaking, most pre-modern societies were agrarian or nomadic pastoralist, which whether they were Greek, Roman, ancient Egyptian, Christian, Islamic, Hindu, Buddhist or animist, shared a view of man essentially different from the 'modern' view propagated by the 18th-century Enlightenment. As Charles Taylor puts it:

> Philosophically speaking, most earlier notions of man defined his 'normal' or optimal condition at least partly in terms of his relation to a larger cosmic order, with which he had to be in tune. The 'modern' view sees him rather as an agent who optimally would use the surrounding world as a set of instruments and enabling conditions with which to effect the purposes which he either found within himself (as 'drives' or desires) or chose freely.[3]

The scientific revolution of the 16th century undercut the metaphysical basis of the pre-modern view of man. The 18th-century Enlightenment provided a rationale for a new view of man, based on 'reason.' The Industrial Revolution — building partly on the scientific one — provided the basis for the material and military progress which so swiftly led to the domination of the world by the West.

The disjunction in men's lives resulting from the Industrial Revolution was matched by that in their minds, flowing from the scientific revolution that undermined the set of beliefs on which men based their identity and conduct in the world. First in the West, and more recently in the South, the pre-modern pictures of the world have been or are being shattered by the progress of industrialization, and the economic growth based on it, which in the words of a French historian: 'began as a European accident and has become an obligatory command for the Whole World.'[4]

But in both the West and the non-Western world there has been a reaction against what Max Weber called the 'disenchantment of the world' flowing from the Enlightenment. This reaction, though it has common roots — insofar as it seeks to rehabilitate some of the pre-modern views of man — has taken different forms in the Western and non-Western world. This is why the beliefs current in the South appear to many Westerners to be recognizable, but confused, and to some extent attractive as well as repellent.

The central ideas of the Enlightenment were: (1) the universality of human nature; and (2) the possibility that at least in principle, scientific methods could be used to discover universal human goals and effective means to subserve them, so that a single, unified and coherent structure of knowledge embracing both questions of fact and value could be discovered. At almost the same time as this view was being formulated, what Berlin has called the 'Counter-Enlightenment,' and others, the 'Romantic Revolt' in Western thought and culture had its beginnings. This was a sustained attack against the universalist, rationalist schema of the Enlightenment and its view that man's relationship to the surrounding world is purely manipulative. As opposed to the Enlightenment ethic (whether utilitarian or Kantian), which ultimately looked upon the human self as being disembodied,[5] the Romantics and all the other counter-movements against the Enlightenment, asserted 'some elementary sense of identity, dignity and worth, against all that patronises and diminishes men, and threatens to rob them of themselves,[6]

> In all cases the organization of life by the application of rational or scientific methods, any form of regimentation or conscription of men for utilitarian ends or organized happiness, was regarded as the philistine enemy.'[7]

It was from this Romantic reaction that European nationalism was born. It initially arose as the reaction of wounded German pride, following the French Revolution and the success of Napoleon's armies, 'against the French cultural domination of the Western world' (Berlin, *op. cit.*). Though nationalism, both in Europe and more recently in the ex-colonies, was in part the reaction of actual or potential elites to military defeat, this can by no means be considered to be a sufficient explanation for this new idea to have arisen. For as Kedourie and Berlin have emphasized, throughout history the cultural or political pride of various people has been wounded without entailing a nationalist response. The special ingredient which led to the nationalist response was the rapid modernization of traditional societies. This modernization was imposed by leaders who were by no means Romantics — such as Frederick the Great in Prussia, Peter the Great in Russia — to acquire the modern material basis of economic and more importantly, military power. The same response was elicited by the westernization imposed by colonialism or those indigenous elites who sought to imitate the West (for instance the Japanese after the Meiji Restoration) in our time.

This modernization disrupted traditional ways of life, and

> left men, and especially the most sensitive among them — artists, thinkers, whatever their professions — without an established position, insecure and bewildered. There is then an effort to create a new synthesis, a new ideology, both to explain and

> justify resistance to the forces working against their convictions and ways of life, and to point in a new direction and offer them a new centre for self-identification.[8]

But, as Plamenatz (1973) has emphasized, the resulting nationalism was of at least two different types, which he labels 'Western' and 'Eastern.' The former was that of the Germans and the Italians, the latter that of the Slavs, the Asians and the Africans. The major difference was that, whereas the 'Western' nationalists already had the cultural appurtenances and skills to put them on a par with the French and English, the 'Eastern' nationalists have had to re-equip themselves culturally with the ideas and practices of an alien civilization.

Moreover, nationalism in Asia and Africa has grown within the arbitrarily defined territorial boundaries of the colonial state. This was no accident. For it was within these colonial boundaries that the West had succeeded in erecting a state:

> a legal and administrative entity which worked, an entity which the West had succeeded in identifying with the nation. As nationalists they felt secure in inheriting such an entity and felt challenged to preserve this entity and make it strong, just and prosperous as the colonial power had never done . . . It is perhaps fitting that nationalism which began as anti-western should end by throwing off western rule in the name of the most western institution of the new order.[9]

Thus, whereas the task as seen by German, Italian and to some extent Slav nationalists was to create a state for a pre-existing cultural and political 'nation,' most African and some Asian nationalists inherited and cherished states created by colonialists, within which they have since sought to create a 'modern' nation.

Thus, Afro-Asian nationalism unlike that of the West has involved two sets of ambivalent rejections:

> rejection of the alien intruder and dominator who is nonetheless to be imitated and surpassed by his own standards, and rejection of ancestral ways which are seen as obstacles to progress and yet also cherished as marks of identity.[10]

After its repudiation of the militarist attempt to challenge the West, Japan is the only country to succeed in this contorted balancing act in establishing a state with a modern identity rooted in traditional culture. Most of the nationalist elites of the Third World are still struggling to find ways of achieving their primary objective of securing their power and prestige against any future challenge from either external foreign intrusions or from any internal subversion by the upholders of the traditional societies they seek to remould. They are all aware of the need both for economic progress as well as for the making of nations out of their subject people, so that they can better defend their sovereignty. 'Socialism' has usually been the formula chosen albeit clothed in indigenous garb, such as 'African socialism' or 'Arab socialism' or Nehru's 'socialistic pattern of society,' to reconcile the ambivalent rejection as well as affirmation of both the native/traditional and alien/modern civilizations.[11]

This is most clearly expressed by Nehru in his *Autobiography*:

> . . . right through history the old Indian ideal did not glorify political and military triumph, and it looked down upon money and the professional money-making class. Honour and wealth did not go together, and honour was meant to go, at least in theory, to the men who served the community with little in the shape of financial reward. Today (the old culture) is fighting silently and desperately against a new all-powerful opponent — the *bania* (Vaishya) civilization of the capitalist West. It will succumb to the newcomer . . .. But the West also brings an antidote to the evils of this cut-throat civilization — the principle of socialism, of cooperation, and service to the community for the common good. This is not so unlike the old Brahmin ideal of service, but the Brahminization — not in the religious sense, of course — of all classes and groups and the abolition of class distinctions.[12]

But why socialism, and is this 'socialism' the same as the Marxist–Leninist doctrines of the East?

II

Again, the Romantic Revolt against the Enlightenment provides the answers. The parentage of the amorphous and fiercely contested set of beliefs labeled as 'socialism' is to be found both in the ideas of the Enlightenment as well as in its Romantic reaction. One strand of socialism has endorsed the Enlightenment view of man. It sees all social and economic structures as open to rationalist manipulation to subserve universal human goals. But an equally important strand has adopted the Romantic critique of the modernization based on the rationalist ideas of the Enlightenment. For as Taylor points out, the Romantic view of man does not return to pre-modern models of man; instead it develops a view of man which Berlin has called 'expressivist.'

> Human life is seen as the external expression of man's potential . . .. [But] the potential which man

> develops is very much his own; it develops out of him, and is not defined by some relations of harmony with a larger order . . .. The expressivist view developed an ideal of communion between men, and between men and nature . . . so that we get with the Romantic peiod something which resembles the pre-modern notions of man as part of a larger order; with this vital difference, that on the earlier views man could only come to himself by finding his right relation to the larger order, whereas now men reach communion with nature by discovering what they really have it in them to express[13]

This expressivist critique of 'modern society as a desert in which everything has been levelled, and all beauty been stamped out to create a mudane servicable world of use-objects'[14] has been taken up by a major strand of the socialist movement, starting with the young Marx, and culminating in the indigenous English socialist tradition represented by William Morris and R. H. Tawney. As the British Fabian socialist tradition combines these two faces of socialism — the manipulative, utilitarian socialism of the Webbs (descendents of the Enlightenement), with the passionate critique of a dehumanizing capitalist society of Morris and Tawney (adherents of the romantic, expressivist tradition) — it is not surprising that some adapted version of Fabianism has been the 'socialism' with most appeal in the Third World; for its formula best reconciles the two ambivalent rejections of the traditional and the modern that is a unique feature of the search for a new identity by the nationalist elites of the Third World.

By contrast, Soviet communism, which in Lenin's apt phrase equals 'Soviet power + electrification,' has only wholeheartedly embraced the Enlightenment strand of socialism. The socialist example set by contemporary communist states has not had much influence in Third World countries, if this influence is measured by imitation,[15] except in those countries which have been directly absorbed into the Soviet ambit or — to use an old-fashioned phrase — empire. This is not because of any squeamishness about the despotism involved in the totalitarian state that the Soviets have established to project their power. For the majority of Third World states are authoritarian — very often military dictatorships. Yet communism is unattractive for most governments, people and armies in the South.

> Most governments in the new states . . . see communists as another of the divisive forces in society, along with tribalism and communalism and so forth.[16]

This is partly because communism is increasingly and correctly perceived as the embodiment of an alien nationalism — Soviet or Chinese — and partly because it does not provide that reconciliation of what Geertz has termed 'essentialism' and 'epochalism' in creating a new national identity.[17]

Instead the socialism espoused by the new states is more likely to degenerate into various forms of populism — for instance Peronism in Argentina, or the '*garibi hatao*' (remove poverty) election sloganeering of Mrs. Gandhi's Congress party. Moreover, in their search for a 'nation' (both traditional and modern) to fit the territorial states they have inherited from the colonial period, Southern political elites find it increasingly useful to revert to the politics of their pre-colonial past, though, of course, suitably refurbished in modernist ideological garb. Thus the proliferation of 'guided' and 'basic' democracies, 'African,' 'Tanzanian,' 'Islamic' socialism, 'Consciencism,' 'Humanism,' and all the other faintly ridiculous official ideologies of the Third World. But these are charades to conceal the reality of a reversion to more indigenous political forms — the tribal chief (but where the different tribes in the territorial state are to be merged into a single party representing a nation) of Africa; the 'chakravartin' ruler of ancient Hindu India, overcoming the perpetually feuding monarchies of the sub-continent; the 'caudillo' of Latin America, and, of a slightly different variety, of traditional Islam.

> It is in fact just this confusion [Geertz reminds us] of the more recognizable voices of the present with the stranger, but no less insistent voices of the past which makes it so difficult to determine just what the politicians, civilian or military, of any particular Third World state think they are up to.[18]

But it is becoming *less* (rather than as some may believe more) likely that these states are, however imperfectly, seeking to construct a bourgeois democratic polity.

This is hardly surprising, for despite their attachment to liberal ideals in their own polities, most colonial powers constructed and bequeathed essentially authoritarian and bureaucratic states to Afro-Asian political elites.[19] Apart from being closer to the states of their older indigenous traditions than the liberal democratic states of the West, this form of bureaucratic state was also perceived to be suited to the task of modernization, where the 'modernizers' considered themselves to be a minority charged with the task of forcing their people to be free. But in subserving this end through promoting economic development, and the development of a truly national consciousness, the 'nationalism' and 'socialism' espoused by these elites have both proved to be double-edged swords, but for different reasons.

III

The process of economic development which all Third World elites seek to foster involves profound changes over time in existing patterns of income distribution, where the latter is not to be thought of in the purely statistical sense, but in terms of what happens to the incomes (and status) of particular households over time. Even without any marked change in the statistical measure of this distribution, economic growth is likely to lead to a considerable, and often rapid shuffling of the relative economic position and prospects of particular individuals. In a genuine nation-state, the ensuing resentment of the 'losers' may be mitigated by the solace they may find in the accompanying national gains. The resentment is, however, unlikely to turn into the deadly conflicts to be found in the pseudo nation-states of the South, with their ancient and still pervasive cleavages of race, religion or tribe, where these shufflings can be so easily identified as the humiliation of one sub-nationality by another. The nationalist rhetoric of the political elite can then rebound (as it has done quite often in the recent past) into demands to dismember the territorial state, whose preservation was the prime end for which nationalism had been conjured up in the first place.[20]

Early German and Italian nationalism was largely integrative and economically beneficial, both because of the larger common market created out of the German and Italian principalites, and the partial containment of political discontent arising from the distributional shuffling involved in economic development. By contrast 'Eastern' nationalism, seeking to build a 'nation' out of the sub-national groups within an inherited state, can lead to a breaking up of the common market, with all its attendant economic damage. Not surprisingly therefore, it is in the relatively homogenous polities of East Asia that nationalism has performed the integrative emotional and economic function that it did in the West. In the more fragile and pluralistic polities of Southeast Asia, South Asia and Africa, by contrast, nationalist rhetoric used to gain independence from colonialism has created as many problems of 'national integration' as it was hoped it would solve.

Nor has the type of Fabian socialism espoused in many Third World countries proved helpful in establishing an economically progressive nation-state. This is in part because of the Enlightenment strand in this form of socialism, which has come to be associated with the notion of 'planning' — a term that like 'socialism' seems to have as many different meanings as adherents. Though for some socialists, planning is synonymous with Soviet practice, this form of detailed material balance planning has not — outside India — had many Southern adherents.[21] However, two aspects of Soviet practice have struck a deep chord and been embodied in the economic policies of many of these countries. The first is a suspicion of the price mechanism, accompanied by attempts to supplant or control its workings. The second is a suspicion of international trade and a preference for the forced industrialization (usually termed 'self-reliance') seemingly so successfully pioneered by the USSR. This suspicion of foreign trade was not purely ideological, but the lesson drawn from the effects of the inter-war collapse of world trade on the economies of those countries most integrated into the world economy.[22]

As a result, the economic policies of most Southern countries have involved supplanting the price mechanism by bureaucratic allocative mechanisms in the form of price controls, industrial licensing, exchange controls and quantitative restrictions on foreign trade. These policies have now become synonymous in these countries with 'planning' and the promotion of 'socialism.'[23] The harm that this irrational dirigisme has done to the end of promoting growth as well as equity (an aim shared by all types of socialists), has now been copiously analyzed and documented for a myriad Third World countries.[24] In practice, therefore, the type of 'socialist planning' usually adopted has made promotion of the economic progress required to provide the material basis for the desired national self-autonomy all that more difficult. But despite this mounting evidence against the dysfunctional nature of much Southern dirigisme, there is a reluctance to alter their economic policies. Why?

IV

Part of the reason lies in the sheer element of plunder which the 'rent-seeking' policies[25] of these modern Revenue Economies allows,[26] a motive of some importance in most pre-modern polities, as well as in some modern ones. But, there is a deeper reason in my view why both Third World elites, as well as many of their Western economic advisers (not to mention many Western governments), find it difficult to accept the utility of what is usually termed a 'market economy' in promoting economic development.

Without singling it out as the prime cause, most economic historians attach great importance in the development of capitalism and that vast expansion in productive potential called the Industrial Revolution to the rise in economic power and social status of the merchant and the financier from the 16th to 18th centuries.[27] However, this rise was not uncontested in the realm of ideas, as it posed severe problems for the existing 'Aristotelian' ethical beliefs of these societies. These essentially concerned the ethical problem of ascribing virtue to the acquisition of wealth by the lending of money.

As Max Weber (1904) has emphasized, at least for pre-modern agrarian societies, 'the canonical prohibition on interest has an equivalent in almost every ethical system in the world.' Whatever functional justifications may be provided for the ban on usury,[28] the ethical revulsion was based on Aristotle's quite unequivocal statement: 'Usury is detested above all and for the best of reasons. It makes profit out of money itself, not for money's natural object . . . .. Money was intended as a means of exchange, not to increase at interest.'[29] This ban on interest, particularly as it related to trade was gradually lifted in the West, if for no other reason than the need for rural credit which, given climatic uncertainty and the time lag between sowing and harvesting, could not be eliminated. 'One went as furtively to visit the moneylender as one went to visit a "whore" — but one went all the same.'[30]

However, ethical worries about the 'unreality' of credit, and of the socially unproductive nature of interest were to surface with a vengeance in early 18th-century England. The Financial Revolution of 1694–96 based on the establishment of the Bank of England and the National Debt, created a vastly expanded credit mechanism, leading to the rise of the rentier. 'The stocks which were his title to a return upon the loans he had made became themselves a commodity, and their value was manipulated by a new class of stockjobbers.'[31]

In the ensuing Augustan debates, this posed a severe problem for the traditional value system shared by both opponents and friends of the new goddess Credit. For the traditional ethical system 'the moral foundation for civic virtue and moral personality is taken to be independence and real property.'[32] Property in the form of land was the most real, and though the trader and the merchant's wealth was moveable, and hence not as reliable in inducing civic virtue as the landlord's, it at least consisted of real things. By contrast, the wealth of the stockholder and the stock jobber created by the new system of public credit appeard to be unreal and fantastical:

> When the commodities to be bought and sold were paper tokens of men's confidence in their rulers and one another, the concept of fantasy could more properly be applied, and could bear the meaning not only of illusion and imagination, but of men's opinions of others' opinions of them.[33]

This is a view of commerce and the speculation it necessarily engenders, which survives to our day — as witness the continuing attacks on speculation in commodity or foreign exchange markets by politicians in the South as well as the West. Lest this be thought to be the untutored prejudice of economic illiterates, one only has to remember Keynes's peroration on the stock market in his *General Theory*,[34] which clearly echoes the above Augustan critique of commerce.

The friends of credit tried to make it seem as much like trade as possible. As Pocock states:

> The more capitalist man's perception could be of real goods in circulation, instead of the mere fluctuating tokens of the exchange media, the more he could perceive other men and himself as real; and this was in itself a powerful motive for depicting mercantile society as based upon trade rather than credit.[35]

The development of the labor theory of value was the next stage in anchoring economic value in reality in the vastly expanded exchange economy made possible by the new credit mechanism.

> If men created by their labor the values of the goods they exchanged, the reality of a world of commodity and commerce would be assured.[36]

It was left to Marx to draw the implication that the labor theory of value far from overcoming the problem of rooting Credit in 'reality,' justified the Augustan critique of the rentier. As Alfred Marshall saw clearly:

> If we admit that it is the product of labor alone, and not of labor and waiting, we can no doubt be compelled by inexorable logic to admit that there is no justification for interest, the reward of waiting; for the conclusion is implied in the premise.[37]

Despite the obvious unacceptability of the labor theory of value in a world of multiple factors of production,[38] the Augustan revulsion against the 'fantasy' of 'interest' and pure 'profit' not tied to concrete productive activity has by no means abated; as witness the heat generated by the contemporary 'Cambridge debates' on capital theory.[39] This was less attributable, in my view, to divergent views about the determinants and ethical justification of the distribution of income in capitalist societies; rather, it occurred because Cambridge, England, thought it had found a flaw in the modern neoclassical theory of general equilibrium, by establishing that, in a capitalist economy 'the rate of profit was purged of any contamination with the technological productivity of plant and equipment' (Solow, 1975). The rentier and the financier were once again shown to be economic parasites, with no economic or moral justification based on the 'real world.' The elimination of these intermediary parasites is, of course, official policy in communist countries, but their euthanasia, along with the pursuit of equality, would also seem to be a shared belief among various feuding socialist sects. I would, however, argue it is an atavistic impluse, as is made transparently clear in the earlier quotation from Nehru.

The reason for the continuing resonance of this atavism in not only Southern, but also many Western breasts, is found in my view, in the new, unparalleled and seemingly man-made uncertainties in economic (and thereby also in social) life that the wholly new type of economic change flowing from the industrial, commercial and financial revolutions since the Renaissance has entailed. There were and are uncertainties primarily connected with the climate (but also with disease and warfare) in relatively closed pre-modern subsistence agrarian economies. These uncertainties could, at least in principle, be reduced to actuarial risk based on the objective probabilities associated with repetitive natural cycles. Moreover, this type of uncertainty could be readily rationalized within that circular and cyclical view of time and history that has seemed to accompany most pre-modern views of man's relationship to the cosmic order. By contrast, the Industrial Revolution led to the introduction of wholly new processes and eventually products. Not only were these based on man's inventions, but also their introduction or eventual viability could not be predicted. For who could tell when some new invention or change in tastes would not make the fixed capital in which the existing technique was embodied redundant? And one distinguishing feature of the new industrialization was its appetite for 'hostages to fortune' in the form of fixed capital. The future in many ways had become irreducibly (uninsurably) uncertain. The world was no longer enclosed in the relatively stable natural cycles of the closed agrarian economy; it had become 'all awhirl,' being subject to all sorts of unforseeable and uninsurable disturbances imposed by the 'Unbound Prometheus.' History was no longer the working of an inexorable natural or cosmic cycle, it was now seen as 'the play of the contingent, the unexpected and the unforeseen' (Fisher, 1936). The Knightian risk associated with the closed stochastic (in the modern statistical sense) processes of Nature, were overtaken by largely new and more incomprehensible and incommensurable Knightian uncertainty attached to the open-ended but now 'stochastic' (in the original literary sense — 'pertaining to conjecture') processes resulting from man's increasing control over Nature.

Shackle (1972) has observed that, in the entire history of economic thought from Adam Smith to Keynes, there is a pervasive 'fear of uncertainty.' This has by no means disappeared even in our own day. The two modern responses to this 'new' irreducible uncertainty of the industrial world are 'planning' — which assumes away the problem by implicitly postulating an omniscient committee of experts which can foretell the future[40] — and more recently theories based on 'rational expectations'[41] — which seek to reduce the Knightian uncertainty of the modern world to the Knightian risk of the closed pre-agrarian world of natural cycles.[42] Both responses are implicit in the Enlightenment program — with its hope of finding social laws of motion similar to those of the natural sciences. What may be termed the epistemological weaknesses of planning are by now well known, but those involved in parts of the rational expectations program of reading the entrails through statistical time series analysis less so.[43] This is not the place to go into these technical debates. I would only like to note that the atavism of denying the Knightian uncertainty involved in the process of modern economic growth is to be found on both sides of the ideological divide.[44]

Is it then surprising that there should be continuing suspicion and misunderstanding of the role of the 'speculator,' the 'financier,' the 'entrepreneur' — those modern agents who live by making money out of Knightian uncertainty? One historian of Western capitalism finds the role of two social types as being central to industrialization — the entrepreneur and the technologist 'one devoted to searching exclusively for profit and the other to scientific and technical progress.'[45] One distinctive feature of much of the South (and the East) is its rejection of the entrepreneur while embracing the technologist or engineer. In particular, they have tended to maintain what McKinnon (1973) has labeled 'financially repressed' economies, so that the mechanisms of commerce and credit, the very lifeblood of the mercantile capitalism that seemed so 'fantastic' to the Augustans, are grossly attenuated. But in giving in to this atavistic impulse, are they not harming their prospects of economic development? Is it a mere coincidence that, as many economic historians have noted, the establishment or a shift of financial centers has marked the spread of economic growth — first from the Mediterranean to the Netherlands, to Britain, to the United States and, in time perhaps to Japan? Is it purely accidental that in the so-called Gang of Four, East Asian countries — the star economic performers in the South — the reduction or absence of 'financial repression' preceded or accompanied their spectacular economic transformation?

V

I have argued that the persuasiveness of all three ideas explored in this paper depends in large part upon their Janus-faced characteristics. They combine the 'modern' aspects of the rationalist Enlightenment with those of a partly 'pre-modern' rural nostalgia embodied in the Romantic movement. This seeming integration of the past with the present is particularly appealing to Southern minds disjointed by foreign domination, seeking both to reject and imitate their 'oppressors' and to repudiate as well as affirm their own traditions. Moreover, it is the atavism in the resulting attitudes in the South that most appeals to many people in the West.

But this rural nostalgia is misplaced in the South. Whatever its role in providing an emotional salve to bruised psyches, it is dysfunctional in terms of the desired aims of 'nation-building' and attaining material progress. Nationalism, far from being an adhesive, can become a disintegrative force in plural Southern societies. Planning becomes the means of suppressing the agents of the economic modernization that is desired. The waving of the Enlightenment and socialist banner of equality in suppressing the merchant, financier and entrepreneur in the South is a smokescreen. The suppression reflects more atavistic impulses that amount to a denial of, or turning their face against, the irreducible uncertainty which unavoidably attends commercialization, monetization and industrialization.

In the West, the appeal of these atavistic impulses reflect its own increasing reluctance to accept change; but this is to repudiate the central value that has led it to its extraordinary material position and influence in the world. It would indeed be ironic if the West were to catch the Southern infection that holds most of the Third, as well as the Second, World in thrall. But that in itself need not mean a worldwide disaster, for there are a number of countries on the Pacific rim that have accepted change as a value. The torch of material civilization might then pass to these mercantile states, if the West decides to repudiate the world it has made in the name of the world it has lost.

NOTES

1. The discussion of nationalism will deal mainly with Asia and Africa. This is because nationalism in Latin America has meant (except for Mexico) that local *white* elites have continued to exercise power over 'a sea of color' (except for the three Southern cone countries), unlike Afro-Asia, where local non-white elites wrested power. Latin America continues to be neocolonial, in a precise sense that is not true of Afro-Asia (see Stein and Stein, 1970). However, as I have argued elsewhere (Lal, 1978) there are enough similarities in the attitude of Latin America and Afro-Asian elites, that for the other ideas we can include them in the South.

2. Its importance in the formation of social attitudes since the mid 19th century in Britain is documented by Weiner.

3. Taylor (1974), p. 49.

4. Baechler (1975), p. 108.

5. See Sandel and Macintyre, who have both shown how the utilitarian and Kantian tradition (the latter encompassing the modern works of Rawls and Nozick) imply a view of man as that of the disembodied self. This allows them to divorce ethics from politics. As Sandel (1982) writes: 'not egoists but strangers sometimes benevolent, make for the citizens of the deontological republic . . . .By putting the self beyond the reach of politics, it makes human agency an article of faith rather than an object of continuing attention and concern, a premise of politics rather than its precarious achievement' (p. 183). By contrast, the Aristotelian tradition, which Macintyre (1981) champions in a powerful book, did not divorce politics from ethics in this way.

6. Hausheer (1979), p. xiv.

7. Berlin (1979), p. 20.

8. *Ibid.*, p. 349.

9. Gungwu (1973), p. 92.

10. Plamentaz (1973), p. 34.

11. There has also been another response, historically, that of the clam. Gandhi's attempt to resurrect a traditional but refurbished Hindu society under the banner of Satyagraha, was only one of many such failed attempts to use tradition to challenge the West. That Gandhi failed in his challenge is cogently argued by Judith Brown. However, it should be noted that this traditional challenge is not exhausted, as witness its most virulent recent eruption in Khomeini's Iran. Whether it will succeed is doubtful.

12. Nehru (1962), p. 431–2.

13. Taylor (1974), p. 50.

14. *Ibid.*, p. 51.

15. See Wiles (1967).

16. Finer (1975), p. 217.

17. 'Essentialism' is defined by Geertz (1973) (pp. 240–1) as: 'to look to local mores, established institutions and the unities of common experience — to 'tradition', 'culture', 'national Character' or even race — for the roots of a new identity.' 'Epochalism' is to look to the general outlines of the history of our time, and in particular what one takes to be the overall direction and significance of that history.'

18. Geertz (1973), p. 340.

19. See Worsley (1964), and Lal (1978).

20. The violent civil wars surrounding the issues of Biafra and Bangladesh are explosive examples, while the various 'quasi-secessionist' movements in India, most recently of the Sikhs, are more mundane, almost workaday, examples; nor are such subnational feuds confined to the South, as witness the conflicts within Canada, Belgium, Nothern Ireland and Yugoslavia.

21. See Wiles (1967).

22. See Lal (1983).

23. See Lal (1980) for India, Killick (1978) for Ghana and Coulson (1982) on Tanzania for three case studies of the outcome in countries which have recently taken the notion of 'socialism' and 'planning' relatively seriously in the formulation of economic policy.

24. See Little, Scitovsky, and Scott, (1970); Krueger, (1979); Bhagwati, (1979); Balassa, (1971); Lal, (1983).

25. This is the term used in Krueger (1974) to explain and characterize these dirigiste policies.

26. See Hicks (1969) on traditional and modern Revenue Economies.

27. See Braudel (1982), Hicks (1969), Baechler (1975), Weber (1904).

28. See Hicks (1969), pp. 72ff, for a possible explanation for the ban or usury. Also see Braudel (1982) and Schumpeter (1959).

29. Aristotle, n.d., pp. 20–21.

30. Braudel (1982), p. 562.

31. Pocock (a) (1975), p. 72.

32. *Ibid.*, p. 71.

33. *Ibid.*, p. 76.

34. See Keynes (1936), pp. 155 and following.

35. Pocock (a) (1975), p. 80.

36. Pocock (b) (1975), pp. 457–8.

37. Marshall (1922), p. 487.

38. See Arrow and Starrett (1973).

39. See Harcourt (1972), and Blaug (1974), for two very different accounts of these debates.

40. See Lal (1980).

41. See Lucas and Sargent (1981), for a collection of the basic scriptures. I provide my own account and critique in Lal (1982).

42. This is explicitly noted in Lucas (p.13). See Lal (1982), pp. 95–96.

43. See Hicks (1979) and Georgescu-Rogen (1971), for critiques of the implicit notions of causality on which the econometric analysis of historical time series are based. Also see Hendry (1980) and Friedman and Schwartz (1982), p. 630.

44. Another important part of the Augustan critique of credit emphasised by Pocock but not dealt with in this paper concerned the potential for corruption flowing from the vast expansion in the government's financial resources that supposedly accompanied the establishment of the UK's National Debt. Not only did this increase the power of the government to finance armies and placemen without explicit taxation, but also, it was argued, it now suborned the independence of men of financial property whose fortunes were increasingly tied to those of the new government bonds. These ideas are, of course, still alive in the libertarian critique of 'big government,' as well as in various objections to the so-called 'inflation tax' levied by modern governments.

45. Baechler (1975), p. 94.

REFERENCES

Aristotle, *Politics* (Everyman Edition).

Arrow, K. J. and D. A. Starrett, 'Cost — and demand — theoretical approaches to the theory of price determination,' in J. R. Hicks and W. Weber (Eds), *Carl Menger and the Austrian School of Economics* (Oxford: Clarendon Press, 1973).

Baechler, J., *The Origins of Capitalism* (Oxford: Blackwell, 1975).

Balassa, B., *The Structure of Protection in Developing Countries* (Baltimore, Maryland: Johns Hopkins, 1971).

Berlin, I., *Against the Current — Essays in the History of Ideas* (London: Hogarth Press, 1979).

Bhagwati, J. N., *Anatomy and Consequences of Trade Control Regimes* (National Bureau of Economic Research, 1979).

Blaug, M., *The Cambridge Revolution — Success or Failure*? (London: Institute of Economic Affairs, 1974).

Braudel, F., *Civilisation and Capitalism, Vol. II: The Wheels of Commerce* (London: Collins, 1982).

Brown, Judith, *Gandhi's Rise to Power* (Cambridge: University Press, 1972).

Brown, Judith, *Gandhi and Civil Disobedience* (Cambridge: Univeristy Press, 1977).

Coulson, A., *Tanzania — A Political Economy* (Oxford, 1982).

Finer, S. E., *The Man on Horseback — The Role of the Military in Politics*, 2nd edn (Harmondsworth: Penguin, 1975).

Fisher, H. A. L., *A History of Europe* (London: Arnold, 1936).

Friedman, M., and A. J. Schwartz, *Monetary Trends in the United States and the United Kingdom — Their Relation to Income, Prices and Interest Rates, 1867–1975* (Chicago: National Bureau of Economic Research, 1982).

Geertz, C., *The Interpretation of Cultures* (Basic Books, 1973).

Georgescu-Roegen, N., *The Entropy Law and the Economic Process* (Harvard: University Press, 1971).

Gungwu, Wang, 'Nationalism in Asia,' in E. Kamenka (Ed.), *Nationalism* (London: Arnold, 1973).

Hausheer, R., 'Introduction,' in I. Berlin, (1979).

Harcourt, G., *Some Cambridge Controversies in the Theory of Capital* (Cambridge: University Press, 1972).

Hicks, J. R., *A Theory of Economic History* (Oxford, 1969).

Hicks, J. R. *Causality in Economics* (Oxford: Blackwell, 1979).

Hendry, D. F., 'Econometrics — alchemy or science?,' *Economica* (November, 1980).

Kedourie, E., *Nationalism* (London: Hutchinson, 1966).

Kedourie, E., (ed.), *Nationalism in Asia and Africa* (London: Weidenfeld & Nicholson, 1970).

Keynes, J. M., *The General Theory of Employment, Interest and Money* (Basingstoke: Macmillan, 1936).

Killick, T., *Development Ecomics in Action — A Study of Economic Policies in Ghana* (London: Heinemann, 1978).

Knight, F., *Risk, Uncertainty and Profit* (London: Harper Torchbook edition, 1965).

Krueger A. O., 'The political economy of the rent-seeking society,' *American Economic Review* (June 1974).

Krueger, A. O., *Liberalisation Attempts and Consequences* (Ballinger: National Bureau of Economic Research, 1979).

Lal, D., *Poverty, Power and Prejudice — the North–South Confrontation* (London: Fabian Research Series 340, 1978).

Lal, D., *Prices for Planning — Towards the Reform of Indian Planning* (London: Heinemann Educational, 1980).

Lal. D., 'Do Keynesian diagnoses and remedies need revision?,' in A. Maddison and B. S. Wilpstra (Eds.), *Unemployment — The European Perspective* (London: Croom Helm, 1982).

Lal, D., *The Poverty of 'Development Economics,'* (London: Institute of Economic Affairs, 1983).

Little, I. M. D., T. Scitovsky, and M. Fg. Scott, *Industry and Trade in Some Developing Countries* (Oxford, 1970).

Lucas Jr. R. E., 'Understanding business cycles,' in K. Brunner. and A. Meltzer (Eds.), *Stabilization of the Domestic and International Economy* (Amsterdam: North Holland, 1977).

Lucas, Jr. R. E., and T. J. Sargent (Eds.), *Rational Expectations and Econometric Practice* (London: Allen & Unwin, 1981).

Macintyre, A., *After Virtue — A Study in Moral Theory* (Duckworth, 1981).

Marshall, A., *Principles of Economics*, 18th edn (Basingstoke: Macmillan, 1922).

McKinnon, R. I., *Money and Capital in Economic Development* (Brookings, 1973).

Nehru, J., *An Autobiography* (Allied Publishers, Indian edition, 1962).

Plamenatz, J., 'Two types of nationalism,' in E. Kamenka (Ed.), *Nationalism*, (London: Arnold, 1973).

Pocock, J. G. A., (a) 'Early modern capitalism — the Augustan perception,' in E. Kamenka and R. S. Neale (Eds.), *Feudalism, Capitalism and Beyond* (London: Arnold, 1975).

Pocock, J. G. A., (b) *The Machiavellian Moment — Florentine Political Thought and the Atlantic Republican Tradition* (Princeton: Univesity Press, 1975).

Ricardo, D., *The Works and Correspondence of David Ricardo*, ed. P. Sraffa, Vol. 1 (1951).

Sandel, M. J., *Liberalism and the Limits of Justice* (Cambridge: University Press, 1982).

Schumpeter, J. A., *History of Economic Analysis* (Oxford, 1959).

Shackle, G. S., *Epistemics and Economics. A Critique of Economic Doctrines* (Cambridge: University Press, 1972).

Solow, R., 'Cambridge and the real world,' *Times Literary Supplement*, (14 March 1975).

Stein, S. J., and B. H. Stein, *The Colonial Heritage of Latin America* (Oxford, 1970).

Taylor, C., 'Socialism and Weltanschaung,' in L. Kolakowski and S. Hampshire (Eds.), *The Socialist*

Idea — A Reappraisal (London: Weidenfeld & Nicholson, 1974).

Wiener, M. J., *English Culture and the Decline of the Industrial Spirit, 1850–1980* (Cambridge: University Press, 1981).

Weber, M., *The Protestant Ethic and the Spirit of Capitalism* (1904).

Wiles, P., 'Power without influence — the economic impact,' in Royal Institute for International Affairs, *The Impact of the Russian Revolution 1917–1967 — the Influence of Bolshevism on the World Outside Russia* (Oxford, 1967).

Worsley, P., *The Third World* (London: Weidenfeld & Nicholson, 1964).

12 The Political Economy of Industrialisation in Primary Product Exporting Economies: Some Cautionary Tales

Deepak Lal*
UNIVERSITY COLLEGE, LONDON AND WORLD BANK

1 INTRODUCTION

Ever since the collapse of primary commodity prices during the Great Depression and the attendant balance of payments problems faced by most of the primary product export economies of the third world, industrialisation has been viewed as the major panacea for developing most of these economies. Much of the resulting industrialisation has been import substituting – some of it naturally induced as the relative profitability of domestic import substitutes rose with the terms of trade and accompanying real exchange rate changes which resulted from the inter-war collapse of primary commodity prices and the subsequent disruption of international trade during the Second World War. But in many countries both the inter-war difficulties with primary product export-led growth and the rise of economic nationalism – which has been a characteristic of most of the Third World since the Second World War – has led to the institution of protective systems which have pushed industrialisation beyond these 'natural' levels by tariff- and quota-induced 'hothouse' import-substituting industrialisation.

However, one of the best researched and well-established stylised facts about postwar economic development is the inefficiency and inequity associated with this hothouse industrialisation.[1] Some countries have recognised this and have established more 'neutral' trade regimes, others have had cycles in their trade regimes – with partial trade liberalisation followed by a backsliding to controls and vice-versa – while some, despite the accumulating evidence of the dysfunctional nature of their protectionist trade and payment regimes, have tenaciously clung to them even though it is apparent that liberalisation would help to improve the rate as well as the quality of their economic growth.

These differences in public behaviour would seem to pose a problem for those who like Keynes believe that: 'Madmen in authority, who hear voices in the air, are distilling their frenzy from some academic scribbler of a few years back . . . soon or late, it is ideas not vested interests which are dangerous for good or ill' (Keynes, *General Theory*, p. 384). Memories may be long, but there are new hungry generations waiting to tread on those whose ideas were set in the thirties and forties. More seriously, while the influence of ideas on public policies is undeniable, a belief in their primacy over interests depends upon assuming a State which is moved entirely by the best arguments of the day (when its mind was formed), and with no autonomous ends of its own. This is a view of the *benevolent State* as a committee of ageing Platonic Guardians closeted in their studies reading and cogitating on the essays in persuasion written by their technocratic peers. It is a view which is becoming less and less persuasive.

By contrast the emerging 'new political economy' takes a more even-handed view of the motives of the State and its citizens, regarding them as being equally self-regarding. Ideas clearly play a role but the interests (possibly shifting) of those who comprise the State must be equally important. Moreover, as a result of the State's conversion of certain ideas into policies, particular interest groups may be created which make it impossible to reverse policies even when the ideas on which they are based are generally recognised to be hollow. The 'irrational' policies that are then followed can be said to be ideological, where ideology is used in its literal sense, viz. 'thinking or theorising of an idealistic abstract or impractical nature; fanciful speculation'.

In sorting out these more subtle interactions between ideas, ideology and interests it is useful to consider the determinants and outcomes of policies in countries where 'ecological' conditions could be expected to favour the emergence of interests more conducive towards those 'outward-oriented' development policies which past research has shown aid development. In this paper therefore I consider the long-run development policies and outcomes of five export economies with abundant land and natural resources relative to their past and current populations. Their comparative advantage has clearly been in primary product exports.[2] Two of these are in Latin America – Argentina and Peru; two in Africa – Ghana and Tanzania; and one in Asia – Thailand.[3]

All five countries have in the past been highly successful primary product export economies, but their contemporary fortunes have diverged sharply (see Table 12.1).[4] Three of these countries, Thailand, Ghana and Tanzania have traditionally been peasant economies. Their output of export crops grown by peasant households rose with the growth in export demand following their integration in the world economy in the last century. Argentina by contrast is a land-abundant country where the main primary commodities – wool, wheat and meat – are produced mainly by medium- and large-scale agricultural units with hired labour. Peru is the classic dual economy, with a largely untouched subsistence peasant sector in the Sierra, co-existing with wage based farms (in the coastal plain) and mining and fishing enterprises which have produced most of the primary product exports which have been the basis of Peruvian growth since about 1850.

One of our major theses is that these initial 'ecological' conditions provide a strong predisposition towards a particular path of development. In this paper therefore I will tell some analytical 'political economy' stories for these different 'types' of export economies which will seek to sort out the different effects over time of the interactions between interests and ideas in explaining their development policies and outcomes. A major purpose of the paper is also to show how the new political economy can be used to analyse some important aspects of long-run development. Thus the countries chosen also typify three different types of 'polity' – what I label respectively the predatory, factional and oligarchic state – in terms of the differing objectives subserved by the controllers of the 'polity'.

Our core analytical model is the so-called specific factors Ricardo–Viner model of trade theory (see Jones, 1971; Snape, 1977; Ruffin and Jones, 1977) and its extensions in analyses of: (a) the Dutch Disease (see Corden and Neary, 1982); (b) the political economy of tariffs – where the political process which yields protection is endogenised – (see the series of models by Findlay and Wellisz, 1982, 1983, 1984 and by Mayer, 1984); combined with the emerging literature on the political economy of fiscal policies (see Brennan and Buchanan, 1980; Findlay and Wilson, 1987; Lal, 1984). Another purpose of this paper is to show how an analytical framework devised from the above can be represented by three simple diagrams which can be used in analysing various aspects of the political economy of long-run development.[5]

Section 2 provides some stylised facts about the five economies. Section 3 deals with the cautionary tale based on the Thai, Ghanian and Tanzanian experience of the predatory state. Section 4 with that of Argentina and the factional state, and Section 5 with Peru and the oligarchic state. As with all cautionary tales it is for the reader to draw the relevant moral. Hence it would be presumptuous to append any conclusions!

2 FIVE EXPORT ECONOMIES – SOME STYLISED FACTS

For a number of developing countries Lloyd Reynolds (1985) has dated the beginning of what he labels intensive growth – when, after a period of population and output growing at the same rate, there is a sustained rise in per capita incomes. For our five countries Reynolds' dates for these turning points are:

1850 – Thailand
1860 – Argentina
1880 – Peru
1895 – Ghana
1900 – Tanzania.

The great world-wide boom associated with the establishment and spread of the nineteenth-century liberal trading order – from 1850 – drew these primary producing economies into an expanding world economy. Their export-led growth was based in Peru on a combination of mineral and agricultural products, in Argentina on temperate zone products such as wool, wheat and meat, in Tanzania on sisal and coffee, and in Thailand and Ghana on the expansion of smallholder peasant agriculture producing respectively rice and cocoa for export.

In both Peru and Argentina there was both a sequencing and impressive diversification of primary product exports. Except for some foreign-owned Peruvian mineral exports, much of the value added from the expanded production of primary commodities was retained within the country. This was particularly true of the peasant smallholder economies, where the spread effects of this export-led growth on mass levels of living were also more favourable.

For Argentina Carlos Diaz–Alejandro (1970) estimated that, in the 50 years before the First World War, GDP grew at about 5 per cent per annum, population at about 3·4 per cent, leaving a substantial improvement in per capita income. The domestic capital and labour markets were increasingly integrated with world factor markets, and there was also growth in 'natural' import-competing manufacturing based on processing primary products as well as from the introduction of light industry with the expansion of the domestic market. By 1929, 19 per cent of Argentinian GDP originated in manufacturing.

In Peru, Webb (1986) has estimated that between 1913 and 1941, real GDP grew at about 3·8 per cent per annum and population at 1·5 per cent per annum, yielding a per capita growth rate of about 2 per cent. Exports grew at about 3·8 per cent per annum between 1900 and 1930 and manufacturing output by 4·8 per cent per annum between 1918/19 and 1950.

In Thailand there was a steady rise in population and an even greater rise in rice exports from 1850. There was also a steady rise in per capita income (see Ingram, 1971; Reynolds, 1985, p. 158). Population grew from 6 million in 1850 to 18·15 million in 1950, while rice exports increased from 990 000 piculs (1 picul = about 60 kgs) in 1958–9 to 25 370 000 piculs in 1935–9. The State shared in this prosperity through export taxes. Peasant producers on average received only half the export price. There was very little manufacturing before the Second World War and most of it was in handicrafts. Thus in 1937 only 1·6 per cent of the labour force was employed in manufacturing. The country was ruled by an absolute monarch until 1932, when the king became an influential constitutional ruler, and the country has since been ruled in effect by an oligarchy.

Ghana was a British colony from 1874. Exports primarily of smallholder cocoa and gold expanded rapidly, the average rate of growth being 9·2 per cent per annum between 1882 and 1913 (Reynolds, 1985, p. 219). The colonial government's main economic function was to provide improved infrastructure.

Tanzania developed as an export economy from 1900, first as a German and later as a British colony. The major exports were sisal grown on plantations, and coffee, rubber and cotton grown both on settler farms and by peasant smallholders. There was virtually no growth in manufacturing during the colonial period. In all our countries the growth of the export economy was also associated with a rise in public expenditures on infrastructure (see Birnberg and Resnick, 1975).

Table 12.1 provides summary statistics on various aspects of socio-economic performance in our five countries in the post-Second World War period. As is apparent from Table 12.1(A), the growth performance has diverged sharply as between the 5 countries and for all except Thailand over time in each country. Argentina's postwar performance has been much worse by its own pre-war standards, as has Peru's since the mid-1960s, Tanzania's since the early 1970s and Ghana's since the early 1960s.

Each of these 'slumps' in economic performance was associated with the pursuit of policies of 'hot house' industrialisation, by governments keen to break out of the 'colonial' pattern of trade and development. In Argentina this 'turning-point' can be associated with Péron, in Ghana with Nkrumah, in Tanzania with Nyerere's Arusha Declaration in 1967.

Manufacturing as a share of GDP rose in all our countries (seeTable 12.1(B)) the largest change being in Thailand which alone of our five countries industrialised relatively 'naturally' in the postwar period after a brief flirtation with import substituting industrialisation in the mid-1960s. Thus Meesook *et al.* (1986) estimate that, between 1960 and 1972, the sources of growth in domestic industry were: domestic demand, 77·9 per cent; export expansion, 14·3 per cent; and import substitution, 7·8 per cent. For the period 1972–5 the figures were: domestic demand, 90 per cent; export expansion, 9·0 per cent; and import substitution, 1·0 per cent.

Except in Thailand and Argentina, food availability per capita declined (Table 12.1(C)), and except for Thailand and Peru so did the share of exports to GDP (see Table 12.1(D)). There was an increase in the share of public consumption in all our countries, the largest increases being in Tanzania and Peru, while domestic investment collapsed in Peru and Ghana – in the latter country spectacularly.

Ghana and Tanzania also saw a large increase in public employment. In Ghana, Ansu (1984) estimates that 64·8 per cent of the total work force was in public employment in 1964, and this rate rose to 77·8 per cent in 1978. In Tanzania there was a rapid growth in parastatals from 1969. All the growth in regular wage employment of 137 000 between 1969 and 1974, was in parastatals and the public services (see Coulson, 1982, Table 23.2). Public servants accounted for 72 per cent of the total of 363 000 in regular wage employment in 1974. There were improvements in social indicators in all five countries (Table 12.1(C)), the most dramatic being the increase in primary school enrolment in Tanzania.

3 THE PREDATORY STATE

In our first cautionary tale the government is assumed to be controlled by a single ruler – a monarch, a dictator, or a charismatic leader. In the first two forms of government, the monarch or dictator may change, but the form of government is not altered, as we assume the changes result from mere palace coups, and not because of any change in the 'interest groups' controlling the State. Put differently, in this model, the constellation of domestic interest groups has little direct effect on the policies of the sovereign who is more autonomous therefore than in the models in the two following sections. The objective of the State is net revenue maximisation. This is thus a model of the *predatory* State (Lal, 1984). The model will also apply to countries ruled by a charismatic leader who may often also be a dictator; but the model will be applicable only during his/her lifetime, unless a quasi-monarchical dynastic succession can be assured. The model would also apply to a country ruled by a colonial power, which is not beholden to the interplay of domestic interest groups.

The State can be identified in this story with an absolute ruler, who provides the public goods of law and order, and possibly some directly productive inputs such as irrigation, roads, and so on. The cases we have in mind are Thailand since 1850 and Ghana and Tanzania from colonial times. In Thailand the absolute monarch was replaced in 1932 by an oligarchy. The king became a constitutional ruler but with considerable influence. In Ghana and Tanzania the colonial rulers were replaced by charismatic leaders – Nkrumah and Nyerere.

All three are also peasant economies where family-'owned' peasant farms produce the major export commodities. Consider a traditional peasant economy with a very favourable land–man ratio. With traditional techniques, the existing labour force in agriculture is L_A

Table 12.1 (A) Per capita GDP growth rates 1950–80

	Real per capita GDP			*Average of decades*
	50–60	*60–70*	*70–80*	
Thailand	3.3	5.1	4.2	4.2
Argentina	1.2	2.8	1.0	1.7
Tanzania	1.4	5.0	2.0	2.8
Peru	2.9	1.9	0.4	1.7
Ghana	2.4	0.0	−2.1	0.1

(B) Output by sector of origin (% of GDP)

	Agriculture			*Industry*			*Manufacturing*			*Services*		
	50	80	Δ	50	80	Δ	50	80	Δ	50	80	Δ
Thailand	58	25	−57	16	29	+81	10	20	+100	26	46	+76
Argentina	14	12	−14	38	41	+8	29	33	+14	48	39	−19
Tanzania	63	54	−14	16	13	−18	6	9	+50	22	33	+54
Peru	35	8	−77	24	45	+88	15	27	+82	41	47	+15
Ghana		n.a.			n.a.			n.a.			n.a.	

Continued overleaf

Table 12.1 (continued)

(C) Change in welfare indicators

	Food availability (per capita calories/day)			Primary school enrolment (% of age going)			Life expectancy at birth (years)		
	1964–6	*1978–80*	*△*	*1950*	*1980*	*△*	*1960*	*1980*	*△*
Thailand	2 220	2 301	+81	52	96	+44	51	63	+12
Argentina	3 241	3 386	+145	66	112	+46	65	70	+5
Tanzania	2 140	2 025	−115	10	104	+94	42	52	+10
Peru	2 256	2 166	−90	43	112	+69	48	58	+10
Ghana	2 160	1 862	−298	19	69	+50	40	49	+9

(D) Export performance

	Growth of Merchandise Exports (% p.a.) 1950–80	Exports/GDP		△% of GDP
		1950–52	*1978–80*	
Thailand	10.1	18.2	18.8	+0.6
Argentina	7.9	15.8	10.8	−5.0
Tanzania	5.7	26.0	10.9	−15.1
Peru	9.0	18.0	25.6	+7.6
Ghana	5.4	32.2	10.4	−21.8

Source: Reynolds (1985).

(E) Output by end uses (% of GDP)

	Gross domestic investment			Public consumption			Private consumption			Resource balance	
	51–60	80	%Δ	51–60	80	%Δ	51–60	80	%Δ	51–60	80
Thailand	14	27	+93	10	12	+15	77	66	−15	−2	−5
Argentina		n.a.			n.a.			n.a.			n.a.
Tanzania	14	22	+57	9	14	+56	72	78	+8	+5	−14
Peru	24	16	−33	8	13	+55	70	68	−3	−3	+3
Ghana	15	5	−66	8	9	+18	75	86	+14	+2	0

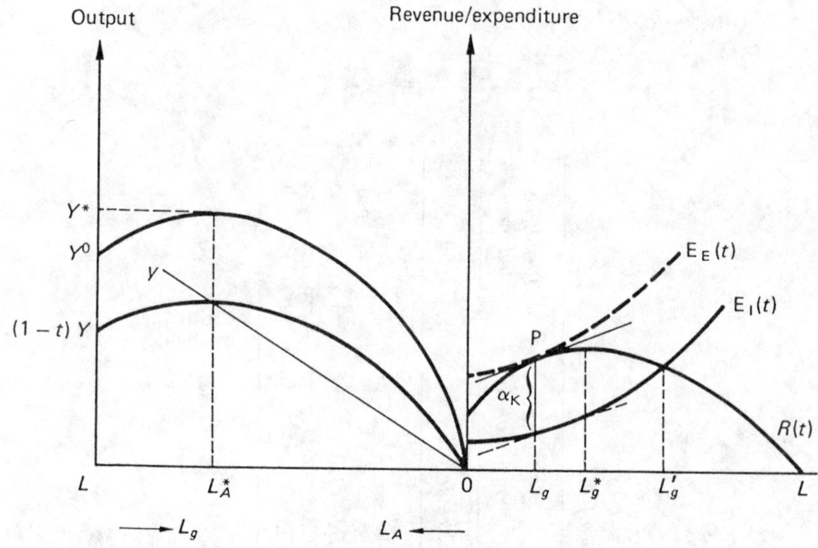

Figure 12.1

working on a fixed quantity of land N ($N < \bar{N}$ the total land available) and through equal work and income sharing each worker receives the (net of tax) average product of labour y in agriculture as his income. There is a sovereign who imposes a fixed proportionate tax at the rate t on rural output to finance his court, army, and law and order institutions. Thus, part of the revenue the sovereign receives is used to hire public servants providing public goods – the police, judges, army, engineers. The rest is used for the sovereign's own purposes – courtiers, palaces, mistresses and the accumulation of 'royal' treasure. Following Findlay and Wilson (1987) we assume that the provision of public goods raises the productivity of the economy above the level that would exist without the State – viz. in anarchy.

Thus in Figure 12.1 we depict the total agricultural output curve of the economy with respect to the given total labour force OL, working on a given fixed acreage. If there are no government employees (L_g) then the total population is in the rural private sector (L_A) and produces output LY^o. This is the 'anarchy' level of output. With some government employees being hired to provide public goods for the rural sector, the rural labour force shrinks but total output increases until the allocation of the labour force given by L_A^* is reached where $LL_A^* = L_g^*$ workers are government employees and OL_A^* are left in the rural sector, producing the maximal output Y^* (which is higher than Y_o, because of the public goods provided by the L_g^* public employees).

For a *given* tax rate t on rural output, the vertical distance between the Y and $(1-t)y$ curve in Figure 12.1, gives the total revenue available for a particular level of public (L_g) and private (L_A) employment. This revenue function $R(t)$ is plotted in quadrant II of Figure 12.1. It reaches a maximum when $L_g^* = L - L_A^*$ workers are employed in the public sector. The government must pay its employees the competitive wage equal to the supply price of rural labour, which is *ex hypothesi* the net of tax average product in agriculture. This is given by the slope of the ray Oy when the level of rural private employment is L_A^* and public employment is L_g^*. Thus by a similar construction for each level of L_g, and for the given tax rate (t) the variable cost component of the public expenditure function $E(t)$ can be derived in quadrant II. In the absence of any fixed costs (on which more below), the variable cost function and $E(t)$ function will be the same. Let us assume that this is so.

The sovereign we have also assumed is a net revenue maximiser. This means – for any given tax rate (t) – that he will seek to maximise the distance between the $R(t)$ and $E(t)$ functions, that is, equate the marginal cost of L_g public employees with the marginal tax revenue from the output produced by the remaining L_A rural workers. It is clear from the shapes of these functions that, irrespective of the tax rate t chosen, the net revenue-maximising sovereign will provide less public employment than the socially optimal level L_g^*.

The net tax revenue will rise as t is raised, as the $R(t)$ and $E(t)$ curves shift outwards. The net of tax income of labour declines with rises in t as the $(1-t)Y$ curve shifts downwards. But there is an upper limit to t, given by the level at which the net of tax average product of labour is equal to subsistence income. Even a revenue-maximising predatory state is unlikely, however, to raise taxes to the level which reduces peasant incomes to the subsistence level, as well before that the current controllers of the multiproduct natural monopoly providing the public goods of 'law and order' and 'security', which is the State, will find that their industry is contestable (in the sense of Baumol *et al.*, 1982. See Lal, 1984, for this interpretation of the limits on the behaviour of the predatory state). The contestants could be either internal or external rivals. The level of taxes which will be sustainable depends upon the barriers to entry – including physical (geographical), technological (military) as well as ideological (including religious) – which allow the maximum 'natural' rent to be extracted by any controller of the State (see Lal, 1984).

These ideas can be formalised as follows. A large part of the costs incurred by an incumbent sovereign in capturing his/her estate will be sunk costs. Say these fixed capital costs are K, and the variable costs of providing the public goods and maintaining the sovereign in power are V. If α is the proportion of the fixed capital costs which are sunk, then the 'advantage' the incumbent has over a new entrant is that whereas its total costs TC_I

$$TC_I = f((1-\alpha)K, V)$$

that of the new entrant (who has access to the same military and civil technology, say)

$$TC_E = f(K, V)$$

and as $\alpha < 1$, TC_E will lie above TC_I by the fixed amount αK.

Assume that the total variable costs V, are incurred entirely on hiring public employees (these are the same for the incumbent and the entrant) then V for a given tax rate t are (as in Figure 12.1)

$$V = y(L_g) \,.\, L_g$$

where y is the net of tax *average* product in agriculture = public sector wage rate, and L_g are the number of public employees hired. Then the total expenditure function for the new entrant $E_E(t)$ for a given tax rate t, can be drawn in Figure 12.1, quadrant II, as a vertical displacement by αK of the total expenditure function of the incumbent $E_I t$.

The maximum profit the incumbent can then earn is π and given by

$$\pi = (V + K) - (V + (1 - \alpha K)) = \alpha K.$$

The optimal tax rate (t) for the net revenue-maximising predatory state will be determined by the tangency of the *entrants* expenditure function $E_E(t)$ with the revenue function $R(t)$ for this optimal rate, as at p in quadrant II of Figure 12.1. For suppose the tax rate were higher ($t' > t$), then the incumbent's and entrant's expenditure functions ($E(t')$) would shift downwards and the revenue function ($R\ (t)$) upwards (not drawn). The incumbent's monopoly would no longer be sustainable as the entrant could charge a marginally lower tax rate and still make a net profit. Similarly, if the tax rate were lower ($t'' < t$) then the revenue function would shift downwards and expenditure functions would shift upwards and the incumbent would not be maximising net revenue. Thus there will be a unique tax rate, and fiscal cum public employment equilibrium, determined by the underlying production function, and the net barrier to entry costs facing a new entrant. That is, in Figure 12.1, the vertical distance at the sustainable and surplus-maximising point between the $E_E(t)$ and $R(t)$ curves when the $E_I(t)$ curve is tangential to the $R(t)$ curve must equal αK. Thus in the general equilibrium model of the fiscal and employment decisions of a predatory state depicted by Figure 12.1, quadrant II, the surplus-maximising sovereign will set the tax rate t, such that the surplus generated at the public employment level L_g, where the marginal costs and marginal returns (to the sovereign) from public employment are equated, is equal to the net 'barrier to entry' costs facing a new entrant coveting the State.

Suppose this economy has been conquered by a colonial power. Being foreign it will face higher internal costs in terms of its legitimacy than potential internal rivals. This means that, as compared with the indigenous rulers it replaces, the colonial power will only be able to extract a smaller net surplus, as in terms of Figure 12.1, the net 'barrier to entry' costs for its potential contestants will be lower. The $R(t)$ curve in Figure 12.1 quadrant II will be lower and the $E(t)$ curve higher than for the indigenous ruler it displaces, and hence its surplus-maximising tax rate (where the marginal revenue and expenditure are equal, and the surplus is equal to ($\alpha' K$, with ($\alpha' < \alpha$)) will be lower. More importantly the level of public good provision and public employment will be higher than for the indigenous 'predatory' state. This prediction of the model seems to conform to the stylised fact, noted in Section 2, that there was a marked expansion of public expenditures in colonial export economies.

Over time, this economy expands with population growth and the extension of export crop agriculture onto new lands, as in various vent for surplus-type models (see Myint, 1958; Caves, 1965). The foreign exchange earned by the economy will be used to import consumer goods. Depending upon transport costs, there may be – as a result of the increased demand associated with the rise in national income – a viable market for the domestic manufacture of some imported consumer goods. Such 'natural' import substitution can be expected to accompany the growth of the primary producing export economy. Our main concern, however, is to provide some political economy type of reasons why the government might wish to promote industry, particularly in the public sector, beyond these natural limits.

Suppose at some stage the absolute ruler is replaced by a government subject to more popular pressures. This can be said to have happened in Thailand with the 1932 coup and the conversion of the King from absolute to constitutional monarch, and in Ghana and Tanzania with the ending of colonial rule. To the extent that these changes increase the legitimacy of the new incumbents controlling the state, they will *ceteris paribus* increase the costs of rival entrants seeking to capture the State. In Figure 12.1, the $R(t)$ curve will shift upwards and the $E(t)$ curve downwards till a new equilibrium at a lower level of L_g is reached where the 'surplus' is equal to $\alpha^1 K$ with the higher 'net barrier to entry' costs as $(\alpha^1 > \alpha)$.

However, unlike the absolute ruler, the new 'constitutional' rulers – albeit dictators – will find it difficult openly to appropriate the net surplus for themselves. They may seek to expand their patronage instead by hiring more retainers. If in addition, as in post-independence Ghana and Tanzania, the new leaders seek to 'modernise' their countries by social engineering through a technocracy, they may have ideological reasons for expanding the bureaucracy beyond the net revenue-maximising point L_g in Figure 12.1. The objective of this post-independent predatory state would be 'bureaucrat maximisation'.

Thus, as is argued by the recent rent-seeking literature (see Krueger, 1974 and Buchanan *et al.*, 1980) the professional bureaucracy and its hangers-on will themselves seek to garner the State's surplus by exerting pressure to expand government expenditure. Findlay and Wilson (1984) describe this as the Parkinson–Niskanen law that 'Government expenditure expands to absorb all the resources available to finance it'. Public employment will expand to L_g^1, well beyond the socially optimal level L_g^* in Figure 12.1.[6] But in this process, with the increase in the provision of public goods, output could be higher than when the State is run by an absolute monarch or colonial power.

So far we have implicitly assumed that the relative prices of the commodities in our model economy have remained unchanged. Now suppose export prices and that portion of the government's revenue derived from export taxes fluctuate. Once it has hired public servants *pari passu* with the past rise in its revenues, it will be very difficult for the government either to cut current wages or the numbers of public employees when revenues fall. It is thus likely to face a fiscal crisis with every fall in export prices (as R_t shifts downwards and $E(t)$ remains unchanged in Figure 12.1).[7]

One way for the government to insulate itself from the incipient fiscal crises that the periodic collapse in export prices generates is to put some of the revenues at good times in foreign financial assets (reserves) to be used to finance fiscal expenditures when times are bad. But for most third-world states this has proved virtually impossible because of the pressures that arise for the State to spend the windfalls, most often by hiring the relatives of its retainers. To the extent that this increase in public employment also exerts upward pressure on the economy-wide wage rate, the benefits from such spending could be quite wide and hence popular. But the dangers of succumbing to these pressures is the fiscal crisis during the downside of the export cycle. Furthermore during the downside of the cycle as peasant earnings have also fallen, there will be pressures from them to get the State to spend any reserves it has accumulated to stabilise peasant incomes. The state may thus not be able to use the surpluses, accumulated during the upswing of the export cycle and held as publicly visible reserves, to fulfil its objective of stabilising public employment.

An alternative policy for the government to escape its fiscal bind and subserve its bureaucrat-maximising objective would be to insulate the financing of public employment from fluctuating export price-induced changes in revenues. It could use the export tax proceeds in good times to import capital goods to set up import substitute industries (beyond the 'natural' extent that has occurred because of the income growth associated with export led expansion). As long as the domestic demand for the products of these industries is relatively stable, and the products can be sold at a domestic price sufficient to cover *variable costs* (including, above all, those of the public labourers employed), the government will have succeeded in providing a stable means of financing public employment from the fluctuating export tax revenues. It being noted that as efficiency *per se* is not a goal of this net revenue or bureaucrat-maximising state, there is no presumption that the government will choose to maximise the profits of these public enterprises. As far as it is concerned the capital imports financed by the export taxes may well be a sunk cost, and as long as the public employees are paid out of the net revenues (taking account of other variable costs), the State would have achieved its predatory objectives, though by conventional or social accounting criteria most of these public enterprises could well be making losses.

Alternatively, the government may seek to augment its revenues by providing tariff protection to private sector manufacturers. The revenue from the tariff supplements that from the export tax. As long as there is a subsistence sector in the economy which fixes the supply price of labour to the rest of the economy, the introduction or expansion of import substituting industries will merely mean a reduction in output and employment in the subsistence sector, with no change in the wage rate (or in the rents accruing to landlords in the export sector – if agriculture is commercially organised rather than being based on peasant household labour) (see Findlay and Wellisz, 1984). Thus the State may face no 'costs' in the short run from this policy of promoting some 'hot-house' import substituting industrialisation through a combination of both public and private enterprises and the institution of some non-prohibitive revenue tariffs.

This seems to be the story (by and large) of the economic development of Thailand since 1850, of Ghana till about 1961 during the Nkrumah regime, and of Tanzania from colonial times to Nyerere's regime until the Arusha Declaration in 1967. Though introducing well-known inefficiencies in production, the mild protection to promote (in particular public sector-based) industrialisation could have been justifiable from a net revenue and public employment maximising government's viewpoint. This is true even if account is taken of the indirect effects on government revenue from the well-known Lerner symmetry theorem whereby an import tariff is equivalent to an export tax. The revenue tariff is likely to affect export output and hence export tax revenue adversely. But this loss in mean export revenues (in the face of fluctuating export prices) has to be balanced, from the public employment maximising government's viewpoint, against the stability (reduction in the variance of tax revenues) thereby bought in the financing of public employment – essentially by substituting a more stable form of 'revenue' generation through public enterprise-based industrialisation. There will be some optimum level of public enterprise-based industrial employment provision at which these costs and benefits will be equal.

Suppose, however, that on the basis of current ideas (Ghana under Nkrumah)[8] or ideology (Nyerere's Tanzania after the Arusha Declaration)[9] the State seeks to promote public sector-based industrialisation beyond this 'optimal' level: that is, in terms of Figure 12.1, it seeks to increase public employment beyond the level L_g'. As tariffs on final consumer goods become prohibitive and most intermediate and capital goods are allowed into the country at low or zero tariffs to provide high effective protection to public sector industries, tariff revenue is likely to fall, as is the revenue from export crops, with the increase in the direct and indirect tax burden on the sector.

Then, given the interrelationship between export taxes, export output, the rural–urban terms of trade, and the subsistence based supply price of peasant household labourers, there could be a complete elimination of the peasant export crop, as the peasants move to the untaxable subsistence sector. They may still be willing to exchange domestically produced manufactured import substitutes for some subsistence output. But this reduced domestic demand for import substitutes may no longer be sufficient to employ all the existing 'entitled' public sector workers. Furthermore the collapse of domestic export supply following its increased direct and indirect taxation, will have led to a reduction in the supply of foreign exchange required to finance even the imported intermediate inputs required by domestic industry. The State will have a fiscal, foreign exchange and domestic output crisis. The predator will have a problem of surviving as it has virtually destroyed its prey! This seems very much to be the story of Ghana after 1961 and Tanzania in the 1970s and 1980s (see Ansu, 1984; Collier *et al.*, 1987). But this denouement is not inevitable as the more favourable outcome in Thailand illustrates, although this requires a pragmatic and non-ideological State![10]

4 THE FACTIONAL STATE

The second analytical story is roughly based on the Argentinian case. It is of a land-abundant economy *without* a subsistence sector. Agriculture produces for both domestic consumption and exports, and is conducted on medium- or large-scale commercial farms making use of hired labour. In addition there may be a small import-competing manufacturing sector, as well as a non-traded goods services sector.

Unlike the 'absolute' rulers who controlled the State in the story in Section 3, we now have a State which serves the interests of that coalition of pressure groups which succeeds in its capture. The method of capturing the State need not be majoritarian democracy, even though this form of government would be compatible with our story. The interests served are narrowly defined to be the economic self-interests of the constituents of the government. The income effects induced by the economic policies adopted and hence of concern to a particular government will depend upon the returns to the primary factor endowments of its constituents. A recent model of endogenous tariff determination in a voting polity due to Mayer (1984) is helpful in providing an analytical framework for the behaviour of what we may call the factional State.

The basic idea can be explained fairly simply. Suppose that there are only two factors of production, capital (K) and labour (L) and that all individuals in the economy can be described by their respective capital labour ($k_i \equiv K_i/L_i$) endowments. The *mean* of the distribution of these individual k_i endowments will be the aggregate capital–labour endowment $K/L = \bar{k}$ of the economy.

Next we define the set of individuals who are *decisive*, in the sense that they can compete for the capture of the State and thus the determinants of economic policies subserving their interests. Suppose initially that *all* economic agents in the population form part of the decisive set of the polity and the political mechanism is democratic – with 'one man one vote', and the majority capturing the State. All voters vote their economic interests. Then from the well-known median voter theorem, the median voter's capital/labour endowment (k_m) will determine the interests that will be served by the coalition of majoritarian interest groups who capture the state. If the distribution of individual factor endowments is symmetric so that its median and the mean are the same, the median endowment will be identical to the average for the economy as a whole ($\bar{k} = k_m$). Then from the law of comparative advantage we know that the income of the median individual will be maximised by free trade. If, however, the median individual endowment is more (less) capital intensive than the average, the median voter's income-generating interests will be in a tariff (subsidy) on capital intensive imports or a subsidy (tariff) on labour-intensive imports. Thus in this form of the pressure group model what we need to know is the mean of the national factor endowment and median of the distribution of the income-generating factor endowments of the set of decisive individuals.[11]

The economic model we use to tell our story of the factional state is the simple Ricardo–Viner version of the Heckscher–Ohlin model of trade theory with three goods: an agricultural export, non-traded services, and import-competing manufactures. Initially the output of the latter is negligible. We are interested in medium- and long-term changes, and so we assume that all three goods use mobile labour and 'capital' for their production. The land which is in surplus and is specific to the production of the agricultural good (X) can be made 'effective' only with complementary capital (see Kenen, 1965) and hence the output of the agricultural commodity too depends upon the mobile capital and labour used in its production.[12] The agricultural sector is the most capital intensive. The capital–labour ratio in manufacturing (M) is higher than that in services S. A large part of the latter consists of government services. (This stylised economic structure seems to correspond pretty well to Argentina's. See Diaz-Alejandro, 1970, Essay 1.)

This 3 factor-3 commodity model can be depicted in Figure 12.2 (see Corden and Neary, 1982), where L_S is the demand curve for services L_M for manufactures, and the difference between the L_T (the curve for both the traded goods) and L_M the implicit curve for agriculture L_X. These curves in quadrant I are drawn for a given set of relative prices between services, agriculture and manufacturing, and for given stocks of land 'cum capital' in agriculture and capital in the manufacturing and services sectors. We take the domestic price of manufactures as the numeraire.

Initially, the State levies export taxes which it uses to finance non-traded government services. Apart from this trade cum fiscal intervention there is free trade. The economy is linked to both world capital and labour markets, such that (apart from a given constant risk cum transport premium) there is a perfectly elastic

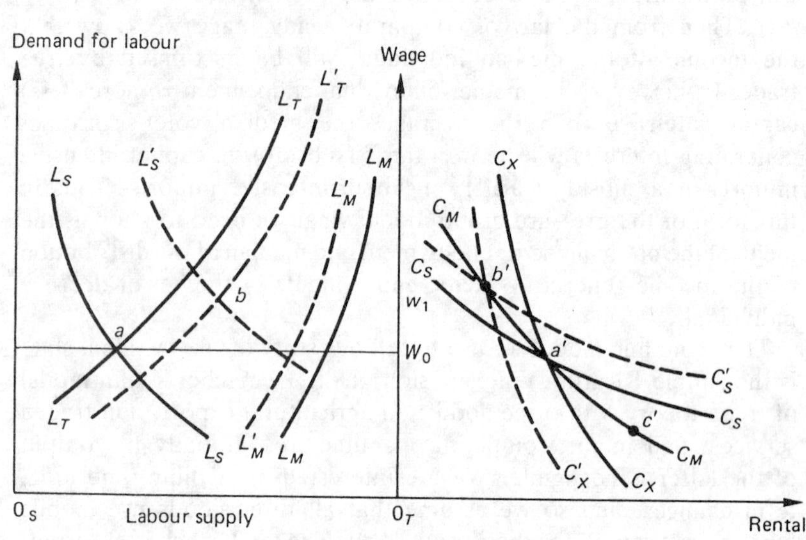

Figure 12.2

supply of both capital and labour at given world interest (r) and wage (w) rates to the economy. Full employment at the given world wage rate of w is constantly maintained through immigration (and emigration), whenever aggregate domestic labour demand exceeds (falls short) of supply. Thus the domestic labour supply O_sO_T in Figure 12.2 varies with the level of aggregate demand for labour.

We start our story in the heyday of the nineteenth-century's liberal trade regime. There is no manufacturing sector. Agricultural export-led growth shifts the L_T schedule to the left. This increased demand for labour is met at the unchanged wage rate of w_o by an expansion of the labour supply by OT' (not drawn). As both the wage and rental rates are *ex hypothesi* constant, the factor proportions in producing both services and agricultural goods remain unchanged, and hence there will also be a capital inflow into the economy, which will lead to an expansion in the outputs of both sectors. With factor prices fixed, the domestic relative price of services and agriculture (the real exchange rate – e in our model) is also fixed. Thus the requisite amounts of foreign capital and labour flowing into the economy will be such as to shift the production possibility frontier between the tradable-agriculture, and non-traded service sectors in a balanced manner.[13]

During this period, corresponding to the second half of the nineteenth century to the early 1920s, the 'decisive' individuals in Argentina are the landlords. As a large proportion of both capitalists and labourers are foreign, they do not form part of the 'polity'. The median endowment of 'land-capital'/labour of the set of decisive landlords is likely to be greater than the average endowment for the economy as a whole. This implies that the interests of the median 'decisive' individual in the polity will be best served by maintaining free trade.

In time, with the expansion of incomes resulting from primary product export-led growth, there will be a sufficient domestic market for the products of some light industries. Competitive domestic import-competing industries will be established. The L_M demand curve for labour will then emerge in the economy as shown in panel I of Figure 12.2. Given our assumptions about the elastic supply of foreign capital and labour, the factor proportions of all three industries remain unchanged and they expand *pari passu* in line with increased domestic incomes (and hence demands).

During the succeeding decades of primary product-induced growth there will also be an increase in the economy's endowments of manufacturing specific capital as 'natural' import-substituting industrialisation begins. Some of this capital will be owned by the landlords, and some by domestic capitalists who will increasingly also become part of the 'decisive' set of individuals whose interests may need to be taken into account by the State.

Now suppose there is a collapse in the world price of the country's export good, and the economy also gets delinked from world labour and capital markets. This happened to Argentina during the Great Depression. We use Figure 12.2 to analyse the outcomes. The second quadrant of this Figure shows the unit cost curves of the three industries drawn in wage-rental space. As exportables (X) are assumed to be the most 'capital'-intensive good the slope of their unit cost curve (which shows the capital–labour ratio) at every wage–rental ratio is steeper than for importables (M) which are of intermediate capital intensity and services (S) which are the least capital-intensive commodity. The initial equilibrium is depicted for given commodity prices and factor supplies by points a and a' in the two quadrants.

With the fall in the price of exportables the C_X curve in quadrant II shifts downwards, as does the L_T curve in quadrant I as labour demand in exportables (L_X) falls while that in importables (L_M) remains unchanged.

For factor market equilibrium the new equilibrium must be at the intersection of the C_X' and C_M curves, viz. b'. This must imply that the unit cost curve for services C_s must shift upwards to intersect the other two curves at b'. Hence the price of services and the real exchange rate (the relative price of non-traded to traded goods) must *rise*. The real wage rises, and the rental on capital falls. In quadrant I, employment and output in the agricultural export sector will fall and in the import-substituting manufacturing sector and services will rise, as will the real wage (see Corden and Neary, 1982 for a formalisation of such a model). Thus, in this process of what may be termed neoclassical adjustments to the collapse of agricultural export prices, further 'natural' import-substituting industrialisation will be promoted as part of the adjustment. This happened in Argentina during the Great Depression (see Diaz–Alejandro, 1970). The only 'losers' from this adjustment are the landlords, but as protection does not serve their interests, they will not oppose the continuation of free trade.

Over time, however, the set of decisive individuals in the economy has been expanding with individuals who have non-traded (services) sector-specific capital and/or labour as their primary endowment increasingly entering the political process. At some stage the median of the distribution of endowments (of 'land-capital' to the other factors), of this expanded set of 'decisive' individuals is likely to become less than the economy-wide average. The state will then seek to subserve the interests of the landless, particularly those with 'non-traded' good capital as they will increasingly have become the 'median' voters. This sector might also come to include those import-competing industries which have succeeded by using arguments based on economic nationalism to obtain the imposition of either import quotas or prohibitive tariffs to convert their outputs in effect into non-traded goods.

With the median of the distribution of the endowments of decisive individuals shifting towards those employed in home goods production there would be political pressures for a squeeze on tradables and in particular on export agriculture. The resulting pressures for a relative expansion of non-traded goods will require an appreciation of the real exchange rate. Diaz–Alejandro provides some estimates which suggest that the combined effect of various domestic policies was a sustained real exchange rate appreciation from about 1929 to well into the postwar period with the extent of 'overvaluation' varying over time.

If, however, the fundamentals of the macroeconomic situation do not require such an appreciation of the real exchange rate there would be a balance of payments problem. As noted above, given the factor intensities of the three goods, the full adjustment to the collapse of primary product prices during the Great Depression would have required some real exchange rate appreciation. However, now consider the situation in the late 1940s or early 1950s when with another turn in the primary product cycle, there is a *rise* in primary product exportable goods prices. The whole process of adjustment analysed in Figure 12.2 goes into reverse.

We continue to examine the medium- to long-term adjustment pressures that arise. In Figure 12.2, given that exportables are the most capital intensive, and services the least with import-substituting manufactures in between, the rise in the price of exports shifts the C_X curve upwards (not drawn). Its new intersection with the C_M curve, at c', is the new long-run equilibrium point. For factor market equilibrium the C_S unit cost curve must also pass through this point, which means that the price of services must fall, that is, there needs to be a *real depreciation*. The money and real wages will fall in the new long-run equilibrium.

This required cut in real wages accompanying the real exchange rate depreciation, will obviously be resisted by those whose factor endowments are dominated by labour, and also by the owners of capital in the import-competing (or tradable) manufacturing sector. For, with the postulated factor intensities, the new equilibrium will entail an expansion in the output of exportables and non-traded goods at the expense of importables.

Given the shift in the distribution of factor endowments of decisive individuals towards a median value which is biased towards labour and non-agricultural capital, the state will be captured by those whose interests lie in preventing the real exchange rate depreciation and hence the real wage cut. This seems to provide an explanation of the rise of Péronist populism, which interestingly, as our model suggests, should have been expected to occur as it did when Argentina's external terms of trade *improved* in the late 1940s, and not when they collapsed during the Great Depression!

However the attempt to maintain an overvalued real exchange rate is not sustainable. With given reserves, the ensuing balance of payments deficit will need to be cured. This inevitably requires the usual expenditure – switching and reducing remedies, and the accompanying distributional shifts in real incomes. If the latter are not however accepted by the workers, then after stability is restored they would seek to restore their *status quo ante* real wages. Domestic price inflation which raises the domestic price of non-traded goods would validate this for a while, but as the resulting real exchange rate appreciation once again leads to a crisis, it is not sustainable. We then get the post-Second World War cycles of Argentinian economic history where devaluation becomes the major focus for the distributional deadlock which is due in our stylised model to a polity which is in inherent conflict with the consequences of its comparative advantage.[14]

This dynamic distributional conflict can be depicted in Figure 12.3[15] in which *LL* shows the combinations of the real tradable wage (that is, the money wage deflated by the price of traded goods – which is a composite of the importable–exportable goods) and the real exchange rate (which is the relative price of non-traded to traded goods) which equates the demand for labour. It must be upward sloping as a rise in the real wage at a constant real exchange rate will generate unemployment while a rise in the real exchange rate at a constant real wage will lead to excess demand for labour. The slope of the curve must be less than unity (the slope of a ray from the origin). For suppose there is a movement along the ray from the origin, this means an equiproportionate rise in both the *tradable* real wage and real exchange rate (say with the nominal wage and price of non-traded goods rising in equal proportions). The real product wage in non-tradable production remains unchanged and hence its output remains unchanged, but traded-good producers face a rise in their real product wage and will reduce their demand for labour, creating excess supply, and these points must then lie below the equilibrium *LL* locus.

The *NN* locus shows the combinations of the real tradable wage and real exchange rate for which the non-traded good market is in equilibrium. This curve will slope upwards as a rise in the real exchange rate (keeping the real tradable wage constant) leads to excess supply of the non-traded good, which is cured by a rise in the real wage to discourage production and thereby restore equilibrium in the non-traded good market. The *NN* curve must have a slope steeper than a ray from the origin (greater than unity), as an equiproportionate rise in the real tradable wage and the real exchange rate leaves output of the non-traded good unchanged but leads to a reduction in its demand and hence to excess supply. These points must therefore lie above the *NN* locus.

The intersection of the *LL* and *NN* loci determines the equilibrium values of the real tradable wage and real exchange rate. The arrows show the direction of movements in the two variables when the economy is not in equilibrium.

With the rise in the price of exportables, there will be excess supply of labour at the initial equilibrium point *a*, as the labour use per unit of output falls in all three sectors, with the capital intensive sector – exportables – expanding. Hence *LL* will shift downwards.

Furthermore, as depicted in Figure 12.2, panel II, the relative price of services must fall in the new equilibrium, implying that there will be excess supply of non-traded goods at the old equilibrium point *a* in Figure 12.3, and hence the *NN* curve must shift to the left (see Corden and Neary, 1982, p. 836). At the new equilibrium point *b* both the real tradable wage and the real exchange rate will be lower.

However, suppose that labour resists the real wage cut. Then there will be a short-run equilibrium at *c*, with the real exchange rate appreciating. This appreciation will lead to a worsening of the

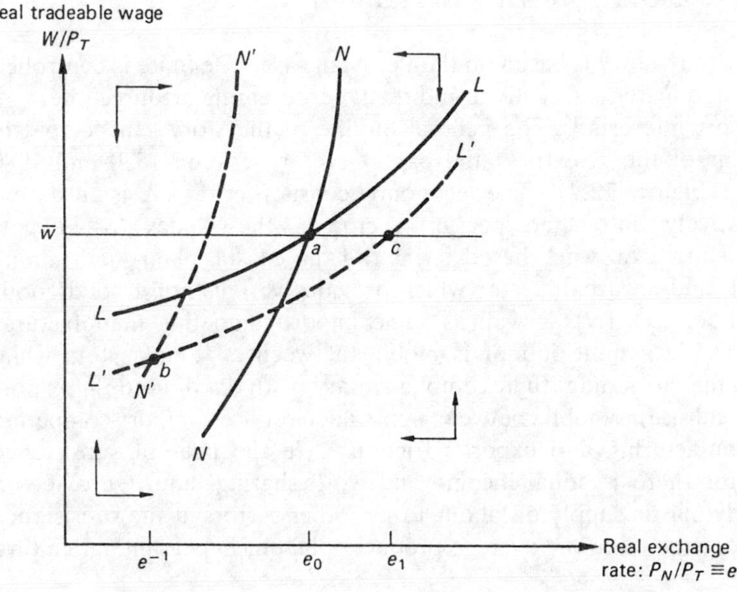

Figure 12.3

balance of payments, and at some stage as part of a package to resolve the stabilisation crisis real wage cuts and a devaluation (to lower the real exchange rate) will become inevitable. The economy will then move towards *b*. However, if subsequently an attempt is made to restore the old real wage, the economy will move back towards *c*, and the crisis will be resurrected.

We thus get the paradoxical result that a combination of the natural industrialisation induced by export led growth; the successful neoclassical adjustment during the Great Depression with the further natural growth of both non-traded good services and import-substituting industries; and the delinking from world capital and labour markets, has created a polity in Argentina where the interests of the median 'decisive' individuals no longer coincide with those which would subserve development along the lines of its comparative advantage.[16] Equally important, our model illustrates how a polity entirely determined by the changing interplay of factional interests may be worse for the social weal than a different form of polity where, as in our previous model of the predatory state, there is a non-ideological 'absolute' ruler with autonomous self-serving ends.

5 THE OLIGARCHIC STATE

Our third story is based on the Peruvian case. The State is controlled by an oligarchy, directly or indirectly representing resource intensive export interests.[17] The general outline of the story can be told in terms of the growth of the export sector between 1830 and 1980 (see Figure 12.4). The economy consists of a subsistence and relatively untouched peasant sector in the Andes (S), export agriculture on wage based farms (on the coastal plain) and mining (X), and an urban sector which provides various non-traded goods and services (N) as well as some import-competing manufactures (M). We assume labour is mobile between all four sectors while capital (including that complementary with land used in export agriculture) is mobile between non-traded services, import-competing manufacturing and export agriculture. In the peasant subsistence sector there is equal income and work sharing, and it provides a fairly elastic supply of labour to the other sectors at the subsistence income equal to the average product of labour in peasant agriculture (y_s).

The model can be depicted by Figure 12.5, which is identical to Figure 12.2, except that there is L_N L_s of labour in the subsistence

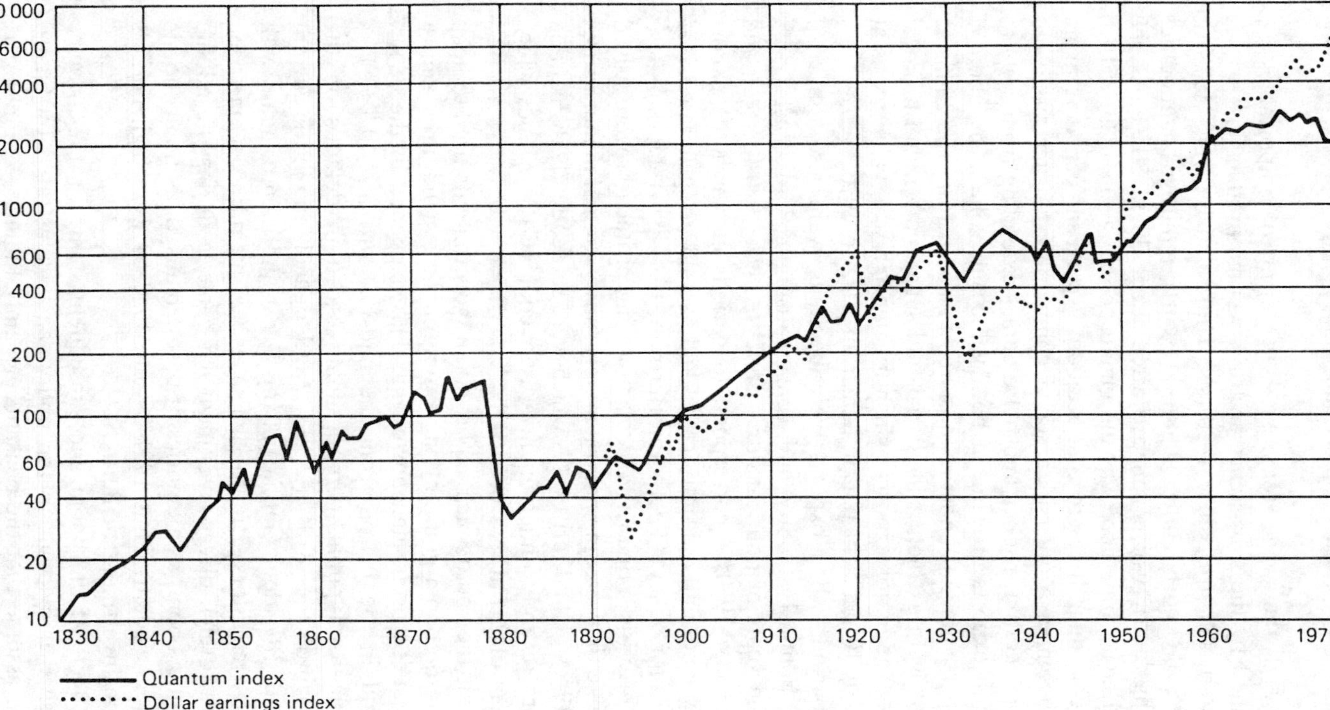

Figure 12.4 Exports 1830 to 1975: indices of volume and dollar value (1900=100)
Source: Figure 1.1, Rosemary Thorp and Geoffrey Bertram, *Peru 1890–1977 Growth and Policy in an Open Economy*, (New York: Columbia University Press, 1978, p. 5).

sector, and the wage (expressed in terms of importables) is determined by the subsistence sector's average product y_s.

The Peruvian story since 1830 (see Thorp and Bertram, 1978) is of a series of export booms in natural resource-intensive commodities (including land), which collapse after about 20 to 30 years (see Figure 12.4). Thus there was the guano boom[18] from 1830 to 1870 with export quantities growing at about 7 per cent per annum; an export boom of a diversified set of commodities – sugar followed by copper, cotton, rubber and petroleum – extending from 1890 to 1929, with exports growing in both value and volume by about 7 per cent per annum; and the most recent boom from the 1940s to late 1960s with extractive industries and sugar, cotton and fishmeal providing the major exports, which together grew in value terms at the rate of 10 per cent per annum from 1942 to 1970.

The periods when exports were booming were also those 'of greatest political stability and conservatism in Peru's history. . . whilst the years of political flux – 1882 to 1895, 1930 to 1948, and since the late 1960s – correspond to periods in which the export economy had entered into crisis and ceased to generate clear guidelines for policy' (Thorp and Bertram, 1978, p. 4). During these periods of crisis, populist voices advocating protection were raised at the same time as some natural import substitution of manufactures (in the 1940s behind tariff walls which were subsequently dismantled and more recently under quantity restriction (QR) regimes which are still in place) always occurred.

Towards the end of each export boom, governments tried to keep the domestic boom going by increasing public expenditures – most often financed by foreign borrowing. This happened in the 1870s, 1920s and in the period from the mid-1960s to mid-1970s. This foreign-financed public pump priming ended in defaults on the foreign debt in the 1870s and 1920s, and arguably too in the current cycle, with President Garcia playing a 'cat and mouse' game with his foreign creditors. But foreign investors' memories seem to be short and foreign direct investment has come in during the middle of each new boom, as memories of past defaults fade and economic recovery is evident. Thus 1901–29 and 1950–68 were high periods of foreign investment of Peru.

The effects of the boom and subsequent slump on the incomes of 'decisive' individuals in the polity can be illustrated by Figure 12.5. We assume that the peasants – mainly Indians – are not part of the 'decisive' set. As they are also, in large part, the mobile migrant labour used in the other sectors, the only 'interest' that will be represented in the polity is that of mobile 'capital', which coincides with the requirements for development in line with the country's comparative advantage. This seems to have been the case in Peru till fairly recently (see Webb, 1986). Over time, with the growth of the export economy and the absorption of labour in the 'modern' sector, the average product and hence incomes and supply price of labour in the subsistence sector will rise (y_s in Figure 12.5 will shift upwards). With the tradable wage and the relative price of importables to exportables fixed exogenously, the internal adjustments required during the export cycles will come about through changes in the rental rate on capital and the price of non-traded goods.

Thus with an export boom, the C_x curve in quadrant II of Figure 12.5 shifts outwards. As the wage is fixed, a differential is opened up in the rental rates in capital used in the export sectors (point *b*) and the import competing manufactures and non-traded good sectors (still given by point *a*). As the price of the import competing sector is fixed, C_M cannot shift; so at the given real wage y_s capital will begin shifting from the import competing sector into exportables. As the import-competing good cannot be produced at its exogenously fixed price with the same real wage and higher rental rate, the industry will shut down. (The curve L_M disappears in quadrant I.)

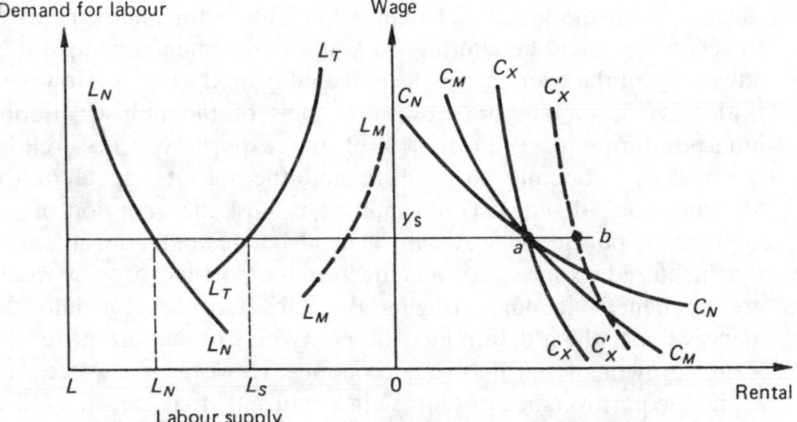

Figure 12.5

What of the non-traded good? The rise in real income and hence in the demand for the non-traded good, as well as the factor price changes represented by point *b*, imply that the C_N curve will have to shift upwards to intersect the C_x^1 curve at *b*. The price of the non-traded good must rise, and the real exchange rate appreciate. This seems to have happened in each of the Peruvian export booms (see Thorp and Bertram (1978) for the evidence on real exchange rate movements).

There will thus be a rightward shift in the L_T and L_N curves in quadrant I, with the L_M curve disappearing, and its labour being partly absorbed by the expanding exportable and the non-traded good sector. As the rental rate has risen, the 'decisive' capitalists in the polity will be content with export-led growth, as will labour to the extent that there is an increase in the demand for labour of the modern sector which, by reducing the labour force in the subsistence sector, raises y_s.

With the collapse of the export boom the above process will go into reverse, but if the 'slump' is not long-lasting the next export cycle can begin without any damage to the process of export-led growth. The main difference between the most recent 'slump' of the Peruvian economy and earlier ones is that it seems (see Thorp and Bertram, 1978; Webb, 1986) that the sources of future primary product-based export-led growth seem to be drying up as a result of the exhaustion of natural resources that could be exploited relatively cheaply, as well as the limits being reached for extending irrigation and hence the extension of the land frontier on the coast (which has produced most of the agricultural exports). Taken together with the growth of population, the factor endowments of the economy could be altering, so that the incremental comparative advantage of the country may lie in manufactured exports. However, if this is so, the import-substituting bias of the industrialisation induced during past downturns of the export cycle as well as the rise of economic nationalism and the recent appeal of the 'dependencia' ideology, could militate against the adoption of the appropriate policies which would be needed to foster labour-intensive manufactured exports. As manufactured export-led growth would greatly benefit labour, bringing the subsistence sector into the 'decisive' set which determines the polity may be important for the future growth of the Peruvian economy. However, the effects on economic performance of the rise in populism[19] that the integration of 'labour' might entail – as outlined in the second of our cautionary tales: that of the factional state – could give one cause to pause!

Notes

* The research on which this paper is based forms part of an ongoing comparative study of 'The Political Economy of Poverty, Equity and Growth', which the author is co-directing with Hla Myint, for the World Bank under RPO 673–73. Comments by participants at seminars at Duke University and the University of Texas at Austin have helped to improve the paper. The World Bank does not accept responsibility for the views expressed herein which are those of the author and should not be attributed to the World Bank or to its affiliated organisations. The findings, interpretations, and conclusions are the results of research supported by the Bank; they do not necessarily represent official policy of the Bank. The designations employed, the presentation of material and any maps used in this document are solely for the convenience of the reader and do not imply the expression of any opinion whatsoever on the part of the World Bank or its affiliates concerning the legal status of any country, territory, city, area, or of its authorities, or concerning the delimitation of its boundaries, or national affiliation.

1. See Little (1982); Lal (1983) for summaries of the evidence.
2. In Lal (1985) I have attempted to analyse the political economy factors underlying the contrasting industrial policies and outcomes in two labour-abundant economies – India and Korea.
3. Three of these countries are part of a larger set being studied in an ongoing multi-country comparative study of 'Poverty, Equity and Growth' in developing countries, which I am co-directing with Hla Myint for the World Bank. I owe Hla Myint a particular debt for the origin of some of the ideas which are common to the analytical framework underlying the comparative study and this paper.
4. See Reynolds (1985) for a good summary account of the evolution of these economies since the 1850s. The stylised facts used in telling the tales in the next 3 sections are based on the following economic histories of the countries: Argentina: Diaz–Alejandro (1970); Mallon and Sourrouille (1975); Peru: Levin (1960); Thorp and Bertram (1978); Webb (1986); Thailand: Ingram (1971); Meesook *et al.* (1986); Ghana: Killick (1978); Roemer (1984); Ansu (1984); Tanzania: Coulson (1982); Lele (1984); Collier *et al.* (1987).
5. Though in this paper we have not included monetary aspects, they can be readily incorporated into Figure 12.3, as is shown in Lal (1986a). To have included them in this paper would have led to unnecessary complications without providing any further useful insights.
6. Thus Coulson writes of the adverse effect on economic performance of the recent expansion of the bureaucracy and its *de facto* takeover of the State in Tanzania: 'The contradiction which has not been recognised is that of implementing a radical programme with a "bureaucratic bourgeoisie" – the servants of the State (with an obvious interest in expanding its services) in the paradoxical position of controlling the State. Either a section of the bureaucracy will

have . . . to pursue a more ruthless capitalist accumulation or else the workers and peasants will have to use Nyerere's ideology to take control of the State through democratic organisations . . .. By 1980 it was clear that Nyerere and the Tanzanian leadership would countenance neither alternative, and that the contradictions and stagnation of the 1970s were likely to continue' (Coulson, 1982, p. 33).

7. See Levin (1960) for a detailed discussion of this aspect of the export economy.
8. See Killick (1978) for an interpretation of irrational dirigiste economic policies under Nkrumah which emphasises that they were influenced by and based on the development economics current at that time.
9. See Coulson (1982) for a discussion of the ideological factors underlying Tanzanian policy.
10. Not seeking to expand public employment beyond the 'sustainable' level L_g' in Figure 12.1 (quadrant II).
11. In this paper the set of decisive individuals and the distribution of their factor endowments is taken to be given exogenously. However, it should be possible using simple growth economics and results from the literature on changing wealth distributions to generate the distribution of individual factor endowments endogenously.
12. See Lal (1986) for the application of a similar model to explain postwar real wage movements in the Philippines.
13. This implies that the tangency between the new production possibility curve and the highest attainable indifference curve occurs at the same unchanged real exchange rate e_o.
14. A recent historian has summarised this deadlock which focuses on devaluation as follows: 'At best devaluation was a short-term expedient, one that invariably prompted urban recession and increased political friction. After each devaluation food and import prices rose and consumption fell, which caused manufacturing output to fall and urban unemployment to increase. Recession, in turn, provoked a decline in government revenues, as the tax base narrowed and tax evasion spread. Government spending then declined, helping to hasten and deepen contraction throughout the economy. When spending did not drop quickly enough, the economic depression was accompanied by inflation. As events in 1954 first showed, political responses to devaluation were usually most potent in the aftermath of recession, once the balance of payments was improving, manufacturing again reviving, and unemployment falling. At this point, as the labour market tightened, the trade unions led strike campaigns to restore the predevaluation wage share in national income. But then as wages rose, so too did production costs and soon prices. The mounting inflation again channelled exportables into the home market. While manufacturers increased production, imports were also rising, which renewed the balance-of-payments crisis and required another devaluation. Through this chain of intersectoral income shifts, changes in relative prices, and inflation, each

devaluation thus carried the seedling of its successor' (Rock, 1985, pp. 327–8).

15. See Neary (1985), Prachowny (1981), Lal (1986a) for further details about this diagram.
16. The model also illustrates how the changing structure of the polity impinges on the precommitment of the State to free trade. Thus in the post-1942 period in Argentina the State's earlier precommitment to free trade can no longer be taken for granted.
17. The earlier phase of the Argentinian study can also be taken to be one of the 'oligarchic state'.
18 See Levin (1960) for a detailed discussion.
19. It could be argued that populism has already captured the State in the form of President Garcia. But it is doubtful whether the Andean peasants have been integrated into the polity by APRA, whose 'populism' is therefore likely to be rhetorical, and similar to the rhetoric which has been dominant at each downturn in past Peruvian export cycles.

References

Ansu, Y. (1984) 'Comment' in Harberger, A. C. (ed.).

Baumol, W. J., Panzar, J. C. and Willig, R. D. (1982) *Contestable Markets and the Theory of Industry Structure*, (San Diego: Harcourt Brace Jovanovich).

Birnberg, T. B. and Resnick, S. A. (1975) *Colonial Development* (Yale University Press).

Brennan, G. and Buchanan, J. M. (1980) *The Power to Tax* (Cambridge University Press).

Buchanan, J. M. *et al.* (eds) (1980) *Towards a Theory of the Rent-Seeking Society* (Texas A and M University Press).

Caves, R. (1965) ' "Vent For Surplus" Models of Trade and Growth', in Baldwin, R. E. *et al.*, *Trade Growth and the Balance of Payments* (Amsterdam: North Holland, 1966).

Collier, P., Bevan, D. and Gunning, J. (1987) 'East African Lessons on Economic Liberalization', Thames Essay No. 48, Trade Policy Research Centre, London.

Corden, W. M. and Neary, J. P. (1982) 'Booming Sector and De-Industrialisation in A Small Open Economy', *The Economic Journal*, December.

Coulson, A. (1982) *Tanzania – A Political Economy*, (Oxford: Clarendon Press).

Diaz–Alejandro, C. (1970) *Essays on the Economic History of the Argentine Republic* (Yale).

Findlay, R. and Wellisz, S. (1982) 'Endogenous Tariffs, the Political Economy of Trade Restrictions and Welfare' in Bhagwati, J. N. (ed.) *Import Competition and Response* (University of Chicago Press).

Findlay, R. and Wellisz, S. (1983) 'Some Aspects of the Political Economy of Trade Restrictions', *Kyklos,* Vol. 36, Fasco 3, pp. 469–81.

Findlay, R. and Wellisz, S. (1984) 'Protection and Rent-Seeking in Developing Countries' in Colander D. (ed.) *Neoclassical Political Economy* (Cambridge, Mass: Ballinger).

Findlay, R. and Wilson, J. (1987) 'The Political Economy of Leviathan', in Razin, A. and Sadka, E. (eds) *Economic Policy in Theory and Practice* (New York: St Martin's Press).

Harberger, A. C. (ed.) (1984) *World Economic Growth* (San Francisco: Institute for Contemporary Studies).

Hopkins, A. G. (1973) *An Economic History of West Africa* (Columbia University Press).

Ingram, J. C. (1971) *Economic Change in Thailand, 1850–1970* (Stanford University Press).

Jones, R. (1971) 'A Three Factor Model in Theory, Trade and History' in Bhagwati, J. *et al.* (eds) *Trade, The Balance of Payments and Growth* (Amsterdam: North Holland).

Kenen, P. B. (1965) 'Nature, Capital and Trade', *Journal of Political Economy*, October, Vol. 73, no. 5, pp. 437–60.

Killick, T. (1978) *Development Economics in Action – A Study of Economic Policies in Ghana* (London: Heinemann Educational Books).

Krueger, A. O. (1974) 'The Political Economy of the Rent-Seeking Society', *American Economic Review*, June.

Lal, D. (1983) *The Poverty of 'Development Economics'* (IEA, London, 1983, American Edition, Harvard, 1985).

Lal, D. (1984) 'The Political Economy of the Predatory State', DRD discussion paper no. 105, mimeo, World Bank.

Lal, D. (1985) 'Ideology and Industrialisation in India and East Asia' in Hughes, H. and Riedel, J. (eds) *Industrialisation in East and Southeast Asia*, proceedings of a conference at ANU, Canberra, September 1985, to be published by Cambridge.

Lal, D. (1986) 'Stopler–Samuelson–Rybczynski in the Pacific: Real Wages and Real Exchange Rates in the Philippines 1956–1978', *Journal of Development Economics*, April. Vol. 21, no. 1, pp. 181–204.

Lal, D. (1986a) 'A Simple Framework for Analyzing Various Real Aspects of Stabilization and Structural Adjustment Policies', mimeo, VPERS, World Bank, September, *Journal of Development Studies* (forthcoming).

Lele, U. (1984) 'Tanzania: Phoenix or Icarus?', in Harberger, A. C. (ed.).

Levin, J. V. (1960) *The Export Economies* (Cambridge, Mass: Harvard University Press).

Little, I. M. D. (1982) *Economic Development – Theory, Policies and International Relations* (New York: Basic Books).

Mallon, R. D. and Sourrouille, J. V. (1975) *Economic Policymaking in a Conflict Society: The Argentine Case* (Cambridge, Mass: Harvard University Press).

Mayer, W. (1984) 'Endogenous Tariff Formation', *American Economic Review*, December. Vol. 74, no. 5, December, pp. 970–85.

Meesook, O., Tinakorn, P. and Vaddhanaphuti, C. (1986) 'The Political Economy of Poverty, Equity and Growth – Thailand', draft mimeo paper presented to the Lisbon workshop July 7–16, 1986, VPERS, World Bank, June.

Myint, H. (1958) 'The "Classical Theory" of International Trade and the Underdeveloped Countries', *Economic Journal*, vol. 68, no. 270, June, pp. 317–37.

Neary, J. P. (1985) 'Theory and Policy of Adjustment in an Open Economy', in Greenway, D. (ed.) *Current Issues in International Trade: Theory and Policy* (London: Macmillan).

Prachowny, M. (1981) 'Sectoral Conflict Over Stabilization Policies in Small Open Economies', *The Economic Journal*, vol. 91, no. 363, September, pp. 67–84.

Reynolds, L. G. (1985) *Economic Growth in The Third World 1850–1890* (New Haven, Conn.: Yale University Press).

Rock, D. (1985) *Argentina 1516–1982* (California).

Roemer, M. (1984) 'Ghana 1950–80: Missed Opportunities' in Harberger A. C. (ed.).

Ruffin, R. and Jones, R. W. (1977) 'Protection and Real Wages: The Neoclassical Ambiguity', *Journal of Economic Theory*, Vol. 14, no. 2, April, pp. 337–48.

Snape, R. H. (1977) 'Effects of Mineral Development on the Economy', *Australian Journal of Agricultural Economics*, vol. 21, no. 3, December, pp. 147–56.

Thorp, R. and Bertram, G. (1978) *Peru 1890–1977* (Columbia University Press).

Webb, R. (1986) 'The Political Economy of Poverty, Equity and Growth – Peru 1948–1985', draft paper for the Lisbon workshop, June 1986, mimeo, VPERS (Washington, DC, World Bank).

4

After the Debt Crisis: Modes of Development for the Longer Run in Latin America

Deepak Lal

1 Introduction

My brief in this chapter is to consider alternative modes of development for the longer run after the debt crisis has been solved. In discussing this issue, it is clearly of some importance to know whether the solution will involve confrontation between lenders and borrowers, and the long-run disruption of international trade and investment flows, or whether some middle way will be found which allows Latin America to adjust and grow out of its debt burden without severance of its international ties. Being an optimist by nature, I shall assume the latter more hopeful outcome of the debt crisis.

Moreover, there is also an emerging professional consensus that in the face of similar external shocks, the severity of the Latin American debt crisis (as compared with that in East Asia for example) was primarily due to its mistakes (often long-standing) concerning trade and exchange rate (macroeconomic) policies. As Sachs (1985), Balassa (1985), Mitra (1986) have shown, the external shocks faced by Latin America in the 1979–83 period were no greater than those faced by various East Asian countries. Yet the latter (with the exception of the Philippines) managed to adjust fairly smoothly to the global interest rate and terms of trade shocks, without impairment of their medium- and long-term growth processes. The decisive difference was that, for similar debt to GDP ratios in the two regions, Latin America had much higher debt to export and, *ipso facto*, debt service ratios. It is now conventional wisdom that this was due to Latin America's failure to use its foreign borrowing to expand its output of tradables sufficiently to meet future debt-servicing needs.

The question about future modes of development, at least at a technocratic level, can be answered fairly simply. The major lesson of the debt crisis, which I believe most professional observers would accept, is the need

Table 4.1 Openness index in selected Latin American countries, 1965–1985*

	1965	1970	1975	1980	1985
Argentina	–	–	33.8	12.8	18.4[a]
Bolivia	40.2	33.6	41.4	30.9	14.6[b]
Brazil	12.5	13.7	19.3	21.0	20.2[b]
Chile	18.6	29.2	61.1	35.5	38.0
Colombia	22.0	22.5	23.8	27.2	21.0
Costa Rica	48.9	55.6	60.5	52.6	56.8
Dom. Republic	23.3	37.2	49.5	39.2	47.7
Ecuador	28.6	33.1	45.5	40.3	33.4[b]
Guatemala	31.3	30.6	37.1	40.0	25.6[b]
Mexico	13.0	10.9	10.8	18.9	13.3
Panama	43.6	45.7	64.0	50.8	37.4
Peru	33.0	26.6	31.4	41.9	31.6[b]
Uruguay	34.8	19.3	29.3	29.0	34.8[b]
Venezuela	45.2	38.3	53.7	52.4	51.6[b]

*This index was constructed as the ratio of total trade (imports plus exports) to GDP.
[a] 1983
[b] 1984
Source: Edwards (1987), constructed from data from the IMF

to improve Latin America's "capacity to transform." As defined by Kindleberger, "capacity to transform is capacity to react to change, originating at home or abroad, by adapting the structure of foreign trade to the new situation in an economic fashion" (Kindleberger, 1967, p. 99). Trade and exchange rate policies are important determinants of this capacity to transform. Latin American experience, as well as that of other developing countries, attests to this fact. An important indicator of Latin America's failure to create this "capacity to transform" – as compared to the so-called Gang of Four (South Korea, Taiwan, Singapore and Hong Kong) – is provided by their different responses to the "transfer problem" associated with the debt crisis. A good measure is provided by an openness index constructed by Edwards (1987) and reproduced in table 4.1. This shows that, during the 1970s, Latin America had been moving away from the "inward orientation," which had been seen since the mid-1960s to be inimical to its growth prospects. This is shown by the rise in the openness index between 1965 and 1980 in most Latin American countries seen in table 4.1. This in turn was due to various measures of trade liberalization undertaken by many countries, partly as a response to the first oil crisis. But this liberalization was half-hearted and (except in Chile) incomplete (see Edwards and Teitel, 1986; Corbo and de Melo (1985) for an overview of the Southern Cone liberalization programs during this period). Hence, when the debt crisis hit, the required adjustment was made by a reversal of these liberal policies, through import contraction rather than export expansion. The openness index then fell for most Latin American countries.

This in turn, as is now commonly accepted, is due to the "inward oriented" development strategy that Latin American countries have by and large followed during the post-war years. It has been recognized (at least since the 1960s), that Latin America needed to move away from import-substituting towards export-promoting industrialization.[1] This has either not been done, or done only belatedly in many cases. At the same time, in large part because of this failure to develop in line with its changing comparative advantage, Latin American countries have relied on various fantastic "macroeconomic fixes" to reconcile the irreconcilable, with dire consequences for the stability of income growth over the long run.

As numerous observers have emphasized, this failure to create the "capacity to transform" is not due to ignorance of the policies required, or because of a lack of professional consensus on the desirable policies. These have been successfuly summed up by Harberger (1984) in a set of policy rules which development professionals would endorse (even though they might disagree about the precise sequence and timing of the requisite policy reforms). Those which are uncontroversial are:

1 avoid false technicism in economic policy-making;
2 keep budgets under adequate control
3 keep inflationary pressures under reasonable control;
4 take advantage of international trade;
5 some types and patterns of trade restriction are far worse than others . . . only a given uniform rate of tariff can automatically avoid capricious and distorting variations in the effective rates of protection actually achieved;
6 if import restrictions become excessive, and reducing them directly is politically impossible, mount an indirect attack on the problem by increasing incentives to export;
7 Make tax systems simple, easy to administer, and (as far as possible) neutral and non-distorting. (Harberger, 1984, pp. 428–32)[2]

The continuing failure to apply known remedies requires an explanation. Increasingly, many observers realize that these explanations must lie in the realm of political economy. Thus Sachs, in his 1985 survey of responses of Latin America and East Asian countries, rightly notes, "the foundations for export promotion policies in Asia and for import-substitution policies in Latin America are political. It is essential to understand the political economy of export promotion in order to understand the continuing paralysis of Latin American economies" (Sachs, 1985, pp. 525–6). I agree – though, as we shall see, not with Sachs's political economy! The rest of this chapter, therefore is concerned with considering various answers to the question, what, if any, are the impediments, in terms of its political economy which would prevent Latin America from adopting the mode of development – outward orientation – which is generally agreed to be necessary for equitable and stable growth in the long run?

In the next section, I survey various answers to this question, and, not surprisingly, find them wanting. The following section presents a simple trade–theoretic political economy model of that brave abstraction – a "typical Latin American country", which provides some explanations for what I have elsewhere (Lal, 1986) labelled a continent with "a political economy in conflict with its comparative advantage."

2 The Political Economy of Latin America's Trade Regime

Sachs (1985) argues that it is the relative weight of rural versus urban interests in Latin America compared with East Asia, which explains why an export-led strategy has been possible in the latter but not the former region. For "trade restrictions tend to shift income from the agricultural and mineral producing sectors toward the industrial and service sectors." Hence if, as he argues, the weight of rural interests (as judged by the inverse of the degree of urbanization) is decisive in the polity, the country will be successful in developing exports. But, as Williamson and others noted in commenting on Sachs's paper, the political power of rural interests is not necessarily correlated with their relative share in the total population. As Olson (1982) has argued, because of the "free rider" problem, the larger the potential beneficiaries from the activities of a pressure group, the more difficult it is to organize such a group. This partly explains why more developed countries, with a low share of their population in agriculture tend to subsidize, whilst developing countries with a larger share of their population in rural areas, tend to tax agriculture (see Lipton, 1977, for a documentation of the urban bias in most developing countries). Hence Sachs's argument is unconvincing.

Hirschman, as the doyen of Latin American political economists, can be expected to have a view on the factors which have inhibited an outward-oriented development policy in Latin America, though over the years he seems to have changed his mind. In Hirschman (1968) he argues that, because of the power of dominant rural interest groups, it was not possible for the export sector directly to subsidize the industrial sector – the "optimal" policy if the noneconomic objective (presumably) of promoting industry is accepted. Instead, inadvertently and unnoticed, Latin American governments discovered the expedient of maintaining inflationary regimes with an overvalued currency, as an indirect method of achieving the same end.

However, when it was no longer in the interest of industrialists to maintain overvaluation, they were not able to reverse the bias against exporting; they were not influential partly because they did not export. Hence Hirschman's vicious circle: "industrialists are not influential because they do not export, and they do not export because they are not influential" (p. 30). But as with most "vicious circle" type arguments, this is unconvincing.

For underlying these Hirschman Mark 1 arguments is a very peculiar view of the typical Latin American state.[3] It is an aloof and whimsical despotism.

But this view is surely implausible. First, as political scientists have emphasized (see the excellent survey of this literature by Wynia, 1984), though appearing strong, Latin American states are weak – in large part because of the lack of any agreement on the rules of the political game. This leads to a diversity of political rules within many Latin American countries and "is primarily the product of a failure to solve the fundamental problem of political legitimacy that arises in all political systems" (Wynia, 1984, p. 30). This lack of consensus on a legitimate set of political rules means that "groups and individuals who discover that the prevailing rules favour others more than themselves may prefer to undermine the rules rather than obey them" (p. 36).

It also means that every incumbent of the national monopoly, i.e. the state (providing rents for the incumbent and the public goods – hopefully – of law and order for its citizens), will find his monopoly contestable[4] (in the sense of Baumol et al., 1982).[5] The typical Latin American president "plagued by a lack of agreement on the rules of the game . . . may claim as much legal authority as do his more secure neighbours, but in practice he often finds himself constrained by the uncertainties created by the lack of political consensus and his vulnerability to the use of political resources by his opponents" (Wynia, 1984, p. 37). This is a vision of a *harried* ruler "pinned and wriggling on the wall"[6], whose thrashings for survival impart that unpredictability to Latin American economic policy that Hirschman rightly laments.

By 1981, Hirschman views that Latin American state's autonomy as being relatively limited. He distinguishes between an "autonomous state": "the state is endowed with a will of its own . . . [it] has an *interest*, a *raison d'état* which it pursues single-mindedly" (Hirschman, 1981, p. 147), and a "coping state": which for him is "a state which does not act but reacts".

The autonomous state is a "maximizer" whilst the coping state is a "satisficer".

I do not find Hirschman's distinctions between a maximizing "autonomous" and a satisficing "coping" state altogether cogent. It would take me too far afield to explain my doubts about his typology of the state in any detail. Instead, let me present my own typology, which I have found particularly useful in the context of a multi-country comparative study of the political economy of poverty and growth, which I am co-directing with Hla Myint (Lal, 1984, 1986).

The *first* of the types of state, rarely observed but implicitly assumed by much of the technocratic economic policy literature, is the "benevolent state", run by selfless Platonic guardians or a benevolent dictator, maximizing the social welfare of its citizens. The *second*, I label the "predatory state". This is a state run by a self-serving absolute ruler, such as a monarch, dictator or charismatic leader. This sovereign, too, is autonomous, insofar as the constellation of domestic interest groups has little direct effect on his/her policies. For analytical purposes the selfish predatory sovereign is assumed to maximize either net revenue (treasure) or courtiers (bureaucrats).

The *third* type of state I call "factional." This is a state which subserves the interests of the coalition of pressure groups which succeeds in its capture. The interests served are narrowly defined (again for analytical simplicity) to be the economic self-interests of the constituents of government. The method of capturing the state need not be majoritarian democracy, even though such a form of government would be compatible with this type of state.[7]

I would contend that the Latin American state is typically a factional state, though the other types are also observed. Thus, controversially, it can be argued that Pinochet's Chile fits the model of the "benevolent state". It has set itself above the hurly-burly of pressure group activity and seeks to subserve the commonweal – as it sees it. From the scanty evidence available and summarized in the recent World Bank report *Poverty in Latin America*, Chile stands apart, as the one state which has met the adjustment needs of the debt crisis by preserving targetted social welfare programs, whilst cutting back on other inefficient public expenditure and in liberalizing the economy, much as mainstream economic policy advisers would recommend.[8]

Of our second "ideal" type, Mexico under the Partido Revolucionario Institucional (PRI), I contend, provides an example of the "bureaucratic maximizing" variety of "predatory state". But most of the other Latin American states are factional. In a few of these, where there is a political consensus, as in Costa Rica, a relatively stable majoritarian democracy is the form of the factional state. In most of the others, the lack of political consensus has meant a constant shuffling of different coalitions of interest groups capturing the state by fair means or foul.

In all these models the controllers of the state are maximizers – though the maximand clearly differs from one type of state to the other. There is no place for "satisficing" which, as Hahn (1985) for instance has recently noted, is not a well-defined notion.[9] But to delineate the lack of political consensus as a "characteristic trait" of Latin American polities still does not explain it, nor tell us if, and how, it can be changed.

Here Hirschman (1979) is more useful. He now finds a major source of the failure of Latin America to adopt the necessary outward oriented policies to be the fickleness of its intellectuals, and the ideological polarization of proponents of what he calls the "entrepreneural" and "reform functions" in the course of economic development.[10]

He argues that Latin American intellectuals have been wedded to the "structuralist" school's desire to "search for the deep problems – such as certain land tenure conditions – that were believed to underlie the surface problems of inflation and balance of payments disequilibrium". But they have probably gone too far. The resulting barrage of fundamental remedies proposed to cure Latin American ills by this school – planning in the 1950s, economic integration in the early 1960s, domestic redistribution of income and wealth, and restructuring international economic relations to reduce *dependencia* (in the late 1960s) – has sapped the will of Latin American states. For "now, more difficult tasks were continuously presented to the state and society *whether or not* the previous task had been succesfully disposed of. . . This strange process of ideological escalation may well have contributed to that pervasive sense of being in a desperate predicament which is a precondition for radical regime change" (p. 86).

But this will not do. For surely, apart from any frustration arising from the overloading of the state's agenda, created by this structuralist factory of panaceas, there is the more important question, were the proposed remedies sound? One has only to read Ian Little's (1982) devastating critique of structuralism to recognize that, at least, it is arguable whether Latin American countries would have been better served if the structuralist program had been presented at a measured sequential pace, and been adopted.[11]

I would, however, agree with Hirschman that ideas and ideology do matter, if for no other reason than *my* obvious self-interest in believing this to be the case! But I think the role of ideas and ideology in determining policies can be overdone. Ideas to be fruitful must fall on fertile ground. An important task of social science must, in my view, be to explain why certain ideas, in certain places and at certain times, seem to command attention by delineating the factors which lead to changes in the climate of opinion. For though we may all be persuaded by Keynes's argument about the hysteresis in the process whereby new ideas are accepted by "madmen in authority", nevertheless, the important turning-points in human history have (at least) been correlated with changes in the climate of opinion.

It is in this context that the implicit explanation provided by Veliz (1980) for the failure of Latin America to adopt the required outwardly-oriented industrialization policies is of some interest. Veliz contrasts the centralist Iberian tradition – which, he argues, has moulded the actions of all the incumbents of Latin American states – with the more decentralized tradition based on Lockean rights and the ideas of the Scottish enlightenment, which provided the ideological ballast for the states of Anglo-Saxon extraction during their period of industrialization.[12]

Veliz considers the liberalization of trade in the nineteenth century open economies of Latin America as merely "a liberal pause" in the deep-seated centralizing tendencies inherited by Latin America from its Iberian conquerors. The Great Depression and its aftermath greatly enhanced the role of the central state, which became the main financier of private industrial ventures, the "arbiter in the process of income redistribution through the implementation of a variety of social policies; and it assigned a dynamic role to the public sector" (Veliz, 1980, p. 259).

The role of the intellegentsia in the subsequent decades, however, was to aid and abet the centralizing state because of the "redistributive bent of [the] populism and social democracy" many of them supported. "By the early sixties, the populist and social democratic cornucopia had consolidated huge pressure groups that regarded their better interests as identical with those of a prosperous central State" (ibid, p. 290).

As the means of funding these growing entitlements declined, "the social democratic regimes had to face growing discontent, especially among the middle sectors whose expectations had risen highest during the decades of largess and were consequently more vulnerable to rising inflation and declining economic fortunes. Their appeals, however, were not for a revolutionary change of the social and economic system, but for more state intervention along the same lines as before" (ibid, p. 292). Meanwhile the intellegentsia, Veliz contends, adopted the fashionable view of the Cuban Revolution current amongst the radical intellegentsia in the West at the time, namely that "Latin America [had] become the revolutionary frontier" (p. 295). The terrorist campaigns they launched changed the attitudes "of the urban middle sectors . . . and opened the door to the current process of authoritarian recentralization", (p. 293). It is particularly pertinent in this context that "in Latin America the military have traditionally been drawn not from the upper strata of society, but from the middle and, increasingly, from the lower middle sectors. . . . To the violent revolutionary actions of the extreme left wing terrorists, the middle sectors responded first with legal repressive measures administered by social democratic regimes. When these appeared insufficient to stem the tide of violence or when the parallel economic deterioration threatened general institutional collapse, the middle sectors appealed to the military for help" (p. 297).

But Veliz notes two paradoxes in the economic policies of economic liberalization that the subsequent military governments have espoused (though not always followed).[13] The first is that "it was precisely those [failed] policies that greatly enlarged and consolidated the vast urban clientele that called them to power, to dismantle the public sector built over the past three or four decades would risk their disaffection" (ibid, p. 299). The second paradox is that "absolute central power is exercised absolutely in the name of liberal economic theories and schemes whose obvious pre-requisites are diversity and freedom of choice" (ibid, p. 301).

Veliz seems to me to provide a more cogent picture of the intellectual and social forces underlying the continuing Latin American crisis than that presented, for instance, by Hirschman. It is these forces which I seek to examine more analytically in the next section, to show why even though the technocratic remedies for long-term growth in Latin America are by now uncontroversial, it may be difficult for Latin American governments to follow these policies consistently.[14]

3 The Political Economy of the Factional State

The starting point for any political economy of the factional state in Latin America has to recognize an important but paradoxical difference between Latin America and East Asia (for instance), This is the former's relative "embarrassment of riches". An excellent picture of this is provided in figure 4.1, which reproduces Leamer's (1987) depiction of the factor endowments of a sample of countries in a triangular endowment simplex which has three factors of production – land, labor and capital as its three vortices.[15]

One striking fact is that, whereas most of the East Asian "Gang of Four" are on, or close to, the labor–capital axis, most Latin American countries – being relatively land and natural resource abundant, both with respect to labor and capital – are positioned towards the land vortex. This is their "embarrassment of riches" which in a 3-factor–*n* good model can lead to some surprising and, from the viewpoint of political economy, difficult development paths, as compared with the land-scarce East Asian countries. In her Graham lecture, Krueger (1977) emphasized the importance of explicitly accounting for land as a separate factor of production in models of trade and growth. Leamer's work (1984, 1987) has provided further empirical and analytical support for her insights.[16]

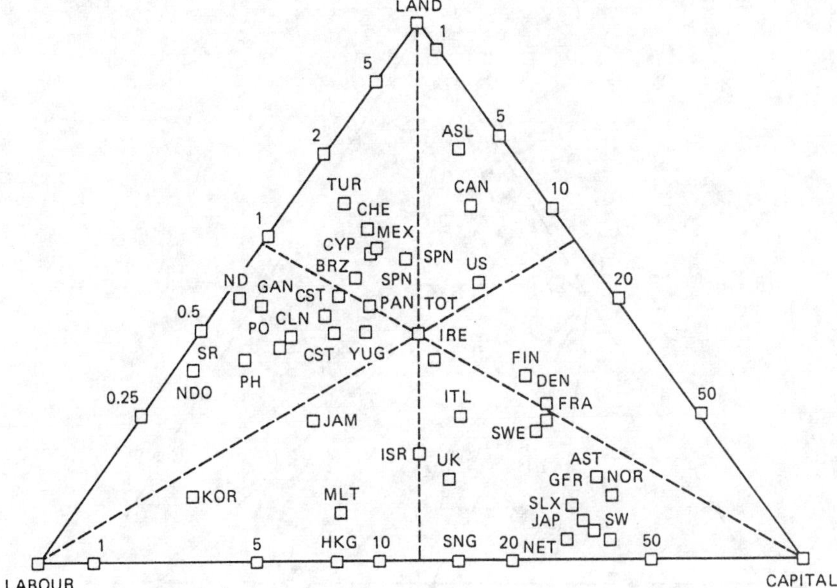

Figure 4.1 Endowment ratios displayed in an endowment triangle

Source: Edward Leamer (1987)

It is the political economy of industrialization that we consider in this 3-factor–n good model, and show how natural resource riches can turn out to be "a precious bane".[17] We follow Leamer (1987) and assume for simplicity that all goods are produced through fixed proportions techniques, so that there is a single input vector corresponding to each commodity. The production functions are the same all over the world, in keeping with the Hecksher–Ohlin tradition. Free trade is assumed. For simplicity we also assume that all goods are traded.[18]

Let us assume that in the world economy, there are five manufactured goods indexed from 1–5, produced with only labor and capital. They are of increasing capital intensity and their input vectors are shown as $M_1 \ldots M_5$ along the labor–capital edge of the Leamer endowment triangle in figure 4.2. In addition there are two agricultural goods. The first A_1 is produced with only labor and land, and lies on the labor (L) and land (T) edge of the endowment triangle. The second A_2 uses all three factors of production, but it is more land-intensive than the agricultural good A_1.

The seven points representing the input vectors and the three axis co-ordinates are connected by line segments to divide the endowment triangle into seven "regions of diversification",[19] for a given set of com-

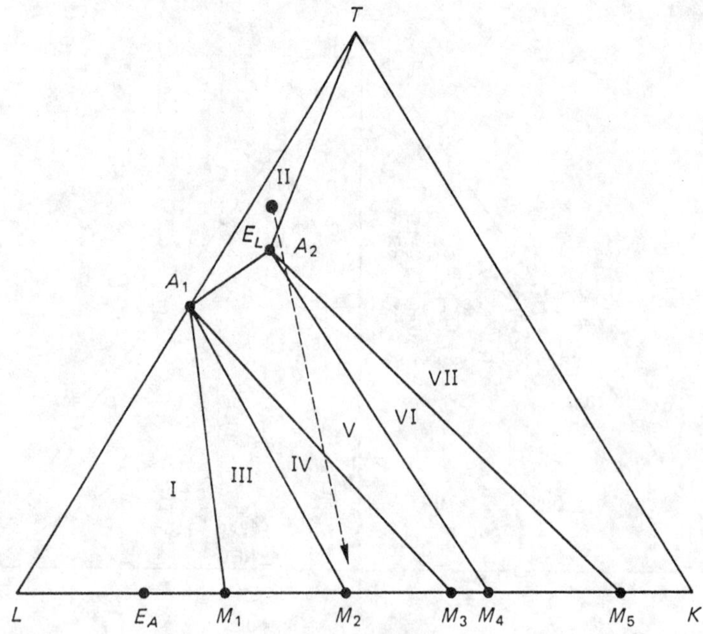

Figure 4.2 Regions of diversification in the Leamer endowment triangle

	Outputs produced	*Wage rate*
Region I	A_1, M_1	W_1
Region II	A_1, A_2	$W_2 > W_1$
Region III	A_1, M_1, M_2	$W_3 > W_1$
Region IV	A_1, M_2, M_3	$W_4 > W_3$
Region V	A_1, A_2, M_3, M_4	$W_5 > W_4$
Region VI	A_2, M_4, M_5	$W_6 > W_5$
Region VII	A_2, M_5	$W_7 > W_6 > W_2$

modity prices for the seven commodities. The factor endowment vectors of different countries can also be represented by points in land–labor–capital space in the endowment triangle. Then it can be shown that countries with endowment points in the same region of diversification will have the same factor prices and produce the same commodities with the vector inputs given by the vertices of the regions of diversification. The commodities produced in the seven regions are listed in the notes to figure 4.2. Given commodity prices, relative factor intensities determine factor prices in each of these regions.

Now consider two possible paths of development in this model. The first is that of the typical East Asian "Gang of Four", whose endowment point E_A is on, or close to, the labor–capital axis. With capital accumulating faster than the growth of the labor force, the country moves from region I, to III to IV. In this process it moves up the ladder of comparative advantage with respect to manufactured goods, with rising capital intensity. Hence, on this development path the wage rises and the rental on capital falls.

The second path is for a land abundant Latin American country whose endowment point E_L lies in the region of diversification II, where it produces both the relatively labor-intensive agricultural good A_1 and the land-cum-capital intensive good A_2. We concentrate on one possible path of development, which seems plausible for a number of Latin American countries. We assume that, as in the previous case, both capital and labor are growing. Over time the economy's land–labor ratio will be falling, and its capital–labor ratio rising. Suppose this path of the economy's changing endowments is given by the dashed line from E_L. Over time, the economy will then move from region II to VII to VI to IV. In this process it will begin to industrialize as soon as it moves into region VII, *but in the most capital-intensive* manufacture. Over time it will move into regions of specialization in which *specialization in increasingly more labor-intensive* goods is required. The factor price consequence of this development path, in line with the emerging and changing comparative advantage of the economy, is that the wage rate will fall, and from the time the economy moves into region VII, the rental rates on capital and land will keep rising. Clearly, as compared with the stylized East Asian case (with rising wages), the distributional implications of this stylized Latin American development path (with a falling or constant wage) for an open economy would seem to be politically hazardous. But note that even though the wage might be falling on the Latin American development path, it will still be higher than on the East Asian path till they converge on the region of specialization in region IV.[20, 21]

It is time to introduce the political features of the factional state. I do this following Lal (1986), using certain ideas developed by Mayer (1984) in endogenizing tariff formation for the political economy of trade policy in developed countries.

Suppose, initially, that there are only two factors of production, capital (K) and labor (L). All individuals in the economy can be described by their respective capital – labor ($k_1 = K_1/L_1$) endowments. The *mean* of the individual k_1 endowments will be the aggregate capital–labor endowment $K = k$ of the economy.

Next we define the set of individuals who are *decisive*, in the sense that they can compete for the capture of the state and thus the determinants of economic policies subserving their interests. Suppose, initially, that *all* economic agents in the population form part of the decisive set of the polity, and the political mechanism is democratic – with "one man one vote" – and the majority capturing the state. All voters vote according to their economic interests. Then from the well-known median voter theorem, the median voter's capital–labor endowment (k_m) will determine the interests that will be served by the coalition of majoritarian interest groups who capture the state. If the distribution of individual factor endowments is symmetric, so that its median and the mean are the same, the median endowment will be identical to the average for the economy as a whole ($k = k_m$). Then, from the law of comparative advantage, we know that the income of the median individual will be maximized by free trade. If, however, the median individual endowment is more (less) capital-intensive than the average, the median voter's income-generating interests will be in a tariff (subsidy) on capital-intensive imports or a subsidy (tariff) on labor-intensive imports. Thus, in this form of the pressure group model, what we need to know is the mean of the national factor endowment, and median of the distribution of the income-generating factor endowments of the set of decisive individuals.

Initially, in our typical Latin American polity with factor endowments given by E_L in figure 4.2 the "decisive" individuals are the landlords. This is the oligarchic phase of Latin American development. The oligarchs' median endowment of land to labor is likely to be greater than the average endowment for the economy as a whole (in region II). This implies that (as in the nineteenth century), the interest of the median "decisive" individual in the oligarchic polity will be served by free trade. As the economy grows, with capital accumulating and population expanding, but without any expansion of the "polity", the median endowment of the land and capital of the landed oligarchy will still be higher than the average of the economy, and so the oligarchy will still wish to maintain free trade.

However, suppose that over time, with the introduction of manufacturing and the growth of the labor-force, pressures grow for enlarging the polity, and a coalition (populist) dominated by individuals with more labor, relative to capital or land, comes to capture the factional state. Suppose this happens during the transition of the economy from region VI (where the wage was higher than in region II) to region V. During this phase, as relatively more labor-intensive manufacturing comes into the "region of specialization", there will be inexorable downward pressures on the real wage. It is in the interest of the median member of the enlarged polity (whose endowments are dominated by labor) to *prevent* this outcome. This end may be achieved by placing a tariff on the more labor-intensive of the two goods produced in region VI, namely M_4. This will, *ceteris paribus*, raise the equilibrium capital-labor ratio in M_5, lower that in M_4, and raise the land-labor ratio in the production of the agricultural good A_2[22] Thus the A_2 point will shift north-eastwards the K vortex, and M_4 towards the L vortex. This will enlarge the region of specialization VI, and allow the new endowment point which would otherwise have fallen in region V to remain in region VI, with a higher wage and lower rental rates on capital and land (Deardoff, 1984, p. 740).

Over time, however, for well-known reasons, the inefficiencies associated with protection will lower the efficiency of the economy. If this also leads to a lowering of the rate of capital formation relative to the labor supply, then the future transition to a lower real wage economy will be accelerated.

Similar pressures for protection can be expected to arise in a factional state, where the median individual in the ruling coalition of interests controlling the state has an endowment dominated by labor relative to capital or land, when there is a terms-of-trade improvement. For in a country whose exports are more capital-intensive than its imports, the rise in relative export price will put downward pressure on the real wage, as the expanding capital-intensive sector creates incipient excess supply of labor, and excess demand for capital and land (see Lal, 1986a, for the details).[23] It is not surprising therefore that the populist phase in Latin America, by and large, coincided with the terms-of-trade improvements for primary product producers associated with the Korean War boom of the early 1950s. *Mutatis mutandis*, periods of terms-of-trade losses would also be periods where the interest of the median member of the enlarged polity is no longer at odds with a reduction in protection. For the terms-of-trade decline would mean that the relative profitability of the more labor-intensive goods would rise, and this would enlarge the region of specialization in figure 4.2, where the more labor-intensive good would be viable at the continuing high wage (previously validated by protection) without protection. Apart, therefore, from the swings in Latin American politics based on conjunctural factors (primarily of a macroeconomic nature),[24] these considerations based on our model of the long-run development of the Latin American factional state, provide some further reasons why periods of marked terms-of-trade improvements should be associated with pressures for protection and those with terms-of-trade losses with moves towards liberalization.

There are a number of other features of Latin American political economy (touched upon briefly in the preceding section) which I hope the model of the Latin American factional state can illumine. First, as we have noted, the development path charted by the dashed arrow in figure 4.2 can be deflected towards the (*K*) vortex, the higher the rate of capital accumulation relative to the economy's rate of population growth. The greater this deflection, the more likely it is that the development path will follow the normal course (as in East Asia) with wages rising with capital accumulation and growth. One way to raise the rate of capital accumulation is to supplement domestic savings (which in any case are low in Latin America by East Asian standards, see Lal and Wolf, 1986) through foreign borrowing. Most Latin American countries have attempted to do so. However imprudent this course may seem, with hindsight its temptations for the harried factional states of Latin American are obvious, as are the consequences of the closing of these borrowing opportunities. The worsening in the terms of borrowing are partly due to the development policies which were part and parcel of the same imperatives which compelled over-borrowing.

A second illustration of the uses of the model concerns the political economy of Latin American inflation. Even if it is true, as Hirschman argues, that the "inflation cum overvalued exchange rate" policies were initially adopted as an expedient for taxing the agricultural sector, it is less implausible that the wild inflationary component of these policies still serves the same purpose. For many developing countries have maintained overvalued exchange rates, and a host of other microeconomic distortions have the net effect of indirectly taxing the agricultural sector. But these policies have not been accompanied by Latin American rates of inflation. Thus the inflation tax is not likely to be an integral part of the arsenal to tax the agricultural sector. In an environment of high inflation, the inflation tax will ultimately be borne by those who cannot take pre-emptive action. These are invariably the poorest, who rely purely on their labor and do not have sufficient financial assets to use the various ingenious devices that are increasingly available to richer citizens, to allow them to substitute some indirect or direct form of foreign currency-based assets for domestic money as a store of value (including, of course, capital flight!). The inflation tax is therefore better viewed as an indirect method of legislating the cut in the real wage that may be periodically required on some of the land and natural resource abundant economy's paths of development.

In this context it is interesting to consider the consequences for our Latin American factional state if it could not periodically – and at least for a brief moment – reconcile the dynamic distributional conflict it has inherited from factor endowments increasingly at odds with the polity.[25] There is one example where the country's geography in effect imposes a constraint on the levying of the inflationary tax – Mexico. This case is also of interest because it provides an example of an exception to the story of the typical Latin American factional state we have been trying to develop in this section. Because of its contiguous border with the US – a country with a strong currency and no exchange controls – it is virtually impossible for Mexico to levy the inflation tax for any considerable period, for currency smuggling across contiguous borders is likely to be easier than smuggling goods and people (if for no other reason than bulk). High inflation in Mexico sustained over a number of years would lead to the virtual dollarization of the economy. The non-inflationary policies of postwar Mexico, the absence of exchange control and the relative stability of the peso, are not therefore completely inexplicable in the Latin American context.

The Mexicans, however, like all the other land and natural resource rich Latin American polities, have to face the incipient and actual social conflict which is inherent in the efficient and growth promoting development path charted in figure 4.2. The Mexicans have succeeded, partly because of historical accident, in bucking the Latin American trend by establishing and maintaining what I like to call a "bureaucrat maximizing" predatory state. The PRI provides an elaborate spoils system to buy out, co-opt, and coerce those who might seek to undermine its hegemony. The secret lies in the public sector's use of various direct (through the expansion of government enterprises) and indirect methods (though creating microeconomic distortions), to garner a large share of the rents which accrue in a land and natural resource rich economy. These are then used to buy off discontent and create a political consensus legitimizing PRI hegemony, whose disruption might lead to the conversion of the polity into, perhaps, a populist factional state.

The recent reduction of the resources available to the state to finance the enhanced entitlements created by President Lopez-Portillo following the oil boom, has put this method of mediating the possibly inherent conflict between "growth and equity" present in most land rich economies, under considerable strain. Thus it remains an open question whether the Mexican predatory states' method of suppressing this conflict is viable in the longer run.

4 Concluding Remarks

I hope I have shown why in many Latin American countries there is likely to be a *tendency* towards a conflict between their comparative advantage and politics. It is based essentially on the discordance between the economy's factor endowments, and those of the set of median individuals comprising the possibly changing polity. Radicals have been right (though for the wrong reasons) in sensing the consensual benefits that might follow from land reform. But, if the polity is to be democratic, such a reform would need to give entitlements to rents from land to *the whole population*. By thus bringing the median individual factor endowments closer to the economy's, such a land reform might mitigate the pressures for policies which go against the region's comparative advantage. But the production losses of such a reform could be considerable. It is also difficult to see how the urban "middle sectors" of Latin America could be provided with an incentive for the productive use of any land entitlements they may receive. Thus, this is not likely to be a fruitful line of attack. With population growth, however, the economy's land–labor ratio is likely to fall, and it is of greater importance that in the future the median individual in the democratic polity has an increasing share in the manufacturing capital in the economy. For, then, even if the "outward oriented" development path – so essential for Latin America's long-term progress – implies lower capital–labor ratios and *ipso facto* lower or constant wages in industry during the growth process, this income effect on the labor endowment of the median individual will be counterbalanced by the rising earnings on his industrial capital endowment. It is in this context that the liberalization of domestic financial markets and the widespread dispersal of share-ownership could become an important means of creating and sustaining the political underpinning for the liberal economic policies that Latin America needs for sustained long-run development.[26]

NOTES

The research on which this chapter is based forms part of a multi-country comparative study of "The Political Economy of Poverty, Equity and Growth", financed by the World Bank. The views expressed are personal and should not be identified in any way with the World Bank.

1 See Lal and Rajapatirana (1987) for a survey of the links between foreign trade regimes and economic growth.
2 There is also the need to roll back inefficient and loss-making public sectors, but some may still consider this to be controversial. So I have not included the final set of Harberger's rules concerning the control of the public sector in the above list.
3 Thus he states: "policymakers positively cultivate unpredictability and distance from interest groups" and at the same time they are highly manipulative. These are the socio-political traits that account, perhaps more fundamentally than the cost price structure of the new industries, for their poor export performance".
4 See Lal (1984, 1986) for this interpretation of the constraints, facing the "predatory state".
5 The big exception to these generalizations of course is Mexico. But see section 2.
6 T. S. Eliot: "The Love Song of J. Alfred Prufrock".
7 But note that, because of Arrow's impossibility theorem, even the majoritarian democratic version of the factional state will not become a benevolent state, because of the lack of a majoritarian social welfare function!
8 It *has* made various technical errors in its economic policy. An excellent and balanced account of the Chilean economy, post-Allende, is in Edwards and Edwards (1987).
9 For instance Hahn notes that the new economics of information have emphasized that the "time and effort spent in discovering the set of possible choices . . . [will itself be] an element of [the] domain [of preferences]" (Hahn

(1985). Hence apparently "satisficing" behavior need not contradict the assumption of rational maximizing behavior.

10 He rightly in my view discounts O'Donnell's (1973) thesis as being empirically invalid. O'Donnell argues that the emergence of Latin America authoritarianism in the 1960s was due to the difficulties of "deepening the industrialization process. Deepening is defined as the putting into place through backward linkage of the intermediate input and capital goods industry once the 'last-stage' industries making consumption or final demand goods are established" (Hirschman 1979, p. 69).

11 See also Lal (1983, 1984) for a critique of these views.

12 This contrast is also noted by some authors and used with the formation of dependency systems to explain the different outcomes in the Northern and Southern parts of the land abundant Americas.

13 Veliz argues that the rhetorical espousal of economic liberalization by the military is the result of their desire to curry favor with their social superiors – the upper class business and land-owning groups – "their new upper-class friends who hold the key to their social advancement (their wives and families as well as their own)" (p. 299). He finds the upper classes in Latin America "culturally dependent" on the West. The constituents of these upper classes are the intellectual and old "oligarchs". He writes, "the bastions of Latin American cultural dependence are well manned by the radical intellegentsia and the upper-class business and land-owning groups. The loyalty that the former have demonstrated to the doctrines of violent revolutionary action, the latter have shown to the tenets of free-trading liberalism their forefathers embraced during the prosperous days of the liberal pause" (Veliz, n22. p. 299).

In Lal (1987) I have also argued (in explaining the North–South confrontation of the 1970s) that the similarities between Latin American and other Third World elites in seeking self respect, lie in the continuing sense of inferiority felt by "white" Latin American elites towards the dominant power and life-styles of white Anglo-Saxons.

14 On the political economy of liberalization see Lal (1987).

15 The endowment triangle "represents graphically the relative endowments of three factors (physical capital, labor and arable land). In the three-dimensional factor space, straight lines emanating from the origin contain all endowment vectors with the same ratio of factors. These lines in three dimensions can be represented by points in two dimensions intersecting the positive orthant with a plane to form the endowment triangle. The three co-ordinates in the three-dimensional factor space are represented by the corners of an endowment triangle, and the endowment vectors of each of the countries are represented by points. . . . The main point to keep in mind is that *every endowment point on a straight line emanating from one corner of the triangle has the same ratio of the other two factors*. For this reason the scales of the three factor ratios can be placed on the edges of the triangle" (Leamer, 1987, pp. 963–4).

16 See also Deardoff (1984) for a geometric presentation of Krueger's model.

17 This evocative phrase is due to Hla Myint.

18 For a model that includes non-traded goods see Lal (1986a).

19 These regions of specialization will depend upon commodity prices, and will alter as commodity prices change.

20 It might seem paradoxical that, whilst the *economy's* capital-labor ratio is rising it is falling in manufacturing. But remember that the rate of growth of labor for the *economy* is not the same as that in *manufacturing*. There it is possible for the agricultural labor force to grow more slowly (because of fixed land) than for the economy as a whole, thereby allowing and requiring the labor force in the manufacturing sector to grow more rapidly than for the economy as a whole. Thus a rising capital–labor ratio for the economy as a whole can be associated with a falling capital–labor ratio in manufacturing. Of course there will be some rate of capital growth at which the capital–labor ratio for manufacturing will also be rising along with that for the economy as a whole, and this paradoxical development path would not occur.

21 This is the basis for Krueger's statement that: "first, the distinction between poor and underdeveloped countries emerges clearly from the model, A poor country is one with an unfavorable land–man endowment. An underdeveloped country is one with a relatively small endowment of capital per person. An underdeveloped country, however, could conceivably have a higher per capita income and real wage than a 'more developed' but poor country. Second, a country abundantly endowed with land and therefore with a relatively high wage would not necessarily have a comparative advantage in labor-intensive manufactures, even in its early stages of capital accumulation: the real wage at which persons would leave agriculture might too high. In such an instance, the capital–labor ratio in manufacturing would be higher in the early stages of development in a poorer country, whilst the output per unit of capital and the rate of return on capital would be lower than in the low-wage country" (Krueger, 1977, p. 15).

22 This follows from the simple observation that, with the tariff on M_4 producers will attempt to expand the output of M_4. As it is the most labor-intensive good being produced, an expansion in its output will create excess demand for labor, and excess supply of the land and capital used in producing the other two goods. Full employment of the three factors will be maintained only as producers switch to using more land and capital-intensive techniques, which save on labor producing the other two goods M_5 and M.

23 This can also be seen in terms of figure 4.2, but this exercise is left to the reader! In an earlier paper (Lal, 1986b) I have used a similar model to explain the long-term decline in real wages in the Philippines – another land abundant country, whose political economy is closer to that of Latin America than its East Asian neighbors.

24 A model of these the factional state is provided in Lal (1986a).

25 This dynamic distributional conflict is modelled more explicitly in Lal (1986a), which provides an explicit role for the real exchange rate, and the non-traded goods sector – an aspect I have ignored in this article.

26 I take it that various dirigiste alternatives such as the creation of welfare states based on taxing the rising rents on land and capital are not likely to be efficient, in part because of their incentive effects on both the rulers and the ruled! For

anyone who doubts this, Uruguay would provide the appropriate cautionary tale.

REFERENCES

Balassa, B. (1985), *Change and Challenge in the World Economy*. London: Macmillan.

Baumol, W. Panzar, J. C., and Willig, R. D. (1982) *Contestable Markets and the Theory of Industry Structure*. San Diego: Harcourt Brace Jovanovich.

Collier, D. (ed.) (1979), *The New Authoritarianism in Latin America*. Princeton, New Jersey: Princeton University Press.

Corbo, V. and de Melo, J. (1985), "Overview and Summary: Liberalization and Stabilization in the Southern Cone of Latin America", *World Development*. Vol. 13, no. 8.

Deardoff, A. (1984), "An Exposition and Exploration of Krueger's Trade Model", *Canadian Journal of Economics*. Vol. 17, November.

Edwards, S. (1987), "The United States and Foreign Competition in Latin America". Dept of Economics, Discussion Paper No. 431, UCLA, February.

Edwards, S. and Edwards A. C. (1987), *Monetarism and Liberalization – The Chilean Experiment*. Cambridge, Mass.: Ballinger.

Edwards, S. and Teitel, S. (1986), "Introduction to Growth, Reform and Adjustment: Latin America's Trade and Macroeconomic Policies in the 1970s and 1980s, *Economic Development and Cultural Change*. Vol, 34, No. 3, April.

Hahn, F. (1985), "*In Praise of Economic Theory*". Oxford: Oxford University Press.

Harberger, A. (1984), "Economic Policy and Economic Growth" in Harberger (ed.) *World Economic Growth*. San Francisco: Institute for Contemporary Studies.

Hirschman, A. (1968), "The Political Economy of Import-Substituting Industrialization in Latin America", *Quarterly Journal of Economics*. Vol. LXXXII, No.1, February.

Hirschman, A. (1979), "The Turn to Authoritarianism in Latin America and the Search for Its Economic Determinants", in D. Collier (ed.)

Hirschman, A. (1981), "Policy making in Latin America", in A. Hirschman (ed.) *Essays in Trespassing*. Cambridge: Cambridge University Press.

Kindleberger, C. (1967), *Foreign Trade and the National Economy*. Yale, New Haven: Yale University Press.

Krueger, A. (1977), "Growth, Distortions, and Patterns of Trade among Many Countries", *Princeton Studies in International Finance*. No. 40, Princeton, New Jersey: International Finance Section, Department of Economics, Princeton University.

Lal, D. (1983), "*The Poverty of Development Economics*" Hobart Paperback No. 16. London: Institute of Economic Affairs.

Lal, D. (1984), "The Political Economy of the Predatory State". Development

Research Department, Discussion Paper 105, Washington D.C., mimeo. (Revised April 1988, University College London).

Lal, D. (1986a) "The Political Economy of Industrialization in Primary Product Export Economies". Paper for the IEA Conference in Delhi, to be published in the conference volume by Macmillan.

Lal, D. (1986b): "Stolper–Samuelson–Rybczynski in the Pacific Real – Wages and Real Exchange Rates in the Philippines, 1956–1978", *Journal of Development Economics*. Vol. 21, April.

Lal, D. (1987), "The Political Economy of Economic Liberalisation", *World Bank Economic Review*. Vol. 1, No. 2, January.

Lal, D. and Rajapatirana, S. (1987) "Foreign Trade Regimes and Economic Growth in Developing Countries", *World Bank Research Observer*, Vol. 2, July.

Lal, D. and Wolf, M. (eds) (1986), *Stagflation Savings and the State – Perspectives on the Global Economy*. New York: Oxford University Press.

Leamer, E. (1984), *Sources of International Comparative Advantage*. Cambridge, Mass.: MIT Press.

Leamer, E. (1987), "Paths of Development in the Three-Factor, *n*-Good General Equilibrium Model", *Journal of Political Economy*. Vol. 95, No. 5, October.

Lipton, M. (1977), *Why Poor People Stay Poor*. London: Temple Smith.

Little, I. (1982), *Economic Development*. New York: Basic Books.

Mayer, W. (1984), "Endogeneous Tarrif Formation", *American Economic Review*. December.

Mitra, P. (1986), "A Description of Adjustment to External Shocks: Country Groups", in D. Lal and M. Wolf (eds).

O'Donnell, G. (1973), *Modernization and Bureaucratic-Authoritarianism: Studies in South American Politics*. Politics of Modernization Series No. 9, University of California, Berkeley: Institute of International Studies.

Olson, M. (1971), *The Logic of Collective Action*. Cambridge, MA: Harvard University Press.

Olson, M. (1982), *The Rise and Decline of Nations*. Yale; New Haven: Yale University Press.

Sachs, J. (1985), "External debt and Macroeconomic Performance in Latin America and East Asia", *Brookings Papers on Economic Activity*. No. 2

Veliz, C. (1980), *The Centralist Tradition of Latin America*, Princeton, New Jersey: Princeton University Press.

Wynia, G. (1984), *The Politics of Latin American Development*. 2nd edn, Cambridge: Cambridge University Press.

[5]

THE WORLD BANK ECONOMIC REVIEW, VOL. 1, NO. 2: 273–299

The Political Economy of Economic Liberalization

Deepak Lal

Two of the major policy problems facing governments of developing countries in the 1980s have been unsustainable external and internal disequilibria, and implementation of politically feasible stabilization cum liberalization programs which become necessary to correct these imbalances. This article discusses these "crises" and subsequent policy reform. The analysis suggests that balance of payments and fiscal deficits are frequently the result of use of an incorrect accounting system in a fixed exchange rate economy, and of public sector expansion beyond its economically feasible size; that governments usually seek to liberalize their economies during a crisis to regain control when the growth of the "transfer State" has led to generalized tax resistance, avoidance, or evasion; that reduction of the government role will be required to alleviate these crises; that sharp departures from past policies rather than gradual reform may be politically necessary; and that, contrary to the current technocratic opinion on this matter, the sequencing of a consistent and credible package of reforms which will most effectively reduce the costs of adjustment is initial liberalization of domestic capital markets simultaneous with cuts in the fiscal deficit, followed by floating the exchange rate and then commodity market liberalization.

With the growing importance of Internal Monetary Fund (IMF) stabilization and World Bank structural adjustment programs, there has been concern about the proper sequencing of the standard stabilization cum liberalization measures contained in these packages. In particular, there is grave concern at the very mixed and in some cases disastrous effects of liberalization attempts on incomes and employment in the Southern Cone of Latin America in the late 1970s and early 1980s. Much of the existing discussion of the order of liberalization is conducted within the traditional technocratic framework,[1] which seeks to determine the welfare-cost-minimizing deployment of policies in the standard stabilization and

1. This assumes a benevolent and well informed government maximizing a social welfare function subject to resource and technological constraints.

Deepak Lal, on leave from the University of London, is at the World Bank. This article is a revised version of parts II and III of Lal (1984b), part I of which now forms a revised and independent companion piece hereinafter cited as Lal (1986a). The author is grateful to Peter Kenen, Assar Lindbeck, and Joseph Stiglitz for valuable comments on earlier drafts of this article.

adjustment packages. Not surprisingly, no clear-cut answers are possible to the unavoidably second best welfare questions that arise.

In a companion paper (Lal 1986a) these issues are analyzed using a standard two-good, two-factor Australian model of "real" trade theory, supplemented by a monetary model.[2] The effects of alternative policies on real wages and rental and exchange rates in the short and long run were examined. Here also, no absolute and generalizable answers about the optimal set of policies was found. The comparative static effects depend upon the relative factor intensities of the two goods (traded and nontraded), the degree of wage flexibility, and the extent of sectoral capital mobility. Comparative static results derived within this framework are summarized in the appendix for the case where the traded good is capital intensive (compared with the nontraded) and receives a subsidy to the use of capital. The apparent variations in these effects are compounded on the dynamic path of the real variables, which, depending upon the relative speeds of adjustment in the relevant markets, can lead to over- or undershooting from their relevant "equilibrium" values.

Nevertheless, based on the recent experience of the Southern Cone, there seems to be an emerging consensus that in liberalizing the foreign exchange, domestic credit, and labor markets, the capital account of the foreign exchange market should be liberalized last. Capital inflows should actively be discouraged (or held at a low constant level) while the other markets are being liberalized. (Edwards 1984 provides a good survey; see also Krueger 1984.)

In this essay I take issue with this emerging consensus on the order of liberalization. I argue that it is based on an implausible model of the attributes and behavior of the State and its citizens, and I suggest that a different, positive "political economy" approach may be more useful in answering questions concerning the sequencing and timing of measures of economic liberalization.

The typical stabilization cum adjustment program is launched when a country is in a "crisis," usually an incipient or actual balance of payments crisis[3] that necessitates a reduction in the level of current expenditures. If there is underutilization of domestic capacity, an expenditure switching policy such as a devaluation may partly (or even fully) offset the extent of the cut in domestic absorption that may be required. Also, if the proper policy measures are taken, the country may be able to obtain some foreign resource inflows which could allow a grad-

2. The real models within this framework are based on Jones (1971), Mussa (1974), Burgess (1980), Neary (1978, 1982, 1985), and Corden and Neary (1982); the monetary model on McKinnon (1981), McKinnon and Mathieson (1981), Dornbusch (1974, 1980), and Krueger (1974); and the integration of the real and monetary aspects on Corden (1977), Corden and Jones (1976), and Prachowny (1981, 1984). Lal (1986b) provides an application of the real model to the Philippines and Lal (1985) of the real cum monetary model to Sri Lanka.

3. For our purposes, it makes little difference whether the crisis is caused by an increase in domestic expenditure, or, say, a decrease in the terms of trade facing the country. It also makes little difference whether the crisis arises from what are sometimes referred to as "insolvency" problems or to "liquidity" problems (though the validity of the conceptual framework underlying this distinction has recently been criticized by Eaton, Gersowitz, and Stiglitz 1986).

ual rather than sudden reduction in real expenditures. With any rate of social time preference greater than the cost of the foreign borrowing, the gradual approach must dominate any sudden shock treatment, if the former is feasible.[4] But it is this very feasibility which is usually in question, essentially on grounds of the likely behavior of particular governments.

It may be possible to alleviate the crisis by persuading foreign creditors to extend more credit. This in turn may require that the foreign creditors believe that the country will actually carry out the proposed adjustment measures. This credibility will in turn be based on the reputation derived from the government's past policies.[5] Thus, in the 1970s and 1980s the newly industrialized Southeast Asian countries (unlike many Latin American countries) have found it relatively easy to obtain external credit to smooth consumption following external shocks (from changing interest rates, commodity prices, and world demand). This is because the adjustment programs announced by these countries are credible given their reputations. By contrast, the announcements made by many Latin American and African countries may not be credible. If in the past a government has reversed preannounced plans because the costs of reversal (say, increased inflation) seemed to be lower than the benefits (say, financing a public sector deficit), then an announced adjustment program which is reversible may be unsustainable. Even if the "new" government has in fact changed its character, before outside creditors are willing to provide capital for smoothing intertemporal consumption, the government may have to demonstrate its newfound resolution by undertaking more Draconian disabsorption measures than would have been required if its announcements were credible. To improve its credibility, a government might choose to precommit itself to the new regime through external commitments, such as the binding covenants signed by Austria and Hungary with the Council of the League of Nations in the 1920s. These covenants reordered their fiscal and monetary systems, raised the costs to the governments of reversing their preannounced policies, and thus made the stabilization plans credible, which succeeded in stopping their hyperinflations almost immediately (see Sargent 1985).

Moreover, the announced speed of adjustment may be an important factor in determining the credibility of the stabilization cum structural adjustment program. For while from a technocratic viewpoint a gradual cut in expenditures may be desirable, the government may find that gradualism allows time for

4. This assumes concave adjustment costs. If adjustment costs are convex, discrete adjustments may be optimal.

5. Fellner (1976, 1979) stressed the importance of the credibility of macroeconomic policymakers. Kreps and Wilson (1982) have provided one formalization of the notion of reputation. The formalization closest in spirit to that presented in the text, however, is that of Shapiro (1983). The literature arising from the problems of time inconsistency of optimal programs (see Kydland and Prescott 1977; Calvo 1978; Barro and Gordon 1983a, 1983b; Fischer 1980) has been extended by Backus and Driffill (1985a, 1985b, 1985c) in a series of papers which model dynamic games in which the credibility of the government's announcements is a central issue, as private agents are uncertain about the government's preferences.

those hurt by the cuts to combine and exert irresistible pressure for their reversal. Politically, a long drawn out cut in real expenditures may thus be more difficult for a government to implement than a single, quick cut. One would expect that certain patterns of government behavior would be discernible which could provide some guidance on the question of the credible speed of adjustment. While this issue is of importance, I do not discuss it in any great detail in this article. But there is a presumption, given the fragility of many governments in the developing world, that long drawn out expenditure cuts will not be feasible in many developing countries.

There is another variant of the "easing of the pain" argument for gradualism in reducing real expenditures and removing policy-induced microeconomic distortions in the economy. These distortions place the economy well within the potential production possibility frontier (PPF). The various policy reforms undertaken to improve the overall efficiency of the economy are likely to induce growth in future real income and output (from the ongoing processes of growth—shifts in the PPF—as well as those increments induced by the improved policies—movement from inside the PPF to the frontier). As aggregate supply rises to eliminate the excess aggregate demand, this growth may preclude real cuts in current or future expenditures.[6] Again, theoretically this would be uncontroversial. Controversy arises because of differing judgments on the *credibility,* tenacity, and political will of governments to complete a phased program of policy reform when the pain experienced by various sectional groups hurt by the removal of various "distortions" from which they have benefited is more immediate and more vocally expressed than the promised future joys from greater efficiency. This is also an empirical question of positive political economy.

Underlying these questions is a prior one: why countries get into a "crisis," and why some then choose and even succeed in not merely stabilizing but also liberalizing their economies. Section I considers this issue. The directions for the sequencing and timing of economic liberalization measures suggested by this discussion are used in section II to reexamine the question of the order of liberalization prescribed by the usual technocratic framework,[7] which seeks to determine the welfare-cost-minimizing adjustment cum stabilization package for countries in "crisis." A brief final section summarizes my conclusions.

I. Why Do Governments Undertake Economic Liberalization?

Most of the existing literature on the order of liberalization is based on the economist's traditional picture of disembodied, altruistic policymakers maximizing some social utility function subject to the usual resource and technological

6. This seems to be the argument underlying many of the contributions in Killick (1982).

7. I have found a specific factor version of the standard trade theoretic Australian model, supplemented by a simple monetary model, a useful heuristic device in answering these technocratic questions, as in Lal (1986a).

constraints. This view of the State is highly misleading, particularly when one considers the heterogeneous group of countries that comprise the developing world.

By contrast, it is more useful to follow the "new political economy" and view the State as composed of a group of self-regarding individuals and groups interacting strategically with private agents (see Staniland 1985; Findlay 1986; Lal 1984a; Srinivasan 1985). The State is then seen as seeking to maximize its own utility (including incomes, perquisites, and power) and not necessarily the welfare of its citizens. Nevertheless, in the resulting game between the State and its citizens (which will at different times have both cooperative as well as noncooperative elements), the latter may undertake various strategies which lead the State to serve the interests of its citizens.[8] Thus, there may be mutually beneficial outcomes in some, perhaps most, circumstances.

Without setting out a formal model, I show in this part how a particular interpretation of past development experience may help to explain why and when States in the developing world choose to undertake economic liberalization (particularly structural adjustment programs) and also suggest the essential elements which must underlie a sustainable stabilization cum liberalization program. This analysis also leads to some empirical judgments about the order of liberalization.

Some Stylized "Crises," and When is a "Crisis" a Crisis?

It is useful to begin by presenting a taxonomy based on three sources of the excess absorption which usually leads to "crises." First, consider the case of excess absorption generated by monetary expansion accompanying increased government expenditure during the political cycle.[9] With flexible money wages, the increase in absorption will initially lead to a rise in real wages.[10] But with the ensuing leakage of the domestic money supply through the resulting payments deficit (at a fixed exchange rate), or else a contraction of real money balances

8. See Barro and Gordon (1983b); and Backus and Driffill (1985b, 1985c), for game theoretic models which provide a formal analysis of the problems of credibility and sustainability of a new policy regime when the reputation of the government is uncertain. However, while providing some useful insights, the robustness of these models may be questioned. Backus and Driffill (1985b), in an interesting paper which attempts to provide an endogenous explanation of the "political cycle" (as outlined by Nordhaus 1975; Lindbeck 1976; and Frey 1978), develop a two-person, noncooperative model in which an inflation conscious private sector is uncertain if the government which cares about output and employment will stick to its preannounced plan to disinflate (or not to inflate) on coming to office. "Instead of having a government create a pre-election boom in order to increase its chance of reelection, our analysis generates a pre-election boom as the solution to a game with a wet lame-duck government. In fact, if there were a chance of reelection, the incentive to preserve reputation may actually restrain the spending spree" (p. 536). They show that inflating at the end of its term is the rational response of a "wet" government that cares about employment. I doubt whether this conclusion is at all a plausible reason for the usual political business cycle; even if particular governments are mortal, parties are not!

9. Lal (1983, 1986b) provides an illustration from the Philippines.

10. This assumes that wages are more flexible (upward) than prices.

through a devaluation, all real variables would eventually return to their original values. In the process, the initial rise in real wages would eventually be reversed, as absorption falls back to its original, sustainable level. During this process of temporary excess absorption, the country will lose reserves, which may present a problem for the government. If the excess absorption is not reversed, however, or if reserves (which for this purpose should include access to external borrowing) are insufficient, at some stage the country will face a crisis. Appropriate expenditure reducing and (if there is nominal wage or price rigidity) expenditure switching policies such as a devaluation will be part of the resolution of the crisis. All this is well known. What is of concern here is why some countries, mainly in Latin America, are prone to follow highly inflationary macroeconomic policies which lead to dramatic periodic crises of overabsorption.

Second, one can consider another stylized case exemplified by the group of countries, mainly in South Asia, which have by and large followed fairly conservative macroeconomic policies. They have introduced a host of policy induced distortions in the working of the domestic price mechanism, however, which have led to rigidities in employment and output. Periodic stabilization crises arise when one of these countries faces a shift in taste or technology or some exogenous shock such as a harvest failure or a terms of trade deterioration.[11] Any of these changes requires an alteration of domestic relative prices to smoothly switch expenditures and outputs to maintain internal and external balance. The country may then suffer from an unsustainable excess of absorption, at the old unchanged relative prices. As is well known, an appropriate combination of policies to switch and reduce expenditures may be able to resolve the crisis. Again, what is of concern here are the reasons why and when such microdistorted economies are likely to reduce the rigidities which lead to their intermittent stabilization crises.

Third, windfall losses and gains of foreign currency are another common cause of "crises"; these are dealt with in greater detail in this section. Here, it is useful to distinguish between those windfalls which accrue directly to the public as contrasted with the private sector. Two recently occurring types of windfall are the foreign currency rents from minerals accruing to the public sector (for example, oil exporters such as Indonesia and Nigeria)[12] and the foreign currency receipts of the private sector derived from remittances by their relatives working abroad (as in Pakistan, Philippines, Sri Lanka, and Turkey).[13] In the following

11. It has been argued within the technocratic literature that *temporary* falls in income should be partly financed by external borrowing, while if the fall in income is expected to be *permanent,* the country should adjust (see Cooper and Sachs 1985). The problem in practice is that except possibly for harvest failures it will be very difficult to judge whether a particular adverse shock to national income is temporary or permanent.

12. See Gelb (1986) for a discussion of the uses and abuses of these rents by various oil producers in the 1970s and 1980s.

13. See Swamy (1981) for some estimates of these remittances in the 1970s.

subsections, I assume with the technocratic literature that the government is optimizing and benevolent but nevertheless gets into a crisis if it is myopic or badly informed.

Private Sector Windfalls. First, consider *remittances.* Assume the exchange rate is fixed and there are exchange controls. The private sector receives foreign exchange remittances, which it exchanges for domestic currency at the central bank. This rise in the bank's foreign currency assets is initially matched by an equivalent increase in the currency and demand deposit component of the domestic money supply. High powered money has risen, however, and the domestic money supply pari pasu will expand, unless the government takes some countervailing action, by either reducing its own demand for credit through a reduction of the fiscal deficit or reducing commercial credit by raising the reserve ratio.

Suppose it does not sterilize the effects of these inflows on the domestic money supply. All other things being equal, at the fixed exchange rate, the expansion in money supply will lead to a rise in the price of nontraded goods and a trade deficit. In the standard trade theoretic framework, the effect on the real wage will be ambiguous. But with the loss of foreign exchange reserves accompanying the trade deficit, the high powered money base and thus the domestic money supply will contract automatically until the initial equilibrium is restored. In this process the "real goods" counterpart of the foreign remittance transfer on the capital account will have been affected through the trade deficit.

Is there any problem or "crisis" for such a country? It will experience an initial boom with inflation and a balance of payments deficit. Though these are usually symptoms of a crisis, in this case such a diagnosis would clearly be mistaken.

Suppose, however, as is likely, that there is some time lag between the receipt of the remittances on capital account and their subsequent implicit spending through the trade account. In the interim, foreign exchange reserves would have risen. Suppose, as is common in many developing countries, the government does not use the notion of high powered money in its budgetary planning. The treasury is advised by various economists that it should use the rising foreign exchange reserves for development purposes by running a larger budget deficit than it would have otherwise. If, as is usual, the government has not sterilized the foreign exchange inflows, the increase in high powered money entailed by the larger budget deficit provides a further boost to the money supply. Without this increase in the government's fiscal deficit, both the domestic inflationary process and the trade deficit would have been self-correcting, but this further expansion will entail more inflation and a larger trade deficit. Their correction through the "money-specie" flow mechanism will entail a *loss of foreign exchange reserves greater than those that had been received through the remittances.* The government, which had not intended to run down its initial level of reserves, de facto finds itself with an incipient rundown. It *now* has a balance of payments problem, the cure of which will require the disabsorption we have already discussed.[14]

But this crisis is due to a misperception of the correct accounting system in a fixed exchange rate economy, with a government which is unable or unwilling to sterilize foreign currency flows. In particular, it arises from a misunderstanding about the relationship between high power money, the fiscal deficit (properly defined), and the movements in foreign reserves. Unless these are understood and the proper accounting framework is adopted, even though the government may (through financing or adjustment) adequately manage this crisis, it is likely that such problems will continually recur. The failure to adopt the correct accounting framework for budgetary and monetary management may thus be as important a factor in the generation of crises as any shocks administered by nature or by the external world.[15]

Public Sector Windfalls. The second type of "crisis" arises from windfall foreign currency gains or losses accruing to the *public sector.* Consider two radically different ways in which the government could in principle spend these rents. First, suppose it decides to distribute them annually, based on some suitable criterion of equity.[16] A seemingly equivalent policy would be for the government to expand its expenditures by the annual inflow of these rents or to reduce general taxation. If the social value of increased government expenditure is considered to be greater than that arising from giving a form of national dividend or tax cuts to its populace, then the direct public use of these rents would seem to be desirable. Moreover, as long as the increase in government expenditure is covered by sales of the foreign currency to the central bank, the fiscal deficit which needs to be covered by domestic borrowing need not rise. Nevertheless, high powered money will increase with these inflows of foreign currency, unless the government actually reduces domestic credit, that is, unless they are sterilized.

The consequent rise in domestic money expenditure will raise the price level as (at a fixed exchange rate) the money prices of nontraded goods rise; part of the excess money demand will spill over into a trade deficit, financed by running down the newly built up foreign currency reserves. Assuming downwardly flexible prices of nontraded goods, this will tend to reduce the domestic money supply and bring the prices of nontraded goods down to their original level, and with it the overall price level.

But at a fixed exchange rate, if the inflow of foreign currency rents continues, the size of the domestic tradables sector will decline as demand for tradables is met by imports, and the relative price of nontraded goods will remain higher. To

14. Fry (1980) provides an illustration from Turkey in the early 1970s.

15. Of course, from the "political economy" perspective which I discuss in the next section, governments may deliberately choose not to employ a fully informative accounting framework, as this may allow them to conceal the implicit or explicit politically determined entitlements they wish to generate.

16. The U.S. state of Alaska did this with its oil revenues.

induce and then maintain the relative expansion of nontradables, *the real exchange rate (defined as the relative price of nontraded to traded goods) will remain at an appreciated level* for some time, depending upon how long it is expected to take the foreign currency rents to run out. The requisite rise in the relative price of nontraded goods need not come about through this inflationary process, if instead the government chose to *appreciate* the nominal exchange rate by the appropriate amount.

A problem would arise if the increased level of government expenditure was unsustainable over the long run. This could happen if the government misjudged the size of the annual foreign exchange flows and committed itself to long maturing investments or unsustainable consumption support programs, which would need to be cut back if there were any falling off in expected foreign exchange rents. The public sector expenditure program may thus be unsustainable.

If, however, the rents had been transferred to the general populace, each individual would have had his or her current income increased and expectations of future rises in income improved. The resulting decentralized decisions concerning the privately optimal consumption/investment mix would, in an open economy, involve portfolio choices between different domestic and foreign financial assets. The associated patterns of deficits and surpluses on the current/capital accounts of the balance of payments would have no overall welfare significance.

Dirigisme, Fiscal Crises, and Government Control

The above examples illustrate how most so-called balance of payments crises are in large part crises for the public sector and reflect misjudgments about its appropriate and feasible size and composition.[17] They also suggest the reasons why self-regarding governments may choose to reverse their previous dirigisme (inducing macro and/or micro distortions) and liberalize an economy they have hitherto repressed.

One of the paradoxical dynamic effects of the past dirigisme of many countries in the developing world (as, of course, in some developed countries) has been that attempts to exercise political control over ever-increasing areas of economic life have often led, after a certain stage, to a diminution of the government's effective areas of control as private agents find numerous ways of avoiding them. What concerns us is the empirical observation that there appears to be a sort of "Laffer curve" of government intervention, so that after a certain stage, increased government intervention, instead of increasing the area of government control, diminishes it. It is rare for liberalization to follow some intellectual conversion of policymakers who, having seen the errors of their ways, seek to find a second best welfare maximizing transition from a controlled to a market economy. Rather, various measures of economic liberalization and/or stabiliza-

17. This is the important insight contained in Corden (1977).

tion are most often sought in order to reassert government control over the economy. It is important to determine the *costs to the State* of *not* liberalizing the economy. For sustained liberalization to be undertaken, these must be greater than the apparent costs of liberalization, namely, the inevitable political pressures which will follow from the changes in distributional rewards and rents which are entailed in any measure of liberalization.[18] This subsection elaborates on these points.

A major motivation for liberalization from the viewpoint of many States in the developing world lies in an attempt to regain control over an economy which seems to be less and less amenable to the usual means of government control. Usually the most important symptom of this malaise is a creeping but chronic fiscal crisis (also reflected sometimes but not always in a balance of payments crisis), which has in different forms beset most economies—including developed ones—in the last decade (see Lal and Wolf 1986 for a fuller discussion). Its origins lie in the creation of politically determined "entitlements" to current and future income streams for various groups in the economy (the deserving poor; industrial labor; regional interests; old age pensioners; infant, declining, or sick, industries—to name just a few). As these entitlements are implicit or explicit subsidies to particular groups, they have to be paid for by implicit or explicit taxation of other groups in the economy. However justifiable on grounds of social welfare, the gradual expansion of this "transfer State" leads to some surprising dynamic consequences.

The gradual expansion of politically determined entitlements creates specific "property rights." The accompanying tax burden to finance them leads at some stage to generalized tax resistance, avoidance, and evasion and to the gradual but inevitable growth of the parallel or underground economy. This has been the case with both developed and developing countries in the past decade. Faced with inelastic or declining revenues but burgeoning expenditure commitments, incipient or actual fiscal deficits become chronic. These can only be financed by three means: domestic borrowing, external borrowing, or levying of the inflation tax.

Many countries, particularly those in Latin America, have tried all three—with dire consequences. Domestic borrowing to close the fiscal gap may crowd out private investment (see Blejer and Khan 1984) and diminish the future growth of income—and thus the future tax base. The fiscal deficit may be financed by foreign borrowing for a time, particularly as in the mid-1970s, when

18. One could, following the "State as pressure group" school of political economy, seek to explain the move to liberalization as resulting from a new pressure group equilibrium (see Becker 1983). But this model of political economy relies on political institutions corresponding to those in Western democracies. Its applicability to the varied authoritarian regimes in the developing world would seem to be limited. Hence my attempt to explain why a developing world government which is *relatively* (but not completely) immune to democratic pressure group activity would seek to liberalize its economy. Another way of making this point is that instead of considering the State to be a passive transmitter of pressure group activity, one looks upon it as an autonomous agent with its own goals (see De Jasy 1984).

real interest rates were low and even negative. But this form of financing is inherently unstable. The debt service ratio can become unviable if, as in the late 1970s, world interest rates rise and the ability of the economies to generate the requisite export and fiscal surpluses to service the higher interest costs of publicly guaranteed debt is limited. This is often due to policy induced distortions inhibiting exports—for example, the maintenance of overvalued exchange rates and high and differentiated effective rates of protection which are an indirect tax on exports—and the difficulty in generating fiscal surpluses to match the interest on the debt. Thereupon, foreign lending can abruptly cease, leading to the kind of "debt crisis" which has plagued Latin America in the 1980s. The third way of financing the deficit, through the use of the inflation tax, is also unviable over the medium run, for it promotes a further growth of the parallel economy and a substitution of some indirect or direct form of foreign currency based assets for domestic money as a store of value. The tax base for levying the inflation tax thus shrinks rapidly.

With taxes being evaded, with domestic and foreign credit virtually at an end, and with private agents having adjusted to inflation to evade the inflation tax, the government finds its fiscal control of the economy vanishing. The growth of entitlements, moreover, reduces the *discretionary* funds available to the government, and it is discretionary funds which give the government power. It may not even be able to garner enough resources to pay the functionaries required to perform the classical State functions of providing law and order, defense, and essential infrastructure. This dynamic process whereby the expansion of the transfer State leads to the unexpected and very unMarxian withering away of the State has rarely reached its full denouement, although in some Latin American countries it may be close.[19]

But well before things come to such a dire pass, attempts are usually made to regain government control. Two responses by the government are possible—an illiberal and a liberal one. The former (which is rarely observed) consists of a further tightening and more stringent enforcement of direct controls. Tanzania provides an example of this response. If this tightening is effective, and the private utility of after-tax income received from legal productive activity declines to the level at which untaxed subsistence activities are preferable, however, producers may seek to escape the controls by ceasing to produce the taxed commodities altogether. The tightening and enforcement of controls could lead to an implosion of the economy.[20] The government might then find that as producers return to untaxable subsistence activities, the very production base over which it seeks control has shrunk or disappeared.

19. For example, in Peru it is estimated (by Hernando de Soto in private communication) that over 70 percent of the labor force in Lima works in "illegal" activities, the government has no domestic or foreign credit, inflation is high and rising, and nearly 70 percent of the money supply is in dollar denominated deposits.

20. See Collier and others (1985) for such an interpretation of recent Tanzanian economic policy and its outcomes.

The more usual response is to regain a degree of fiscal control through some liberalization of controls on the economy. Typically, however, these liberalization attempts are half-hearted and include some tax reform, monetary contraction, and some measures of export promotion. Their aim is to raise the economy's growth rate as well as the yield from whatever taxes are still being paid and to improve the debt service ratio in the hope that this will lead to a resumption of voluntary foreign lending. But unless the underlying fiscal problem (which is largely that of unsustainable public expenditure commitments) has been tackled, these liberalization attempts have usually been aborted.[21]

Without a commitment to reducing unviable levels of entitlements, the liberalization attempts have tended to worsen the fiscal situation. With the lowering of tax rates and lags in supply response, revenues do not rise and may even fall initially. The necessary reductions in money supply to contain inflation reduce the limited seigniorage previously being extracted.[22] Government unwillingness to allow either public or private enterprises to fail entails absorbing the deficits of public enterprises as well as any newly sick units taken over, as the liberalization exerts competitive pressures on unviable firms. Moreover, where liberalization has been accompanied by large public or private capital inflows (often to finance the public sector deficit), there has been an appreciation of the real exchange rate sometimes accompanied by inflationary pressures arising from inappropriate nominal exchange rate policies (as in Sri Lanka; see Lal 1985). This appreciation thwarts potential export growth, so that as capital inflows diminish, the incipient fiscal deficit is once again reflected in a chronic balance of payments problem which the government then seeks to control in the old unviable ways—and the liberalization process is reversed.

The above patterns have been observed in a large number of countries which have attempted to liberalize in the 1970s.[23] The major lesson to be drawn is that liberalization is often undertaken to gain fiscal control, but if nothing is done to rescind unsustainable public expenditure entitlements a stabilization cum balance of payments crisis eventually emerges which undermines the attempt to liberalize the economy. It would thus seem that a sine qua non of a sustainable liberalization attempt must be the prior establishment of fiscal control through a reduction of unsustainable public expenditure commitments.[24] The stabilization

21. Some examples are the Sri Lankan 1977 liberalization episode (see Lal and Rajapatirana, forthcoming); the 1978 Argentina liberalization (see Nogués 1981, Calvo 1986); and the latter part of the 1974 Uruguay reform episode (see Hanson and de Melo 1985).

22. At the end of a period of hyperinflation, however, the demand for money will increase, as will the seigniorage associated with any increase in money supply to meet this incremental demand for the newly stable money.

23. This experience is being analyzed in two sets of multicountry comparative studies undertaken by the Trade Policy Research Centre and the World Bank. My reading of their preliminary findings provides empirical support for the following remarks.

24. Unless, of course, there are sufficient underemployed domestic resources so that an expenditure switching policy such as a devaluation can rapidly increase aggregate supply and thence public revenues by the requisite amount.

of the economy no less than any prospective liberalization also entails a willingness to overcome the resistance of those whose entitlements will be rescinded.

The *political* problem governments most usually face when considering economic liberalization is that the pressures from the potential losers from the liberalization tend to antedate the support which will subsequently be provided by all those who gain. As can be readily shown, under many circumstances there will be losers in the short run from the changes in relative prices and/or disabsorption flowing from stabilization and structural adjustment programs, particularly those whose relative returns on sector specific human and physical capital fall as a result of these changes. If the liberalization is sustained, however, it is likely to yield higher and more efficient growth in income, which will benefit most groups in the economy. Given the government's own rate of discount (which may be much higher than that of society), even if the resulting purely technocratic economic welfare integral is positive, policymakers may still be reluctant to undertake the reforms if they feel uncertain about their ability to survive the political pressures during the transition.[25]

II. Minimizing the Welfare Costs of Adjustment

Consider now the problems facing the government of a developing country which finds itself in a "crisis" but has the requisite political will to implement the policy recommendations commonly contained in stabilization and adjustment programs.[26] These are (a) measures to reduce absorption by cutting the fiscal deficit, limiting overall domestic credit and devaluing the currency (if expenditure switching is required), and (b) measures to improve the supply side of the economy by reducing foreign trade and wage-price controls and by removing interest rate ceilings, changing reserve requirements, and possibly eliminating exchange controls.

The first group of disabsorption measures is unavoidable in a crisis situation. Only their extent is an issue, which (as was argued in the beginning of this article) depends upon the level of foreign financial accommodation available. The desirable level of this accommodation is a matter of judgment, and I have little to add to the earlier discussion.

The remaining questions concern the sequencing of the supply-side policy reforms and whether there are accompanying policies which might be able to minimize the inevitable costs of adjustment during the process of economic liberalization.

25. The "optimal" subsidy route for cushioning the transition for "losers" does not make much sense in this context, for it again assumes an omnipotent and omniscient government. The *political* difficulties I am emphasizing arise precisely because the government does not possess these attributes. Moreover, even if the government were able to implement this gradual adjustment policy, such a policy may not be time consistent and hence feasible.

26. Discussion of these will be found in Guitian (1981) on the IMF's conditionality, and in Stern (1983) on the World Bank's structural adjustment programs.

Optimal Sequencing of Policy Reforms

This subsection addresses welfare theoretic questions posed in the usual technocratic framework, which assumes a benevolent government concerned with maximizing some social welfare function. It is obvious that for an economy in which adjustments in both capital and labor markets are rapid, each of the policy changes proposed in the package must necessarily improve efficiency and hence lead monotonically to higher level of real national income until the new undistorted equilibrium is reached.

Moreover, within the standard trade theoretic Australian model the effects on real wages, particularly in the long run, of all these possible policy reforms is positive if, as one would expect, the factor market distortions are in the capital-intensive traded good sector. At least for the fairly flexible textbook economy outcomes which correspond to the Marshallian long run, the standard adjustment package will not lead to any efficiency or equity losses.[27] In these circumstances, there would be little sense in examining the sequencing and timing of liberalization measures, as there should be a simultaneous and instantaneous liberalization of all the relevant markets.

Short run immobilities of capital and rigidities in wages, however, can lead to short run falls in real income or real wages. This is one reason why governments seem unwilling to liberalize all markets simultaneously (see Krueger 1984). Two questions then arise: first, whether there are feasible supplementary policies which could minimize these efficiency and/or equity losses during the transition, and second, whether there is a policy sequence within the adjustment package which will reduce the pain of the transition. Arguments are presented below in favor of *one* plausible sequencing of policies which runs counter to the currently favored sequence (namely, opening the capital account last). This is to underline the fragility of much of the current argument for particular orders of liberalization being derived in the technocratic literature.

On the first question, consider the case of wage rigidity. It is well known from the literature on project evaluation that, given certain assumptions, any stickiness or rigidity of wages may make the shadow wage lower than the actual wage rate (see Lal 1974 for a summary of the literature on the determinants of the shadow wage rate). In theory, a wage subsidy financed by lump sum taxes would yield the best outcome during the transition. If this is not possible, then some suitable tax-subsidy combination which essentially subsidizes the output of the labor-intensive industry may be desirable. Because self-employment predominates in most developing countries, it will not be feasible to institute a general wage subsidy, and a tax-subsidy scheme on output may be the only feasible policy. The required general subsidy to the labor-intensive sectors can be provided by in effect taxing the output of the capital-intensive sector, that is, by appropriate changes in the real exchange rate. Bhagwati (1979) and Krueger

27. We assume that there is little weight to be placed socially on the losses suffered by those capitalists who lose from the removal of the capital market distortion.

(1978) detail various ways in which the removal of trade distortions and changes in the nominal exchange rate can be combined to yield the requisite change in the real exchange rate.

The devaluation and reduction in output distortions required to obtain the real exchange rate change is likely to have an ambiguous short run effect on real wages if capital is immobile in the short run (see section 4 of Lal 1986a). By contrast, removing the capital market distortion in the capital-intensive traded good sector (with a given distortion in the labor market, and unchanged trade distortions) will raise both real output and real wages in the short and long run. This suggests the following sequencing of the adjustment package. First, remove the capital market distortion, and as the real output and real wage gains begin to appear, begin a phased program to reduce distortions in the commodity markets (particularly for traded goods). The possible short run declines in real wages resulting from the second phase will be mitigated by the wage increases arising from the continuation of the first phase of policy reform.

Removing the capital market distortion, however, is a tricky problem for a financially repressed economy (see McKinnon 1981). It is clear that, as a first step, interest ceilings on deposits and loans should be removed. If the distributional impact of these changes is to be spread over a period of time, then any quantitative credit controls (which imply capital subsidies to favored borrowers) should be converted into explicit subsidies and shown as part of the government budget. Without an increase in government revenues, the consequent rise in the fiscal deficit will require the levying of a higher inflation tax and a suitable adjustment of the reserve ratio on interest bearing domestic money deposits (this need not necessarily imply an increase in that ratio; see McKinnon and Mathieson 1981).

But most important, it will be necessary to keep the economy at the new steady state inflation rate to alter the nominal exchange rate at the same pace as the steady state inflation rate. A fixed nominal exchange rate would not be sustainable. In time, to reduce the inefficiencies of the financial repression associated with high reserve ratios, it will be necessary to reduce the fiscal deficit and thence the inflation rate. Whether this reduction in the steady state inflation rate will be welfare-improving depends on the alternative net social costs of reducing government expenditure and raising taxes to reduce the fiscal deficit. It may then seem to be better to sequence the inflation control program *after* the removal of interest ceilings, the introduction of flexibility in exchange rates, and the start of a phased program of trade liberalization. As real national income rises in response to the policy changes, government revenue will also rise to some extent. Then, if the government's real expenditure remains unchanged, the real fiscal deficit and hence both the reserve ratio and inflation rate should fall.

Though in theory one can couch arguments in terms of steady state inflation rates, in practice it will be very difficult (even for an omniscient and benevolent government) to maintain this steadiness. It may, therefore, be best to combine the reform of the domestic capital market with the reduction of the fiscal deficit and inflation. The last part of this initial package will be made easier by the likelihood that some deficit cuts will have formed part of the initial disabsorption required to deal with the crisis. So the first stage of the adjustment package should probably combine the reduction of domestic capital market distortions with the reduction of the fiscal deficit and inflation.

What exchange rate regime should be adopted by the liberalizing government during and after the transition? I have argued elsewhere (Lal 1980) that an exchange rate regime with an *automatic* balance of payments mechanism be adopted in a world of irreducible uncertainty, where discretionary government action (required in all forms of managed exchange rate regimes) cannot be expected to achieve convergence or reduce deviations from an unknowable equilibrium. The only two choices are a completely fixed or a fully floating exchange rate regime.

It may be worth noting that Chile—unlike the other two Southern Cone countries, Argentina and Uruguay—followed the conventional sequencing pattern: it first controlled its fiscal deficit, second, liberalized its trade regime, and third, liberalized its domestic capital market and opened the capital account of its balance of payments. The Chileans also implemented the advice of international monetarists on exchange rate policy to the letter: they progressed from a crawling peg through a preannounced exchange rate regime to a fixed exchange rate system.[28] Prima facie, the subsequent Chilean debacle presents a dramatic real life argument against this exchange rate choice.

In my judgment, a fully floating rate would have served the Chileans much better: it would have choked off some of the short run capital flows which supposedly destabilized the economy in the early 1980s.[29] Moreover, as Black (1976) and Lal (1980) have noted, the institutional requirements of a floating exchange rate system are probably exaggerated, as the recent floating of a number of African currencies demonstrates.

In summary, my suggested sequencing of liberalization would be as follows: first, reduction of the fiscal deficit, accompanied by removal of domestic capital market distortions; second, elimination of exchange controls and free floating of the exchange rate, accompanied by an announcement of a phased program for removing commodity market distortions; and third, the implementation of this preannounced phased program.

On Liberalizing the Capital Account

A number of objections can be raised against this sequencing, however, and in particular against the proposed liberalization of the capital account simultaneously with the initiation of a phased program of trade liberalization. These

28. See McKinnon (1982), who wrote: "the correct order of liberalization . . . approximates the successful Chilean experience after 1975" (p. 159).

29. For alternative views about the role of the pegging of the exchange rate in the Chilean debacle, see Dornbusch (1985) and Harberger (1985).

objections have supposedly gained greater credence as a result of the effects of the liberalization of the capital account in the 1970s in a number of countries in the Southern Cone of Latin America.[30]

But prima facie, it is not obvious that this experience provides arguments against my preferred sequence. As I have noted above, Chile liberalized its trade account before its capital account, and yet it suffered a debacle, arguably because it maintained a fixed exchange rate with real wage indexation and lax regulation of domestic financial institutions. Argentina liberalized its capital account without undertaking either any substantial trade liberalization or (more importantly) fiscal stabilization and instituted the system of preannounced exchange rates (the *tablita*). This program was clearly inconsistent and hence not credible or sustainable (see Fernandez 1985; Calvo 1986). Uruguay started with the opening of its capital account and the deregulation of its domestic financial system before it undertook trade liberalization. As Hanson and de Melo (1985) note, "no major imbalances occurred before 1979, when the financial liberalization was completed and the real exchange rate did not appear to be in disequilibrium from the viewpoint of the allocation of real resources in the long run," and hence "its experience does not seem to support the common view that the current account should be liberalized before the capital account" (p. 934). The debacle occurred because in October 1978, Uruguay adopted the *tablita,* and in 1982 and 1983 its fiscal deficit increased "due to an increase in social security payments and government salaries and a reduction in labor taxes" (Hanson and de Melo 1985, p. 933). These policies were clearly inconsistent. Thus, rather than blame the opening of the capital account for the crises, it would seem that in all three cases the *tablita* and/or pegging of the exchange rate made the programs inconsistent.

The lesson I would draw from this experience is that an appropriate exchange rate regime during the liberalization process and the maintenance of fiscal stability are essential for a sustainable liberalization program. For the reasons given earlier, a floating exchange rate which requires both domestic financial liberalization and the opening of the capital account would seem to be preferable to a fixed or managed exchange rate regime when liberalization is undertaken. We must consider, however, various technocratic a priori arguments that are raised against opening the capital before the current account of the balance of payments.

The first objection concerns the foreign capital inflows which might be induced as a result of the liberalization of the capital account while there are still distortions in domestic commodity markets. Theoretically, it is possible that capital inflows to a domestically distorted economy may be immiserizing (see Brecher and Diaz-Alejandro 1977). In my proposed package, however, the liberalization of the capital account would be accompanied by an announcement of a

30. See the symposium issue of *Economic Development and Cultural Change,* April 1986, and that in *World Development,* August 1985, on the liberalization experience of the Southern Cone.

future (dated) phased program of reduction in commodity market distortions. If one assumes that expectations are rational, and the public announcements credible, it is unlikely that long term capital flows (based on investors' time horizon extending beyond the trade liberalization phase) would be immiserizing. Because some foreign capital with shorter maturities is likely to flow into activities where private and social rates of return diverge during the trade liberalization phase, there may be a case for temporary and preannounced taxes on such flows by maturity, which are gradually reduced to zero as the trade liberalization proceeds.

The second objection relates to the likelihood of an initial appreciation in the real exchange rate with the removal of exchange controls, before trade has been liberalized. The argument can be stated as follows. With the liberalization of the domestic capital market, domestic real rates of interest will rise. Given the relative scarcity of capital in developing countries, they are likely to be higher than foreign interest rates at the original exchange rate. Hence, the removal of exchange control and the institution of a free float will appreciate the nominal exchange rate to establish interest rate parity. If, in the ensuing process of balance of payments adjustment, foreign capital also flows into the country, the real exchange rate will rise as the country runs a balance of trade deficit to match the surplus on the capital account of the balance of payments.[31] This will lead to resource movements opposite to those required during the process of trade liberalization when the real exchange rate is likely to fall. Hence, it is argued that the opening of the capital account before the trade liberalization is completed will lead to unnecessary shifts in resources, in effect away from traded to nontraded goods industries.

Before discussing this resource shifting argument, it is desirable to contrast the alternative sequencing of the opening of the trade and capital accounts. Suppose, instead of floating, a managed exchange rate system requiring capital controls is maintained during the trade liberalization process. The government will have to judge the precise extent of the *nominal* exchange rate change required to yield the appropriate *real* exchange rate at each point during the transition. Suppose it misjudges and at some point during the transition undertakes a nominal devaluation which is *less* than that required to yield the appropriate real exchange rate. This will lead to an incipient or actual balance of payments deficit which the government may be tempted to reduce through import controls—thus aborting the trade liberalization.

Furthermore, as can be readily shown (depending upon the dynamic structure of the economy, the relative factor intensities of traded and nontraded goods and the degree of short run mobility of capital), the trade liberalization process could lead to an initial real depreciation greater than that required in the final equilibrium. In this case also, the real exchange rate would first fall and then rise, with

31. The resulting short and long run resource and real wage movements can be readily derived in the framework provided in Lal (1986a).

unnecessary resource movements similar to those caused by the opening of the capital account. It is not apparent how one could determine the extent, and choose between these two alternative sets of unnecessary resource movements, in advocating one sequencing pattern over the other.

By contrast, one of the major advantages of instituting a free float before trade is liberalized is that the nominal rate changes which are required during the process of liberalization become automatic. Given the uncertainty in the dynamics associated with the process of adjustment, it is very difficult in practice to judge the precise extent—and in some cases even the direction—of the *nominal* exchange rate changes required in a managed exchange rate system as trade liberalization proceeds. Arguments for a crawling peg, to be followed by a fixed exchange rate regime once full liberalization of commodity markets is achieved (advanced for instance by McKinnon 1982), ignore these difficulties. The arguments for this set of policies are based on the erroneous view that the government, by pegging the *nominal* exchange rate for a set period of time, can also peg the *real* exchange rate (see Stockman 1982, p. 189). Because a major cause of the crises in Latin America's Southern Cone was mismanagement of the nominal exchange rate, a floating rate, by obviating the need for discretionary nominal exchange rate management, will relieve the government of concerns about the balance of payments consequences of other measures of economic liberalization.

The third objection to capital market liberalization in the initial stages of liberalization relates to the likely dynamic effects of foreign capital inflows. These are symmetrical with those discussed in connection with the "Dutch disease" (see Corden and Neary 1982). If there is a sustainable level of foreign capital inflows following the liberalization of domestic capital markets and the capital account of the balance of payments, then the resulting real exchange rate appreciation cannot be said to constitute a problem for the country. Real income will be higher, even though the resulting sectoral shifts in resources will entail distributional shifts in the returns to sector specific factors of production. But these shifts will also result from other policies required to liberalize a repressed economy. They cannot in themselves constitute an argument against liberalization, but they do provide an indication of the likely directions from which opposition to particular liberalization measures might be expected.

The real worry of the opponents of the liberalization of the capital account is that it could lead to an overshooting of capital inflows with an accompanying overshooting in the real exchange rate.[32] It is certainly conceivable that such overshooting may occur and that it will entail greater reversals of resource movements than on the "equilibrium" path of the real exchange rate. But with short run immobility of domestic capital, trade liberalization too will entail reversals in resource movements. In fact, in any dynamic economy with changing relative prices, such reversals (or more correctly changes) in resources move-

32. See Edwards (1984) for a summary of this argument, and the references to the Southern Cone experience with liberalization on which this currently dominant view is based.

ments can be expected to be taking place continually. Moreover, *all* resource movements involve adjustment costs. Unless some divergence between the social and private values of the adjustment costs associated with reversals in resource movements can be discerned, their mere existence does not in itself tell one whether moving resources in and out of particular industries during a dynamic process constitutes a policy problem which should determine the order of liberalization.

Consider the case where it is known by private agents (whose expectations are rational) and the government's Platonic advisers that, with my preferred sequencing of capital and current account liberalization, the real exchange rate will first appreciate and then depreciate over time, so that the relative profitability of nontraded relative to traded goods industries will first rise and then decline. Corresponding to this expected real exchange rate movement, private agents can calculate the present value of investments as relative prices change at any date during the transition, including the cessation of current income streams from investments which fail to cover variable costs. This will yield a private profit maximizing allocation of resources in the two sets of industries over time, which may well involve an initial expansion and then contraction of the nontraded good industry.

Moreover, as this dynamic sequence of investments and sectoral outputs is ex hypothesi based on the same expected real exchange rate movements as those foreseen by the government's advisers, this is also the "optimal" sequence.[33] Even a temporary capital inflow, by improving domestic resource availabilities, must raise the current and the discounted present value of future national income as long as either the domestic rate of time preference (if the inflow finances consumption) or the domestic rate of return of investment financed by the inflows is higher than the effective real interest rate on the capital inflows. It is only if one assumes that the government knows the correct time path of the real exchange rate while myopic and/or ignorant private agents do not that an argument against this sequencing can be made based on a divergence between the private and social costs of adjustment in this dynamic process.

Frenkel (1982) does present an argument based on divergences between private and social costs on alternative orders of liberalization. He argues that "if the capital account is opened up first, portfolio decisions are likely to correspond to the long-run undistorted conditions, but real investment will still be carried out in a distorted environment as long as the trade account is not opened up. Due to the distortions, the social cost of the investment is likely to exceed the private cost. These real investments will have to be reversed once the trade account is liberalized. Due to the difference in private and social costs, it is likely that the first order should be preferred" (p. 200).

33. I assume, of course, in this example that there is no divergence between social and private rates of time preference. But I do not seek to imply that this path is necessarily Pareto efficient. The main point is that there is *no policy* which in the postulated circumstances can yield a welfare improvement.

The crucial assumption in this argument is the assumed asymmetry of information between farsighted foreign portfolio investors and ignorant or myopic domestic real investors. Exactly the opposite outcome is likely if both groups are equally well informed. For as Frenkel himself argues, it is much "easier to reverse wrong portfolio decisions than to reverse wrong real investment decisions." Thus, it will be in the self-interest of investors involved in production decisions to have much longer time horizons in considering their real physical investments than do financial investors!

Finally, if this overshooting argument against the removal of capital controls is correct, it should apply to the liberalization of the capital account *at any time*, irrespective of whether or not trade liberalization has taken place. It would imply that permanent capital controls should be maintained because of the presumed suboptimal resource movements which myopic agents will undertake in response to any overshooting accompanying the liberalization of the capital account. This is hardly a credible argument.

I would conclude, therefore, that some of the currently conventional arguments against opening the capital account at the same time as a phased program of trade liberalization is announced must ultimately be based on the erroneous (but also common) assumption of the limited foresight of private agents and the clairvoyance of governments and their advisers.

III. Conclusions

Most of the "crises" which require the stabilization cum structural adjustment medicine are primarily crises of the public sector. For many developing countries in the past three decades, a vast expansion of the government bureaucracy, of the public sector, and of controls on industry, prices, and foreign trade have created a new system of subinfeudation, in which politically created property rights to rents for various groups are financed by implicit or explicit taxation of the general populace. In many countries these groups include a significant portion of the bureaucracy, public sector functionaries, industrial labor, and those who have been granted the monopolistic protection of the use of their labor or capital by the State's prohibitions on entry and exit of economic enterprises.

A crisis arises as the existing means of funding these entitlements become unviable. Economic liberalization is then seen as a way to regain government control of the fiscal accounts and the economy. The process of gaining fiscal control by reducing public expenditure to a sustainable level and the subsequent liberalization program must inevitably entail either confronting these vested interests or buying them out. The latter approach will only be viable, however, if it is ensured that the economic and legal framework contains enough checks and balances to prevent the State from creating future artificial rents for other vested interests. This is the strongest political and practical case—as distinct from that based on the controversial grounds of economic efficiency—for the promotion of a market economy.

Therefore, if a government can demonstrate its political strength in establishing fiscal control, the question of the order of liberalization which minimizes the pain to be suffered by sectoral and sectional interests during the movement to a market economy becomes politically less important. Moreover, for the *credibility* of the process, speed in implementing the liberalization of the various repressed markets may be of the essence. This speed is necessary both because of the time inconsistency of technocratic programs (whereby for the government it is usually optimal to renege on its past commitments)[34] and to preempt the formation of coalitions by the losers from the liberalization. To assure its credibility, the government might wish to institute a speedy bonfire of *all* controls and Ulysses-like tie itself to the mast by signing a stabilization and structural adjustment program with an international organization. If backed by sufficient resource inflows, this *could* provide the restraints necessary to forestall any future temptation for itself or its successors to reverse the liberalization and thus could make its announced program of liberalization sustainable.

Looked at from this perspective, most of the technocratic literature on the order of liberalization does not seem too relevant, though I have provided some arguments against the currently fashionable view that the capital account of the foreign exchange market should be liberalized last. There is still the controversial technical question of the exchange rate regime the liberalizing government should adopt during the transition, and the regime it should aim for when the liberalization is completed (if different). It was the inconsistency of exchange rate policy which largely explains the Southern Cone debacles. I have provided some reasons why an automatically adjusting floating exchange rate system may be desirable. These are essentially to minimize the information required to set particular nominal values at their optimal levels, and hence to avoid the risk of mistakes in the desirable extent and even the direction of changes of the *nominal* exchange rate.

There is, however, one major unresolved issue which the recent Chilean experience in particular highlights. This concerns the desirable form of regulation of domestic financial institutions which a developing country seeking to liberalize its domestic capital market should adopt during the transition, and as part of its ultimate economic framework. Besides wage indexation and exchange rate policy, it is the mishandling of the financial liberalization which many observers see as the third crucial ingredient in the Chilean debacle with economic liberalization (Congdon 1985). But these policies raise issues which go beyond the scope of this article.

34. Kydland and Prescott (1977) is the seminal contribution on this issue; also see Elster (1979).

Appendix. *Stabilization and Liberalization Policies: Direction of Change from Initial Equilibrium*

Policy changes and assumptions	*Flexible wages*								*Sticky wages*			
	Short run, sector-specific capital				*Long run capital mobility*				*Short run, sector-specific capital*			
	Real wage	*Interest: nontraded goods*	*Interest: traded goods*	*Real exchange rate*	*Real wage*	*Interest: nontraded goods*	*Interest: traded goods*	*Real exchange rate*	*Real wage*	*Interest: nontraded goods*	*Interest: traded goods*	*Real exchange rate*
Capital markets: removing nontraded good tax or traded good subsidy	+	0	–	–	+	–	–	–	0	0	–	–
Product markets: remove distortion in traded goods markets (assume no devaluation; demand management keeps nontraded good price constant)	?	+	–	–	+	–	–	–	+	+	–	–
Exchange rate market: devaluation:												
(1) No other change	?	–	+	–	0	0	0	0	?	–	+	–
(2) Increased preference for traded goods	?	–	+	–	–	+	+	–	?	–	+	–
(assume fixed or no distortions)												
Monetary policy: monetary expansion:												
(1) Fixed exchange rates	?	+	–	+	+	–	–	+	–	+	–	+
(2) Flexible rates	0	0	0	0	0	0	0	0	0	0	0	0
(assume fixed or no distortions)												
Capital account: sustained constant addition to capital stock in each period	?	+	–	+	+	–	–	+	–	+	–	+

Note: All prices are real, rather than nominal values. This analysis assumes that the nontraded good is labor-intensive and that the traded good is capital-intensive.

Source: Lal (1986a).

References

Backus, D., and J. Driffill. 1985a. "Credibility and Commitment in Economic Policy." Centre for Economic Policy Research Discussion Paper 63. London. Processed.

——. 1985b. "Inflation and Reputation." *American Economic Review* 75, no. 3 (June): 530–38.

——. 1985c. "Rational Expectations and Policy Credibility Following a Change in Regime." *Review of Economic Studies* 52, no. 169 (April): 211–22.

Barro, R., and D. Gordon. 1983a. "A Positive Theory of Monetary Policy in a Natural Rate Model." *Journal of Political Economy* 91, no. 4 (August): 589–610.

——. 1983b. "Rules, Discretion, and Reputation in a Model of Monetary Policy." *Journal of Monetary Economics* 12 (July): 101–21.

Becker, G. 1983. "A Theory of Competition among Pressure Groups for Political Influence." *Quarterly Journal of Economics* 98, no. 3 (August): 371–400.

Bhagwati, J. 1979. *Anatomy and Consequences of Trade Control Regimes.* New York: National Bureau of Economic Research.

Black, S. 1976. *Exchange Rate Policies for Less Developed Countries in a World of Floating Rates.* Princeton University, Essays in International Finance 119. Princeton, N.J.

Blejer, M., and M. Khan. 1984. "Government Policy and Private Investment in Developing Countries." *IMF Staff Papers* 31, no. 2 (June): 379–403.

Brecher, R. A., and C. F. Diaz-Alejandro. 1977. "Tariffs, Foreign Capital, and Immiserising Growth." *Journal of International Economics* 7, no. 4 (November): 317–22.

Burgess, D. F. 1980. "Protection, Real Wages, and the Neo-classical Ambiguity with Inter-industry Flows." *Journal of Political Economy* 88, no. 4 (August): 783–802.

Calvo, G. A. 1978. "On the Time Consistency of Optimal Policy in a Monetary Economy." *Econometrica* 46, no. 6 (November): 1411–28.

——. 1986. "Fractured Liberalism: Argentina under Martinez de Hoz." *Economic Development and Cultural Change* 34, no. 3 (April): 511–34.

Collier, P., D. Bevan, and J. Gunning. 1985. "The Macro Economics of Liberalisation—with an Application to East Africa." London: Trade Policy Research Centre. Processed.

Congdon, T. 1985. *Economic Liberalism in the Cone of Latin America.* Thames Essays 40. London: Trade Policy Research Centre.

Cooper, R., and J. Sachs. 1985. "Borrowing Abroad: The Debtors' Perspective." In G. W. Smith and J. T. Cuddington, eds., *International Debt and the Developing Countries.* Washington, D.C.: World Bank.

Corbo, V., and J. de Melo. 1985. "Overview and Summary: Liberalisation and Stabilisation in the Southern Cone of Latin America." *World Development* 13, no. 8 (August): 863–66.

Corden, W. M. 1977. *Inflation, Exchange Rates, and the World Economy.* London: Oxford University Press.

Corden, W. M. and R. Jones. 1976. "Devaluation, Non-Flexible Prices, and the Trade Balance for a Small Country." *Canadian Journal of Economics* 9, no. 1 (February): 150–61.

Corden, W. M., and P. Neary. 1982. "Booming Sector and De-Industrialisation in A Small Open Economy." *Economic Journal* 92, no. 368 (December): 825–48.

De Jasy, A. 1984. *The State.* Oxford: Blackwell.

Dornbusch, R. 1974. "Real and Monetary Aspects of the Effects of Exchange Rate Changes." In R. Z. Aliber, ed., *National Monetary Policies and the International Finance System.* Chicago: University of Chicago Press.

——. 1980. *Open Economy Macroeconomics.* New York: Basic Books.

——. 1985. "External Debt, Budget Deficits, and Disequilibrium Exchange Rates." In G. W. Smith and J. T. Cuddington, eds., *International Debt and the Developing Countries.* Washington, D.C.: World Bank.

Eaton, J., M. Gersowitz, and J. Stiglitz. 1986. "The Pure Theory of Country Risk." *European Economic Review* 30 (June): 481–513.

Economic Development and Cultural Change. 1986. April.

Edwards, S. 1984. *The Order of Liberalization of the External Sector in Developing Countries.* Essays in International Finance 156, Princeton, N.J.: Princeton University Press.

Elster, J. 1979. *Ulysses and the Sirens—Studies on Rationality and Irrationality.* Cambridge: Cambridge University Press.

Fellner, W. 1976. *Towards a Reconstruction of Macroeconomics: Problems of Theory and Policy.* Washington, D.C.: American Enterprise Institute.

——. 1979. "The Credibility Effect and Rational Expectations: Implications of the Gramlich Study." *Brookings Papers on Economic Activity* 1: 167–78.

Fernandez, R. B. 1985. "The Expectations Management Approach to Stabilization in Argentina During 1976–82." *World Development* 13, no. 8 (August): 871–92.

Findlay, R. 1986. "Trade, Development and the State." Economic Growth Center Twenty-fifth Anniversary Symposium on "The State of Development Economics: Progress and Perspectives." April, Yale University, New Haven, Conn. Processed.

Fischer, S. 1980. "Dynamic Inconsistency, Cooperation and the Benevolent Dissembling Government." *Journal of Economic Dynamics and Control* 2 (February): 93–107.

Frenkel, J. 1982. "The Order of Economic Liberalization: Discussion." In K. Brunner and A. H. Meltzer, eds., *Economic Policy in a World of Change.* Amsterdam: North-Holland.

Frey, Bruno D. 1978. *Modern Political Economy.* Oxford: Martin Robertson.

Fry, M. J. 1980. "Money, Interest, Inflation and Growth in Turkey." *Journal of Monetary Economics* 6: 535–45.

Gelb, A. 1986. "The Oil Syndrome: Adjustment to Windfall Gains in Oil-Exporting Countries." In D. Lal and M. Wolf, eds., *Stagflation, Savings, and the State: Perspectives on the Global Economy.* New York: Oxford University Press.

Guitian, M. 1981. *Conditionality: Access to Fund Resources.* Washington, D.C.: International Monetary Fund.

Hanson, J., and J. de Melo. 1985. "External Shocks, Financial Reforms, and Stabilisation Attempts in Uruguay During 1974–83." *World Development* 13, no. 8 (August): 917–39.

Harberger, A. C., ed. 1984. *World Economic Growth.* San Francisco: Institute for Contemporary Studies.

——. 1985. "Lessons for Debtor-Country Managers and Policymakers." G. W. Smith and J. T. Cuddington, eds., *International Debt and the Developing Countries.* Washington, D.C.: World Bank.

Jones, R. 1971. "A Three Factor Model in Theory, Trade and History." In J. Bhagwati, R. W. Jones, R. A. Mundell, and J. Vanek, *Trade, The Balance of Payments and Growth*. Amsterdam: North-Holland.

Killick, T., ed. 1982. *Adjustment and Financing in the Developing World*. Washington, D.C.: International Monetary Fund.

Kreps, D., and R. Wilson. 1982. "Reputation and Imperfect Information." *Journal of Economic Theory* 27, no. 2: 253–79.

Krueger, A. O. 1974. "Home Goods and Money in Exchange Rate Adjustments." In W. Sellekaarts, ed., *International Trade and Finance*. New York: Macmillan.

——. 1978. *Liberalization Attempts and Consequences*. New York: National Bureau of Economic Research.

——. 1984. "Problems of Liberalization." In A. C. Harberger, ed., *World Economic Growth*. San Francisco: Institute for Contemporary Studies.

Kydland, F. E., and E. C. Prescott. 1977. "Rules Rather than Discretion: The Inconsistency of Optimal Plans." *Journal of Political Economy* 85, no. 3 (June): 473–92.

Lal, D. 1974. *Methods of Project Analysis: A Review*. World Bank Occasional Papers 16, Baltimore, Md.: Johns Hopkins University Press.

——. 1980. *A Liberal International Economic Order: The International Monetary System and Economic Development*. Princeton University Essays in International Finance 139. Princeton, N. J.

——. 1983. *Real Wages and Exchange Rates in the Philippines, 1956–78: An Application of the Stolper-Samuelson-Rybczynski Model of Trade*. World Bank Staff Working Paper 604. Washington, D.C.

——. 1984a. "The Political Economy of the Predatory State." World Bank Development Research Department Discussion Paper 105. Washington, D.C. Processed.

——. 1984b. *The Real Effects of Stabilization and Structural Adjustment Policies: An Extension of the Australian Adjustment Model*. World Bank Staff Working Paper 636. Washington, D. C.

——. 1985. "The Real Exchange Rate, Capital Inflows and Inflation: Sri Lanka 1970–1982." *Weltwirtschaftliches Archiv*, no. 4 (December): 682–702.

——. 1986a. "A Simple Framework for Analyzing Various Real Aspects of Stabilization and Structural Adjustment Policies." World Bank Economics and Research Staff Research Unit. Processed.

——. 1986b. "Stolper-Samuelson-Rybczynski in the Pacific: Real Wages and Exchange Rates in the Philippines, 1956–78." *Journal of Development Economics* (April): 181–204.

Lal, D., and M. Wolf, eds. 1986. *Stagflation, Savings, and the State: Perspectives on the Global Economy*. New York: Oxford University Press.

Lal, D., and S. Rajapatirana. Forthcoming. *Trade Liberalisation in Sri Lanka*. Thames Essay. London: Trade Policy Research Centre.

Lindbeck, A. 1976. "Stabilization in Open Economies with Endogenous Politicians." *American Economic Review* 66, no. 2 (May): 1–19.

McKinnon, R. 1981. "Financial Repression and the Liberalization Problem within Less Developed Countries." In S. Grassman and E. Lundberg, eds., *The World Economic Order: Past and Prospects*. New York: Macmillan.

——. 1982. "The Order of Economic Liberalisation: Lessons from Chile and Argentina." In K. Brunner and A. Meltzer, eds., *Economic Policy in a World of Change*. Amsterdam: North-Holland.

McKinnon, R., and D. J. Mathieson. 1981. *How to Manage a Repressed Economy.* Princeton University Essays in International Finance 145. Princeton, N.J.

Mussa, M. 1974. "Tariffs and the Distribution of Income." *Journal of Political Economy,* 82, no. 6 (November/December): 1191–1204.

Neary, J. P. 1978. "Short-run Capital Specificity and the Pure Theory of International Trade." *Economic Journal* 88, no. 351: 488–510.

——. 1982. "Capital Mobility, Wage Stickiness and Adjustment Assistance." In J. Bhagwati, ed., *Import Competition and Response.* New York: National Bureau of Economic Research.

——. 1985. *Theory and Policy Adjustment in an Open Economy.* Centre for Economic Policy Research Discussion Paper 61. London.

Nogués, J. 1981. "Politica Commercial y Cambiara: Una Evaluacion Cuantitativa de la Politica Argentina Durante 1961–1981." Buenos Aires: Banco Central de la Republica Argentina. Processed.

Nordhaus, W. 1975. "The Political Business Cycle." *Review of Economic Studies* 42, no. 130 (April): 169–90.

Prachowny, M. 1981. "Sectoral Conflict over Stabilisation Policies in Small Open Economies." *Economic Journal* 91, no. 363 (September): 671–84.

——. 1984. *Macroeconomic Analysis for Small Open Economies.* Oxford: Clarendon Press.

Sargent, T. J. 1985. "The Ends of Four Big Inflations." In T. J. Sargent, *Rational Expectations and Inflation.* New York: Harper and Row.

Shapiro, Carl. 1983. "Premium for High Quality Products as Returns to Reputation." *Quarterly Journal of Economics* 98, no. 4: 659–80.

Srinivasan, T. N. 1985. "Neo-Classical Political Economy, the State and Economic Development." *Asian Development Review* 3, no. 2: 38–58.

Staniland, M. 1985. *What Is Political Economy?* New Haven, Conn.: Yale University Press.

Stern, E. 1983. "World Bank Financing of Structural Adjustment." In J. Williamson, ed., *IMF Conditionality.* Washington, D.C.: Institute for International Economics.

Stockman, A. C. 1982. "The Order of Economic Liberalisation: Lessons from Chile and Argentina—a Comment." In K. Brunner and A. H. Meltzer, eds., *Economic Policy in a World of Change.* Amsterdam: North-Holland.

Swamy, G. 1981. *International Migrant Workers' Remittances: Issues and Prospects.* World Bank Staff Working Paper 481. Washington, D.C.

Williamson, J., ed. 1983. *IMF Conditionality.* Washington, D.C.: Institute for International Economics.

World Development. 1985. August.

PART II

[6]

A LIBERAL INTERNATIONAL ECONOMIC ORDER: The International Monetary System and Economic Development

Introduction

Since the suspension of the convertibility of the dollar into gold in August 1971 and the subsequent collapse of the Bretton Woods system, the world has gradually moved to what is now described as an international monetary "nonsystem." The Jamaica agreement of January 1976 to amend the Articles of Agreement of the International Monetary Fund legalized the managed floating of exchange rates, which has been widespread since 1973. A fierce and voluminous debate continues on whether the existing nonsystem needs to be reformed by the erection of a new system to replace Bretton Woods and, if so, on what form the new system should take. This debate presupposes some agreement on the necessity of any international economic (including monetary) system or order and on the basic objectives of this system. The debate has gained considerable topical interest with the desire of the less developed countries to seek a new international economic order.

Section 1 of this essay briefly surveys the answers that have been provided to these fundamental questions and argues the case for what has been termed "the liberal international economic order." To do so, some well-trodden ground must be covered, but a number of relatively unfamiliar arguments in favor of such an order are also advanced. In particular, I contend that the arguments in favor of free trade in assets parallel those for goods and services. I also take issue with a common argument advanced against the feasibility of a "spontaneous emergence of free trade" in a world where most countries have some degree of monopoly power (see Kindleberger, 1976a). The arguments for a full-fledged liberal international economic order set the stage for the policy discussions in the next two sections.

Policy debates on the international monetary system have centered around the desirability of alternative arrangements for three dimensions of an international monetary system: the role of exchange-rate adjustments, the nature and role of international reserve assets, and the degree of control of international capital movements. Much of the debate on

---

The research for this paper was done while the author was a Visiting Fellow in the Research School of Pacific Studies at the Australian National University. It forms part of an ongoing project on the New International Economic Order, in collaboration with David Henderson, which is funded by the Nuffield Foundation. Discussions with, and comments on earlier drafts by, Heinz Arndt, Max Corden, Ian Little, and David Henderson have proved most useful. The views expressed are the author's and should in no way be identified with those of the World Bank.

these issues has been based on what Corden (1977, p. 43) has termed "target theory rather than optimising theory." This has meant that, unlike other debates on public policy (e.g. concerning alternative tax structures, price-stabilization schemes, investment criteria, and trade policies), those on the reform of the international monetary system are not usually conducted within the explicit framework of welfare economics. In my view, however, it is both possible and desirable to view the choice of an international monetary system in terms of welfare economics. This is the purpose of section 2.

I take issue with the views of both those who believe in the feasibility and desirability of fixed exchange rates and those who want some rules for a system of managed floating. I argue that fixed exchange rates are not feasible in the real world, where monetary independence is identified with national sovereignty and there is some downward rigidity in money wages and the prices of nontraded goods. The advocacy of managed floating is shown to be based on an implicit model in which governments have perfect (or at least greater) foresight than other market participants. In the real world of irreducible uncertainty, I argue, no such assumption is valid. In consequence, free trade in goods and services (including capital flows) and freely floating exchange rates represent the optimal system for the world as it is.

While many, but by no means a majority of, economists might be willing to concede the optimality of such a regime for advanced (OECD) countries, most would seem to argue for some form of managed flexibility of exchange rates and capital controls for less developed countries (see Díaz-Alejandro, 1975; Cline, 1976; Joshi, 1979; Black, 1976). The merits of these arguments are examined in section 3, which also briefly discusses the pros and cons of the demands of developing countries for a link between foreign aid and the creation of international fiduciary money in the form of Special Drawing Rights. I argue that, except for a few of the least developed countries, a currently heretical case can be made for the application of the arguments of the earlier sections of the essay to most of these countries. It would be in their interests to endorse the monetary arrangements of a liberal international economic order—free floating and no capital controls.

1 The Case for a Liberal International Economic Order

The purpose of public policy is to raise levels of economic welfare, usually identified by economists, though not by politicians and diplomats, with the level of individual consumption broadly defined. It is a fact of life that the individuals concerned are organized into nation-states. The question then arises: What should be the economic objectives of a rational nation-state which subscribes to the relatively mild liberal individualistic premises that, *ceteris paribus*, it is better for individuals to be in their own chosen position and that the source of economic welfare (which is of course only a part of total welfare) is consumption by its current and future citizens?

Economic Objectives of "Rational" Nation-States

It is necessary first to define the set of individuals to be counted as members of the nation—those whose economic welfare is the nation's concern. The individuals defining the nation have common rights and duties concerning the provision of various public goods, as well as the attainment of any commonly shared *national* redistributive goals realizable through either voluntary or coercive transfers between citizens of the nation. Furthermore, the rights of noncitizens to join and of citizens to leave the nation (immigration and emigration policies) are under national control and need to be specified, irrespective of whether national rule making concerning these rights is democratic, dictatorial, or oligarchic.

But apart from thus defining the set of individuals whose economic welfare is its concern, should the nation-state care at all about the actual ownership of claims to physical and other assets within its borders, or about the particular composition of output or assets? To set aside for the moment second-best domestic distributional considerations, assume that each nation can enforce its desired domestic income distribution. Then suppose that the citizens of two nations engage in mutually agreeable trades until each group ends up "owning" all of the other's physical assets in economies assumed to be stationary (to avoid complications arising from differential rates of return on savings, which I take up below). Should this be a matter of concern to either national authority?

In these static economies, there would seem to be no reason why it should be (ignoring political problems concerning, for instance, the risks of expropriation, which are discussed below). The respective consumption and income flows will, of course, still depend upon the initial resource endowments of the two countries' citizens, their rates of time preference, and the respective productivities, but the location of the income-generating assets will not in itself be a source of additional benefit. The foreign ownership of a country's assets, moreover, does not diminish the country's capital stock or remove it from the country. It means only that, as a result of national and foreign portfolio preferences, the portfolio of assets has been altered (and in the process of adjustment the relative prices of different assets may have changed). At any point in time, most of a country's capital stock is physically fixed and cannot be shipped out (except in economists' models with perfectly malleable capital goods). The only question is: Who has the rights to the income stream that is generated by the stock? If nationals are willing without coercion to exchange their rights from local assets for those from foreign assets, both sides to the bargain have presumably gained. Hence, from an *economic* viewpoint, the fear of foreigners' buying up local assets would not be rational.

This argument remains unchanged even when the assumptions of a static economy are relaxed. Allow additions to the local capital stock through *flows* of savings (local or foreign). If there are no disparities between private and social rates of return to investment in either nation, there is again little *economic* reason to be concerned with the location of investments made by citizens with current savings. (The case of disparities between private and social returns to investment, domestic and foreign, is considered in section 3. There may also be noneconomic reasons concerning ownership and control that may lead to national concern over foreign ownership, on which more below.)

What would be the optimal international economic order from the viewpoint of such rational nation-states? Would this optimal order emerge spontaneously from the self-interested actions of such nation-states, or would it need to be enforced?

Alternative World Environments

Assume a world of nation-states each of which follows the economically rational objective of being concerned with the consumption levels of its citizens. Further assume for the moment that each state can correct any *domestic* disparities between private and social values and can legislate the optimal domestic income distribution through nondistortionary lump-sum taxes and subsidies. Following Grandmont and McFadden (1973), we can categorize four world environments that are conceivable in principle.

The first consists of centrally planned nations in which a central committee of Platonic Guardians acts as if the nation consisted of a single consumer. The rest of the environments consist of nations with multiple consumers and relatively decentralized national markets, but they differ in the size of the nations. In the second, the nations are "infinitesimal" in international markets in that they cannot influence world prices or dis-

4

turb world trade equilibrium. In the third, they are "small" in that they treat world prices as parameters but influence the determination of world trade equilibrium. In the fourth, they are "large" in that they treat world prices as variables.

In the first world environment, it has been shown that free trade is to the advantage of each nation. The mutual gains from trade for a world of initially autarkic centrally planned nations follows from the fact that "the refuge of [any degree of] autarky remains available when trade is possible" (Grandmont and McFadden, 1973). Starting from any allocation under autarky, the Platonic Guardians can choose from an enlarged feasible set of allocations under free trade, either the original allocation or one that is at least as good for every consumer. Given such a Pareto-optimal allocation under free trade, any alternative allocation that is feasible under autarky can improve the lot of some consumers in the nation only by worsening that of others. The same arguments apply when we consider the whole spectrum of choices while moving from autarky to restricted trade to free trade. Grandmont and McFadden emphasize that this proposition "does *not* require that nations be either 'infinitesimal' or 'small' in international markets, that nonincreasing returns to scale prevail, that all commodities be tradeable, or that factors be immobile."

For the second and third world environments, namely for "small" and "infinitesimal" multi-consumer trading nations, in which consumers are (locally) nonsatiated and externalities are absent, it can be shown that any alternative allocation feasible under varying degrees of autarky will not be Pareto-optimal, as compared with an equilibrium allocation under competitive trade. For any allocation achieved under autarky, a system of *domestic* lump-sum transfers can be found for which a competitive equilibrium exists and will be at least as satisfactory as autarky for every consumer. This conclusion does not require that traders be "small," that nonincreasing returns to scale prevail, or that factors be immobile.

These conclusions for centrally planned nations and "small" and "infinitesimal" multi-consumer trading nations are not restricted to trade in commodities. As Kareken and Wallace (1977) have shown, similar conclusions apply when asset or portfolio autarky is compared with free trade in assets (where autarky means that "the residents of every country are prohibited from owning real assets, by assumption physically immobile, that are located in other countries"). They show that portfolio autarky is not in general Pareto-optimal, while free trade is optimal.

Mutatis mutandis, the free-trade regime will also be superior to various restricted-trade regimes.

Let us now successively relax some of the assumptions underlying these demonstrations of the mutually beneficial effects of free trade in commodities and assets. First, these results are based on models that abstract from uncertainty or else sidestep it by postulating complete Arrow-Debreu-type futures markets. Many authors have argued that in a world of uncertainty about preferences, the terms of trade, or technology, many of the standard theorems of trade and welfare theory do not hold in the standard trade-theoretic model, which abstracts from trade in international securities and hence in international risk-sharing arrangements. (See Helpman and Razin, 1978, for a review of these studies.)

However, Helpman and Razin have shown that the standard theorems are resurrected once international trade in securities is allowed. The basic reason is that the lack of (or restrictions on) international trade in real equities under conditions of uncertainty turns each of the trading countries into a virtual "closed" economy. The stochastic element for every good (including traded goods) for which there is only a domestic market makes every good in effect nontraded or partially traded. Hence, each country's production decisions are tied to its consumption decisions, as in a closed economy. The introduction of trade in securities, opening up extra international "insurance" markets, is required to "open" the economy completely (as purely "goods" trade does in the standard model without uncertainty). This enables the familiar gains from trade to appear. It becomes possible to separate the country's production and consumption decisions at commodity and asset price ratios that differ from those under autarky, so that there are gains from enlarging its potential consumption-possibility set beyond the domestic production-possibilities set.

Keeping within the confines of our first three world environments, let us next relax the assumptions concerning the optimal correction of any domestic divergences between private and social values. As it will not usually be feasible to use neutral fiscal devices, such as lump-sum taxes and subsidies, only a second-best welfare optimum will be attainable in each trading nation. There will then be a hierarchy of policies for dealing with particular domestic disparities, as well as with domestic income distribution. In this hierarchy, many *domestic* policies will dominate those restricting foreign trade in goods and assets. (See Corden, 1974, for an excellent summary of this modern theory of trade and welfare.) Furthermore, as Neary (1978, p. 508) has shown, once the realistic assumption is made that capital is sector specific in the short run, then a "number of paradoxes which have attracted much attention in recent writings, such as a perverse price-output response, and a perverse distortion-output response, will 'almost never' be observed" when a small open economy is opened up to trade. Though free trade will not necessarily be optimal in *all* second-best situations, the combination of some domestic intervention and free trade will dominate a policy of restricted trade in many situations where the feasible set of domestic policy instruments is not so limited as to rule out their deployment in dealing with domestic distortions.

This still leaves one unrealistic assumption, that the domestic distributional effects of alternative trade policies can be dealt with neutrally through lump-sum domestic taxes and transfers. In practice, lump-sum redistribution will generally not be feasible. Once again, however, there will be various second-best *domestic* redistributive mechanisms which, if feasible, will be preferable to protection in tackling the distributional effects that may flow from increased foreign trade. It should also be noted that the distributional effects of any economic change, even if domestic in origin, would also require domestic compensatory policies in line with each country's distributional preferences.

Finally, we have the fourth world environment to consider, with "large" multiple-consumer nations for which world prices are variables. In this world, there is a case for levying an optimal tariff, which equates the marginal costs and revenues of a country's imports and exports. For a country that can affect its terms of trade because of its monopoly/monopsony power in trade in commodities, mobile factors, or assets, such a tariff would be optimal from a national standpoint if other countries were either price takers or else did not retaliate against the tariff-imposing country. Although world welfare would be lower, the country imposing the tariff would gain. Furthermore, Johnson (1953-54) has shown that even if more than one country can affect its terms of trade and all the others retaliate, it is still possible for one of the countries to be better off in the tariff-ridden situation than with free trade.

It may be argued that in the real world many countries have at least *some* influence over their terms of trade. It may therefore be tempting for the smaller nations to levy optimum tariffs on their foreign trade. As their tariffs would have an almost imperceptible effect on the world economy, the dangers of retaliation against them would be minimal and there would be little incentive for rational countries to move unilaterally to free trade. In order to maximize world gains, it would be necessary to enforce free trade through universal agreements to eschew protective devices (see Scitovsky, 1942, and Kindleberger, 1976a). In the absence of any international externalities in consumption, however, rational nations are unlikely to be moved by notions of cosmopolitan gains. They are more likely to prefer *national* gains to any given total of cosmopolitan gains. Why, then, should any such agreement to eschew the use of optimal tariffs be stable?

The Terms-of-Trade Argument for Protection and the Legislation of a Liberal International Economic Order

To answer this question, an application of N-person cooperative game theory is particularly useful. It allows us to look at the traditional two-country–two-commodity optimal-tariff model incorporating retaliation as a two-person non-zero-sum *non*cooperative game (like the Prisoner's Dilemma). If the world economy consisted of two noncooperating trading blocs, the final configuration would be unpredictable and the free-trade equilibrium would have to be enforced. This implicit model underlies much thinking on an international economic order, as is brought out by the following quotation from Kindleberger (1976a, p. 16):

> In the international economy it has long been recognized that the world of the benign invisible hand does not obtain. Unlike the households and firms of the national economy, countries in the international economy and especially in the international polity have power. A country can improve its terms of trade, that is get imports cheaper, by imposing a tariff on goods bought abroad. The fallacy of composition argues that if each country tries to gain at the expense of others, all lose, so that it is useful to simulate the world of the invisible hand by commitments to the rule of free trade and the gold standard.

But since the world economy is *not* (at least as yet) composed of two mutually opposed trading blocs, are the same conclusions valid for a multi-country trading world in which all traders can within limits choose the quantities they want to buy and sell at mutually agreed prices (and hence are implicitly "price makers" in one sense)?

The relevant model is that of N-person cooperative game theory. Within this framework, it can be demonstrated that, following from a famous theorem of Edgeworth's recently revived in the mathematical theory of the "core" of an economy, when there are many trading nations with some "monopoly" power and those nations have the preferences of *homo oeconimicus*, the only stable equilibrium point in the process of higgling and haggling among these "rational" nations will be where they all act as if they were price takers, namely the free-trade, competitive equilibrium.[1] As Arrow and Hahn (1971, p. 186) point out:

[1] This proof holds (see Malinvaud, 1972) under the usual convexity assumptions, in the presence of all markets (absence of externalities), when the costs of bargaining

> Contrary to the view sometimes expressed that competitive equilibrium has an inherent instability in that it would pay, for example, the owners of some one commodity to form a cartel and exploit their monopoly power [the] theorems on the relation between competitive equilibria and the core suggest that any such attempt would be broken up by the formation of coalitions involving some buyers and some sellers of that commodity. The sellers ultimately can depend for sure only on what they can achieve by trade among themselves, and of course, this may be very little indeed.

This line of argument might appear to be a cruel joke to those suffering from the oil prices legislated by the OPEC cartel since 1973. But the theorist, as always, has a way out! The argument depends upon symmetries in expected behavior. As Arrow and Hahn state:

> If a coalition with monopoly power somehow makes it credible to all others that its demands will not be compromised no matter how much it suffers and that none of its members can be drawn off into side bargains, then it may indeed get its way. The difficulty with this type of argument is its asymmetry. If one coalition can threaten in this way, so can the coalition composed of all others. The asymmetry in expected behavior needed for the efficacy of threat strategies is plausible only when based either on *differential bargaining costs* (so that the counter-coalition cannot really form) or on *extra-economic motives* of loyalty to and identification with some group, such as nation, class, or race (p. 187, emphasis added).

Clearly, the success of the OPEC cartel can be sufficiently explained within this framework by the two italicized conditions. It proved impossible to organize a countervailing consumer coalition, despite U.S. efforts, partly because oil-importing developing countries were sympathetic to OPEC and wanted to follow OPEC's lead by organizing similar cartels for other commodities. Among the producers, Saudi Arabia's adherence to the OPEC cartel was to an important extent motivated by its desire to use the "oil weapon" as a lever to obtain perceived Arab rights.

This argument suggests that *if* nations were moved purely by economic self-interest, *if* there were enough of them, and *if* any particular resource (commodity or factor) were not *wholly* owned by a single nation, then the economic power of any individual nation would be so weakened that it might as well behave like a price taker.[2] Free trade would seemingly

---

(and coalition formation) among nations are low or at least uniform, and when expectations of behavior are symmetrical. It is not my purpose to argue for the realism of these assumptions but merely to show that within the conventional framework (which also makes use of these assumptions), there is no presumption, as is often asserted, that free trade will need to be enforced.

[2] To the best of my knowledge, Graham (1948, pp. 10-12) was the only international trade theorist aware of this deficiency (based on game-theoretic considerations) in the classical terms-of-trade argument.

emerge spontaneously as the result of the self-interested actions of rational nations, except when there were nonconvexities or market failures of one kind or another in the world economy as a whole. Thus Kindleberger and others are wrong to assert that a plurality of self-interested nations with some "monopoly" power in trade would *for that reason alone* find a conflict of interest between subscribing to free trade in the world interest and levying the optimum tariff in the narrow national interest. In a multi-country framework, and under the usual assumptions of trade theory, some monopoly power in trade would not prevent the spontaneous emergence of a free-trade equilibrium.

This does not mean that free trade (or a liberal international economic order) would not have to be enforced in the real world. My contention is merely that the reason most often cited in support of the argument seems invalid. A departure from one or another of the simplifying assumptions made above is required to prevent free trade from emerging spontaneously. It could be argued, for instance, that economic self-interest is not the primary motive for a nation's actions, despite the economists' assertion that it *should* be so. But Graham (1948, pp. 19-20) had an answer to this objection:

> The description of how men act or the explanation of why they act as they do, in what we are pleased to call the economic phase of their lives, is not economics. On the contrary, how men act in "economic" affairs, and why they act as they do, is often *contrasted* with "truly" economic action. We then say that certain of their actions or motives are uneconomic even though they are concerned with what is generally conceded to be the subject matter of economics. We could, however, not make this assertion without some independent criterion of the economic. This criterion it is one of the functions of economic theory to supply. . . . The departure of the actual from the postulated conditions does not, of course, make the theory any less valid for the situation with which it purports to deal. If the trend of facts is regarded as foreordained, or otherwise unalterable, the center of interest is, of course, bound to shift from a theory that has little relevance to reality to a theory which can more readily be applied to the existing or prospective situation. A fatalistic view of events, however, makes all attempts at amelioration vain. . . . We could not then, indeed, have *any* ends, in the sense of choice between alternatives. Unless free will can play some role in human affairs all aspiration is fruitless. . . . There would, in such a world, be no place for economics, as a superior method of realization of chosen ends, since both the ends and the process of their realization would be prescribed. If, then, the classical theory postulates ideal conditions from which we have been retreating, we are logically bound, in spurning fatalism as fatal to economics as to any other striving, to condemn not the theory but the retreat from the conditions it postulates. . . . If all the world should become less honest than of yore the theory that honesty is the best policy, however un-

heeded, might well, as a social precept, seem more valid than ever before. The fact that prevailing practice repudiated the theory would not, of itself, make the theory bad.

If the "irrationality" is based on ignorance of the true dimensions of a nation's self-interest, it should be possible to convince nations to act rationally by resort to arguments and evidence. Only if the irrationality is in some sense pathological should it be necessary to impose international institutional restraints on national conduct. In practice, this is unlikely to be an important enough reason to require the enforcement of the liberal economic order.

The reasons for resistance to voluntary adherence must be sought in the various other assumptions made above about the actions of otherwise rational nations.

The most important of these, as I have emphasized, concern the optimal or, failing that, the second-best cures for various domestic distortions, as well as the legislation of the optimal or second-best domestic income distribution through the use of *domestic* policy instruments. When it is not feasible to use such domestic policy instruments (e.g. because of very high information and transactions costs associated with their use relative to the costs of restrictions on foreign trade), or when nations fail to perceive the superiority of the feasible set of domestic policy instruments over the use of protection, even the most rational nations may not adhere spontaneously to free trade.

More important, however, the deployment of some of these superior domestic instruments may be hindered by domestic political factors, such as the relative strength of domestic sectional interests which stand to gain from trade restrictions. Particularly in these circumstances, some external enforcement of free trade can help to offset "extra-economic" considerations by stiffening the resolve of the government to resist sectional pressures that go against the national and cosmopolitan interest. External constraints on resorting to protection might also encourage countries to search for superior *domestic* policies to correct various domestic divergences in either an optimal or second-best manner. Thus, some form of external enforcement of the liberal international economic order may be required in the real world. Enforcement may be particularly important for developing countries, where voluntary adherence may be prevented by the perceived weakness of domestic fiscal systems as well as by "rent-seeking" oligarchic power structures.

Furthermore, free trade in assets may be resisted because most developing countries (and some developed ones) appear to be concerned about certain noneconomic aspects of foreign ownership and control. Their chief fear seems to be that foreign investors may attempt to subvert the host country's polity or culture, particularly if their investments are large relative to the size of the economy. Given the inequality of states, the leaders of weaker countries are particularly afraid that foreign investors will be used by their parent governments as a foreign-policy tool to cause economic destabilization of the host country and thus to drive a wedge between its rulers and the ruled. An evaluation of these political fears is beyond the scope of this essay (but see Lal, 1975, Part V, for a fuller discussion). Nevertheless, the importance of these noneconomic fears helps to explain the reluctance of developing countries to subscribe wholeheartedly to the financial and monetary aspects of a liberal international economic order.

The other side of the same coin, of course, is the fear on the part of foreign investors that their investments will be expropriated for political reasons. Since foreign investment flows in the past were mainly from developed to developing countries, this was a factor inhibiting the free flow of capital *from* developed countries. More recently, with the emergence of large OPEC trade surpluses, many oil-producing developing countries also fear expropriation—a fear that has probably been accentuated by the Carter administration's ill-advised freezing of Iranian assets in the United States in pursuit of political ends.

Thus, in the absence of any effective international means to outlaw the expropriation of foreign assets, it would be imprudent for governments or their nationals to ignore the political risks attached to foreign as opposed (most often) to domestic investments. This does not mean, however, that restrictions on foreign trade in assets are necessary in the national interest. The risks of expropriation will obviously reduce the expected rate of return on foreign investments and thus reduce their magnitude, and it would therefore be wrong from the viewpoint of national economic welfare to impose additional restrictions on such investments, unless the social returns were deemed to be even lower than the risk-adjusted private returns.

Lacking a world government, and hence an apparatus for enforcing rules that nations may fail to internalize for various irrational reasons, some have suggested that a rational hegemonic power should force the other nations to be free. One advocate goes so far as to say:

> Americans tend to be overly impressed by the merits of constitution writing, just as the British are caught up in admiration when contemplating the evolutionary growth of law. But both require the content of social cohesion,

> and when that is lacking, order cannot be produced spontaneously; it must be imposed. Benevolent despotism is the best form of government because it permits us all not to pay the price of eternal vigilance (Kindleberger, 1976a, p. 38).

One might add to the last sentence the phrase, "particularly against the irrational impulses in us all"! Historical evidence can be cited in support of the view that the liberal international economic order was never as secure as when it was "enforced" under Pax Britannica in the nineteenth century and Pax Americana after the Second World War (see Lal, 1978, and Calleo, ed., 1976). But Kindleberger rightly notes that this is not necessarily an optimal system, since the "difficulty with any benevolent despotism is to keep it benevolent, or viewed as such" (p. 38). A securer foundation, in my view, would lie in propagating rationality and thereby internalizing the adherence to the liberal international economic order among the nations of the world. Hence this essay.

While there is to some extent an emerging professional consensus on the optimal rules of the game for trade in goods (and some services), namely free trade, there is no similar agreement on the optimal rules and arrangements for the system of international finance and payments. This is the matter to which I turn next. It should first be said, however, that there are other aspects of international economic relations that may call for international cooperation. Cooperation is needed to provide various international public goods, such as the maintenance of the bare minimum of law and order in the international lanes of commerce, for instance by outlawing piracy (see Kindleberger, 1978). The optimal provision of international public goods is ignored in the rest of this essay, except for one good whose provision should be a prime function of any international monetary system, namely an international money, which serves at least as an international medium of exchange, although probably no longer as a store of value!

2 What International Monetary System is Optimal?

Much of the previous argument in favor of a liberal international economic order has been implicitly conducted for economies where money is not essential (as is much of the pure theory of international trade). In the real world, exchanges of commodities and of assets are mediated through various monetary instruments. A country's exchange rate is in an important sense the relative price of different national monies, as monetarists emphisize. Most of the analytical issues connected with an optimal international monetary regime can be sorted out in terms of the determinants of national exchange rates and of the optimal exchange-rate regime.

To sort out those issues, I consider a multi-country world in which each country produces three "goods," its national money, a traded good, and a nontraded good. The exchange rate is the price of foreign money in terms of national money and is determined within a simultaneous-equation system in which there will be both stock and flow equilibria in the monetary (asset) and real (goods) markets.

Now consider the "optimal" exchange-rate regime and the associated policy toward international reserves in two simple models. The first is one in which all changes are perfectly foreseen in each economy: there are *no unforseen* exogenous shocks. The second is one in which many changes are unforeseen and *unforeseeable*; there is a very important element of irreducible uncertainty. In both cases I assume free trade in commodities (which we know is optimal).

A Changing World with Perfect Foresight

Consider a changing world in which all changes in tastes, technologies, and resources are perfectly foreseen by all participants (or else there are universal futures markets in contingent commodities). Free trade in commodities and assets will be optimal from the viewpoint of national and world welfare (assuming, as before, that domestic distortions and the distribution of income are handled by using appropriate domestic policy instruments). Given the changing tastes, technologies, and rates of time preference (which need not be the same in all countries), there will be an equilibrium set of relative prices for commodities, factors, and claims, in each country and each time period.

Exchange-Rate Regimes. If there is perfect price flexibility in commodity, factor, and asset markets, then these real equilibria will be instantaneously established in each time period. Changes in the exchange rate and in monetary policy (which in our simplified model entail changes in the relative supplies of national monies) will not affect any real variable in the world economy. They will merely affect the price level.

Consider a devaluation starting from a position of equilibrium.[3] With everything else unchanged, the devaluation will raise the domestic prices of traded goods immediately, as well as raising the overall domestic price level. This will have the following effects:

[3] This is the pure monetarist model. As Corden (1977) has emphasized, its real-world relevance seems limited, for it is unclear what purpose such a devaluation would serve. For the monetary approach to the balance of payments, see the essays collected in Frenkel and Johnson (1976).

First, with the increase in the relative price of traded to nontraded goods, there will be excess demand for the nontraded goods (associated with an incipient balance-of-trade surplus). In our world of perfectly flexible wages and prices, this will cause an instantaneous increase in the prices of nontraded goods to restore the original equilibrium price ratio—and will also put further upward pressure on the general price level in the home country.

Second, the increase in the general price level will reduce real money balances. As compared with the initial equilibrium situation, this will cause an excess demand for money and hence an excess supply of goods. As capital is assumed to be perfectly mobile, there will be a surplus on trade account matched by an equivalent deficit on capital account; foreign money will be added to domestic cash balances to restore their real value to the original level. At this point, the domestic economy will return to equilibrium, with a lower exchange rate, a higher price level, and a larger component of foreign money in the domestic money base, but with all real equilibria the same. Furthermore, if the home country is "small" in that it faces a given interest rate in world capital markets, there will be no change in any intertemporal variable; with an unchanged interest rate, investment levels will be unaffected.

In this pure monetarist model, a devaluation is thus equivalent to a policy of domestic monetary contraction. If I had told the story in terms of a reduction in the domestic money supply instead of a devaluation, it would have been the same except that there would have been no effect on the domestic price level.

Even in this simple world, however, the effect of exchange-rate change depends crucially on whether or not wages and prices are flexible. Thus it is obvious that changing real conditions will alter through time the equilibrium relative price of traded to nontraded goods. If there is perfect wage and price flexibility, that equilibrium price will be achieved continuously even under a system of rigidly fixed exchange rates (and assuming an unchanged price in foreign currency of traded goods); it will be accomplished through changes in the domestic money costs of factors of production, which ensure continuous full-employment equilibrium in a "flex-price" economy. If, however, there is any stickiness in the prices of nontraded goods or in money (but *not* real) wages, then even in this world of perfect foresight, flexible exchange rates will be superior from a welfare viewpoint than a system of rigid exchange rates (as, for instance, under a gold-standard system).

This is illustrated by the familiar Salter (1959) diagram in the accompanying figure. Suppose the economy is in internal and external balance at *P*. Then there is a shift in tastes toward the traded good. The equilibrium is at point *P′*, where the relative price of the traded good is higher than at *P*. With fixed exchange rates and an unchanged price of traded commodities in terms of foreign currency, the price of traded goods is fixed in domestic currency. Hence the only way to bring about the requisite increase in the relative price of traded goods is to reduce the domestic price of the nontraded good. If this price is sticky or rigid downward, equilibrium at *P′* will be unattainable. Where will the economy end up in this case?

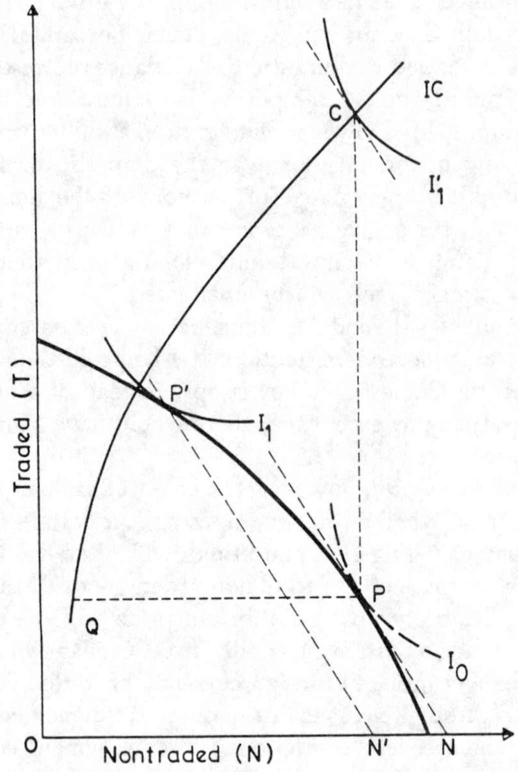

I_0 - indifference curves for old tastes.
I_1 - indifference curves for new tastes.
IC - income consumption curve for new tastes and NP relative price.

16

Suppose the government tries to prevent unemployment from emerging. This will require it to generate enough domestic demand to sustain the full-employment domestic outputs of the two goods at the initial and rigid relative price given by the slope of *NP*. The consumption point will then be at *C*, with an excess demand for traded goods (and hence a current-account deficit) of *PC*. Clearly, this is unsustainable over the long run, as absorption greatly exceeds domestic output. To restore external equilibrium, there will have to be a reduction of expenditure until the point *Q* is reached. At that point, there will be excess supply (and hence unemployment) in the nontraded goods industry, shown by the distance *PQ*. The economy will be at the lower welfare level given by the consumption *cum* production point *Q*, as compared with the welfare optimum at *P′*.

The latter could be attained, however, if the exchange rate were flexible. Given the rigid price of the nontraded good, the relative price of traded to nontraded goods required to reach *P′* can be attained by a devaluation large enough to raise the price of the traded good to the requisite extent. To get to *P′*, of course, the government will also have to reduce domestic expenditure from *ON* to *ON′* in terms of nontraded goods.

This exchange-rate flexibility, moreover, could be of the adjustable-peg type. Under the assumption of perfect foresight, the equilibrium exchange rate would always be known to the authorities. This is a simplified version of the implicit model that justified the Bretton Woods exchange-rate regime, as compared with a rigidly fixed exchange-rate regime of the pure gold-standard type.

With a perfectly flexible exchange rate, the authorities would not need to intervene. Equilibrium exchange rates, *ex hypothesi*, would be perfectly foreseen by speculators. When there is some price rigidity, however, and individual market participants lack the perfect foresight of the Platonic Guardians about the course of the equilibrium exchange rate, then the government should intervene in the interests of real income gains to producers and consumers in all countries. It should smooth out deviations from the equilibrium trend, which is known to the government but not to private speculators. This, in fact, is a simplified version of the implicit model underlying much of the literature on rules for managed floating (see Williamson, 1977, and Ethier and Bloomfield, 1975) as well as the explicit model underlying the literature on price stabilization (see Turnovsky, 1978).

International Liquidity. In a world economy with a perfectly foreseeable flexible-exchange-rate regime, would any international money be needed? It is useful to distinguish between the speculative, precautionary, and transactions demands for international money in answering this question.

There would not be any purely speculative demand based on differences among market participants in their expectations about exchange-rate changes. All exchange-rate changes would reflect real equilibria and would be foreseen perfectly by all market participants. Nor would there be any need for precautionary reserves to tide over temporary adjustment problems. All temporary balance-of-payments adjustment problems would be accommodated by perfectly stabilizing capital flows.

Nevertheless, traders (both public and private) would have transactions demands for foreign monies, and there would clearly be some potential resource gains from pooling the stocks of foreign currencies that traders in each country would otherwise hold for transactions purposes. As Chrystal (1978) emphasizes, the source of these economies lies in the likelihood that the transactions elasticity of demand for any foreign currency will be less than unity and that the variance of net transactions in any particular currency will be smaller for the aggregate of traders than the sum of the individual variances. It does not follow, however, that an international central bank need be created to enforce such pooling. Any intermediary capable of managing the traders' pooled balances would make profits from the potential resource savings. Thus, in the absence of national restrictions on private intermediation, competitive financial centers (i.e. banks) may be expected to emerge to provide the required services.

Drawing an analogy with an argument used to justify foreign-exchange control for a national economy, it might be argued that further gains could be made by substituting an international paper money for the pooled national monies held by various international banks. Instead of having a number of individual banks in any national monetary area competing for traders' deposits of foreign monies, the central bank might enforce a further pooling of the country's external balances through foreign-exchange controls. There could then be a further gain to the country "from the fact that the holding of external money involves an opportunity cost to the economy as a whole, whereas the holding of domestic fiat money does not (assuming an issue of domestic money in excess of reserves)" (Chrystal, 1978, p. 11). But it should be remembered that the administrative costs of enforcing foreign-exchange controls, as well as the loss of convenience to traders, could in many cases outweigh these benefits from exchange control. Furthermore, this "social savings" argument does not apply to the substitution of an international paper money for holdings of national monies. From the viewpoint of the world as a whole, the various national monies are not external to the world economy, which is a closed economy for this purpose. Thus, there are no resource gains to be had by pooling national monies at an international level, for there are no *net* flows of any national currency outside the world economy that would permit savings in transactions balances. As Mundell (1971, pp. 179ff.) emphasizes: "Whilst any individual country can gain by substituting fiat money for 'gold' or 'international reserves' in its domestic money supply, the world as a whole will not benefit beyond the gains accruing from the more efficient exploitation of the advantages of money."

A Changing World with Irreducible Uncertainty

We now enter the real world, where there is no perfect foresight and where transactions costs prevent the emergence of markets for contingent commodities. The underlying world economic system is assumed to be stable (in the formal sense), but there are a series of unpredictable exogenous shocks, monetary and real, including unknowable shifts in tastes, technologies, and resources. To counteract some of these shocks, moreover, governments will be intervening to maintain the fullest utilization of resources compatible with the desired level of price stability. Even though the underlying system may be stable in the face of exogenous shocks, the time it takes the economy to adjust to them could in some cases be speeded up by monetary and fiscal policies. (Governments will also intervene, *ex hypothesi*, to correct domestic distortions and to legislate the desired income distribution in the appropriate second-best manner.)

Assume again free trade in commodities, assets, and mobile factors of production, so that there will be an "equilibrium" relative price of traded to nontraded goods, as well as a portfolio equilibrium in asset markets. But these equilibria will change over time and *they cannot be predicted with certainty by either the Platonic Guardians or market participants.* Williamson (1977, p. 198) argues:

> . . . there is no particular reason for expecting market operators to be more skilled in [the] task [of predicting the equilibrium rate] than national authorities, while there is a compelling reason for expecting authorities to have an advantage: namely that the equilibrium rate depends *inter alia* on the future policies to be pursued by the authorities themselves.

This is a complete nonsequitur. Just because a particular variable—in this case, monetary policy—is supposedly under government control, we cannot conclude that the government *knows* how it is going to use this instrument in the future. The U.K. Chancellor of the Exchequer would be amused to learn that he knew better than market participants how he would alter monetary policy in the future as a result of a constellation of future events, including varying degrees of trade-union militancy!

With any current change in an economic variable, *all* economic participants, including the government, have to make *guesses* about the economy's evolution in the irreducibly uncertain future. The final outcome will be based on the necessarily subjective evaluation of available information, which I assume (not too implausibly) to be the same for all market participants. If the government has better information, it should obviously disseminate it to the market. There is *no* objective way in which the resulting gambles made by anyone (whether a central banker or a currency speculator) can be said *ex ante* to be "better" than someone else's. When the number of "gamblers" (speculators) is large and there is not an infinite supply of "suckers" who enter the market each day to be fleeced by the professionals, the speculators whose guesses turn out *ex post* to be "better" will usually make profits at the expense of the rest. There is thus a presumption that speculation will be stabilizing even though, in principle, the possibility of destabilizing private speculation cannot be ruled out. In other words, speculation can be expected to dampen the deviations from the emerging and only slowly recognizable equilibria.

To sum up, there is little reason to believe that the government can foretell the future better than anyone else, and hence little basis for any action on its part to achieve convergence to an *unknowable* equilibrium (or prevent deviations from it). It can of course speculate, just like any other market participant. But only if its guesses turn out to be better than those of market participants (and there is no particular reason for them to be better) will the government be able to stabilize the relevant variable "faster" than the market. The sign of its success is the profitability of its speculation!

Relative Merits of Alternative Exchange-Rate Regimes. We next examine the relative advantages of alternative exchange-rate regimes in this uncertain environment. Broadly speaking, three exchange-rate regimes can be contrasted: a completely fixed-rate system, as under the gold standard; a fully floating-rate system; and different forms of managed flexibility, including the adjustable-peg system, various crawling-peg regimes, and the current "dirty floating" regimes. Those in the third group differ in kind from the first two regimes because they entail *discretionary* changes in the exchange rate. Under both completely fixed rates and fully floating rates, the balance-of-payments adjustment mechanism is automatic. Under all the managed systems, specific government decisions about the exchange rate are required to trigger the adjustment mechanism.

When considering the relative merits of these alternative exchange-rate systems, it should be remembered that "real" exchange rates will be changing over time with changes in "real" variables, which argues in favor of an adjustment mechanism that imparts flexibility to relative prices, either through domestic wage-price flexibility or through exchange-rate changes.[4] By implication, a flexible exchange rate has great appeal because it enables the economy to adjust speedily to emerging disequilibria. Furthermore, the recent move to managed floating would seem to make the consideration of fully flexible exchange rates, for all independent monetary areas, of more than academic interest.

Instability of floating exchange rates. Many commentators on the present exchange-rate regime (e.g., Williamson, 1977) feel that some public intervention is still needed to combat the instability of floating rates. Others (Kindleberger, 1976b, McKinnon, 1976) want to revert to a completely fixed-rate system.

Two possible sources of exchange-rate instability may be noted. First, the underlying markets for traded goods may be unstable, in the sense that the price elasticities determining flows of traded goods may be low and the Marshall-Lerner stability condition may not be met. This fear underlay various models of foreign-exchange bottlenecks that were built for developing countries in the early 1960s. Export pessimism engendered by the interwar collapse of international trade and the ensuing depression of commodity prices led to the belief that the elasticities of demand were low for most primary products exported by developing countries. It was therefore assumed that these countries faced fixed export earnings and thus a fixed import capacity that could not be altered by exchange-rate changes. Import substitution, working back to more and more elemental stages of production, was seen to be the only solution (see Lal, 1972, for a critique of these models). The growth of exports by these countries, particularly in the 1960s and 1970s, has belied this elasticity pessimism (see World Bank, 1977, and Cline *et al.*, 1978). The empirical assumptions underlying the bottleneck view and, *mutatis mutandis*, concerns about the instability of flexible exchange rates are not supported by the evidence.

[4] I do not deal in this essay with the assertions of the so-called "New Cambridge" school, who argue from an assumption of *real* wage rigidity that exchange-rate changes are ineffective, so that protection may be desirable to achieve external and internal balance. The illogicality of their position is shown in Corden, Little, and Scott (1975) and Lal (1979).

The second source of instability comes from the possibility of destabilizing speculative capital flows. To assess this possibility, a system of flexible exchange rates must be contrasted with a system of genuinely fixed exchange rates (as under a pure gold standard), and both must be contrasted with the adjustable-peg system established at Bretton Woods.

It is conceivable in principle that destabilizing speculation might occur in a free foreign-exchange market. As many economists have emphasized (e.g. Friedman, 1962, and Meade, 1951), however, such destabilizing speculation cannot continue for any length of time unless the body of speculators is continually fed by a stream of amateurs who lose their money. If there is a relatively large and stable body of speculators, destabilizing speculation would mean that they were buying when prices were relatively high (with reference to the notional equilibrium rate) and selling when prices were low. Hence, they would be taking losses as a group. It is not surprising, therefore, that it has been impossible to document obvious periods of destabilizing speculation in either foreign-exchange or commodity markets (see Willett, 1977).

This does not mean that a flexible exchange rate will not fluctuate. Changes in technologies, resources, and public policies (e.g. monetary policies) alter underlying short-period equilibria in goods and assets markets, often in unpredictable ways. We would therefore expect the exchange rate to change in unforeseeable ways. The efficient-market hypothesis states that a large group of profit-maximizing speculators will stabilize the price in a particular market by making the best use of *available information*. Only someone with *better information* can do better than market participants whose actions are based on rational expectations. The fluctuations of a flexible exchange rate are therefore reflections of the underlying fluctuations in various economic variables whose origins, timing, and effects are, and *can only be*, dimly perceived by mere mortals.

Given these unforeseeable fluctuations in economic variables, a rigidly fixed exchange rate of the gold-standard type would necessitate (a) that no country attempt to follow an independent monetary policy and (b) that changes in real economic variables in every economy entail quantity adjustments (e.g. unemployment and unanticipated inventory changes) in the absence of instantaneous and perfectly flexible wages and prices in domestic commodity and factor markets. If, in particular, the domestic relative price of traded to nontraded goods is sticky, any excess supply emerging in the market for nontraded goods must lead to unemployment.

As long as there are national governments that want monetary autonomy to attain various employment goals, a strict gold-standard mechanism, with its genuine international monetary integration, will be unacceptable.[5] A genuine worldwide monetary union would confer efficiency gains, flowing from the convenience and reduced transactions costs of a stable monetary unit. But those who have been mesmerized by these gains and thus advocate a system of genuinely fixed exchange rates are burying their heads in the sand. The international political prerequisites for monetary integration—an implicit world state with a single monetary authority—and hence for the institution of a true gold standard do not exist at present. The alternatives, therefore, are some form of adjustable peg (fixed but changeable), of which managed floating is merely a more flexible variant, or freely floating exchange rates.

The Bretton Woods type of adjustable peg offered the worst of all possible worlds for the authorities, as far as destabilizing speculative capital flows are concerned. As is well known, it gave speculators a one-way bet in currencies whose par values were expected to change. In a flexible-exchange-rate system, by contrast, the speculators bet against each other. When underlying forces appear to require that a flexible exchange rate depreciate, moreover, speculators will try to profit by anticipating the new "equilibrium" rate and in the process will push the rate to this new value faster than would otherwise be the case.

It has been argued (see Kindleberger, 1976b, and McKinnon, 1976) that the large fluctuations in exchange rates seen since the world moved to floating rates are a sign that speculation has been destabilizing, or insufficiently stabilizing. Critics have also blamed floating rates for the rise in transactions costs and the poorer performance of forward rates as predictors of spot rates. But if underlying economic conditions are volatile (as they have been in the 1970s), one would expect exchange rates to be volatile. It is illegitimate to argue that speculation has been destabilizing because exchange rates have been volatile. Willet (1977, p. 37) points out that empirical tests that have attempted to identify destabilizing speculation (by finding systematic cycles or patterns in exchange rates) in general suggest that the major foreign-exchange markets have not been characterized by persistent and systematic poorly

[5] This, of course, assumes that there is a nonvertical long-run Phillips curve for each country. If this is denied, as it is by monetarists, then governments cannot affect employment levels by independent monetary policies, and the arguments against a full-fledged gold standard and world monetary integration are weakened. I shall not enter into the debate about the feasibility of affecting employment levels. It is enough to note for my purposes that, at least at present, governments consider it both feasible and desirable to use monetary policy to affect employment. My views on monetarism, etc., for what they are worth, are stated in Lal (1977).

behaved speculation. He has derived a similar view on balance from his discussions with exchange-market participants.

Increased uncertainty and the J-curve. Two other criticisms of floating rates should be considered: (a) that floating rates have increased uncertainty in international trade and (b) that a depreciation can become cumulative because of so-called J-curve effects.

There are a number of counterarguments to the first criticism. First, as argued above, the instability of floating rates is due to the underlying instability of economic conditions. Discontinuous but large exchange-rate changes under an adjustable-peg regime would not reduce this underlying uncertainty. Second, in the absence of perfect wage-price flexibility, genuinely fixed rates would transform exchange-rate instability into real income (and employment) instability. Third, stabilizing speculative flows in a floating-rate system will provide speedier adjustments to real disequilibria and hence contribute to a lowering of uncertainty. Finally, it appears that traders have learned from experience to cope with floating rates by making more use of forward-exchange markets (see Dreyer *et al.*, 1978).

This leaves the J-curve argument. It states that if traders price their exports in terms of domestic currency while their imports are priced in foreign currency, then the impact of a devaluation will be to worsen the balance of trade. The relatively inflexible quantities of imports and exports in the very shortest of short runs will lead to a fall in foreign-currency receipts from exports without any change in foreign-currency payments for imports. Over time, of course, and assuming that demand elasticities at home and abroad are sufficiently high, the quantity of exports will rise and that of imports fall, improving the balance of trade. Hence the latter can be expected to follow a J-shaped path after a devaluation. The twist in a floating-rate world is as follows: The initial deterioration in the balance of trade after a depreciation will put further downward pressure on the currency. There will not be sufficient time for the stabilizing effect of the upturn in the J-curve to work itself out in the currency market, and the exchange rate will depreciate still further, leading (it is feared) to a cumulative depreciation.

There are two objections to this argument. First, it assumes that domestic exporters are extremely short-sighted. They are assumed to be unaware that, given high price elasticities of foreign demand, they are losing money by pricing their goods in a depreciating currency. If they are not short-sighted, they will change their currency of invoicing. In fact, there is some evidence that traders *have* adjusted their pricing behavior following the advent of floating (see Grassman, 1976). Second, the argument assumes that speculators are unaware of the J-curve effect (if it exists) and do not seek to make profits by buying the currency on the downswing in order to sell it on the upswing of the trade-balance movements. If they do so, they will arrest any cumulative depreciation.

Hence, it would seem that Willett (1977) is right in concluding:

> Unless variability in exchange rates is due to poorly behaved speculation, the costs [in terms of the reduced information content of current prices and exchange rates] cannot be reduced by official intervention to peg the exchange rate. . . . In well-behaved markets, variability in prices and exchange rates is a symptom not a cause of uncertainty and instability. . . . International trade will inevitably be riskier between countries which have greatly disparate macroeconomic policies than between countries with similar underlying economic conditions.

The law of one price. A completely different argument against flexible exchange rates is made by various "monetarist" proponents of fixed exchanges rates. They claim that exchange-rate changes are ineffective in correcting disequilibria in the balance of payments because of the high degree of substitutability between traded and nontraded goods. They believe that strict purchasing-power parity (PPP) holds in the form of what is labeled the "law of one price" (Laffer, 1975). Their view is thus based on assumptions diametrically opposed to those of the elasticity pessimists but leads to similar conclusions about the ineffectiveness of exchange-rate adjustments.

If the law of one price (or strict PPP) did hold, then effectively all goods in every economy would be tradeables, and there would be no relative price of traded to nontraded goods for the exchange-rate to affect. Moreover, domestic macroeconomic policy would affect only the world price level and not exchange rates or the level of domestic activity.

Assume that there is an increase in the supply of money in the home economy. This will lower domestic interest rates as people bid for bonds to attain portfolio balance. But, given perfect international capital mobility, reduced domestic interest rates will lead people to attempt to substitute foreign bonds for domestic money and bonds. As the supply of foreign bonds is fixed, their price must be bid up until domestic and foreign interest rates are again equal. Equilibrium in the world economy is attained when all world prices are higher and exchange rates are unchanged.

This whole argument hinges on the empirical assumption about the law of one price. But recent research (Isard, 1977; Houthakker, 1978; and Kravis and Lipsey, 1978) shows that there is little evidence to support strict PPP. Thus the alleged ineffectiveness of exchange-rate adjustments following from this monetarist argument can at best be regarded as a theoretical curiosity.

Relative insulation from shocks. Finally, arguments have been advanced for or against flexible exchange rates on the basis of the relative insulation that alternative exchange-rate regimes are likely to provide from internal or external shocks. On the whole, a fixed-rate regime will transmit both domestic disturbances to the world economy and foreign disturbances to the domestic economy. By contrast, a flexible rate will to some extent insulate the domestic economy against foreign disturbances but will also tend to bottle up domestic disturbances. In a world of high capital mobility, however, and with stickiness of prices or exchange-rate expectations, insulation is not complete. It has been argued that the international transmission of some types of domestic disturbances can be even stronger under floating than under fixed exchange rates (Dornbusch, 1978).

Nevertheless, Black (1976) has argued that the types of insulation provided by the two regimes can provide a basis for a particular country's choice between fixed and flexible exchange rates. A country should choose a flexible exchange rate if it expects that most of the shocks likely to affect it will be external in origin. If, instead, it expects most of the shocks to be internal (for instance, domestic harvest failures in a primarily agricultural country), it should opt for a fixed exchange rate, because a fixed rate will confer greater stability on the domestic economy by dissipating internal disturbances abroad.

In my view, this criterion is inadequate. First, it assumes that it is possible to *predict* which type of shock is likely to be important for a particular country. Little faith can be placed in such predictions. Second, a fixed exchange rate adopted to dissipate domestic disturbances internationally is an invitation to continual international friction, as was in fact the case under the Bretton Woods system. Third, as has been emphasized above, a *genuinely* fixed exchange rate would require either a supra-national monetary authority charged with running a world monetary policy or passive acceptance of the national employment levels engendered by the requirements of external balance under a gold-standard regime. It is not at all clear that the resulting abdication of national monetary control would be in the interests of (or even acceptable to) most countries.

This does not imply that, in an ideal world, the optimal currency area (within which there is the full integration afforded by a common currency) would be coterminous with the existing nation-states. A case can be made for multinational integrated monetary areas. But particularly in newly independent developing countries, where nationalism is fierce and newly acquired national status jealously guarded, any forfeiture of national sovereignty is strongly resisted. This is borne out by the dismal record of various attempts to organize common markets among developing countries, the latest casualty of this economic nationalism being the East African Community. For all practical purposes, then, we have to accept that most nations will continue to be independent monetary areas in the world economy.

Finally, and most important, the choice between alternative exchange-rate regimes turns on the optimal response in terms of borrowing and lending to any internal or external shock, given the degree of domestic wage-price flexibility. Suppose that our economy has some downward rigidity in money wages and nontraded-goods prices. There is a one-period exogenous shock (say a harvest failure), which leads to excess demand for traded goods at the constant level of money expenditure maintained by the government to assure full employment in the non-traded goods industries. If the exchange rate is fixed and there are no private capital flows or official foreign borrowing, the temporary balance-of-payments deficit will have to be financed by running down official reserves. Because of its exchange-rate commitment and its desire to maintain full employment, the country will have to maintain current consumption (at the fixed relative price of traded to nontraded goods) by running down its assets at the expense of future consumption.

If, however, the exchange rate is flexible and there are no restrictions on private capital flows, but money expenditure is still maintained at the level required to assure full employment in the nontraded-goods industries, the outcome will be some combination of exchange-rate depreciation, foreign borrowing, and running down of "reserves" by both the private and public sectors. The last two portfolio choices will affect both how much the exchange rate depreciates and how much future consumption is foregone to maintain current consumption.[6] It is unlikely, however, that the optimal rundown of reserves (or foreign borrowing) will be just large enough to maintain the exchange rate unchanged.

In a world of flexible exchange rates and capital mobility, optimizing agents will be able to choose through their portfolio behavior many pos-

[6] This does not mean that I advocate "dirty floating." For the public sector, the relevant choice is between using reserves to buy foreign currency to hold and using reserves to buy foreign currency to spend. The first choice can be the result either of a portfolio decision or of a deliberate effort to manipulate the exchange rate. The choice between reserve use (borrowing) and depreciation examined in the text corresponds to the former case, since foreign currency purchased with reserves for spending purposes will not be motivated, *ex hypothesi*, by a desire to manipulate the exchange rate.

sible combinations of exchange rates, ratios of traded to nontraded goods prices, and present versus future consumption choices. Only some of these will correspond to the choices they would *have* to make if they were committed to a fixed exchange rate. The fixed-rate combinations are always open even under a flexible-rate system. If they are not chosen by optimizing agents, we can assume that the alternative choice is better. Put differently, a commitment to a fixed exchange rate (or to particular rules for managed floats) is a constraint, and it will necessarily reduce the range of present and future consumption choices. It will therefore be inferior in a welfare sense to a system that allows not only the fixed-rate combinations but others that are ruled out under a fixed-rate constraint.

In line with these arguments, I must come down squarely on the side of exchange-rate flexibility in the debate on the optimal exchange-rate regime. In a world of irreducible uncertainty, the path of the exchange rate is likely to be unpredictable; governments and speculators alike will be able only to guess at the extent and direction of changes. Many commentators and officials have convinced themselves of the feasibility and desirability of managed exchange rates by implicitly (and illegitimately) subsuming this real-world case in the artificial case of perfect, or greater, governmental foresight. In a world where the values of the relevant variables are irreducibly uncertain, such a belief is unwarranted.

International Liquidity. The so-called problems of international liquidity can be dealt with more summarily. It is obvious that with freely fluctuating exchange rates there would be no need for international reserves as such for managing the balance-of-payments adjustment process. The problem of managing international liquidity was peculiar to the Bretton Woods adjustable-peg system. With its commitment to maintain par values, except under conditions of "fundamental" disequilibrium, when exchange-rate changes were allowed, countries needed international reserves to tide them over short-term, reversible disequilibria in their balance of payments. Since exchange-rate changes could not be used to deal with such disequilibria, domestic income and employment changes were the only alternative to financing deficits by reserve movements. As such measures entailed the welfare costs of foregone output, an adequate level of reserves was considered desirable to avoid them. The pre-1971 debates then centered on the adequacy of the aggregate level of international reserves—whether reserves were sufficient to meet the sum of unavoidable short-run deficits and the desire of all countries to hold an increasing volume of reserves in some rough ratio to the rising volume of foreign trade.

The ensuing debate, triggered by a famous book by Triffin (1960), concentrated on the inherent instability of the form of international reserve creation that came to be an integral part of the post–World War II gold-exchange standard. This was the role played by reserve currencies (initially sterling and the dollar, but, with the relative decline of the U.K. economy, mainly the dollar) in supplementing the major reserve asset, gold.

Triffin pointed out that this form of reserve creation would be unstable because it depended upon the belief that U.S. dollars held as reserves by other central banks could always be converted into gold at a fixed dollar price. The confidence problem lay in the fact that, with an increase in the dollar component of the international reserve stock, it would become increasingly clear that the United States could not redeem dollars held as reserves using its own gold stock. Moreover, as the world's gold stock could not be expected to increase at the same pace as the demand for international reserves, there would be continual pressure on the United States to run a balance-of-payments deficit in order to supplement the level of international reserves. This process would grant the United States some seignorage gains, since the United States could obtain real resources by printing its own currency. (These seignorage gains were quite limited in practice, because of the interest paid by the United States on foreign holdings of dollars.) It also meant, however, a deterioration in the net reserve position of the United States until the time came when the U.S. gold stock would not be large enough to finance a sustained conversion of dollars into gold by other central banks.

Growing awareness of the asymmetry of the system—of the special position of the reserve-currency countries in obtaining seignorage, however limited—as well as of its potential instability led to numerous plans for increasing world liquidity (see Williamson, 1977, and Machlup, 1964, for surveys). These need not concern us in any detail, as most of them now lie on the garbage heap of history. The major objective was to overcome the international liquidity problem by permitting the International Monetary Fund to issue an international reserve asset—Special Drawing Rights, or SDRs, as they were to be called—that would replace gold as the basis of the international monetary system. But soon after agreement was reached at Rio in 1967 on the setting up of a facility to issue this so-called "paper gold" as the centerpiece of the international monetary system, events overtook its advocates.

With President Nixon's ending of gold convertibility in 1971 and the subsequent movement to a system of managed floating, the old debates about the adequacy of international reserves became muted. Although reserves were still "needed" in the managed floating system, this need was not as pressing as under the old Bretton Woods system. Moreover, it became apparent that a move to a system of fully flexible exchange rates would make discussions of the adequacy of reserves irrelevant. Under completely flexible exchange rates, the exchange market can clear in each time period and there is no need to hold precautionary reserves, as under the Bretton Woods regime. The public sector might still want to hold "reserves" for portfolio-balance reasons, and the motivation could be termed "precautionary." But there is no need to hold reserves to maintain a particular exchange-rate commitment.

Transactions and asset demands for an international means of payment did not disappear. But now it was clear that, given the relative strength of the U.S. economy and the widespread use of the dollar as a vehicle currency, countries and traders were willing to hold dollars for these purposes. Instead of fading away as the centerpiece of the international payment system, the dollar came out even stronger after the movement to the current "nonsystem." The real casualty has been the SDR and the dreams of those supporters of the IMF who wanted it to become a world central bank running a truly SDR-based international monetary system. This is no accident and, in my view, is as it should be.

It is vain to hope that in a world without an international government the IMF can become the central bank of an integrated worldwide monetary union. To establish such a union, governments would have to relinquish national control over policy instruments, such as monetary policy, which are jealously guarded in the present world of nation-states. Nor, even in principle, is the world likely to be the optimum currency area (see the review of the rather ambiguous literature on this issue by Tower and Willett, 1976). It is thus difficult to see what purpose SDRs might serve in a world where full exchange-rate flexibility is not ruled out and may even come to exist in the near future.

As Chrystal (1978, p. 20) has rightly noted,

> [The] SDR is an unconditional right to borrow "real" convertible currency from another central bank at a specified rate of interest. It should be thought of as an unused overdraft facility rather than as [an] interest-bearing checking account. . . . The SDR is basically a credit instrument. Users of the SDR would prefer the rate of interest to be low. . . . Net holders would prefer the rate to be high. . . . If capital markets were perfect and the SDR bore the market rate of interest, the SDR stock would be irrelevant, since loans would already be available at the market rate of interest.

There are two reasons why the interest rate paid on SDRs entails a loss of income for net holders. First, the SDR interest rate is only four-fifths of the weighted average of the rates in five major financial centers. Second, even if the rate were equal to this weighted average, the SDR would be an unattractive asset to hold unless the portfolio preferences of net holders matched the weights used to compute the SDR interest rate. At the same time, the SDR "overdraft facility" is attractive to net users, because the interest rate is lower than the world interest rate. But, as Chrystal (1978, p. 20) points out,

> To rectify the position for net holders would be to destroy the usefulness of SDR credit for all but the least creditworthy, i.e., those who find it difficult to borrow at market rates. An SDR yielding competitive interest rates would simply be a means of channeling loans to the weakest countries, with the Fund acting as guarantor.

Nor does the SDR appear to be a useful unit of account, comprising as it does a basket of fluctuating currencies. The value of the SDR may be more stable than the values of the component currencies taken individually, but it is no easier to predict than the value of any single currency (Chrystal, p. 21). Moreover, as most traders live in a particular currency zone or area, there is always *some* currency other than the SDR in which prices will be set in practice. Finally, as Chrystal emphasizes, though the SDR must be more stable than some of the currencies in the basket, it can be less stable than others, which will then be preferred to the SDR as a numeraire.

These arguments are devastating, in my view, for the future of the SDR. They explain why the SDR has declined as a proportion of total international reserves since the advent of floating. Though some, like Chrystal himself, still hanker after an international money, it is not clear that an international money is required once the straitjacket of exchange-rate fixity of the adjustable-peg type is removed and free capital movements are allowed, together with the associated intermediation by various "banks." The reasons are given in the previous section, and the argument in favor of private intermediation is supported by the explosive growth and development of the Eurocurrency market, in which at least some developing countries have been important participants (see Wellons, 1977, and Díaz-Alejandro, 1975).

Thus, I conclude that, because nation-states exist and desire to maintain sovereignty over national monetary policy, it is vain to hope for an integrated worldwide monetary system of which the IMF would be the centralized monetary authority. The best course would be to ignore the whole question of international liquidity and to encourage countries to remove controls on both capital flows and trade, as well as to permit full flexibility of exchange rates. No rules for managing the exchange rates can be laid down—not even to exclude central banks from acting as exchange-market participants, from holding desired portfolios, and from gambling from time to time on the foreign exchanges!

31

3 The Relevance for Developing Countries

Many economists may be willing to grant the optimality of an international monetary system based on fully flexible exchange rates and free movements of commodities and assets. Nevertheless, it has been asserted that the arguments presented in this essay are not relevant for many developing countries, which might find it "optimal" to restrict short-term capital flows and eschew full flexibility of their exchange rates (see Cline, 1976; Díaz-Alejandro, 1975; Black, 1976; and Joshi, 1979). Furthermore, at least some observers (e.g. Joshi, 1979) feel that it is in the interests of developing countries to lend their support to the establishment of an SDR-based international monetary system in which there would be effective international control over alternative forms of international liquidity such as that provided through the Eurocurrency markets.

The Exchange-Rate Regime

Some of the arguments against full flexibility for the exchange rates of developing countries are based on the misconceptions that I analyzed in the previous section. Thus Joshi claims that floating rates lead to an anti-trade bias "which they engender as a result of the *extra* uncertainty of engaging in foreign exchange transactions" (emphasis added).[7] As I argued, there is little reason to believe that floating exchange rates increase the instability of the underlying economic variables that are responsible for exchange-rate fluctuations. Since some degree of instability is unavoidable, fixed exchange rates are not viable when domestic wages and prices are at all sticky and "full employment" is to be maintained; any attempt to maintain exchange-rate fixity will lead only to large discrete changes in the rates. It is not at all clear why traders should find dealing in an overvalued currency, susceptible of devaluation by a large amount at any time, less uncertain than dealing in a floating-rate system where adjustment takes place over a period of time.

Another set of arguments advanced against floating rates for developing countries is based on the expectation that, since the exchange rate is determined simultaneously by demand and supply conditions in commodity and asset markets, "in the short run, it is this asset price aspect of the exchange rate which dominates over its commodity price aspect, . . . so that the exchange markets have often behaved rather like a stock market with asset holders speculating about the views of other asset holders and the intentions of the foreign exchange authorities" (Joshi,

[7] Joshi (1979) sets out very clearly the conventional wisdom on these issues. My remarks on his paper thus apply to a whole body of thinking of which his paper is succinctly representative.

1979). The implication, presumably, is that this will lead to greater instability.

It is wrong, however, to assume that, because it follows a "random walk," the behavior of the stock market is irrational (a view going as far back as Keynes) and that a foreign-exchange market that behaves like a stock market will also be irrational. As various theoretical and empirical studies have argued, stock-market behavior follows a random walk because the underlying shocks follow a random walk (see Samuelson, 1972, and Fama, 1970). Only by unjustifiably assuming that the underlying system is predictable and that there are thus "correct expectations" about exchange-rate movements (Joshi, 1979) can we judge fluctuations in exchange rates to be "excessive." If, for some reason, there is a wave of excessive optimism or pessimism that pushes the exchange rate "too far" in one direction in the government's judgment, the government can undertake *profitable* counterspeculation. The success of its speculation (i.e. whether it *is* stabilizing or not) can be judged by its profitability. No other general rules can be given for central-bank intervention.

The third set of arguments against freely fluctuating exchange rates for developing countries is based on the lack of active and well-developed capital and forward-exchange markets, which are necessary for a flexible exchange rate to function efficiently. There is no doubt that domestic financial retardation is a feature of many developing countries, which means that the functioning of a flexible exchange rate will be relatively less efficient. But this is an argument not against flexible exchange rates for developing countries but for institutional reform that would strengthen domestic capital markets and enable the floating rate to function more efficiently. As McKinnon (1973) has argued, moreover, such reform is needed to foster domestic development in many developing countries irrespective of the exchange-rate regime.

Furthermore, as Black (1976) has argued, the institutional reforms needed to make a floating exchange rate work are probably exaggerated. The forward market, for instance, need be developed vis-à-vis only *one* international currency, and the international banking system can then be used to purchase or sell other foreign currencies forward. The capital mobility that may be required to stabilize a floating rate is discussed below in connection with the control of capital movements. Nevertheless, some of the least developed countries may not find it feasible to develop the currency and financial markets required by an efficient free-floating system. For these few countries, some of the "basket of currency" schemes advocated and discussed by Black (1976) and Joshi (1979) may be desirable.

Another set of arguments concerns the allocative and income effects that are supposed to flow asymmetrically from alternative exchange-rate systems. Thus Joshi (1979) argues that "freely floating exchange rates are efficient only if they do not lead to violent short-run exchange fluctuations, which are wasteful and expensive in terms of resource movements." Black (1976) argues for that exchange-rate system which reduces the variance of domestic relative prices of tradeable goods, on the grounds that risk-averse producers and consumers with diminishing marginal utilities would prefer less variability in prices.

There are a number of problems with these arguments. The "resource movements" argument of Joshi assumes that producers are extremely short-sighted; they shift resources around purely on the basis of current exchange rates and prices, taking no account of the *expected* future values. This assumption is unwarranted. It is similar to the assumption often made in the older development literature that "static comparative advantage" rules because businessmen look only at current prices.

As for Black's arguments, they assume that it is possible to predict the type of shock that an economy is generally likely to suffer and thereby to choose the exchange-rate regime that will minimize domestic instability. I have already given reasons why this is not likely to be "optimal" or practical. But suppose that the authorities can predict the probable nature of shocks and other market participants cannot. The authorities can then stabilize both the domestic economy and the exchange rate by undertaking profitable countercyclical speculation under a floating-rate regime.

It should be noted, moreover, that a government which chooses a freely floating rate and free capital mobility provides its citizens with the largest access to what are, in effect, insurance markets. Taking advantage of this access, private and public sectors can make consumption and production decisions according to their degrees of risk aversion, given the degree of uncertainty associated with variable prices. A case could even be made for public intervention in favor of risky activities if social risk aversion is (or should be) lower than private risk aversion. But complete price stability, or even increased price stability, is not necessarily welfare optimal (see Turnovsky, 1978).

Capital Controls

The standard development economist's view of capital controls (and the associated exchange controls) is provided by Joshi (1979): "It seems neither feasible nor desirable that LDCs should, over the foreseeable future, relax their exchange controls on capital movements and expose themselves to the vagaries of short-run movements of funds." On the feasibility of controls, Friedman (1963, p. 57) has noted:

> Full-fledged exchange controls and so called "inconvertibility of currencies" are an exception to the rule [that there is seldom anything truly new under the sun in economic policy]. . . . To the best of my knowledge they were invented by Hjalmar Schacht in the early years of the Nazi regime. On many occasions in the past, of course, currencies have been described as inconvertible. But what the word then meant was that the government was unwilling or unable to convert paper currency into gold or silver, or whatever the monetary commodity was, at the legally stipulated rate. It seldom meant that a country prohibited its citizens or residents from trading pieces of paper promising to pay specified sums in the monetary unit of that country for corresponding pieces of paper expressed in the monetary unit of another country —or for that matter for coin or bullion.

It would be possible to do without controls. The world, with countries at all stages of development, lived without them until the 1930s. Some developing countries—Mexico, Hong Kong, and more recently Indonesia —have found it feasible to do without capital controls in the postwar period.

On the desirability of controls, I have already argued that free trade in both long-term and short-term assets is welfare optimal. Some accept this argument for long-term flows but say that it hardly applies to short-term flows—movements of hot money that can be readily reversed, with supposedly disastrous effects on the domestic economy. In assessing the desirability of controls on short-term capital movements, it is necessary to be clear about the exchange-rate regime under which they are applied, as well as about the motives for the capital movements.

Under an adjustable-peg regime, it is essential to maintain controls on short-term capital flows in order to prevent the one-way gambles that it affords to speculators. This was in fact the reason that the Bretton Woods agreement sanctioned controls on short-term capital flows, although it was not seen that such controls were necessary to make the system work. But it became progressively clearer over the post-war period, in a world of growing interdependence and increasing foreign trade not subject to controls, that controls on short-term flows cannot prevent the speculation that threatens countries whose pegged rates are seen by the market to be out of line. It is difficult to separate short-term from long-term capital flows. How do we classify investments in short-term foreign bonds that are held for genuine long-term investment purposes? Furthermore, seemingly speculative flows can be generated by the "leads and lags" resulting from normal hedging by traders. These can to some extent be limited by subjecting *all* foreign-trade transactions to controls. But many developing countries have found that trade controls can be evaded by over-invoicing imports and under-invoicing exports (see Bhagwati, 1974, and Government of India, 1971). More important, the institution of Draconian controls, with their well-known inefficiencies and invitations to corruption, merely to make the adjustable-peg system work, would seem to be a classic case of the tail wagging the dog. This is particularly so if, as I have argued, pegged exchange rates are inappropriate in principle to a world of continual change, sticky prices, and irreducible uncertainty.

Thus the relevant question is whether, with flexible exchange rates, it is desirable purely from the viewpoint of national economic welfare to allow complete freedom for all capital movements.

Capital flows may be motivated by three broad types of considerations: fear of domestic political or economic crisis; differences in rates of return at home and abroad, net of tax differentials; and expectations of exchange-rate movements. All three types of flows can be financed not only from current savings but also from idle cash balances and sales of domestic bonds, equities, and physical capital assets.

It is the fear of politically motivated flows that has perhaps been most important historically in creating a climate of opinion favorable to capital controls. Haberler (1976, p. 74), has pointed out:

> [It was the] politically induced capital . . . from Hitler-Europe to the U.S. during the last years before the outbreak of the Second World War which strongly influenced Keynes' views on capital controls. He said: "There is no country which can, in the future, safely allow the flight of funds for political reasons or to evade domestic taxation or in anticipation of the owner turning refugee. Equally, there is no country that can safely receive fugitive funds."

As Friedman (1963) noted, it was Hjalmar Schacht who invented exchange controls in the 1930s. However, Haberler goes on to note, such capital flight is the exception rather than the rule.

Moreover, for a number of reasons the removal of exchange controls is unlikely to substantially increase politically motivated capital flight from third-world countries. First, to enjoy the fruits of such capital, the owner would have to "flee" too, changing his actual residence. With the nearly universal tightening of controls on immigration from third-world countries by both developed and developing countries, any large-scale movement of people with their capital is unlikely. Second, the elites in the third world, for whom immigration restrictions may not apply, have probably already taken advantage of both legal and illegal methods to build up foreign assets. They have moved their capital despite controls.

Third, under a floating exchange rate any massive attempt to move out of the domestic currency would cause that currency to depreciate, imposing what is in effect a heavy capital levy on the fleeing capitalists. Finally, for reasons spelled out above, there is no way in which much of the physical capital stock of the country could be reduced by a capital flight, which means that capital flight is unlikely to have disastrous effects under a system of floating rates.

I have already argued that there is no welfare reason for prohibiting the second category of capital flows, those reflecting differences in rates of return at home and abroad, except when there are disparities in relative private and social returns from domestic and foreign investment. If the social return from foreign investment is less than the private return, there is a case for a "second-best" tax on capital outflows. The optimal height of this tax, however, is unlikely to be prohibitive.

Turning to the third motive for capital movements, speculation on the exchange rate, we have merely to recall one of the advantages of a floating-rate system as opposed to an adjustable-peg system. Under a floating rate this type of capital movement is likely to be stabilizing rather than destabilizing, and there is thus no reason to resist it.

The conclusion is inescapable. Except for correcting disparities between the private and social returns from investments abroad, there is little justification for restricting capital flows under a floating-rate system. A welfare-economic rationale for controls can be provided only if it is explicitly or implicitly assumed that the world *should* be on an adjustable-peg system. But there is no reason to believe that such a system is more desirable than a floating-rate system.

International Reserves and the Link

Under a floating-rate system, the case for creating SDRs to provide an adequate level of international reserves is greatly diminished, for the reasons set out earlier. Central banks and the private sector will still hold parts of their portfolios in foreign currencies and assets denominated in foreign currencies. The SDR as presently constituted will probably not be attractive as a reserve instrument to most countries, as they can obtain higher returns on other assets, such as deposits in the Eurocurrency market. Many developing countries are now important depositors as well as borrowers in this market (see Wellons, 1977), and it appears from the evidence to be relatively efficient.

Moreover, the present system has a noneconomic advantage. Under a pure SDR-based international monetary system, the decisions of the supranational central bank must by their very nature be political. Under the present system, developing countries have access to a relatively apolitical market for both their reserve placements and their borrowing. For this reason, developing countries are right to insist on retaining the freedom to place their reserves in the Euromarkets and to resist proposals to control that market put forward by those who want to strengthen the IMF rather than the world economy and establish a politically determined SDR-based monetary system. I therefore disagree with Joshi (1979), who observes:

> It must be recorded that LDC's played their part in frustrating progress on [the imposition of controls on reserve placements by central banks in Euro-markets] by insisting on the freedom to place their reserves in Euro-markets to profit from the interest rates offered. This was a short-sighted position. Interest earnings on reserves are less important from the LDC point of view than moving towards an SDR based monetary system.

His position would seem to be exactly the opposite of that required to serve developing-country interests!

What of the SDR link? This is at best an academic issue, because of the decreasing importance of SDRs in the world monetary system—a trend that I cannot lament, for the reasons given earlier. For completeness, however, I cite the conclusion of Cline (1976, pp. 93-94), who has made the most thorough study of the issue:

> The expectations, discussion, and acrimony generated by link proposals have been completely out of proportion to the significance of the instrument itself. . . . As currently proposed by the LDC's the link would be an inefficient aid instrument, conferring on developing countries already too prosperous for IDA eligibility 40 cents out of every dollar of gross link aid. . . . The arguments for and against the link on economic grounds are weak. Some are misconceived (SDR's are not a complete windfall that should go to the poor), some are outdated or at least inapplicable for a permanent instrument (world unemployment is not an argument that justifies a link), some dubious but comfortably unverifiable (the confidence issue), and some directionally correct but empirically of negligible importance (inflation and payments imbalance aggravation).

This argument is still valid.

In conclusion, developing countries would be well advised to support the financial and monetary aspects of a liberal international economic order by allowing free capital mobility and freely floating exchange rates. They would also do better to resist controls on their reserve placements and borrowings in the Eurocurrency markets than to accept the evolution of an SDR-based international monetary system. This essay, although heretical, has at least shown that there are strong arguments in support of these views.

38

References

Arrow, Kenneth J., and Frank H. Hahn, *General Competitive Analysis*, San Francisco, Holden-Day, 1971.

Bhagwati, Jagdish, *Illegal Transactions in International Trade*, Amsterdam, North-Holland, 1974.

Black, Stanley W., *Exchange Policies for Less Developed Countries in a World of Floating Rates*, Essays in International Finance No. 119, Princeton, N.J., Princeton University, International Finance Section, 1976.

Calleo, D. P., ed., *Money and the Coming World Order*, New York, New York University Press, 1976.

Chrystal, K. Alec, *International Money and the Future of the SDR*, Essays in International Finance No. 128, Princeton, N.J., Princeton University, International Finance Section, 1978.

Cline, W. R., *International Monetary Reform and the Developing Countries*, Washington, The Brookings Institution, 1978.

Corden, W. M., *Trade Policy and Economic Welfare*, Oxford, Clarendon Press, 1974.

———, *Inflation, Exchange Rates and the World Economy*, Oxford, Clarendon Press, 1977.

Corden, W. M., I. M. D. Little, and M. F. Scott, *Import Controls versus Devaluation and Britain's Economic Prospects*, Guest Paper No. 2, London, Trade Policy Research Centre, 1975.

Díaz-Alejandro, Carlos F., *Less Developed Countries and the Post-1971 International Financial System*, Essays in International Finance No. 108, Princeton, N.J., Princeton University, International Finance Section, 1975.

Dornbusch, Rudiger, "The Theory of Flexible Exchange Rate Regimes and Macroeconomic Policy," *Scandinavian Journal of Economics*, 78 (May 1976), reprinted in Jacob Frenkel and Harry G. Johnson, eds., *The Economics of Exchange Rates: Selected Studies*, Reading, Mass., Addison-Wesley, 1978.

Dreyer, Jacob, Gottfried Haberler, and Thomas D. Willett, eds., *Flexible Exchange Rates and the International Monetary System*, Washington, D.C., American Enterprise Institute, 1978.

Ethier, Wilfred, and Arthur I. Bloomfield, *Managing the Managed Float*, Essays in International Finance No. 112, Princeton, N.J., Princeton University, International Finance Section, 1975.

Fama, Eugene F., "Efficient Capital Markets—A Review of Theory and Empirical Work," *Journal of Finance*, 25 (May 1970), pp. 383-417.

Frenkel, Jacob, and Harry G. Johnson, eds., *The Monetary Approach to the Balance of Payments*, Toronto, University of Toronto Press, 1976.

Friedman, Milton, *Capitalism and Freedom*, Chicago, University of Chicago Press, 1962.

Government of India, *Report of the Study Team on Leakage of Foreign Exchange through Invoice Manipulation*, New Delhi, Ministry of Finance, 1971.

Graham, Frank D., *The Theory of International Values*, Princeton, N.J., Princeton University Press, 1948.

Grandmont, J. M., and D. McFadden, "A Technical Note on Classical Gains from Trade," *Journal of International Economics*, 2 (May 1972), pp. 109-125.

Grassman, Sven, "Currency Distribution and Forward Cover in Foreign Trade: Sweden Revisted 1973," *Journal of International Economics*, 6 (May 1976), pp. 215-221.

Haberler, Gottfried, "The Case against Capital Controls for Balance of Payments Reasons," in Alexander K. Swoboda, ed., *Capital Movements and Their Control*, Leiden, Sijthoff, 1976.

Helpman, Elhaman, and Assaf Razin, *A Theory of International Trade under Uncertainty*, New York, Academic Press, 1978.

Houthakker, Hendrik S., "Purchasing Power Parity as an Approximation to the Equilibrium Exchange Rate," *Journal of Economic Letters*, 1 (No. 1, 1978), pp. 71-75.

Isard, Peter, "How Far Can We Push the 'Law of One Price'?" *American Economic Review*, 67 (December 1977), pp. 942-948.

Johnson, Harry G., "Optimum Tariffs and Retaliation," *Review of Economic Studies*, 21 (No. 2, 1953-54), pp. 142-153.

Joshi, V. R., "Exchange Rates, International Liquidity and Economic Development," *The World Economy*, 2 (May 1979), pp. 243-275.

Kareken, John, and Neil Wallace, "Portfolio Autarky: A Welfare Analysis," *Journal of International Economics*, 7 (February 1977), pp. 19-43.

Kindleberger, Charles P., "Systems of International Organization," in Calleo, ed. (1976a).

———, "Lessons of Floating Rates," *Journal of Monetary Economics*, 3 (Conference Number, 1976b), pp. 51-77.

———, *Government and International Trade*, Essays in International Finance No. 129, Princeton, N.J., Princeton University, International Finance Section, 1978.

Kravis, Irving B., and Robert E. Lipsey, "Purchasing Power Parity—Under Fixed and Flexible Exchange Rates," *Journal of International Economics*, 8 (May 1978), pp. 193-246.

Laffer, Arthur B., "The Phenomenon of World-wide Inflation," in D. I. Meiselman and A. B. Laffer, eds., *The Phenomenon of World-wide Inflation*, Washington, American Enterprise Institute, 1975.

Lal, Deepak, "The Foreign Exchange Bottleneck Revisited: A Geometric Note," *Economic Development and Cultural Change*, 20 (July 1972), pp. 722-730.

———, *Appraising Foreign Investment in Developing Countries*, London, Heinemann Educational Books, 1975.

———, *Unemployment and Wage Inflation in Industrial Economies*, Paris, OECD, 1977.

———, *Poverty, Power and Prejudice—The North-South Confrontation*, Fabian Research Series No. 340, London, Fabian Society, 1978.

———, "Comment" on the paper by Robert Nield in R. Major, ed., *Britain's Trade and Exchange Rate Policy*, London, National Institute of Economics and Social Research, Heinemann, 1979.

Machlup, Fritz, *Plans for Reform of the International Monetary System*, Special Papers in International Finance No. 3, Princeton, N.J., Princeton University, International Finance Section, 1964.

Malinvaud, E., *Lectures on Micro-economic Theory*, Amsterdam, North-Holland, 1972.

McKinnon, Ronald I., *Money and Capital in Economic Development*, Washington, D.C., The Brookings Institution, 1973.

———, "Floating Exchange Rates, 1973-74: The Emperor's New Clothes," *Journal of Monetary Economics*, 3 (Conference Number, 1976), pp. 79-114.

Meade, James E., *The Balance of Payments*, London, Oxford University Press, 1951.

Mundell, Robert A., *Monetary Theory*, Pacific Palisades, Goodyear, 1971.

Neary, J. Peter, "Short Run Capital Specificity and the Pure Theory of International Trade," *Economic Journal*, 88 (September 1978), pp. 488-510.

Salter, W. E., "Internal and External Balance: The Role of Price and Expenditure Effects," *Economic Record*, 35 (August 1959), pp. 226-238.

Samuelson, Paul A., "Proof That Properly Anticipated Prices Fluctuate Randomly," in *Collected Scientific Paper of Paul Samuelson*, Vol. 3, Chap. 198, Cambridge, Mass., MIT Press, 1972.

Scitovsky, Tibor, "A Reconsideration of the Theory of Tariffs," *Review of Economic Studies*, 9 (No. 2, 1942), pp. 89-110.

Tower, Edward, and Thomas D. Willett, *The Theory of Optimum Currency Areas and Exchange-Rate Flexibility*, Special Papers in International Finance No. 11, Princeton, N. J., Princeton University, International Finance Section, 1976.

Triffin, Robert, *Gold and the Dollar Crisis*, New Haven, Yale University Press, 1960.

Turnovsky, Stephen J., "The Distribution of Welfare Gains from Price Stabilization: A Survey of Some Theoretical Issues," in F. G. Adams and S. A. Klor, eds., *Stabilizing World Commodity Markets*, Lexington, Mass., Lexington Books, Heath, 1978.

Wellons, P. A., *Borrowing by Developing Countries on the Euro-Currency Market*, Paris, OECD, 1977.

Williamson, John H., *The Failure of World Monetary Reform, 1971-74*, London, Nelson, 1977.

Willett, Thomas D., *Floating Exchange Rates and International Monetary Reform*, Washington, American Enterprise Institute, 1977.

World Bank, *Prospects for Developing Countries 1978-85*, Washington, D.C., World Bank, 1977.

[7]

FOREIGN TRADE REGIMES AND ECONOMIC GROWTH IN DEVELOPING COUNTRIES

Deepak Lal
Sarath Rajapatirana

The static case for free trade is as simple as it is powerful. The removal of barriers to foreign trade expands the feasible set of consumption possibilities. It does so by providing, in effect, an indirect technology for transforming domestic resources into the goods and services that yield current and future utility for consumers. This static case does not involve any commitment to laissez-faire;[1] the law of comparative advantage, as well as the gains from trade it underpins, applies to both socialist and capitalist economies. The dynamic version of the law incorporates investment in line with a country's changing comparative advantage, which minimizes the present value of the resource costs of its future demands. By widening the market, foreign trade also allows a country to exploit economies of scale. Furthermore, the competitive pressures exerted by imports prevent the emergence of welfare-reducing domestic monopolies and induce domestic producers to improve quality and reduce costs. To the extent the static gains are saved and invested efficiently, they will grow over time, while the introduction of new goods and (more important) new technology through foreign trade can affect an economy's rate of technical progress.

Apart from this last factor, the result of moving toward free trade is a higher level of per capita income, not a permanently faster rate of growth. This is one argument currently being used to denigrate the case for free trade as a means of enhancing growth (see Lucas 1985); it will be discussed in the last section of this paper. Longer-standing skepticism includes, first, the claim that the static gains are fairly small for even large reductions in tariffs and, second, that dirigiste foreign trade regimes (which in 1945–65 encouraged import substitution and then, after 1965, export promotion) are likely to do more to boost a country's growth rate.

This article surveys empirical studies that seek to demonstrate the limited static gains from freer trade and then reviews studies of the dynamic effects of growth of exports on that of per capita income. The following section summarizes the results of comparative studies of developing countries undertaken in the 1960s and early 1970s, which show fairly conclusively that "outward orientation" seems to be positively associated with faster growth and greater equity. The article then examines whether the conclusions of these studies hold for the more volatile conditions since then. It considers the various arguments that cast trade as an "engine of growth." The final section introduces certain insights of the classical writers—in particular Adam Smith—which have reemerged in the neo-Austrian, as well as the more recent neoclassical "new political economy" schools, which might explain the stylized facts about the links between trade and growth. These emphasize the importance of the nonquantifiable aspects of a free trade regime in creating (in an irreducibly uncertain world) an economic framework that encourages entrepreneurship, productivity, and thrift. We argue that free trade is thus the handmaiden of growth, as it indirectly constrains the state from going beyond the bounds of providing those public goods essential for development.

The Static Gains from Trade

Early studies of the costs of protection measured the static gains from trade in terms of the familiar welfare triangles associated with complete or partial trade liberalization (as in the case of customs unions). Harberger (1959) estimated that the cost of protection in Chile amounted to "no more than 2½ percent of the national income" (p. 135). Scitovsky (1958) estimated the gains to the European Community from increased specialization at "less than one-twentieth of one percent of the gross social product of the countries involved" (p. 67). Johnson (1958) estimated the gain to Britain from the formation of a free trade area as at most 1 percent of national income.

Recently, several models have been developed to examine the general equilibrium effects of trade liberalization (*AB* in figure 1).[2] These estimates are based on the standard Heckscher-Ohlin model with constant returns to scale. The gains are estimated as Hicksian-equivalent variations as percentages of gross domestic product (GDP) in a base period. The gains from trade liberalization appear to be small: Whalley (1984) estimates a global *net* gain of about 0.3 percent of world GDP in 1977, and the maximum for any region or country is 0.5

percent of GDP (see Srinivasan 1986a, 1986b). Moreover, in Whalley's model, with a move to world free trade, the developing countries *lose* 4 percent of their GDP.

As Srinivasan (1986a) has argued, however, the results of these models are not credible, partly because of how they manipulate data to make an internally consistent equilibrium set (when the data themselves come from nonequilibrium situations) and partly because of how they specify some crucial elasticity parameters. In particular, they all make use of estimated trade elasticities (see Stern and others 1976), which have a well-known bias to underestimation (see Orcutt 1950, Kemp 1962, Kakwani 1972).[3] Most of these models also do not take account of scale economies and imperfect competition. An exception is a model for Canada by Harris (1983), which shows that a multilateral reduction of all tariffs yields welfare gains of more than 5 percent of GDP.

Figure 1

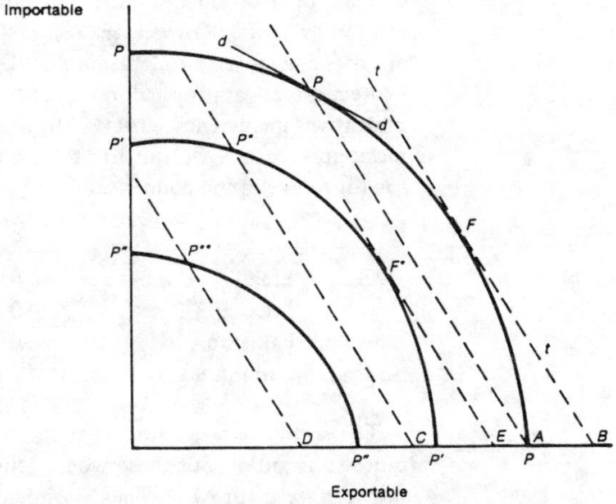

Note: *PP* is the production possibility frontier. *F* is the free trade output when world prices are given by *tt*. With a tariff and no lobbying or rent seeking, the production point is *P*, with the domestic price ratio being given by *dd* and the welfare cost by *AB*. With lobbying for the tariff, the production possibility curve shifts to *P'P'*, the production point to *P**, and the welfare loss is *CB*. To avoid various "immiserizing paradoxes" (which depend on the relative slopes of the Rybczynski line between *P* and *P**, and the world price ratio *tt*), which could imply a welfare gain from the lobbying equilibrium at *P** as compared with *P*, it is better to decompose the welfare loss *CB* into the loss due to the tariff *CE* (this is the usual triangle estimate) and that due to lobbying *EB* (see Bhagwati 1980). With rent seeking, the production possibility curve shifts inward to *P"P"*, the production point to *P***, and the welfare loss at world prices is *DB*.

Furthermore, most of these models do not take account of the "rent seeking" and "directly unproductive" activities triggered by protectionism (see Tullock 1967, Krueger 1974, Bhagwati 1980). In the case of rent seeking, the deadweight loss associated with, for instance, a tariff, is not merely the conventional net change in the consumer and producer surplus triangles, but also the spending by lobbies for and against the tariff and by those who aim to capture the rent for themselves. Thus in figure 1 the lobbying costs shift the production possibility (*PP*) curve inward, with an associated welfare cost of protection *CB*.[4] If there is a struggle over the rents associated with the tariff, the welfare costs rise to *DB*, as the *PP* curve shifts further inward (see Srinivasan 1986b). One study by Grais and others (1984) has attempted to estimate the costs of rent seeking (but not lobbying) associated with quotas in Turkey. It found that if tariffs were removed but quotas maintained, there was little effect on real GDP; if quotas were also eliminated, real GDP rose between 5 and 10 percent.

So far we have excluded the deadweight losses of domestic monopoly and X-inefficiency associated with protection (see Leibenstein 1966, Corden 1974, Krueger 1984). Thus "a reduction in tariff levels might be expected to result in a downward shift in industry supply curves. The welfare costs of protection would then consist of the conventional production cost, plus an inefficiency cost and possibly a monopoly cost" (Krueger 1984, p. 544). The only attempt to measure all these costs is by Bergsman (1974). He found that the costs of protection as a proportion of GNP, consisting of the conventional allocative inefficiency costs (A), the X-inefficiency combined with monopoly costs (X), and the total costs ($T = X + A$) were as follows for four developing countries:

	A	X	T
Brazil	0.3	6.8	7.1
Mexico	0.3	2.2	2.5
Pakistan	0.5	5.4	5.9
Philippines	1.0	2.6	3.6

The static welfare gains from trade liberalization could therefore be quite substantial. But these would still affect only the level of income, not its rate of growth. They do not explain why the growth rates of free-trading countries should be higher on a sustainable basis, as seems to have been the case.

Statistical Tests of Exports and Growth

The links between trade and growth have many statistical studies, which are summarized in tables 1 and 2. Michalopoulos and Jay (1973) estimated an aggregate neoclassical production function for thirty-nine countries. Exports were found to be highly significant, and GNP growth was significantly correlated to the growth rate of exports.

By studying the change in the proportion of exports to GNP relative to the rate of GNP growth in forty-one countries during 1950–73, Michaely (1977) found a significant relationship at the 1 percent level for the Spearman rank correlation. The study attempted to avoid autocorrelation between exports and GNP by using the change in the share of exports in GNP to represent the growth of exports which was then regressed against the rate of change of per capita income (Michaely 1977, p. 50).

In her study for the National Bureau of Economic Research (NBER) on foreign trade regimes and economic development, Krueger (1978)

Table 1. ***Estimated Spearman Rank Correlation Coefficients between Export Growth and Output Growth in Developing Countries***

Author	*Average annual change in export GNP ratio vs. average annual per capita GNP growth*	*Export growth vs. GNP growth*	*Incremental export GNP ratio vs. GNP growth*	*Increments in export GNP ratios vs. GNP growth*
Michaely				
For 41 observations, 1950–73	0.380**	—	—	—
For 23 middle-income countries, 1950–73	0.523**	—	—	—
For 18 low-income countries, 1950–73	−0.04	—	—	—
Balassa: for 11 semi-industrial countries, 1960–73	—	0.888**	0.813**	0.776**

**indicates 1 percent level of significance.
Source: Michaely 1977, pp. 51–52, and Balassa 1978, p. 184.

regressed GNP growth for each of ten countries against the rate of export growth. She found a positive and significant relationship between the two. Similarly, Balassa (1978), by reestimating Michaely's equations and incorporating the Michalopoulos-Jay factors, noted a robust relationship between exports and GNP growth for eleven countries. He recognized that it understated the effects of export growth. And Feder (1983) not only found a positive correlation between exports and GNP growth, but also provided evidence to support the hypothesis that export-oriented policies both led the economy to an optimal allocation of resources and generally enhanced productivity.[5]

All these studies confirm a statistical relationship between export and income growth. But at best this provides a stylized fact, not a theory. As in most statistical matters however, even this association is disputed—a reflection of the emerging "law" that all econometric evidence is equivocal. Thus Helliner (1986) in a study of low-income countries heavily weighted toward Sub-Saharan Africa, concluded that the results for 1960–80 "show no statistically significant link between the change in export share of GDP and growth. Indeed, the sign on this relationship is consistently negative" (p. 146). Similar results were also reported by Michaely (1977): "the positive association of the economy's growth rate with the growth of the export share appears to be particularly strong among the more developed countries, and not to exist at all among the least developed . . . This seems to indicate that growth is affected by export performance only once countries achieve some minimum level of development" (p. 52).

Table 2. *Estimated Relationship between Export Growth and Output Growth in Developing Countries*

Author	Dependent variable,[a] $\left(\frac{\Delta Y}{Y_1}\right)$	Independent variables[b] $\frac{\Delta K_d}{Y_1}$	$\frac{\Delta K_f}{Y_1}$	$\frac{\Delta L}{L_1}$	$\frac{\Delta X}{\Delta Y}$	$\frac{\Delta X}{X_1}$	$\frac{\Delta X}{Y_1}$	$D_{i1}t$	$D_{i2}t$	R^2
Michalopolous and Jay: for 39 observations, 1960–66	—	0.25	0.20	0.66	—	—	—	—	—	0.53
		(7.81)	(3.35)	(2.44)						
	—	0.24	0.12	0.60	0.04	—	—	—	—	0.71
		(9.62)	(2.33)	(2.81)	(4.82)					
Balassa: for 10 observations, 1960–73	—	0.18	0.30	1.09	—	—	—	—	—	0.58
		(3.23)	(2.42)	(1.74)						
	—	0.15	0.23	0.97	0.04	—	—	—	—	0.77
		(3.33)	(2.40)	(1.99)	(3.57)					
Feder: for 31 observations, 1964–73[c]	—	0.284		0.739	—	—	—	—	—	0.37
		(4.311)		(1.990)						
	—	0.178		0.747	—	—	0.422	—	—	
		(3.542)		(2.862)			(5.454)			0.689
	—	0.124		0.696	—	0.131	0.305	—	—	0.809
		(3.009)		(3.399)		(4.239)	(4.571)			
Krueger: for 10 observations, 1950–70[d]	—	—		—	—	0.11	—	0.08	0.16	0.99
						(4.29)		(0.85)	(1.70)	

Note: Numbers in parentheses are *t* values.

a. The dependent variable ($\Delta Y/Y_1$) is the GNP growth in Michalopoulos and Jay, Balassa, and Krueger. In the Feder study, it refers to GDP growth.

b. The independent variables are $\Delta K_d/Y_1$, domestically financed investment as a proportion of the GNP in the initial period; $\Delta K_f/Y_1$, foreign-financed investment as a proportion of GNP in the initial period; $\Delta L/L_1$, increase in population as a proportion of the population in the initial period; $\Delta X/\Delta Y$, incremental export-GNP ratio; $\Delta X/X_1$, increase in exports as a proportion of the exports in the initial period; $\Delta X/Y_1$, increase in exports as a proportion of GNP in the initial period; D_{i1} a dummy variable which takes the value of 1 during Phases 1 and 2 of the trade regimes; D_{i2}, a dummy variable which takes the value of 1 during Phases 3 and 4 of trade regimes; and *t* which is a time variable.

c. The export variables in Feder are $(\Delta X/X)(X/Y) = (\Delta X/Y)$ and $(\Delta X/X)$.

d. In Krueger's study log refers to a pooled sample of ten countries in which log GNP is regressed on a time trend and log *X*, a dummy variable for the country's Phases 1 and 2 trade regime (that is, $D_{i1}t$), and another dummy variable for Phases 3 and 4 trade regime.

Source: Michalopoulos and Jay 1973; Balassa 1978, p. 186; Feder 1983, pp. 65, 68; Krueger 1978, p. 273.

As most of the low-income countries in the sample used by Helliner (using data from the *World Development Reports*[6]) can hardly be classified as having followed outward-oriented policies, the failure to find a link between exports and growth is not surprising. We would expect, however, that in the turbulent decade after the first oil shock of 1973, even among these dirigiste low-income countries, the *relatively* more outward-oriented would have had a better growth record. Using data from the *World Development Report 1986*, on GDP, labor force growth, and the growth of export and investment shares in GDP, we estimated the following regression for eighteen low-income countries for which statistics were available:

$$\begin{array}{lcccccc} \text{GDP} & = 2.251 + 0.225 & \text{Investment} & -0.963 & \text{Growth} & +0.152 & \text{Growth of} \\ \text{growth} & & \text{share of} & & \text{of labor} & & \text{export share} \\ \text{rate,} & & \text{GDP,} & & \text{force,} & & \text{of GDP,} \\ \text{1973–84} & & \text{1984} & & \text{1973–84} & & \text{1965–73} \\ & (0.064) & & (0.786) & & (0.079) & \end{array}$$

$$r^2 = 0.30;\ F = 3.2$$

The figures in brackets are standard errors. This equation shows that there was a positive and statistically significant association between income growth rates in the turbulent decade after the oil shock and the growth of exports in GDP in the preceding period (1965–73).

All the studies reviewed above use conventional statistical tests for establishing an association between exports and growth. Following classical statistical methodology, these correlations by themselves reveal nothing about causation. To make causal inferences, an underlying theoretical model is required, whose validity is then tested by standard econometric techniques. Recently, however, a new school of econometrics has sought to make causal statements purely on the basis of a particular statistical technique called vector auto regression (VAR) and of a Granger-Sims causality test, which seeks to establish whether over time a particular variable regularly precedes another. Jung and Marshall (1985) have applied the Granger causality test to data for thirty-seven developing countries in 1950–81 to determine whether exports "Granger-cause" growth, or vice versa. They find that only Costa Rica, Ecuador, Egypt, and Indonesia provide evidence in favor of export promotion; "more interestingly, many of the countries most famous for the miraculous growth rates that appeared to arise from export promotion policies (e.g. Korea, Taiwan, Brazil) provide no statistical support for the export promotion hypothesis" (p. 10). Darrat (1986) has also applied the Grangercausality test to the time series for exports and growth between 1960 and 1982 for Hong Kong, Korea, Singapore, and Taiwan and finds that for the first three "neither exports cause economic growth nor economic growth causes exports." For Taiwan he finds that "economic growth unidirectionally causes exports" (p. 697).

Several points need to be made against this recent counterrevolution. First, even within the atheoretical Grangercausality framework, the results showing that output growth causes export growth are not inconsistent with the export-growth link found by the more conventional studies. Consider this comment by Darrat: "The economic growth that Taiwan enjoyed during the estimated period (1960–82) appears to be an internal process perhaps due to domestic technological advancement and enhanced accumulation of human capital (Jung and Marshall 1985). *Given the country's limited market capacity, Taiwan's producers were probably compelled to turn to foreign markets for exports.* It seems therefore, that economic growth (generated internally) has caused higher exports in Taiwan, contrary to the implication of the export-led growth hypothesis" (p. 697–98, emphasis added). However, it is obvious that, if a small country is developing efficiently in line with its comparative advantage, it will specialize and hence be "compelled to turn to foreign markets for exports" of goods that use its most abundant factor of production most intensively. The statistical establishment of this fact hardly disproves the validity of the outward-oriented development strategy; in fact, it supports it. Thus in the Jung and Marshall (1985) study if the cases in which output growth causes export growth are also included as supporting the outward orientation theory (as they should be on the above argument), the list of countries rises to fourteen and also includes Bolivia, Greece, Iran, Israel, Kenya, Korea, Pakistan, Peru, South Africa, and Thailand.

Second, it is clear from the test of precedence (which is what the the Grangercausality test amounts to) that the statistical counterrevolutionaries are testing for the growth-enhancing effects of a development strategy that *biases* incentives toward exports. They are not concerned with the neutral free trade equilibrium point—*F* in figure 1—whereas (as we argue below) most proponents of outward orientation do not favor this biased export-led growth. The same criticism applies to Fishlow's (1985) interpretation of the case for outward orientation as identical with that for export-led growth. To test this hypothesis, he rightly argues, "requires calculation of the relationship between aggregate performance and the extent to which the rate of growth of exports *exceeds* overall growth"; not surprisingly, he finds that "with such a specification, there is no statistically significant relationship" (p. 139). But again, it is clearly unwarranted to identify the case for outward orientation (or, more precisely, for neutral trade policies) with that for an export bias.

Third, the statistical studies based on Granger causality, which test for the precedence of one variable over another, do not in fact reveal anything about causation as the term is normally understood. Leamer (1985), in a review of the new econometric fashion that uses vector autoregressions alone for causal inferences, rightly notes that: "this concept should be called 'precedence'. . . We can all think of contexts in which precedence is suggestive of causation and also contexts in which it is not . . . It is altogether clear that precedence is not sufficient for causality. Weather forecasts regularly precede the weather, but few of us take this as evidence that the forecasts 'cause' the weather" (pp. 259, 283).[7]

There is one other, more compelling reason why judgments based solely on statistical tests (both conventional and novel) of dynamic effects of trade regimes must remain inconclusive. Economics, as Hicks (1979) has put it, "is on the edge of science and of history" (p. 38). The historical aspects are particularly important for what he terms "sequential causality"—which is the relevant notion of causality for analyzing the dynamic effects of trade regimes. But in studying such dynamic historial processes, techniques of statistical inference may not be very useful, because "when we cannot accept that the observations along the time series available to us are independent or cannot by some device be divided into groups that can be treated as independent, we get into much deeper water. For we have then, in strict logic, no more than one observation, all of the separate items having to be taken together. We are left to use our judgment, making sense of what has happened as best we can, in the manner of the historian. Applied economics does then come back to history after all" (p. 126).[8]

Evidence on Trade Regimes

This section looks at five comparative studies of particular developing countries' trade regimes undertaken in the 1960s and 1970s (Little and others 1970, Balassa 1971, Donges 1976, Bhagwati 1978, and Krueger 1978). The studies provide fairly firm evidence that countries that adopted or moved toward an export-promoting (EP) strategy did much better in growth of per capita income and equity than those with an import-substituting (IS) strategy. These terms, EP and IS, have caused some confusion. The most common definition now is that a movement from the neutral free trade position is IS, and a movement toward it (that is, from *P* to *F* in figure 1) is EP. Thus the EP strategy does not imply any subsidization of exports beyond the level that restores equality between the effective exchange rates on imports and exports.[9]

For our purpose we need only note that the five comparative studies have established that IS regimes produce a misallocation of resources. Although there are analytical doubts about the use of domestic resource cost (DRC) measures as indicators of static efficiency in some of these studies, the general conclusion is reinforced by more appropriate indicators of allocative efficiency: the divergences between Little-Mirrlees (LM) shadow prices and market prices for several developing countries.[10] More significantly, these studies (in particular the NBER study) showed that countries that reduced or removed the bias against exports had accelerated their growth rates of per capita incomes; those with an IS strategy did not.

In this context it is important to distinguish between the degree and pattern of protection. It has been argued that the existence of some highly protected industries in an economy whose trade regime *on average* shows little IS bias (for example, Korea) invalidates drawing any inferences from its experience in favor of neutral trade (see Wade 1985). Jagdish Bhagwati (1986) has given the correct response to this argument:

> Thus, within the broad aggregates of an EP country case, there may well be activities that are being import-substituted (i.e., their EER_m exceeds the average EER_x) [where EER_m is the effective exchange rate for imports, and EER_x is the effective exchange rate for exports]. Indeed there often are. But one should not jump to the erroneous conclusion that there is therefore no way to think of EP versus IS and that the distinction is an artificial one—any more than one would refuse to acknowledge that the Sahara is a desert, whereas Sri Lanka is not, simply because there are oases (p. 93).

Tables 3 and 4 summarize the divergence between market and LM shadow prices for traded goods in India and Korea.[11] Though there are highly protected activities in both countries, even casual inspection shows that Korea's trade regime is much more neutral than India's, and the dispersion of its protection is lower.[12]

Of the five studies, only the one from the NBER explicitly sought to quantify the possible effects of alternative trade regimes on savings rates, technical progress, and entrepreneurship—the dynamic factors that affect a country's growth rate. The evidence (surveyed in Bhagwati 1978) on entrepreneurship, innovation, and technical change is inconclusive, though none of these factors is shown to benefit from IS regimes. On savings, Bhagwati concludes that the evidence does not support the view that restrictionist exchange control regimes "will or are likely to contribute to increased domestic savings, and/or to augmented capital formation. If anything, much of our evidence—at least on the domestic savings issue—suggests an opposite relationship" (p. 174).

The NBER study also emphasized the importance of appropriate macroeconomic and exchange rate policies to maintain a realistic real exchange rate. As Krueger (1978) put it:

> It seems a fair conclusion that one of the policy mistakes of the two decades covered by the country studies was using devaluation to a new fixed exchange rate as an instrument designed to attain both domestic price stabilisation and a liberalised trade regime (p. 297).

Exogenous Shocks in the 1970s and 1980s

The 1970s and 1980s produced two oil shocks, the worst recession since the Great Depression, and a huge switch in real interest rates (low or negative for most of the 1970s, unprecedentedly high in the 1980s). These shocks were common to all developing countries, yet the relative performance of the EP countries was far superior (see Lal and Wolf 1986).

Table 3. *Accounting Ratios for Traded Commodities in India, 1973*

Sectoral code number	*Commodity*	*Accounting ratio*
T1	Electrical equipment	0.36
T2	Nonelectrical equipment	0.65
T3	Transport equipment	1.28
T4	Metal products	0.29
T5	Iron and steel	1.00
	Pipes and tubes	1.00
	Pig iron	1.00
T6	Cement	0.66
T7	Nonferrous metals	0.59
T8	Other minerals	0.61
T9	Rubber	0.60
T10	Leather	0.50
T11	Other leather products	0.50
T12	Leather footwear	0.81
T13	Animal husbandry	0.37
T14	Sugar	0.52
T15	Gur and khandsari	1.08
T16	Vegetable oils	1.14
T17	Vanaspati	0.65
T18	Starch	0.87
T19	Milk products	0.29
T20	Breweries and soft drinks	0.68
T21	Confectionery	0.60
T22	Cigarettes and cigars	0.39
T23	Other tobacco products	0.39
T24	Fruits and vegetables	0.32
T25	Cashew nut processing	0.27
T26	Cotton	0.51
T27	Cotton yarn	2.04
T28	Cotton textiles	0.46
T29	Jute	0.57
T30	Jute textiles	0.44
T31	Woolen yarn	0.60
T32	Woolen textiles	0.61
T33	Raw silk	0.71
T34	Silk textiles	0.50
T35	Man-made fiber (rayon)	0.13
T36	Artificial silk	0.43
T37	Other textiles	0.44
T38	Tobacco	0.43
T39	Fertilizers	1.00
T40	Ceramics and bricks	0.44
T41	Glass and glassware	0.72
T42	Wood products	0.97
T43	Timber	0.80
T44	Chinaware, pottery	0.50
T45	Wood, others	0.56
T46	Other forest products	0.27
T47	Petroleum products	0.65
T48	Rubber footwear	0.73

(Table continues on next page)

Table 3 *(continued)*

Sectoral code number	*Commodity*	*Accounting ratio*
T49	Synthetic rubber	0.73
T50	Other rubber products	0.48
T51	Paper and paper products	0.44
T52	Plastics	0.47
T53	Dyestuff	0.39
T54	Paints and varnishes	1.35
T55	Insecticides and pesticides	0.91
T56	Drugs and pharmaceuticals	0.32
T57	Soaps and glycerine	0.57
T58	Perfumes and cosmetics	0.39
T59	Miscellaneous chemicals	0.53
T60	Coal and coke	0.72
T61	Matches	0.76
T62	Plantations	1.00
T63	Aluminum primary product	0.80
T64	Zinc	0.61
T65	Lead	0.58
T66	Tin	0.57
T67	Manganese	1.00
T68	Sulfur	0.65
T69	Sulfuric acid	0.65
T70	Rock phosphate	0.87
T71	Salt	1.00
T72	Wheat	0.87
T73	Soda ash	0.76
T74	Dry cells	0.52
T75	Ball bearings	0.40
T76	Electric fans	1.00
T77	Radio receivers	0.52
T78	Nonferrous metal alloys	0.69
T79	By-products of foodgrains	0.87
T80	Gypsum	1.00
T81	Limestone	1.00
T82	Iron ore	1.00
T83	Bauxite	1.00

Note: The accounting ratio is the ratio of the social price to the market price; see note 11 to the text for a fuller definition. The unweighted means of these accounting ratios is 0.675, with a standard deviation of 0.294.

Source: Lal 1980.

The starting point for explaining this conclusion is a simple one: all countries need some foreign trade. In dealing with external shocks, the more inward-looking countries face greater costs of output forgone through compressing imports (which are mainly capital goods), and they have more difficulty in expanding exports because of a smaller proportion of their output is tradable. For these reasons, IS countries have not only had slower growth but also more serious debt

Table 4. *Accounting Ratios for Traded Commodities in Korea, 1973*

Sector number	*Commodity*	*Accounting ratio*
1	Rice, barley, and wheat	0.84
2	Vegetables, fruits	0.79
3	Industrial crops	0.84
4	Livestock breeding	0.87
5	Forestry products	0.88
*6	Fishery products	1.27
7	Coal	0.85
8	Metallic ores	0.95
9	Nonmetallic minerals	0.87
10	Slaughtering, dairy products	0.85
11	Canning and processing	0.81
12	Grain polishing and milling	0.81
13	Other food preparations	0.80
14	Beverages	0.47
*15	Tobacco	0.95
*16	Fiber spinning	1.16
*17	Textile fabrics	1.08
*18	Apparel and fabrications	1.08
*19	Leather and leather products	1.04
*20	Lumber and plywood	1.03
*21	Wood products and furniture	1.00
22	Paper and paper products	0.67
23	Printing and publishing	0.93
24	Inorganic chemicals	0.77
25	Organic chemicals	0.68
26	Chemical fertilizers	0.93
27	Drugs and cosmetics	0.80
28	Other chemical products	0.68
29	Petroleum refining	0.80
30	Coal products	0.91
31	Rubber products	0.69
32	Nonmetallic minerals	0.77
33	Iron and steel	0.86
34	Primary iron and steel manufactures	0.76
35	Nonferrous metal manufactures	0.79
*36	Fabricated metal products	1.05
37	Nonelectrical machinery	0.84
38	Electrical machinery	0.76
39	Transportation equipment	0.83
40	Measuring, medical	0.67
*41	Miscellaneous manufactures	1.33
*56	Unclassifiable	1.33

Note: These ratios have been derived as described in Lal (1978b). The asterisked items were taken to be export sectors. The unweighted mean of these ratios is 0.883 with a standard deviation of 0.178.

problems than EP countries: witness the contrast between the newly industrializing countries (NICs) in Southeast Asia and the Latin American Southern Cone countries.

For comparative purposes, three groups of economies have been selected. Group A consists of Hong Kong, Korea, Singapore, and Taiwan, which have followed EP strategies as defined in the Bhagwati-Krueger studies.[13] Group B includes the Southern Cone countries—Argentina, Chile, Uruguay—plus a South Asian country, Sri Lanka. They are referred to as moderately IS countries, which made some effort to liberalize their trade regimes in the late 1970s.[14] Group C consists just of India, an IS country in which the effective exchange rate for imports markedly exceeds that for exports.

Group A: Export-Promoting Countries

The four economies in this group have been the most dynamic exporters in the world. During 1970–79, their exports grew at an annual average rate of 25 percent, with manufactured exports growing at 30 percent. During 1978–81 their exports grew at 19 percent a year; then, with the world recession of the early 1980s, they actually declined. But they recovered more rapidly than the exports of any other group, despite experiencing greater external shocks than most other developing countries. The shocks were equal to 18 percent of GNP for Singapore, 10 percent for Taiwan, and 9 percent for Korea; for developing countries as a whole, the shock was 6 percent of GNP (Balassa 1984). By 1983, the GDP growth rates of all four economies were back to the 1970–82 average; so were their trade balances and export growth.

The four EP economies adjusted in two ways. First, they expanded exports by raising their market shares even when world demand was depressed. Second, they raised domestic savings. Korea was an exception to this rule, because its financial market was repressed. It financed part of the temporary loss in income by increasing its external borrowings—but, unlike most heavily indebted countries, it was able to service its debt without cuts in domestic output.[15]

Group B: Moderately Import-Substituting Economies

The countries in this group tried to liberalize their trade regimes between the mid-1970s and the early 1980s. They are the Southern Cone countries of Argentina, Chile, and Uruguay and one South Asian country, Sri Lanka. All were initially successful in liberalizing their trade regimes. They speeded up their GDP and export growth and improved their external accounts. In the 1980s, however, they ran into crises of macroeconomic stabilization.

The Southern Cone countries shared a common path up to the mid-1970s. By that stage, Argentina's GDP growth was slow (averaging 0.5

percent a year during 1965–73), and its trade heavily protected. Inflation was high—around 180 percent in 1975—so was unemployment. Effective rates of protection ranged from 111 percent for manufacturing to −13 percent for agriculture. Since the 1930s it had followed an IS strategy.

For Chile, too, the initial conditions were very difficult. GDP shrunk by 5.6 percent in 1973 on the eve of the reforms. Inflation had reached 1,000 percent. In trade, rates of protection averaged 217 percent, varying from 1,140 percent for petroleum and coal products to −7 percent for agriculture.

Uruguay had experienced prolonged stagnation during 1950–70. In 1965–73, GDP growth averaged 2.0 percent a year. Inflation had reached 97 percent, capital flight was substantial, and the currency was overvalued. By 1970 its IS strategy had hit the limits of the small domestic market.

All three countries undertook substantial economic reforms during 1975–80, of which a principal feature was trade liberalization. In Argentina, taxes on exports were reduced;[16] so were import tariffs, thus lowering both the average level of effective protection and the variance. Following these reforms GDP growth averaged nearly 4 percent a year between 1978 and 1980. Manufactured exports increased by 216 percent in 1975–80. In 1978 the government started to preannounce exchange rates (the *tablita*). But it had failed to curb the fiscal deficit. The ensuing domestic inflation, coupled with a slowly adjusting nominal exchange rate, led to a rise in the real exchange rate, capital flight, and the collapse of the banking system (Calvo 1986). Because of this stabilization crisis, by 1982 the trade reforms had been reversed.

The Chilean trade reforms were the most far-reaching. All quotas were eliminated except those on motor vehicles. All tariffs were reduced to a uniform 10 percent by 1979. By 1977–78, the budget was balanced. The exchange rate was first put on a crawling peg, and then in 1979 fixed against the U.S. dollar. Also by 1979 the capital account was liberalized. The results of these reforms were dramatic. During 1976–81 GDP grew by 8 percent a year and manufactured exports by 30 percent a year. However, the opening of the capital account and the fixing of the nominal exchange rate led to a large appreciation in the real exchange rate. As in Argentina, this was followed by a balance of payments crisis, capital flight, and the collapse of the domestic banking system. In 1982 GDP declined by 14 percent, and unemployment reached 22 percent of the labor force.

In Uruguay, taxes on traditional exports were lowered in the mid-1970s. Nontraditional exports were given additional incentives. Price controls were reduced sharply, and restrictions on the inflow of private capital were eliminated. The results of these reforms were impressive. Having averaged 1.0 percent a year in 1955–73, GDP growth rose to an average of 4.5 percent during 1974–80. In 1982, however, the worldwide rise in interest rates, combined with an appreciation in the real exchange rate (because of its tablita) and an increase in the fiscal deficit, led to a balance of payments crisis. GDP declined by nearly 10 percent in 1982.

The Southern Cone experience provides several lessons. The trade reforms were successful in raising export and GDP growth, particularly in Chile and Uruguay. But the overall attempt at economic liberalization failed eventually, because of unsustainable macroeconomic and real exchange rate policies (Corbo and de Melo 1985, de Melo and Tybout 1986). Compared with the Southeast Asian NICs, the Southern Cone countries faced more difficult conditions initially and made errors in macropolicy when it came to dealing with external shocks.

In Sri Lanka, the trade liberalization of 1977 reversed a long-standing IS strategy. By that stage, the economy was highly distorted—but not subject to the inflationary instability of the Southern Cone. For many years the economy was sluggish: in 1965–77, for example, GDP growth averaged 2.9 percent a year. The country's share of world trade declined, as did its volume of exports—by 1.5 percent between 1970 and 1977.

The wide-ranging reforms of 1977 mainly involved the trade regime and led to a dramatic economic recovery. Sri Lanka's GDP grew by 6 percent a year in 1978–85, and unemployment fell from 24 percent of the labor force in 1973 to 12 percent in 1981 (Bhalla and Glewwe 1986). By 1983, however, macroeconomic imbalances forced the government to slow down its reform program. Heavy public expenditure and a reluctance to close loss-making public enterprises proved to be incompatible with the trade reforms (Lal and Rajapatirana 1987). As in the Southern Cone, macroeconomic imbalances—in this case brought about by the financing of public expenditure by capital inflows—led to a real appreciation of the rupee and to a balance of payments and fiscal crisis.

The experience of this group of countries points to three lessons for trade liberalization. First, appropriate macroeconomic policies are vital to maintaining a more liberal trade regime. Second, an appropriate real exchange rate plays a bigger role in trade reform than was realized in the five comparative studies. Third, the order in which the various repressed markets are reformed seems to be important. In both Chile and Uruguay the liberalization of financial markets was destabilizing. It is still an open question whether this was due to the structure of the domestic financial market, or to poor macroeconomic and exchange rate management, or is an inherent property of financial liberalization itself.

Group C: Import-Substituting Countries

India's relative immunity to the external shocks of the 1980s is often used to suggest that, over the long haul and despite the acknowledged productive inefficiencies of the country's trade regime, India's "delinking" from the world economy has allowed it to maintain much steadier growth in the past two turbulent decades.[17] This view is mistaken, because any stability of domestic incomes achieved by delinking can also mean that average income is lower than if the international roller coaster is ridden efficiently.

India proves this point. Its trend rate of GDP growth has been 3–4 percent a year for three decades—much lower than the growth that could have been obtained by integration into a world economy, which boomed for two decades. To illustrate this loss, in 1960 the absolute size of Korea's manufacturing industry was a quarter of India's; in 1980 it was almost two-thirds of the size. Korean manufactured exports rose from virtually nothing in 1960 to more than $15 billion in 1980. In the same period India's manufactured exports rose from $600 million to only $4.1 billion. "Even tiny Singapore has managed to export more manufactures in value terms ($11.7 billion in 1981) than India! India's share in world exports has declined steadily from 2.4 percent in 1968 to a minuscule 0.41 percent in 1981" (Srinivasan 1986). Since labor-intensive manufacturing is a major means of providing employment and alleviating poverty in countries with a rapidly growing labor force and a scarcity of land, India's inward-looking policies have done long-term damage to both growth and equity.

Though it is now fashionable to castigate Latin American countries for having followed "debt-led" growth in the late 1960s and 1970s, the subsequent income losses they may have suffered to service their debts have to be set off against the enormous previous gains in real incomes that debt-financed growth entailed (see Bhagwati 1986).

Income Effects of Trade and Growth

Two of the most influential development economists, Nurkse (1961) and Lewis (1980) have adduced a link between trade and growth in terms of the transmission of rapidly growing world demand to an open developing country: "trade as the engine of growth."[18] Nurkse (1961) argued that in the nineteenth century, trade had been such an engine for white settler communities, but predicted that it would no longer be so for developing countries in the second half of the twentieth century.

Nurkse's historical analysis and his forecasts both proved false. The view that international trade assisted the growth of the countries of new settlement in the nineteenth century has been questioned by Kravis (1970). Essentially, he argues that economic growth is determined by internal factors. Foreign trade provides an extension of the domestic opportunities available for converting resources into goods and services. Furthermore, by widening the market, it enables a country to produce goods with decreasing costs of production. Probably most important of all, exposure to international competition is the best antimonopoly policy—and thereby prevents the development of high-cost industries.

Most of these benefits concern the efficient use of available resources and hence the supply side of an economy. The demand factors that preoccupied Nurkse and others cannot be as influential, because the countries that shared in the nineteenth century expansion of trade developed in such different ways. For instance, Australia seemed to develop whereas Argentina did not, despite similar natural resource, "white" populations (Argentina had none of the problems of assimilation posed for other countries in Latin America by an indigenous population), and a similar stimulus from the rise in foreign demand for their primary products. Thus, as Kravis emphasizes, though strong external demand for a country's exports may be helpful,

> it is neither a necessary nor sufficient condition for growth or even trade to play a helpful role in growth . . . The term "engine of growth" is not generally descriptive and involves expectations which cannot be fulfilled by trade alone; the term "handmaiden of growth" better conveys the role that trade can play (p. 869).

More recently, Lewis (1980) has presented another model in which trade serves as an engine of growth. He bases his theory on the following empirical regularity:

> The growth rate of world trade in primary products over the period 1873 to 1913 was 0.87 times the growth rate of industrial production in the developed countries; and just about the same relationship, about 0.87, also ruled in the two decades to 1973. World trade in primary products is a wider concept than exports from developing countries, *but the two are sufficiently closely related for it to serve as a proxy.* We need no elaborate statistical proof that trade depends on prosperity in the industrial countries (p. 556, emphasis added).

The italicized words contain by no means an innocuous assumption: whereas manufactures accounted for only 10 percent of developing countries' nonfuel exports in 1955, their share had risen to over 40 percent by 1978. Primary product exports can no longer serve as a proxy for developing country exports, as Lewis asserts. Nor, except for Sub-Saharan Africa, does the picture change much when the figures are disaggregated. There are big differences in the export structures of developing countries: manufactures now account for 75 percent of the exports of the four East Asian superperformers, for example. But most countries in South Asia plus Brazil, Egypt, Mexico, Tunisia, and some smaller Latin American countries (together accounting for about two-thirds of the population of the developing world) have also raised the share of manufactures in their exports (on a trade weighted basis) from an average of 15 percent in 1950 to above 50 percent in 1978.

Disaggregation also greatly weakens Lewis's link coefficient of 0.87 between the rate of growth of industrial production in industrial countries and developing country exports (see Riedel 1984). Broadly speaking, Lewis's hypothesized link is unstable over time, and the only commodities to which it seems to apply are tea and sugar. For manufactures, the dominant and growing element in developing country exports, Riedel concludes that "the evidence . . . suggests that supply rather than demand factors have principally determined LDC export performance in manufactures." This is also the conclusion of the numerous historical studies of the trade and industrialization policies of developing countries cited earlier (Little and others 1970, Balassa 1971 and 1982, Bhagwati 1978, and Krueger 1978). Despite creeping protectionism and the slowdown in industrial countries, Reidel noted that

> whereas in the 1960s LDC exports of manufactures grew almost twice as fast as DC [industrial country] real GDP . . . in the 1970s, despite a general slowdown of growth after 1973, LDC exports maintained their rapid pace, growing four times as fast as DC real GDP. (p. 67).

Thus the view of trade as the engine of growth cannot adequately explain the link between neutral or liberal trade regimes and growth.

Other studies (Streeten 1982, Cline 1982) have argued that there is a fallacy of composition in generalizing the example of the East Asian NICs to the rest of the world. They claim that if all developing countries were to switch to export promotion, the industrial countries would become protectionist in an effort to stave off a surge in developing country exports. Ranis (1985) provides a thorough critique of these views (see also Havrylyshyn 1987). Ranis writes that, with the adoption of an EP strategy, "the much more substantial growth of per capita income resulting in the exporting countries would enable them to increase their imports from the North as well as each other" (p. 544). Unless developing countries were to run continual and massive trade surpluses, the industrial countries would boost their exports to them—a powerful counterweight to any protectionist lobbies. Despite the fears expressed about the "new protectionism" in industrial countries, the fact is that protectionism has by and large been kept at bay during the deepest recession since the 1930s.

Level and Growth Effects

It seems to be as firm a stylized fact as any in the economics of developing countries: a sustained movement to an outward-oriented trade regime leads to faster growth of both exports and income. How can this be explained? Krueger (1978) argues that mere neutrality of the trade regime is not enough:

> There are numerous countries where incentives for export and import substitution have been about equal, and the results have not been spectacular . . . Although economic theory suggests that incentives for exports and for import substitution should be equated at the margin, in fact neither Brazil nor South Korea did so; during the rapid growth years [Korea after 1964 and Brazil after 1968] the bias in their regimes was toward exports (p. 282–83).

Krueger then compares two activist policies to encourage growth ("the alternative of a strictly laissez-faire regime is not explored") and argues that "a growth strategy oriented toward exports entails the development of policies that make markets and incentives function better, while an import-substitution strategy usually involves policies designed to frustrate individuals' maximizing behaviour under market incentives" (p. 284).

These statements have misled some economists (see Streeten 1982 and the riposte by Henderson 1982) to suggest that an outward-oriented strategy necesssarily involves an export bias. Of course, export promotion can be as inefficient and chaotic as protection, as India has shown (Lal 1979c). The liberal position on trade and growth (which we support) is different. As a first step it entails a neutral trade regime. The fact that such a regime does not necessarily lead to growth merely underlines the Kravis view of "trade as the handmaiden of growth," which sees internal factors as the biggest determinants of growth, with trade a helpful though not dominating influence.

However, a liberal trade regime (and an export-biased one) can help more directly than Kravis allowed to create a domestic economic system conducive to growth. This was one of Tumlir's insights developed in a series of papers in the late 1970s and early 1980s but unfortunately not consolidated into the book he was planning to write when his life was so tragically cut short. Analytically, he accepted that the case for government intervention in foreign trade can be separated from that in the domestic economy—so that, whatever view one takes of the latter, the former is unjustifiable (except for the optimal tariff case). But he argued that the analytical separation in this "management economics for governments" was misguided (Tumlir 1981). Though it mitigated some of the irrational dirigisme of governments, it nevertheless implied that market failure was ubiquitous. The canons of second-best welfare economics then allowed benevolent, omniscient, and omnipotent governments to intervene in the social interest.

There is another, clearer view of government motives and foresight. It is associated with Adam Smith and the classicists, whose modern votaries are the so-called neo-Austrians, and it recognizes the ubiquitousness of government failure. The case for a liberal trade regime then becomes part of the general case for markets against mandarins. The ideal balance between the two is discussed in Lal (1986), not in this article. But, if one accepts the need for restraints on the natural and often irrational dirigisme of mandarins in most developing countries, then the adoption of a liberal trade regime (irrespective of the ensuing gains from trade, static and dynamic) becomes an important means to this end.

This line of thought can be developed by making use of some ideas attributable to Maurice Scott on investment and growth (see Scott 1976). They also provide an antidote to the criticism by Lucas that static gains from free trade merely affect the level of income, not its rate of growth.

In the standard neoclassical growth model (Solow 1956, Swan 1956), the steady state growth of an economy—its "natural rate of growth"—is determined by the exogenously given growth rate of population (n), plus the rate of labor-augmenting (Harrod-neutral) technical progress (t) which falls like manna from heaven. Several authors, starting with Kaldor (1957), Kaldor and Mirrlees (1962), and including Arrow (1962),[19] have argued that this exogeneity of productivity growth does not explain one of the mainsprings of economic growth. In various forms they have sought to introduce the rate of investment (which in the neoclassical model only affects the level and not the rate of growth) as an endogenous determinant of technical progress. In the standard neoclassical framework, an improvement in allocative efficiency in economy A compared with (otherwise identical) economy B leads to a higher level of income per person in A; it is as if A had saved more. But income does not grow faster. This result also holds in the Arrow (1962) and Kaldor-Mirrlees (1962) type of growth models, which seek to endogenize technical progress through a technical progress function that assumes a direct link between the growth of capital per person and the rate of labor-augmenting technical progress. However, as Eltis (1973) has argued,[20] it is more plausible in endogenizing technical progress to include in the technical progress function the saving ratio instead of the rate of growth of capital. In that case an increase in allocative efficiency, which is equivalent to an increase in savings, will raise the growth rate.[21]

These ideas have been further developed by Scott (1976). He argues that "investment is . . . by definition . . . the cost of *change*, and so will cover all activities associated with growth" (p. 317) and that "growth due to capital and technical progress are *both* the result of investment" (p. 330) in the sense of "the cost, in terms of consumption forgone, of propelling the economy forward instead of leaving it in a stationary state" (p. 318). "Incurring capital expenditure leads to a rearrangement of the things of this world. It does not lead to there being any more of some substance 'capital'... There is then simply *change* which is due to investment, and to population growth. We cannot separate change which is 'more capital' from change which is 'technical progress.' We must abandon the attempt to distinguish between movements along a production function whose arguments are labor, land and *all* capital, and a shift in that function due to technical progress" (p. 331). Within his proposed framework, "the rate of increase of static income is a function of only two variables: total savings and labor force growth. There is no independent technical progress" (p. 331).

The key aspect of Scott's analysis is its emphasis on "the importance of allocation" for the growth rate. Unlike the conventional framework, which views allocative improvements as providing "a once-and-for-all increase in output and a temporary boost to the growth rate while it is occurring," Scott argues that "if, however, investment is essentially a matter of incurring costs to reallocate resources, then the efficiency with which this is done must affect the yield of investment, and so the *proportionate* rate of growth in the *long run*. So long as investment is occurring, reallocation is occurring. It is *not* once-and-for-all, but a continuing process, and, indeed, the principal source of growth in many countries" (p. 332–33).

Moreover, argues Scott, "investment at any given time is undertaken in a state of ignorance about the future. We make changes whose consequences we cannot wholly foresee, and, simultaneously, others are making changes of which we can only become aware after they are made. In the light of these changes we are then in a better position to make the next round of changes." This implies "that there is an externality to investment" (p. 334).[22] But "if the externality exists just because we are *ignorant* of the future effects of investment, it may be impossible to discover very much about the characteristics of investment that produce the externality" (p. 325).

This argument needs to be extended. It suggests the importance of an economic environment that is conducive to this ignorance-based, externality-creating form of investment. This is the place for the neo-Austrian insights concerning the role of the entrepreneur in an economic environment characterized by *ignorance* (see Lal 1986 for references and a fuller discussion). The entrepreneur is redundant in neoclassical economics, which assumes an environment of purely actuarial Knightian risk. But he is at the center of the neo-Austrian stage—creating and searching out investment opportunities and gambling on the future. Like the speculator and middle man, the entrepreneur is an economic agent who lives by making money out of irreducible Knightian uncertainty. This entrepreneurial function must, for reasons to do with incentives and information, be decentralized. To the extent that an EP strategy has to rely on this entrepreneurial function (as export markets cannot be ensured by local mandarins), it will induce the creation of that economic framework in which Scott's externality-creating investments will lead to faster growth.

The case for a free trade regime (or, as a second best, an export biased one) is thus close to that argued by the classical and neo-Austrian economists. As Keynes emphasized, the classical case against mercantilism was *not* based on laissez-faire, but rather on limiting state action to areas where such action was indispensable. These, broadly speaking, are to provide the public goods essential for the efficient functioning of market processes—law and order, stable money—and those infrastructural activities that affect public goods. The modern variant of the classical case, while accepting the need for an activist state, would seek to limit its activities. The state would be prevented from creating those policy-induced distortions that supposedly are there to cure endogenous distortions in the working of the price mechanism but which merely aggravate the level of distortions in the economy. Such distortions have led to large, though unquantifiable, losses, through diverting energies and resources from productive activities into the wasteful lobbying and rent-seeking activities so common in most developing countries. In this task of confining public action to its proper place, a free trade regime could be an important component. It would help to create an economic framework that provides the necessary incentives for entrepreneurship, productivity, and thrift. In a formal sense, these qualities are only dimly understood by economists. But they are, at bottom, the mainsprings of sustained and sustainable economic growth.

Abstract

This article surveys empirical studies of the static gains from a movement toward free trade and studies of the dynamic effects of growth in exports on per capita income. It also summarizes comparative studies of the trade regimes of developing countries undertaken in the 1960s to 1970s, which show fairly conclusively that "outward-orientation" is associated with better economic performance. The conclusions of these studies are then tested for the more volatile global environment of the 1970s and 1980s. Various arguments are weighed about the dynamic income effects of the growth in world income and trade on a free-trading country's economic growth rate—the "trade as an engine of growth" view. The closing section introduces insights of the classical writers that have reemerged in the neo-Austrian and the more recent neoclassical "new political economy" schools, which might explain the links between trade and growth performance. These emphasize the importance of the nonquantifiable aspects of a free trade (as compared with a protectionist) regime in creating a general economic framework conducive to individual entrepreneurship, productivity, and thrift. In this context we argue that free trade is the "handmaiden of growth," as it indirectly constrains the state from going beyond the bounds of necessary public action for the provision of those domestic public goods that are essential for development.

Notes

The authors wish to thank Jagdish Bhagwati and Soogol Young for valuable comments on the draft of this article and Sophie Kim, Fayez Omar, and John Wayem for research assistance. This is a revised and considerably expanded version of a paper prepared for the conference on "Free Trade in the World Economy" organized by the Institute for World Economics, Kiel. This article is dedicated to the memory of Jan Tumlir.

1. Thus it is recognised that endogenous domestic distortions may require appropriate domestic public interventions for their correction; where the country has monopoly (monopsony) power in trade and can feasibly influence its terms of trade, taxes or subsidies on trade may be justified.

2. See Srinivasan and Whalley (1986) for a comprehensive discussion and evaluation of the principal models in this genre. Also see Srinivasan (1986a, 1986b, and 1987).

3. Also see Krueger (1984), Taylor and Black (1974), and de Melo (1978), for other model-based estimates of these static gains.

4. But see the note to the figure for the decomposition of this loss into that due to the tariff and lobbying.

5. See also Tyler (1981), Heller and Porter (1978), Michaely (1979).

6. The World Bank's *World Development Report* is published annually by Oxford University Press.

7. Leamer is also quite caustic about Granger's defense that: "provided I define what I personally mean by causation, I can use the term." Leamer rightly castigates Granger for misusing common language and for misleading persuasive definitions. He writes: "I detect a certain lack of concern for the human capital that is invested in our language. If I were to continue in that tradition I would propose that we henceforth refer to this notion of precedence by the word pair: fool's causation. This substitutes a loaded word 'fool' for the neutral 'Granger' just as 'causation' has replaced the neutral 'precedence.' Moreover, 'fool' is decidely simpler than 'Granger"—it contains only four letters, one of which is repeated—and, like 'cause,' it is rather difficult to define precisely. One man's fool is another man's genius. My definition of a 'fool' would be a friend of mine living in San Diego" (Leamer 1985, p. 284). But, as Leamer is at pains to emphasize, this does not mean to imply that the atheoretical statistical technique of vector autoregressions underlying the new econometrics cannot be useful as a descriptive and perhaps a forecasting device.

8. See also McKloskey (1983) who rightly argues that the evidence adduced in support of particular economic propositions must be ecclectic and cannot be confined to the positivist statistical testing that is currently so fashionable. As Hicks argues, "the usefulness of 'statistical' or 'stochastic' methods in economics is a good deal less than is now conventionally supposed. . . Thus it is not at all sensible to take a small number of observations (sometimes no more than a dozen observations) and to use the rules of probability theory to deduce from them a 'significant' general law. For we are assuming, if we do so, that the variations from one to another of the observations are random, so that if we had a larger sample (as we do not) they would by some averaging tend to disappear. But what nonsense this is when the observations are derived, as not infrequently happens, from different countries, or localities, or industries—entities about which we may well have relevant information, but which we have deliberately decided by our procedure to ignore. By all means let us plot the points on a chart and try to explain them; but it does not help in explaining them to suppress their names. The probability calculus is no excuse for forgetfulness" (p. 122).

9. See Lal (1981), and for an emphatic reassertion of this point see Bhagwati (1986). This point is also emphasized in the last chapter of Bhagwati (1978).

In this context it may also be useful to distinguish a liberal trade regime from a neutral one. A failure to do so has caused some confusion about the nature of what different developing countries have done to liberalize their trade. A neutral trade regime is one where incentives for import substitution do not outweigh those for export promotion; but it does not rule out (essentially offsetting) trade interventions. A liberal trade regime ensures this neutrality of trade incentives, because of the absence of trade intervention. We owe this point to Soogil Young's comment on our paper at the conference.

10. For these LM shadow price estimates see the references in Little and Scott (1976); in addition see Little and others (1979) for Pakistan, Lal (1978a) for the Philippines, Lal (1978b) for Korea, Lal (1979a) for Jamaica, Lal (1980) for India, and Lal (1979c) for Sri Lanka.

11. These LM accounting ratios are the commodity-specific ratio of the domestic to border price (c.i.f./f.o.b.) of the traded good, with the dollar value of the border price converted into local currency at the official exchange rate. The effective exchange rate on exports (imports) is the units of domestic currency that can be obtained for a dollar's worth of exports (imports). Thus the rates are weighted averages of the relevant accounting ratios of traded commodities, where the weights are the actual shares in exports (imports) of the relevant commodities.

12. Wade in a private communication has stated that we have misrepresented his position, which he says is from Wade (1985): "In the comparison between Taiwan and Korea, on the one hand, and India and Latin America, on the other, the first important fact about trade regimes is that the East Asia type is more 'liberal' in the sense that the average level of protection is much lower. But the second important fact, which the neoclassical argument has tended to ignore, is that dispersion around the average is much higher in East Asia, because selective promotion of some industries requires high protection to a small number" (p. 27). However, as can be seen from tables 3 and 4, the dispersion around the average protection is also lower in Korea than India, as measured by the respective standard deviations of the accounting ratios in the two countries.

13. This is in relation to the effective exchange rates for exports and imports.

14. These countries attempted to move from Phase II to Phase III of the restrictive trade regimes in the Bhagwati-Krueger sense. See Krueger (1978).

15. Balassa's studies (1981, 1982, 1984) of forty-three countries subject to shocks in 1974–76 and 1979–81 confirm the superior response of the NICs to external shocks.

16. The export tax on wheat was reduced from 56 percent to 5 percent, on corn from 46 percent to 16 percent, and for wool from 33 percent to 16 percent from July 1976 to July 1977 (Nogues 1981).

17. The external shock to India was 2.1 percent of GNP in the 1974–78 period. See Balassa (1981).

18. Much of this is based on Lal (1983).

19. See Hahn and Matthews (1965) for a more complete survey.

20. See Dixit (1976, p. 81 and following) for a lucid discussion of the models that seek to endogenize technical progress. See also Hahn and Matthews (1965).

21. Formally in the standard Solow-Swan model, the determinants of the steady state growth rate are:

$$g_y = g_k = s/v = n + t$$

where g_y = growth rate of output
g_k = growth rate of capital
s = savings rate
v = capital output ratio
n = rate of population growth
t = rate of Harrod neutral (labor-augmenting) technical progress.

With $n + t$—the natural rate of growth—determined exogenously, changes in the savings ratio will not effect the steady state growth rate of output or capital, but through countervailing changes in the capital output ratio (v) merely lead to changes in the *levels* of capital and output per capita.

In the Eltis framework, the exogenously given technical progress term t, is replaced by an endogenously determined term whose argument is savings (s), hence in this alternative framework,

$$g_y = g_k = s/v = n + \phi(s)$$

where ϕ is an increasing concave function (see Dixit 1986, ch. 4). Actual and "as if" increases in savings because of improved efficiency will now lead to a rise in the growth *rates* of output and capital (y and k).

22. Lucas (1985) presents a neoclassical model of economic development in which a central element is an externality in human capital investment. Many of his insights would seem to complement those of Scott, except that he draws unwarranted dirigiste implications from them.

References

Arrow, K. J. 1962. "The Economic Implications of Learning by Doing." *Review of Economic Studies* 29, no. 3: 155–73.

Balassa, B. 1971. *The Structure of Protection in Developing Countries*. Baltimore, Md.: Johns Hopkins University Press.

_____. 1978. "Exports and Economic Growth: Further Evidence." *Journal of Development Economics* 5, no. 2 (June): 181–89.

_____. 1981. "The Newly Industrializing Development Countries after the Oil Crisis." *Weltwirschaftliches Archiv* 117, no. 1: 142–94.

_____. 1982. *Development Strategies in Semi-Industrial Economies*. Baltimore, Md.: Johns Hopkins University Press.

_____. 1984. *Adjustments to External Shocks in Developing Countries*. World Bank Staff Working Paper 472. Washington, D.C.

Bergsman, J. 1974. "Commercial Policy, Allocative and 'X-Efficiency.'" *Quarterly Journal of Economics* 58 (August): 409–33.

Bhagwati, J. 1978. *Foreign Trade Regimes and Economic Development Anatomy and Consequences of Exchange Control Regimes*. Cambridge, Mass.: Ballinger.

_____. 1980. "Lobbying and Welfare." *Journal of Public Economics* 14, no. 3 (December): 355–64.

_____. 1986. "Rethinking Trade Strategy." In J. P. Lewis and V. Kalleb, eds. *Development Strategies Reconsidered*. Washington, D.C.: Overseas Development Center.

Bhalla, S., and P. Glewwe. 1986. "Growth and Equity in Developing Countries: A Reinterpretation of the Sri Lankan Experience." *World Bank Economic Review* 1, no. 2: 35–63.

Calvo, G. A. 1986. "Fractured Liberalism: Argentina under Martinez de Hoz." *Economic Development and Cultural Change* 34, no. 3: 511–34.

Cline, W. R. 1982. "Can the East Asian Model of Development Be Generalised?" *World Development* 10, no. 2: 81–90.

Corbo, V., and J. de Melo. 1985. "Overview and Summary: Liberalization and Stabilization in the Southern Cone of Latin America." *World Development* 13, no. 8: 863–66.

Corden, W. M. 1974. *Trade Policy and Economic Welfare*. Oxford: Oxford University Press.

Darrat, A. F. 1986. "Trade and Development: The Asian Experience." *Cato Journal* 6, no. 2: 695–700.

de Melo, J. 1978. "Protection and Resource Allocation in a Walrasian Trade Model." *International Economic Review* 19, no. 1: 25–44.

de Melo, J., and J. Tybout. 1986. "The Effects of Financial Liberalization on Savings and Investment in Uruguay." *Economic Development and Cultural Change* 34, no. 3: 561–88.

Dixit, A. K. 1976. *The Theory of Equilibrium Growth*. Oxford: Oxford University Press.

Donges, J. 1976. "A Comparative Study of Industrialisation Policies in Fifteen Semi-Industrial Countries." *Weltwirtschftliches Archiv* 112, no. 4: 626–59.

Eltis, W. A. 1973. *Growth and Distribution*. London: Macmillan.

Feder, G. 1983. "On Exports and Economic Growth." *Journal of Development Economics* 12, no. 1/2 (February/April): 59–74.

Fishlow, A. 1985. "The State of Latin American Economics." In Inter-American Development Bank. *Economic and Social Progress in Latin America: Annual Report*. Washington, D.C.

Grais, W., and others. 1984. "A General Equilibrium Estimation of the Reduction of Tariffs and Quantitative Restrictions in Turkey in 1978." In T. N. Srinivasan and J. Whalley, eds. *General Equilibrium Trade Policy Modelling*. Cambridge, Mass.: Cambridge University Press.

Hahn, F. H., and R. C. U. Matthews. 1965. "The Theory of Economic Growth: A Survey." In American Economic Association. *Surveys of Economic Theory*, vol. 2. London: Macmillan.

Harberger, A. C. 1959. "The Fundamental of Economic Progress in Underdeveloped Countries: Using the Resources at Hand More Effectively." *American Economic Review* 49, no. 42: 134–46.

Harris, R. 1983. *Trade, Industrial Policy and Canadian Manufacturing*. Toronto: Ontario Economic Council.

Havrylyshyn, O. 1986. "Penetrating the Fallacy of Export Composition." Background paper to the *World Development Report 1987*. Washington, D.C.: World Bank, Economics and Research Staff.

Heller, P. S., and R. C. Porter. 1978. "Exports and Growth: An Empirical Re-Investigation." *Journal of Development Economics* 5, no. 2: 191–94.

Helliner, G. 1986. "Outward Orientation, Import Instability and African Economic Growth: an Empirical Investigation." In S. Lall and F. Stewart, eds. *Theory and Reality in Development*. London: Macmillan.

Henderson, P. D. 1982. "Trade Policies and 'Strategies': Case for a Liberal Approach." *World Economy* 5, no. 3: 291–302.

Hicks, J. R. 1979. *Causality in Economics*. Oxford: Blackwell.

Johnson, H. G. 1958. "The Gain for Free Trade with Europe: An Estimate." *Manchester School* 26, no. 3: 241–55.

Jung, W. S., and P. J. Marshall. 1985. "Exports, Growth and Causality in Developing Countries." *Journal of Development Economics* 18, no. 1: 1–12.

Kakwani, N. C. 1972. "On the Bias in Estimates of Import Demand Parameters." *International Economic Review* 13, no. 2: 239–44.

Kaldor, N. 1957. "A Model of Economic Growth." *Economic Journal* 67, no. 268: 591–624.

Kaldor, N., and J. A. Mirrlees. 1962. "A New Model of Economic Growth." *Review of Economic Studies* 29, no. 3: 174–92.

Kemp, M. C. 1962. "Errors of Measurement and Bias in Estimates of Import Demand Parameters." *Economic Record* 38, no. 83: 369–72.

Kravis, I. B. 1970. "Trade as a Handmaiden of Growth—Similarities between the 19th and 20th Centuries." *Economic Journal* 80, no. 320: 850–72.

Krueger, A. O. 1974. "The Political Economy of the Rent-Seeking Society." *American Economic Review* 64, no. 3: 291–303.

_____. 1978. *Foreign Trade Regimes and Economic Development: Liberalization Attempts and Consequences*. Cambridge, Mass.: Ballinger.

_____. 1984. "Trade Policies in Developing Countries." In R. W. Jones and P. B. Kenen, eds. *Handbook of International Economics*, vol. 1. New York: North Holland.

Lal, D. 1978a. *Men or Machines*. Geneva: International Labour Office.

_____. 1978b. *Estimates of Shadow Prices for Korea*. Discussion Papers in Public Economics 10. London: University College, Department of Political Economy.

_____. 1979a. "Accounting Prices for Jamaica." *Social and Economic Studies* 28, no. 3: 534–82.

_____. 1979b. "Estimates of Accounting Prices for Sri Lanka." London: University College, Department of Political Economy.

_____. 1979c. "Indian Export Incentives." *Journal of Development Economics* 6, no. 1: 103–17.

_____. 1980. *Prices for Planning*. London: Heinemann.

_____. 1981. Review of Bhagwati (1978). *Journal of Political Economy* 89, no. 4: 826.

_____. 1983. *The Poverty of Development Economics*. London: Institute of Economic Affairs.

_____. 1986. "Markets, Mandarins and Mathematicians." Paper prepared for Cato Institute Conference in Honor of Lord Bauer, May 1986. To be published in *Cato Journal*, forthcoming.

Lal, D., and S. Rajapatirana. 1987. *Impediments to Trade Liberalization in Sri Lanka*. Thames Essay No. 51. London: Gower for the Trade Policy Research Centre.

Lal, D., and M. Wolf, eds. 1986. *Stagflation, Savings and the State: Perspectives on the Global Economy*. Oxford: Oxford University Press.

Leamer, E. E. 1985. *Vector Autoregressions for Causal Inference?* Carnegie Rochester Series on Public Policy 22. Amsterdam: North Holland.

Leibenstein, H. 1966. "Allocative Efficiency vs. X-Efficiency." *American Economic Review* 56, no. 3: 392–415.

Lewis, W. A. 1980. "The Slowing Down of the Engine of Growth." *American Economic Review* 70, no. 4: 555–64.

Little, I. M. D., and others. 1970. *Industry and Trade in Some Developing Countries*. Oxford: Oxford University Press.

Little, I. M. D., and M. F. Scott. 1976. *Using Shadow Prices*. London: Heinemann.

Little, I. M. D., and others. 1979. "Shadow Pricing and Macro Economic Analysis: Some Illustrations from Pakistan." *Pakistan Development Review* 18, no. 2: 89–112.

Lucas, R. E., Jr. 1985. "The Mechanics of Economic Development." University of Chicago, Department of Economics.

Mckloskey, D. 1983. "The Rhetoric of Economics." *Journal of Economic Literature* 21, no. 2: 481–517.

Michaely, M. 1977. "Exports and Growth an Empirical Investigation." *Journal of Development Economics* 4, no. 1: 149–53.

_____. 1979. "Exports and Growth: A Reply." *Journal of Development Economics* 6, no. 1: 141–43.

Michalopoulos, C., and K. Jay. 1973. "Growth of Exports and Income in the Developing

World: A Neoclassical View." Discussion Paper 28. Washington, D.C.: U.S. Agency for International Development.

Nogues, J. 1981. "Politica Comercial y Cambiaria: Una Evaluacion Cuantitativa de la Politica Argentina Durante 1961–1981." Technical Study 52. Buenos Aires: Banco Central de la Republica Argentina.

Nurkse, R. 1961. *Equilibrium and Growth in the World Economy*. Cambridge, Mass.: Harvard University Press.

Orcutt, G. H. 1950. "Measurement of Price Elasticities in International Trade." *Review of Economics and Statistics* 32, no. 2: 117–32.

Ranis, G. 1985. "Can the East Asian Model of Development be Generalised?" *World Development* 13, no. 4: 543–45.

Riedel, J. 1984. "Trade as the Engine of Growth in Developing Countries, Revisited." *Economic Journal* 94, no. 373: 56–73.

Scitovsky, T. 1958. *Economic Theory and Western European Integration*. London: Allen and Unwin.

Scott, M. F. 1976. "Investment and Growth." *Oxford Economic Papers* 28, no. 3: 317–63.

Solow, R. M. 1956. "A Contribution to the Theory of Economic Growth." *Quarterly Journal of Economics* 70, no. 1: 65–91.

Srinivasan, T. N. 1986a. "Development Strategy: Is the Success of Outward Orientation at an End?" In S. Guhan and M. Shroff, eds. *Essays on Economic Progress and Welfare*. New Delhi: Oxford University Press.

_____. 1986b. "International Trade and Factor Movements in Development Theory, Policy and Experience." Twenty-fifth Anniversary Symposium on The State of Development Economics, April 11–13, 1986, Yale University, New Haven, Conn.

_____. 1987. "Structural Change, Economic Interdependence and World Development." In J. Dunning and M. Usui, eds. *Economic Independence*. London: Macmillan (forthcoming).

Srinivasan, T. N., and J. Whalley, eds. 1986. *General Equilibrium Trade Policy Modeling*. Cambridge, Mass.: MIT Press.

Stern, R. M., and others. 1976. *Price Elasticities in International Trade: An Annotated Bibliography*. London: Macmillan for the Trade Policy Research Centre.

Streeten, P. 1982. "A Cool Look at 'Outward-looking' Strategies for Development." *World Economy* 5, no. 1: 159–70.

Swan, T. W. 1956. "Economic Growth and Capital Accumulation." *Economic Record* 32, no. 2: 334–61.

Taylor, L., and S. L. Black. 1974. "Practical General Equilibrium Estimation of Resource Pulls under Trade Liberalisation." *Journal of International Economics* 4, no. 1: 37–58.

Tullock, G. 1967. "The Welfare Costs of Tariffs, Monopolies and Theft." *Western Economic Journal* 5, no. 3: 224–32.

Tumlir, J. 1981. "The Contribution of Economics to International Disorder." Second Harry G. Johnson Memorial Lecture. Trade Policy Research Centre, London.

Tyler, W. 1981. "Growth and Export Expansion in Developing Countries: Some Empirical Evidence." *Journal of Development Economics* 9, no. 1: 121–30.

Wade, R. 1985. "The Role of Government in Overcoming Market Failure: Taiwan, South Korea and Japan." In Helen Hughes, ed. *Explaining the Success of East Asian Industrialisation*. Cambridge: Cambridge University Press.

11

International Capital Flows and Economic Development

DEEPAK LAL

Introduction

The role of international capital in economic development has been one of Ian Little's major interests. His 1965 book, *International Aid*, with Juliet Clifford still provides one of the few balanced discussions of 'the flow of public resources from rich to poor countries' (as stated in its subtitle). Since then he has developed the well-known Little–Mirrlees method of project analysis (Little and Mirrlees, 1969, 1974) which is now widely used in the appraisal of aid-financed projects in developing countries. He has also provided clear-headed accounts of the costs and benefits of direct investment in developing countries in Little (1972), and his 1972 study with David Tipping of the Kulai palm-oil estate was one of the first empirical social cost benefit analyses of a major foreign investment in a developing country.

All these discussions and analyses were timely, as official capital flows and direct investment have been the major forms of international capital available to the Third World since the Second World War. But since the mid 1970's (see Fig. 11.1 and Table 11.1) these have been overshadowed by private portfolio lending in the form of syndicated bank loans (which in the late 1970s were almost of the same magnitude as official flows) and private export credits (which were almost of the same magnitude as direct investments in the same period).

These new forms of foreign capital have, however, turned out to be a mixed blessing for their recipients, many of whom are now in a 'debt crisis' which has dominated discussions of the international economy in the 1980s. Not surprisingly, much of the analytical and empirical work by economists in the last decade has therefore been concerned with various aspects of this 'debt crisis'. But given the continuing importance of official capital flows in the overall flow of capital to developing countries, and the growing 'aid fatigue' of the major donors in the 1980s, there has been revived interest in justifying and evaluating the contribution that official capital flows can make to development. There has also been a revival of interest in promot-

I am grateful to Maurice Scott for comments on an earlier draft which greatly helped to improve this chapter.

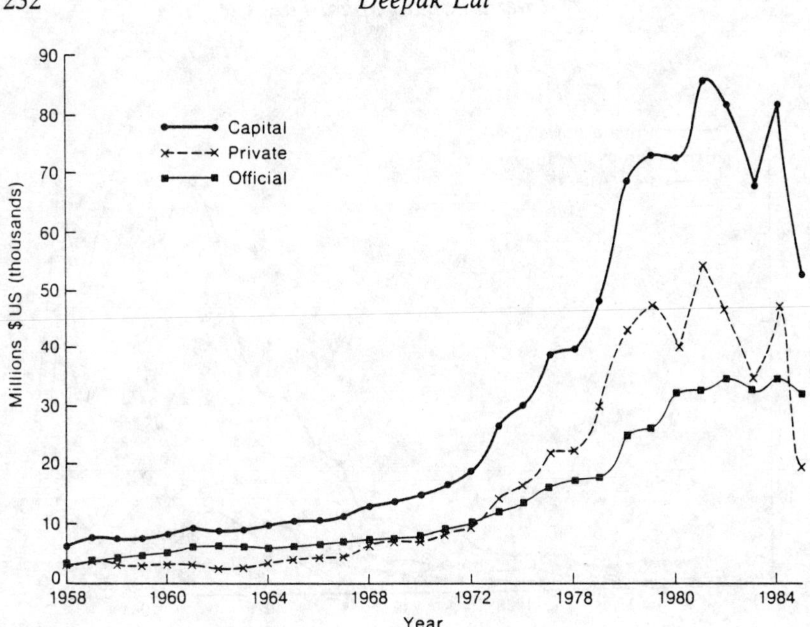

Fig. 11.1 (*a*) Capital, official and private flows, 1956–1985

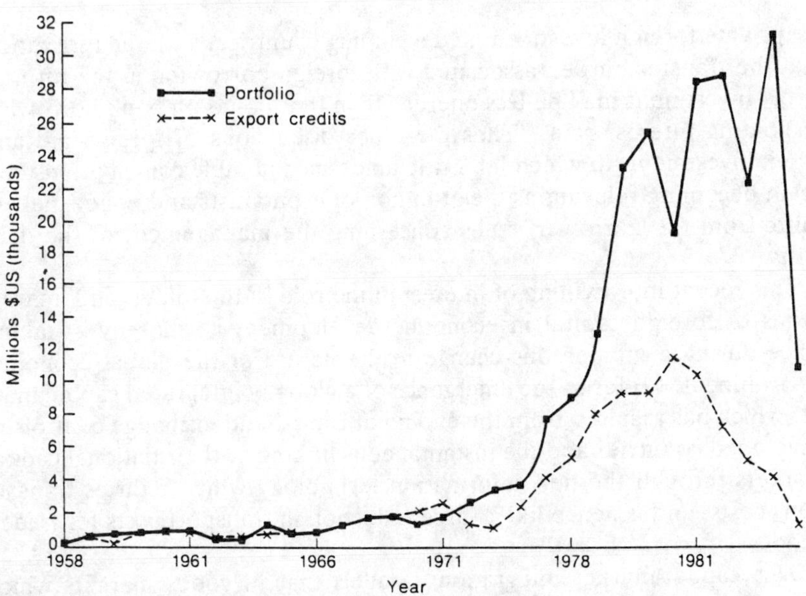

Fig. 11.1 (*b*) Portifolio and export credits, 1956–1985

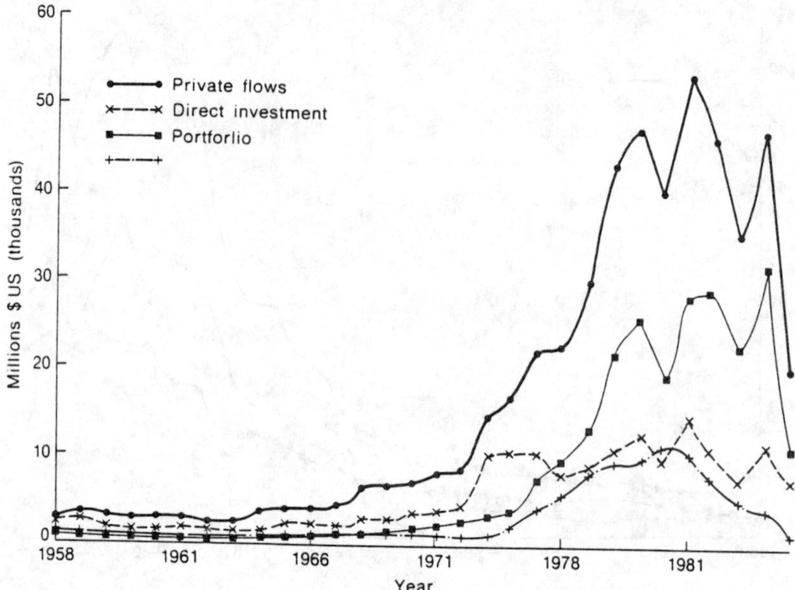

Fig. 11.1 (*c*) Private flows, 1956–1985

ing private foreign investment in developing countries, with the realization that the transfer burden associated with foreign borrowing in the form of direct investment may be less onerous than that based on bank borrowing at floating interest rates. Thus the older discussions of foreign aid and direct investment, to which Ian Little made such notable contributions, are again becoming relevant as the attention of economists and policy-makers shifts from the narrower issues concerning the management of the debt crisis.

This recent intertwining of interest in the role of the 'older' and 'newer' forms of foreign capital in economic development is, moreover, taking place during a momentous change in the nature of the global economic environment. I refer to the emergence of a globally integrated capital market which has resulted from the ending of capital and exchange controls in developed countries and the instantaneous linking of their national capital markets through the new information technology which reduces transactions costs, and is hence like a large reduction in transport costs for traded goods.

This capital-market integration parallels that in goods markets which was achieved in the first two decades after the Second World War as a result of various GATT rounds of multilateral tariff reductions. We know,

TABLE 11.1. Private capital flows and official grants and loans from DAC countries to developing countries, 1956–1985 (million $US)

Year	Direct investment	Portfolio and bank lending	Private export credits	Total private flows	Total official flows (inc. grants)	Total capital flows (inc. grants)
1956	2,350	190	458	2,998	3,260	6,258
1957	2,724	601	454	3,779	3,856	7,635
1958	1,970	733	214	2,917	4,387	7,304
1959	1,782	691	347	2,820	4,311	7,131
1960	1,767	837	546	3,150	4,965	8,115
1961	1,829	704	573	3,106	6,143	9,249
1962	1,495	386	572	2,453	5,984	8,437
1963	1,603	296	660	2,557	6,015	8,572
1964	1,572	1,298	859	3,729	5,916	9,645
1965	2,468	902	751	4,121	6,199	10,320
1966	2,179	625	1,124	3,959	6,431	10,390
1967	2,105	1,269	1,007	4,381	7,060	11,441
1968	3,043	1,738	1,596	6,377	7,047	13,424
1969	2,910	1,630	2,047	6,587	7,192	13,779
1970	3,557	1,251	2,211	7,019	7,984	15,003
1971	3,874	1,617	2,724	8,215	9,030	17,245
1972	4,306	2,695	1,429	8,430	10,195	18,625
1973	10,254	3,543	1,196	14,993	11,841	26,834
1974	10,350	3,795	2,482	16,627	13,499	30,126
1975	10,494	7,792	4,142	22,428	16,611	39,039
1976	7,824	9,169	5,424	22,417	16,971	39,388
1977	8,792	13,096	8,100	29,988	18,015	48,003
1978	10,906	23,265	9,400	43,571	25,381	68,952
1979	12,745	25,537	9,408	47,690	25,714	73,404
1980,	9,769	19,171	11,490	40,430	32,536	72,966
1981	14,639	28,548	10,593	53,780	32,243	86,023
1982	10,385	28.843	7,328	46.556	35,191	81,747
1983	7,792	22,370	5,249	35,411	32,471	67,882
1984	11,269	31.815	4,239	47,322	34,934	82,256
1985	7.690	10,927	1,506	20,123	32,783	52,906

Note: Private flows = Direct investment + Portfolio and bank lending + Private export credits

Capital flows = Total official flows + Total private flows.

Sources: OECD *Development Co-operation Review* (1986) and earlier editions of the same.

largely as a result of Ian Little's pioneering research (Little *et al.*, 1970) that the relative economic performance of many developing countries in the 1960s and 1970s was in part determined by their reaction to the vastly expanded and growing opportunities for foreign trade. Hence, we may hypothesize that the future prospects of particular Third World countries will depend upon how they react to the new opportunities presented by the integration of world capital markets.

It may, therefore, be useful to provide an eclectic, but by no means comprehensive, survey of the insights to be gleaned from the large literature on foreign capital and economic development to see how public policy in developing countries can best be adapted to these new emerging trends in the global economy. This is the purpose of this chapter, which is in three sections. The first, examines analyses which attempt to explain the determinants and effects of capital flows at an aggregate level. Our purpose in this section is also to provide a translation of various recent theoretical models whose mathematical virtuosity is rarely matched by expository clarity. We attempt to show that they can be integrated fairly simply into the standard geometric tool-kit employed by more old-fashioned economists! It might therefore serve a heuristic purpose. It also attempts to judge these models in terms of the historical evidence on capital flows.

Section 2 of the chapter examines the arguments surrounding the determinants, and costs and benefits, of particular forms in which capital has been transferred to developing countries.

Section 3 looks at the role capital flows could play in development in an increasingly integrated global economy, from the more novel viewpoint of 'neo-classical' political economy.

1. Theoretical Determinants and Effects of Aggregate Capital Flows

At its simplest, foreign capital flows transfer savings from one group of countries to another. Writing in 1961, Sir Alec Cairncross noted:

> When we turn to the theory of international capital flows we are struck at once by its astonishing formalism. . . . I doubt whether even today we have formulated a theory of investment that does justice to the historical experience. . . . Existing theory does not even pose, much less answer the questions. . . . What governs the division of a country's savings between home and foreign investment? What determines which countries will lend and which will borrow? What causes the total volume of international investment to expand or contract? . . . Why do countries that are not inherently incapable of mastering the techniques of modern industry fail to obtain from abroad the resources that might transform them? (Cairncross, 1961, p. 50).

In this section we outline the answers which have or could be provided to Cairncross's questions, as well as our judgements on their validity in the light of the historical record. As Cairncross noted, it is useful to categorize the answers in terms of two different approaches. The first is the mainstream neo-classical general equilibrium framework in which 'we make comparisons between the marginal productivity of capital in different countries and relative rates of interest and profit in order to bring out the market forces governing the international flow of capital' (Cairncross, 1961, p. 51). The second is what nowadays would be called the 'structuralist' approach, which views 'capital requirements as a more or less fixed proportion of output, without much regard to interest rates or variations in capital/output ratios' (Cairncross, 1961).[1]

As much of conventional development economics has been formulated within the second framework we briefly outline the rationale for capital inflows it has provided before examining recent explanations within the former neo-classical framework.

1.1. 'Structuralist' Theories

The structuralist rationales are in a direct line of descent from neo-Marxist theories of the determinants of capital flows between developed and developing countries, due to Hobson and Lenin. They expound what Cairncross calls the 'sink' theory of capital flows. It is assumed that there are fixed capital/output ratios in each country, and that at some stage rich capitalist countries save more than they can invest at home. They then 'need a convenient "sink" for [these surplus savings] such as foreign investment could provide' (Cairncross, 1961, p. 51). There is a large neo-Marxist literature on the resulting economic imperialism towards which developed countries are impelled. It has a modern garb in 'dependency theory' of which Ian Little provided a masterly critique in his book on *Economic Development*. We cannot appraise these neo-Marxist theories in this chapter, (but see Lal, 1983). However, it is important to note that the dominant 'structuralist' theory which even today views developing countries as being endemically short of capital, harks back to this neo-Marxist origin. Keynes, too, flirted with this view because of his fears about secular stagnation in developed countries resulting from over savings (see Cairncross, 1961). Such views seem particularly strange today, when the largest capitalist economy, the USA, is currently suffering from an acute shortage of savings (see Lal and Wolf, 1986).

In developing countries this neo-Marxist and neo-Keynesian 'structuralist' view is used 'to demonstrate that. underdeveloped countries have a

[1] The latter approach looks at the world as being relatively inflexible in production and consumption. I like to call it, 'kinky', as it is based on assuming kinky production and consumption sets, such that there is little substitutability in production or consumption. See Little (1982) and Lal (1983, 1985) for critiques.

chronic shortage of capital and would develop more rapidly if they could borrow more abroad or find an assortment of fairy godmothers, preferably of international extraction, to bless them with grants and low interest loans' (Cairncross, ibid.).

The most famous of the structuralist explanations for a chronic need in developing countries for capital inflows is the so-called 'two gap' or 'foreign exchange bottleneck view' propounded by Chenery-Strout (1966) and McKinnon (1964).[2] This was enshrined in various formulae for determining 'aid requirements' by international and bilateral aid agencies. Its logic and limitations can be readily explained (see Lal, 1972).

In these two-gap theories, Nurkse's (1961) pessimism about the post-war export prospects of developing countries was carried to its logical extreme by assuming that the export proceeds of developing countries could not be increased. Furthermore it was assumed that domestic production required imported inputs, in the form of capital and intermediate goods, in set proportions. Production could not, therefore, be increased above a level determined by the quantity of imports which the fixed export earnings could finance. Even if a country was willing to save and invest a larger proportion of its income to finance growth, it would not be able to transform the savings into higher income and output because of the inexorable limit set by the 'fixed' export earnings. The incremental savings could not be transformed into the foreign exchange to finance the import requirements of additional investment.[3] The country was now stuck in a foreign exchange bottle-neck independent of any savings constraint.

This chronic balance-of-payments constraint on a country's development could not be cured by the orthodox means of raising the price of foreign exchange (through a devaluation) to induce an increase in the supply of and a reduction in the demand for this 'good' which was inhibiting growth. For both these effects had been ruled out by assumption. Either the volume of exports was limited by world demand; or an increased volume of exports could be sold only at declining prices on world markets without any rise in foreign exchange earnings. Thus, raising the price of foreign exchange would not increase its supply, whilst the technologically fixed import requirements of domestic output meant that, for any quantity of output, raising the price of foreign exchange would have no effect on demand for it.

[2] Ian Little, indeed, can be looked upon as an early proponent of this view, see Little (1960). But he has since eschewed it. See Little (1982).

[3] There are four assumptions which must hold simultaneously for a country to be in a foreign exchange bottle-neck: (i) the import content of current production must be unalterable; (ii) there must be no further possibilities of import substitution; (iii) export earnings must be completely inelastic, and (iv) the marginal social utility of current consumption must be zero. If *any* of these assumptions is relaxed the country cannot be in a foreign exchange bottle-neck. See Lal (1972).

The only available options were for government to husband its foreign exchange fund for use in 'essential' industries and to seek to augment it through concessional foreign loans and grants.

The assumptions required to generate a foreign exchange gap independently of a savings gap are highly unrealistic. First, even if export earnings from traditional primary commodities are inelastic it is possible to diversify exports into lines where foreign demand is more elastic, as many countries have done (see Riedel, 1984). Second, it is only in the very short run that the import intensity of domestic production will be fixed. Over the medium term import substitutes can be readily developed. Third, it is difficult to believe that the social utility of current consumption in countries which are poor could ever fall to zero—another necessary assumption for the foreign exchange bottle-neck to exist. Thus, the 'foreign exchange' gap aspect of the 'two gap' theories is extremely implausible. In fact, as the development of the Gang of Four—whose significance was first noted in Little *et al.* (1970)—and many other countries has shown, those which have maintained relatively open trade regimes and developed broadly in line with their comparative advantage have faced no chronic foreign exchange shortage. Instead, it is those 'inward-looking' countries of which India remains a prime example whose protectionist trade and exchange rate policies have created an artificial scarcity of foreign exchange. For these countries the theory of the foreign exchange bottle-neck became a self-fulfilling prophecy by *leading* to the very retardation of export earnings and irreducibility of minimum import requirements which were its premises (see Lal, 1983, 1985).

In historical perspective, even the 'savings gap' version of the 'two gap' view as an explanation of the determinants of capital flows is puzzling. First, as Lewis (1978) has emphasized, in the nineteenth century when some of the current developed countries were developing, the flow of international capital was not always from rich to poor countries. Thus nineteenth-century per capita income was higher in the major borrowing countries (the United States, Australia, and Argentina) than in the lending countries (the UK, France, and Germany). Second, it is likely that saving rates were higher in the borrowing countries of new settlements than in Europe in the nineteenth century. It is not evident that capital has necessarily flowed from high-to low-savings countries (see Kuznets, 1966, Table 5.3). Third, the savings performance of developing countries in the post Second World War period (see Lluch, 1986) shows that nearly all the developing countries (including those in Africa until the early 1970s) have steadily raised domestic savings rates since the 1950s. Whilst an economic explanation of this unexpected and remarkable savings behaviour is still awaited, it would seem to undermine the view that foreign capital is necessarily required to supplement fixed and inadequate domestic savings. Finally, differences in economic performance (in terms of growth rates) seem to be related more to the differences in the productivity of investment than its level.

1.2. Neo-Classical Theories

We therefore turn to the neo-classical, general equilibrium explanations for the determinants of international capital flows. The basic framework used has been an extension of the autarkic Solow–Swan neo-classical growth model (with one or two sectors) to two large countries (or regions) with perfect capital mobility between them, or to one small country which shifts from portfolio autarky and is faced by an exogenously determined world interest rate. To set ideas, it is useful to consider the simple static version of these two-country models due to MacDougall (1960), Kemp (1966), and Jones (1967). Differences in the autarkic interest rates (which are assumed equal to the respective marginal products of capital) in the two countries lead to capital flows between them until a common interest rate (and hence marginal productivity of capital) is established. There are the normal 'gains from trade' depicted in Fig. 11.2 (whose note provides an explanation), and this establishes the superiority of foreign trade in capital services to portfolio autarky within the standard neo-classical framework. Also, in parallel with the results from trade theory, if a country can influence the terms on which it can borrow or lend, then there is an 'optimum tariff'-type case for an optimum tax on the relevant capital flows (see Jones, 1967). This is the basis of Harberger's (1986) argument that as most developing countries face an upward-sloping supply of syndicated bank credit, they should levy an optimal tax on such borrowing to equate its tax-inclusive average cost to the higher marginal cost.

1.3. Steady-State Growth Theories

A dynamic version of the Kemp–MacDougall model can also be readily provided (Ruffin, 1979). There are a number of other dynamic models which have been propounded, but most of these are, in Ian Little's words, 'useless theoretical toys'. We provide an outline of the simplest of these steady-state models, which establishes whatever insights there are to be gleaned from this literature.[4]

Consider two standard Solovian economies with *differing* technologies but *identical* growth rates of the effective labour force, producing a single traded commodity which can be consumed or invested either at home or abroad. The accumulated investments of the commodity represent the capital stocks (K and K^*) *owned* by the two countries (but not necessarily located in them). The savings rates are constant and a fixed proportion s and s^* of the per capita income y and y^* in the home and foreign countries

[4] See the surveys in Jones and Kennen (1984) by Ruffin (1986), Findlay (1984).

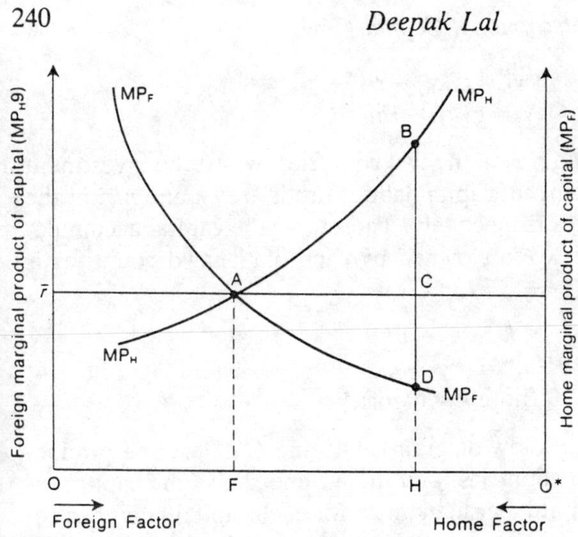

Fig. 11.2

Note: MP_H is the home country and MP_F the foreign country's marginal product of capital curve. Before capital mobility the foreign country's capital stock is OH, the home country's O*H. With capital mobility a common interest rate of r is established and HF of the foreign country's capital stock is placed in the home country. The foreign country gains ACD and the home country ACB. For the foreign country loses output ADHF (the area under the MP_F curve) and it gains capital income of ACHF (the capital flow HF times the interest rate r) whilst the home country gains output ABHF (area under MP_H curve) but has to pay area ACHF for the capital inflow.

respectively. Labour in efficiency units, L and L^*, in the home and foreign country is assumed to be growing at the same rate n. Assume that the home country locates D units of its capital abroad. The per capita capital stocks producing output in the two countries are then:

$$\begin{aligned} k_h &= k - d \quad (\text{where } k = K/L \text{ and } d = D/L) \\ k_f &= k^* + bd \quad (\text{where } b = L/L^*). \end{aligned} \tag{11.1}$$

Output in both countries is a function of the capital stocks *located* in the two countries $(f(k_h);\ g(k_f))$. With perfect capital mobility, as in the Kemp–MacDougall theory, the rate of interest (r) is equated to the marginal products of the capital stocks *located* in the two countries that is

$$r = f^1(k_h) = g^1(k_f). \tag{11.2}$$

Per capita incomes in the home (y_h) and the foreign (y_f) country are then the domestic output plus (minus) the interest payments on the capital stock located abroad (at home). That is

$$y_{\mathrm{h}} = f(k_{\mathrm{h}}) + rd$$
$$y_{\mathrm{f}} = g(k_{\mathrm{f}}) - rbd. \tag{11.3}$$

Per capita savings is sy_{h} and s^*y_{f} in the two countries, whilst the investment required to maintain the current capital/labour ratios are nk and nk^* in the home and foreign countries respectively. Therefore, the capital accumulation or decumulation per worker owned by each of the two countries is given by

$$\dot{k} = sy_{\mathrm{h}} - nk$$
$$\dot{k}^* = s^*y_{\mathrm{f}} - nk^* \tag{11.4}$$
$$(\text{note } \dot{k} = \mathrm{d}k/\mathrm{d}t).$$

In Fig. 11.3 (the standard Solow diagram), OZ and OZ* are the production functions for the two countries, and the nk line shows the capital requirements to maintain capital per man intact for each capital/labour ratio, given the *common* rate of growth of the effective labour force of n. Initially assume that, under autarky, the two economies are in steady-state equilibrium with capital/labour ratios (both owned and those nationally located) of k_1^*, in the foreign and k_1 in the home country. Output and income per head is $Z_1^* = y_{\mathrm{f}1}$ and $Z_1 = y_{\mathrm{h}1}$ respectively, and savings per head are s_1^* and s_1 which are just sufficient to maintain the respective autarkic capital/output and capital/labour ratios constant with effective labour growing at the rate n. The marginal product of capital at Z_1^* is greater than that at Z_1.

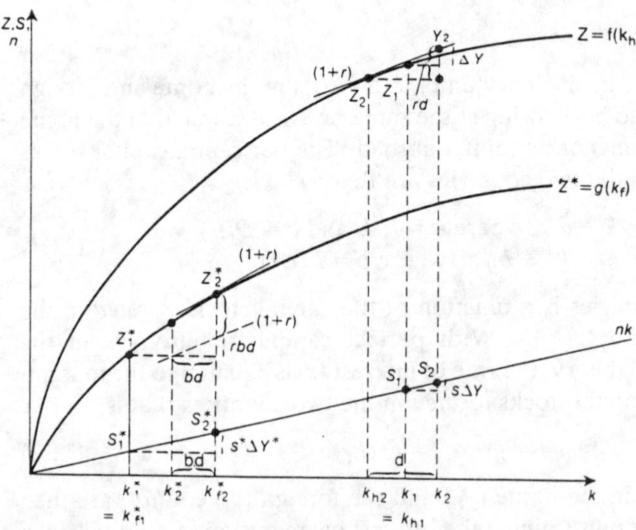

Fig. 11.3

Once free trade in capital is allowed the two economies will converge to the new output equilibrium given by Z_2^* and Z_2; with *owned* capital/labour ratios of k_2^* and k_2, and domestically located capital/labour ratios of k_{f2}^* and k_{h2} for the foreign and home country respectively. This new steady state will have come about as a result of steady-state capital flows per head of d (the difference between k_{h2} and k_2) for the home country, which are equivalent to inflows of bd (the difference between k_2^* and k_{f2}^*—also note that as drawn we are assuming that $b = L/L^* < 1$, namely that the capital-importing country is more populous than the exporting one).[5] The marginal product of capital on the *nationally located* capital stocks is the same and equal to the common world interest rate r. Per capita income is given by $Z_2 + rd = Y_{h2}$ for the home country, and by $Z_2^* - rbd$ for the foreign country. In the new open-economy steady state the extra savings generated by the increases in per capita income Δy^* and Δy, namely $s^*\Delta y^*$ and $s\Delta y$ are just sufficient to maintain the new steady-state capital/labour ratios constant in the two economies.

Clearly, as a result of capital mobility, income per head, as well as *owned* capital per head will be higher in both economies. However, as in the capital-exporting economy, the marginal product of nationally located capital rises (from the slope at Z_1 to Z_2), the wage rate will fall. The converse change in factor prices will occur in the capital-importing country.

1.4. *Stages in the Balance of Payments*

This is as much as can be learnt from this steady-state analysis. As with much of growth theory its relevance to the real world is likely to be tenuous. For instance, these models seem to suggest that there would be a tendency for some countries to be perpetual capital exporters and others to be capital importers. However, from the historical evidence this has not been true—most dramatically in the case of the US, which was a large borrower for much of the nineteenth century, became a lender for much of this century, and has recently become the world's largest borrower of foreign capital.

[5] Stated in terms of the capital stocks *located* in the two countries the flows of investment between the two countries are:

$$\text{for the home country } I_h = [sy_h - nk_h]L$$
$$\text{for the foreign country } I_f = [s^*y_f - nk_f]L^*.$$

Using (11.1) we have the investment flows in terms of *owned* capital stocks.

$$I_h = [sy_h - n(k - d)]L$$
$$I_f = [s^*y_f - n(k^* + bd)]L^*.$$

In the steady state as $\dot{k} = \dot{k}^* = 0$, we have from (11.4) that

$$sy_h = nk \text{ and } s^*y_f = nk^*,$$
$$\text{so } I_f = I_h = dL = bdL^*.$$

These fluctuations in the status of particular countries as importers or exporters of capital have to be matched by equivalent fluctuations in their balance of payments on current account to effect the necessary transfers on the capital account. Cairnes (1874) was the first to suggest a theory of stages in the balance of payments corresponding to various stages in the development of an economy. This idea has been developed by Kindleberger (1968) and a number of models have been devised to explain this supposedly historical phenomenon (see Fischer and Frenkel, 1972). This 'stages' approach also underlies the various arithmetic models of debt cycles (see Domar 1950, and Avramovic *et al.* 1964) which have been popular in the literature on developing countries, and have recently been revived to outline adjustment paths for the major debtor countries (see Selowsky and van der Tak, 1986).

In a sense the 'stages' approach to the determinants of capital flows and the evolution of debt and the balance of payments follows from a purely mechanical arithmetic model, which is in effect the basis of most current 'debt cycle' models. Recent theoretical models (see Fischer and Frenkel, 1972) by contrast have attempted to provide some general equilibrium analyses which would generate the 'debt cycles' as part of the endogenous evolution of a growing economy as it approaches the steady state. It is argued that a developing country will pass through various stages, from being a debtor to a mature creditor. During this transition, initially the debtor will run deficits on both its trade and current accounts. Then as it becomes an adult debtor it will have a surplus on trade but a deficit on current account because of debt-service obligations. In the following stage as the country repays its debt it will still be a net debtor but will run a current account surplus till it becomes a net creditor when both its trade and current accounts are in surplus, and then the final stage is reached when the country is a mature creditor with a trade deficit, but current account surplus based on its interest earnings from its foreign assets.[6] Ruffin (1979) and Engel and Kletzer (1987) show how the interaction of savings and investment decisions in each country can lead to the balance-of-payments stages in the approach to the steady state. In terms of the model depicted by Fig. 11.3, this would involve a cyclical adjustment of the *owned* capital stocks (k, k^*) in the approach to the steady state (see Ruffin, 1979). We cannot go into the details but the economics of these models are rather contrived. Moreover, it does seem that these models are probably

[6] Bazdarich (1978) in an optimal savings model shows that these stages cannot exist! This is because he assumes a constant rate of time-preference. Engel and Kletzer (1987) show how the 'stages' in the balance of payments can be generated if the dubious Uzawa (1968) assumption that the rate of time-preference increases with the level of steady-state consumption is incorporated into a two-sector model consisting of traded and non-traded goods.

trying to explain a non-existent historical phenomenon. Even in his 1968 resurrection of the 'stages' notion Kindleberger noted that the historical experience of the UK and US does not fit the model too well—a conclusion which is strengthened with the 'mature' US currently a big borrower running a massive current account deficit.

1.5. Urbanization and the Need for Foreign Capital

More interesting for our purposes are two empirical features of the historical record of foreign borrowing emphasized by Lewis. The first as we have noted is that, unlike most of the models discussed above, capital flows have not necessarily been from 'rich' high-saving and, therefore, presumably low time-preference to 'poor' low-saving and hence high time-preference countries. In fact, as Lewis puts it: 'If Britain and France were saving enough to be lending in the middle of the 19th century, when they were not much richer than Ceylon or Brazil is today, why cannot the developing countries now save for themselves all the capital they need?' (Lewis, 1978, p. 39). His answer to this rhetorical question is that it is differences in rates of urbanization which explain which countries in the past were lenders or borrowers—the second feature of past foreign capital flows. In the ninetheeth century, European countries whose urban populations were growing by less that 3 per cent p.a. loaned to the countries—mainly of 'new settlement'—where urban populations were growing well above that rate. Urbanization Lewis claims is intensive in the provision of infrastructure which uses both more physical and human capital per unit of output than equivalent rural infrastructure. Thus, in Lewis's view, the urbanization induced by population growth in the Third World since the Second World War is the prime determinant of their excess demand for capital and hence for foreign borrowing.

Prima facie, this view has some plausibility. Consider a standard neoclassical two-good two-factor model of an open economy, where the two goods are a composite tradable good (assuming a small country which faces given world prices for its exports and imports) and a non-traded good, produced by capital and labour. Assume that there is perfect capital mobility so that the domestic rental on capital is equated to the world interest rate. With the world price of tradables and the interest rate given by world markets, the price of non-traded goods and the real wage will also be fully determined.

Assume that, initially, at this relative price of the two commodities the economy is in internal and external balance with no net capital inflows and outflows, and hence the desired and actual domestic capital stocks are the same. Now assume with Lewis that there is an increase in urbanization and hence in the demand for the non-traded good, *which is more capital-intensive* than the tradable good. The emerging excess demand for the non-traded good cannot, *ex hypothesi*, be met through foreign trade. It requires an expansion of non-traded good output. If, however, non-traded good output were to expand, induced by an increase in the short run in the relative price of the non-traded good, the real wage would have to fall and the rental on capital to rise. For the labour-intensive tradable good sector will be releasing less capital relative to labour than is required by the expanding non-traded good sector. The rise in the domestic rental rate on capital would induce an inflow of capital to restore the original wage/rental ratio and permit the old relative price equilibrium to be restored, but (following Rybczynski, 1955) with an absolute increase in the output of non-traded and fall in the output of traded goods. Fig. 11.4 illustrates the argument. It shows how in a general equilibrium framework there can be an excess demand for capital generated by a pattern of domestic demand which is biased towards non-traded capital-intensive goods.

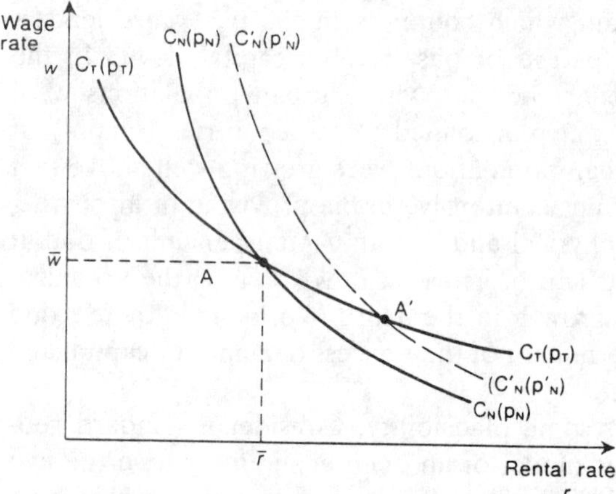

Fig. 11.4

Note: C_T and C_N are the iso cost curves for the two composite commodities, 'tradables' and the 'non-tradables' respectively. It is assumed that, the non-traded good is more capital-intensive than the traded good, and hence C_N has a steeper slope at every wage–rental combination than C_T. The price of the traded good P_T and the rental rate $\overline{r}$ are given by the world market. This then determines P_N and $\overline{W}$. Initially, equilibrium is at A. With a rise in the demand for non-traded goods, the D_N curve shifts outwards. The short-run equilibrium is at A′ with a lower wage and higher rental rate. The latter induces a capital inflow which expands non-traded good output, reducing its price, and thus restoring the initial equilibrium (in factor prices space) at A, but with (following Rybczynski) a reduction in the output of the traded and expansion in that of the non-traded good.

1.6. Foreign Finance of Public Sector Deficits

Moreover, if as is common in most developing countries, a significant portion of non-traded goods in the form of infrastructure services are publicly provided there will be an excess demand for capital in the *public sector*. As I have argued elsewhere (Lal and van Wijnbergen, 1985) endemic public sector deficits may then emerge which cannot be financed through domestic taxation or borrowing. Governments may then seek to close the deficits either through levying the inflation tax (as has been common in many developing countries) or through foreign borrowing. We would therefore expect that there would be a positive association between urbanization and public expenditure and between government deficits and the growth of the debt/GDP ratio across developing countries. The evidence on the former is discussed in Lluch (1986), which broadly confirms that the level of urbanization and the share of government expenditure are correlated in a sample of 50 countries (Mitra, 1978). The evidence on deficits and debt was recently examined in the World Bank's *World Development Report 1985* and is reproduced in Fig. 11.5. This confirms a statistically significant positive association between the growth of debt and of government budget deficits in many developing countries between 1972 and 1982.[7]

Just as there are demographically determined pressures for capital-intensive urbanization which create an excess demand for capital in the provision of publicly provided infrastructure in developing countries, in recent years demographic pressures arising from the ageing of OECD populations, related to old-age-related public expenditures on health and pensions, have also put pressure on public finance in developed countries. In Lal and van Wijnbergen (1985) we have developed and calibrated a global model in which the interaction of the public sectors in developed and developing countries is the major determinant of world interest rates (as well as the terms of trade between the North and the South) in an integrated world economy.[8]

Consider a world consisting of three regions, the OECD, OPEC, and LDC's. Each is completely specialized in producing its 'own' good. OPEC produces oil, which is used as an intermediate input in the production of

[7] The mechanism envisaged in the *World Development Report* is that the growth in government expenditure leads to *growing* fiscal deficits which lead to balance-of-payments crises which in turn lead to the *growth* of debt.

[8] The discussion of global interactions in Part I of the *World Development Report 1984* was based on this model, whilst an updated econometrically estimated version by van Wijnbergen (1985) formed the basis for the global projections in the *World Development Report 1985*. The econometrics, not surprisingly, can be questioned as is usual of this genre. See the discussion of van Wijnbergen (1985) in particular by Wickens (1985). But I would still stand by the argument justifying the structure and the qualitative conclusion concerning the global outcomes resulting from the interactions of public sectors analysed by the model, as discussed at length in Lal and van Wijnbergen (1985, 1986).

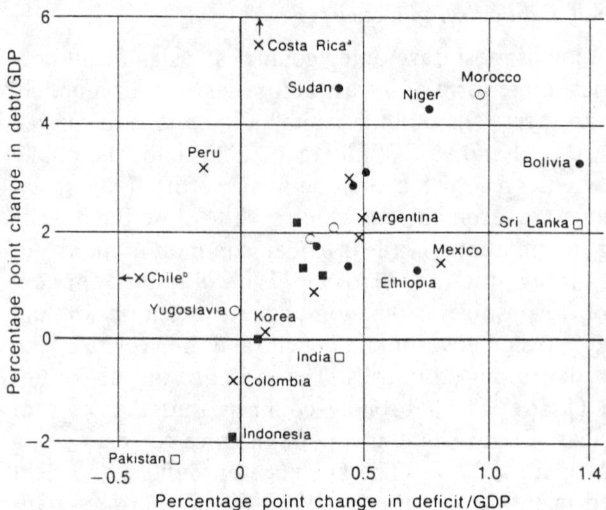

× Latin America and Caribbean
□ South Asia
○ Europe and North Africa
● Sub-Saharan Africa
■ East Asia and Pacific

Fig. 11.5 Growth of debt and government budget deficits in selected developing countries, 1972–1982

[a] Percentage point change in debt/GDP for Costa Rica equals 7.0.
[b] Percentage point change in deficit/GDP for Chile equals −1.3.
Note: Percentage point changes in debt/GDP and deficit/GDP are annual averages based on trend line calculations. Deficit data are not available for all countries for each year in the period shown. The positive relationship between growth of deficits and debt is significant at the 99 % confidence level, with $R^2 = 0.51$ for a sample of 25 countries.

Source: IMF *Government Finance Statistics* 1984; World Bank data.

From *World Development Report 1985*, OUP, 1985, p. 62.

the single, final consumer-good produced by each of the other regions. It is assumed that savings rates are highest in the OPEC region, followed by those in the OECD region, with LDC's being the lowest net savers. There is free trade in commodities and capital. There are two endogenous variables which are determined as part of the world equilibrium—the world rate of interest (r), and the terms of trade of the LDC's *vis-à-vis* the OECD (t). Two basic equations can be derived for the world equilibrium, one of which requires the *world* current account W to be equal to zero. The other requires excess demand for OECD (D) goods to be zero.

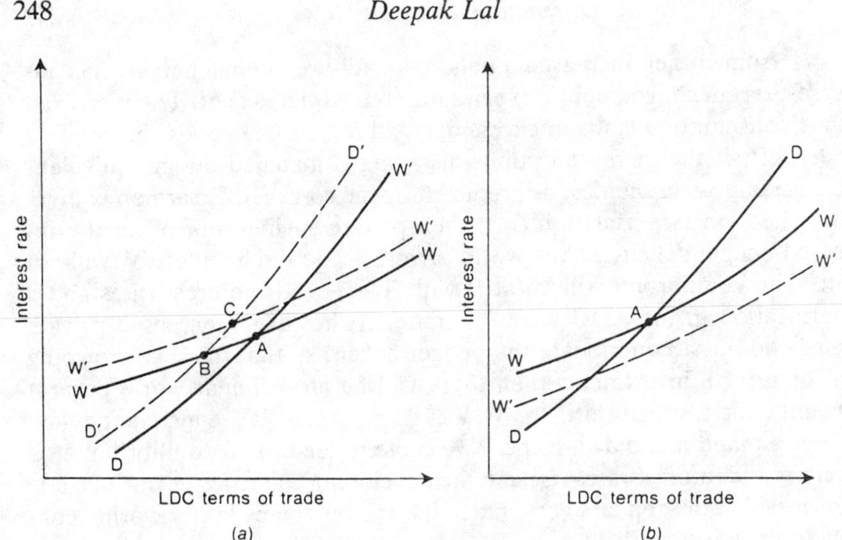

Fig. 11.6

$$W\underset{(+)}{(r}, \underset{(-)}{t)} = 0,$$

$$D\underset{(-)}{(r}, \underset{(+)}{t)} = 0.$$

(The signs below the variables indicate the expected signs of the partial derivatives.)

As regards the current account equation, higher world interest rates (r) lead to an incipient current account surplus, whilst an improvement in the LDC's terms of trade leads to a deficit as they imply a transfer of income from high to low savers. The WW curve in Fig. 11.6 therefore slopes upwards, as the incipient deficit due to a rise in interest rates requires an improvment in LDC terms of trade to eliminate the deficit.

The second equation sets the excess demand for the OECD good to be zero. Higher world interest rates reduce expenditure and hence lead to excess supply for OECD goods, whilst higher relative prices of LDC goods switch expenditure towards OECD goods and cure the excess supply. The DD curve in Fig. 11.6 will therefore also be upward sloping, but for the equilibrium to be stable (as it is assumed to be) the curve must be steeper than the WW curve, so that an incipient world current account surplus pushes down interest rates and an excess demand for the OECD goods pushes up their relative price.

Now consider an increase in the budget deficit in the OECD region resulting from either increased public expenditure unmatched by tax increases, or unchanged public expenditure but with a tax cut. The increased public consumption leads to excess demand for OECD goods shifting DD to the left. If the increased public dissaving is matched by an equivalent increase in private savings, as predicted by the so-called Ricardian equivalence theorem (see Barro, 1974), then private savings will offset the increased budget deficit and the world current account schedule WW will not shift. The equilibrium will be at B with lower world interest rates and a deterioration in the LDC terms of trade. If, however, increased private savings do not accommodate the budget deficit, so that there is 'crowding out' of private investment, then there will be an incipient world current account deficit, which shifts the WW curve upwards. If the incipient deficit *is large enough* it could shift the WW curve to lead to an equilibrium at C where world interest rates *rise* and the developing countries' terms of trade deteriorate. This appears very much like the outcomes in the world economy in the early 1980s.

A second shock to the world economy—a rise in oil prices—which was of importance in the 1970s can also be examined with the model. Higher oil prices transferred income from low- to high-savings countries leading to an incipient world current account surplus so the WW curve shifts down in Fig. 11.6(*b*). Depending upon whether as a result of the rise in the price of oil (a 'co-operative' factor of production in OECD output) OECD supply falls more than demand, there could be excess demand or supply for OECD goods. Hence the DD curve could shift to either the left or the right. In either case, however, world interest rates *fall* (unless there is a large shift to the right in the DD curve), but the LDC terms of trade could go either way. This scenario seems to be close to the outcomes in the world economy after the oil shock of 1973–4.

2. Determinants and Effects of Alternative Forms of Foreign Capital Flows

Whilst the above models provide some rationale for the flow of capital to developing countries, and effects in raising their per capita output and consumption, much of the policy debate has concerned the quality of the particular *forms* of capital flows and their presumed side-effects that are not captured by these highly aggregative models.

As Table 11.1 shows, the three major forms of capital flows to LDCs are official foreign aid, direct foreign investment, and—more recently—syndicated bank loans. In this section we briefly outline the reasons adduced for the determinants of these particular forms of capital flows and their presumed costs and benefits.

2.1. Official flows

Foreign aid has aroused the fiercest passions. This form of capital flow both in its magnitude and global coverage is novel. Though there are numerous historical examples of countries paying 'bribes' or 'reparations' to others, the continuing large-scale transfer of capital from official sources to developing countries is a post-Second World War phenomenon. Humanitarian, political, and purely economic justifications have been provided for the transfer of capital on concessionary terms through bilateral or multilateral agencies. The efficiency of concessional flows in subserving these multiple ends has been questioned (see, in particular, Bauer, 1972).

The most balanced discussion still remains that in Little and Clifford (1965). They recognized (p. 93) early on that the humanitarian motives for giving aid justified transferring Western taxpayers' money to poor *people* not poor *countries* and that giving money to the latter may have no effect on the former. Nor can the poor of the world claim a moral *right* for welfare transfers from the rich, on the line of argument used to justify *domestic* welfare payments. For the latter depends upon the existence of *national* societies with some commonly accepted moral standard. No similar *international society* exists within which a *right* to aid can be established (see Lal, 1978, 1983).

On the political reasons for giving aid, little can be said except to recognize the partial truth of Bauer's contention that, by and large Western Political interests have not been well served by foreign aid, which has instead fostered the formation of anti-Western coalitions of Third World states seeking 'bribes' not to go communist. As a recent study by Mosley (1987) concluded 'as an instrument of *political leverage*, economic aid has been unsuccessful' (p. 232). So it is by its broad economic effects that foreign aid needs to be judged.

The early justifications for aid were based on the two-gap type theory we discussed in the previous section. As these models are no longer credible this form of justification of aid has worn thin.

Recent attempts have therefore been made to assess the general impact of foreign aid on the growth prospects of recipient countries including the redressal of poverty (see Cassen, 1986; Mosley, 1987; Krueger *et al.*, 1988). The results of the statistical study by Mosley concluded unsurprisingly that 'at the world level' the efficiency of aid in *promoting growth* in the recipient country 'appears to be neutral: neither significant and automatically positive, as many defenders of aid assume, nor negative, as argued both by Bauer and by many writers on the extreme left' (Mosley, 1987, p. 233).[9]

[9] By 'neutral' Mosley seems to mean the effects differ with the circumstances, and no broad generalization of positive, negative, or zero effects of aid can be deduced.

The growth impact seems to depend on 'public sector behaviour [which] is not subject to general laws of behaviour which predetermine the effectiveness of aid; rather it varies from country to country and from period to period' (p. 23–4). On the poverty redressal effects of aid Mosley concludes from his empirical analysis that 'it appears to redistribute from the reasonably well-off in the West to most income groups in the Third World *except* the very poorest' (p. 233). Another finding of some importance is that 'over the last fifteen years aid has had a significant effect on development in Asia and very little in Africa' (p. 234).

The last point is important in forming judgements on the future role that aid can and should play in economic development. Apart from the dubious structuralist reasons given for aid programmes in the 1950s and 1960s, a straightforward welfare case for capital mobility exists in the context of differential rates of return in the neo-classical models discussed in the previous section. However, immediately after the Second World War, Western private capital markets—of which the US was the most important—were in effect shut to LDC borrowers. This was the consequence of the widespread defaults in the 1930s on Third World bonds (the major form of international capital flows before the Second World War), and the imposition of the so-called 'blue sky law' by the US which forbade US financial intermediaries from holding foreign government bonds. Meanwhile European markets were closed through exchange controls. In this environment official flows to LDCs at *commercial interest rates* (for instance through the non-IDA lending of the World Bank) would have been justifiable, purely on grounds of global efficiency.

This argument for official financial intermediation may seem to have become weaker with the explosion in bank lending in the 1970s. However, with the onset of the debt crisis and the cessation of voluntary commercial lending to at least the high-debt countries,it is argued that in effect the 'debt overhang' will prevent the commercial capital market functioning efficiently. The 'debt overhang' implies that current debts are so high relative to current income that future income increases will have to be used to finance current obligations. Hence as Krueger (1986 p. 65) has argued:

> because foreigners correctly perceive this claim on future income, they will not lend even for new projects that would yield acceptable returns. This inability to insulate new claims from existing debt leaves countries in a vicious circle: they cannot restore creditworthiness without growth, and they cannot grow till creditworthiness is restored. The private capital market may thus fail despite the rational behaviour of all participants, and there is a strong analytical case for official assistance on commercial terms.

This argument would seem to provide a justification for the continuing financial intermediation of multilateral agencies like the World Bank.

The case for continuing official *concessional* assistance is less secure. If, as the evidence suggests, its growth and poverty-redressing impact is at best neutral, and given the declining political support for such programmes in developed countries, particularly as they are seen not to serve selfish political or economic interests, we can expect the share of concessional aid flows in the capital flows to LDCs to decline.

It is arguable that, at least in the early stages of development, much of the infrastructural investment which is required for growth has to be publicly provided—partly because of significant externalities (education, health) and partly because of the difficulty of levying user charges (because of low and slowly growing utilization of lumpy investment projects). If the domestic tax and financial systems are also underdeveloped, governments may not be able to finance public infrastructure through taxation. Borrowing on commercial terms is infeasible because, for the same reasons which preclude domestic financing, the government would not be able to meet the debt-service charges on the foreign loans. Concessional offical assistance is then advocated. Against this, we have to set Bauer's (1972) argument that 'the view that a substantial infrastructure is a precondition of development is unhistorical, as it ignores the fact that the infrastructure develops in the course of economic progress, not ahead of it' (Bauer, 1972, p. 111). Moreover, he emphasizes that the difficulty in financing infrastructure has been due in part to the poor treatment many developing countries have offered to foreign capital, and for their 'tendency to divert resources into subsidised manufacture, which reduces the funds available for the construction and maintenance of the social overhead capital' (Bauer, 1972, p. 111).

There are various other issues concerning the impact of aid on domestic savings, whether it should be given to programmes or projects, and what, if any, form of 'conditionality' should be attached to it. These have been discussed *ad nauseam* in the aid literature. I have reviewed some of these debates elsewhere (see Lal, 1978, 1983). They are not particularly relevant for the argument which I am trying to develop in this subsection, namely that whilst there is likely to be a continuing role for official (chiefly multilateral) capital flows at *commercial* interest rates (at least till the 'debt crisis' unwinds), the economic and political case for official *concessional* capital flows has become weaker.

2.2. *Direct Investment*

Private capital flows comprise (*a*) portfolio lending in the form of bonds (the predominant nineteenth-century and early twentieth-century form) and syndicted bank lending (the major form of lending in the 1970s), and (*b*) direct foreign investment.

Direct foreign investment (DFI) arouses even stronger passions than foreign aid. The malign as well as the benign effects attributed to DFI are completely disproportionate both to its past and likely future role in Third World development. Historically, DFI has been important in the development of natural (mainly mineral) resources and public utilities in the Third World. These traditional avenues for foreign investment have been steadily blocked by the rise of economic nationalism and the desire of host countries to acquire all the rents from the exploitation of their natural resources. The current conventional wisdom is that utilities should be in the government sector. DFI is today increasingly found in manufacturing industry where its virtues and vices are seen to stem from the associated attributes it brings of managerial expertise, new technology, and modern marketing methods, including advertising and foreign marketing connections.

Whereas the determinants of portfolio lending need to be sought in the interest rate differentials emphasized by the aggregative open-economy models discussed in Section 1, those for DFI are to be found in the strategic game-theoretic factors underlying the decisions of firms to invest in oligopolistic industries in different national markets (see Hymer, 1977; Kindleberger, 1969; Caves, 1971, 1982; Vernon, 1977).[10]

Vernon (1977) has shown that imperfections in the 'markets' for knowledge (due to increasing returns and/or externalities in its production and dissemination) and in those for organization (due to imperfections in information) are probably the most important reasons for DFI flows between developed countries. In developing countries, on the other hand, it is the imperfections in product markets created by their tariff structures which are the primary reason for the type of defensive DFI which predominates in their manufacturing sectors (see Reuber, 1973; Lal, 1975; Lall and Streeten, 1977).[11] The major determinants of DFI flows into natural resource based industries, as well as in the development of the international 'putting out' system in some industries, such as electronics, are the increasing returns to scale that can be attained by global vertical integration in some oligopolistic industries based in developed countries. In the latter industries, traditonal relative factor price differentials within

[10] As Caves (1971, p. 1) notes: 'In the parlance of industrial organisation, oligopoly with product differentiation normally prevails where corporations make "horizontal" investments to produce abroad the same lines of goods as they produce in the home market. Oligopoly, not necessarily differentiated, in the home market is typical in industries which undertake "vertical" direct investments to produce abroad a raw material or other input to their production process at home. Direct investment tends to invoke market conduct that extends the recognition of mutual market dependence—the essence of oligopoly—beyond national boundaries'.

[11] The recent examples of Japanese 'quid pro quo' investment in the US studied by Bhagwati (1986) and Dinopolous (1987) would also be examples of defensive investment to forestall the introduction of tariff barriers on Japanese goods.

the Hufbauer–Posner–Vernon 'product cycle' model of international trade are the major determinants of the DFI flows.

More recently there has been DFI by developing countries mainly in other developing ones (see Wells, 1983). Much of this investment, like a considerable part of so-called South–South trade, is from countries which have created heavily subsidized heavy industries (such as India), in which there is chronic excess capacity. The direct foreign investment is then based on acquiring equity on the basis of exporting the excess capacity of these heavy industries (Lal, 1978*d*). It is the counterpart of what can be termed bureaucratically created, artificial 'vent for surplus' trade (see Havrylshyn, 1987).

The passions surrounding DFI and other forms of capital flows concerns their welfare effects on the host country. In the 1960s, statistical demonstrations were provided of the inimical effects of capital inflows (both official aid and DFI) on domestic savings and thence on the growth rate of developing countries (e.g. Griffin and Enos, 1970; Weisskopf, 1972). These exercises were soon shown to be spurious since the definition of 'domestic savings' they used tautologically required 'domestic savings' to fall whenever there was a capital inflow (Papanek, 1972; Miksell and Zinser, 1973; Lal, 1978). But since it is the rate of investment that influences the growth rate, and no evidence was provided that foreign capital inflows reduce domestic investment, no harmful effects can be deduced from this fall in 'domestic savings'.

The next attack was based on estimates of the so-called 'balance-of-payments' effects of DFI flows. These also were shown to be illogical on the ground that the balance-of-payments effects of DFI which, *ex hypothesi*, raises national income and hence is socially desirable, can be whatever a government chooses (Little, 1972; Lal, 1975, 1978*d*). For, in a fundamental sense, the balance of payments reflects the difference between domestic output and domestic expenditure. Even if domestic output rises as a result of DFI—which is a good thing—a government can, through fiscal and monetary means, raise domestic expenditure by even more and thus engineer a balance-of-payments deficit—a bad thing! But the 'problem', if there is one, is with the government's fiscal and monetary policies, and not with DFI.

The cost-benefit framework, ideally of the Little–Mirrlees variety, does however provide an adequate measure and evaluation criteria to determine when foreign borrowing is desirable. Such criteria which take account of current and future constraints on saving, taxation, and terms-of-trade effects induced by making the requisite transfers have been derived (see Lal, 1971, 1975). Empirical studies of the effects of DFI on host country welfare based on these social cost-benefit welfare criteria can be found in Lal (1975) and Lall and Streeten (1977). These show that the welfare effects of DFI are by and large negatively correlated with the degree of effective protection provided to the industry in which the DFI takes place.[12]

If the deleterious effects of DFI are exaggerated by its opponents, so are its beneficial effects by its proponents, As noted above, compared with other forms of foreign capital inflows, DFI brings 'extras' in the shape of technology and managerial expertise. Since, however, most developing countries in the early stages of manufacturing are likely to have a comparative advantage in either light consumer goods or the simpler capital goods (like lathes, hammers, and other products of light engineering), their need to scale any great technological and managerial heights requiring DFI is doubtful. The technology of textile mills, and even steel mills, is fairly well known and can be readily purchased without having to rely on DFI. Korea, for instance, though it made use of foreign technology, which it bought, and foreign capital, which it borrowed, has made little use of DFI in its spectacular development. Thus, whilst there may be a valid case for more reliance on private enterprise in developing countries, it is by no means co-terminous with that for DFI.

2.3. *Portfolio and Bank Lending*

Commercial bank loans are the third major form of foreign capital inflows into developing countries. From modest beginnings in the mid to late 1960s, they became the principal source of external capital for LDCs in the 1970s.

The major nineteenth-century and early twentieth-century source of foreign capital for development—portfolio lending from the richer to poorer countries—was blocked to developing countries until fairly recently because of their widespread defaults in the 1930s. Bilateral and multilateral aid flows in the 1950s and 1960s can thus be justified as providing alternatives to the traditional channels of capital to developing countries. However, these forms of capital transfer (aid and DFI) share the disadvantage, in contrast with portfolio lending, of requiring a fairly intimate relationship between the borrower and lender with all the accompanying misunderstandings and politicization of economies. The old form of portfolio lending was anonymous and apolitical; lenders were only concerned that their interest payments were made on time.

The same American banking regulations which had led to the demise of the old portfolio lending were responsible for the development of the offshore banking facilities known as the Euro-currency markets. These were based on deposits in banks outside the USA, initially in dollars but later in other currencies also. In the early years, the main depositors were East

[12] Various deleterious 'social' effects due to the inappropriateness of the products produced or technology used have also been adduced against DFI (see Stewart, 1977; Lall and Streeten, 1977). However, there is little logic or empirical evidence to substantiate these—see Lal (1975, 1983).

European countries, but more recently they have been OPEC countries worried about opening deposits in US banks. The lending based on these deposits has become one of the major sources of external capital, at least for the semi-industrialized developing countries and those poorer ones with some readily exploitable mineral resources.

By the 1970s many middle-income developing countries particularly those in Latin America which for the reasons cited earlier had endemic public finance problems made ample use of this market. As real interest rates were low and for some years negative this borrowing could have been justified even to finance public consumption if the decision had taken in account risk and the future ability to repay the loans. Despite the undoubted waste associated with some of this foreign borrowing, Sachs (1981) concluded that by and large much of the borrowing went into public investment with social rates of return above the cost of borrowing.

In the late 1970s as a result of the common attempts to control inflation in OECD countries, there was a world-wide deflationary shock, which raised world interest rates to historically unprecedented levels and also led to depression in the prices of primary commodities of importance for many debtor countries in Latin America. The Mexican Government's inability to continue debt service in 1982 precipitated the debt crisis.

The problem arose because most of the borrowing was made by countries with weak fiscal systems through commercial bank loans of short maturity and with a floating rate of interest. The changes in the world capital market in the late 1970s exposed the fiscal weakness in the major borrowing countries. The debt crisis was and remains in large part a crisis of confidence in the ability of the *public sector* in many borrowing countries to generate the requisite net resources (either by cutting back public expenditure or by raising taxation) to meet the rising cost of real public debt service.

That the cause was these differences in domestic circumstances rather than the global recession or because debt-service ratios were intolerably high is borne out by the differential incidence of the 'debt crisis'. Thus many countries in South-East Asia (for instance Korea) suffered the same global shock as the 'debt crisis' countries of Latin America, Africa, or Eastern Europe, and yet did not become crisis debtors (see Balassa, 1985, Mitra, 1986). This was because their ability to generate the required domestic surpluses and to convert them into foreign exchange (by relatively smooth switching of output and employment from non-traded to traded goods production) was not in doubt. By contrast the crisis debtors, due to their endemic fiscal deficits and policy-induced inflexibilities in the working of their price mechanisms, found that the *costs* of meeting their higher debt-service obilgations had become intolerable.

Many observers argued that the 'debt crisis' reflected the inability to pay of the affected countries. But, as has been increasingly emphasized, it is not the *inability* of *sovereign* debtors to repay (either because they are illiquid or insolvent) but their *unwillingness* to repay (which will occur before they are unable to do so) which leads them to default—or reschedule their debts.

The distinction between unwillingness and inability to pay is crucial for all forms of sovereign lending, and explains why the current series of defaults is only one in a long historical series of 'boom–bust' cycles in private lending to sovereigns. The Bardi and Peruzzi banks were ruined by Edward III's default in the fourteenth century, whilst the British Council of Foreign Bondholders, formed in 1868, continued till 1988,[13] to seek compensation for the losses suffered in the repudiation by a number of American state governments in the 1840s of their bonds held by British investors (see Makin, 1982). Yet lending to princes has continued. Thus despite their heavy losses in the fifteenth century to King Edward IV, 'rather than refuse deposits, the Medicis succumbed to the temptation of seeking an outlet for surplus cash in making dangerous loans to princes' (de Roover, cited in Makin, 1984, p. 28). As Lewis (1978) notes, since the defaults on sovereign loans or 'rescheduling' as they are now called were common in each of the major recessions since the 1820s, 'The European capital market took such defaults in its stride. It knew that borrowers would have to come back for more money, and could then be made to recognize outstanding obligations before becoming eligible for new borrowing' (Lewis, 1978, p. 49).

Do these 'boom–bust' cycles in private international lending suggest that there is some market failure which requires corrective public action? There is one view due to Minsky (1972, 1982) recently popularized by Kindleberger (1978) which views these 'boom–bust' cycles as being endemic in capitalist economies due to the supposedly 'irrational' behaviour of private speculators, so that speculative bubbles in which there is overlending are followed by collapse and crisis. A lender of last resort is then advocated to mitigate the deflationary impact of the financial crisis.[14]

Whatever the merits of the view in the domestic context (and that too is

[13] It was finely disbanded in April 1988, even though there was still one US state which was in default on its 19th-century bonds. Most other defaulters have come to terms with their bondholders!

[14] The following is the mechanism envisaged: 'Suppose an economy is subject to random shocks generated in a stationary way. A chance period of stability will be misinterpreted as implying that fewer precautions need to be taken, thus increasing the economy's vulnerability to the next "normal" shock. As applied to financial structures, enterprises adopt excessively exposed geared, levered positions in a period of stability that does not in fact reflect a favourable shift in the economy's stochastic environment' (Flemming, 1982, p. 40). As Flemming goes on to note: 'the argument depends on agents failing to distinguish a run of good luck from a favourable structural shift in their environment. Such errors are not only identifiable but also optimal if agents attach the correct non-zero probability to structural changes. If Minsky believes that people are too willing to believe that such changes have occurred, he should consider suggesting to the authorities that they intervene randomly in financial markets—by increasing their variance, such intervention would hinder the recognition of genuine shifts and should also inhibit false inferences.'

doubtful for the reasons given in the previous footnote) is it valid in international lending? To sort out ideas it is useful to see the essential differences between domestic credit markets and those for sovereign loans. As Eaton *et al.* (1986) have emphasized, both sets of markets have to deal with problems of enforcement, moral hazard, and adverse selection. The major difference lies in the lack of any legal means of enforcement in international lending as opposed to the legal framework which is available within most national frontiers. Nor is there an equivalent of bankruptcy at the international level. Nevertheless, there are various penalties—withdrawal of trade credit, moratorium on future lending, sequestration of foreign assets—which would influence the sovereign's decision to default.

The sovereign borrower will continue to service the debt incurred as long as the expected utility from his income stream if he repays is greater than if he defaults. This implies (sec Eaton and Gersovitz, 1981; Kletzer, 1984; Eaton *et al.*, 1986) that because of sovereign risk there will be credit rationing in the international capital market, and that lenders are unlikely to extend credit to levels that would exist if contracts were enforceable. Instead, with sovereign risk, 'long before a country's ability to pay would become relevant, its willingness to pay constrains its access to credit' (Eaton *et al.*, p. 499). In that sense it is unlikely that there will be an over-extension of credit in the presence of sovereign risk.

What of panics? Following Diamond and Dybvig (1983), Eaton *et al.* (1986) argue that sovereign borrowers are rather like domestic banks with illiquid assets and liquid liabilities, and their commercial bank creditors are like the depositors in the domestic banking system. Bank runs arise when the 'bank' has short-run liabilities and many creditors. Then there may be an externality in that, when some creditors run, they may increase the likelihood that other creditors will be unable to recoup their loans. Moreover, these runs can be avoided if the loan contracts have a well-defined seniority structure, or as in the case of mutual funds the value of the debt is continuously revalued. If panics can thus be easliy forestalled, it is likely that the appropraiate adjustments to this form of lending would have been taken by rational actors given repeated runs. If they have not, perhaps the 'boom–bust' cycles are not best represented by the 'mania–panic' model.

In fact an alternative interpretation can be given of defaults or reschedulings. Rescheduling or defaults will only arise if it is impossible to contract completely against all possible contigencies. Eaton *et al.* (1986) report an unpublished model due to Ozler (1984) in which in a two-period model there are two uncertainties about the second period—the borrower's income and the default penalty. Once the loan is made under competitive conditions in the first period, the sovereign borrower and syndicated bank lender face each other as bilateral monopolists in the second period. Apart from the case where the debtor's second-period income and default penalty exceed the repayments due when debt service is met (when repayment will be made in full), there are two other situations. The first favours the lender—the borrower faces a pure liquidity problem and the default penalty is still higher than the repayment obligations. In this case the loan will be rescheduled at more favourable terms to the lender than the original loan. This seems to have been the case according to Ozler for the reschedulings in the 1970s, and was reflected in higher interest rate spreads on the rescheduled loans than on voluntary lending. The second situation arises where the default penalty falls below the repayment obligation. This favours the borrower who can use the threat of default to secure better terms than the original loan. This seems to have been the character of the recent 'debt crisis' reschedulings with interest rate spreads on rescheduled loans being lower than on voluntary loans.

Ozler's model therefore suggests that the 'bust' phase of the 'debt cycle' can be expected to be a natural (but not inevitable) part of sovereign lending. Given the impossibility of complete contingent contracting and the problem of sovereign risk, rescheduling can be expected to be part of the only feasible loan contracts that can be devised. In that sense contracts which lead to periodic 'panics' may be second-best Pareto-efficient.

Some support for this view is provided by the empirical estimates that Eichengreen and Portes (1986) have derived on the realized rates of return to maturity (including periods in which they were in default) on various US and UK bonds with government guarantees (issued between 1924 and 1930 for the US and between 1923 and 1930 for the UK bonds). They find that for the UK, the internal rate of return of 5.41 per cent exceeded the average yield on consols of 4.48 per cent, whilst for the US the returns were 3.25 per cent compared with a 5.3 per cent on Aa corporate bonds. Moreover they found 'that [as] the return on continuously serviced sterling loans was lower than that on comparable dollar loans whilst the cost of the average default on dollar loans was higher it reinforces the hypothesis that this differential default risk was recognized in the 1920s and incorporated into the required rate of return on the two categories of assets' (p. 628)

Secondly Edwards's (1984, 1986) econometric excercises on the pricing of bonds and bank loans to LDCs in the 1970s tends to confirm the hypothesis that this lending did take account of the changing default risk. In particular he found that the continuing risk premiums were positively related to the debt/output ratio and negatively to the ratio of investment to GDP. He also found that, on the basis of yields on Mexican and Brazilian bonds in the secondary market, the Mexican crisis of 1982 was anticipated though only by a few weeks by the financial market, which after the onset of the crisis heavily discounted Brazilian and Mexican debt.

If the above argument and evidence is accepted, then the reschedulings associated with the 'debt crisis' are part of the 'normal' cycle of sovereign lending. There is still no case for public concern or intervention. However it has been argued (see Cline, 1984) by analogy with domestic banking panics that the debt crisis raises the spectre of bank failures (amongst the most heavily exposed commercial banks). This in turn through the interaction of the global interbank market could lead to a collapse of the international system of finance and credit. Hence, analogously to the role of domestic central banks as lenders of last resort, it is argued that there should be an application of Bagehot's rule at the international level. Bagehot's rule to guide a central bank during a generalized financial panic was to discount the bills of those firms which were illiquid because of the general panic, but to liquidate those firms which were insolvent as the value of their assets was below their liabilities.

In the recent international debt crisis, however, there has been no general panic and the issue of illiquidity or insolvency should (following Bagehot) relate to the paper assets of the banks, not to the liabilities of the sovereign debtors. There is no reason to believe that financial markets would not correctly value the assets of banks. If the total market value is sufficiently below the total face value of their assets (by the amount of bank capital), the relevant banks are insolvent. As in any other case of insolvency, the stockholders should bear the resulting losses and if necessary the bank should be taken over or allowed to fail. Cline (1984, p. 132) disagrees with this 'solution'; he asserts these 'proposals apper naïve in that they do not address their dire implications for bank capital'. But this is a *non sequitur*. Consenting adults make all sorts of contracts, some of which lead to a loss of all their capital. Does this mean that Cline would support the public underwriting of any loss from all such private gambles? None of the dire consequences of allowing insolvent banks to be liquidated is stated. I take it, of course, that central banks know how to prevent any reduction in the overall national money supply from bank bankruptcies, and that in most countries small depositors are protected against bank failures by suitable provision, including deposit insurance.

By confusing the potential insolvency of some banks, with the liquidity problem of some debtor countries, Cline is able to argue that there should, in effect, be a global application of Bagehot's rule through an implicit international 'bail-out' of the banks, albeit through individual 'deals' with particular debtor countries. But it is arguable that it is precisely the moral hazard associated with such expected bail-outs which has led to the protracted debt crisis. Given the temper of the times, both the debtors and commercial banks had hoped after 1982 that, playing on the historical memories of the bank failures during the 1930s, they could force a bail-out by Western governments, ideally through the concealed means of intermediation by an international agency such as the World Bank. The 'willingness to pay' model suggests that, because of the 'moral hazard' associated with such perceptions, the perceived penalties of default and hence the willingness to pay of the borrowers would decrease. At the same time the banks by holding back on calling a default could avoid the inevitable downward revaluation of their assets.

In May 1987 the major New York banks with high exposure to Third World debt decided to set aside larger reserves against their Third World loans. Since then, various methods, like the recent Mexican swap arrangement to, in effect, buy back part of its existing debt at close to its value in the secondary market, reflect the growing realization of both the debtors and lenders that they will not be bailed out by the world's taxpayers. They are now negotiating the terms of the rescheduling which will determine how the losses embodied in the changed present value of past promises (contracts) will be shared.

The most important lesson for public policy of the 'debt crisis' for developed-country action therefore would seem to be—forbear. The 'debt crisis' in our judgement would have been resolved much earlier if today's Western governments had explicitly stood by the position expressed by Britain in the nineteenth century in the face of spectacular defaults on foreign bonds. In a famous circular of 1848 Palmerston, whilst eschewing any public action, noted: 'The British government has considered that the losses of imprudent men who have placed mistaken confidence in the *good faith* of foreign governments would provide a salutary warning to others' (cited in Lipson, 1985).

3. The Political Economy of Global Financial Integration

Despite the current debt crisis the future flow of capital to the Third World is most likely to be private (see Section 2.1). Its dimensions will inexorably be tied to expectations about the willingness to pay of sovereign nations. This is just another way of defining the political risks associated with foreign investment. The great nineteenth-century booms in foreign lending were promoted by the extension of norms of conduct based on European capitalist individualism—in particular the sanctity of private property rights—to much of the Third World, through the expansion of *Pax Britannica*, and its influence on the local legal institutions even of many independent states, as in Latin America. A strict set of legal rules was established through a number of commercial treaties between European states (see Lipson, 1985). The legitimacy of these nineteenth-century rules was not challenged until the Soviet and Mexican revolutions, and the explicit introduction of *étatist* policies by Turkey (under Atatürk) as a means of national economic development. Since then, there has been a gradual erosion of public acceptance of the sanctity of private property rights when faced with social policies designed to promote the general—usually nationalist—weal.

There was a partial restoration of these international property rights which underpinned the nineteenth-century economic order with the establishment of *Pax Americana* after 1945. But it has not successfully withstood the explosion of economic nationalism, following decolonization and the formation of numerous Third World nation-states determined to assert their rights of national sovereignty against any purported international property rights.

As direct foreign investors provide more local hostages to fortune, they have borne the brunt of the deleterious effects of this disintegration of the legal order. Moreover, most governments of developing countries, being both nationalist and *dirigiste*, have sought to regulate, tax, or nationalize particular foreign investments on grounds of national social utility rather than out of any general antagonism towards private property as such. This has meant that the US has been unable to identify expropriation of foreign capital with ideology (communism or socialism), as the nationalization of companies in the late 1960s and early 1970s by right-wing regimes in the Middle East proved.

This inexorble erosion of the old standards of international property rights might however be ending. The recent emergence of Third World multinationals, the importance of many OPEC countries as portfolio lenders, and with the US becoming the world's largest debtor, the old distinction between the divergent interests of developed capital-exporting countries interested in protecting international property rights, and of Third World capital-importing countries keen to circumscribe them, is becoming less valid. In the future the interests of developed and developing countries may converge and lead to an increasing acceptance of rules protecting international property.

This is all the more likely because of the rapid and remarkable integration of world capital markets that is currently taking place. This has resulted from: the ending of capital and exchange controls and the accompanying deregulation of domestic capital markets in most developed countries; the instantaneous linking of national capital markets through the new information technology which reduces transaction costs and is alalogous to a large reduction in transport costs for traded goods; the introduction of new financial instruments—the 'securitization' of all forms of debt—so that, even those forms of debt, such as house mortgages, which were previously considered to be intrinsically non-traded outside national boundaries, can now be traded internationally. At the same time many institutional investors—particularly pension funds, whose beneficiaries increasingly include a large portion of the developed countries' labour force—are holding an internationally diversified portfolio. These trends have a number of interesting implications for the conduct of public policy in developed countries, and point to the required changes in developing countries' policies which would help them to make the best use of these emerging global opportunities.

As far as developed countries are concerned, recent political economy models have sought to endogenize the pressures for protection in these countries. One such model due to Mayer (1984) is particularly useful for our purpose. He considers an economy described by the standard two-good, two-factor Hecksher–Ohlin model. The political system is based on majority voting, and it is assumed that voters vote their economic interests. The latter are determined by the income they receive from their individual endowments of the two factors of production—capital and labour. The *mean* of the distribution of factor ownerships is just the average capital/labour ratio of the economy (k). Under majority voting, with no voting costs and if voters have 'singled-peaked' preferences, then as Black (1948) demonstrated, public policy will be determined by the *median* voter's preferences. If, *ex hypothesi*, voters seek to serve their narrow economic interests, namely to raise the returns to the factor which is more abundant in their individual factor endowment, then the policy pursued will depend upon the *median* voter's factor endowment (k_m). Assuming that the distribution of factor ownership is unimodal, a tariff (subsidy) on capital-intensive imports will be voted in if the median (k_m) is greater (less) than the mean (k) of the distribution of factor ownership. If this distribution is symmetric then the median and mean are the same ($k_m = k$), and the voters will support free trade (as that from standard trade theory maximizes the real income of a 'country'). However 'for most non-socialist countries there is strong evidence that capital–labour ownership distributions are not symmetric, but skewed to the right. Accordingly, one would expect a built-in tendency towards protection of labour's interests, through subsidies on capital-intensive imports or tarriffs on labour-intensive imports' (Mayer, p. 338).[15]

But now suppose there is complete global capital market integration.

[15] Strictly speaking the model would establish labour's interest in various non-tariff domestic subsidies to expand the domestic output of the labour-intensive industry, as these will dominate the tariff as second-best methods of achieving the non-economic objective of raising labour's share in national income. Also as Mayer emphasizes this is a long-run model and would explain 'long run tariff trends, especially in relationship to changes in voter eligibility rules, voting costs, or overall factor ownership distributions. It is much less suitable, however, in explaining more short-term attempts by individual industries to gain tariff protection. In particular, it sheds no light on the frequently observed phenomenon that a single industry succeeds in raising tariffs on its product, even though the vast majority of eligible voters do not benefit from such a policy.' He then goes on to develop 'a many industries model with specific factors to show how majority voting can result in tariff protection of a small industry'. It would take us too far afield to outline this short-run model which shows how 'a small minority of gaining factor owners can become a majority of actual voters for a tariff increase on a given commodity' (Mayer, p. 338). For our relatively long-term purposes, the above long-term version of Mayer's model will suffice to make the major point we wish to make in this section.

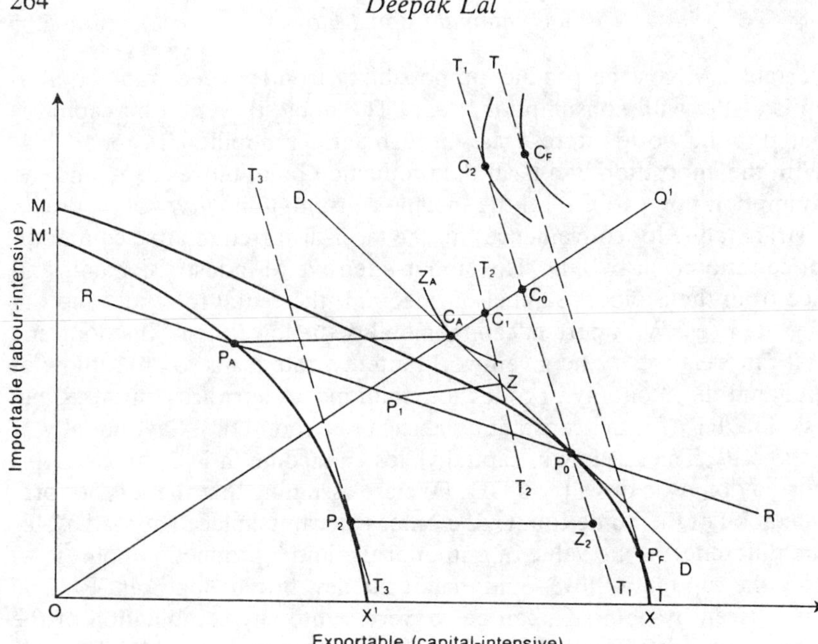

Fig. 11.7

One of the consequences will be that the interest rate on domestic capital will be exogenously determined for each 'small' country by the world economy. With given world prices for the two traded goods in the model, the wage rate will also then be fully determined. Suppose under majority voting in a capital-abundant country, the median voter has a factor endowment *less* capital-intensive than the economy. An imposition of a tariff on the labour-intensive import good would cause an incipient rise in the wage and fall in the rental rate. The latter would immediately lead to an outflow of capital, and the unviability of the capital-intensive export industry at the given world rental rate, as the economy's output shrinks along its Rybczynski line with the outflow of domestic capital.[16] As Mundell (1957) showed in his model of international trade and factor mobility in the new equilibrium, the free trade commodity and factor/price ratio would be restored, but with the elimination of commodity trade.

Fig. 11.7 sets out the argument. It depicts the standard Hecksher–Ohlin model, in which the home country faces given terms of trade TT, and produces both an exportable good (X) which is more capital-intensive than the

[16] The Rybczynski line would show the absolute decrease in the outputs or the capital-intensive good (at the new tariff inclusive commodity price) as capital fled, with the production possibility frontier for the two goods shifting inwards.

importable. MX is the production possibility frontier, free trade equilibrium is at P_F, with consumption at C_F. The domestic rental on capital is equated to the world interest rate through perfect mobility of capital.

With the imposition of a tariff the production point moves to P_0 and the consumption point to C_0, on the income consumption curve OQ^1 (drawn as a straight line for convenience) for the tariff-distorted relative commodity price ratio given by DD. The labour-intensive M industry expands and hence from the Stolper–Samuelson theorem, the rental rate falls and the wage rate rises. With perfect capital mobility the lowering of the domestic rental rate relative to the given world interest rate leads to an outflow of capital and the economy's production point moves leftwards on the Rybczynski line RR (for the constant domestic price ratio DD). Say, initially, it moves to P_1. The outflow of capital yields an income of P_1Z_1 at the tariff-distorted domestic price ratio DD. (We are assuming that there is no foreign taxation of the home country's earnings on capital placed abroad.) This is the difference in the value of output at the initial production point P_0—before the capital outflow—and that at the new production point P_1. The income given by point Z_1, can be converted into any combination of the two traded goods along the unchanged terms of trade, given by T_2T_2. Consumption will therefore be at C_1, on the income consumption curve OQ^1.

However, as at P_1, where the domestic tariff-distorted price ratio DD still rules, the rental on capital is still below the world interest rate, capital will continue to flow out until the point P_A on the Rybczynski line RR on the shrunken production possibility frontier X^1M^1 is reached. At P_A income from the capital placed abroad is P_AZ_A, and the income corresponding to Z_A will also be the consumption point C_A, as Z_A lies on the income consumption curve OQ^1. *There will be no trade at* C_A, and thus the domestic price of the importables, will no longer be determined by the world price plus the tariff. If there is an infinitesimal outflow of capital at P_A, and rise in the output of the importables its relative price will fall, which in turn will *raise* the domestic rental rate, thereby reducing its gap from the world interest rate and hence the inducement for capital outflows. The relative fall in the price of importables will continue until *domestic relative prices have returned to their initial free-trade ratio given by DD.* Production will then be at P_2, income from capital abroad will be P_2Z_2 and consumption at the domestic price ratio (now equal to the free trade one) will be at C_2. There will of course still be no trade in commodities, but as far as the factor-price configuration is concerned it will have returned to its original free-trade one. (Also see Minabe, 1974, and Brecher and Diaz-Alejandro, 1977.) For our purpose the lesson of the model is that, with perfect capital mobility, within the (admittedly unrealistic) Heckscher–Ohlin framework, labour's attempt to raise its wage above the free trade level by voting in protection of the labour-intensive good would have been foiled!

Clearly, in practice well before the economy reaches the trade-extinguishing point, P_A, in Fig. 11. 7 the collapse of the exportable industry and any attendant balance-of-payment crisis that may ensue in the absence of the smooth adjustment assumed in the Mundell model, would lead in this world of perfect capital mobility to attempts by the polity to return to the status quo ante by rescinding the tariff. Thus by making it difficult for the median voter to achieve the desired distributional changes associated with a tariff 'equilibrium' (which can be achieved when capital is *immobile*), essentially because of the capital flight that would be induced by squeezing domestic returns to capital, global capital-market intergration could provide that essential bulwark against the inevitable long-run political pressures for tariffs in developed countries as modelled by Mayer. It could thus provide most democratic developed economies a means of 'tying themselves to the mast' to save themselves from the siren calls of their politics.

What of developing countries? Given the differential incidence of the debt crisis, it is clear that differences in domestic policy were largely responsible for the divergent performance of highly indebted countries when faced by the global rise in interest rates and primary commodity price falls in the early 1980s. The two major policy failures of the past have been the tendency to run unsustainable fiscal deficits and the maintenance of inward-looking trade regimes. It is essential that, if developing countries are to utilize foreign borrowing efficiently in the future, they will first have to set their domestic house in order. Paradoxically, global capital-market integration can help in stiffening the spine of Third World governments to undertake this economic liberalization and to stick by more liberal economic policies in the future.

Elsewhere, we have argued (see Lal, 1987) that Third World governments have usually undertaken sustained economic liberalization only when the costs of maintaining repressed regimes to *them*, in terms of their control over the economy, had become too high. The past *dirigisme* of most Third World states has led to the gradual expansion of politically determined entitlements to current and future income streams to favoured groups. The accompanying (implicit or explicit) tax burden to finance them leads at some stage to generalized tax resistance, avoidance, and evasion. With taxes being evaded, with domestic and foreign credit virtually at an end, and with private agents adjusting to inflation to evade the inflation tax, the government finds its fiscal control of the economy vanishing. It is to restore this control that, most often, liberalization is undertaken.

In the 1980s, the integration of the global capital markets accelerated this dynamic process whereby the expansion of what can be called the 'transfer state' leads to the unexpected and very un-Marxian withering away of the state. For one important feature of the debt crisis was that the macroeconomic imbalances which in part were its cause, also led in many countries to capital flight (see Cuddington, 1986). For despite exchange controls, economic agents sought to protect their capital against the domestic depredations of asset values arising from the endemic inflation that accommpanied macro mismanagement. With improved domestic prospects, and particularly with macroeconomic stability and more realistic exchange rates, flight capital has returned in many countries. But the important lesson is *not* that tighter capital controls should be maintained by developing countries. For with the expansion of trade and the growing familiarity of at least the richer residents of developing countries with international capital markets, capital controls are at best a short-term palliative. As Cuddington (1986) rightly concludes:

> over expansive monetary and fiscal policies, an incompatible exchange-rate policy, and a repressive set of financial policies designed to divert resources toward the public sector will cause widespread distortions and imbalances even in the short run. Capital flight is an important symptom of these policy-induced distortions. While attacking this symptom directly by imposing capital controls may be essential in a crisis, it hardly represents a long-term antidote for destabilizing exchange-rate, fiscal and financial policies. Without capital controls, the threat of capital flight might impose much needed discipline on policy makers.

Thus, again as in the case of developed countries, integrated capital markets may be able to tie the hands of developing-country governments so that they no longer act to subserve base interests but the common weal. The major benefits for the economic development of Third World countries from free world-wide capital movements are therefore likely to come not primarily from the conventional sources of a better allocation of the world's savings, as is emphasized in most of our traditional economic models (surveyed in earlier sections), but from this political economy of global capital-market integration.

It is increasingly being realized that the role of open foreign trade regimes is probably more important in terms of their effects in inducing the establishment of a domestic economic system which is conductive to growth (see Lal and Rajapatirana, 1987). As Keynes (1926) emphasized, the classical case against mercantilism was essentially based on limiting state action to areas where such action was indispensable. What I have been arguing in this section is that free capital movements are likely to provide an even more effective shackle on the irrational *dirigiste* impulses of governments in both developed and developing countries.[17] The direct

[17] The political importance of capital-market integration in overcoming the territorial instincts of states is also of importance and is argued in a brilliant book by Rosecrance (1986). His arguments and those of the Luddites who wish to prevent capital-market integration in order to foster national autonomy in public policy are reviewed in Lal (1988).

effects of capital flows on growth (as of trade) are not likely to be substantial, as Cairncross (1962) perceptively noted. Thus we can extend Kravis's (1970) view of 'trade as the handmaiden of growth', to trade not merely in commodities but more importantly to the services of capital.

The handmaiden's primary role is to create incentives for our rulers to maintain a domestic economic framework where the state provides the indispensable public goods—law and order, stable money, and social overhead capital—for development, without over-extending itself and generating those policy-induced distortions which have done more damage to Third World prospects than the so-called endogenous distortions in these economies that the policies were meant to cure. Many economists have become hoarse preaching these economic virtues to states—but with little effect. But as most states seem to agree with the Bard that, 'there is no virtue like necessity' (*Richard II*), the 'political economy' consequences of the global integration of capital markets may yet force them to make a necessity of these virtues!

References

Avramovic, D. *et al.* (1964), *Economic Growth and External Debt* (Baltimore: Johns Hopkins Univ. Press).

Balassa, B. (1985), *Change and Challenge in the World Economy* (London: Macmillan).

Barro, R. (1974), 'Are Government Bonds Net Wealth?' *Journal of Political Economy*, Nov.–Dec.

Bauer, P (1972), *Dissent on Development* (London: Wiedenfeld & Nicolson).

——(1981), *Equality, the Third World and Economic Delusion* (London: Methuen).

——(1984), *Reality and Rhetoric: Studies in the Economics of Development* (London: Weidenfeld & Nicolson).

Bhagwati, J. N. (1986), 'Investing Abroad', Esmée Fairbairn Lecture, Univ. of Lancaster.

Brecher, R. A., and Diaz-Alejandro, C. F. (1977), 'Tariffs, Foreign Capital and Immiserizing Growth', *Journal of International Economics*, 7 (Nov.).

Buiter, W. H. (1981), 'Time Preference and International Lending and Borrowing in an Overlapping-Generations Model', *Journal of Political Economy*, 89 (Aug.).

Cairncross, A. K. (1962), *Factors in Economic Development* (London: Allen & Unwin).

Cairnes, J. E. (1874), *Some Leading Principles of Political Economy* (London: Macmillan).

Cassen, R. *et al.* (1986), *Does Aid Work*? (Oxford: Clarendon Press).

Caves, R. E. (1971), 'International Corporations: The Industrial Economics of Foreign Investments', *Economica* 38 (Feb.).

——(1982), *Multinational Enterprises and Economic Analysis* (Cambridge: CUP).

Chenery, H. B., and Strout, A. M. (1966), 'Foreign Assistance and Economic Development', *American Economic Review*, 56 (Sept.).

Cline, W. R. (1984), *International Debt: Systemic Risk and Policy Response* (Washington, DC: Institute for International Economics).

Crawford, V. P. (1987), 'International Lending, Long-Term Credit Relationships and Dynamic Contract Theory' *Princeton Studies in International Finance*, no. 59, (Princeton).

Cuddington, J. T., (1986), 'Capital Flight: Estimates, Issues and Explanations', *Princeton Studies in International Finance*, no. 58 (Princeton).

Diamond, P. A. (1965), 'National Debt in a Neo-classical Growth Model', *American Economic Review*, 55 (Dec.).

Diamond, D., and Dybvig, P. E. (1983), 'Bank Runs, Deposit Insurance and Liquidity', *Journal of Political Economy*, 91 (June).

Dinapolous (1987), 'Quid Pro Quo Foreign Investment', paper for World Bank conference on Political Economy, June 1987.

Domar, E. (1950), 'The Effect of Foreign Investment on the Balance of Payments', *American Economic Review*, 40 (Dec.).

Eaton, J., Gersovitz, M., and Stiglitz, J. E. (1986), 'The Pure Theory of Country Risk', *European Economic Review*, 30 (June).

Eaton, J., and Gersovitz, M. (1981), 'Poor Country Borrowing and the Repudiation Issue', *Princeton Studies in International Finance*, no. 47 (Princeton).

Edwards, S. (1984), 'LDC Foreign Borrowing and Default Risk: An Empirical Investigation', *American Economic Review*, 74 (Sept.).

——(1986), 'The Pricing of Bonds and Bank Loans in International Markets', *European Economic Review*, 30 (June).

Eichengreen, B., and Portes, R. (1986), 'Debt and Default in the 1930s', *European Economic Review*, 30 (June).

Engel, C., and Kletzer, K. (1987), 'Saving and Investment in an Open Economy with Non-traded Goods', *NBER Working Paper No. 2141*, (Cambridge, Mass.: NBER).

Findlay, R. (1978), 'An "Austrian" Model of International Trade and Interest Rate Equalization', *Journal of Political Economy*, 86 (Dec.).

——(1984) 'Growth and Development in Trade Models', in Jones and Kenen (1984), Vol. i.

Fischer, S., and Frenkel, J. (1972), 'Investment, the Two-Sector Model, and Trade in Debt and Capital Goods', *Journal of International Economics*, 2 (Aug.).

Fisher, I. (1930), *The Theory of Interest*, reprint, 1965 (New York: Augustus M. Kelley).

Flemming, J. S. (1982), 'Comment on Minsky', in Kindleberger and Laffargue (1982).

Griffin, K., and Enos, J. (1970), 'Foreign Assistance: Objectives and Consequences', *Economic Development and Cultural Change*, 18 (Apr.).

Harberger, A. C. (1986), 'Welfare Consequences of Capital Inflows', in A. Choksi and D. Papageorgiou (eds.), *Economic Liberalization in Developing Countries*, (Oxford: Blackwell).

Havrylshyn, O. (ed.) (1987), *Exports of Developing Countries—How Direction Affects Performance*, (Washington, DC: World Bank).

Houthakker, H. S. (1965), 'On Some Determinants of Saving in Developed and Underdeveloped Countries', in E. A. G. Robinson (ed.), *Problems in Economic Development*, (London: Macmillan).

Hymer, S. (1977), *The International Operations of National Firms: A Study of Direct Foreign Investment* (Cambridge, Mass.: MIT Press).

Ihori, T. (1978), 'The Golden Rule and the Role of Government in a Life Cycle Growth Model', *American Economic Review*, 68 (June).

Jones, R. W. (1967), 'International Capital Movements and the Theory of Tariffs and Trade', *Quarterly Journal of Economics*, 81.

——(1979), *International Trade: Essays in Theory* (Amsterdam: North-Holland).

——and Kenen, P. B. (eds.) (1984), *Handbook of International Economics*, 2 vols. (Amsterdam: North-Holland).

Kemp, M. C. (1966), 'The Gain from International Trade and Investment: A Neo-Hecksher–Ohlin Approach', *American Economic Review*, 56.

Keynes, J. M. (1926), *The End of Laissez-Faire* (London: Hogarth Press).

Kindleberger, C. P. (1958), *International Economics* (Homewood: R. D. Irwin).

——(1969), *American Business Abroad* (New Haven: Yale Univ. Press).

——(1978), *Manias, Panics and Crashes* (New York: Basic Books).

——and Laffargue, J. P. (eds.) (1982), *Financial Crises—Theory, History & Policy* (Cambridge: CUP).

King, M. A. (1985), 'The Economics of Saving: A Survey of Recent Contributions' in K. Arrow and S. Honkapohja (eds.), *Frontiers in Economics* (Oxford: Blackwell).

Kletzer, K. M. (1984), 'Asymmetries of Information and LDC Borrowing with Sovereign Risk', *Economic Journal*, 94 (June).

Kravis, I. B. (1970), 'Trade as a Handmaiden of Growth-Similarities between the 19th and 20th centuries', *Economic Journal*, 80 (Dec.).

Krueger, A. O. (1986), 'Aid in the Development Process', *World Bank Research Observer* 1 (Jan.).

——(1987), Michalopoulos, C., and Ruttan, V. (1987), *The Impact of Development Assistance to LDCs* (Baltimore: Johns Hopkins Univ. Press).

Kuznets, S. (1966), *Modern Economic Growth* (New Haven: Yale Univ. Press).

Lal, D. (1971), When is Foreign Borrowing Desirable? '*Bulletin of the Oxford University Institute of Statistics*, 71 (Aug.).

——(1972), 'The Foreign Exchange Bottleneck Revisited: A Geometric Note', *Economic Development and Cultural Change*, 20 (July).

——(1975), *Appraising Foreign Investment in Developing Countries* (London: Heinemann Educational).

——(1978*a*), 'On the Multinationals', *ODI Review*, no. 2.

——(1978*b*), *Poverty, Power and Prejudice—The North-South Confrontation*, Fabian Research Series no. 340 (London: Fabian Society).

——(1978*c*), 'Industrial Co-operation Agreements', in *Industrial Co-operation*, Commonwealth Economic Papers No. 11, (London: Commonwealth Secretariat).

——(1978*d*), 'The Evaluation of Capital Inflows', *Industry and Development*, no. 1 (reprinted in *World Bank Reprint* Series, 84).

——(1983, 1985), *The Poverty of 'Development Economics'*, Hobart Paperback 16 (London: Institute of Economic Affairs). American edn. with new preface and additional Appendix (Cambridge, Mass: Harvard Univ. Press 1985).

——(1987), 'The Political Economy of Economic Liberalisation', *World Bank Economic Review*, (Jan.).

——(1988), 'By Land or by Sea, the Merchant Shall Inherit the Earth', *World Economy*, 11 (Mar.).

——and Rajapatirana, S. (1987), 'Foreign Trade Regimes and Economic Growth', *World Bank Research Observer*, 2 (July).

——and van Wijnbergen, S. (1985), 'Government Deficits, the Real Interest Rate and Developing Country Debt: On Global Crowding Out', *European Economic Review*, 29 (Dec.); reprinted with extensions in Lal and Wolf (1986).

——and Wolf, M. (eds.) (1986), *Stagflation, Savings and the State* (New York: OUP).

Lall, S., and Streeten, P. (1977), *Foreign Investment, Transnationals and Developing Countries* (London: Macmillan).

Lewis, W. A. (1978), *The Evolution of the International Economic Order* (New York: Princeton Univ. Press).

Lipson, D. (1985), *Standing Guard—Protecting Foreign Capital in the 19th and 20th Centries* (Berkeley: Univ. of California).

Little, I. M. D. (1960), 'The Strategy of Indian Development', *National Institute Economic Review*, 9 (May).

——(1972), 'On measuring the value of private direct overseas investments', in G. Ranis (ed.), *The Gap Between Rich and Poor Nations* (London: Macmillan).

——(1982), *Economic Development* (New York: Basic Books).

——and Clifford, J. M. (1965), *International Aid* (London: Allen & Unwin).

——and Mirrlees, J. A. (1969), *Manual of Industrial Project Analysis*, vol. 2, (Paris: OECD Development Centre).

——(1974), *Project Appraisal and Planning for Developing Countries*, (London: Heinemann Educational).

——Scott, M. FG., and Scitovsky, T. (1970), *Industry and Trade in Some Developing Countries* (London: OUP).

——and Tipping, D. G. (1972), *A Social Cost-Benefit Analysis of the Kulai Oil Palm Estate* (Paris: OECD Development Centre).

Lluch, C. (1986), 'ICORs, Savings Rates and the Determinants of Public Expenditure in Developing Countries', in Lal and Wolf (1986).

Makin, J. H. (1984), *The Global Debt Crisis* (New York: Basic Books).

Mayer, W. (1984), 'Endogenous Tariff Formation', *American Economic Review*, 74 (Dec.).

MacDougall, G. D. A. (1960), 'The Benefits and Costs of Private Investment from Abroad: A Theoretical Approach', *Economic Record*, 36, special issue; also published in *Bulletin of the Oxford Institute of Statistics*, 22/3 (1960).

McKinnon, R. I. (1964), 'Foreign Exchange Constraints in Economic Development', *Economic Journal*, 74 (June).

Minabe, N. (1974), 'Capital and Technology Movements and Economic Welfare', *American Economic Review*, 64 (Dec.).

Mikesell, R. F. and Zinser, J. E. (1973) 'The Nature of the Savings Function in Developing Countries—A Survey of the Theoretical and Empirical Literature', *Journal of Economic Liternature*, 11 (Mar.).
Minsky, H. P. (1977), 'A Theory of Systematic Fragility', in E. I. Altman and A. W. Sametz (eds), *Financial Crisis: Institutions and Markets in a Fragile Environment* (New York: Wiley).
Mitra, A. K. (1978), 'An Intertemporal Cross-country Analysis of the Impact of Economic and Demographic Factors on Growth Expenditure Share', PhD dissertation, Duke University, North Carolina.
Mitra, P. (1986), 'A Description of Adjustment to External Shocks: Country Groups', in Lal and Wolf (1986).
Modigliani, F. (1970), 'The Life Cycle Hypothesis of Saving and Inter Country Differences in the Saving Ratio', in W. A. Eltis, M. FG. Scott & J. N. Wolfe (eds.), *Induction, Growth and Trade* (Oxford: Clarendon Press).
——(1975), 'The Life Cycle Hypothesis of Saving Twenty Years Later', in M. Parkin and A. R. Nobay (eds.), *Contemporary Issues in Economics* (Manchester: Manchester Univ. Press).
Mosley, P. (1987), *Overseas Aid* (Brighton: Wheatsheaf Books).
Mundell, R. A. (1957) 'International Trade and Factor Mobility', *American Economic Review*, 47 (June).
Ozler, S., (1984), 'Rescheduling of Sovereign Government Bank Debt, (Stanford: Stanford University), mimeo.
Papanek, G. (1972), 'The Effects of Aid and Other Resource Transfers on Savings and Growth in Less Developed Countries', *Economic Journal*, 82 (Sept.).
Reuber, G., Crookell, H., Emerson, M., and Gallais-Hamonno, G. (1973), *Private Foreign Investment in Development* (Oxford: Clarendon Press).
Riedel, J. (1984), 'Trade as the Engine of Growth in Developing Countries, Revisited'. *Economic Journal*, 94 (Mar.).
Roover de R. (1948), *The Medici Bank* (New York: New York Univ. Press).
Rosecrance, R. (1986), *The Rise of the Trading State* (New York: Basic Books).
Ruffin, R. J. (1979), 'Growth and the Long-Run Theory of International Capital Movements', *American Economic Review*, 69 (Dec.)
——(1984), 'International Factor Movements', in Jones and Kenen (1984), Vol. i.
Rybczynski, T. (1955), 'Factor Endowments and Relative Commodity Prices', *Economica*, 22 (Nov.).
Sachs, J. (1981), 'The Current Account and Macroeconomics Adjustment in the 1970s', *Brookings Papers on Economics Activity*, no. 1.
——(1984) 'Theoretical Issues in International Borrowing', *Princeton Studies in International Finance*, no. 54 (Princeton).
Samuelson, P. A. (1958), 'An Exact Consumption Loan Model of Interest with or without the Social Contrivance of Money', *Journal of Political Economy*, 66 (Dec.).
Selowsky, M., and van der Tak, H. G. (1986), 'The Debt Problem and Growth', *World Development*, Sept.
Stewart, F. (1977), *Technology and Underdevelopment* (London: Macmillan).
Uzawa, H. (1968), 'Time Preference, the Consumption Function and Optimum

Asset Holdings' in J. N. Wolfe (ed.): *Value, Capital and Growth* (Edinburgh: (Edinburgh Univ. Press).

Van Wijnbergen, S. (1985), 'Interdependence Revisited: A Developing Countries Perspective on Macroeconomic Management and Trade Policy in the Industrial World', *Economic Policy*, Nov.; also comments by R. Dornbusch and Michael Wickens.

Vernon, R. (1977), *Storm over the Multinationals* (London: Macmillan).

Weisskopf, T. E. (1972), 'The Impact of Foreign Capital Inflow on Domestic Savings in Underdeveloped Economies', *Journal of International Economics*, 2 (Feb.).

Wells, Jr., L. T. (1983), *Third World Multinationals* (London: MIT Prerss).

World Bank (1984), *World Development Report 1984* (New York: OUP).

——(1985), *World Development Report 1985* (New York: OUP).

33

Industrialization Strategies and Long-Term Resource Allocation

Deepak Lal

Introduction

Since the so-called "industrial revolution" in Britain, which began in the mid-18th century, industrialization has come to be identified with modernization and self-sustaining economic growth. Most governments in developed and developing countries have sought to promote industrialization, partly for nationalist and militarist reasons and in part for the sound economic reason that it often provides another means for raising output, productivity and incomes even in countries which are not blessed with the older sources of national wealth — fertile land and natural resources.

Since the beginnings of industrialization, debates concerning its proper public promotion have been intimately linked with questions of foreign trade policy, and hence the validity of various arguments for protection.

This paper provides a broad historical perspective on the pattern of industrialization and ideas about industrialization strategies in terms of different historical phases over the past 200 years. This is done in the first two sections. In the third section, we restate the classical case for free trade as it has been reformulated in the modern theory of trade and welfare, and then examine its relevance in fostering efficient industrialization in the light of various "new" arguments being advanced for dirigiste industrial and trade policies.

I. Historical Phases in Global Industrialization

Broadly speaking, six phases of global industrialization can be delineated, with their distinctive policy discussions and stances.

The first was the mercantilist period during which industrialization first took root in Britain. This was based on innovations in cotton textiles, iron smelting and the steam engine. The removal of internal barriers to trade around 1700 in the UK aided this nascent process of industrialization. But as Adam Smith noted in classic work, the mercantilist system with its controls on foreign trade militated against the productivity gains that were available from a further widening of the market through a growing international division of labour and the specialization it entailed.

Partly due to the internal contradictions of the mercantilist system (see [Hecksher, and Lal & Myint, 1990, Ch. 11]), a process of liberalization of internal controls and trade barriers had also spread across Europe after the French Revolution. After the Napoleonic War, with the developments in steel, and the growth of railways and later steamships, the industrial revolution began to spread beyond Britain. The fall in transport costs and the growing integration of the world economy facilitated a growing international division of labour. It led to the progressive industrialization of Western Europe and the United States whilst various peripheral areas of white settlement (Canada, Australia and Argentina) began to specialize in producing raw materials and agricultural products for these growing industrial areas.

This period also saw the emergence, under British leadership, of the first liberal international economic order. From 1820 onwards external trade was progressively liberalized in Britain, many European countries and the US. This process culminated in the espousal of unilateral free trade as part of its economic ideology by Britain after the repeal of the Corn Laws in 1846. The next 20 years were the heyday of world-wide free trade.

The classical writers in Britain had meanwhile produced the intellectual justification for universal free trade in Ricardo's famous law of comparative advantage, which, as we shall see, despite attacks and counterattacks still provides the enduring justification for the ideal long term pattern of resource allocation for maximising global welfare, and thence the pattern of industrialization in the world economy.

However, with the rise of protection in the US after the Civil War in 1865, Germany which, by 1877, had abolished most tariffs faced the famous coalition of "rye and steel" which led it to abandon free trade soon afterwards, in 1879. France soon followed suit. But a newcomer to the world stage, Japan, was forced under the unequal treaties imposed on it by the opening of the country by Commander Perry to develop under a virtual free trade regime from 1858 – 98. This free trade regime together with the removal of various internal barriers to trade and labour mobility after the Meiji restoration provided the impetus for early Japanese industrialization, which seemed to follow the first steps on the "ladder of industrialization" began in Britain, with simple light manufactures such as textiles as its major engine.

It was during this phase too, that the so-called "second industrial revolution" consisting of a cluster of innovations based on the greater use and institutionalization of applied science and research became important. What is now called total factor productivity (TFP) (or the Solow residual) came to exert a major influence on overall growth rates, and thence on differences in growth performance between countries. In Britain between 1899 – 1913, TFP (as estimated by [Crafts, 1985, p. 159]) was nought, whereas in the US it rose from 0.35% p.a. before 1890 to 0.84% in 1890 – 95 and 1.52% p.a. in 1905 – 22 [David & Abramovitz, 1973]. In Germany, TFP in industry and commerce rose from 1.13% p.a. in 1870 – 1900 to 1.46 p.a. in 1900 – 13. These differences in UK and US & German performance have in turn been ascribed to "under investment in education especially scientific and technical education" [Crafts, ibid]. But as Crafts (1984) has emphasized in his study of the patterns of development in 19th century Europe (on the lines of Chenery and Syrquin (1975) for contemporary developing countries), it appears that in the 19th century "a plausible picture of Britain's comparative advantage ... is that it was based on exports of horse-power intensive products [in turn dependent on the availability of cheap coal] exchanged for imports of human-capital intensive products" (p. 454). If this resulted in lower TFP and thence a worse growth performance (than its competitors), we would have an early instance of a case where dynamic comparative advantage and hence potential growth might have been altered by public policy (in this case through greater provision of technical training and education). This is a theme which will recur in our later discussion.

The post 1870 period also saw the emergence of new arguments for protection, and what Schumpeter called "the defeat of liberalism." The most important argument for protection advanced was for infant industry (or infant economy) protection associated with the names of Hamilton in the US and Liszt in Germany. This still finds an echo in our day (see Section 3 below).

The period from 1913 to 1950 encompassing two world wars, and the Great Depression, can be looked upon as one in which the international trading system, which had transmitted the growth impulse around the world (through the liberal economic order) broke down. Many developing countries particularly those in Latin America which had been integrated into the 19th century world economic order suffered disastrous collapses in their terms of trade. They thereafter became suspicious of the classical case for free trade and increasingly turned inward, progressively using more direct controls to foster import substituting industrialization. This period also saw the rise and implementation of the model of autarkic and forced industrialization pioneered by Stalin in the Soviet Union, which, too, was to have considerable resonance in the industrialization policies of many developing countries after the Second World War.

The post Second World War period till the first oil shock of 1973, marked a new golden age of world-wide growth, industrialization and expanding international trade. Based in part on the backlog of innovations which had not been converted into new products and processes in the interwar period, there was another "industrial revolution" based on the development of consumer durables for mass consumer markets. The rise of the multinational corporation led to the evolution of international trade and specialization based on the product cycle (see [Vernon, 1966]).

During this post war golden age, industrialization spread across the world. But initially there was a paradox. Nearly all the OECD countries participated in the booming global economy through a process of *liberalizing* the controls on foreign trade and payments they had instituted during the inter-war period. This process was underwritten by explict agreements for liberalizing trade under the auspices of various GATT trade rounds. By contrast most developing countries turned inwards. In this they were influenced in part by their experience of the collapse of world trade in the 30s; the seemingly shining example of successful industrialization under dirigisme in the Soviet Union; the almost universal economic nationalism to be found in particular in the newly independent countries; and by the emerging "new development economics" which appeared to denigrate the classical case for free trade in favour of import substituting industrialization not merely under state direction but also state ownership. In the 1960s some countries, notably the so-called Gang of Four (S. Korea, Taiwan, Hong Kong and Singapore) bucked this trend and switched policy. The dramatic effects of the resulting outward orientation in leading to rapid industrialization and equitable growth in these economies is now part of the folklore of the economics of development.

The subsequent two decades can be looked upon as the marking intermittent but gradual movement away in most of the Third World from "inward" to "outward" looking policies. This was accompanied by what has been called the "neoclassical resurgence" in development economics, which seemed to provide the intellectual basis for the reapplication of the classical prescriptions for economic development, most memorably developed in *The Wealth of Nations.* But given the pendular swings in opinion that have characterized the free-trade versus protection debate which lies at the heart of the question of industrial strategies for efficient long run resource allocation, new "protectionist" arguments which go under the name of the "new trade theory" and "selective industrial strategy" are being presently propounded.

II. Industrial Growth, Productivity and Structure

Figure 1 charts the post-war rates of manufacturing value added in developed and developing countries (1950 – 85). Since 1960 the growth rates in manufacturing have been much higher in the South than the North. The Southern growth rate was maintained till the second oil shock (1979) whereas that in the North faltered after the first oil shock of 1973. The growth rates of total output and of labour productivity in the North in the period 1950 – 73 were "higher than in the whole of period 1870 – 1950, and in the case of the war damaged economies of Europe and Japan, sometimes twice or three times as high" [UNIDO, 1985, p. 9].

The growth rates of manufacturing output and employment by ISIC categories

Table 1-1. Growth Rate of MVA; North and South Compared by Industrial Branch, 1963 – 1981[a]

(Percentage per annum)

ISIC	Branch	Growth Rate of Value Added 1963 – 1979[b] North	South	1980[c] North	South	1981[c] North	South
	Total manufacturing	5.0	6.7	0.5	4.7	1.0	−0.1
311/2	Food products	3.7	5.1	1.4	5.7	0.5	4.1
313	Beverages	4.4	7.2	1.6	9.4	1.2	5.6
314	Tobacco	2.7	4.9	1.8	3.2	0.2	8.0
321	Textiles	3.4	3.9	−0.7	2.7	−2.1	0.4
322	Wearing apparel	3.8	5.1	−0.7	1.4	0.1	3.9
323	Leather and fur products	2.3	4.3	−5.0	3.1	1.5	6.5
324	Footwear	2.2	3.2	−1.1	3.7	−0.6	3.4
331	Wood and cork products	3.1	5.2	−4.4	5.1	−3.7	−1.7
332	Furniture and fixtures	4.9	4.6	−0.6	6.7	−2.2	−5.8
341	Paper and paper products	4.0	6.1	0.9	5.1	0.1	0.3
342	Printing and publishing	3.3	4.3	2.1	4.3	0.5	3.0
351	Industrial chemicals	7.4	10.4	−2.1	3.4	1.9	1.5
352	Other chemicals	5.7	8.7	1.7	8.8	2.9	−1.1
353	Petroleum refineries	5.9	7.6	−5.0	3.9	−4.3	2.0
354	Misc. petroleum and coal products	2.2	6.3	−2.6	8.0	−1.3	3.7
355	Rubber products	4.8	7.0	−3.0	7.3	−0.3	−3.3
356	Plastic.products	10.7	7.9	−0.8	5.4	2.2	−2.2
361	Pottery, china and earthenware	4.6	6.4	4.1	5.1	−0.7	−6.9
362	Glass and glass products	5.7	8.5	2.4	4.2	−1.5	0.6
369	Other non-metal mineral products	4.7	8.2	−2.0	7.7	−1.9	2.6
371	Iron and steel	3.3	7.4	−5.1	3.7	−1.2	−1.0
372	Non-ferrous metals	5.1	6.3	1.1	−1.1	−1.4	−7.1
381	Metal products	5.2	7.0	0.0	3.8	0.6	−4.7
382	Non-electrical machinery	5.6	11.0	3.3	5.8	2.9	−7.1
383	Electrical machinery	7.2	10.3	4.7	4.8	3.8	−0.9
384	Transport equipment	5.2	8.2	−1.5	4.0	1.7	−6.0
385	Professional and scientific goods	7.9	9.5	5.5	−1.5	3.2	−6.6
390	Other manufactures	5.7	4.6	3.5	−0.4	1.2	−1.0

Source: UNIDO (1985) p. 11.

[a] These growth rates differ from those shown in figure 1.II because the latter are an estimate from national accounts GDP components while those in this table are based on manufacturing surveys. Disaggregate data before 1963 are not available.

[b] Compounded annually between 1963 and 1979 (by semi-log regression).

[c] Growth over the previous year.

Table 1-2.. Growth Rate of Manufacturing Employment North and South Compared by Industrial branch, 1963 – 1980

(Percentage per annum)

		Employment Growth Rate			
		1963 – 1979[a]		1980[b]	
ISIC	Branch	North	South	North	South[c]
	Total manufacturing	1.2	5.1	−0.3	1.5
311/2	Food products	0.9	5.1	0.4	3.0
313	Beverages	0.4	4.0	−1.9	0.4
314	Tobacco	−0.6	4.8	−0.3	3.6
321	Textiles	−0.7	3.0	−2.4	2.2
322	Wearing apparel	1.0	9.1	0.0	−1.7
323	Leather and fur products	−0.3	6.1	−1.1	−3.8
324	Footwear	−0.3	6.2	0.5	0.9
331	Wood and cork products	−0.3	5.8	−2.3	1.1
332	Furniture and fixtures	1.5	5.0	−0.8	1.4
341	Paper and paper products	0.3	5.7	−0.5	1.8
342	Printing and publishing	1.0	2.8	2.2	1.3
351	Industrial chemicals	1.3	6.1	0.1	2.7
352	Other chemical	0.6	5.2	1.3	0.7
353	Petroleum refineries	1.4	4.8	1.6	4.1
354	Misc. petroleum and coal products	1.5	4.5	−1.3	−4.6
355	Rubber products	1.1	5.5	−2.7	2.4
356	Plastic products	4.9	7.9	1.9	0.3
361	Pottery, china and earthenware	0.6	4.3	−0.4	5.0
362	Glass and glass products	0.9	4.6	−1.3	0.3
369	Other non-metal mineral products	1.1	5.4	−0.9	1.6
371	Iron and steel	0.1	5.2	−1.8	0.7
372	Non-ferrous metals	0.8	5.7	0.9	1.9
381	Metal products	1.3	4.7	0.3	1.1
382	Non-electrical machinery	1.5	7.3	1.0	2.3
383	Electrical machinery	3.4	8.4	1.4	0.3
384	Transport equipment	1.7	3.7	1.2	0.2
385	Professional and scientific goods	2.0	8.4	0.1	7.2
390	Other manufactures	1.2	8.0	2.1	5.6

Source: UNIDO (1985) p. 12.
[a] Compounded annually between 1963 and 1979 (by semi-log regression)
[b] Growth over the precious year
[c] Estimate

for the period 1963 – 79 for the North and South is given in Table 1. The "South outperformed the North in all the branches of manufacturing except furniture and fixtures, plastic products and other manufactures" [UNIDO, op. cit. p. 12].

But this average performance conceals large divergences in performance amongst the group of Southern countries. Table 2 gives the growth rates in industry and export for a sample of 21 developing countries which are part of a multi-country

Table 2.

	6	7		8		9			10			11
Country	Distortion Index	Total Factor Productivity Gwth %	%Va	Industrial Growth Rates 1965–80	1980–85	Export Growth Rate % P.A. 1970–80	1980–85	1960–85	Ratio X: GDP 1950	Ratio X: GDP 1985	% CH in Ratio	Ag Prod Growth Rate 50–85
A. Labour Abundant												
Hong Kong	na	4.28	47	na		9.4	9.4	10.71	79.3 (1960)	106.6	34.4	−1.10 (60–84)
Singapore	na	−0.01	−0.1	12.2	5.9	12	5.9	7.6	163 (1960)	196 (1982)	20.2	1.3 (60–85)
Malta	na	na	na	na					65.4 (1955)	72.5	10.9	na
Median		2.1	23.5			10.7	7.7	9.2	79.3	106.6	20.2	0.1
Mean		2.1	23.5			10.7	7.7	9.2	102.6	125	21.8	0.1
Variance		4.6	554.6			1.7	3.1	2.4	1858.3	2711.9	93.4	1.4
B. Land Abundant												
Malaysia	1.57	na	na	na	6.7	7.4	10.7	7.4	54.8 (1955)	54.8	0	3.7
Thailand	1.43	1	na	9.5	5.1	11.8	8.4	8.44	21.8	26	19.3	4.3
Brazil	1.86	2	53.7 21.9	10.0	0.3	7.5	6.6	6.4	9.6	12	25	4.1
Mexico	1.86	2	28.3 37.5	7.6	0.3	13.4	10.1	9.4	14.1	16.1	14.1	4.1
Turkey	2.14	2.23	34.8	7.2	6.0	5.5	25.3	10.14 (65–85)	8.2	20.6	151.2	3.2
Costa Rica	na	na	na	8.7	−0.1	3.5	0.4	5.0	27.4	31.5	15	3.4 (60–85)
Columbia	1.71	2.1	20.7	5.5	2.9	1.9	1.6	1.96	10.9	14.7	34.9	3.3
Nigeria	2.71	na	na	13.4	−5.8	2.6	−9.9	1.5	20.7	16.7	−19.3	2.2
Ghana	2.86	na	na	1.4	−5.5	−8.4	−7.9	−4.9	33.5	9.6	−71.3	3.2
Uruguay	2.29	na	na	3.1	−7.2	4.8	(.)	2.8	3.7	23.5	535.1	0.7
Median	1.86	2	34.8			5.5	6.6	6.4	14.1	20.6	19.3	3.4

Continued overleaf

Table 2. (Continued)

Country	6 Distortion Index	7 Total Factor Productivity Gwth %	7 Total Factor Productivity %Va	8 Industrial Growth Rates 1965–80	8 Industrial Growth Rates 1980–85	9 Export Growth Rate % P.A. 1970–80	9 Export Growth Rate % P.A. 1980–85	9 Export Growth Rate % P.A. 1960–85	10 Ratio X: GDP 1950	10 Ratio X: GDP 1985	10 % CH in Ratio	11 Ag Prod Growth Rate 50–85
Mean	1.92	1.87	33.5			5	4.5	4.7	20.5	20.5	65	3.2
Variance	0.3	0.2	127.9			36.2	103.2	20.6	231.1	168.4	28752.7	1
C. Intermediate												
Egypt	2.14	1.66	na	7.0	7.0	−0.7	3.9	1.8	19.5 (1960)	21.5	10.3	2.9
Indonesia	1.86	0.6	na	11.9	1.0	8.7	1.1	5.3	13.3 (1960)	22.9	72.2	3.5
Sri Lanka	1.86	na	na	5.1	4.2	−2.4	7.3	2.3	38.9	25.6	−34.2	3.1
Malawi	1.14	na	na	na	1.3	5.7	2.9	7.4	20.8 (1955)	23.5	13	3.5 (60–85)
Peru	2.29	1.5	28.3	4.4	−3.0	3.9	1.4	2.6	20.8	21.6	3.8	2.1
Jamaica	2.29	na	na	−0.1	−1.6	−6.3	−7.2	−2.5	30.5	58.2	90.8	1.3
Mauritius	na	na	na	na	4.3	3.4	7.4	4.4	46	53.5	16.3	0.09 (60–85)
Madagascar	na	na	na	na	−6.8	−1.2	−2.8	1.02	11.9 (1960)	14.5	21.8	2.3
Median	2.14	1.5	28.3			2.6	1.4	2.3	20.8	22.9	1.3	2.3
Mean	2	1.3	28.3			1.5	0.4	2.6	24.7	28.7	19.4	2.3
Variance	0.19	0.32	0			14.2	32.2	4.9	117.4	222.6	1404.3	1.1

Figure 1. Manufacturing Value Added

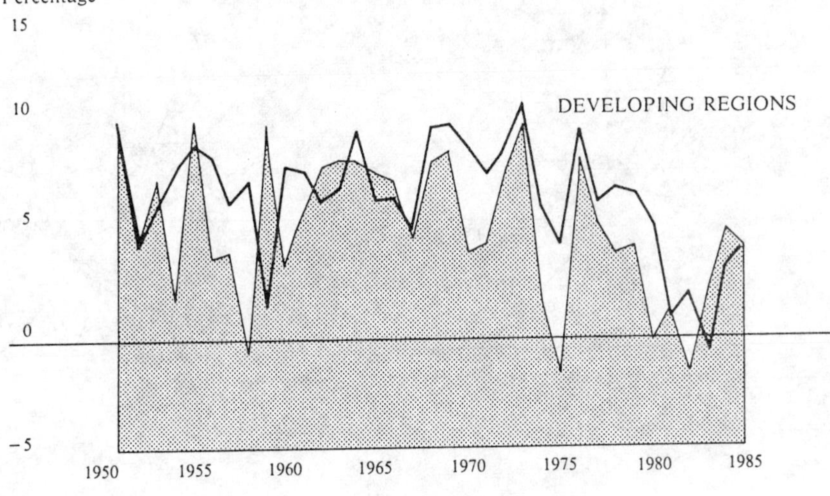

Source: UNIDO (1985) p. 10

comparative study of the political economy of poverty and growth co-directed by the present author and Hla Myint. Two points need to be made. First, the growth rates given are at market prices, and as Little, Scitovsky, Scott showed in their classic study of trade and industrialization in protected economies, these growth rates at distorted market prices overstate the true contribution of industrial growth to national welfare. For that estimates of value added at world prices would be required and these are not available. But from Little et al.'s estimates for 1950–64 for their 6 countries (Argentina, Brazil, Mexico, Pakistan, Philippines, Taiwan) (see their Table 2.13) it is apparent that this factor can be of considerable importance in forming any judgement about industrial performance in various developing countries. Thus protection besides lowering the efficiency of resource allocation and thence the long run rate of industrialization, also implies that observed rates of growth in protected economies would be overstated.

Second, in the post war "golden age" the world-wide boom pulled most developing countries along, irrespective of the policy induced distortions in the working of their price mechanisms resulting from the almost universal protectionism they had adopted in the first decade after 1950. It was in the more turbulent conditions in the world economy (beginning in 1973 but accentuated after the second oil crisis of 1979), that the inflexibilities in production and trade structures engendered by their past dirigiste trade and industrial policies, led to differences in overall and industrial growth performance. A rough and ready indicator of this (for our sample of 21 countries) is provided by correlations between the industrial growth

Figure 2. Structural Change: the World, Developed Countries and Developing Countries, 1965 – 80
(Index of value added: 1965 = 100)

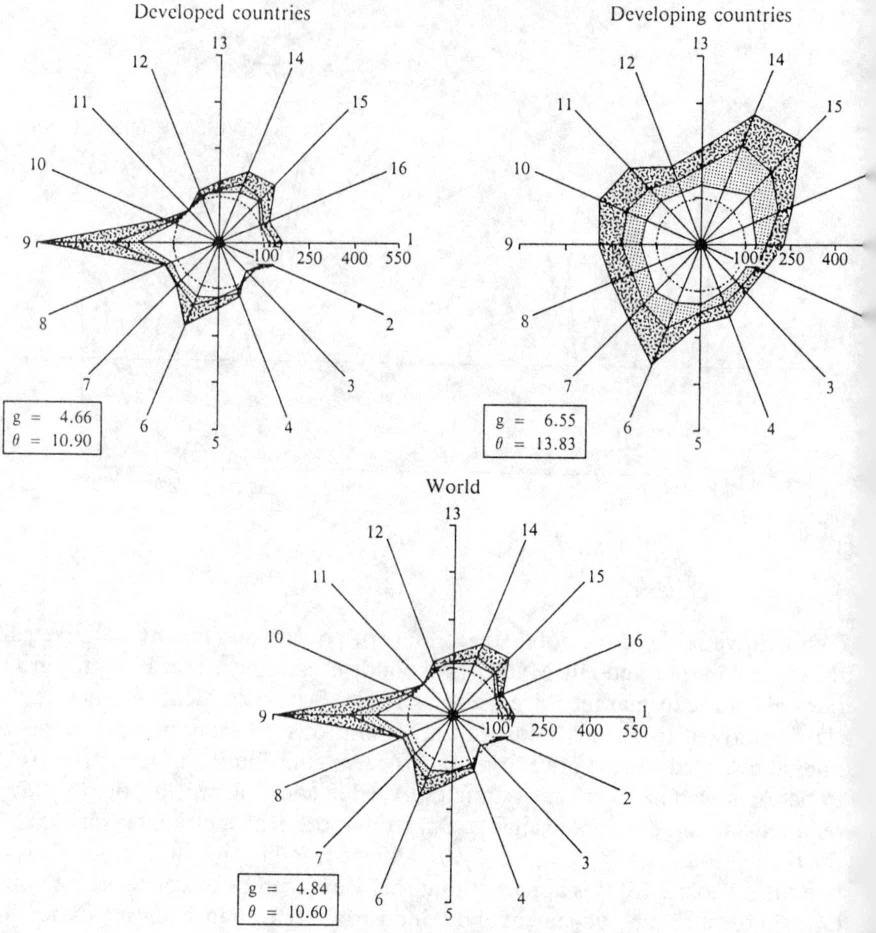

Developed countries

13 12 14 11 15 10 16 9 1 100 250 400 550 8 2 7 3 6 4 5

g = 4.66
θ = 10.90

Developing countries

13 12 14 11 15 10 9 100 250 400 8 7 3 6 4 5

g = 6.55
θ = 13.83

World

13 12 14 11 15 10 16 9 1 100 250 400 550 8 2 7 3 6 4 5

g = 4.84
θ = 10.60

Key:
Branches (ISIC code):

1 Food products (311/2, 313, 314)
2 Textiles (321, 322)
3 Leather industries (323, 324)
4 Wood and furniture (331, 332)
5 Paper and printing (341, 342)
6 Chemicals (351, 352)
7 Petroleum and coal (353, 354)
8 Rubber products (355)
9 Plastic products (356)
10 Non-metal mineral products (361, 362, 369)
11 Iron and steel (371)
12 Non-ferrous metals (372)
13 Metal products, excl. machinery (381)
14 Non-electrical machinery (382)
15 Electrical machinery (383)
16 Transport equipment (384)

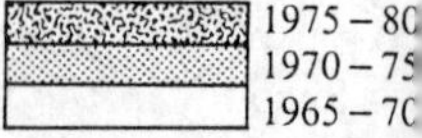

g Average annual growth r
1965 – 80 (percentage)
θ Index of structural chang
1965 – 80
(constant prices in 1975 do

Source: UNIDO (1985) p. 33

Figure 3. Relationship between Total Factor Productivity Growth and Total Factor Input Growth

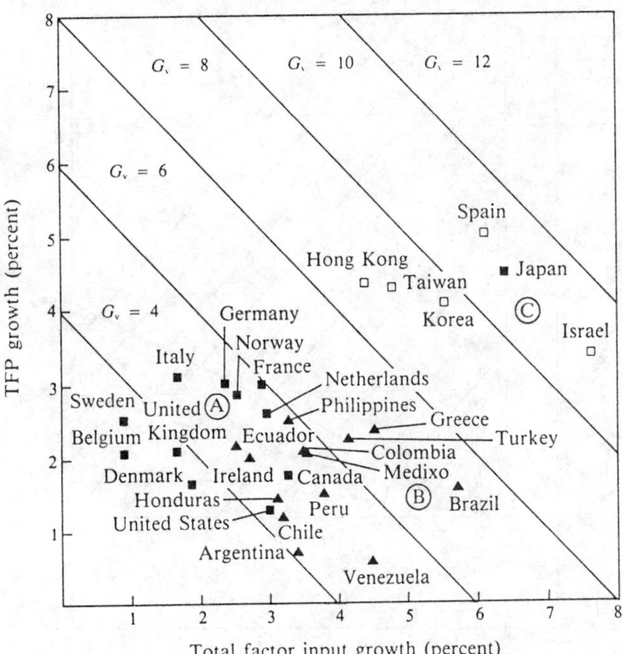

Source: Chenery et al (1986) Fig. 2.5, p. 25

rates (g_I) in 1965 – 80 and 1980 – 85 and a distortion index (D) developed by Aggarwal, and also shown in Table 2. The estimated OLS regressions are:

$$\begin{aligned} 1965-80: \quad G_I &= 12.83 \quad - \; 2.96\,D \\ &\quad\;(2.09) \qquad (1.03) \\ R^2 &= 0.09 \\ 1980-85: \quad G_I &= 17.35 \quad - \; 8.13\,D \\ &\quad\;(3.14) \qquad (3.14) \\ R^2 &= 0.47 \end{aligned}$$

(Figures in brackets are T ratios)

Finally, we can obtain some idea of the changing industrial structure in developing countries, developed countries and the world in terms of a schema devized by UNIDO and reproduced in Figure 2. This shows the changing value shares of 16 manufacturing branches in the overall change in manufacturing output, along 16 rays.[1]

As the UNIDO report notes, plastic products are growing in value share at world level, largely because this was the fastest growing branch in developed countries.

Figure 4. Relationship between Total Factor Productivity Growth and Total Factor Input Growth by Country

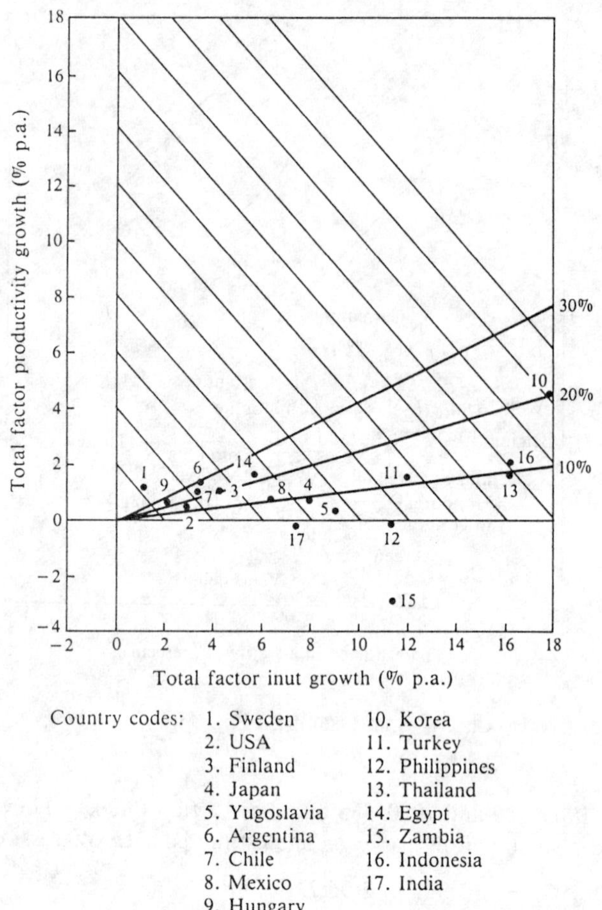

Source: Page (1990) p. 113

Industrial growth appears to be much more balanced in the developing countrie taken as a whole. But again this aggregate hides important differences betwee countries. (see [UNIDO, op cit]).

Ever since the pace of technical innovations was determined by institutiona ized R & D in the post 1870 period, a crucial question concerning industrializatio strategies has been the role of technical progress in determining the overall (an in particular the industrial) growth performance of economies. The growth ac counting techniques pioneered by Solow and extensively applied and refined b Dennison and others, has been applied to a number of developing and develope countries. Chenery et al. (1986) have provided a useful summary of the availab

Figure 5. Relationship between Total Factor Productivity Growth and GNP per Capita

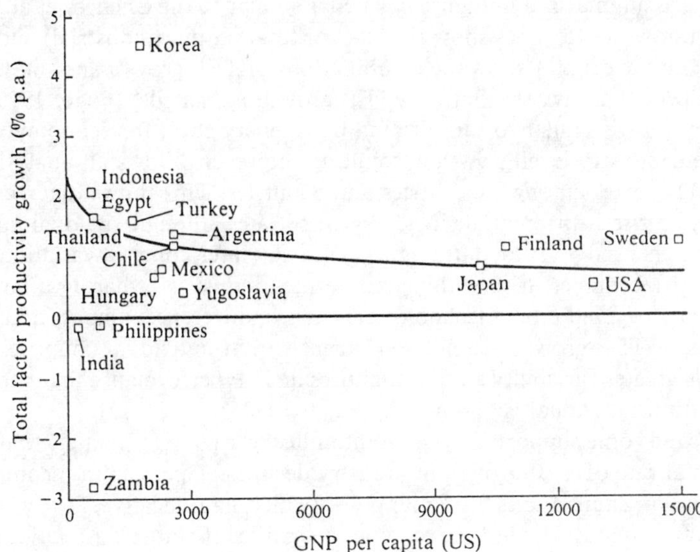

Source: Page (1990) p. 114

7 country studies, covering 39 countries around the world, of the sources of 'owth. Figure 3 provides a summary picture of the results. This shows that most eveloped countries fit within the "A" cluster, with relatively low growth of the rimary factors (labour and capital) and with total factor productivity (TFP-the olow residual) accounting for 50 to 70 percent of overall growth. Japan, as in much else, is an exception, in both having double the average growth rate (G_v) r a developed country and a higher proportion being accounted for by growth factor inputs.

The developing countries fall into two groups. The larger one, group B, has w TFP growth (between 0.5 and 2.0 percent) and most of the output growth due to increased factor inputs. The smaller group C, consisted of 3 of the 4 -called Gang of Four, SE Asian high performers and Japan. They had much gher rates of overall growth (G_v) over 10%, based on both higher factor inputs nd TFP than other developing countries. It is the purported industrial targeting two of them (Korea and Japan) which it has recently been argued led to their gh TFP growth rates, and which is being used to resurrect a variant of the Listi- n argument for infant industry protection.

Whilst Chenery et al. looked at the contribution of TFP and factor inputs in verall growth, Nishimizu and Page (1987) have looked in terms of growth ac- ounting at the performance of particular industries at the ISIC two digit level for 18 countries between 1956–82.[2] Their results on the sources of overall industrial growth are summarized in Figure 4 which is similar to the Chenery et al. diagram, except now the 45° lines show the level of total output (industrial) and the three rays from the origin "show the combinations of TFP growth and total factor input growth that give the share of TFP growth indicated" [Page, 1990, p. 113]. The results are similar to those found by Chenery et al. for economy wide growth. Their industry level growth accounting, however, allows an analysis of variance in TFP rates amongst industries and countries. This shows that "as income per capita rises, differentials in TFP growth rates among individual industries decrease markedly. And, although significant inter-country variations in productivity performance arise within well-defined industries, sharing a largely common technology and rate of technological change, differences among industry-specific rates of TFP growth are not significant within individual countries. In short, there is greater variability among countries in TFP performance than among industries within individual economies." [Page, 1990, p. 112–13].

They also find some support for the infant industry argument, namely that the average annual rate of TFP growth in industry declines as per capita income increases. If India, Zambia and the Philippines (which had negative TFP growth in industry) are excluded from their sample, a significant statistical relationship between TFP growth in industry and GNP per capita (shown by the solid line in Figure 5) emerges.

But this then requires some explanation for the "outliers." One of these, India, in terms of its initial conditions in 1950 — an early start in industrialization in the mid-19th century leading to a substantial and relatively diversified industrial sector by the time of independence, an elastic supply of skilled labour, and a potentially large domestic market — could have been expected to have had high TFP growth. Moreover, its dirigiste system of controls was based in part on the type of "industrial strategy" which, it has been recently suggested, accounts for the better productivity performane of NICs such as Korea and Taiwan [Wade, Amsden] and Japan [Chalmers-Johnson]. Yet this "industrial strategy" has clearly failed in India. (See [Ahluwalia, Lal, 1989]). As Little et al. and the subsequent comparative studies by Bhagwati and Krueger, Donges et al., and Balassa and associates have shown, and as Page (1990) rightly sums up: "within the group of developing countries, ... the extreme variability of both average and industry-specific rates of productivity change — as well as their relative contributions to output growth — point to policy-based as opposed to structural explanations." We, therefore, need to examine the changing views about the appropriate industrial strategy which is closely linked to trade policy.

III. Industrial and Trade Policy

Following the publication of the magisterial comparative study by Little, Scitovsky and Scott in the late 1960s, both subsequent theoretical development and further comparative work on trade and industry seemed to have led to the so-called neo-classical consensus on the appropriate policy for trade and industry. The starting point is the classic case for free trade, modified by possible second best considerations. This was the theory of trade and welfare developed in the 1950s and 1960s.[3]

The static case for free trade is simple and powerful. The removal of barriers to foreign trade expands the feasible set of consumption possibilities, by in effect providing an indirect technology for transforming domestic resources into the goods and services that yield current and future utility to consumers. This static case does not involve any necessary commitment to laissez-faire. It is recognized that so-called ''endogenous'' domestic distortions may require appropriate domestic public interventions for their correction, but these interventions will not include interventions in foreign trade. Industrial promotion may hence be justified, protection will not be. It is also recognized that when a country has monopoly (monopsony) power in its foreign transactions and can (on either current or capital account) feasibly influence its relevant terms of trade, taxes or subsidies on trade may be justified. This ''optimal tariff'' argument provides the only ''first best'' justification for foreign trade intervention from the viewpoint of national welfare (in the absence of foreign retaliation). The so-called ''new'' or ''strategic'' trade theory (see [Krugman]) will be seen to be in essence a variant of this argument.

The dynamic version of the law of comparative advantage incorporates investment in line with a country's changing comparative advantage, which minimizes the present value of the resource costs of its future demands. By widening the market, foreign trade also allows a country to exploit economies of scale. Furthermore, the competitive pressures exerted by imports (or the need to export from increasing returns to scale industries for which the domestic market is too small) prevent the emergence of welfare-reducing domestic monopolies and induce domestic producers to improve quality and reduce costs. In terms of the recent theory of industrial organization, foreign trade increases contestability in existing or incipient monopolistic industries (see [Baumol et al., 1982], [Helpman & Krugman, 1985]).

Finally, to the extent the static gains are saved and invested efficiently, they will grow over time, while the introduction of new goods and (more important) new technology through foreign trade can effect an economy's rate of technical progress and thence its long run equilibrium rate of growth.

This neo-classical consensus which seemd to have been vindicated by the growing empirical evidence on the effects of alternative foreign trade regimes on economic performance,[4] has recently come under attack from various directions.

The first is a resurrection of the Listian type of argument for infant industry protection. As is well known (see [Corden, Baldwin, 1969]) the infant industry argument requires some form of dynamic external economies for its justification. If these exist, there will be grounds for government intervention. But the first best policy will be some appropriate domestic subsidy rather than protection from foreign trade, following the central tenet of the modern theory of trade and welfare that in dealing with domestic distortions it is best to deal directly with the distortion; intervention in foreign trade being at best a third or fourth best policy.

A necessary condition for infant industry intervention to be justified is that the inputs per unit of outputs decrease more rapidly in that industry (or in other words its total factor productivity increases) both relatively to (a) its foreign competitors, and (b) other industries in the country. But this condition is not sufficient, for in addition it is necessary that the discounted net present value of the losses incurred during the high cost phase are recouped during the post infancy phase to earn at least the social rate of return to investment in the economy. (see [Krueger-Tuncer, 1982], [Bell et al., 1984]).

The TFP test, which provides only the necessary conditions for justifying infant industry promotion was applied by Krueger and Tuncer to a sample of Turkish industry for 1963 – 76. They found there was no tendency for input per unit of output to fall more rapidly in more protected industries. Similarly in a survey of the productivity performance of infant industries in a number of developing countries, Bell et al. (1984) concluded:

> "There is little evidence about productivity growth among infant industries in todays less developed countries. But the evidence does suggest that many infant firms have failed to reach international competitiveness — or if they have once reached it, have failed to maintain it. This inference is consistent with the record of overall industrial performance in these countries. It is also consistent with findings from various studies of the costs of protection in developing countries" (p. 123).

However, as Bell et al. note, none of the studies they surveyed, explicitly estimated any externalities generated by the relevant firms for other firms (and vice versa). One of the more important externalities that is adduced in support of the infant industry case is labour training. Assuming that workers cannot borrow against the returns to prospective human capital, they will be unable to finance the costs of any on the job training that develops general skills. If firms are to bear the cost of training in general skills, they may suffer a loss and hence be unwilling to provide the training, which, nevertheless, is socially (at shadow prices) desirable. A social cost benefit study of labour training in the public sector in India [Charkvavarati, 1972] did find that the social rate of return to training was positive (and greater than the social discount rate) even though the private rate of return (to the firm) was negligible or negative. Public subsidization of labour training in industrial enterprises may thus be a valid form of industrial promotion, even though protection of industry (for the usual reasons of "getting to the heart of the matter") will not be.

But it is important to note that the presumed externality — often labelled a pecuniary externality — in the case of labour training, actually turns out to be a case of a distortion in the working of the capital market. It is the correction of this *distortion* which requires government intervention and not the existence of a pecuniary externality *per se*.

This illustrates the slippery notion of externalities, namely the uncompensated side effects of a producers or consumers activity on other economic agents. Two theoretical points need to be kept in mind in their identification.

The first is a distinction made by James Buchanan and Craig Stubblebine between Pareto-relevant and Pareto-irrelevant externalities. Pareto-relevant externalities are said to be present when, in a competitive equilibrium, the marginal conditions of optimal resource allocation and hence for Pareto-efficiency are violated. Then government intervention may be required. But not all the side-effects on consumers and producers in a highly interdependent market economy will result in Pareto-relevant externalities.

The second distinction, due to Jacob Viner, is between pecuniary and technological externalities. Pecuniary externalities are those in which one individual's activity level affects the financial circumstances of another. But this does not imply any resulting misallocation of resources. Consider, for example, a perfectly competitive economy in which there are continuous shifts in tastes and technology. Suppose that some group increases its consumption of whisky, the price rises, and that this affects the welfare of other consumers of whisky. This has no significance for the efficiency of the economy, which ex hypothesis is perfectly competitive and hence (in the jargon) Pareto-efficient. Or suppose there is a cost-saving invention by one producer. He increases his output and reduces his price. Through market interdependence other producers lose rents and are hurt, and consumers gain (consumer's surplus). It is readily shown that the consumer gains and those of the cost-reducing producer are always greater than the losses of the inefficient producers. What is more, the cost-reducing producer must not take account of the losses of the inefficient producers, for if he did, he would restrict output and would therefore be behaving as a quasi-monopolist; thus the industry's output level would be sub-optimal.

Pecuniary externalities are therefore synonymous with market interdependence and the price system. They must be Pareto-irrelevant. By contrast, technological externalities are interdependencies between economic agents which are not mediated through the market, and hence not reflected in relative prices. A well-known example is the smoke emitted by a factory which raises the costs of a nearby laundry.

Apart from technological externalities (non-market interdependence) the other main potential cause of market failure is "increasing returns due to indivisibilities or peculiarities of the production function" [Arrow & Scitovsky, 1969, p. 183]. The discussion of externalities particularly as regards industrial policy in developing countries was greatly muddled by Scitovsky's definition of "pecuniary externalities" which cause market failure owing primarily to economies of scale (increasing returns) and the long lag with which market prices transmit information about investment decisions." [Arrow & Scitovsky, op. cit. p. 184]). These are *not* pecuniary externalities in Viner's sense. These sources of potential market failure are more properly described as being due to the presence of increasing returns and what may be called imperfections in futures markets, so that future prices, on whose estimates investment must be planned, do not exist.

Both these sources of potential market failure are of importance in the recent revival of the case for what is called selective government intervention in industrial policy (see for instance Pack & Westphal (1986) for the most cogent statement of this case). It may, therefore, be useful to see what theory tells us about the relevance of these two sources of potential market failure in an open economy, before we turn to the examples of Japan and South Korea which are usually cited as cases of successful industrial dirigisme.

It has been well known since Graham (1923) (and proved by [Grandmont and McFaden, 1972]) that in the standard neo-classical open economy general equilibrium model, increasing returns that are *external* to individual firms but internal to an industry still allow a perfectly competitive equilibrium, but that domestic output valued at constant prices may be lower in a trading equilibrium compared to autarky if with trade there is a decline in the output of industries with increasing returns to scale.

With increasing returns to scale *internal* to the firm (that is with decreasing costs over the relevant range of output for an individual firm) it is well known that the market for its output cannot be perfectly competitive (with price equal to marginal cost). There has been a recent flurry of theoretical activity to model the ensuing imperfect market structures and their implications for both the positive and normative theories of trade (see [Helpman & Krugman]). Some development economists ([Stewart, 1984] [Helliner, 1988]) have drawn the implications from this so-called ''new'' or ''strategic'' trade theory that the policy prescription of the post 1970s neo-classical resurgence (namely outward looking policies are optimal for developing countries)is invalid.

In an important paper Markusen and Melvin synthesize the results on the gains from trade in the presence of increasing returns and differentiated products (a summary of the various models is available in Helpman (1984), whilst Srinivasan provides a survey which looks in particular at the relevance of these models for developing countries). They identify three types of models that have been developed. The *first,* are with homogeneous goods and with increasing returns to scale (IRS) *external* to individual firms. The *second,* are with homogeneous goods and with IRS *internal* to individual firms and *third* models with differentiated products produced under monopolistic competition. They show that in all three cases GFT may not occur for the same two reasons. As is well known, in the standard neo-classical trade model with constant returns to scale and perfect competition, the free trade price line is tangential to the economy's production frontier (implying marginal cost pricing) and also forms a separating hyperplane to the production set. In all the three type of ''new'' trade theory models, the IRS goods have marginal costs lower than price, so the tangency condition breaks down, with the free trade price line cutting the production set at the free trade point. Second, even if the tangency condition is satisfied (that is marginal costs equal price), IRS could lead to non-convexities in the production set, so that even a price plane which is tangential may not form a separating hyperplane to the production set. They then show:

> "With respect to the tangency conditions, results (generally well known) show that losses from trade may occur if trade contracts the IRS industries. The intuition is fairly straightforward. With prices greater than marginal costs in autarky, the economy is already under-producing the IRS goods. If trade reduces production further, the economy may be moving away rather than towards its optimal production mix. We suggested that a sufficient condition for GFT is that trade have a certain rationalizing effect on production. This is a rather crude notion to the effect that surviving industries expand output more than in proportion to the number of IRS industries lost due to the opening of trade. We argued that this is in fact a reasonable outcome (although hard to define rigorously) provided that trade does not decrease the total resources devoted to the IRS industries.
>
> Non-convexities present a more difficult problem. On the one hand, we are able to show that the same expansion of all IRS industries that is sufficient for GFT in the convex case continues to be sufficient in the presence of non-convexties. Further, this result does not rely on restrictive functional forms, specialization in production, or on average-cost pricing in the IRS industries. On the other hand, the weighted increase in the outputs of the IRS industries that is sufficient in the convex case is no longer sufficient with non-convexities. We are thus still without a sufficient condition for GFT in the realistic case in which trade expands some IRS industries and contracts others."

If theory is inconclusive, what of the empirical evidence?

An OECD study surveying the empirical research on trade liberalization and imperfect competition found that the gains from trade were greater under imperfect as compared with perfect competition. No empirical support was found for the view that there would be greater gains from trade intervention when there was imperfect competition (see [Richardson, 1989]).

There is little comfort for protectionists or dirigistes in this conclusion.

However, protectionist policy conclusions have been drawn from the "new" strategic trade theory models, particularly in the notorious "Kodak" papers.[5] These are in essence based on a very simple notion (most sharply brought out in [Krugman, 1987]), namely that as the monopolistic or oligopolistic firms (which exist under IRS) enjoy excess profits (with prices above marginal costs), the government is in a position to shift profits from foreign to domestic firms by either subsidizing domestic firms or else by putting import restrictions on the products of their foreign competitors. As Krugman, one of the progenitors of this theory argues, the relevance of the theory is however likely to be limited. First, it is necessary to have reliable models of oligopolistic behaviour (which are unavailable) to determine the optimal policy. Second, the general equilibrium effects on the rest of the economy of the targeted industries need to be known. Third, there is (as with the optimal tariff argument) the threat of tariff retaliation and a trade war. Fourth, with the ubiquitous rent seeking by special interests, the Olson problem arises: "The kinds of interventions that the new trade theory suggests ... will typically raise the welfare of small, fortunate groups by large amounts, while imposing costs on larger, more diffuse groups. The result ... can easily be that excessive or misguided intervention takes place because the beneficiaries have more knowledge and influence than the losers." [Krugman, 1987]. As a general policy free trade, he therefore argues correctly, is likely to be second best even from the viewpoint of the national weal!

The new trade theory, however, is claimed [Helliner, 1985] to have even greater relevance for "small" developing countries which have some foreign oligopolies earning rents in the home market. The government can through an appropriate tax-subsidy policy (like a two part tariff) not only shift these rents to domestic consumers but also get the foreign monopolist to finance the subsidy. (See Srinivasan for an outline of the model and why it is unrealistic). Various other arguments that have been advanced in the context of the new trade theory are surveyed by Srinivasan, and need not concern us. As he concludes, most of these recent outpourings "do not contradict the presumption that outward orientated policies that promote competition and efficiency will be beneficial. Indeed, given that concentration in industry and oligopolistic behaviour by *firms* in the *domestic market* have often been *created* by the set of policies pursued as part of the import-substituting industrialization, it is not profit diversion from foreign, but the promotion of competition and improvement in the efficiency of the operation of domestic firms that is important" (p. 21).

This leaves the "pecuniary" externalities associated with increasing returns which were used by Scitovsky and Rosenstein-Rodan to advocate programmes of "balanced growth" and "big pushes" in the 50s. The arguments being advanced for industrial strategies for instance by Pack & Westphal (1986) are of the same ilk. But these "pecuniary" externalities are Pareto-irrelevant . If they were Pareto-relevant, then as Scitovsky noted "the complete integration of all industries would be necessary to eliminate all divergences between private profit and public benefit" (p. 249) or, as Rosenstein-Rodan advocated, "the whole of industry to be created is to be treated and planned like one huge firm or trust" (p. 204). This so-called co-ordination of investment plans is, of course, nothing else but the planning syndrome — the search for a centrally determined investment plan which takes account not merely of current but all future changes in the demand supply of a myriad of goods. It is now known that because of imperfect information and irreducible uncertainty no market economy can ever attain the inter-temporal Pareto efficient outcome of the Utopian Arrow-Debreu theoretical construct, where there are markets for all "commodities" indexed by date and state of nature till Kingdom come. But neither can the planners achieve this outcome, as Hayek & Mises pointed out years ago in the debate about the efficiency of Soviet type central planning.[6] The recent collapse of this system world-wide is a resounding empirical confirmation of the validity of the Austrian insight that in the real world imperfect markets are superior to imperfect planning.

The reason lies in the role of entrepreneurship and decentralized forecasting in a world of irreducible (Knightian) uncertainty. Unless planners can foretell the future better than entrepreneurs there is no reason to believe, and plenty of evidence from the gigantic mistakes[7] by planners to disconfirm the view that investment decisions based on planners forecasts will be better than those of a myriad of entrepreneurs about the likely *future* changes in technology, tastes and resources, and hence on the demand and supply and relative prices of different goods.

How can this be squared with the purported perfection of "planners" in Japan and South Korea.[8] It is undoubtedly the case that these economies (unlike Hong Kong for instance) are not examples of classical laissez-faire. Dirigiste industrial policies have been followed, and seemingly have been highly successfully given their exceptional growth performance. But this begs the question whether the good performance has been due to or in spite of their industrial dirigisme. To assume that the two are causally linked is like assuming that because quite often witch doctors are seen to and believed to have made efficacious cures, their remedies are the causes of the patient's recovery.

This last statement is not merely rhetorical. For the advocates of successful industrial dirigisme in Japan and S. Korea have singularly failed to provide any evidence of a *replicable* mechanism whereby the industrial planners in these countries succeeded in efficient "industrial targeting" whereas others (most notably in India, but also countries like Brazil, Turkey or Mexico) have failed. Unless Korean and Japanese bureaucrats are more prescient than their fellows in other countries — and why should they be — there is no logical reason provided for their success.[9]

In fact, there is evidence that far from bring prescient the South Korean planners clearly made mistakes, particularly in promoting the development of heavy industry in the 70s. But unlike their counterparts in other developing countries, they saw and corrected their policy errors fairly quickly. Similarly Singapore, another relatively dirigiste but outward looking country sought to jump a few rungs on the ladder of comparative advantage by legislating higher wages. The adverse impact on its growth performance led to a speedy correction of its mistake.

The important and interesting question about the dirigisme found in many NICs is not, as is often alleged (against all logic and whatever patchy and inconclusive evidence on relative TFP rates etc. that is available), the nature of the superior skills of their industrial planners in picking industrial winnners, but why they did not make the mistakes of many other countries in promoting inappropriate industrialization (that is not in line with their dynamic comparative advantage) and when they did, why was there swift recognition and rectification of these mistakes. The results from a multi-country comparative study of growth and poverty that Hla Myint and I have recently completed for the World Bank suggest some possible answers.

We have used an open economy theoretical framework with three factors of production (land, labour and land) due to Krueger and Leamer. This allows a classification of countries in terms of their initial resource endowments (c 1950) into labour abundant, land abundant and intermediate with reference to the aggregate world endowment of the three factors of production.

The resulting model provides a richer menu of possible efficient development paths than the standard 2 × 2 Hecksher-Ohlin model. The latter is mainly relevant for labour abundant economies. For them it implies the standard prescription of developing labour intensive industries, and then moving up the ladder of comparative advantage with capital accumulation. On this development path, real wages rise and hence there is unlikely to be any conflict between the needs of the economy and the polity (irrespective of its different forms). The major task for the government is to provide an adequate infrastructure to reduce the transaction costs of the relatively small scale organizational units which will predominate in the earlier stages of this development path. In a sense this growth path is the easiest to follow. This is largely because the incremental comparative advantage of the country is self-evident, as are the infrastructural requirements. Moreover, if the country is small, the limited size of the domestic market makes reliance on foreign trade inevitable. This makes it less likely that any grave departures from the free trade resource allocation will emerge—irrespective of the degree of "dirigisme" of the government. There seem to be two reasons for this. First, given the small size of the domestic market, any departures from the free trade allocation, is unlikely to lead to vertical import-substitution (into the inputs required by domestic industry). Hence, when the costs of inappropriate import-substitution become clear, it will be easier to switch the policy regime, by creating an "as if" free trade regime for exporters by allowing them to obtain their inputs at world prices. For there will be no domestic import substitute producers of such inputs and hence their lobbies preventing their competitive import. By contrast, in larger countries, or those with more intermediate resource endowments, such a switch in policy regime will be politically difficult as it would hurt the interests of inefficient import substitute intermediate goods producers.[10] Mistakes can thus be more easily rectified as part of a learning process, because the political costs of rectification are likely to be low.

A labour abundant country's growth path is likely to be easier for a second reason. Its incremental comparative advantage is readily apparent to economic agents both in the public and private sector. In this sense "industrial winners" are more obvious, and the consequences of picking losers (or policies which stimulate losers) more immediate — as with Singapore's ill-advised and ill-fated attempts to jump a few rungs on the ladder of comparative advantage through an artificial raising of wages. The propensity towards dirigisme of most Third World states can thus be satisfied at low cost in such countries, and their governments can gain the kudos of visiting academics for their rational dirigisme in having promoted the obvious winners. But as any dirigisme has deadweight costs, there will still be some, though perhaps small costs, of substituting public for private action. But there may be additional costs if hubris sets in and the "planners" depart from the obvious and seek to promote industries which do not fit the country's incremental comparative advantage.[11]

Similarly, the comparative advantage of a large land-abundant country is also likely to be relatively obvious, but much more difficult, to realize. This is for two reasons. First, with a high supply price of labour (compared with the labour abundant countries) due to its more favorable labour-land ratios, once such a country seeks to industrialize, its incremental comparative advantage is likely to lie on the relatively capital intensive rungs of the ladder of comparative advantage. As the development of such industries is likely to require lumpy investments, scarce skills and imported technology, it may be difficult to develop such industries without at least some public promotion. The dangers of "bureaucratic failure" endemic in such promotion may then lead to a failure to realize their economic potential.

Second, with increasing population, if the rate of capital accumulation is not high enough, then their efficient development path could contain segments where real wages need to fall. Thus, unlike the unilinear (rising wage) development path of the labour abundant countries, land abundant countries might find that they first have to move onto a higher rung of the ladder of comparative advantage, then slide down a few rungs (if capital growth is not rapid enough), before proceeding on a similar unilinear path as their labour abundant cousins. This required "equilibrium" time-path of real wages could, however, pose some serious political problems if the polity is subject to factional democratic pressure. We could get a polity which seeks to resist the "equilibrium" real wage adjustments by turning "inward" and thence comes to be at odds with its comparative advantage.

The intermediate group of resource endowment countries have the most difficult development paths. For, first, their incremental comparative advantage is not so apparent. Hence, "mistakes"[12] are not easily recognized, nor rectified — particulary if the "mistakes" have been made by the public sector, which in the absence of any bankruptcy constraint, resists the exit of inefficient firms. Second, like the land-abundant countries the intermediate groups are also likely to face situations in which their polities are at odds with their comparative advantage.

Conclusion

Our conclusion can be brief. In the by now long history of industrialization around the world, it is apparent that by and large an outward orientated trade regime which embodies the classical law of dynamic comparative advantage aids efficient industrialization. But there is still an important role for government in providing that essential economic framework — a legal system ensuring clear property rights, a monetary constitution which assures monetary stability — which allows the entrepreneur (who is ultimately at the heart of the growth process) to do his/her job. In addition, it is in the provision of these essential public goods and quasi public goods such as infrastructure, together with the development of human resources (education, training, health) that governments should ideally confine their necessarily limited capabilities. To urge them to undertake selective industrial policies, as many voices are currently recommending, is a snare and a delusion.

NOTES

1. Along each of the sixteen rays, 1000 measures the base year (1965) level. If the overall growth was taking place evenly in all branches, then one would observe a series of concentric circles. Thus the distortion of the shape away from a perfect circle tells us where change is occurring.
2. There is, however, one general issue raised by these growth accounting studies which needs to be considered. This is whether so-called "outward orientations" in trade policy leads to higher TFP and hence overall growth performance. As Bhagwati and Srinivasan have argued, there is no reason to believe that TFP rates in import substitution industries are lower than in export industries, and hence no conclusive evidence on the *efficiency* of outward orientated reforms can be derived in this way. For a survey of studies of TFP and trade reform see Havrylshyvn (1990).
3. The pioneers of this theory were Meade, Haberler, Bhagwati-Ramaswami, Johnson and Corden. The latter still provides the best synthesis and summary of the theory.
4. A survey is provided in Lal & Rajapatirana (1987). Also see Havrylyshyn (1990) for a survey of the literature looking more explicitly at the connection between TFP growth and trade regimes.
5. By Krugman & Dornbusch. A concise and hard-hitting critique of the "new" trade theory is Haberler (1989).
6. For the continuing skeptics one need only note that recent estimates of TFP growth in the USSR show that from 1970 TFP (which was never more than 1.6% pa) became stagnant and from 1975 was negative. (See [Ofer, 1983]). This is increasingly seen both by the Soviets themselves and outside observers as a systemic problem flowing in large part from that dirigiste form of industrial planning whose justification was the "coordination failure" highlighted by Scitovsky and Rosenstein-Rodan. Desai & Martin (1983) have moreover estimated the inefficiency arising from interbranch misallocation of capital and labour deployed in Soviet Industry and find it ranges from a low of about 3 – 4 percent to a high of 10 percent of efficient factor use. Moreover, this inefficiency is rising over time. For China, another command economy, also presumably capable of overcoming the "co-ordination failure," Chow (1985) found that the increase in industrial output was mainly due to an increase in capital inputs, rather than of improvement in technology, or efficiency.
7. For UK examples in the promotion of high tech industries, see Henderson.
8. See Chalmers-Johnson, Amsden.
9. The best assessment of Japan's astonishing post-war economic resurgence remains the collection of essays in Patrick & Rosovsky ed. (1976). The essay by Trezise & Suzuki clearly shows that there is little merit in the arguments of Chalmers Johnson, Wolfren et al., about the omniscience of Japanese bureaucrats, and MITI in particular, in Japan's

post-war industrialization. The crucial ingredient according to Caves and Uekusa was the importance of entrepreneurship. As Trezise & Suzuki note:

> "It is not credible that these talented men [the numerous business innovators and managers] really could have been closely guided and directed by a cadre of civil servants, however well educated, or that their vision and skills could have been adequately exploited within a tightly managed, essentially bureaucratic system" (p. 810).

They also note the many mistakes made by the bureaucracy and they aptly conclude:

> "Considerations of this kind suggest a healthy scepticism toward assigning to Japan's civil service capabilities not visible in other bureaucracies" (p.778).

10. For a discussion of the relative difficulties of India adopting Korean tactics to switch trade regimes, see D. Lal: "Ideology and Industrialization in India and East Asia" in H. Hughes ed.: *Achieving Industrialization in East Asia,* Cambridge, 1988.
11. An example is the promotion of heavy industries in S. Korea in the mid-70s. See K.W. Kim: 'South Koreas' in C. Saunders (ed): *The Political Economy of New and Old Industrial Countries,* Butterworth, 1981. Also of the Gang of Four, the efficiency of capital seems to be the highest in Hong Kong. See Findlay and Wellisz (1990). Moreover, as Scitovsky has noted, the particular form of Korean dirigisme has led to needless concentration of wealth and power in a few major industrial groups favoured by the planners compared with Taiwan.
12. The reason for putting the term in inverted commas is that if incremental comparative advantage is not apparent, then the mistakes cannot be *ex ante* ones. They can only be identified with hindsight and so it becomes doubtful if they are mistakes!

REFERENCES

Aggarwal, R. *Price Distortions and Growth in Developing Countries,* World Bank Staff Working Paper, No. 575.

Ahluwalia, I.J. *Industrial Growth in India Stagnation Since the Mid-Sixties* (New Delhi: Oxford University Press, 1985).

Amsden, A.M. *Asias Next Giant: South Korea and Late Industrialisation* (New York: Oxford University Press, 1989).

Arrow, K.J., and Scitovsky, T. ed. *Readings in Welfare Economics* (London: Allen & Unwin, 1969).

Baldwin, R.E. "The Case Against Infant Industry Tariff Protection," *Journal of Political Economy,* Vol. 77 (May – June 1969).

Balassa, B. *the Structure of Protection in Developing Countries* (Baltimore: Johns Hopkins, 1971).

Baumol, W.; Panzer, J.C.; Willig, R.D. *Contestable Markets and the Theory of Industry Structure* (New York, 1982).

Bell, M.; Ross-Larsen, B.; Westphal, L.E. "Assessing the Performance of Infant Industries," *Journal of Development Economics,* Vol. 16 (Sept./Oct. 1984).

Bhagwati, J.N. *Anatomy and Consequences of Trade Control Regimes* (New York: Ballinger, 1979).

Bhagwati, J.N.; and Srinivasan, T.N. *Foreign Trade Regimes and Economic Development in India* (Columbia University Press, 1975).

Bhagwati, J.N.; and Ramaswami, V.K. "Domestic Distortions and the Theory of Optimum Subsidy," *Journal of Political Economy* (Feb. 1973).

Buchanan, J.M.; and Stubblebine, C. "Externality," Economica, Vol. 29, 1962; reprinted in K.J. Arrow and T. Scitovsky eds. Readings in Welfare Economics (London: Allen and Unwin, 1969).

Chakravarti, A. "The Social Profitability of Training Unskilled Workers in the Public Sector in India," *Oxford Economic Papers,* Vol. 24, No. 1, March 1972.

Chenery, H.; Robinson, S.; and Syrquin, M. *Industrialisation and Growth — A Comparative Study* (New York: Oxford University Press, 1986).

Chenery, H.; and Srinivasan, T.N. *Handbook of Development Economics Vol. I* (North Holland, 1988).

Chow, G.C. *The Chinese Economy* (New York: Harper & Row, 1985).

Corden, W.M. *Trade Policy and Economic Welfare* (Oxford: Clarendon Press, 1974).

Crafts, N.F.R. "Patterns of Development in 19th Century Europe," *Oxford Economic Papers,* Vol. 36, No. 3, Nov. 1984.

__________. *British Economic Growth During the Industrial Revolution,* (Oxford: Clarendon Press, 1985).

Desai, P.; and Martin, R. "Efficiency Loss from Resource Misallocation in Soviet Industry," *Quarterly Journal of Economics,* Vol. XCVIII, Aug. 1983.

Donges, J.B. "A Comparative Study of Industrialisation Policies in 15 Semi-Industrial Countries," *Weltwirtschaftliches Archiv,* Band 112, Heft 4, 1976.

Eaton, J.; and Grossman, G. "Optimal Trade and Industrial Policy Under Oligopoly," *Quarterly Journal of Economics,* 1986.

Graham, F. "Some Aspects of Protection Further Considered," *Quarterly Journal of Economics,* Vol. 37, 1923.

Grandmont, J.M.; and McFadden, D. "A Technical Note on Classical Gains From Trade," *Journal of International Economics,* Vol. 2, 1972.

Haberler, G. "Strategic Trade Policy and the New International Economics: A Critical Analysis" in R.W. Jones and A.O. Krueger (1989) ed.

Haberler, G. "Some Problems in the Pure Theory of International Trade," *Economic Journal,* 1950.

Havrylyshyvn, O. "Trade Policy and Productivity Gains in Developing Countries: A Survey of the Literature," *World Bank Research Observer,* Vol. 5, No. 1, Jan. 1990.

Hecksher, E. *Mercantilism,* 2 vols. (London: Allen & Unwin, 1955).

Helliner, G. "Industrial Organisation, Trade and Investment: A Selective Literature Review for Developing Countries" mimeo, paper presented at conference on "Industrial Organisation Trade and Investment in North America, Merida, Mexico, 1985.

Helpman, E. "International Trade in the Presence of Product Differentiations, Economies of Scale and Monopolistic Competition: A Chamberlin-Hecksher-Ohlin Approach," *Journal of International Economics,* Vol. 11 (1981).

Helpman, E.; and Krugman, P. *Market Structure and Foreign Trade: Increasing Returns, Imperfect Competition and the International Economy* (Cambridge, Mass.: MIT, 1985).

Henderson, P.D. "Two British Errors: Their Probable Size and Some Possible Lessons," *Oxford Economic Papers* (July 1977).

Johnson, C. *MITI and the Japanese Miracle* (Stanford, 1982).

Johnson, H.G. "Optimal Trade Intervention in the Presence of Domestic Distortions" in R. Baldwin et al. eds. *Trade, Growth and the Balance of Payments (Chicago, 1965).*

Jones, R.W.; and Krueger, A.O. eds. *The Political Economy of International Trade* (Oxford: Blackwells, 1989).

Kierzkowski, H. ed. *Monopolistic Competition and International Trade* (Oxford: Clarendon Press, 1984).

Krueger, A.O. *Growth, Distortions and Patterns of Trade among Many Countries,* Princeton Studies in International Finance, No. 40 (Feb. 1977).

Krueger, A.O.; and Tuncer, B. "An Empirical Test of the Infant Industry Argument," *American Economic Review,* Vol. 72, No. 5 (Dec. 1982).

Krueger, A.O. *Liberalisation Attempts and Consequences* (New York: Ballinger, 1978).

Krugman, P. ed. *Strategic Trade Policy and the New International Economics* (Cambridge, Mass.: MIT, 1986).

_________. "Is Free Trade Passe," *Journal of Economic Perspectives,* Vol. i, No. 2 (1987).

Lal, D.; and Rajapatirana, S. "Foreign Trade Regimes and Economic Growth in Developing Countries," *World Bank Research Observer* (July 1987).

Lal, D. "Ideology and Industrialisation in India and East Asia," in H. Hughes ed.: *Achieving Industrialisation in East Asia* (Cambridge, 1988).

Lal, D.; and Myint, H. *The Political Economy of Poverty, Equity and Growth,* mimeo (London, 1990).

Lal, D. *The Poverty of 'Development Economics,'* Institute of Economic Affairs (London, 1983), (Cambridge Ma.: Harvard University Press, 1985).

_________. *The Hindu Equilibrium,* 2 vols. (Oxford: Clarendon Press, 1989).

Lau, L.J. ed. *Models of Development: A Comparative Study of Economic Growth in South Korea and Taiwan* (San Francisco: ICS Press, 1986).

Little, I.M.D. *Economic Development* (New York: Basic Books, 1982).

Little, I.M.D.; Scitovsky, T.; and Fg. Scott, M. *Industry and Trade in Some Developing Countries* (Oxford University Press, 1970).

Markusen, J.; and Melvin, J. "The Gains-from-Trade Theorem with Increasing Returns to Scale," in H. Kierzkowski ed. (1984).

Meade, J. *Trade and Welfare* (London: Oxford University Press, 1955).

Ofer, G. "Soviet Economic Growth 1928 – 1985," *Journal of Economic Literature,* Vol. XXV, No. 4 (Dec. 1987).

Pack, H. "Industrialisation and Trade" in Chenery; and Srinivasan ed. (1988).

Pack, H.; and Westphal, L.E. "Industrial Strategy and Technological Change: Theory Versus Reality," *Journal of Development Economics,* Vol. 22 (June 1986).

Page Jr., J.M. "The Pursuit of Industrial Growth: Policy Initiations and Economic Consequences," in Scott & Lal 1990 ed.

Patrick, H.; and Rossovsky, H. ed. *Asia's New Giant: How the Japanese Economy Works* (Washington DC: Brookings, 1976).

Rhee, Y.W.; Ross-Larsen, Bruce; and Pursell, G. *Korea's Competitive Edge: Managing the Entry into World Markets* (Baltimore: Johns Hopkins, 1984).

Richardson, J.D. "Empirical Research on Trade Liberalisation with Imperfect Competition: A Survey," *OECD Economic Studies,* No. 12 (Spring 1989).

Rosenstein-Rodan, P.N. "Problems of Industrialisation of Eastern and South-Eastern Europe," *Economic Journal,* Vol. LIII (1943).

Scitovsky, T. "Two Concepts of External Economies," *Journal of Political Economy,* Vol. 17, 1954, reprinted in Arrow & Scitovsky ed.

_________. "Economic Development in Taiwan and South Korea, 1965 – 1981" in Lau ed. (1986).

Scott, M. Fg.; and Lal, D. eds. *Public Policy and Economic Development* (Oxford: Clarendon Press, 1990).

Srinivasan, T.N. "Recent Theories of Imperfect Competition and International Trade: Any Implication for Development Strategy?," *Indian Economic Review,* Vol. XXIV, No. 1, Jan. – June (1989).

Stewart, F. "Recent Theories of International Trade: Some Implications for the South" in H. Kierzkowski 1984 ed.

Stigler, G.J.; and Boulding, K.E. eds. *Readings in Price Theory* (London: Allen & Unwin, 1953).

UNIDO, *Industry and Development: Global Report 1985* (New York: United Nations, 1985).

van Wolfren, K. *The Enigma of Japan* (London: Macmillan 1989).

Vernon, R. "International Investment and International Trade in the Product Cycle," *Quarterly Journal of Economics,* Vol. 80 (1966).

Viner, J. "Cost and Supply Curves," Zeitschrift fur Nationalekonomie, Vol. III, 1931, reprinted in G.J. Stigler and K.E. Boulding eds., *Readings in Price Theory* (London: Allen and Unwin, 1953).

Vogel, E.F. *Japan as Number 1* (Harvard University Press, 1979).

Wade, R. *Governing the Market: Economic Theory and the Role of Government in East Asian Industrialisation* (Princeton, 1990).

Westphal, L.E. "The Republic of Korea's Experience with Export-led Idustrial Development," *World Development,* Vol. 6 (March 1978).

__________. "Industrial Policy in an Export-Propelled Economy: Lessons from S. Korea's Experience," *Journal of Economic Perspectives,* Vol. 4, No. 3 (Summer 1990).

World Bank, *World Development Report 1987* (New York: Oxford University Press, 1987).

PART III

World Development, 1976, Vol. 4, No. 9, pp. 725–738. Pergamon Press. Printed in Great Britain.

Distribution and Development: A Review Article

DEEPAK LAL
University College, London

INTRODUCTION

From the recent proliferation of books and articles on the subject, it appears that there is a great surge of interest in problems of income distribution in both developed and developing countries. (See Chenery *et al.* [7], Adelman and Morris [1], ILO [14], Atkinson [2], Blinder [5], Meade [26], Tinbergen [35], Wiles [37] and Cline [9].) The three books specifically concerned with development and distribution, and reviewed in this article, are the Chenery et al volume, *Redistribution With Growth* (RWG), the Adelman-Morris book, *Economic Growth and Social Equity in Developing Countries* (AM), and the ILO's report to the recent tripartite World Employment Conference entitled *Employment, Growth and Basic Needs* (ILO). All three books make grandoise claims to have discovered new insights into the development process and to propose new strategies for development. Thus Chenery, in the introduction to RWG, claims that the book 'leads to several conclusions which . . . differ markedly from traditional approaches to development policy' ([7], p. xiii). In assessing these claims, particularly those made by RWG and AM, it will be useful to consider the reasons for this resurgence of interest in distributional problems, for this will enable us to judge to what extent traditional approaches to development were blinkered about income distribution. This is our purpose in Section I.

Section II deals more specifically with RWG and AM's analysis of the relationship between growth and income distribution. It also contrasts their explanation of the determinants of income in developing countries with those presented in the other recent books on distributional problems, but which are chiefly concerned with developed countries [2, 5, 26, 35, 37].

From describing the effects on distribution of growth, it is a small step to making prescriptions for equitable growth. RWG, AM and ILO are much concerned with prescribing a 'new' development strategy. Any such prescriptions must, however, grapple with the problems of 'distributive justice' and the related themes of the rights of individuals versus the State. These have been the traditional concerns of political philosophy, which too has seen a recent revival. The two great philosophical works by Rawls [33] and Nozick [29] take one back to the 18th and 19th centuries in their scope, depth and (often) modes of argument about the basic principles on which the 'Good Society' should be based. As there is an underlying moral fervour in the prescriptions of RWG, AM and ILO, it will be useful to see to what extent the ethical preconceptions of these volumes are soundly based. Nozick's [29] discussion of the principles of distributive justice provides an interesting counterpoise to these preconceptions, and is also of relevance in assessing the ethical validity of the system of distributional weighting recommended in RWG for intercountry comparisons of economic performance. This is the subject matter of Section III.

Section IV discusses the specific policy prescriptions of the three books – RWG, AM and ILO – whilst the final section briefly summarizes our conclusions.

I

Climate of opinion

Ever since the storming of the Bastille to the chant of 'Liberty, Equality and Fraternity', these three concepts have, to varying degrees informed 'modern' discussion (whether in socialist or capitalist societies), though the meaning and the relative importance attached to them have differed widely (see Becker [3], Plamenatz [31]). As 'whether arguments command assent or not depends less upon the logic that conveys them than upon the climate of opinion in which they are sustained' (Becker [3], p. 5), it is the current relative increase in emphasis on the contemporary preconception in favour of equality which conerns us. There are in my view three major strands in recent Western history which explain this increased concern with distributional problems.

The first of these, which is probably of greatest importance in putting RWG and AM in historical and intellectual perspective, is what may be termed the crisis of American politics and society of the mid-1960s.

Since the rise of Marxist doctrines and the Russian revolution, Western-style liberal democracies have been haunted by the possible irreconcilability of two of the central ideals of the Enlightenment, liberty and equality. However, the growth of the welfare state and the historically unprecedented rates of stable growth (until the mid-1960s) in most OECD countries, led many (particularly American) political commentators to the conclusion that:

> the fundamental political problems of the industrial revolution have been solved: the workers have achieved industrial and political citizenship; the conservatives have accepted the Welfare State; and the democratic left has recognized that an increase in over-all State power carries with it more dangers to freedom than solutions for economic problems (Lipset [22], p. 406).

For many American writers, the liberal democratic political system as epitomized by the USA was supposed to have established the 'good society' in which any residual problems of class and group conflict could easily be handled.

> For Berle, Riesman and Lipset contemporary America *is* the good society. 'What is there in Pericles' famous praise of Athens that does not apply to us, in some or even extended measure?' asks Riesman rhetorically, while Lipset declares that democracy as practised in the United States 'is the good society itself in operation' (Lukes and Arblaster [25], p. 13).

In order to establish the good society in the Third World, which was seen to be the remaining ideological battleground, many American analysts felt that the primary task was to create the preconditions for American-style democracy through rapid economic growth [22, 32]. Moderately reformist governments subscribing to socialist rhetoric, like Nehru's India and Nasser's Egypt, were looked upon by many American policy-makers with suspicion if not hostility. The 'ideal' developing country from their perspective was in some ways Ayub's Pakistan. Mason, in his foreword to Papanek's book on Pakistan, in 1967, concluded: 'Pakistan *has* had a remarkable record, although it is much too soon to talk of self-sustaining growth . . . partly by accident and partly by design . . . Pakistan has found a successful combination of private initiative and government intervention' ([30], p. viii, ix). But towards the end of the 1960s there occurred 'a series of disasters . . . in countries in which development seemed to be vigorously under way. The civil war in Nigeria and the bloody falling apart of Pakistan are only the most spectacular instances of such "development disasters", (Hirschman [13], p. 544). Since in both cases one of the stated grievances of the secessionists was distributive injustice, the lesson which was drawn was that the 'old' development economics was bankrupt, 'with its accent on growth rates, industrialization and international assistance, and the need [was felt] for a wholly new doctrine that would emphasize income distribution, employment and self-reliance' (Hirschman, *ibid.*). This inference, of course, does not follow, at least in the case of the two 'development disasters' cited by Hirschman. For nationalism provides an equally (if not more) plausible explanation for both the Nigerian civil war and the partition of Pakistan than any worsening of the regional (or tribal) distribution of income *per se*.

But the proposition that domestic disorder results from increases in relative or absolute deprivation was being strengthened by experience in the USA and many other Western democracies. The failure of various traditional attempts to solve the problems of poverty and race in America; the questioning of a basic tenet of the 'American dream' that equality of opportunity through equal access to education could reduce inequalities [see 15 and 20]; the sharpening of domestic conflict, in particular during the Vietnam war, with cities and campuses aflame – all these made the views of the previous decade about the end of ideology and conflict in America appear complacent. While some advocated a policy of 'benign neglect' for seemingly insoluble problems, (Moynihan [27]), others advocated a direct assault on inequality, which appeared persuasive to those who were too ready to identify the prevailing domestic disorder with continued (or increased) relative deprivation, in particular of the blacks (Valentine [38]). Thus, by the early 1970s, in many influential circles in the USA, the solution to the problem of equity seemed to be the most important in mitigating what appeared to be increasing threats to domestic and international order.

The second set of factors leading to an increasing emphasis on equity was connected with the inflationary pressures in most OECD countries, which reached their peak in 1973–1974. Apart from the resurgent monetarists, many commentators saw these as the result of a constant 'war of all against all' for a larger share of the national income.[1] This is also the view taken by Tinbergen, who writes: 'while definitely part of the problem resides, as before, in a lack of financial discipline, another and maybe the larger component is an aspect of income distribution, even of labour income distribution' (Tinbergen [35], p. 145).

Thirdly, the capital-theoretic debate conducted around the problem of reswitching of techniques, whose outcome was taken to vindicate the Cambridge (England) view that the classical writers, in particular Ricardo and Marx, were right in asserting that 'income-distribution (e.g. the wage–profit ratio) was a precondition of the formation of relative prices' (Dobb [10], p. 35), has been used to assert that conventional (i.e. neo-classical) economic theory is mere apologetics for the inequalities of capitalism.[2] The alternative theory of the Cambridge (England) school appears at least to one observer 'as considering income distribution (to be) the result of an *autonomous political decision*, and technology as well as demand for final products being flexible enough to adapt itself to any income distribution desired' (Tinbergen [35], p. 9). And Harcourt concludes:

> if one were told whether an economist was fundamentally sympathetic or hostile to basic capitalist institutions, especially private property and the related rights to income streams, or whether he were a hawk or a dove in his views on the Vietnam war, one could predict with a considerable degree of accuracy both his general approach in economic theory and which side he would be on in the present controversies ([12], p. 13).

The ensuing fillip given to the critique of what was pejoratively labelled neo-classical economics centred around its supposed lack of interest in distributional problems, a charge on which Lindbeck in his critique of the 'New Left' concluded:

> As a general statement, however [despite the extensive analyses of the functional and personal distribution of income amongst economists since Ricardo and Pareto], I think it is safe to say that the development of the theory and analysis of distribution problems has been considerably weaker than the development in many other branches of economics *during the period since World War II* ([21], p. 10).

'Traditional' development theory

The two books, RWG and AM, reflect this changed climate of opinion in western countries, but particularly in the USA with its domestic political and social crisis of the mid-1960s. For at least in the discussions of development policy (apart from one particular 'school', on which more below) distributional and equity questions had always been recognized to be of crucial importance.

However, Jolly, seeking to argue for the novelty of his (and his collaborators') work in RWG states:

> in the world of international economic analysis three major paradigms exist at present: the neo-classical, the structuralist and the dominance/dependence.... Every man has his own examples of archetypes, perhaps archangels or archdevils. Mine [in this area] ... would include: neo-classicals Harry G. Johnson and Jagdish Bhagwati; structuralists Hollis Chenery, Gunnar Myrdal and Dudley Seers; dominance/dependence analysts Paul Baran and Gunder Frank ([7], p. 162).

Presumably, as only two of the above names also feature in RWG, the new approach to development emphasizing distribution is by implication that of the 'structuralists' and as the dominance/dependence 'school' has still 'to arrive', the inference must be that the 'traditional approaches to development policy' (Chenery [7], p. xiii) which neglected distributional issues must be those of the neo-classicals. But if one glances at the contents of a 1966 *textbook* by one of Jolly's archetypical neo-classicals, Jagdish Bhagwati, one will find that the first chapter of the book is entitled 'Poverty and income distribution', which clearly states: 'What lends poignancy to the situation in which underdeveloped countries find themselves is not merely their poverty but also its uneven distribution among their citizens' ([4], p. 20–1). By contrast, consider the following statement from one of Jolly's archetypical structuralists, Hollis Chenery's introduction to a 1970 collection of studies from the Harvard Project for Quantitative Research in Economic Development:

> There are two other important areas to which we feel insufficient attention has been given [in the studies] – the nature of technical change and the redistribution of income. Their neglect in this

> volume is due to the lack of quantitative information and perhaps to *our too ready acceptance of the notion that the economist's role is to prescribe policies designed to maximize output, leaving questions of income distribution and technology to politicians and engineers* ([8], p. 10, emphasis added)!

Thus if we can label some of these 'structuralists' as another school, that of the mathematical programming-planning model builders, it is they who have traditionally neglected distributional issues, and who are now discovering redistribution and equity as important aspects of development policy, as represented by their writings in the RWG and AM books. As they have also been influential in the American foreign aid establishment, it would be correct to say that these volumes also mark a change in emphasis in American foreign aid policy, towards questions of equity. In both of these specifically American intellectual Odysseys, the factors which have led to the marked change in the climate of opinion in the USA about distributional questions have obviously played some part.

It is only some such explanation which enables us to make sense of what otherwise seem to be outrageous statements in the RWG and AM volumes. Who, unless imbued with the American political science model of the 1950s, could write: 'We had also not greatly questioned the relevance today of the historical association of successful economic growth with the spread of parliamentary democracy' (Adelman and Morris [1], p. vii)? And Chenery's statement in RWG, that 'on the theoretical side, it is necessary to discard the conceptual separation between optimum growth and distribution policies that lies at the heart of traditional welfare economics' ([7], p. xiii), must seem astounding to anyone brought up on the traditional welfare economics of Bergson, Meade, Samuelson and Little. I find it inconceivable how anyone claiming to study *optimum* growth, which is essentially concerned with the intergenerational distribution of welfare, could maintain a conceptual separation between growth and distribution. It was the planning model 'school' (and the economists in USAID), as the above quotation from Chenery [8] shows, which maintained the conceptual separation of growth and distribution, and it is their belated recognition of the illegitimacy of this separation, rather than any conceptual shortcomings of traditional welfare economics, which are highlighted in the RWG and AM volumes.

II

Past growth and distribution

But what of the substantive conclusions reached by Chenery [7] and Adelman and Morris [1]? These, alas, betray the traditional failings of over-enthusiastic converts to 'the cause'. Thus, at the start of the Chenery introduction we are told: 'It is by now clear that more than a decade of rapid growth in underdeveloped countries has been of little or no benefit to perhaps a third of their population' (p. xiii); and Adelman and Morris conclude 'that development is accompanied by an absolute as well as relative decline in the average income of the very poor' (p. 189). Neither conclusion can be deduced from the evidence presented.

The Chenery volume contains a useful summary of the available data on income distribution by Ahluwalia. The variety of sources, and limited reliability of the data, are stressed, and an apparently reasonable position is maintained, namely 'that until better data become available, *cautious* use of existing data – with all its limitations – provides some perspective on the nature of the problem' ([7], pp. 6–7, emphasis added). Though the above qualification is borne in mind in dispelling some of the wilder 'conclusions' of the Adelman–Morris book (on which more below), it is perhaps not sufficiently taken to heart.

On relative inequality Ahluwalia concludes:

> Most of the *underdeveloped countries* show markedly greater relative inequality than the developed countries. About half of the underdeveloped countries fall in the high inequality range with another third displaying moderate inequality. The average income share for the lowest 40% in all underdeveloped countries as a group amounts to about 12.5%, but there is considerable variation around this average ([7], p. 7).

However, the evidence presented in RWG's Fig. I.1 on the influence of GNP growth on the growth rate of income of the poorest 40% of the population does not square with the 'conclusion' quoted above from the book's Introduction. From Fig. I.1, the only place in RWG in which time series data are given about the growth rate of income of the poorest 40% of the population in 18 countries (of which 14 are developing countries), the unexceptionable conclusion is drawn that it does not show 'any marked relationship between income growth and changes in income shares' (p. 13), a conclusion which undercuts the whole Adelman–Morris thesis about growth and inequality. But the more important conclusion concerning the influence of growth on the absolute levels of living of the poor, which this figure suggests, is not drawn. This is of considerable importance because of some of the preconceptions (buttressed by writings such as AM) which lie behind current discussions of growth-promoting strategies such as the Green Revolution (see Lal [18]).[3] For what Fig. I.1 shows is that in none of the countries cited was there a zero or negative growth rate of income of the poorest 40%, and that, moreover, the growth rate of income of these groups was greater than the rate of growth of population (with the possible exception of Peru and Panama, countries which, from Ahluwalia's Table I.1, accounted for only 3.5 million of the 578 million poor below the $75 poverty line in 1969). Thus India, which accounts for 62% of the Third World's estimated population below $75 ([7], p. 12), appears to have had a rate of growth of income of the poor (in 1954–64) of about 3.8% ([7], Fig. I.1), while the rate of growth of population was only about 2.5%. Moreover, as I have argued elsewhere (Lal [18]), India's poor would have benefited even more from faster agricultural growth. Chenery's conclusion in RWG's introduction (quoted above) is thus misleading, and unsupported by the evidence RWG itself provides.

The basis for the Adelman–Morris results is even more questionable. As the above summary shows, their conclusion about the worsening absolute and relative position of the poor with past growth is not borne out by the data assembled by Ahluwalia, and which appears to be similar to that used by Adelman–Morris. The reason is that Adelman–Morris seem to make no use of time series data, whereas the above conclusions, which contradict theirs, are based on such data (imperfect though they be). Instead, they use cross-section data to carry out a step-wise variance analysis. They find that the GNP share of the poorest 60% of the population in their group of countries with a zero *per capita* growth of GNP is 34%, while in the group of countries with *per capita* GNP growth rates of about 3%,

> the average income share of the poorest 60% [is] 20%. *If we hypothesize* that the typical path of change is represented by a movement [from the first to the second group of countries] *and assume* that the income share of the poorest 60% drops from 34 to 20%, *it follows* that almost a generation would be needed for the poorest 60% in a country with a hypothesized increase in growth rate of 3 percentage points to recover the *absolute* loss associated with a decline in income share of 14 percentage points ([1], p. 180, emphasis added).

This 'logic' is breathtaking, particularly when one turns to Appendix C, Table C2, which presents their regression results for the same cross-section data on which the step-wise variance analysis was done, and finds that these show *no statistically significant decline in the absolute level of income with rising per capita GNP*, for the poor income groups!

It would be tedious to go on labouring this point, but clearly the RWG and AM volumes do *not* show that growth has led or must lead to the immiserization of the poor in developing countries, despite their claims to the contrary. Neither do they provide evidence for any necessary conflict between growth and equality. As Ahluwalia rightly sums up: 'There is little firm empirical basis for the view that higher rates of growth inevitably generate greater inequality. This may have happened in particular cases but an explanation for this must be sought in the circumstances of each particular case and not in terms of a generalized relationship' ([7], pp. 15–16). This is not to deny the importance of problems of equity in development, and so we turn to the analysis these studies make of the determinants of distributional changes during the development process.

The determinants of poverty and inequality

Adelman and Morris, in their mechanistic way, use a statistical technique based on analysis of variance, which seeks to 'explain' the cross-sectional data on income distribution in terms of 35 independent variables ranging from 'degree of modernization of outlook' to 'extent of leadership commitment to economic development'. Various ordinal indices of these are reported to have been derived (but are not given) on the basis of the subjective judgments of various experts (who are not cited), and it is found that the most 'significant' independent variables associated with reductions in income inequalities are the rate of improvement in human resources, direct government activity, and a reduction in socio-economic dualism. Whilst I am not competent to judge the merits of the statistical technique employed, the conclusions do appear rather banal.

AM's theoretical explanations for their (unproven) contention of the immiserization of the poor, however, are a veritable *pot pourri*:

> Inflation, population growth, technological change, the commericalization of the traditional sector, and urbanization all combine to reduce the real income of the poorest 40% of the population in

very low-income countries in the before-take-off stage of development ([1], p. 183).

What is the mechanism whereby these heterogenous factors are supposed to lead to the immiserization of the poor or to greater inequality? Would a *lack* of growth in the 'pre-take-off' stage of development, in a situation of population growth, *not* lead to this immiserization and inequality? Is *all* technological change (including that which is land-augmenting, or which raises the demand for labour) inimical to the income levels of the poor? Would the poor be better off if barter was the common mode of transaction in the traditional sector? The AM volume provides no economic analysis to answer these questions, merely assertions, which, moreover, are often inconsistent with the 'facts'.

The RWG volume, at least, though patchy in its contents, does attempt some analysis. Ahluwalia rightly emphasizes that the cross-section results seeking to explain the determinants of income distribution (his results are similar to AM's, but they take two pages to report, as compared with a whole book by AM) do not provide any basis for policy formulation. So, Chenery *et al.*[7] instead attempt to outline the economic characteristics of the poor and the determinants of their income. There are no surprises: the poor are mainly in rural areas, and are small farmers, landless labourers and various self-employed artisans, as well as those in the urban informal sector. Their poverty is explained chiefly in terms of the unequal distribution of assets, particularly land, and of limited access to capital, in particular human capital. There is nothing new in this 'analysis'.

Moreover, by comparison with some of the other recent books on income distribution, but chiefly concerned with developed countries, this approach to the determinants of income does appear to be rather shallow. Not surprisingly, one of the founders of the programming-planning model school of economists, Tinbergen, also places primary emphasis on human capital formation in explaining existing patterns, as well as for changing the distribution of income in developed countries. Within a demand and supply framework for different types of labour he 'sees the reduction of inequality not as an *automatic* consequence of rising average incomes, but possible only if the expansion of *education overtakes* the expansion required by technological development' ([35], p. 8).

Atkinson's [2] excellent summary of alternative theories of the determinants of the distribution of income and wealth, and of the empirical evidence for the different theories, however, concludes that the evidence for developed countries 'suggests that the human capital theory explains part, but far from all, of the earnings dispersion. One reason for this is that the human capital approach leaves out important elements: differences in individual abilities and background, and the fact that the labour market does not necessarily operate in the smooth, perfectly competitive way posited' (p. 86). Ahluwalia [7] in a contribution which seems lukewarm about the emphasis otherwise given in RWG to human capital, acknowledges this, but adds weakly that these studies which have been done for developed countries may not be relevant for skill-short developing countries, and that 'the problem is not whether education is desirable but to determine what is the right kind of education and how to ensure that broadening educational programmes will benefit the lower-income groups'. With this we can all agree.

However, as Atkinson [2] and Meade [26] (in a characteristically pellucid and important book) emphasize, the observed pattern of income and wealth distribution in any country is likely to be the result of a complex interaction of genes, fortune, assortative mating and differential fertility as much as of inequalities of opportunity and the workings of labour and capital markets. And Blinder [5] has developed a simulation model for the US income and wealth distribution using models 'based on utility maximizing behaviour [which] yield solutions for each person's wage rate, labour supply, rate of return (to investment) and net worth, contingent upon his tastes and endowments of human and non-human capital' (p. 7). For the US he finds that 'inheritances account for surprisingly little overall inequality, (and that) . . . dispersion in wage rates is always the principal cause of inequality' (p. 158).

The explanation of existing inequalities of wealth and income is thus more complex than RWG and AM would suggest. Though the broad features of the causes of these inequalities are known and obvious, the interaction of the various factors is complex (see Meade [26]), while their relative contribution to any existing unequal distribution remains controversial (see Atkinson [2]).

III

Ethics

The mere recognition of the importance of

distribution in development does not by itself enable us to make prescriptions for public policy. Though any *universalistic* prescriptions must ultimately be based on some ethical premises, for particular countries, considerations of *realpolitik* may be particularly important in formulating distributional policies, at least from the viewpoint of their rulers seeking to maintain themselves in power. All three volumes, RWG, AM and ILO, are very prescriptive. Moreover, they seem to be laying down *universal* prescriptions, but show no evidence of having thought through the implicit ethical premises of their recommendations. Thus Chenery and Ahluwalia [7] argue for the use of distributional weights which would 'enable us to set development targets and monitor development performance not simply in terms of growth of GNP but in terms of the distributional pattern of income growth' (p. 39). The 'us' presumably refers to international agencies like the World Bank, to which these two authors belong, and to judge from their worked examples in RWG, it seems that this system of distributional weighting is to be used to assess the extent of income redistribution *within* countries, rather than that *between* them. The ILO, in equally prescriptive mood, has laid down a strategy for *all* the countries in the world for 'the achievement of a certain specific minimum standard of living before the end of the century' ([14], p. 6).

This raises two issues: first, whether our concern for distribution in development policy should reflect a concern for the poor or for equality; secondly, whether there are valid *ethical* grounds for universalist policies which concentrate on national redistribution rather than on the international redistribution of incomes and wealth. This is of particular importance in assessing both the validity of the type of distributional weighting for intercountry comparisons advocated in RWG, and the appropriateness of *international* agencies advocating particular measures of *national* redistribution of income and wealth.

On the first question, Chenery *et al.* seem to be concerned at times with poverty and at others with inequality. Adelman and Morris seem to concentrate on the poor, as does the ILO more explicitly. I think this objective is right, though others with more egalitarian prejudices might think otherwise. On this opposing viewpoint it would be necessary to maintain that it would be better for Bangladesh to concentrate on achieving complete equality of income and wealth, even if this meant no income growth, as compared with a policy which led to some growth which was poverty redressing, but which was also accompanied by a worsening of the Gini coefficient. It would also require approving the bloody redistribution of assets by the Khmer Rouge in Cambodia, which seems to have taken to heart the lesson of the role of human capital in generating inequalities, and instituted the speediest equalization of these assets by the elimination of anyone with any education!

The latter example lends poignancy to the arguments of Nozick [29] in a brilliant book, which is profoundly disturbing to the egalitarian preconceptions of social democrats about distributive justice. This book is also useful as a counterpoise which shows up the relative superficiality of the ethical underpinnings of RWG, AM and ILO. Nozick's arguments are also useful in demonstrating the need for consistency in the principles of distributive justice as applied to both national and international redistribution, an issue of importance in answering the second of the questions posed above. A bald summary does injustice to the subtlety of his argument, but the following might give some idea of its flavour.

Nozick propounds an entitlement theory of distributive justice according to which a person's holdings are just if acquired through just original acquisition or just transfer (as in voluntary exchange or gift) or through the rectification of injustice in the above two senses. One weakness of the book is that he does not provide a detailed account of these principles of justice, and seems to be more concerned with using its broad outline to contrast this historical theory of distributive justice with traditional theories, which justify state intervention (coercion) to achieve some end result or patterned distribution ('to each according to his moral merits, or needs or marginal product, or how hard he tries, or the weighted sum of the foregoing. . . .' ([29], p. 156)). He rejects these end-pattern theories on the ground that any enforcement of a patterned distribution must conflict with liberty (in a fairly minimal sense) which any individualistic ethic must reject; for any patterned distribution can be upset by people's voluntary actions in exchange, and hence 'no end-state principle or distributional patterned principle of justice can be continuously realized without continuous interference with people's lives. . . . The socialist society would have to forbid capitalist acts between consenting adults' ([29], p. 163) – a point which Mao at least has acknowledged! For suppose we have what you consider to be a just distribution, *D*1, and people voluntarily, through exchange, moved from it to a different distribution, *D*2 (say, through transferring part of their just holdings to hire the services of a pop singer or basketball player in his spare time), then is not *D*2 also just? The adherent to the patterned distributional principle would have to say it was not, and to *force* a return to the original just distribution, *D*1.

The basic trouble with end-state theories of distributive justice, according to Nozick, is that they are based on an implicit notion that 'holdings' fall like manna from heaven, so that they 'are theories of recipient justice'. They ignore the fact that 'things' come attached to people. As a result, as for instance in Rawls's theory, they rule out almost by assumption any entitlement theory of justice. But, asks Nozick: 'May all entitlements be relegated to relatively superficial levels? For example people's entitlements to parts of their bodies?' (p. 206). Would the forcible redistribution of bodily parts be justified to satisfy an end-state principle of distributive justice, say Rawls's maximin, or one based on relative needs? The trouble lies in that 'end-state and most patterned principles of distributive justice institute (partial) ownership by others of people and their actions and labour. These principles involve a shift from the classical liberals' notion of self-ownership to a notion of (partial) property rights in *other* people' ([29], p. 172). Thus a theory of property rights is central to any theory of justice.

> It is not only persons favouring *private* property who need a theory of how property rights legitimately originate. Those believing in collective property, for example those believing that a group of persons living in an area jointly own the territory, or its mineral resources, also must provide a theory of how such property rights arise; they must show why the persons living there have the rights to determine what is done with the land and the resources there that persons living elsewhere don't have (with regard to the same land and resources) ([29], p. 178).

This last point is of particular importance in assessing the ethical validity of the strident calls made by RWG, AM and ILO for *national* redistribution, and their relative silence on the issue of *international* redistribution of income and wealth. The resulting inconsistency is perhaps best brought out by the following quotation from an official Polish journal, concerning the recent demand of the Third World for a new economic world order necessitating 'redistribution of wealth on a world scale'. Discussing the demands of the Group of 77, the author says:

> So long as the Group demands compensation for hundreds of years of colonial exploitation; ... so long as it presents its claims to those who truly bear the historical and therefore material responsibility for the pitifully low starting level at which their former colonies commenced their independent existence; so long as it does this it can count on our solidarity. But this cannot be the case when the conception of 'industrialized countries' suddenly ceases to be treated by the Third World within its historical context and is increasingly used by it as a synonym for describing all the countries that have succeeded in climbing above the level of say $1,500 annual income a head. When this happens, we get an unacceptable and immoral confusion of the amount of national *per capita* income with the sources of income; we get an insulting comparison of the poor nations whose people with clenched teeth and by their own efforts have managed to build the foundations of industrial civilization, with the white sahibs who for a number of generations grew fat on the blood and sweat of the colonial peoples.... Treating all the 'industrialized countries' as though there were no inherent differences among them is only one step away from some very odd and disquieting ideas. One of them, for instance, is that all industrialized countries should pay a tax depending on their national income irrespective of the historical origins of their present levels of national income.... Such reasoning ... will not be accepted by any socialist country ([11]).

A more clear-cut adherence to a Nozick-type historical entitlement theory of distributive justice in judging the ethics of international redistributive policies would be hard to come by.[4] But then the question arises, if on these grounds we reject a patterned principle of distributive justice which would lead to *international* land reform, and/or income and wealth redistribution, how can these be ethically justified on this entitlement view as regards *national* distributive justice?

If, however, RWG, AM and ILO are more 'socialist' than the socialist countries, and adhere to a patterned principle of distributive justice both nationally and internationally, then, apart from Nozick's objections quoted above, they are faced with two other ethical problems. First, it would be easy to show that in terms of any mildly egalitarian distributional weights, *international* redistribution of income and wealth would increase world welfare much more than any purely *national* redistribution. On universalistic ethical grounds, therefore, the emphasis should be on international rather than national redistribution. Here both RWG and ILO, which deal to some extent with international redistribution, are lukewarm. Why? Presumably because they feel that it is *unrealistic* to expect any international redistribution given the current world system. But, then, why is it more realistic to expect any national redistribution, given the current socio-political systems in most developing countries? Thus, on both ethical and *realpolitik* grounds the relative emphasis on national rather than international redistribution seems inconsistent.

Secondly, the members of the organizations represented by RWG and ILO, as well as the authors of these works and AM, are faced by a further problem if they believe in some patterned principle of distributive justice. For, it is always open to them *personally* to improve the existing distribution of their *own national* and the international distribution of income and wealth towards their desired distribution by making voluntary transfers. They could all transfer their assets and income above the ILO's basic minimum needs (defined in terms of local standards) to raise some of the world's poor towards their national basic needs target. This is in fact a personal dilemma which, Nozick has noted, faces any adherent to a patterned egalitarian principle of distributive justice. I have heard the argument advanced by some wealthy socialists that personal transfers as such cannot alter the existing inequalities in any marked measure; the important thing is to alter the system which generates inequalities, rather than to rely on private charity; and hence, while continuing to fight for a more just system, they are entitled in the meantime to continue enjoying their wealth. This argument has always seemed to me to be rather hypocritical. In an international context it becomes morally repulsive. Armed with their new-found moral fervour in aid of some patterned principle of distributive justice, I have seen agents of international agencies hectoring civil servants in at least one developing country about the need to reduce the incomes of people in the top decile in the country. The implication, never very far off, is that this must include cuts in the inequitable income being received by the civil servant being lectured to. A simple comparison, at least in India, would, however, show that the high-level national civil servant being lectured to receives a *weekly income* which is lower than the *daily allowance* of the international civil servant in the country he is advising. It is only some rigid separation between the supposed application of a patterned distributive principle nationally, but not internationally, which could explain such morally offensive, but I expect not uncommon, behaviour on the part of international civil servants.

These general and personal inconsistencies which are apparent in the ethical preconceptions of RWG, AM and ILO, moreover, have more serious implications. For nearly two decades after World War II, many Western countries, and particularly the USA, sought to intervene directly and indirectly in many Third World countries, in the name of preserving one of their cherished ideals: liberty. These interventions were resented and labelled imperialistic by Third World countries. International agencies were accused of abetting this imperialism. Whatever our feelings about the preservation of freedom around the world, it has sadly become apparent that this cause is not necessarily served by the intervention (covert or overt) of third parties. Now, we are being asked to endorse the international legislation (but within national boundaries) of another principle of the Enlightenment: equality. As long as this endorsement is merely in the form of resolutions and international charters (to be compared with those concerning human rights and freedom which most countries endorsed at the founding of the United Nations), no international friction will obviously arise from this source. But there is a danger that, as in the case with freedom, zealots will try to intervene (or argue for such intervention) in order to promote their cherished ideals in other countries. Would the imperialism to promote national equality be more justified than that to promote liberty or democracy, particularly if, as seems to be case, the egalitarianism (unlike libertarianism) only applies within and not between nation-states?

These are just some of the issues which arise if international distributive prescriptions are to be laid down by international agencies, such as the World Bank or the ILO. But neither RWG nor ILO give any indication of having even considered them, let alone having thought through the answers.

Distributional weighting

This shallowness is particularly transparent in RWG's recommended use of distributional weighting for comparing inter-country economic performance. As the quotation from Chenery and Ahluwalia showed, these weights are supposed to help the international agencies like the World Bank in setting 'development targets' and 'monitoring development performance'. The system of distributional weighting, as they admit ([7], p. 39), has been taken over from the theory of project analysis (UNIDO [36], Little–Mirrlees [23], Lal [16]), and whose basis is lucidly discussed in Meade [26]. However, in project analysis, the system of distributional weighting is not based on any external ethical preconceptions about what constitutes distributive justice. It is, rather, based on the more practical observation that in the business of domestic politics governments *are* often concerned with the distributional effects of their actions. An explicit set of distributional weights which reflects *their* distributional objectives is then seen as an aid in their decision-making when they are weighing up the distributional effects, on a large number of different groups, of a large number of different projects. Explicit distributional weights which reflect the government's distributional preferences enable the vectors of the particular distributional effects of each project to be reduced to a scalar, making possible both consistency in project choice as well as the decentralization of many investment decisions.

The justification for the type of distributional weighting recommended by Chenery and Ahluwalia is, however, obscure. Will the weights reflect national distributive preferences, or those of an international agency such as the World Bank? If the latter, then this implies some universalistic patterned principle of distributive justice, which (as we have noted above) in turn implies that the problems of inconsistency in emphasizing national rather than international redistribution must be squarely faced. Furthermore, it is arguable that even if the weights reflect national distributive preferences, it is more important at the level of judging *national* economic performance (in terms of stated *national* objectives) to have the full array of incomes, particularly as Wiles [37] has noted, the spread between the extremes of the income or wealth distribution. Distributional weighting at a national income level, as a measure of economic performance, will probably obscure many aspects of social and economic policy which are of practical importance in evaluating any particular country's socio-economic policies. As Wiles notes, 'we need techniques for following the fates of individuals and small groups: we need to know *who* is gaining on *whom*, not merely how anonymous statistical units are spread out' ([37], p. xi). The use of distributional weighting by an international agency to evaluate national economic performance must, however, build on ethical preconceptions, which, as we have tried to show in the previous sub-section, are questionable. For its purposes therefore, it would be better to follow Wiles's prescription of giving and examining the whole array, or its more important components (as is in fact done in Table I.1 of RWG), leaving the ethical conclusions to be derived according to alternative welfare predilections. The alternative recommendation of RWG remains open to the charge of being a rather naive form of 'mathematical politics'.

IV

Policies

What policy prescriptions, then, are made by the authors of the three books on development, RWG, AM and ILO, for fostering more equitable development?

Both RWG and ILO, but not AM (for reasons we have mentioned and rejected as invalid), emphasize the continued importance of economic growth for poverty redressal. Chenery and Ahluwalia in RWG develop a simple three-class Harrod–Domar type simulation model of distribution and growth. Given the simple 'sausage machine' nature of such models, the conclusions follow fairly obviously from the assumptions, which include fixed capital-output ratios, savings rates and population growth rates for the three 'sectors': rich, medium and poor. Amongst the three alternative policies considered – consumption transfers to the poor, wage restraint and investment transfers to the poor – not surprisingly, the policy which transfers investment assets to the poor wins hands down on grounds of both equity and growth. For compared with the alternatives such transfers improve the distribution of assets and cause no reduction in aggregate investment and hence, growth.

The ILO, not to be outdone, presents its own model to achieve basic needs defined in terms of *per capita* physical targets for food, education and housing for different regions by the year 2000, through the alternative policies of (a) rapid growth alone, and (b) through some redistribution combined with growth. Both these policy options are found to require historically unprecedented growth rates ranging from 6 to 11% per annum to achieve the basic-needs targets by the year 2000. With a policy of national redistribution the required growth rate falls from 11 to 8–9% for Africa, from 9.7 to 7.2% for Asia (excluding China), and from 9.4 to 7% for Latin America, whilst for China and the Middle East oil-producing countries it remains unchanged at 6 and 11.3% respectively. Hence ILO too supports the Chenery *et al.* title *Redistribution with Growth.*

For both ILO and RWG, however, this asset redistribution is to be confined within national boundaries, and both assume that there is no feedback between growth and distribution.

Both RWG and ILO agree that transfer payments on any large scale to alleviate poverty are not feasible, and that land reform is desirable. RWG particularly stresses the importance of an incremental redistribution of assets (basically education and health services), and the inputs of the rural development package, towards the poor during the growth process. RWG underplays the role of reforming existing relative factor and commodity price structures to raise the demand for labour, on the grounds that 'several empirical studies of the degree of substitution between capital and labour have come up with elasticities of substitution greater than zero but substantially less than unity for a wide range of industries' ([7], p. 75). The ILO, by contrast, emphasizes substitution policies in some sectors like construction which remain unexploited. Both RWG and ILO, however, with their concentration on substitution possibilities within *particular* industries, do not take sufficient account of the possibility that the *aggregate* labour intensity of production can be raised even if particular industries have fixed coefficients, if in aggregate a more labour-intensive 'bundle' of industries is adopted. The reform of the existing price structure in many developing countries would aid this move towards the selection of more labour-intensive *industries* (rather than just labour-intensive *techniques* in existing industries), as would the reversal of the conventional policy emphasis on import substitution in favour of export promotion.[5]

Moreover, the emphasis that RWG lays on education for promoting equality and redressing poverty seems to me to place the cart before the horse. Despite the case in some countries for changing the educational mix in favour of elementary education, not much hope can be placed on the mere upgrading of the skills of the poor for redressing their poverty. It is more important to increase the overall demand for their labour. The by now conventional wisdom is surely right in emphasizing that this increased demand for labour will be generated by efficient growth which makes use of the comparative advantage of the abundant labour in the capital-and-natural-resource-scarce poor countries. There is nothing in RWG or ILO which suggests that there are any other panaceas for alleviating poverty in developing countries which would obviate their need for rapid growth in line with their comparative advantage. In the incessant search for some 'new strategy for development', which seems to have become an endemic disease amongst international agencies, it would be a great disservice to the world's poor if development policy lost sight of these 'old' verities. This is particularly important in view of the evidence RWG presents in its case studies of Taiwan and India. As these show, the former followed what is labelled the conventional wisdom by RWG, the latter (though imperfectly) its supposedly new strategy, with the well-known results that Taiwan has had poverty-redressing growth, whilst India has had little growth and little poverty redressal. As I have argued elsewhere (Lal [18a], if only India had followed the so-called conventional wisdom of fostering growth in line with its comparative advantage, it would have done more for its poor (who are also the bulk of the Third World's poor) than by any feasible measure of redistribution of assets.

Finally, there is the difficult problem for anyone trying to influence the actions of national governments, of what one is to assume about the nature of the state. Both RWG and ILO, like most economists, tend to view the state or 'planners' as comprising a group of 'Platonic guardians'. Though an unrealistic assumption, as both RWG and ILO recognize, it seems that they cannot avoid making it if they hope to change the world by mere exhortation. Thus the ILO states:

> The main prerequisite for the effective implementation of this approach would thus appear to be an effective, decentralized and democratic administrative structure to translate policies into decisions and action, and mass participation in the development process by the poverty groups ([14], p. 6).

And what happens to poverty redressal if these preconditions are not met? In how many developing countries can these prerequisites be said to exist, even in small measure? And, if this structure does not exist, who is to set it up, and how and with whom? For listen to Bardhan in RWG:

> In sum, the problems of poverty in India remain intractable, not because redistributive objectives were inadequately considered in planning models, nor because general policies of the kind prescribed in this volume were not attempted. . . . The major constraint is rooted in the power realities of a political system dominated by a complex constellation of forces representing rich farmers, big business, and the so-called *petite bourgeoisie*, including the unionized workers of the organized sector. In such a context it is touchingly naive not to anticipate the failures of asset distribution policies or the appropriation by the rich of a

> disproportionate share of the benefits of public investment. . . . The second set of constraints . . . relates to the nature of the local bureaucracy which administers the poverty programmes. More often than not the local administrative machinery is manned by people belonging to the families of the rural oligarchy and the urban élite. One does not have to believe in conspiracy theories to note that good-intentioned redistributive programmes are sometimes negated by the local vested interests with at least tacit administrative connivance. To quote a Bengali rural proverb, 'if there are ghosts inside your mustard seeds, how would you use them to exorcise the ghosts?' (pp. 261–2).

So the radicals are probably right in stressing that any substantive redistribution of assets would require a revolution. But revolutions cannot be manufactured by the exhortations of external agencies. Nor should egalitarians concerned with poverty jump to endorse the funding of revolutionary movements in Third World countries by international agencies. For, apart from the ethical dilemmas this would pose (see Section III), the benefits to the poor from revolution are not obvious. As Wiles [37], in an extremely interesting book notes, revolutions (at least judging from past experience) impose economic costs (apart from those in terms of the freedom which at least some of us liberals still value). These costs flow from 'the unlikelihood of non-violent redistribution' ([37], p. 96), and the consequent costs of economic and social dislocation. Wiles presents a cost–benefit analysis of revolutions, by comparing five development sequences, for a stylized developing country represented by Colombia in 1968. He assesses the effects of the five development sequences, on the average income of the rich, the poor and the average income recipient. The development sequences, themselves, reflect what actually happened in a number of historical development sequences, but with the *Idealtypen* being assumed to be more favourable than reality in the case of the two revolutionary scenarios based on Soviet and Polish experience. The three other scenarios are based on (i) the standard Western prescription for a mixed economy, (ii) the Chicago School's tough minded non-welfare capitalism with its trickling down of benefits to the poor, and (iii) a populist policy which is based on the policies of Pazos in Cuba in 1959 before Castro went Communist. Comparing the *undiscounted* values of the consumption of the poor in the five sequences, Wiles finds from his simulation exercise that the populist path dominates the Chicago and mixed economy paths at all times. The Chicago path catches up with the mixed economy path during the 10th year. The Polish path catches up with the mixed economy path in the 19th, the Chicago path in the 27th and the populist path in the 43rd year. The Soviet path behaves very much like the Polish one, catching up with the mixed economy path for instance only in the 26th year. If any time discount is applied to consumption along the alternative paths then the two revolutionary sequences (Polish and Soviet) 'become quite untenable policies' ([37], p. 103), from the viewpoint of the welfare of the poor.

Of course, future revolutions *may* turn out to be more favourable to the poor than the historical experience of Poland and Russia. Wiles offers various qualifications and warnings (p. 104), but does not appear to think that the Chinese experience alters his conclusion (p. 105). Whilst the actual numbers used by Wiles (as he recognizes) can be questioned, nevertheless his simulation exercise should at least make potential revolutionaries, interested in serving the interests of the poor, think of the economic costs of past revolutions.

CONCLUSIONS

Our conclusions can be briefly summarized. The current concern with distributional issues amongst the international agencies and American development economists marks more their acknowledgment of *their* past neglect of what a number of Third World governments and many development economists have for a long time recognized to be a major area of concern, rather than any 'new' insight into the development process. The broad reasons for the continuing inequities in the development process are fairly well known, and the books by Chenery *et al.* and Adelman and Morris do not extend the frontiers of our knowledge in this respect. Instead Adelman and Morris argue that past growth has (and must have, in the absence of redistribution) actually harmed the poor. If anything, their own evidence does not support this assertion, and the evidence in Chenery et al. actually suggests the opposite. Further, the various, admittedly crude, simulation exercises of Chenery *et al.* and ILO suggest that growth remains of primary importance for poverty redressal. Redistribution of assets could aid this process, but the magnitude of the beneficial effects of some of this redistribution (particularly of education) is overstated. In any case, it is probably politically naive to expect any substantial redistribution of assets in most developing countries (or in most countries, or in the world!) as is recommended by both Chenery *et al.* and ILO. The radicals are at least right in stressing that revolution may be required to achieve a substantial measure of equality, though whether the poor benefit more from revolution than from certain reformist strategies seems dubious. Moreover, despite these practical *realpolitik* grounds, the presumption that the pursuit of equality through redistribution should be the primary aim of public policy is also open to objection on ethical grounds. The ethical preconceptions underlying Chenery *et al.* and ILO are particularly shallow. Finally, there is the danger that in creating the false impression that growth in the past has harmed or not benefited the poor and in overstating the case for (and feasibility of) redistribution, all three books (RWG, AM and ILO) may perhaps do indirect damage to the prospects of the poor by not emphasizing enough that efficient growth which raises the demand for labour is probably the single most important means available for alleviating poverty in the Third World.

NOTES

1. The empirical evidence from surveys about attitudes to income distribution does not, however, support this view. See Lal [17] for a survey of the evidence; also Mary Jo Bane in [20].

2. It should be noted that if these debates have any relevance for the distribution of income, it is for the functional distribution and not the personal distribution of income; though to the extent that the latter is influenced by the former, the two are related. Also the reswitching controversy itself is not relevant even for the determination of factor shares, except for that version of neo-classical theory which depends upon assuming the existence of an aggregate production function, for it only demonstrates that with the usual neo-classical assumptions it is not true that, in general, steady states with lower interest rates have higher consumption per worker. But, as Solow notes, it is not clear how this result is so subversive of standard theory. 'Suppose that, long ago and in another country, I had accepted the standard theory of consumer behaviour – utility maximization subject to a budget constraint – but I had somehow thought that this theory implied that all demand curves were downward-sloping. Then someone showed me that the Giffen good was a clear possibility within the theory. . . . [or] suppose that from study of the two good case I had concluded that all commodities were substitutes in the Slutsky sense; and then I learnt that as soon as there are three or more goods complementarity is possible. I would have to kiss a neat generalization goodbye, and its immediate consequences too, but the theory of consumer demand would evidently not tumble on that account' ([34], pp. 51–2). Moreover as Bliss [6] has shown, Dobb's statement is false if it means that the neo-classical theory too requires that the income distribution be specified prior to the determination of prices, for the neo-classical general equilibrium theory of capital, excellently expounded by Bliss, shows the distribution of income to be the outcome of the balancing of a large number of mutually interacting forces ([6], p. 352), in which given initial endowments, tastes and technology, factor shares, factor and commodity prices are simultaneously determined. Of course, as is obvious, it can provide no *justification* of the distribution of income.

3. This paper also shows how sensitive are the conclusions about rising or falling real wages, incomes, etc., during a period of agricultural growth, to the end points of the comparisons being made. In particular it argues that, given the lag of money wages behind prices, studies using end-period data from an inflationary period are likely erroneously to conclude that the *trend* of real wages is downwards. Thus it shows that the pessimistic conclusions about the effects of the Green Revolution in India on rural real wages and poverty redressal were based on using terminal date wage data which ended in a period when money wages were still adjusting to price rises. With price stability, the conventional hypothesis that agricultural growth does lead to rises in real wages (*ceteris paribus*) is borne out by the Indian data.

4. Nozick also discusses and dismisses many of the arguments for forcible redistribution based on equality of opportunity (where his case, as he himself admits, is weak), self-esteem, envy, social co-operation and Marxian exploitation. The case for redistribution would rest purely on the rectification of injustices caused by the violation of the principles of just acquisition and transfer. As Nozick admits:

> Some patterned principles of distributive justice [may be viewed] as rough rules of thumb meant to approximate the general results of applying the principle of rectification of injustice. . . . An important question for each society will be the following: given *its* particular history, what operable rule of thumb best approximates the results of a detailed application in that society to the principle of rectification? These issues are very complex and are best left to a full treatment of the principle of rectification. In the absence of such a treatment applied to a particular society, one *cannot* use the analysis and theory presented here to condemn any particular scheme of transfer payments, unless it is clear that no considerations of rectification of injustice could apply to justify it ([29], p. 231).

One could, of course, discard the individualistic premises on which Nozick's theory is based, and this presumably is the line of attack that holists, seeking to justify collectivist action beyond that justified by

Nozick's analysis, might want to take. (Lukes [24], O'Neill [28]).

5. This substitution pessimism probably reflects the general understating of substitution possibilities in the work of the programming-planning model school of development economists. Thus, where Chenery and Raduchel (in Chenery [8]), do examine the issue of substitution, they construct a model in which it is *assumed* that the typical developing country is faced by declining terms of trade, an assumption which is not borne out by the available evidence, and which, moreover, neglects the possibilities of diversification of exports into a large number of labour-intensive manufactures, for which developing countries would not face declining export prices (Lary [19]). Furthermore, in their model, Chenery and Raduchel assume low capital-labour substitution elasticities on the basis of CES production function estimates from Japan and the USA, which is surely not a realistic assumption for developing countries with very different industrial structures (both actual and potential) from these two countries. Having *built in* these assumptions, the 'sausage machine' (their model) turns out the expected answer that 'our results suggest ... that the possibilities for indirect factor substitution via demand and trade may not be extensive enough to accomodate very wide variations in factor proportions' ([8], p. 47).

REFERENCES

1. I. Adelman and C. T. Morris, *Economic Growth and Social Equity in Developing Countries* (Stanford, 1973).
2. A. B. Atkinson, *The Economics of Inequality* (Oxford, 1975).
3. Carl L. Becker, *The Heavenly City of the Eighteenth-Century Philosophers* (Yale Paperbound, 1959).
4. J. Bhagwati, *The Economics of Underdeveloped Countries* (World University Library, Weidenfeld & Nicholson, 1966).
5. A. S. Blinder, *Toward an Economic Theory of Income Distribution* (MIT, 1974).
6. C. J. Bliss, *Capital Theory and the Distribution of Income* (North Holland, 1975).
7. H. Chenery, M. S. Ahluwalia, C. L. G. Bell, J. H. Duloy and R. Jolly, *Redistribution with Growth* (Oxford, 1974).
8. H. Chenery (ed.), *Studies in Development Planning* (Harvard, 1971).
9. W. R. Cline, 'Distribution and development: a survey of literature', *Journal of Development Economics* (February 1975).
10. M. Dobb, *Theories of Value and Distribution Since Adam Smith* (Cambridge, 1973).
11. W. Gornicki, article in *Kultura*, abridged and published under title 'Who's being taken for a ride?', *The Sunday Times* (28 March 1976).
12. G. C. Harcourt, *Some Cambridge Controversies in the Theory of Capital* (Cambridge, 1972).
13. A. O. Hirschman, 'Changing tolerance for inequality in development', *Quarterly Journal of Economics* (November 1973).
14. ILO, *Employment, Growth and Basic Needs* (ILO, 1976).
15. C. Jencks, *Inequality* (Basic Books, 1972).
16. D. Lal, *Methods of Project Analysis – A Review* (Johns Hopkins, 1974).
17. D. Lal, *Unemployment and Wage Inflation in Industrial Economies* (OECD, 1976).
18. D. Lal, 'Agricultural growth, real wages and the rural poor in India', *Economic and Political Weekly*, Review of Agriculture (June 1976).

18a. D. Lal, *New Economic Policies for India*, Fabian Research Series 311 (London, 1973).

19. H. B. Lary, *Imports of Manufactures from Less Developed Countries* (NBER, 1968).
20. D. M. Levine and M. J. Bane, *The 'Inequality' Controversy* (Basic Books, 1975).
21. A. Lindbeck, *The Political Economy of the New Left* (Harper & Row, 1971).
22. S. M. Lipset, *Political Man* (Heinemann, 1960).
23. I. M. D. Little and J. A. Mirrlees, *Project Appraisal and Planning for Developing Countries* (Heinemann, 1974).
24. S. Lukes, 'State of nature', *New Statesman* (14 March 1975).
25. S. Lukes and A. Arblaster (eds.), *The Good Society* (Methuen, 1971).
26. J. E. Meade, *The Just Economy* (Allen & Unwin, 1976).
27. D. P. Moynihan, *Maximum Feasible Misunderstanding* (Free Press, 1969).
28. J. O'Neill (ed.), *Modes of Individualism and Collectivism* (Heinemann, 1973).
29. R. Nozick, *Anarchy, State and Utopia* (Blackwell, 1974).
30. G. F. Papanek, *Pakistan's Development* (Harvard, 1967).
31. J. Plamenatz, *Democracy and Illusion* (Longman, 1973).
32. W. W. Rostow, *The Stages of Economic Growth*, 2nd edition (Cambridge, 1971).
33. J. Rawls, *A Theory of Justice* (Oxford, 1971).
34. R. M. Solow, 'The unimportance of reswitching – comment', *Quarterly Journal of Economics*, (February 1975).
35. J. Tinbergen, *Income Distribution* (North Holland, 1975).
36. UNIDO, *Guidelines for Project Evaluation* (United Nations, 1972).
37. P. Wiles, *Distribution of Income – East and West* (De Vries lectures, North Holland, 1974).
38. C. A. Valentine, *Culture and Poverty* (Chicago, 1968).

7

Public Enterprises

Deepak Lal

The purpose of this chapter is to analyze the role of public enterprises in the industrialization process in developing countries. The first section discusses the objectives that industrial public enterprises have been intended to fulfill. It leads to an assessment of the economic argument for public enterprises in promoting efficient industrialization, the subject of section II. Once a government has decided to set up public enterprises in manufacturing, the important questions are: (1) how the enterprises should make investment decisions and (2) what pricing policies they should adopt. These questions are discussed in sections III and IV. Section V turns to various organizational and managerial problems of public enterprises and shows how an analytical framework can be used to devise appropriate policy.

PUBLIC ENTERPRISES PLAY a significant role in the industrialization process in many developing countries. They are most important in such socialist countries as Algeria and Tanzania, but their contribution to total manufacturing production is also marked in such mixed economies as India. They are even used as an instrument of government policy in countries such as Korea and Brazil that are following basically capitalistic roads to development. In recent years there has been a resurgence of public enterprises in manufacturing, particularly in oil-rich countries and those seeking to increase local ownership of manufacturing firms.

Public enterprises include a variety of management-ownership forms. In mixed economies the extent of public ownership of the means of production and control over firms' internal decisionmaking can be present in differing mixtures. Normally public control of an enterprise requires that the government own a majority of the equity, but there are cases where control of a firm's internal decisionmaking may be exercised without equity (as, for instance, in the so-called sick mills in India). Conversely, in the worker-managed firms of Peru, though the government may own the capital, control over decisionmaking rests with the workers or managers. It is therefore necessary to distinguish between arguments for public control of enterprises and those for public ownership of the means of production, even though in practice most public enterprises in developing countries are both publicly owned and publicly controlled.

I. The Objectives of Public Enterprises

Countries that consider private entrepreneurs to be unwilling or unable to take a lead in industrialization turn to public enterprises for an essentially promotional role. Such an entrepreneurial function may be important if there is a lack of domestic entrepreneurs—typically the situation in rural subsistence economies just emerging from colonial domination—or if, after periods of war, entrepreneurs are excessively averse to risk. Similarly, where, for historical and institutional reasons, the supposedly middle-class "virtues" fundamental to entrepreneurial drive are found only in the military or bureaucracy, reliance on public enterprise may be the only feasible method for initiating industrialization.

Public enterprises may also be used to correct racial imbalances in entrepreneurship. Entrepreneurs are often confined to a racial minority whose relatively high returns from entrepreneurship are resented by the racial majority. In such countries, public enterprises can provide opportunities to build up the entrepreneurial and managerial skills that some groups lack.

In the early stages of industrialization there is likely to be a dearth of capital, even though there may be no shortage of entrepreneurs. The funding required for such large, capital-intensive industries as steel and fertilizers cannot be assembled because an efficient capital market is lacking. The private banking sector may not yet be able to intermediate between savers and entrepreneurs. (See Chapter 5 for a discussion of monetary and credit policies and how these may assist or hinder investment in manufacturing.) Public involvement in the financing of enterprises either through public ownership or through public control by loans from public financial institutions may be unavoidable. However, it must be noted that if involvement by government in the direct or indirect financing of industries is not carefully handled, it may inhibit the promotion of an efficient equity market in the future.

When promotional public industrial enterprises are developed, the question arises whether they should be sold to the private sector once established. Such sales were usual in Japan in the past; Korea, the Philippines, Brazil, Pakistan, and Singapore have also followed that policy at some stage. The basic argument in favor of selling is that it is difficult for governments to run public enterprises in manufacturing because of the constant changes in demand and supply conditions. These make manufacturing very risky, particularly in market economies that are trade oriented, and require continual adaptation to that changing environment. The concomitant risk, the very essence of entrepreneurship in manufacturing, raises the danger of failure. It is difficult for a government to declare a public enterprise bankrupt even though the costs of keeping it in operation are generally much higher than those, such as severance payments to workers, in closing it down. The same logic of course applies to private enterprises. Some inefficient firms are propped up by the government through tariffs, quantitative restrictions on imports, or protection against the entry of new firms, as indicated in previous chapters. Sometimes—and not only in developing countries—they are taken over by the government and, as public enterprises, become a burden to the public purse, reversing the disinvestment process. However, in most market economies, bankruptcy is usually the ultimate fate of unsuccessful entrepreneurship, and the entrepreneur, as the risk-taker, bears the brunt of the costs just as he enjoys the high profits when successful.

Public enterprises have also been established on purely economic grounds. It is often argued that a developing country cannot afford the misallocation of resources created in a market system as a result of the imperfections that arise when market prices do not coincide with social prices. It is assumed that a public enterprise can avoid such pitfalls by careful evaluation of social as well as economic and financial objectives in the context of national planning.

Noneconomic political objectives have also been of some importance in the establishment of public industrial enterprises. A large body of socialist thought identifies socialism with public ownership of the means of production. In predominantly socialist developing countries, the bulk of medium- and large-scale manufacturing activity is accordingly publicly owned and managed. The belief that direct government control over the "commanding heights" of the economy is a necessary condition for the establishment of socialism was stated explicitly in the Indian Industrial Policy Resolutions of 1948 and 1956, which demarcated the industries which were to be exclusively reserved for public enterprise. The "commanding heights" were identified as large-scale, capital-intensive "base" sectors which were important in the early stages of production in manufacturing activity. Public enterprises have accordingly been established in steel, fertilizer, heavy engineering, basic chemicals, and petrochemicals. This policy is typical of many developing countries. A number of other countries, though not committed to socialism, have also felt that the political consequences of a concentration of private wealth are undesirable and need to be countered by public ownership or control of key enterprises. The belief is that by owning basic industries the government can avoid the political opposition from industrial groups that emerged in Europe, North America, and Japan in the past. It can also supply inputs to the private sector on socially optimal lines. The economic reasons for the establishment of public enterprises are thus frequently underlined by and intertwined with political objectives.

Not all socialists would agree that ownership of the means of production is an essential component of socialism. Substantial numbers of those of the social democratic persuasion argue that the basic end is equality and that public ownership of the means of production (or of the "commanding heights") must be judged purely as a means toward that end. Efficiency then becomes the criterion in production, with the emphasis on equality in the distribution of public and private goods that compose the national product. In this view, public ownership need not be identified with socialism, but should be judged along with various other public policy alternatives for the achievement of equality. Not to do so would be to confuse means with ends.

Public enterprises have also been used to avoid the buildup of foreign capital interests or to nationalize them when they have been deemed inimical to a country's economic or political interests. Despite ideological differences, public enterprises are seen in this and other contexts in many developing countries as a useful means of extending state political power per se; it is arguable whether, among the alternatives that are available, the public enterprise mechanism is the most appropriate for this end. Indeed, it is even questionable whether the extension of state political power leads to increased welfare and hence whether even that end is justifiable.

II. The Economic Rationale for Public Enterprises

Market Failure and "Optimal" Intervention

For economists, the failures of the market that give rise to the necessity for government intervention are failures relative to the performance of a utopian model of a perfectly competitive economy. The conditions for the existence of a competitive equilibrium, one which is Pareto-efficient (that is, for a given income distribution it is not possible to make one person better off without making someone else worse off), have been rigorously worked out by recent theoretical work in welfare economics. If any of the conditions are absent, that in itself could provide a case for government intervention.

In a perfectly competitive world, consumers and producers face prices they cannot influence by their own actions. Wanting to maximize utility and profits, they will choose the optimal consumption and production bundles of commodities. These bundles will be consistent in that in each time period aggregate consumption will equal aggregate production plus initial endowment. The result is that for any given initial endowment, a Pareto-efficient allocation of commodities will exist, and it will entail the fulfillment of the so-called marginal welfare equivalences, namely: (1) the marginal rates of transformation in production of different commodities are equal to their marginal rates of substitution in consumption; (2) the marginal rates of substitution between any pair of factors are the same in all the industries in which they are used; and (3) the marginal rates of substitution of any pair of commodities are the same for all individuals consuming both goods. By treating the same physical commodity at different dates as many different commodities, intertemporal marginal equivalences for an efficient intertemporal program of commodity inputs and outputs can be derived. Furthermore, if universal futures markets exist, there will be a Pareto-efficient competitive equilibrium even in the presence of uncertainty about the future. Economic agents will be able to make contingent contracts for different commodities which are now differentiated not only by physical and temporal characteristics but also by whether or not certain conditions or states exist in the world at particular times. They will then be able to maximize their expected utilities according to their own subjective estimates of the probability of various unknown future states of the world.

If the income distribution associated with a particular Pareto-efficient competitive equilibrium is considered to be socially just, a full social welfare maximum (a Pareto optimum) will be achieved. At such a Pareto optimum, market prices of goods and factors would equal the marginal social cost of producing and the marginal social value of using the relevant goods and factors. In this case market prices would be the social prices, and decentralized investment and production and consumption decisions taken on the basis of such prices would be socially optimal.

Even if the conditions required for achieving an optimal income distribution are ignored, all the assumptions necessary to assure a competitive Pareto-efficient allocation are not likely to exist in the real world. In particular, the assumptions relating to the independence and convexity of consumption and production sets and the universality of markets are unrealistic. The existence of externalities in production and consumption rules out the independence of production and consumption sets; indivisibilities in consumption and production (increasing returns to scale) rule out convex consumption and production sets. It is also obvious that, in the real world of uncertainty, universal contingent commodity markets are notable for their absence. As long as the nonconvexities in the consumption and production sets are not large relative to the economy, then an approximate competitive equilibrium is likely to exist. However, without universal markets it is not likely to be Pareto-efficient.

In a sense, therefore, it is the lack of universal markets that is most likely to prevent the unfettered market mechanism from achieving a Pareto-efficient allocation. Externalities really constitute a special case of the nonexistence of markets. The problems arise because it is difficult (if not impossible) to create a market for these external "commodities," chiefly because pricing a commodity in any market requires the exclusion of nonbuyers from obtaining the commodity; in the case of many externalities, it may be technically impossible or extremely resource-intensive to ensure such exclusion. Clean air or water, for example, cannot be treated as separate commodities to be supplied to some individuals and not to others. For other types of externalities for which exclusion may be possible, the number of buyers and sellers in the market for externalities is likely to be small, and hence the market would necessarily be imperfectly competitive. More generally, transaction costs, which are attached to any market and indeed to any mode of resource allocation, mean that not all possible markets exist. This in turn leads to inefficiency in the competitive allocation. Market failure is the particular case where transaction costs are so high that the existence of the market is no longer worthwhile.

Thus any real world market economy is not likely to be Pareto-efficient, first (and less plausibly), because of the existence of technological indivisibilities which lead to increasing returns in production over a range that is large relative to the economy;[1] and second (more certainly), because of the transaction costs attached to markets (including the costs of exclusion, as well as those of acquiring and transmitting information). For these reasons, many markets will not exist or else will be imperfect. This will mean that the marginal welfare equivalences, whereby the market prices of goods and factors equate the marginal social cost of producing and the marginal social value of using the relevant goods or factors, will no longer hold.

Furthermore, even if the economy were perfectly competitive, there would be different Pareto-efficient allocations associated with different income distributions. As it is the initial endowments which will determine the particular Pareto-efficient allocation and its associated income distribution, the actual equilibrium of a competitive economy, though Pareto-efficient, may not yield the maximum social welfare. It may thus be necessary, even in a perfectly competitive Pareto-efficient economy, for government to intervene. By using neutral fiscal devices in the form of lump-sum taxes and subsidies, it can reallocate the initial endowments suitably in order to attain that Pareto-efficient, competitive equilibrium which achieves the full social welfare optimum (the so-called first-best welfare or full Pareto optimum).

Given the breakdown of the assumptions of perfect competition, there would appear to be a similar prima facie case for government intervention to correct the divergences that may exist between the marginal social value and the marginal social cost.[2] As in the case of legislating the optimal income distribution, if neutral fiscal devices are avail-

1. "Less plausibly" because, for an open economy facing given terms of trade, most goods will be tradables and hence in the absence of government intervention could be "produced" through the (indirect) foreign trade "technology," with constant returns to scale. Even in this case, where there are increasing returns in production in some industries, though they are not large relative to the economy, government intervention may be required to legislate the optimum production and investment decision rules for the industries subject to increasing returns.

2. These divergences between marginal social value and marginal social cost can generally be said to result from distortions in the conditions that would prevail under perfect

(*Note continues.*)

able and can be used to eliminate the divergences between marginal social costs and marginal social values, then again through government intervention a first-best social welfare optimum could be achieved.

However, governments are not likely to find any feasible neutral fiscal devices, either to legislate the optimal income distribution or to correct divergences between marginal social costs and marginal social values. The use of other than neutral fiscal devices (whether these be in the form of price-reliant instruments such as income or indirect taxes and subsidies or in the form of administrative controls) would lead to new wedges being driven between some other marginal social costs and marginal social values. These will in turn entail welfare losses, which will have to be counterbalanced against the welfare gains that would result from curing the initial divergences between marginal social costs and marginal social values. There will thus in general be a second-best optimum at which, by using the distortionary instrument of public policy to correct an initial divergence between the marginal social cost and the marginal social value, the *net* gain in social welfare is maximized. As is obvious, welfare will be lower at the second-best than at the first-best welfare optimum, and at a second-best welfare optimum it may not be optimal to eliminate completely the initial divergence between marginal social cost and marginal social value.

This absence of first-best corrective devices to cure market failures can in turn be ascribed to the transaction costs associated with the use of these instruments of government intervention. Moreover, the transaction costs associated with alternative instruments, which can be differentiated into those which work indirectly through the price mechanism and those which are more direct, such as bureaucratic controls, will also differ. Thus it is possible that, even in the presence of well-known cases of market failure, there may be no feasible instrument of government intervention which would yield a net increase in social welfare, as compared with that produced by the imperfect market mechanism. More important, when comparing alternative feasible in-

---

competition. Any distortion, then, can be looked upon as driving a wedge between marginal social value and marginal social cost and hence causing a divergence between them (and market price). Thus transaction costs drive a wedge between the buyer's price (marginal social value) and the seller's price (marginal social cost) of the relevant good. A market for a particular good (for instance, a futures, contingent commodity market) will fail to exist if the wedge between the buyer's and seller's price is large enough to make the lowest price at which anyone is willing to sell the commodity above the highest price anyone is willing to pay for the commodity.

struments of public policy, in particular those relying on the price mechanism and alternative direct methods of allocation, the differential transaction costs must be taken into account. It cannot be assumed that welfare losses resulting from the existence of transaction costs in a price system of allocation will necessarily be eliminated by an alternative direct method of allocation. The latter may fail for bureaucratic reasons (to be contrasted with market reasons) in terms of equally high, if not higher, transaction costs, for example, in acquiring information on demand and supply conditions in the absence of markets.

The Case for Public Enterprise

Government regulation or direct ownership is called for in industries which are natural monopolies, that is, industries such as railways or electric power supply utilities which are subject to increasing returns to scale. Manufacturing industries, on the other hand, for the most part produce traded goods, and their effective supply curve to the economy is characterized by constant returns to scale. Trade is generally an alternative to government regulation of an incipient or actual monopoly, as foreign competition will eliminate this possibility on the part of domestic producers. Public utilities are classic examples of natural monopoly industries, and not surprisingly most countries, developed and developing, have found it desirable either to nationalize them or to subject them to close regulation. For many public goods, state provision not only may be desirable, but it may be the only feasible means at the optimal level. The difficulties of nonexclusion and/or the limited numbers involved on either side of the market for externalities in such goods may result in the absence of a market or one that is inherently imperfect. (Because such public goods are outside the scope of this study, they are ignored in the rest of this chapter, even though much of the theoretical literature has been concerned with the various aspects of public policy required to optimize the provision of these goods.)

This then leaves various distortions in the economy which cause divergences between marginal social value and marginal social cost and the continuance of which implies that the allocation of investment and production through laissez-faire will not achieve optimal use of resources. Moreover, as noted above, with the restrictions on the availability of neutral fiscal devices, any form of government intervention to cure these divergences will lead to by-product distortions. Thus the most that can be attained is a second-best welfare optimum in which the net gain from the removal of the initial divergence between marginal social value and marginal social cost is partially offset by the loss caused by the creation of some other divergence.

Nationalization of industry will be one of the various instruments of public policy that government can use to intervene in order to attain a second-best welfare optimum. Other alternative instruments can in general be made equivalent to various tax and subsidy policies. The important question is: *can nationalization of industries (other than natural monopolies or those producing public goods) result in outcomes which affect the efficiency and equity of the economy in an essentially different way from what could be achieved by taxes and subsidies?*

In principle, the government could, through appropriate taxes and subsidies, achieve any pricing of inputs and outputs in the economy that a public enterprise is meant to achieve. The difference must therefore ultimately flow from the difference in ownership and control of public and private enterprises. In countries where stock markets and other institutional devices for dispersing private industrial ownership are not likely to exist and where, if they do, they are unlikely to be used by the bulk of the population, public ownership could be a feasible means for incremental industrial asset redistribution. There may thus be an equity justification for public ownership in industry that makes the use of this particular policy instrument desirable.

Similarly, even though in principle the government could achieve its second-best social welfare objectives through the use of an appropriate mix of distortionary (and hence quasi-optimal) taxes and subsidies for the inputs and outputs of private industry, in practice the available set of second-best taxes and subsidies may also be severely restricted. More important, even if the appropriate taxes could be levied, the administrative costs associated with their levy (or disbursement in the case of subsidies) may make the alternative of public ownership more cost effective.

Against these arguments in favor of nationalization must be set various practical difficulties in the actual management and operation of public enterprises, which have arisen in most countries, developed and developing. These problems relate to the suppression by nationalization of the twin functions of the market of providing the incentives and information (virtually at no cost) required for maintaining productive efficiency. These market forces tend to be sluggish or absent when public enterprise investment and pricing policies become part of a bureaucratic process. One purpose of the discussion of investment and pricing policies in the next part of this chapter is to provide rules which enable the government to decentralize these decisions effectively; another purpose is to show which tools will both provide the requisite incentives to managers and allow the monitoring of their performance.

III. Investment Policies

The experience of public enterprise management in developing countries suggests that it is of central importance that the government be clear as to the basic objectives public enterprises are supposed to serve. Investment and pricing rules should be devised for purely entrepreneurial purposes for public enterprises which will operate in an otherwise market-oriented economy, so that public enterprises will function as private enterprises would if they existed. However, where public enterprises are set up to achieve second-best efficiency and equity objectives, the recent developments in what may be termed the "welfare economics of imperfect economies" are most relevant. It is in this area of public sector investment and pricing rules that economic analysis can be of considerable assistance. This section therefore focuses on the determination of investment rules for the public sector in an imperfect economy, where it is assumed that existing distortions between marginal social values and marginal social costs are pervasive and are unlikely to be removed in the near future.

Any non-lump-sum tax or subsidy will lead to a divergence between the marginal social value and marginal social cost of a commodity or factor. It is useful to think of the existing divergences between marginal social values and marginal social costs in the economy as equivalent to given fixed taxes or subsidies, even though the source of the divergence could be a variety of distortions, such as those relating to increasing returns, externalities, monopoly power, or fragmented markets.

Investment Decisions and Shadow Pricing

Given the existing distortions in factor and commodity prices, investment decisions based on market prices would not lead toward the second-best welfare optimum. The first question to ask is therefore: in such an economy, how should the government make public sector investment decisions, taking into account the effects of its actions not merely on economic efficiency, but also on equity (both interpersonal and intergenerational)?

Social cost-benefit analysis provides a systematic approach to this problem. Just as financial cost-benefit analysis provides a framework for the comparison of the financial (private) profitability of alternative investments, given existing market prices, so social cost-benefit analysis provides a systematic basis for comparing the likely social returns on projects, essentially by shadow pricing the relevant quantities by their social values. Two basic variants of social cost-benefit analysis have been developed: the method suggested in the UNIDO *Guidelines*, and that in Little and Mirrlees, *Project Appraisal and Planning for Developing Countries*. They differ partly in their choice of numeraire, which in the Little-Mirrlees method is uncommitted social income expressed in foreign exchange, as compared with that of the *Guidelines* of aggregate consumption in domestic currency. They also differ in their relative need for averaging across the multiplicity of exchange rates at which traded commodities exchange in the domestic markets of most developing countries, as well as in their treatment of the shadow prices of non-traded goods.

The choice of numeraire can be of some importance when distributional objectives need to be taken into account, for the numeraire must be homogeneous (and hence invariant to the system of distributional weights) if it is to be an accurate yardstick. An elastic ruler would be pretty worthless in measuring length. If the interpersonal distribution of consumption is to be taken into account, then the value of aggregate social consumption will vary with the system of distributional weights chosen.

The Little-Mirrlees numeraire (uncommitted social income) provides a relatively homogeneous numeraire (at least from the viewpoint of the government) for the alternative items of national income from which it could be chosen. It also has the merit, as seen below, of enabling various public sector pricing rules to be put systematically into the same framework as in the case of investment decisions.

Given this numeraire, the Little-Mirrlees rules for public sector investment decisions can be outlined briefly. Any investment project entails changing the time stream of consumption in the economy. An evaluation of these inter- and intratemporal changes raises two types of weighting problems which are part of the difficulty of making different types of costs and benefits commensurable. As social welfare is usually taken to be a function of the consumption accruing to various individuals in a country, there is the need to make the consumption gained or lost as a result of an investment project at different dates commensurable. If, moreover, the consumption accruals to different groups at a point in time are not equally valuable socially, it will also be necessary to make them commensurable. As public income can be used to provide consumption to any group currently (through consumption transfers) or in the future (through investment), the various consumption changes that occur can be converted into public income equivalents if a set of weights (rather like prices) is available which translates the consumption changes of a specific group at a particular date into current public income values.

In addition, however, the investment project's costs and benefits will involve different currency items—those in foreign and in domestic currency. The exchange rate normally converts the foreign currency values into domestic currency. If, however, as is typical in most developing countries, the exchange rate is overvalued and not unified (implying a multiplicity of effective exchange rates as a result of the tariff and quota system), then the domestic currency valuation of foreign currency items at the official exchange rate will not give their relative social value. It will therefore be necessary to convert the various foreign currency items into their equivalent social values by using the implicit exchange rates for each commodity. This process is greatly simplified if all commodities are valued (in a relatively open economy) in terms of their foreign exchange value. Little and Mirrlees suggest that relative social values of commodities are most easily measured in terms of relative "border" prices, that is, the prices the country has to pay for imports or gets for its exports. (This assumes a country cannot influence its terms of trade, in which case the relevant marginal costs or revenues in foreign trade of the commodities will be their accounting prices.) These border prices will be the relevant accounting prices for fully traded goods, that is, for goods for which the impact of marginal changes is taken to be on foreign trade. For goods that do not enter foreign trade at all because of prohibitive transport costs, the accounting prices will be given by the cost of producing these nontraded goods in terms of the numeraire, namely uncommitted social income expressed in terms of foreign exchange. This is the Little-Mirrlees method for valuing nontraded goods, for which increased demand is met by increased production.

There will be, however, a third category of goods—which can be labeled partially traded—for which an increase in demand could affect domestic production, foreign trade, and domestic consumption. It will be necessary to determine the proportion in which the extra demand is met from each of the above three sources. This done, the social costs of meeting the demand will be the weighted average of the social costs of a marginal increase in domestic production, decrease in domestic consumption, and increase (decrease) in imports (exports) of the goods, the weights being the estimates of the proportionate share of these alternative sources in meeting the increase in demand.

For the proportions which come from foreign trade and domestic production, the above general principles for determining social costs can be used. But what of the proportion that comes from decreased consumption? The effect of the increased demand for the partially traded goods would have led to some bidding up of their domestic prices, and hence the switching of consumer expenditure away from them to other goods and services. The accounting cost of providing these alternative goods and services to consumers will then be the social cost of obtaining the goods from domestic consumption for use on the project. It will normally not be possible to determine the "other goods and services" to which consumers shift their expenditures. However, if it is assumed that they consist of the same goods and services that make up the average consumption bundle for the economy, then by revaluing the components of this bundle at accounting prices, it is possible to determine its total accounting value. The ratio of the value of the consumption bundle at market prices to that at accounting prices will be the average aggregate consumption conversion factor for the economy. If the groups whose consumption is affected by the increase in project demand for a particular good can be identified, then, given their expenditure pattern, specific consumption conversion factors can be derived for any particular group of consumers.

These rules do not apply only where the economy is at, or moving toward, free trade. They can be derived within a second-best general equilibrium framework in which public sector investment decisions have to be made on the basis of given distortions between marginal social value and marginal social cost, some of which could be due to the existence of nonoptimal tariffs.

Having determined the social values of the commodity inputs and outputs, it is still necessary to take account of any distortions that may exist in labor markets and the general problem of weighting the various consumption changes (at shadow prices) which the investment project entails, intra- and intertemporally. For labor, it will be necessary to determine the accounting prices of types of labor which are differentiated from each other both by differences in quality and by their location in space and time. The shadow price of seasonally unemployed agricultural labor will be different from that of skilled urban labor employed in modern factories. In determining the accounting prices of a particular class of labor in general, two main sets of considerations will have to be taken into account. The first is the output forgone in earlier employment, valued in terms of foreign exchange (the numeraire used here), resulting from the employment of a laborer on the investment project being appraised. The second is to weight any income gains which the worker or his family might receive if the wage paid in his new employment is greater than that received in previous employment. These weights will have to reflect such social objectives as the desired change in both the intratemporal and intertemporal distribution of income and consumption. These weights must ultimately depend upon value judgments, and there are obvious advantages to deriving them from an explicit and consistent set of value judgments. Given these weights, the net social cost of the increase in workers' consumption in terms of the numeraire (public income expressed in foreign exchange) can be determined and added to the social cost of the output forgone by their employment on the project to yield the accounting wage.

The discount rate in the Little-Mirrlees procedures—the accounting rate of interest—is given by the rate of change in the value of their numeraire (uncommitted public income) and will normally be different from the social discount rate used in methods which take aggregate consumption as their numeraire.

The derivation and application of appropriate shadow pricing rules is a means of improving public sector investment decisions. It is particularly important that a social evaluation of public sector industrial projects be institutionalized. Project appraisal has become common within ministries and departments as well as in central planning offices to evaluate major investments in both the private and public sectors. A centralized approach to the estimation and updating of the relevant shadow prices has become essential in many countries. Past experience suggests that, in making investment decisions about public enterprises, exclusive reliance on macroeconomic projection models and on techniques of the type used in material balance-planning models can be misleading. The investment choices suggested by such macroeconomic models should be checked by detailed appraisals.

Much of the art of good project analysis consists of forming judgments about national parameters. As these involve the specification of and choice between conflicting objectives, it is important that these judgments be made centrally. The development of national income accounts provided a powerful tool for devising sensible macroeconomic policies. Similarly, it is hoped, the derivation of economy-wide shadow prices, once institutionalized in the same way as national income accounting, will enable the various microeconomic interventions of the government (whether they be in the form of its choice of alternative public sector investments or its pricing policy) to be made more rationally and consistently.

IV. Pricing Policies

Even more than public investment criteria, the pricing policies of public enterprises in most developing countries offer much scope for improvement. Particular pricing rules adopted by a public enterprise may have a pervasive effect on the economy through the market mechanism, distorting the use of resources and having social impacts other than those intended. Various ad hoc rules are often adopted, and the economic rationale behind many pricing policies is hard to discern. In some countries where public sector pricing policies are considered to be an instrument in anti-inflationary policies or income distribution, public sector prices are kept artifically low. At other times prices have been raised to whatever level the market will bear to generate public sector surpluses.

Two conflicting forces usually press on those who set prices: (1) the need to finance continuing public investment through public sector surpluses, which leads to pressures to adopt some form of average cost (or break-even) pricing formula; and (2) the desire to take account of the social effects, which normally means selling at prices lower than average cost and, in some cases of basic goods such as textiles, even below marginal cost.

The principles underlying the system of shadow pricing discussed above also enable these various conflicting objectives to be taken into account systematically and consistently in the quasi-optimal pricing policies of public enterprises. To see the general principles involved, as well as the link with the Little-Mirrlees shadow pricing rules, consider the problem of setting the price for nontraded consumer goods produced in the public sector. Clearly, the government should not set a price for this good which is below its marginal social cost. Suppose, however, that the government does set a price which is marginally greater than marginal social cost. In addition to distributional effects, this will entail a loss of consumers' utility equal to the difference between the price set and the marginal social cost. Against this, however, must be balanced the change in public income (over and above that taken into account in deriving the Little-Mirrlees shadow prices) which results if the price set by the government is greater than the marginal costs of production at *market* prices—that is, marginal social cost *plus* the price effects of all distortions (net taxes). In other words, the marginal gains in terms of public income resulting from charging a price higher than the marginal cost of production at market prices has to be traded off against the marginal loss in terms of consumption which a marginal increase in the public sector output entails. Note that the gain is in terms of public income (the Little-Mirrlees numeraire), but the loss is in terms of private consumption. However, as part of the Little-Mirrlees shadow price set, there will be an estimate of a national parameter (the premium on public income in terms of private consumption) whose value enables private sector consumption changes to be translated into their equivalent public income value—taking into account the aggregate public income (and savings) constraint on the economy as a whole. On this basis it can be said that, at the second-best optimum, the quasi-optimal price of the public sector output will be achieved when the marginal loss in consumption converted into its equivalent public income value equals the marginal gain in public income.[3]

In the extreme case, if the premium on public income (savings) is infinite, the optimal price will be that at which marginal revenue is equal to the marginal cost of production at market prices—that is, the full monopoly price. In this case the public sector should behave as a private monopolist would in its pricing policy. If, on the other hand, there is no utility attached to public income (that is, there are no constraints on public income and hence on generating the desired level of savings over time), then the public sector's output price should be equated to the marginal social cost of production.[4]

3. As the price of the public sector output increases, the marginal increase in public revenue will reach a maximum when the marginal costs of production at market prices equal marginal revenue. It would never be optimal to set a price such that marginal revenue would be greater than the marginal cost of production at market prices. The marginal *increase* in public revenue is, therefore, given by the difference between marginal cost of production at market prices and marginal revenue.

4. Thus if q is the price set for the public sector unit output, whose marginal *social* costs of production are p and whose marginal cost of production at *market* prices is

Normally, however, the value placed on public sector income will fall between zero and infinity, and hence the quasi-optimal price will lie between the marginal social cost of production and the full monopoly price. The quasi-optimal divergence of the price from the marginal social cost of production is greater, the higher the value set on public sector income (savings) and the lower the elasticity of demand for the good.[5]

The value placed on public sector income (savings) takes account of the second-best intergenerational distributional problems and the extent to which current public income (and savings) are constrained. Within the same Little-Mirrlees framework, the interpersonal (intratemporal equity) aspects can also be easily taken account of when determining the optimal price for a public sector output. The same framework can be readily extended to take account of interdependent demand curves in the public and private sectors or within the public sector, as well as in the pricing of public sector intermediate goods for sale to the public and private sector.

In fact, for nontraded producer goods produced in the public sector, the public sector pricing rules are relatively straightforward. In general, taxation on transactions between producers is undesirable, a condition which suggests that the price charged for public sector producer goods sales within the public sector should be the marginal social cost divided by the average divergence between accounting and market prices in the economy (the Little-Mirrlees standard conversion factor). This is based on the following argument. The price paid by private producers for the public sector's intermediate output will reflect its marginal value product at market prices for its use in the private sector. The marginal social benefit of the intermediate output's marginal use in the private sector will then be the value of the marginal physical product of the output evaluated at shadow prices. If the standard conversion

---

$(p + t)$, then, if s is the premium on public income in terms of private consumption and e the elasticity of demand for the good, the optimal pricing formula will be:

$$q[1 - (1/k \cdot e)] = p + t/k$$

where $k = (1 + s)/s$. As s approaches infinity, k approaches 1, and hence the optimal price is $q(1 - 1/e) = p + t$, that is, the full monopoly price. However, if s approaches 0, k will approach infinity and $q = p$.

5. This last aspect of the rule, the so-called inverse elasticity rule for optimal public sector pricing, as well as for optimal distortionary taxation to raise a given government revenue, is well known in the literature of second-best pricing policies for public enterprises.

factor measures the average difference between shadow and market prices, then the marginal social benefit will equal the price multiplied by the standard conversion factor. The second-best optimum will be where the marginal social benefit is equal to the marginal social cost, that is, where the price is equated to the marginal social cost divided by the standard conversion factor.

For public sector outputs which are tradables, pricing rules can also be readily formulated within this framework. With given tariffs and the production of a tradable consumer good by both the private and public sectors, clearly the given tariff-inclusive price will be the right one to charge. If, however, the tariff can be altered or the government is the sole producer of the good under a prohibitive tariff (so that it is in effect a nontradable), then the same considerations as are relevant in setting the price for a nontraded consumer good, discussed above, would apply.

In fact, to the extent that the quasi-optimal public sector pricing rules involve pricing the goods above the marginal social cost, they are equivalent to the determination of the quasi-optimal taxes on public sector outputs. These quasi-optimal tax rules under a variety of constraints have been studied by various authors, but obviously the precise rules will vary with the particular constraints that are specified. Nevertheless, the basic principles will be linked to the shadow pricing framework discussed in this part, and hence the particular rules for specific cases can be readily derived within this framework.

V. Management and Control

The problems of management and control have persistently bedeviled public sector enterprises. They are in essence the problems of assessing public sector performance and of providing managers with adequate incentives to attain technical efficiency in their operations. Poor financial performance is a common feature of many public enterprises. Both the proponents and opponents of private enterprise use the lack of financial profitability to grind their own axes. The proponents argue that public enterprises which are set up to subserve social objectives should not be judged by crude financial profitability, while opponents claim that not to do so at all is an open invitation to perpetuate waste and inefficiency.

As it happens, both groups are to some extent correct. Where private and social profitability diverge because of the various divergences between market and shadow prices, it is social profitability that is the relevant criterion for judging public sector performance. But it is not necessarily the case that all socially profitable public investments need be financially unprofitable. It also cannot be assumed, without doing the necessary sums, that a financially unprofitable public enterprise is necessarily socially profitable. Public sector company accounts must present both the social and financial profitability accounts of various enterprises, for it is by its social profitability that a public enterprise's performance should be judged.

In a sense, the maintenance of social profitability accounts would be equivalent to the government's actually making the prices facing public enterprises equal to the relevant shadow prices. Thus, for traded goods, the public enterprise's social accounts would show the social cost as the border price of the goods, that is, as if the various import duties had been rebated. As such rebates would be merely transfer payments within the public sector, the government instead of actually transferring the money could equally well tell the public sector accountants to assume they had received the rebates. The same argument applies for any implicit taxes or subsidies in the difference between the market and shadow prices of nontraded inputs, as well as for the implicit wage subsidy in the difference between the shadow and market wages paid for labor by the public enterprise. Where public enterprises provide a form of unemployment relief by employing an excessive number of workers, such subsidies should be evaluated. Other forms of employment assistance are often much less costly.

However, in practice it may be better for these transfers actually to take place. Most managers prefer clear-cut financial objectives. The actual payment of the necessary subsidies (or taxes) to public firms would make their financial cash flows identical with the social cash flow, and conventional management tools for judging performance could then be readily applied. This desire of managers to see their shadow profits converted into something more substantial should not be a cause for worry, as it would not involve any net change in the government's financial situation. (This is not true, of course, if the implicit tax paid by the public enterprise is in effect a monopoly rent paid to a private producer for an input.) Similarly, if the industry would suffer a loss when the optimal price to be charged does not cover average social cost, as is the case with nontraded goods subject to increasing returns to scale, the appropriate subsidy should be paid to the enterprise.

If these practices became common, a much more meaningful appraisal of public sector performance would be possible. Furthermore, to the extent that the transfers were actually made, the incentives for managers to base their productive decisions on shadow prices would be restored. This should also aid public sector efficiency.

Such an approach would require new attitudes toward the training of managers for public enterprises in manufacturing. At present managers are recruited either from the private sector or from other public service institutions and services. In the former case they do not appreciate the difference between social and private costs and returns and tend to run the enterprises to maximize financial returns, even if it means social subsidies through protection, price controls, or similar instruments. At the same time they tend to minimize risk in their new circumstances, thus combining the worst of the private and public enterprise worlds. Those managers who come from customs, education, or other administrative posts, on the other hand, have no experience in the dynamics of manufacturing and of the importance of risk taking. They are not familiar with the difference between private and social costs and returns. In some of the least developed countries they even lack such basic skills as double-entry bookkeeping. A country that is seriously concerned with establishing public enterprises in manufacturing has to give attention to the training of existing and new managers in the special skills required in public service business management.

It is necessary to reinforce further the incentives for management by ensuring that their material and psychic rewards are directly linked to social profitability. This is likely to be the most intractable aspect of public sector control and management. For even though in principle there may not appear to be much of a difference in the separation between ownership and management in the large public or private corporation, in practice there is likely to be an important difference because of the differing natures of the owners. As the literature on the modern private corporation has emphasized, there is still a powerful stimulus for managers of corporations to behave in the profit-maximizing way posited by theories of the firm which assume the existence of owner-managers. The threat of takeovers, which would be likely to occur if the stock market valuation of the company falls too low, reinforces such behavior because takeovers are normally followed by the sacking of top management. The latter are naturally anxious to prevent such a disaster. In this way owners (stockholders) can exert some influence on managers to maximize profits.

The problem with a public corporation is that there is no obvious source of such influence on its managers. True, public sector managers will be subject to pressures from their "owners," the departments and ministries who often control their policies, but unlike stockholders, public sector owners are likely to be swayed by many objectives other than the social profitability of the enterprises under their control. The relatively anonymous pressures of the stock market on private corporation managers are replaced by powerful political pressures which often have little to do with efficiency. The problem of eliminating inefficient public enterprises is thus much more difficult.

To suggest that politicians and civil servants should judge public sector managers in terms of social profitability just as private managers are judged by stockholders in terms of private profitability is likely to be a counsel of perfection. For better or for worse, public enterprises are more likely to remain subject to the political process. This is inherent in their very form of ownership and control. To the extent that in many cases productive efficiency is likely to be sacrificed to political expediency, there could be a strong case against public enterprises. Hence, if a feasible system of government intervention could be designed which would manage the price mechanism so that private enterprises would subserve social ends, it would be preferable. It could tend, purely on grounds of second-best economic welfare, to serve the commonweal much better than the public enterprises whose efficiency is eroded by changing political forces.

Bibliography

Much of the literature on public enterprises in developing countries is descriptive and lacks a clear analytical base. As representative of this literature, see Asian Centre for Development Administration (ACDA), *Approaches to Public Enterprise Policy in Asia on Investment, Prices, and Returns Criteria* (Kuala Lumpur, September 1976), and Werner Baer, Isaac Kerstenetzky, and Annibal V. Villela, "The Changing Role of the State in the Brazilian Economy," *World Development* (November 1973).

An exception is Leroy P. Jones, *Public Enterprise and Economic Development* (Seoul: Korean Development Institute, 1976), and, to some extent, John B. Sheahan, "Public Enterprise in Developing Countries," in William Geoffrey Shepherd, ed., *Public Enterprise* (Lexington, Mass: Lexington Books, 1976).

On the dispute among socialists about the role of public enterprises in subserving the end of equality, see Charles A. R. Crosland, *The Fu-*

ture of Socialism (London: Jonathan Cape, 1956), and Deepak Lal, *New Economic Policies for India*, Research Series no. 311 (London: Fabian Society, 1973).

For an excellent account of contemporary general equilibrium competitive theory, see Kenneth J. Arrow and Frank H. Hahn, *General Competitive Analysis* (San Francisco: Holden-Day, 1971), and Gerard Debreu, *Theory of Value* (New York: Wiley, 1959). Kenneth J. Arrow, "Political and Economic Evaluation of Social Effects and Externalities," in Julius Margolis, ed., *The Analysis of Public Output* (New York: National Bureau for Economic Research, 1970), provides a succinct account of the reasons for market failure within this framework. For an extension of welfare economics to a growing economy, see Robert Dorfman, Paul Samuelson, and Robert Solow, *Linear Programming and Economic Analysis* (New York: McGraw-Hill, 1958).

A useful general textbook on the economics of public enterprises is Raymond Rees, *Public Enterprise Economics* (London: Weidenfeld and Nicolson, 1976).

On the analytics of deriving shadow prices for public sector investment, see Partha Dasgupta, Stephen Marglin, and Amartya Sen, *Guidelines for Project Evaluation* (New York: UNIDO, 1972); Ian Little and James A. Mirrlees, *Project Appraisal and Planning for Developing Countries* (London: Heinemann Educational Books, 1974); and Stephen Marglin, *Value and Price in the Labour Surplus Economy* (London: Oxford University Press, 1976). Deepak Lal, *Methods of Project Analysis—A Review* (Baltimore: Johns Hopkins University Press, 1974), provides an analytical comparative review of the alternative methods.

A fuller discussion of public sector pricing rules within the Little-Mirrlees framework is found in Deepak Lal, *Prices for Planning* (London: Heinemann Educational Books, 1979), while Rees, *Public Enterprise Economics*, is a useful source for rules based on the conventional numeraire of aggregate consumption. There is a large literature on second-best taxation structures, deriving from the work of Marcel Boiteux, "On the Management of Public Monopolies Subject to Budget Constraints," *Journal of Economic Theory* (September 1971). Other important references are William J. Baumol and David F. Bradford, "Optimal Departures from Marginal Cost Pricing," *American Economic Review* (June 1970); Peter A. Diamond and James A. Mirrlees, "Optimal Taxation and Public Production," *American Economic Review* (March and June 1971); and Martin S. Feldstein, "Distributional Equity and the Optimal Structure of Public Prices," *American Economic Review* (March 1972).

On the importance of exit in a dynamic economy, see Albert O. Hirschman, *Exit, Voice and Loyalty* (Cambridge, Mass.: Harvard University Press, 1970); while Robin Marris, *The Economic Theory of Managerial Capitalism* (London: Macmillan, 1964), and Robin Marris and Adrian Wood, eds., *The Corporate Economy* (Cambridge, Mass.: Harvard University Press, 1971), provide analyses of the role of profit maximization when ownership and control are separate in modern corporations.

Finally, a number of case studies have used the Little-Mirrlees and UNIDO methods; some of these also derive the economy-wide shadow prices which are required for public investment appraisal and price setting. The following studies use the Little-Mirrlees method:

Deepak Lal, *Wells and Welfare* (Paris: OECD Development Centre, 1972).

Deepak Lal, *Appraising Foreign Investment in Developing Countries* (London: Heinemann Educational Books, 1975).

Deepak Lal, *Men or Machines* (Geneva: ILO, 1978).

Deepak Lal, *Prices for Planning* (London: Heinemann Educational Books, 1979).

Ian Little and David G. Tipping, *A Social Cost-Benefit Analysis of the Kulai Oil Palm Estate, West Malaysia* (Paris: OECD Development Centre, 1972).

Ian Little and Maurice FG. Scott, *Using Shadow Prices* (London: Heinemann Educational Books, 1976).

Maurice FG. Scott, John D. MacArthur, and David M. G. Newbery, *Project Appraisal in Practice* (London: Heinemann Educational Books, 1976).

Francis Seton, *Shadow Wages in the Chilean Economy* (Paris: OECD Development Centre, 1972).

Nicholas H. Stern, *An Appraisal of Tea Production on Small Holdings in Kenya* (Paris: OECD Development Centre, 1972).

Two studies by the International Labour Organisation use the UNIDO method:

George W. Irvin, *Roads and Distribution: Social Costs and Benefits of Labour-Intensive Road Construction in Iran* (Geneva: ILO, 1975).

William A. McCleary, *Equipment versus Employment: A Social Cost-Benefit Analysis of Alternative Techniques of Feeder Road Construction in Thailand* (Geneva: ILO, 1976).

[12]

Shadow Prices and Political Economy (Comment on Harberger)

Deepak Lal

SINCE I FIRST MET ARNOLD HARBERGER in the late 1960s, I have been arguing with him on the subject of his present paper. Arguing with a pioneer—which Harberger assuredly is—cannot but be good training for one's intellectual muscles, and over the years I have learned a great deal from him and his writings.

The present paper lucidly summarizes his well-known views on social project evaluation. Their centerpiece is his so-called three basic postulates of applied welfare economics, which he says he derives from the grand tradition of Marshall, Pigou, and others. The only recent and probably less well-known addition to this corpus comes as the result of his conversion to "basic needs externalities" as a form of merit good, which he includes in his recommended method of social project evaluation.

He has always justified the rules and procedures he advocates on the pragmatic grounds of their simplicity and ease of communication, and for being derivable from the grand tradition of welfare economics. I have never had any worries about their simplicity, but the claim that his rules follow from the grand tradition has always troubled me—as I suspect it has others. It still does, despite my having come to accept many of his specific rules (those on the shadow price of labor and the social opportunity cost of public funds, but *not* on the shadow pricing of commodities, discussed below). After the ebbing of the passions (which surprisingly this subject generates) of my misspent youth, I think I now know where the trouble lies, and these comments will provide an elucidation!

As in Harberger's paper, the starting point must be to ask: What are social project evaluators supposed to be doing? Harberger describes

Deepak Lal is professor of political economy at University College, London, and research administrator, Economics and Research Staff, the World Bank.

them as people "who strive *selflessly* to see to it, insofar as they can, that projects not meeting adequate standards are rejected, while those in the *social interest* are accepted" (emphasis added). This seemingly bland and unexceptionable statement conceals a number of assumptions, two of which I have emphasized, but others are implicit and unclear. The most important one concerns the nature of the government or state which the project evaluators are to serve or advise.

A detailed typology of actual and possible government forms (in terms of the objectives they seek to subserve) is beyond the scope of this paper. But I have recently found it useful to think of two polar types: the benevolent (platonic guardian) and the self-serving (predatory) state. The objectives of the former are well known as they form the staple of every elementary economics textbook. The objectives of the latter are more murky but must by analogy with biological predator-prey models involve the self-serving extraction of the maximum continuing flow of resources (which includes intangibles such as power and prestige) for the members and associates of the government. Predators will share an interest in enlarging the incomes of their prey (say, through economic growth) insofar as this raises the potential flow of their own income. For the predatory state the welfare of its subjects—as conceived by economists—may be at best only a very minor direct component of the state's objective function. More important, however, is the likely opportunistic nature of government behavior in the predatory state, which in turn implies that compared with the more principled benevolent state, its orderings over social states are likely to be fickle.

In reality, most states will of course not fall into either of these extreme categories, but for the purpose of clarification it will be useful to maintain this stark contrast. The most important point which follows from it is that in what Harberger calls the grand tradition of Marshall, Keynes, Pigou, and others the implicit assumption was that, by and large, the economics were being worked out for a benevolent state. This in itself was not an unreal or absurd assumption. As Skidelsky's biography of Keynes shows—by its excellent description and dissection of the intellectual and social milieu of Edwardian and post-Edwardian Britain—English economists of the day could reasonably assume that the governments they were advising were either benevolent (made up of people like themselves) or, even more important, could be directly influenced to serve the commonweal as viewed by these self-proclaimed platonic guardians.[1]

The consequent "social welfare planning" approach of Pigou and

1. Robert Skidelsky, *John Maynard Keynes*, vol. 1, *Hopes Betrayed, 1883–1920* (London: Macmillan, 1983). Despite the major contributions of French and American economists, the grand tradition was developed primarily by English—and even more narrowly, by Cambridge—economists.

Meade in England and a host of mathematical economists, beginning with that celebrated animal DOSSO[2] in the United States, has indubitably been fruitful. It has erected an elegant, sophisticated, and subtle body of theory. This body of thought leads from Ramsey, Samuelson, Meade, Little, and Diamond-Mirrlees to Atkinson and Stiglitz, to the derivation of second-best welfare theoretic rules for most aspects of public policy—including optimal taxation and, more important for present purposes, the appraisal of public investments.

Most theorists will not dispute that *in principle* the correct set of rules for project appraisal in a distorted economy being run by platonic guardians is the manual put together by Little and Mirrlees—the "Arthashastra" for the benevolent state.[3] There are obvious variants of their general shadow pricing rules, which can be derived by making special or simplifying assumptions concerning this or that aspect of a particular economy; Little and Mirrlees themselves provide a number of useful ways of doing so. But these are all variations on a theme, which at the most general and theoretical level must conform to the so-called Little-Mirrlees rules.[4]

It may be useful to recapitulate these, because it will allow me to make the few purely technical points I have against Harberger's position. The most important, distinctive, and in my judgment useful of the Little-Mirrlees rules is the border price rule for shadow pricing tradable commodities (and its foreign exchange equivalent derivation for the shadow price of nontraded goods). Given Harberger's desire to advocate and use simple rules derivable from the grand tradition, it is strange that this rule is not even mentioned in his paper.

On the shadow pricing of labor, I believe there is no difference between the rules advocated by Little-Mirrlees and by Harberger. Furthermore, his modified supply price rule for the shadow wage *has* incontrovertibly been shown by Christopher Heady to be derivable from the grand tradition.[5] When we come to inter- and intratemporal distributional shadow prices, however, more serious problems arise.

The most serious is for Harberger's third postulate—in effect to

2. Robert Dorfman, Paul Samuelson, and Robert Solow, *Linear Programming and Economic Analysis* (New York: McGraw-Hill, 1958).

3. I. M. D. Little and J. A. Mirrlees, *Project Appraisal and Planning for Developing Countries* (New York: Basic Books, 1974); see Deepak Lal, *Prices for Planning* (London: Heinemann Educational Books, 1980), and references therein for support for this assertion. The "Arthashastra" is an ancient Indian text written to advise a prince on the best ways to stay in power.

4. This of course means accepting the usual simplifying assumptions of neoclassical theory—but this is not generally the point disputed by the various manuals in this debate.

5. "Shadow Wages and Induced Migration," *Oxford Economic Papers*, vol. 33, no. 1 (March 1981).

neglect income distributional effects—which he claims is derived from the grand tradition. The trouble with this is that in *The Economics of Welfare*, for instance, which is surely part of the grand tradition, A. C. Pigou unequivocally states "it is evident that any transference of income from a relatively rich man to a relatively poor man of similar temperament—must increase the aggregate sum of satisfaction.[6] Pigou's utilitarian summation of interpersonal utilities was discarded by the subsequent Paretian welfare economics, which introduced its own rigamarole of compensation tests.[7] Subsequent developments in the grand tradition culminated in the general adoption by theorists of some form of Bergson-Samuelson social welfare function in their study of welfare economics. The modern literature on investment planning and optimal taxation for a benevolent state builds on this work, and it is this work with its explicit concern with distribution which *is* in the grand tradition. Harberger's third postulate clearly is *not*. But does that matter?

To answer this we need to get back to our forlorn project evaluator. Clearly if he is a servant or adviser of a benevolent state of platonic guardians, the government will have informed him of its social welfare function and the implicit or explicit distributional weights it would like applied to the changes in its citizens' income induced by the project. The project evaluator would still have to choose between the two leading manuals of project evaluation that take account of the distributional effects. If he chose the UNIDO *Guidelines*[8] and adopted their numeraire (consumption) and discount rate (the social rate of discount or consumption rate of interest) he would face the paradox noted by Harberger: there would be a multiplicity of consumption rates of interest (CRIs), one for each of the income groups. For this reason Little and Mirrlees chose investment (or more precisely income in the hands of the government) as their numeraire; it is relatively homogeneous compared with a consumption aggregate that depends on a changing distributionally weighted average of consumption by different individuals or

6. London: Macmillan, 1974, p. 89.

7. Pigou in fact straddles the classical and neoclassical branches of welfare economics in the grand tradition. As J. R. Hicks notes ("The Scope and Status of Welfare Economics," *Oxford Economic Papers*, vol. 27, no. 3, November 1975, p. 237), Pigou is concerned "like the Classics, with the Social Product. A Social Product of goods, not of utilities. Where he differs from the Classics is in his method of valuation; he does not value by cost, but by marginal utility. He is recasting the classical structure in terms of utility theory." After this move is made, however, at some stage in the resulting neoclassical analysis the distributional implication of economic changes will necessarily arise.

8. United Nations Industrial Development Organization, *Guidelines for Project Evaluation* (New York: UNIDO, 1972).

groups. As I have shown,[9] given the platonic guardians' social welfare function and the relevant technological and resource constraints, a unique accounting rate of interest (loosely speaking, the investment rate of return) can be defined, and the multiple CRIs enter only indirectly in the determination of the intratemporal distributional weights to be used in the cost-benefit calculus.

The happy project evaluator should not rush to assume that, as a result, he can return the UNIDO *Guidelines* to the shelf, however. Using a single CRI or social discount rate on the "consumption as numeraire" method is not necessarily illogical as Harberger suggests. Squire and van der Tak have shown that distributional weights can be used, in effect, to discount each individual's discount rate (a particular CRI of, say, B in Harberger's example) to make it commensurable with that of a reference individual or group (say, A in Harberger's example) in each time period; this reference group's own discount rate (CRI) can then be used as the unique CRI to discount that period's distributionally weighted aggregate consumption.[10]

Thus as long as a project evaluator in the grand tradition does not blindly follow the UNIDO *Guidelines*, but adopts Squire and van der Tak, there would be nothing illogical in using a unique CRI or social discount rate in his calculus. Better still, he could adopt the Little-Mirrlees numeraire and discount rate that finesses this whole problem. An added advantage over the UNIDO *Guidelines* is that he would be able to use the simple border price rule. Despite Partha Dasgupta's undoubted demurral on this point, his own work and that of others have shown this rule to be robust in many second-best conditions.[11] It is surprising Harberger fails to adopt it since it allows the finessing of various conceptual and estimation problems concerning the shadow exchange rate.

But the premise of a benevolent state on which the above discussion has been based is highly unrealistic. Suppose instead that the state which Harberger's still "selfless" project evaluator is advising is predatory (in my sense). Being selfless and keen to serve the social weal, the evaluator is now faced by a serious dilemma. He knows that the

9. Lal, *Prices for Planning*, pp. 146–47.

10. Lyn Squire and Herman G. van der Tak, *Economic Analysis of Projects* (Baltimore, Md.: Johns Hopkins University Press, 1975), p. 139.

11. Partha Dasgupta and J. E. Stiglitz, "Benefit-Cost Analysis and Trade Policies," *Journal of Political Economy* (January-February 1974); P. G. Warr, "On the Shadow Pricing of Traded Commodities," *Journal of Political Economy* (August 1977), and "Shadow Pricing, Information, and Stability in a Simple Open Economy," *Quarterly Journal of Economics* (February 1978).

government's objective function has little resemblance to the social welfare function of which he and his peers are now (more than just merely) platonic guardians! He might decide that by getting the government to accept a procedure (but how?) for investment appraisal that implicitly or explicitly smuggles in the benevolent social welfare function—which necessarily includes distributional weighting—he can still do good by stealth. This seems to be the implicit posture of many real-world project evaluators, and the passage I cited at the beginning of these comments suggests it might also be Harberger's. This would be one way (though highly implausible) of dealing with the obvious dilemma facing the project evaluator when advising quasi-predatory governments whose real objective function is so different from that advocated in the grand tradition on the assumption of a benevolent state.[12]

Of course, as is more than likely, the project evaluator may not be the selfless and socially conscious individual Harberger seeks. The use of flexible distributional weights, camouflaged for rhetorical purposes as deriving from the grand tradition, could then yield what in practice most governments probably seek: social *cosmetic* analysis!

It is in the context of predatory states that the acceptance of Harberger's third postulate makes good sense. As independent auditors and accounts are required to keep self-serving private corporations honest, so an independent project evaluation agency (if it can be established) has the task of keeping the government and its public enterprises honest. In this task, controversial and perhaps elastic ethical judgments—which must be involved in distributional weighting—will inevitably make the results of project evaluation appear to be discretionary and hence arbitrary to a great extent. Business accountants have resisted the use of inflation accounting (despite the economist's impeccable case in its favor) because of the hypothetical and hence speculative estimates of the value of the capital stock at replacement cost that would be required (compared with the verifiable historic cost estimates); similarly, it can be argued that controversial and speculative distributional weighting should be eschewed to maintain the integrity of the auditing function of project evaluation as a routine exercise. This is the "professionalism" I suspect Harberger seeks, much like that of accountants or blacksmiths or dentists.[13]

12. Amartya Sen's well-known discussion of "control areas" in project evaluation is related to this problem; see his "Control Areas and Accounting Prices: An Approach to Economic Evaluation," *Economic Journal*, special issue (March 1972).

13. Keynes looked forward to the day when economists, like dentists, would become involved in merely routine tasks; see his *Essays in Persuasion* (New York: Norton, 1963), p. 373.

This argument in favor of Harberger's third postulate has nothing to do with the grand tradition. In fact, it is relevant precisely because the beautiful and elegant edifice built by the grand tradition is irrelevant for most of the world's states that are not governed by social welfare functions administered by platonic guardians.

A similar rejection of the grand tradition is also required to justify Harberger's recommendation—which, in my view, is correct—that our public expenditure auditors should, in calculating the social opportunity costs of public funds, adopt the "capital market" rather than the "fiscal sourcing" method.[14] The latter, however, is indubitably the correct method in the grand tradition for a benevolent state to adopt. For such a state, on the basis of Atkinson and Stiglitz's excellent textbook on public economics, would have established a second-best optimal set of taxes.[15] It would in its fiscal decisions logically balance the social costs of increasing various distortionary taxes against the social benefits of the uses to which the resulting revenue is put. A marginal increase in public investment (or expenditure in general) would require within this framework of stable taxes (contrary to Harberger and of course the real world) an estimate of the marginal costs of raising the requisite revenue through distortionary taxation (including that implicit in the levying of the inflation tax through inflationary public borrowing). The fiscal sourcing method would be the correct one to use to estimate the social opportunity cost of public finance.

But it is not these platonic guardian states that we observe. Apart from the instability of actual fiscal policy that Harberger cites for his preferred "capital market" route to estimating the social opportunity cost of public funds, there is a much more telling fact against the alternative recommendations based on the grand tradition. Those of us who have been brought up to accept arguments justifying various forms of government action as a solution to the "assurance paradox" must find the recent savings behavior in developing countries paradoxical. It has been argued (and incorporated in the project evaluation literature) that the social rate of discount (CRI) must be lower than the private rate of time preference on the grounds that society as an immortal collectivity would wish to save more than mortal individuals. The latter would thus sign a social compact to save more than they would be willing to do atomistically. Governments as a result were charged by the grand tradition with using the choice of public projects as an indirect means of raising national savings above the suboptimal levels resulting from

14. And surely Harberger is right in wanting to extend the scope of social cost-benefit analysis to the government's current as well as capital account.

15. A. B. Atkinson and J. E. Stiglitz, *Lectures on Public Economics* (New York: McGraw-Hill, 1980).

individual choices. Apart from the obvious "project illusion" on which this argument must be based,[16] it is not applicable if a predatory rather than a benevolent state is assumed as the executing agency of this social compact.

No vast empirical research is required to test the assumptions of this view. All we need point to is the amazing "stylized fact" that (except in Sub-Saharan Africa since 1973) household savings in developing countries have consistently risen over the past two decades to levels which, on Arthur Lewis's view in the *Theory of Economic Growth*,[17] should have led to self-sustaining growth in most of the developing world. At the same time, one distinguishing feature of the past decade has been the prodigal behavior of the public sector nearly everywhere—in the more developed countries as much as in the developing countries.[18] Instead of supplementing national savings, the governments of most developing countries have been depleting the potential savings pool available from households through budget deficits and the losses of public enterprises.

From the perspective that views most states as being closer to the predatory end of the spectrum, this is hardly unexpected. Countries and societies may be immortal (though even that is dubious), but governments certainly are not. Concerned about their tenure, which is probabilistically much shorter than that of the average individual's lifetime (and that of his offspring), the average government's rate of time preference is likely to be much higher (as their recent savings behavior shows) than that of private individuals. The resulting crowding out of private expenditures entailed by their predatory raids on the pool of national savings to finance current public expenditures is best measured, as Harberger rightly argues, through its effects on the capital market. But, concerned as he seems to be with wrapping the mantle of the grand tradition around himself and his rules, he does not state that the capital markets route is to be preferred in estimating the social opportunity cost of public funds precisely because of the irrelevance of that tradition in the real world.

The task of the project evaluator in a predatory state (assuming it allows him a role) is at best analogous to that of the business accountant. He needs relatively uncontroversial rules to allow him to present an audit of the net effects on efficiency and growth of the actions of the public sector. These rules should be precise and simple and not subject

16. Deepak Lal, "Disutility of Effort, Migration, and the Shadow Wage Rate," *Oxford Economic Papers*, vol. 25, no. 1 (March 1973), p. 123.

17. London: Allen and Unwin, 1955.

18. See Deepak Lal and Martin Wolf, eds., *Stagflation, Savings, and the State: Perspectives on the Global Economy* (New York: Oxford University Press, 1986), for empirical substantiation of these assertions.

to elastic interpretation of facts or ethical predilections. Passages in Harberger's paper suggest that this is in effect the role he envisages for his project evaluator, and, as I have argued, his basic three postulates could be justified from this perspective. But I fear it is more than likely that Harberger envisages his project evaluator doing good by stealth—using the grand tradition for both deriving his rules and stiffening his spine. If this is so, then some of the rules Harberger advocates, and in particular his third basic postulate, are clearly illogical. His conversion to basic needs does not meet the objections from the practitioners of the grand tradition. For Harberger, basic needs are included in the social cost-benefit calculus as merit goods, and he seeks to justify this as an alternative to the use of distributional weighting. But this is not an appropriate *either-or* choice. Merit goods as well as distributional weights are required by the grand tradition. If the state is not benevolent the inclusion of both these subjectivist elements in the public sector audit can be questioned on the grounds given above. But if the grand tradition is being appealed to, *both* must necessarily be included. (It is not at all obvious, however—and certainly not uncontroversial—that the basic needs of Harberger and others *are* merit goods.)

Harberger is one of the few economists I know with the imagination and skill to tailor conventional economic theory to the needs of policymaking for a real world in which benevolent states run by platonic guardians are scarce. The rules he has derived for project evaluation (with some exceptions noted above) must be seen in this light.

Perhaps being realistic and keen to influence policy he wants to use the persuasive aura of a particular rigorous and well-established normative tradition of the economics of benevolent policymaking. At the moment there is no other equally well-worked-out system of policy analysis for the alternative model of a predatory state. The positive economics of policymaking in a self-serving state that goes by the name of the "new political economy" is still in its infancy, as is the development of the welfare economic implications of the recent literature on "rent seeking," or as it has come to be relabeled, "directly unproductive activities." The pioneers who develop this will doubtless be honored in future volumes in the "Pioneers" series. We might then have more relevant and robust rules for project evaluation for predatory states than are provided by current manuals in the grand tradition. Meanwhile, we could do worse than accept Harberger's three postulates—for the reasons I have given—as the best rules currently available for project evaluation in quasi-predatory states, but with the explicit incorporation of the one robust, simple, and extremely important rule to be derived from the grand tradition (which does *not* depend on the assumption of a benevolent state): the border price rule.

I hope that these comments may help others to overcome the worries that have plagued me for so long about the Harberger procedures for social cost-benefit analysis. I have tried to show that his rules have wrongly been found unacceptable because he has misleadingly (as in this lecture) wrapped himself in the mantle of the grand tradition. Pioneers are usually heretics, and it would certainly aid understanding, even though it might reduce their worldly influence, if they revealed themselves for what they are. My chief conclusion therefore is that if Harberger's views are to be cogent it would be best if he were to come out of the closet and repudiate the grand tradition.

[13]

A Simple Framework for Analysing Various Real Aspects of Stabilisation and Structural Adjustment Policies

*by Deepak Lal**

This article shows how a simple geometric framework containing a real model based on the standard two-good three-factor trade theoretic model and a monetary model of the domestic banking system can be used to analyse the changes in the real and nominal values of various economic variables of concern resulting from stabilisation and structural adjustment policies

INTRODUCTION

With the expansion of IMF stabilisation and World Bank structural adjustment lending, concern is being expressed about the short and long run effects of these programmes on the real economy. (See Dell [*1981*], Williamson [*1983*], Killick [*1982*], Nowzad [*1981*]. A central question is whether there are policies which can be correctly sequenced to minimise the efficiency and equity costs of the transition.

In answering these questions, a bewildering array of very different theoretical frameworks is available and has been applied to various countries.[1] Surprisingly, in applied work the orthodox trade theoretic framework, using a model of the small dependent economy (the so-called Australian model of balance of payments theory) has been rarely used to answer these questions. Many of the seeming diverse theoretical frameworks being applied to analyse the effects of stabilisation policies turn out to be special cases of this more orthodox model. The assumptions leading to these 'queer cases' from the view point of traditional theory, usually concern odd assumptions about 'substitutability' in production or consumption.[2] Cline (in Williamson (ed.) [*1983*]) has recently provided a compendium of these strange assumptions, and the evidence against them.[3] It may be useful, therefore, to set out a version of the orthodox framework in some detail, as in my view it is sufficiently rich to think through the various issues raised in the current 'stabilisation' debate. In keeping with the purely heuristic purpose of this paper, most of the discussion is conducted in words and through diagrams.

---

*Professor of Political Economy, University College London. This is a substantially revised and extended version of part 1 of Lal [*1984*]. Comments by members of a seminar at the World Bank and by Sebastian Edwards, Peter Kenen and an anonymous referee are gratefully acknowledged.

In outlining this simple framework for analysing stabilisation and structural adjustment policies, we shall be particularly concerned with the effects on the real wage (and real profit rate) in the economy. As their labour is the major endowment of the poor in most developing countries these changes in real wages should also capture the major effects of alternative programmes on the levels of living of the poor. The instruments considered are the disabsorption (expenditure reducing) components of the deflationary fiscal and monetary package, changes in nominal exchange rates, reduction of the foreign trade and other commodity price distortions, and the reduction or removal of distortions in financial (capital) markets.

There are two essential components of the framework: (1) a simple two-good, three-factor trade-theoretic model,[4] which determines the real equilibrium of the economy and the key relative prices; and (2) a simple model of the domestic banking system which determines the nominal values of key variables and their dynamic paths of adjustment. These real and monetary models are spelt out geometrically in the following two sections.[5]

I. THE REAL ECONOMY

Consider a small open economy, facing given terms of trade. Its exportables and importables can be aggregated into a Hicksian composite good labelled 'tradeables'. There is also one non-traded good. Both tradeables and non-tradeables are final consumer goods, and as intermediate inputs can be combined with capital and labour to produce the domestic outputs of the two goods (though for simplicity we shall assume that there are *no* intermediate inputs). Throughout, capital is assumed to be sector-specific in the short run, but in the long run it can be 'shifted' from one 'sector' to the other, through depreciation and new investment. The growth of the labour force and capital stock are assumed to be exogenous.

There are distortions in foreign trade and in the capital and labour markets. Though, to simplify the exposition, we will deal with them sequentially, by assuming that only one or the other is present.

The trade distortions could be due to the presence of either import tariffs, quantitative import controls and/or export subsidies. For simplicity we assume that the distortion is an import tariff which raises the domestic price of importables by t per cent over their world price. The price of the composite tradeable commodity is normalised in terms of the *domestic* price of importables.[6]

The capital market distortion arises from the provision of explicit or implicit interest rate subsidies through the banking system to (say) the traded good sector. The labour market is distorted because the wage paid by the traded good sector is above its social opportunity cost and, hence, higher than that in the production of non-tradeables, either because of 'dual economy' type reasons or because of labour market segmentation. We assume that this particular wage distortion is unalterable. It is a constant fixed markup on the traded good money wage over that in non-traded good production. Thus we can work with an 'as if' uniform wage in both sectors. The analysis of a wage distortion which can be removed, parallels that for the removal of the capital market distortion discussed below.

The domestic price of the traded good (P_T) is determined by the implicit trade tax (t per cent), the exogenously given world prices (P^*_M, P^*_X), and the nominal exchange rate (e), whilst that of the non-traded good (P_N) is determined endogenously by domestic demand and supply. We normalise the price of the traded good at unity ($P_T = 1$).

II. THE MONETARY ECONOMY

From the view point of the consolidated bank system, there are the well known identities in the monetary economy relating domestic credit (DC), money supply (M) and the two components of high powered money (H) – government debt (S) and foreign exchange reserves (F) – which are summarised in Table 1. There are two monetary assets held by the general non-bank public – non-interest bearing cash and short-term interest-bearing deposits with commercial banks. The only other financial instruments are government bonds (S) which are held by the Central Bank or by foreigners.

The essential link between high powered money and the money supply M is given by

$$M = b.H$$

where $b = 1/[cm + (1-m)k]$ is the money multiplier with

- c – the cash ratio, that is, the currency and central bank reserves held against demand deposits;
- k – the reserve ratio against time deposits and
- m – proportion of commercial banks demand for time deposits in the total money supply.

This latter ratio will depend upon the non-bank sector's liquidity preference and the interest rate on time deposits. For simplicity, in much of the following (up to section IV) we assume that government bonds and time deposits bear the same interest rate (i), which is also the common interest rate for both depositors and creditors. Thus the demand for money will be a function of the domestic interest rate (M = M(i)].

The monetary economy is linked to the world capital market by the simplest of portfolio models [*Williamson, 1983: Ch. 9*], in which capital inflows are determined by: first, an international and portfolio distribution effect which depends only on changes in the difference between the domestic (i) and foreign interest rate (i*); second, a portfolio growth effect which depends upon changes in the wealth of 'foreign' investors and, third, creditworthiness which determines the riskiness of the country's liabilities issued to foreigners.[7]

Moreover, we assume that the riskiness for foreign investors of our

TABLE 1
BALANCE SHEETS

Commercial Banks

Assets	Liabilities	
Loans to non-bank sector (L)	Demand deposits	D
Reserves with central bank (R) against time deposits.	Term deposits	T
Currency and reserves (C) apart from deposits		

Central Bank

Assets	Liabilities
Government debt (S)	Currency & reserves against demand deposits (C)
Foreign exchange reserves (F)	Reserves against time deposits (R)

For the consolidated bank sector

$$L + R + C + S + F = D + T + C + R$$

$$L + R + C = D + T$$

$$L = D + T - R - C$$

$$= D + T - kT - C$$

$$(D-C) + (1-k)T$$

$$= (1-c)D + (1+k)T$$

(where c is the cash ratio)

Domestic credit $DC = S + L$

Money Stock $= M2 = D + T$

High Powered Money $(H) = S + F$

country's 'bonds' is measured by the foreign exchange risk attached to likely future movements in our country's exchange rate. As in most developing countries the link between domestic and foreign capital markets is attenuated by exchange controls of defacto varying degrees of severity, we *cannot* use the interest arbitrage condition linking the domestic to international capital market.[8] However, as Edwards and

Khan [*1985*] have shown in a hybrid model where both open and closed economy considerations (the Fisher condition) affect domestic interest rates, the latter still depend upon the foreign interest rate (i*) and the expected rate of devaluation.[9]

Finally we assume rational expectations which in the absence of stochastic shocks implies that agents have perfect foresight. Thus the actual and expected exchange rate will coincide.

The domestic interest rate (i) therefore in our model economy will be determined by the given foreign interest rate (i*) and the domestic exchange rate (e):

$$i = i(i^*, e)$$

Money market equilibrium therefore will entail that

$$(S + F)/P_T y = M(i\ (i^*, e)] \quad (1)$$

where $P_T y$ is the value of domestic income (output) (y is the value of real domestic output measured in units of tradeables).[10]

From the view point of the money market, government debt (S), domestic output (y) and the two foreign currency prices – the interest rate and price of tradeables – are exogenous. Hence only the level of reserves F, or the exchange rate (e) needs to be determined by equation (1). If the exchange rate is *fixed* the level of reserves will alter to equate the demand and supply for money. If the exchange rate is *flexible* then it will vary and change the domestic price level and thence affect the available supply of *real* money balances to bring about market equilibrium.

Finally, we introduce the government budget, where the consolidated budget (B) of the public sector is represented by total government expenditure G less taxes T or

$$B = G - T \quad (2)$$

This budget 'deficit' is financed either by (i) borrowing from the central bank or through (ii) foreign borrowing, so that

$$G - T = \Delta S - \Delta F_g \quad (3)$$

where ΔF_g is the change in foreign reserves due to government borrowing abroad.

We now have all the ingredients we need to put our small model economy to work in sequentially analysing the real effects of various policies which typically constitute an adjustment cum stabilisation package. A series of three diagrams allows us to tell most of the story.

III. THE EFFECTS OF REMOVING OR REDUCING PRODUCT MARKET DISTORTIONS

We consider the case where the tariff on imports is removed. We assume there are no other distortions (for simplicity). With given stocks of capital and income, in Figure 1(A) PP represents the production possibility curve of non-traded into traded goods of the economy, *given the fixed tariff distortion in the traded good sector*. The equilibrium in this Salter [*1959*] diagram is represented by the production point A and the consumption point B (which lies vertically above A). The *domestic* price of importables is the numeraire. The tariff revenue of τ, is assumed to be disbursed to consumers in lump sum fashion.[11] The initial *real exchange rate* (z_0) – the equilibrium relative price of non-traded to traded goods – is the inverse of the common slopes of the tangents at A to the production possibility frontier and at B to the highest attainable community indifference curve. With the fixed tariff rate, domestic income (measured in terms of tradeables = importables) at factor cost = OY_F, which is less than domestic income at market prices = OY_M by the amount of tariff revenue τ.

FIGURE 1

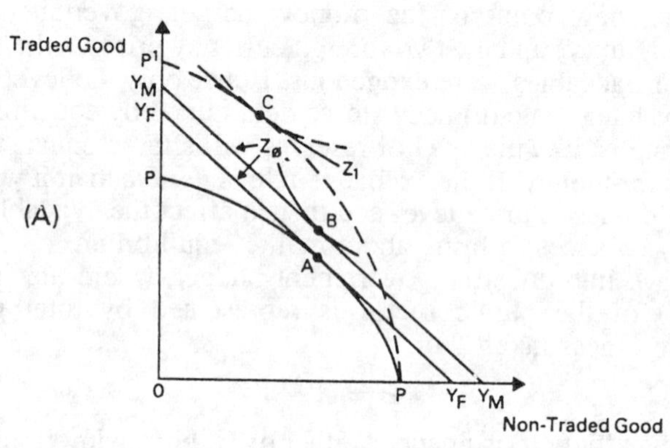

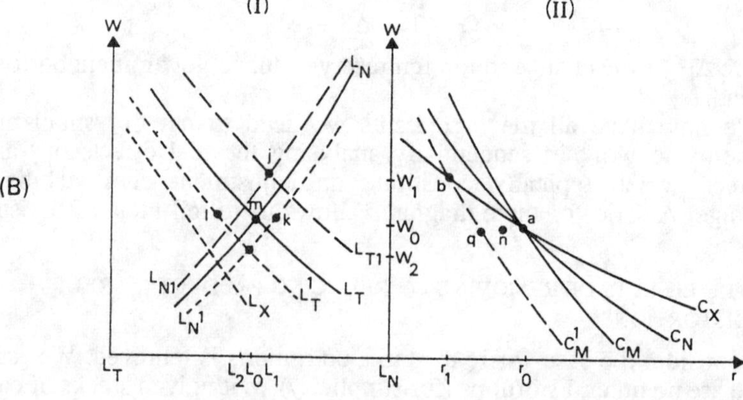

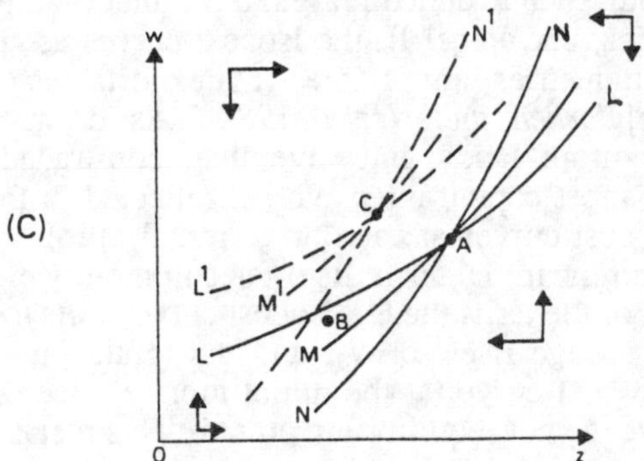

With the removal of the tariff there will be no tariff revenue (τ = O). Also the production possibility frontier will shift outwards to PP^1, as the relative price of exportables in terms of our numeraire (the domestic price of importables) rises and hence at any point on the initial PP curve, the quantity of exportables produced by the given allocation of resources exchanges for more importables. Thus, the overall quantity of traded goods (measured in terms of the numeraire – importables) rises, and the PP curve shifts upwards from P. The extent of the shift will depend upon the relevant elasticities of substitution in production between importables and exportables, and the proportion in which resources are deployed in traded and non-traded good production.

Simultaneously the community indifference curve will shift downwards. For, with the removal of the tariff, consumers can obtain the same quantity of tradeables at a lower cost in terms of the numeraire (the domestic price of importables). The extent of the shift will be determined by the elasticity of substitution in consumption between exportables and importables, and by the proportion of traded goods consumed.

In the new equilibrium, as there is no tariff revenue and ex-hypothesi no remaining domestic distortion, the equilibrium consumption and production point will be the same, given by the tangency of the new PP′ curve and the highest attainable indifference curve from the *new* set of such curves. The inverse of the slope of the common tangent is the new equilibrium real exchange rate (z_1).

(A) Changes in Real Variables

What happens to real wages during the transition from A to C? This will depend upon the direction in which the long-run real exchange rate changes, which in turn depends upon the relative factor intensities of the exportable and non-traded good. If exportables are the most labour-intensive good in the economy then as we show below the real exchange rate will depreciate (as drawn – z_1 is flatter than z_0), and conversely will appreciate if non-traded goods are more labour-intensive than exportables.

(i) Long run – capital mobility: To see this consider Figure 1(B), whose Panel I depicts labour's value added marginal product (vampl) schedules in the three industries, and Panel II, the isocost curves at given product prices for *all* three industries, importables (M) exportables (X) and non-traded goods (N) [*Corden and Neary, 1982*]. As drawn exportables are assumed to be more labour-intensive than non-traded goods and importables are the most capital-intensive (as reflected in the respective slopes of their unit cost curves at each wage rental ratio).

The equilibrium for the initial tariff distorted commodity price ratio is at a. With the removal of the tariff the C_M isocost curve shifts to the left, and the long run money wage rises to W_1, and the rental rate falls to r_1.[12] However, the C_N isocost curve (at the initial money price of non-traded good) now lies above the new equilibrium point b. This means that the real exchange rate – the price of the non-traded good in terms of both exportables, and the lower price of importables – will have to fall to allow the curve C_N price to shift downwards (not drawn) to intersect the C_M and C_X curves at b. The rise in the money wage, and fall in the price of both importables and non-traded goods, will raise the long-run real wage unambiguously in this long-run Stolper–Samuelson equilibrium.

If, however, the non-traded good is more labour intensive than exportables, C_N will lie below b, the intersection of the (now steeper) C_X isocost curve and the C_M curve. This will imply that in the long-run equilibrium the real exchange rate (relative price of non-traded goods) must rise to shift the NN curve upwards to intersect at b.[13]

(ii) Short run with sector-specific capital: The point b describes the long-run configuration of the economy when both capital and labour are mobile between the three sectors. In the short run, however, capital will be immobile. In panel (I) of Figure 1(B) we depict the vampl curves (L_T, L_N) for tradeables and non-traded goods at the initial distorted commodity prices. The tradeable demand for labour (L_T) is disaggregated into that in the exportables (L_X) and in the importables industry (the difference between the L_T and L_X curve). The tariff reduction shifts the L_T curve downwards as demand for labour in the importable industry falls whilst that for exportables is unchanged. Assuming that exportables are the most labour intensive of the three goods, the fall in the non-traded good price shifts the L_N locus downwards, but by less than that of the L_T curve, as the money price of non-traded goods falls less than that of importables.[14] The short-run money wage falls to W_2 by an amount greater than in the money price of importables. As the money price of exportables is unchanged, the short-run wage declines in terms of both exportables and non-traded goods but rises in terms of importables. This is the so-called neo-classical ambiguity in short-run real wage movements when capital is sector-specific and commodity prices change. At the short-run wage W_2, the rental rate on sector-specific capital will decline in the importable industry and rise in the two other industries in terms of all three goods.

These differences in rental rates will induce the shifting of capital from the importable industry to the exportable and non-traded good industries, till the new long-run equilibrium at b (discussed earlier) is reached at a higher uniform real wage and a lower real rental rate. During this process the vampl curve for exportables (not drawn) and hence the L_T curve will shift rightwards but, as the labour force in importables contracts, the shift in the L_T curve will be less than that in the exportable sector. The vampl curve for the non-traded good L_N will also shift upwards. The intersection of the 'long-run' L_T and L_N curves will be at the long-run wage W_1, and to the right of m (in panel I) reflecting the long run contraction in non-traded good employment and output at the expense of the traded good (entirely in exportables).[15] In the process, the economy will move to the point b (the intersection of the 'new' unit cost curves) in panel (II), and j in panel I. In both industries the capital labour ratio (given by the slope of the tangent to the respective isocost curces) will be higher at b than at a. During this process of adjustment there will be a monotonic increase in national income as measured by the new 'distortion free' relative prices of commodities.[16]

(iii) Sticky wages: Hitherto we have assumed that wages are fully flexible. *Suppose the money wage is sticky.* This implies that the labour market will not clear until the long run equilibrium is reached. There is disequilibrium in the short run in both factor markets. In Figure I(B), if with the fall in the relative price of non-tradeables (the real exchange rate), the money wage is sticky, short term equilibrium will be at k and 1 in panel I, and at q, n and a in panel II. There will be unemployment of labour of 1K, and a rental differential in favour of exportables and non-traded goods, which will induce the shifting of capital. As the sticky money wage W_0, is combined *ex-hypothesi* with a fall in the money price of tradeables (following the removal of the import tariff) and in the price of non-traded goods (because of the required fall of the real exchange rate), the *real* wage will be higher in this sticky money wage 'short-run' equilibrium than in the original distorted equilibrium. With time, and the shifting of capital from the non-traded to traded goods industries, the L_T and L_N curves shift upwards in panel I. The money and real wage rise above their 'sticky' level, till the long-run equilibrium is established at b and j.[17]

(B) Dynamics of Adjustment

What of the dynamics of the economy as it moves from A to C in Figure 1(A), and to b in Figure 1(B), and what will be the movements in the nominal exchange rate or foreign exchange reserves, and the overall price level during the transition to the new equilibrium? To determine these, consider Figure 1(C). LL shows those combinations of the *real tradeable wage* (the nominal wage deflated by the domestic price of tradeables $w = W/P_T$ and the *real exchange rate* ($z = P_N/P_T$) which equates the demand and supply of labour.[18] It must be upward sloping as a rise in the real wage at a constant real exchange rate will generate unemployment whilst a rise in the real exchange rate at a constant real wage will lead to excess demand for labour. The slope of the curve must be *less than unity* (the slope of a ray from the origin). For suppose there is a movement along the ray from the origin, this means an equiproportionate rise in both the *tradeable* real wage and real exchange rate (say with the nominal wage (W) and price of non-traded goods (P_N) rising in equal proportions). The real product wage in non-tradeable production remains unchanged and hence its output remains unchanged, but traded good producers face a rise in their real product wage and will reduce their demand for labour, creating excess supply, and these points must then lie below the equilibrium LL locus.

The NN locus shows the combinations of the real tradeable wage and real exchange rate for which the non-traded good market is in equilibrium.[19] This curve will slope upwards as a rise in the real exchange rate (keeping the real tradeable wage constant) leads to excess supply of the non-traded good, which is cured by a rise in the real wage to discourage production and thereby restore equilibrium in the non-traded good market. The NN curve must have a slope steeper than a ray from the origin (*greater than unity*), as an equiproportionate rise in the real tradeable wage and the real exchange rate leaves output of the non-traded good unchanged but leads to a reduction in its demand and hence to excess supply. These points must, therefore, lie above the NN locus.

The intersection of the LL and NN loci determines the equilibrium values of the real tradeable wage and real exchange rate. The arrows show the direction of movements in the two variables when the economy is not in equilibrium. The equilibrium point A corresponds to the initial (distorted) equilibrium in Figure 1(A) and (B). We know from the discussion of Figure 1(B), that with the removal of the tariff, in the *long run* the capital labour ratio and hence labour use per unit of output rises in all three sectors, with the labour intensive sectors (exportables and non-tradeables) expanding at the expense of the capital intensive sector (importables). Hence, LL will shift upwards. A will represent a point of excess demand in the labour market. Also, with the removal of the tariff and the accompanying relative price changes there will be a positive stimulus to the production and negative stimulus to the consumption of the non-traded good, implying an excess supply for it at A.[20] Therefore, the NN curve will also shift leftwards and the new long run equilibrium will be at C with a *higher* tradeable real wage and a *lower* real exchange rate, as we know from Figure 1(B), so that the long-run real wage rises unambiguously in terms of *all* goods.

Finally, to determine the movements in the other nominal variables as the economy moves from A to C in Figure 1(A) and (C), we need to introduce the endogenously determined locus for equilibrium in the money market. This is given by equation 1 above and the MM locus in Figure 1(C). As the money is neutral in the long run in this model, a doubling of the monetary base and the money price of tradeables (the numeraire) leaves all real values unchanged. Also, there is balance of payments equilibrium on the MM curve. Thus, in equilibrium, the MM locus must also pass through the point of intersection of the NN and LL loci. The MM locus must be upward sloping, for a higher real exchange rate at the equilibrium real wage at A implies an excess demand for money (and a trade surplus), whilst a higher real wage at the equilirium real exchange rate at A implies excess supply of money and a trade deficit. The slope of the MM curve can be greater or less than that of the LL curve [*Prachowny, 1984: 70–73*]. We assume it is steeper than the LL line.

(i) Long run with domestic capital mobility: The movements in the nominal variables can now be determined. After the LL and NN loci shift, and the endogenously determined MM locus also shifts to C, the economy, which is still at A, exhibits excess demand for labour and excess supply of the non-traded good, putting upward pressure on the nominal wage and downward pressure on the money price of the non-traded good. The economy's trajectory from A to C and thus the relative movements in the real tradeable wage and the real exchange rate will depend upon the relative speeds with which the money wage and money price of non-traded goods move in response to the respective excess demands and supplies in the two markets. If the non-traded good price adjusts faster, the trajectory will lie closer to the real exchange rate axis in Figure 1(C); with continuing excess demand in the labour market, the money wage begins to rise and there could be a cyclical approach to the point C. Alternatively, if the money wage adjusts faster than the price of non-traded goods, the trajectory could lie closer to the real wage axis. In this process, as the real exchange rate undershoots (trajectory 1) or overshoots (trajectory 2) its equilibrium value at C, there would be periods in which the money price of traded goods was falling and then rising. If there was an ongoing inflation[21] these movements would imply a rising or falling inflation rate as well as unemployment rate as the economy moves in a dampened cycle, criss-crossing the L′L′ and N′N′ curves to the new equilibrium at C.

Furthermore, if the exchange rate is fixed, then in the movement from A to C there is initially excess supply of money and hence a trade deficit and the Central Bank's foreign reserves and thence the monetary base will be falling to provide the reduction in real balances required on the MM locus at C. If there is a flexible exchange rate regime the nominal exchange rate will depreciate as soon as an incipient trade deficit develops because of the excess supply of domestic money. This depreciation will *raise* the domestic money price of tradeables (thereby establishing the required real exchange rate with a *rise* in the general price level), and *decrease* the real value of the existing level of nominal money balances required to correct the excess supply in the money market at A. Once again depending upon the process of dynamic adjustment from A to C, there could be cycles (with under and overshooting) in reserve movements and the balance of trade if the economy is on a fixed exchange rate regime, or in the nominal exchange rate's movements if it has a flexible exchange rate.

(ii) Short run with sector-specific capital: However, in the *short run*, with capital in each of the three sectors bolted down, the economy will move to a point such as B, which lies below the LL but above the MM curve. The reasons for this are as follows. With short-run immobility of capital, the capital labour ratio in each of the three sectors must fall (see the discussion above Figure 1(B)) and this will imply that at A (compared to the short-

run equilibrium point) there is excess *supply* of labour and the LL curve will shift downwards in the short run. The NN curve will for the same reason as in the long-run case shift leftwards but not to the full extent of its long-run shift. So the intersection of the short-run NN and LL curves will be below A with the tradeable wage and the real exchange rate having fallen. Moreover, we know that, compared to A, B must represent a point where there is excess supply of money. For with the removal of the tariff and at an unchanged nominal exchange rate, there is an immediate trade deficit, which implies an excess supply of real money balances. The point B must, therefore, lie *above* the MM locus in the region where there is excess money supply and a trade deficit.

As before, the endogenously determined MM locus will shift upwards first to B and then to C. In the process, depending upon the exchange rate regime, either a loss of reserves and an accompanying reduction in the domestic money supply, or else a depreciation of the nominal exchange rate and a consequent rise in the domestic price level will reduce real money balances to establish equilibrium in the money market. The dynamic paths of the nominal and real variables will once again depend upon the relative speeds of adjustment in the relevant market, and there could be 'overshooting' or 'undershooting' of the real variables as well as cyclical movements in the inflation and unemployment rates in the approach to short and long run equilibrium.

Finally, it should be noted that even if there is smooth adjustment in all these variables, there will nevertheless be conflicting resource movements into and out of the *non-traded* good sectors in the short and the long run, though the exportable sector will expand and importables shrink unambiguously in both time periods.

The same three-diagram apparatus can be used to determine the short- and long-term effects on real and nominal variables of other components of 'structural adjustment' programmes.

IV. THE REAL EFFECTS OF DISABSORPTION

So far we have considered the real effects of some elements of the stabilisation cum structural adjustment packages seeking to reduce or remove policy induced distortions in the working of the price mechanism. These may be called the 'supply side' reforms of the package. Other important components of these packages, particularly if they are undertaken in response to a crisis whose major symptom is an excess of domestic absorption over income, will include some methods of disabsorption. What are those methods, and what are their likely real effects?

There are three potential avenues for affecting money expenditure and thereby domestic absorption. The first two are through the direct reduction of the high powered money base: (a) the automatic reduction arising from any foreign reserve losses, (b) the policy induced reduction of the government budget and (c) the policy induced rise in the reserve ratio. But the automatic effect under (a) *is also a policy variable*, as it assumes a *fixed* nominal exchange rate. If the rate were *fully flexible*, the balance of payments deficit would lead to an automatic devaluation to equilibrate the balance of payments without any loss of foreign reserves.

The real effects of these methods of disabsorption can be analysed in two steps. First, there will be the effects which result from any change in the real exchange rate (the z line in the Salter diagram of the previous section) and the ensuing relative price changes which have already been discussed. Second, there may be further relative price changes induced by alternative methods of disabsorption. In considering these, we assume a fixed or managed rate throughout what follows; though (as discussed in Lal [*1980*]) this should not be taken to mean that a fixed (or discretionary) exchange rate policy is necessarily superior to a fully flexible one in welfare-theoretic terms.

With a fixed exchange rate, the automatic disabsorption resulting from (a) the *foreign currency losses* associated with the payments deficit will not entail any second-round relative price changes. In a sense, this case coincides with the 'neutral' disabsorption policies we had assumed in the previous section. By contrast, reducing the budget deficit, and/or reserve ratios could have further relative price and thence real effects on the economy.

Consider (b), the *reduction of the budget deficit*. In considering the effects of stabilisation policies on income distribution, it is obvious that any change in the composition or levels of transfer payments associated with the reduction of the budget deficit will have direct distributional effects.[22] Moreover, if these changes lead to a different composition of demand for tradeables relative to non-tradeables (at given relative prices of the two), the community indifference curve map in the Salter diagram will alter, and thence the 'new' long-run equilibrium will entail an alteration in the 'real' exchange rate, with accompanying changes in real wages and real profit rates. In addition, any change in the composition or level of government investment or consumption, could also lead to a similar change in the economy's 'tastes' (if these government expenditures are large relative to total domestic expenditure), with similar 'real' effects.

What of (c), *changes in the reserve ratio*? Their real effects will depend upon the relationship between the domestic rate of inflation, the distortion in the market for commercial bank term deposits, and lending to the non-bank public. Most Third World governments levy an inflation tax. This can be readily derived as the real income flow which accrues to the government from increasing high powered money (H), through the budget deficit $B = \Delta H$. Denoting the price level by P, and the absolute rate of change of high powered money by $\dot{H}$, we have

$$B/P = \dot{H}/P = (\dot{H}/H)\ (H/P) = \alpha\ (H/P) \qquad (4)$$

where $\alpha = \dot{H}/H$ is the proportionate rate of change in base money. So the real revenue that the government can extract from the banking system will depend upon the percentage change in high powered money.

Furthermore, assuming that the rate of inflation π is determined by the difference between the rates of growth of money supply and realy income (y), where the former is determined through the money multiplier by the rate of growth of high power money, it follows that:

$$\pi = \alpha - y \quad (5)$$

Hence, for any given rate of real income growth, a steady state inflation rate will be associated with a given steady state budget deficit financed by this inflation tax. *Furthermore*, following McKinnon [*1981*], a relationship can be established between the rate of inflation, the reserve ratio requirements and the nominal and real term deposit and commercial bank lending rates.

Figure 2 illustrates this market for loanable funds. The D_L curve shows the demand for commercial bank loans as a function of the real interest rate on loans ($r_L = i_L - \pi$) for any fiven level of real income (y_O). The D_T curve shows the demand for term deposits as a function of its real interest rate, $r_d = (i_d - \pi)$. Assuming term deposits are the only source of commercial bank loans and that demand deposits have to be fully backed by cash and central bank reserves, the supply of loanable funds is then given by the curve S_L, points on which are (1–k) times the term deposits (on D_T) forthcoming at any real interest rate.

FIGURE 2

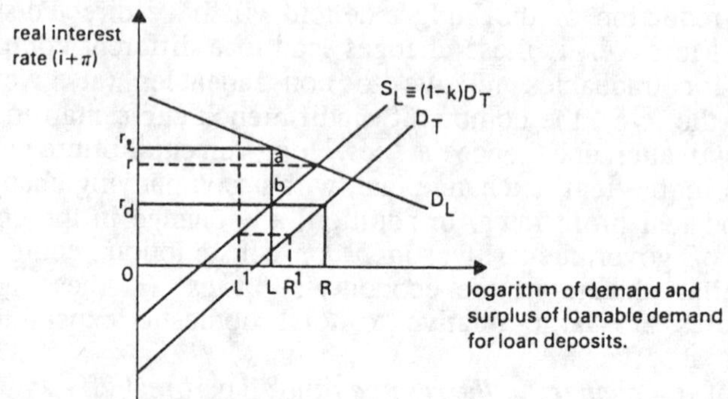

Suppose there are no interest rate regulations. There is steady state inflation at the rate π, which corresponds to a given steady state real budget deficit B/P. The equilibrium is depicted in Figure 2, OR will be the time deposits induced by the equilibrium deposit rate r_d, of which k percent equal to LR, are held as reserves at the central bank, and OL are lent out to the non-bank public at the market clearing real loan rate of r_L. Given the relevant elasticities of demand for term deposits and commercial bank loans, the inflation tax, for the given reserve ratio (k) is shown in this steady state by the distance ab, and is borne by both depositors and borrowers, whose real market returns and costs differ from the non-inflationary equilibrium rate of r.

Assuming the banking system is competitive, it must be the case that as it pays and receives the nominal interest rates,

$$i_d.OR = i_L.OL = i_L(OR)(1-k)$$

or

$$i_d = (1-k)i_L$$

From this and the fact that $r_d + \pi = i_d$ and $r_L + \pi = i_L$ it can be readily derived that:

$$r_L - r_d = \left(\frac{k}{1-k}\right)(\pi + r_d) = i_L - i_d$$

The difference in real and nominal rates will depend directly upon the inflation rate π, and the reserve ratio k, for any given real return on time deposits. For any given reserve ratio, k, an increase in inflation (π) caused by a higher budget deficit will lead to a bigger wedge between r_L and r_d (assuming that the nominal deposit rate i_d rises by the rise in inflation). This can be seen from Figure 2. Furthermore, if there are interest ceilings on the nominal deposit rate, then the real deposit rate r_d declines as much as the increase in the rate of inflation π and the wedge between the real and nominal interest rate remains constant. However, the deposit interest ceilings will, *ceteris paribus*, reduce the size of the loanable funds market, leading to the 'crowding out' of private borrowers, with the obvious inefficiencies that this financial repression entails [*McKinnon, 1981*]. If there are also ceilings on the nominal lending rate, then, with an increase in the inflation rate, the real loan interest rate will decline, and the excess demand for loanable funds will have to be met by rationing, with the attendant distortions that causes in the capital market. Removing interest ceilings, therefore, will both expand the supply of loanable funds and remove the capital market distortions assumed in section I. From Figure 1(B) this will, *ceteris paribus*, raise real wages both in the short and long runs.

Changing the reserve ratio is equivalent to shifting the 'inflation tax' levied to finance the fiscal deficit. For the reserve ratio on interest bearing deposits is a way of levying an inflation tax on the 'loanable funds' of the banking system. However, McKinnon and Mathieson [*1981*] have recently shown that, to finance a given fiscal deficit at minimum cost in terms of the accompanying 'steady state' inflation rate, there will be an optimum reserve ratio. This can be seen as follows. If there were no reserve requirements, the government would have to finance its given fiscal deficit entirely through the inflation tax levied on the 'currency and demand deposits' component of the money supply, as there would not be any contribution from the 'term deposit' component. As the reserve ratio is raised, the term deposit component will contribute its share to the 'tax' and a lower inflation rate will be, therefore, sustainable. But the rising reserve ratio, *ceteris paribus*, also reduces the supply of term deposits because of the changes it induces in the nominal deposit and loan interest rates. This shrinking of the 'term deposit' tax base, means that at some point (depending upon the relevant elasticities of the demand for the two financial assets) the revenue from raising the 'tax' (on a reduced tax base) starts to decline. Hence to finance the same fiscal deficit, a larger 'tax' must be levied on the 'demand deposits' by a further increase in the money supply, leading to a higher inflation rate. Thus, the curve charting the steady state inflation rate and reserve ratios jointly required to provide the 'revenue' to meet a given fiscal deficit will be U-shaped. Any reserve ratio less than or greater than the optimal one (given by the bottom of the U) will entail higher inflation.

The steady-state inflation generated at the optimal reserve ratio for a given fiscal deficit will entail a continuing rise in the price of non-traded goods and, if the nominal exchange rate is fixed, a continuing appreciation in the real exchange rate. If this could be sustained, it would imply a rise in real wages. But the real exchange rate appreciation, through its switching effects, will entail a balance of payments deficit, which cannot be sustained without unlimited foreign exchange reserves.

However, if the government adopted a floating exchange rate, the nominal exchange rate would alter to restore and maintain a constant, real exchange rate (assuming that it is the steady state one), and the steady state inflation process could continue indefinitely. However, there would be obvious real income losses in the financial repression associated with levying the inflation tax. If the fiscal deficit can be financed by other taxes which entail smaller by-product distortion costs, then a reduction in the inflation tax will improve welfare. As the need to finance the fiscal deficit through the 'seignorage' extracted from the banking system declines during this process, both the optimal reserve ratio and the inflation rate will fall.

V. CONCLUSIONS

We have shown how the short- and long-run real effects of stabilisation and adjustment policies can be thought through within a simple general equilibrium framework. It may be useful to put together some of the results we have derived as well as others that can be readily obtained in a schematic table (see Table 2). The major lesson to emerge is that there will be predictable changes in the pattern of production and the distribution of income resulting from the relative price changes associated with adjustment and stabilisation programmes. But the time path of the changing nominal and real variables is likely to be highly uncertain. As policy makers can, at best, control nominal values of the relevant variables, good policies must be based on two important practical considerations. First, problems concering the information required in setting particular *nominal* values at their 'optimal' levels must not be assumed away. Second, policy programmes should be devised to at least minimise the risk of mistakes not merely in the size but even the direction of changes in particular *nominal* variables – for example, the nominal exchange rate. A companion paper [*Lal, 1987*] discusses these questions concerning

TABLE 2

SUMMARY REAL OUTCOME WITH REFERENCE TO INITIAL EQUILIBRIUM (DIRECTION OF CHANGE)

Policy Changes	Flexible Wages: Short Run Sector Specific Capital				Flexible Wages: Long Run Capital Mobility			Sticky Wages: Short Run Sector Specific Capital			
	Real Wage [W]	Real Rental in N $[r_N]$	Real Rental in T $[r_T]$	Real Exchange Rate $[P_N/P_T]$	Real Wage [W]	Real Rental in N+T $[r_N=r_T]$	Real Exchange Rate $[P_N/P_T]$	Real Wage [W]	Real Rental in N $[r_N]$	Real Rental in T $[r_T]$	Real Exchange Rate $[P_N/P_T]$
1 Removing a capital market distortion (subsidy to T or Tax on N)	+	0	–	–	+	–	–	0	0	–	–
2 Removing product market distortion (assumed to be in T) No devaluation and price of non-traded good kept constant, by suitable variations in domestic expenditure	?	+	–	–	+	–	–	+	+	–	–
3 Assuming fixed or no distortions. Devaluation with											
(a) No change introduced	?	–	+	–	0	0	0	?	–	+	–
(b) Changing tastes: increased preference for T	?	–	+	–	–	+	–	?	–	+	–

Continued overleaf

TABLE 2 (cont.)

Policy Changes	Flexible Wages: Short Run Sector Specific Capital				Flexible Wages: Long Run Capital Mobility			Sticky Wages: Short Run Sector Specific Capital			
	Real Wage [W]	Real Rental in N [r_N]	Real Rental in T [r_T]	Real Exchange Rate [P_N/P_T]	Real Wage [W]	Real Rental in N+T [$r_N = r_T$]	Real Exchange Rate [P_N/P_T]	Real Wage [W]	Real Rental in N [r_N]	Real Rental in T [r_T]	Real Exchange Rate [P_N/P_T]
4 Assuming fixed or no distortions. Monetary expansion with fixed exchange rate	?	+	-	+	+	-	+	-	+	-	+
with flexible exchange rate	0	0	0	0	0	0	0	0	0	0	0
5 Capital inflow (sustained constant addition to capital stock in each period)	?	+	-	+	+	-	+	-	+	-	+

Notes: Factor Intensity Assumption:
N – Labour intensive/Non-traded good:
T – Capital intensive/Traded good.

the sequencing and timing of alternative stabilisation and adjustment policies.

final version received May 1988

NOTES

1. For a sample see Cline and Weintraub (eds.) [*1981*].
2. Thus some monetarist models assume the 'law of one price' so that there is perfect substitutability between traded and non-traded goods. No role is left in these models for the determinants and the effects of changes in the real exchange rate, that is, the relative price of non-traded to traded goods, which is central to the workings of the orthodox model. By contrast, many of the so-called 'Keynesian' models assume little if any substitutability in production and consumption so that relative prices play little part in their stories, which are dominated by changes in the level of income.
3. Also see Hanson [*1982*] for a critique of the models of the 'contractionary' effects of devaluations.
4. In section III, we also consider a three by three (short) and three by two (long-run) model.
5. The real models are based on Jones [*1971*]; Mussa [*1974*]; Burgess [*1980*]; and Neary [*1978*]; [*1982*]; [*1985*]; the monetary models on McKinnon [*1981*]; McKinnon and Mathieson [*1981*]; Dornbusch [*1974*]; [*1980*]; Krueger [*1974*]; and the integration of the real and monetary aspects in Corden [*1977*]; Corden and Jones [*1976*]; and Prachowny [*1981*]; [*1984*]. Lal [*1986*] provides an algebraic formulation and an application of the 'real' model to the Philippines, and Lal [*1985*] of the real cum monetary model to Sri Lanka.
6. Thus if Y is the value of output at domestic prices (P_1) and Q_1, the output of the three goods i = X (exportable), M (importable) and N (non-traded), and Q_T is the output and P_T the price of the composite tradeable good, then

   $$Y = P_N Q_N + P_M Q_M + P_X Q_X = P_N Q_N + P_T Q_T;$$

   where $P_T = P_M = e\, P^*_M(1{+}t)$ and $Q_T = Q_M + (P_X/P_M)Q_X$
   with e – nominal exchange rate

   P^*_M – the foreign currency price of importables

   and

   $P_X = e\, P^*_X$ where P^*_X is the foreign currency price of exportables.
7. As is well known, if returns to investments in different countries are not highly correlated, international investors seeking to diversify risk will be prepared to hold more risky developing country liabilities in their portfolios, as long as the risks attached are inversely correlated with those in developed countries.
8. This condition for a fully open economy would be:

   $$i = i^* + (Ee - e)/e$$

   where the last term represents expected capital gains and losses on domestic bonds held by foreigners.
9. That is (Ee – e)/e. In the hybrid model of Edwards and Khan [*1985*] the nominal interest rate is a weighted average (with weights of u and (1–u)) of the interest arbitrage condition and the Fisher condition, namely

   $$i = u\,(i^* + e) + (1 - u)(\rho + \pi)$$

   where in addition to our earlier notation ρ is the closed economy real rate of interest, π the expected rate of inflation.
10. That is, $y = Y/P_T = Q_T + (P_N/P_T)Q_N$

where Q_T and Q_N are the outputs of traded and non-traded goods respectively and $Y = P_TQ + P_NQ_N$.

11. For the formal derivation of this Salter diagram, when there is a fixed tariff on the importable [*Lal, 1985*].
12. The long-run equilibrium factor prices following the change in the relative price of the traded good in this two factor–three commodity model are uniquely determined by the cost conditions in the traded good market. This can be seen as follows [*Batra, 1983: Ch. 12*]: The isocost curves for the three industries are given by:

$$a_{LM}W + a_{KM}r = P_M \quad (1)$$

$$a_{LX}W + a_{KX}r = P_X \quad (2)$$

$$a_{LN}W + a_{KN}r = P_N \quad (3)$$

where P_j is the commodity price, a_i the factor inputs of labour (L) and capital (K) per unit of output in the three industries and W and r are the nominal wage and rental rates.

With P_M and P_X determined exogenously by given world prices and given tariffs, W and r are uniquely determined by (1) and (2), which will then determine P_N from (3).

13. We can determine the required change in the price of non-traded goods and the real exchange rate following a change in the price of traded goods, by totally differentiating equations (1)–(3) in the preceding note and using Jones [*1965*] notation, with $\theta_{ij} = a_{ij}p_i/p_j$, the distributive shares of the relevant factor inputs in industry j, and $x^* = \frac{x}{dx}$ denoting percentage changes, obtaining:

$$\theta_{LM}W^* + \theta_{KM}r^* = P^*_M \quad (1a)$$

$$\theta_{LX}W^* + \theta_{KX}r^* = P^*_X \quad (2a)$$

$$\theta_{LN}W^* + \theta_{KN}r^* = P^*_N \quad (3a)$$

From (1a) and (2a):

$$(W^* - r^*) = (P^*_M - P^*_X)/\,|\,\theta\,| \equiv - p^*/\,|\,\theta\,| \quad (4)$$

$$(W^* - r^*) = (P^*_M - P^*_N)/\,|\,\theta\,| = - z^*/\,|\,\theta_N\,| \quad (5)$$

$$\text{where } |\,\theta\,| = \begin{vmatrix} \theta_{LM} & \theta_{KM} \\ \theta_{LM} & \theta_{KX} \end{vmatrix} \text{ and } |\,\theta_N\,| \equiv \begin{vmatrix} \theta_{LM} & \theta_{KM} \\ \theta_{LN} & \theta_{KN} \end{vmatrix} \quad (6)$$

so $z^* = |\frac{\theta_N}{\theta}|\,p^*$

The signs of $|\,\theta_N\,|$ and $|\,\theta\,|$ depend upon the capital labour ratios (k_i) in the three industries, with $k_i \equiv \frac{a_{Ki}}{a_{Li}}$ (i = X,M,N), then $|\,\theta\,| \gtrless 0$ if $k_x \gtrless k_m$ and $|\,\theta_N\,| \gtrless 0$ if $k_N \gtrless k_M$. We have assumed that $k_X < k_M$ so that $|\,\theta\,| < 0$.
Also, as we have assumed that
$k_N < k_M$, $|\,\theta_N\,| < 0$. Moreover, as

$$\frac{|\,\theta_N\,|}{|\,\theta\,|} = \frac{\theta_{LM} - \theta_{LN}}{\theta_{LM} - \theta_{LX}}$$

and X is more labour-intensive than N, $\theta_{LX} > \theta_{LN}$, hence

$$|\frac{\theta_N}{\theta}|\,1.$$

This implies that $z^* < p^*$, or that the price of non-traded goods will fall relative to that of exportables, but rise with respect to importables, given our factor intensity assumption.

This will involve a real exchange rate depreciation in the long run (of the 'new' composite commodity of importables and exportables at the tariff reduced relative prices of tradeables) [*Dornbusch, 1974*].

14. See the previous note.
15. This can be derived from the familiar Melvin–Edgeworth–Bowley box diagram [*Corden and Neary, 1982*].
16. See Neary [*1982*].
17. This is, of course, the result of our factor intensity assumptions. Thus, if tradeables were labour-intensive, then the long run equilibrium would have entailed a *lowering* of the money and real wage. The initial sticky wage would not have been validated in the process of adjustment with the shifting of capital stocks. The unemployment of 1K associated with the sticky wage would exert downward pressure on it, until the new long-run equilibrium was reached. Moreover, during this transition, the path of national income (measured at the 'new' relative commodity prices) need not be monotonic. It is possible that instead of increasing monotonically, there may be periods of 'falling real national income' or what Neary [*1982*] terms 'immiserising reallocation'. This is due to the fact that, with unemployment, the shadow wage (in this simple model) is zero, and the *shadow* rentals of capital in the two sectors are then given by the *average* product of capital in the two industries. Private agents, however, will earn the *marginal* product of capital (our 'rental' rates), as they still have to pay the slowly adjusting sticky wage, even though there is unemployment. It is possible, therefore, that the relative *shadow* rentals (= relative average product of capital) may not be the same as the relative marginal products of capital, which are influencing the private shifts of capital. There may thus be overshooting with the wage falling below its long run equilibrium level, leading to capital being shifted back to the traded good industry. If, however, private agents perceive the long-run equilibrium wage, or else in the transition the government can provide a wage subsidy which equates the sticky money wage to the 'equilibrium' money wage, this problem will not arise. Given the problems of information, however, it is unlikely that such a second-best policy will be feasible.
18. This curve is given by:

$$L^T (w) + L^N (w/z) = L$$

    where L is the fixed total labour supply and L^T and L^N is the labour demanded by the traded and non-traded good sectors respectively.
19. Setting P_T equal to unity, the equation of this curve is:

$$Q^N (w/z) = C^N (z, y)$$

    where Q^N is the output and C^N the demand for non-traded goods. The former depends only on the real product wage in the non-traded good industry, the latter on domestic relative prices (the real exchange rate) and real national income in terms of traded goods.
20. Note that because the relative prices within the composite 'traded goods' commodity have altered, the slope of N′N′ will not necessarily be the same as that of NN, though it must still be greater than unity.
21. Figure 1(C) can be interpreted in terms of an ongoing steady state inflation in which the nominal exchange rate and hence the money price of tradeables, the money wage and the money price of non-traded goods are all rising at the same rate.
22. See Pfefferman [*1986*] for an analysis of the different forms that public expenditure cuts have taken in the stabilisation programmes in the Southern Cone of Latin America. Chile seems to have been the only country which has succeeded in protecting its poor from the effects of public expenditure cuts.

REFERENCES

Batra, R.N., 1973, *Study in the Pure Theory of International Trade*, London: Macmillan.

Burgess, D.F., 1980, 'Protection, Real Wages and the Neo-Classical Ambiguity with Inter-Industry Flows', *Journal of Political Economy*, Vol.88, No.4, Aug.1980.

Cline, W.R. and S. Weintraub, 1981, *Economic Stabilisation in Developing Country*,

Washington, DC: Brookings Institution.

Corden, W.M., 1977, *Inflation, Exchange Rates and the World Economy* Clarendon Press, Oxford 1977.

Corden, W.M. and R. Jones, 1976, 'Devaluation, Non-flexible Prices, and the Trade Balance for a Small Country', *Canadian Journal of Economics*, Vol.9, No.1, Feb.

Corden, W.M. and P. Neary, 1982, 'Booming Sector and De-Industrialisation in a Small Open Economy', *The Economic Journal*, Vol.92, No.369, Dec.

Dell, S., 1981, 'On Being Grandmotherly: The Evolution of IMF Conditionality', *Princeton Essays in International Finance*, No. 144, Oct.

Dornbusch, R., 1974, 'Real and Monetary Aspects of the Effects of Exchange Rate Changes', in R.Z. Aliber (ed.), *National Monetary Policies and the International Finance System*, Chicago.

Dornbusch, R., 1980, *Open Economy Macroeconomics*, New York: Basic Books.

Edwards, S. and M. Khan, 1985, 'Interest Rate Determinants in Developing Countries – A Conceptual Framework', *IMF Staff Papers*, Vol. 32, No. 3, Sept.

Fry, M.J., 1978, 'Money and Capital or Financial Deepening in Economic Development?' *Journal of Money, Credit and Banking*, Vol.10, No.1, Nov.

Hanson, J., 1982, 'Contractionary Devaluation, Substitution in Production and Consumption and the Role of the Labour Market', mimeo, IBRD.

Harberler, G., 1950, 'Some Problems in the Pure Theory of International Trade', *Economic Journal*, Vol.60, No.38.

Jones, R., 1965, 'The Structure of Simple General Equilibrium Models, *Journal of Political Economy*, Vol.73, No.6, Dec.

Jones, R., 1971, 'A Three Factor Model in Theory, Trade and History', in J. Bhagwati *et al.*, *Trade Balance of Payments and Growth*, Amsterdam: North Holland.

Killick, T., (ed.), 1982, 'Adjustment and Financing in the Developing World, IMF, Washington, DC.

Krueger, A.O., 1974, 'Home Goods and Money in Exchange Rate Adjustments', in W. Sellekaarts (ed.), *International Trade and Finance*, London: Macmillan.

Lal, D., 1980, 'A Liberal International Economic Order: The International Monetary System and Economic Development' *Princeton Essays in International Finance* No. 139, Princeton, NJ.

Lal, D., 1984, 'The Real Effects of Stabilisation and Structural Adjustment Policies: An Extension of the Australian Adjustment Model', World Bank Staff Working Paper, No. 636, Washington, DC.

Lal, D., 1985, 'The Real Exchange Rate, Capital Inflows and Inflation: Sri Lanka 1970–1982', *Weltwirtschaftliches Archiv*, Vol.121, No.4.

Lal, D., 1986, 'Stolper–Samuelson–Rybczynski in the Pacific – Real Wages and Exchange Rates in the Philippines, 1956–78', *Journal of Development Economics*, Vol.21, No.1, April.

Lal, D., 1987, 'The Political Economy of Economic Liberalisation', *World Bank Economic Review*, Vol.1, No.2, Jan.

Magee, S., 1973, 'Factor Market Distortions, Production and Trade: A Survey', *Oxford Economic Papers*, Vol. 25, No. 1.

McKinnon, R., 1981, 'Financial Repression and the Liberalisation Problem Within Less Developed Countries', in S. Grassman and E. Lundberg (ed.), *The World Economic Order – Past and Prospects*, London: Macmillan.

McKinnon, R. and D.J. Mathieson, 1981, 'How to Manage a Repressed Economy', *Princeton Essays in International Finance*, No. 145, Dec.

Mussa, M., 1974, 'Tariffs and the Distribution of Income', *Journal of Political Economy*, Vol.82, No.6, Nov./Dec.

Neary, J.P., 1978, 'Short-run Capital Specifity and the Pure Theory of International Trade', *Economic Journal*, Vol.88, No.351.

Neary, J.P., 1982, 'Capital Mobility, Wage Stickiness and Adjustment Assistance', in Bhagwati (ed.), *Import Competition and Response*, Chicago: NBER.

Neary, J.P., 1985, 'Theory and Policy of Adjustment in an Open Economy', in D. Greenaway (ed.), *Current Issues in International Trade: Theory and Policy* London, Macmillan.

Nowzad, B., 1981, 'The IMF and Its Critics', *Princeton Essays in International Finance*, No. 146, Dec.

Pfefferman, G., 1986, *Poverty in Latin America – The Impact of Depression*, World Bank, Washington, DC.

Prachowny, M., 1981, 'Sectoral Conflict Over Stabilisation Policies in Small Open Economies', *The Economic Journal*, Vol.91, No.364, Sept.

Prachowny, M., 1984, *Macroeconomic Analysis for Small Open Economies*, Oxford: Clarendon Press.

Salter, W.E.G., 1959, 'Internal and External Balance: The Role of Price and Expenditure Effects', *Economic Record*, Vol. 35, Aug., pp.226–38.

Williamson, J., (ed.), 1983, *IMF Conditionality*, Washington, DC: Institute for International Economics.

PART IV

Why growth rates differ: the political economy of social capability in 21 developing countries*

Deepak Lal

Abstract

This paper first summarizes the evidence on the proximate causes of growth in a sample of 21 developing countries studied as part of a large multi-country comparative study. It briefly examines various endogenous growth models and finds only one – due to Scott – to be consistent with the evidence from the 21 countries studied. The paper then outlines a 3 × 2 × 5-fold classification of the countries' initial resource endowments, organizational structure and polities to draw comparative historical judgments on the deeper determinants of growth. The final part outlines the policy framework which on the basis of the country studies is most likely to foster social capability.

Introduction

The organizers of this symposium have asked participants to consider the role of what they have termed social capability as a determinant of the differing growth performance of developing countries over the last three decades. This term, as I understand it, is meant to cover all those causes of growth which go beyond the proximate ones – the level of investment and its efficiency –in explaining differences in growth rates. These include: entrepreneurship, learning by doing, organizational and institutional aspects related to transactions and information costs, as well as the general economic and political framework which determine the relative costs of doing business in different countries, as well as their efficiency of investment, and levels of thrift. A recently completed multi-country comparative study co-directed by the author and Hla Myint for the World Bank, was explicitly designed to provide some answers to a similar set of questions.[1] It was based on in-depth historical studies of 21 developing countries, which explored the role of (a) initial conditions-resource endowment and economic structures; (b) national political institutions and economic organization and (c) economic policies (including alternative policies which might have been undertaken). In this paper some of the results emerging from the synthesis volume (Lal-Myint, 1991) which provides the comparative analysis of the country studies are used to answer some of the questions concerning social capability– what it is, and how it can be fostered.

The paper is in three parts. In the first we examine the evidence on the proximate causes of growth in our sample of 21 developing countries. We also briefly look at various endogenous growth models, recently developed under the rubric of the 'new' growth theory, to see if they can provide the requisite explanations, and find them lacking. In the second part we provide a brief outline of a 3 × 2 × 5-fold classification of our countries' initial resource endowments, organizational structures and polities, which we found useful in making our comparative historical judgments on the deeper determinants of growth. The third part outlines the conclusions on the policy framework which we found best serves to foster social capability.

I. The proximate causes of growth

Table 1 shows the per capita income levels and growth rates of per capita GDP in Kravis dollars for the 21 countries in the Lal-Myint study between 1950 and 1985. Figure 1 charts the real per capita income figures for 1960 and 1985. The wide divergence in growth performance in the sample is obvious. The major qualitative conclusion emerging from the country studies – the building blocks of the comparative analysis – was that relative differences in both the level and efficiency of investment were the proximate causes of the difference in growth performance in

Table 1 Real GDP per capita in 1980 international prices

		1950	*1955*	*1960*	*1980*	*Growth rate 1960–85*
Malawi	MW		212	237	387	2.0
Indonesia	IND			494	1255	3.8
Egypt	EG	427	433	496	1188	3.6
Ghana	GH		511	534	349	−1.7
Nigeria	NIG	478	543	552	581	0.2
Madagascar	MDGR			659	497	−1.1
Thailand	TH	638	516	688	1900	4.1
Sri Lanka	SL	787	868	974	1539	1.8
Brazil	BZ		832	991	3282	4.9
Mauritius	MR	1253	1145	1012	1869	2.5
Malaysia	MLY		1006	1103	3415	4.6
Turkey	TK	822	1132	1255	2533	2.8
Malta	MLA		1087	1282	5319	5.9
Colombia	COL	1188	1376	1344	2599	2.7
Jamaica	JAM		1117	1472	1725	0.6
Singapore	SING			1528	9834	7.7
Costa Rica	CR	1175	1541	1663	2650	1.9
Peru	PR	1235	1501	1721	2114	0.8
Hong Kong	HK			1737	9093	6.3
Mexico	MX	1652	1905	2157	3985	2.5
Uruguay	UR	2864	3523	3271	3462	0.2

NB '1960' Indonesian figure is for 1962

Source: 'A New Set of International Comparisons of Real Product and Prices for 130 Countries 1950–85,' Robert Summers and Alan Heston, in *The Review of Income and Wealth*, March 1988, Series 34, No. 1

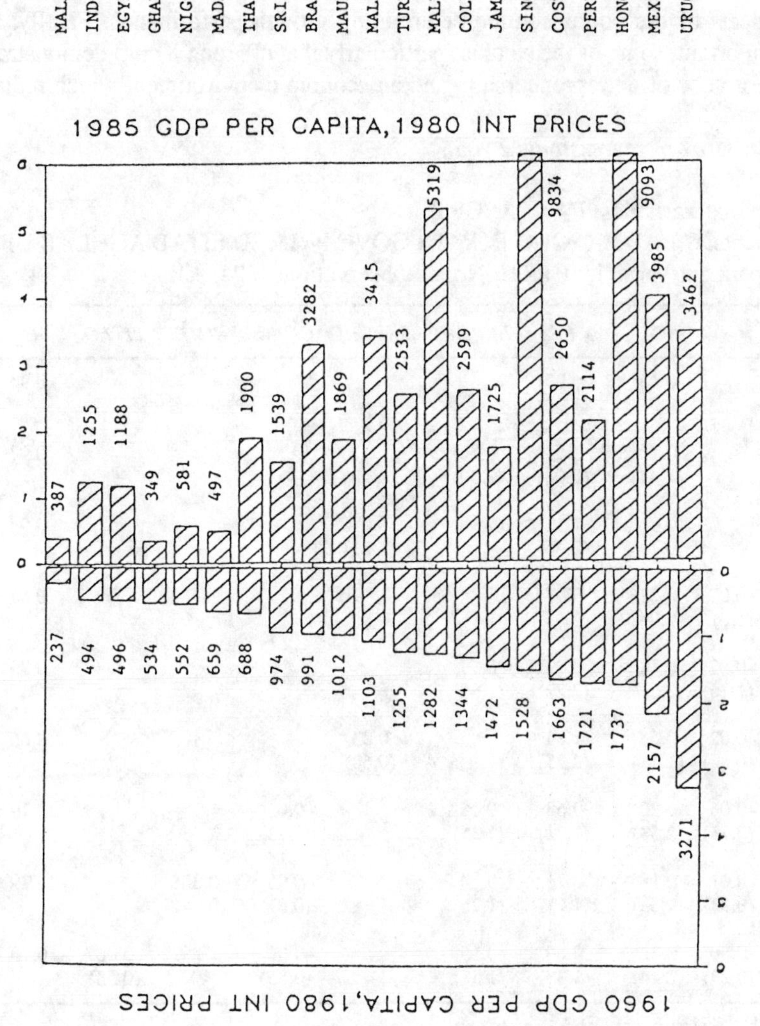

Figure 1 Real GDP per capita in 1980 international prices, 1960 and 1985

our sample. Furthermore, the policy regime was crucial in explaining the differences in the efficiency of investment. Outward orientation, as well as the absence of policy-induced distortions in the working of the price mechanism, were important aspects of the policy regime determining growth performance. Finally, and most important, some of the studies (particularly that of Hong Kong) demonstrated the importance of entrepreneurship, and an economic environment which reduces

Table 2 Growth regressions: TSLS

Endogenous Variables: INV EXPGRT
Instruments: C LAB EXPCHG DUMTR GOVC PRIMED LITAD AGRLAB URBP
(A) Dependent Variable: GRTH; No. of Observations = 21

	C	*INV*	*LAB*	*EXPGRT*	*EXPCHG*	*GOVC*	*PRIMED*	*LITAD*	*Rsq*
R.I		0.13**	0.85*						0.94
		(2.31)	(1.93)						
R.II		0.11**	0.67*	0.22**					0.97
		(2.44)	(2.00)	(2.39)					
R.III		0.06	1.31**		0.05				0.94
		(0.75)	(2.46)		(1.51)				
R.IV	–0.02	0.23***	0.97**						0.67
	(1.7)	(2.94)	(2.35)						
R.V	–0.02	0.18**	0.79**	0.17					0.79
	(1.26)	(2.5)	(2.22)	(1.65)					
R.VI	–0.02	0.15	1.84**		0.03				0.66
	(0.82)	(1.12)	(2.23)		(0.68)				
R.VII	–0.06	0.20*	0.68	0.15		–0.05			0.79
	(0.75)	(2.53)	(1.72)	(1.35)		(0.75)			
R.VIII	–0.01	0.18*	0.76	0.14		–0.05	0.005		0.79
	(0.63)	(1.83)	(1.6)	(1.26)		(0.6)	(0.34)		
R.IX	–0.005	0.22**	0.60	0.15		–0.07		–0.007	0.79
	(0.29)	(2.44)	(1.38)	(1.33)		(0.85)		(0.53)	

Notes: *** – significant at 1%
** – significant at 2.5%
* – significant at 5%

GRTH – annual GDP growth rate 1950–85 (country studies)
INV – average share of investment in GDP 1950–85
LAB – labour force growth rates 1960–85
GOVC – Govt. consumption as share of GDP, average 1965–85
EXPGRT – growth rate of exports 1960–85
EXPCHG – change in ratio of exports to GDP, 1985 and 1960
DUMTR – trade regime dummy (1 – outward, 0 – inward oriented)
PRIMED – Percentage age group in primary education 1965
LITAD – Adult literacy rate in 1960
AGRLAB – percentage of labour force in agriculture 1965
URBP – urban population as percentage of total, 1965

Table 2 (continued) Growth regressions: TSLS

(B) Dependent Variable: GRTK
No. of Observations = 21

	C	*INV*	*LAB*	*EXPGRT*	*EXPCHG*	*GOVC*	*PRIMED*	*LITAD*	*Rsq*
R.I		0.16**	0.70						0.92
		(2.29)	(1.29)						
R.II		0.13**	0.43	0.32***					0.96
		(2.36)	(1.08)	(2.97)					
R.III		0.08	1.22*		0.05				0.92
		(0.78)	(1.83)		(1.37)				
R.IV	–0.04**	0.33***	0.91*						0.68
	(2.52)	(3.57)	(1.86)						
R.V	–0.03**	0.26***	0.66	0.22*					0.81
	(2.2)	(3.21)	(1.64)	(1.91)					
R.VI	–0.04*	0.34*	0.88		–0.003				0.67
	(1.91)	(2.08)	(1.40)		(0.07)				
R.VII	–0.03	0.26**	0.66	0.21		–0.03			0.81
	(1.51)	(2.32)	(1.20)	(1.63)		(0.30)			
R.VIII	–0.03	0.27**	0.61	0.21		–0.02	0.003		0.81
	(1.33)	(3.00)	(1.35)	(1.71)		(0.10)	(0.16)		
R.IX	–0.02	0.31***	0.46	0.22		–0.05		-0.01	0.80
	(0.99)	(2.99)	(0.91)	(1.66)		(0.55)		(0.91)	

Notes: Significance levels as in previous note. Figures in brackets are t ratios. GRTK – annual growth rates of GDP Kravis dollars from Table 1
The other variables are as in previous footnote.
All the regressions in this table have been estimated by the GIVE procedure in the statistical package ECOS.

the costs of doing business as important determinants of better growth performance.[2]

Crude statistical representations of some of these conclusions of the analytical economic histories of the countries on which they were based, are provided by the cross-section, two-stage least-square regressions (TSLS) that we ran on the summary data of their economic performance. Table 2 summarizes these regression estimates for (a) GDP growth rates between 1950-85 from the country studies, and (b) Kravis dollar growth rates of real GDP between 1960-85, as the dependent variables. Various structural and policy variables (listed in the notes to the Table) were used to form instruments for the two independent endogenous variables, the investment rate and the export growth rate (used as a proxy for the openness of the economy).

The investment rate is invariably positively correlated with the growth rate at a highly significant level, as is the proxy for openness. Alternative measures for human capital and the share of government spending in GDP, which for instance

Barro (1991) found were statistically significant in his cross-section regressions of the whole Kravis sample, did not appear to be of any importance in explaining differences in growth rates, in either our country studies or the cross-country regressions. The latter, which included a composite distortion index developed by Aggarwal (1983) as an independent variable, did provide cross-section statistical support for the conclusion of the country studies that the relative level of policy-induced distortions is an important proximate cause of differences in the efficiency of investment and hence in growth performance.

As is well-known, the standard Solow-Swan neoclassical model predicts that in the long run growth is dependent entirely on exogenous factors – the rate of labour-augmenting technical progress and the rate of growth of the quality-adjusted labour force. Neither policy, which determines the efficiency of investment, nor preferences which determine its level, affect the steady state growth rate of GDP. This has troubled theorists. Thus Kaldor (1957) and Arrow (1962) tried to endogenize technical progress by making it depend on the rate of investment. But their models still only led to level rather than growth effects of changes in investment.

After a hiatus of two decades there have been fresh attempts to endogenize growth within the Solow-Swan framework (see in particular Lucas, 1988 and Romer, 1986, 1987). But they are not persuasive, as their key features – a particular value of a parameter which yields increasing returns to investment in Romer, and an unexplained externality to human capital in Lucas – which yield their endogenous growth results seem arbitrary and implausible (see Stern, 1991 for a succinct critique). Moreover as Benhabib and Jovanovic (1991) have shown, the empirical evidence cited in Romer (1987) in support of aggregate increasing returns to capital and labour because of an externality associated with capital investment is not supported by an alternative explanation of the same cross-section evidence. They instead argue that the evidence is consistent with the Solow-Swan model, in which:

> the variation in countries' growth rates is consistent with each country having the same constant returns-to-scale production function and with a stochastic process for technological change that is the same across different countries but starts from different initial positions. (p. 82)

Moreover, they interpret these 'technology shocks':

> broadly to include shifts in institutional and organizational structures, such as shifts in the corporate, legal or bureaucratic structures, or even in attitudes to work. These elements can greatly enhance or retard the effective use and operation of factors of production. (p. 102)

They admit that these technology shocks which are their engine of growth are still another 'black box'. But what they 'have shown is that this engine is fuelled primarily by something other than physical capital' (p. 102).

A more promising model from the 'new' growth theory stable is that of Murphy-Shleifer-Vishny (1991). This endogenizes growth by assuming that there are increasing returns to ability (talent). 'Talented people typically organize production by others, so they can spread their ability advantage over a larger scale' (p. 503). The economic environment then determines whether a country's talented people start firms, innovate and foster growth, or become rent seekers aiming to merely redistribute wealth, thereby reducing growth.

This model fits in well with another 'endogenous' growth model due to Scott (1989). His model is a direct descendant of what Johnson (1964) called the 'generalized capital accumulation' approach deriving from Irving Fisher (1930). This sees capital accumulation broadly defined to include all forms of investment which yields a stream of income over time. But:

> 'investment' in this context must be defined to include such diverse activities as adding to material capital, increasing the health, discipline, skill and education of the human population, moving labor into more productive occupations and locations and applying existing knowledge or discovering and applying new knowledge to increase the efficiency of productive processes. All such activities involve incurring costs, in the form of use of current resources, and investment in them is socially worthwhile if the rate of return over costs exceeds the general rate of interest, or the capital value of the additional income they yield exceeds the cost of obtaining it. (Johnson, 1964, p. 221)

This wider notion of investment as the prime mover of the growth process also makes growth endogenous 'and is a potent simplification of the analytical problem of growth, and one which facilitates the discussion of problems of growth policy by emphasizing the relative returns from alternative investments of currently available resources' (ibid.).

Scott's endogenous neoclassical equilibrium growth model is the fullest working out of this approach. He makes three departures from the Solow-Swan framework. First, he argues that depreciation is essentially a transfer of income from capitalists to workers in a progressive economy. Were the 'appreciation' (in workers' incomes) which results not excluded, as it is in conventional accounting, then 'net investment for society as a whole is (approximately) equal to gross investment as conventionally measured, and not to gross investment minus depreciation' (Scott, op cit., p. 92).[3]

Second, Scott argues that there are no diminishing returns to cumulative gross investment (that is the capital stock measured as the sum of all past gross investments), but there could be diminishing returns to the rate of investment.

Third, he argues (in Scott, 1976) there is no need to invoke any independent or exogenous technical progress to explain growth. He argues that: 'investment is ... by definition ... the cost of change, and so will cover all activities associated with growth' (p. 317) and that 'growth due to capital and technical progress are both the result of investment' (p. 330) in the sense of 'the cost, in terms of consumption foregone, of propelling the economy forward instead of leaving it in a stationary state' (p. 318). He adds

> incurring capital expenditure leads to a rearrangement of the things of this world. It does not lead to there being any more of some substance 'capital'. There is then simply change which is due to investment, and to population growth. (ibid., p. 331)

Scott then provides a detailed empirical analysis of the conformity of the growth experience of the currently developed countries to his model. We carried out a regression analysis similar to Scott's for our sample of 21 countries and found that the estimated equation (using TSLS) (where g is the growth rate of GDP 1950–85; s the average gross investment rate 1950–85; gL- the growth rate of labour force 1960–85 (due to lack of data we could not use the correct variable which adjusts for the quality of the labour force)) was:

Table 3 Determinants of growth

(A) Growth of GDP (g), Investment Rate (s), Growth of Labour Force (G_L), Share of Wages (λ) and Average Rates of Return to Investment (r)

Country	g	s	G_L	λ	r
A. Labour abundant					
Hong Kong	8.9	26.1	3.63	na	na
Singapore	8.3	34.0	3.86	na	na
Malta	5.6	26.1	1.35	na	na
B. Land abundant					
Malaysia	6.9	23.0	3.39	na	na
Thailand	6.7	22.9	3.09	52.0	22.2
Brazil	6.6	21.4	3.25	64.7	21.0
Mexico	5.7	18.2	3.55	64.7	18.7
Turkey	5.6	18.9	1.80	57.0	24.0
Costa Rica	5.0	22.0	3.65	58.5	13.0
Colombia	4.7	19.0	2.49	53.0	17.8
Nigeria	3.7	16.6	2.93	52.0	13.1
Ghana	1.3	11.7	2.58	>100.0	–10.9
Uruguay	1.1	12.9	0.66	34.7	6.8
C. Intermediate					
Egypt	5.4	19.4	2.29	43.4	22.7
Indonesia	5.3	15.2	2.62	na	na
Sri Lanka	4.7	17.2	2.31	69.0	18.1
Malawi	4.3	23.4	2.51	50.1	13.0
Peru	4.1	19.1	2.93	na	na
Jamaica	3.3	22.1	1.97	na	na
Mauritius	2.9	22.3	2.60	na	na
Madagascar	2.0	14.3	1.79	na	na

Note: g – growth rate of GDP (1950–85) from *World Tables* and country study
s – average gross investment rate (1950–85) from country study
λ – share of wages from country studies and Anderson (1990) for Sri Lanka from Lal (1979)
r – estimated from $r = (g-\lambda G_L/s)$

$$g = 0.71gL + 0.15\, s$$
$$(1.8) \qquad (2.99) \qquad R2 = 0.94$$

(t ratios in brackets)

The differences in the efficiency of investment in our sample of countries can be seen from Table 3, which reports the estimated average rate of return (within the Scott framework) for those countries where data on the share of wages – a crucial variable – was available.

It would seem, therefore, that the relative efficiency of investment, even more than its level, was the crucial proximate determinant of growth rate differences. The policy regime was in turn crucial in explaining these differences in efficiency. This raises the deeper question subsumed in the notion of 'social capability', of why countries adopted the policy regimes they did, and why some of them changed these during the 25 years covered in the country studies.

II. The 3 × 2 × 5 comparative framework

The role of initial conditions in determining growth outcomes was captured in the synthesis of the country studies by a three-fold classification of the countries into 'labour abundant', 'land abundant' and 'intermediate' using the three-factor (land, labour and capital) trade theoretic framework of Krueger (1977) and Leamer (1984, 1987). [Essay 4 provides a highly condensed account of the model.] It yields a rich menu of alternative efficient paths of development and the implied patterns of changes in the functional distribution of income over time. Figure 2 depicts the

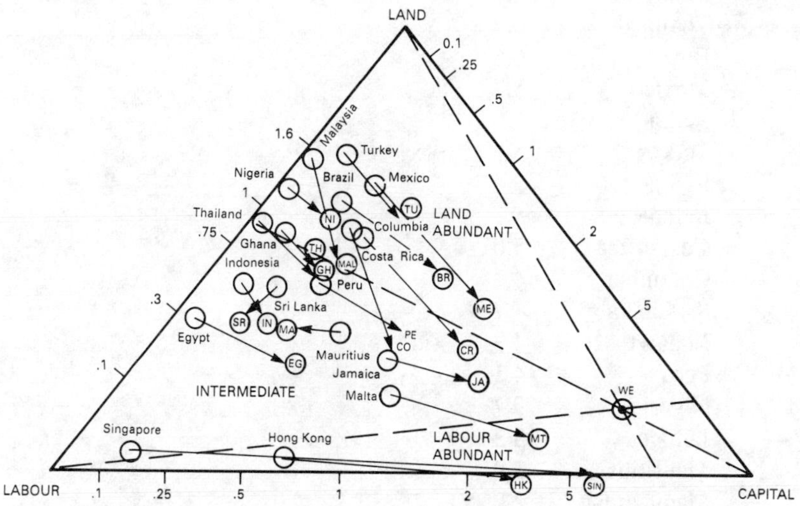

Figure 2 Resource endowments

classification of our countries by their factor endowments in 1958 and 1978 in an endowment triangle devised by Leamer (1987).

Secondly, a two-fold organizational dichotomy was used to qualify the initial adaptations required to realize the potential comparative advantage in small-scale labour-intensive peasant exports and in large-scale plantation and mining exports among the 'land-abundant' and 'intermediate' groups of countries (see Myint, 1985 for details).

Thirdly, a five-fold classification of the polity was found useful. This distinguished between the objectives of the government and constraints on its activities. On the latter distinction, two basic types of state were distinguished – the autonomous state and the factional state. In the former, the State subserves its own ends. The autonomous state classification can be further subdivided by the different objectives of the state. The first is the benevolent state, which is the Platonic Guardian state of public economics. The other is the predatory state,[4] whose self-seeking can take either the form of the absolutist state seeking to maximize net

Table 4 Growth and type of polity

Region		*Growth Rate*	*Autonomous*			*Factional*	
			Plat.	*Predatory*		*Olig.*	*Dem.*
				Author.	*Burec.*		
As	Hong Kong	8.9	x				
As	Singapore	8.3	x				
As	Malaysia	6.9					x
As	Thailand	6.7		x			
LA	Brazil	6.6		x			
LA	Mexico	5.7			x		
ME	Malta	5.6					x
ME	Turkey	5.6	x				
ME	Egypt	5.4		x			
As	Indonesia	5.3		x			
LA	Costa Rica	5.0					x
LA	Colombia	4.7				x	
As	Sri Lanka	4.7					x
Af	Malawi	4.3	x				
LA	Peru	4.1				x	
Af	Nigeria	3.7					x
LA	Jamaica	3.3					x
As	Mauritius	2.9					x
Af	Madagascar	2.0				x	
Af	Ghana	1.3		x			
LA	Uruguay	1.1					x

Ranked in terms of growth performance

revenue for the use of the sovereign, or the bureaucratic state concerned with maximizing public employment.

The factional state by contrast subserves the objectives of the groups who are successful in its capture. Two broad types were distinguished – the oligarchic state and a majoritarian democracy (see Lal, 1989 for details). Table 4 shows how our countries were classified to reflect the central tendency of the polity as identified by the country authors.

Some of the broad patterns emerging within this classificatory framework which are relevant for the discussion in the next section may be noted.

First, apart from Hong Kong, most of our countries followed dirigiste policies to varying extents. However, in the so called postwar golden age of the world economy, with its vast expansion of world trade, this mild dirigisme towards trade and industry did not do great damage to growth performance. It was during the more turbulent world economic environment – post 1973 – that the effects of differing policy regimes on the efficiency of investment and thence their growth became manifest. Many of our countries suffered growth collapses (as judged by our country authors). In our land-abundant group, eight out of ten (i.e., except Malaysia and Thailand) suffered a growth collapse. None of the labour abundant and only three (Jamaica, Peru and Madagascar) in the intermediate endowment group suffered a growth collapse.

The proximate cause of the growth collapses was an inflationary *cum* balance of payments crisis usually generated by unsustainable fiscal commitments. These fiscal crises had two major causes: (a) 'big push' type development expenditures in Brazil, Peru, Nigeria, Ghana, Turkey and Madagascar, and (b) unsustainable social expenditures on income transfers and subsidies in Sri Lanka, Egypt, Jamaica, Mauritius, Uruguay and Costa Rica. Two striking patterns in these sources of fiscal imbalance were, first that most of the 'big push' type fiscal imbalances were in land-abundant countries. Second, except for Egypt, all the countries with unsustainable social expenditures were factional states.

Finally, in dealing with the crises which ensued, the response was found to be conditioned jointly by the country's polity and its underlying resource endowments. Thus, by and large, factional states (particularly of the democratic type) in relatively large, land-abundant countries, where it was economic to have large-scale production, found it more difficult to change the policy regimes which had generated the crises, until economic ruin stared the polity in the face.

The classification according to differing initial resource endowments and the polity was useful in explaining these divergent policy regimes and outcomes. First, the labour-abundant countries irrespective of their polity had the easiest development task. For them the standard policy prescription of the two factor Heckscher-Ohlin model of initially developing labour-intensive industries and then moving up the ladder of comparative advantage is easy to follow. First, this policy leads to politically-desirable factor price movements. With wages rising as capital is accumulated, there is unlikely to be political resistance from the bulk of the populace in factional states to policies which realize the country's comparative advantage. While all types of autonomous state will also find that even their predatory ends are better served by undertaking the development of their only resource – the human – on which their revenues and prosperity depend. The major task of government is to provide an adequate infrastructure to reduce the transaction costs of the relatively small-scale organizational units which will predominate in the earlier stages of their development. Second, if the country is small (as were all three countries in our sample), the limited size of the domestic market makes reliance on foreign trade inevitable. Also, there is unlikely to be vertical import substitution when the ubiquitous dirigisme leads to departures from free trade. This means that when a switch to freer trade is made there will not be lobbies preventing competitive imports of intermediate inputs. The political costs of rectifying past policy mistakes are likely to be lower than in the land-abundant or intermediate group of countries. Third, their incremental comparative advantage is readily apparent to economic agents in both the public and private sectors. It is thus easier to pick 'industrial winners' and the consequences of picking losers or policies which stimulate them are more immediately apparent – as with Singapore's ill-judged attempt to jump a few rungs on the ladder of comparative advantage through an artificial raising of wages.

The comparative advantage of large land-abundant countries is also likely to be clearer than for the intermediate group, but more difficult to realize than for the labour-abundant group of countries. This is for two reasons. First, with a higher supply price of labour than the labour-abundant countries, due to their more favourable land-labour ratios, their incremental comparative advantage is likely to lie on the relatively capital intensive rungs of the ladder of comparative advantage. Public promotion may be required because of the ensuing lumpiness of investments, and the need to develop scarce skills and absorb complex imported technology. The dangers of 'bureaucratic failure' endemic to such promotion may then lead to a failure to realize their economic potential. Second, if the rate of capital accumulation is not high enough, then with growing labour forces, their efficient development path could contain declining real wage segments.[5] If the polity is subject to factional democratic pressures, this 'equilibrium' time path of real wages could lead to political pressures to resist the requisite real wage adjustments by turning inward. The polity could be at odds with the economy, with political cycles of economic repression (during factional political phases) followed by liberalization (during autonomous political periods). Third, given the political imperative of avoiding the 'falling wage' segments of their development path, such countries have attempted 'big push' development programmes (to push their factor endowments towards the capital vortex in the Leamer triangle), often financed by foreign borrowing. This big push has often pushed them into a fiscal and debt crisis and thence a growth crisis.

Finally, the intermediate resource endowment group faces the most difficult development path. Their incremental comparative advantage is more opaque, so 'mistakes' are not so easily recognized nor rectified, particularly by the public sector, which in the absence of any bankruptcy constraint resists the exit of inefficient firms. Secondly, this group was found to be more likely to face situations in which their polities were at odds with their comparative advantage.

One important conclusion arising from our country studies was the importance of stability in property rights (even more than their efficiency) in leading to a successful and sustainable growth performance. This does not mean that a clean (once and for all well-defined) redistribution of property rights is ruled out. What is harmful is uncertainty about such redistribution. Furthermore, the definition of a right to property is in effect to claims on the income streams from the use of that property. Hence property rights are not altered only through asset redistribution, but also through changes in the implicit or explicit set of taxes and subsidies on factors of production and commodities, to which most public interventions are analytically equivalent, and which change the net income stream attached to 'property'. These taxes and subsidies must also include the changes in property rights that occur from the levying of the inflation tax. A stable fiscal and monetary constitution was thus also found to be an important part of a growth promoting economic framework.

III. The promotion of social capability

The mainsprings of growth remain productivity, thrift and entrepreneurship. Their promotion is also synonymous with the creation of social capability. Our country studies provided ample evidence that this capability is best promoted through what can be called the classical liberal economic framework. Its clearest statement was in Mill's *Principles*, and its modern refurbishment is in Hayek's 'Constitution of Liberty'. Before delineating these principles, it is useful to consider why they have until fairly recently been rejected by most Third World countries in the postwar period.

The clue to the widespread dirigiste impulse noted in Part II (also see Lal, 1985) lies in the economic nationalism which has been characteristic of nearly every Third World state. In this they echo the nationalist impulse of the absolutist monarchies after the Renaissance, which also sought to build cohesive nation states through dirigiste policies (see Heckscher, 1955). Their mercantilist system of controls and regulation, set up to pursue the objective of 'nation building', has obvious resonances in the neo-mercantilist policies pursued by most Third World states. But these absolute monarchies found that after some initial success, far from building nations their dirigiste policies were becoming counterproductive, and leading to national disintegration. The consequences of their regulations and controls, particularly of internal trade and industry, were similar to those observed in many developing countries – corruption, rent seeking, tax evasion and the growth of illegal activities in growing underground economies. As has been observed for many developing countries (see Lal, 1987) and is confirmed by our country studies, one paradoxical dynamic effect of attempts to exercise political control over ever-increasing areas of economic life has often been that after a certain stage, there is a diminution of the government's effective areas of control – an unMarxian withering away of the State – as private agents find numerous ways of avoiding them. The most important sign of this for any state is loss of control over its fiscal affairs. With the expansion of politically-determined entitlements as part of the mercantilist system of a politicized economy, the accompanying tax burden to finance them leads at some stage to generalized tax resistance. Faced with inelastic or declining revenues but burgeoning expenditure commitments, incipient or actual fiscal deficits become chronic. It is to regain government control over increasingly ungovernable economies that economic liberalization was undertaken in the great Age of Reform in the 19th century. Paradoxically, as Heckscher notes, the new economic liberalism (though short-lived) achieved the goal sought by mercantilism:

> Great power for the state, the perpetual and fruitless goal of mercantilist endeavour, was translated into fact in the 19th century ... The result was attained primarily by limiting the functions of the state, which task laissez-faire carried through radically. The maladjustment between ends and means was one of the typical features of mercantilism, but it disappeared once the aims were considerably limited. Disobedience and arbitrariness, unpunished infringements of the law, smuggling and embezzlement flourish particularly under a very extensive state administration and in periods of continually changing ordinances and interferences with the course of economic life. It was because the regime de l'ordre bore this impress that disorder was one of its characteristic features. (Heckscher, p. 325)

The same process seems to be occurring today in the neo-mercantilist states of all three worlds, which has led to a new worldwide Age of Reform in the 1980s.

What are the principles of economic liberalism, and how do they differ from those derived within the Arrow-Debreu market failure based view of public policy? The two most important are Gladstonian finance and sound money.[6] The requirements of the latter are self-evident and broadly accepted today. The former, however, would be contested by proponents of contemporary optimal tax theory. The latter embodies two views about the economy whose precursor is J.S. Mill. The first is that questions of allocation can be separated from those concerning the distribution of income (see Mill, pp. 349–50), what Hayek has termed the 'manna from heaven' presumption of contemporary distributivist theory (see Gray, 1984). The second is the neglect of the polity (see Barry, 1978), so that for purely technical reasons, in public economics the government is assumed to be composed of a committee of Platonic Guardians.

As our country studies have shown, and is apparent from the economic history of both Western economies as well as of communist countries, the pre-Mill classical insight is still valid – a point which has been reiterated by the new institutional economics. As Bardhan (1989) notes:

> one of the main pillars of Walrasian neo-classical economics – the separability of equity and efficiency – breaks down when transaction costs and imperfect information are important; the terms and conditions of contracts in various transactions which directly affect the efficiency of resource allocation, now crucially depend on ownership structures and property relations. (p. 1389)

The growth and productivity outcomes of particular institutional forms cannot be separated from their system of property rights, and the distribution of income streams flowing from them. The equity-efficiency trade-off is a chimera.

Nor can the central assumption about the polity underlying optimal tax theory be supported by even casual empiricism. Thus two of the proponents of this theory for developing countries assume that:

> the government has coherent, unified and largely benevolent objectives, captured in the social welfare function, and we search for ways in which the tools available to it can be used to improve the measure of welfare. (Newberry and Stern, 1987, p. 653)

As our country studies have shown, except for rare cases, most polities do not come even close to these assumptions about their character. Once a predatory or rent-seeking polity is accepted as being common, the pattern of optimal taxes envisioned by Ramsey – even from the viewpoint of a neutral outside observer – is no longer desirable. In fact, this yields exactly the set of revenue-maximizing taxes that a predatory state would choose to levy! (See Brennan-Buchanan, 1980; Lee and Tollison, 1988; Lal, 1990.)

An important difference in the neutrality of taxation as envisaged by Ramsey and under Gladstonian finance is that for the former it means reducing the deadweight cost of taxation, while for the latter it refers to the generality or uniformity of the tax. As Harberger (1987) has noted (in a discussion which looks at various arguments for these two forms of neutrality) the main difference of these two approaches is their different philosophies of government, one of which corresponds to the classical liberal view, the other to the social engineering view. That the latter is really a form of neo-mercantilism can be readily seen from the fact that in this modern variant, the objective of economic policy is no longer the welfare of the state but the welfare of citizens as summarized in a social welfare function laid down by the state.

If we thus eschew the social engineering viewpoint underlying much technocratic policy advice as being mercantilism in another garb, and accept that the most important way to promote social capability is to establish a policy framework that emphasizes economic freedom (misleadingly called *laissez-faire*), this does not imply, as some seem to assume, that the government should be 'inert or indifferent'. As Henderson (1986) has noted:

> Liberalism's emphasis is a positive one. It is concerned with economic freedom, including the freedom of individuals and enterprises to enter industries or occupations, to choose their place of residence or operation within a country, and to decide their own products, processes and markets. There is nothing outdated about these principles nor do they operate against the weak. To the contrary, they enable opportunities to be opened up more widely, and thus operate against special privileges within an economic system ... In any case, liberalism is not to be identified with hostility to the state, nor with a doctrinaire presumption that governments have only a minor role in economic life. On the contrary, the liberal view of the role of the state, both internal and external, is strongly positive. (p. 98)

For the Third World the essential tasks of governments from a liberal viewpoint are considerable. As Bauer summarized them:

> the tasks include the successful conduct of external affairs, notably the defense of the country, and also the preservation and encouragement of external communications and contacts; the maintenance of public security; the effective administration of the monetary and fiscal system; the promotion of a suitable institutional framework for the activities of individuals; and the provision of basic health and education services and of basic communications. (Bauer, 1984, p. 28)

That these tasks have so rarely been fulfilled by many Third World states, provides a measure of what still needs to be done to promote social capability from a liberal point of view. But how the different states we observed can be made to undertake these tasks, and not indulge in the predatoriness commonly found, remains an open question. For whatever the contemporary imperatives which may have forced many Third World states to embrace economic liberalism – however reluctantly – if their inherent character has not altered, they will be open to the siren voices of new forms of mercantilism in the future. How to tie a reluctant Ulysses to the mast remains the most important unsettled question of political economy.

Notes

* Paper prepared for Korea Development Institute's 20th Anniversary Symposium, July 1991.

1. The principal authors of the country volumes are as follows. These volumes are currently in press with the publishers' names given in brackets:

   Malawi and Madagascar by Frederic Pryor, Oxford, 1991.
   Egypt and Turkey by Bent Hansen, Oxford, 1991.
   Sri Lanka and Malaysia by Henry Bruton, Oxford, 1992.
   Indonesia and Nigeria by D. Bevan, P. Collier and J. Gunning, Oxford (in press).
   Thailand and Ghana by O.A. Meesook, D. Rimmer and G. Edgren, Pergamon (in press).
   Brazil and Mexico by A. Maddison and Associates, Oxford, 1992.
   Costa Rica and Uruguay by S. Rottenberg, C. Gonzales-Vega and E. Favaro, Oxford (in press).
   Colombia and Peru by A. Urdinola, M. Carrizossa and R. Webb (mimeo, World Bank, Latin American Dept., 1990).
   Five Small Economies (Hong Kong, Singapore, Malta, Jamaica, Mauritius) by R. Findlay and S. Wellisz, Oxford (in press).

   In addition, a collection of essays has been produced:

   G. Pscaharopoulous (ed.): *Essays on Poverty, Equity and Growth, Pergamon, 1991.*

   Finally, the synthesis volume by Lal and Myint (1991) is currently being prepared for publication. This paper is based in large part on this draft synthesis volume.
2. These costs of doing business are part of transactions costs. On their importance in the evolution of institutions as well as determining the historical evolution of Western economies, see Williamson (1979, 1985) and North (1981).
3. See the debate between Scott, Eisner and Bradford on the proper accounting procedures for depreciation in the September 1990 issue of the *Journal of Economic Literature.*
4. The term 'predatory' reflects the symbiotic relationship between the State and its citizens, as in the predator-prey models of the natural world. Though self-seeking, a predator is concerned to some extent with the welfare of the prey, which provides it with its food supply!
5. Of our land-abundant countries, except for the top performers (Thailand and Malaysia), all the rest had 'U' or inverted 'U' shaped time paths of real wages.
6. Schumpeter (1954) lists three basic principles of Gladstonian finance:

   (1) Retrenchment means that 'the most important thing is to remove fiscal obstructions to private activity. And for this, it is necessary to keep public expenditure low.'

(2) Neutrality implies 'raising the revenue that would still have to be raised in such a way as to deflect economic behavior as little as possible from what it would have been in the absence of all taxation.' (3) Balance refers to the principle of the balanced budget, or rather, since debt is to be reduced, 'the principle that Robert Low ... embodied in his definition of a minister of finance: 'an animal that ought to have a surplus' (pp. 403–5).

References

Aggarwal, R. (1983), 'Price Distortions and Growth in Developing Countries,' World Bank Staff Working Paper, No. 575, Washington, DC: World Bank, 1983

Anderson, D. (1990), 'Investment and Economic Growth', *World Development*, **18**.

Arrow, K.J. (1962), 'The Economic Implications of Learning by Doing,' *Review of Economic Studies*, **29**.

Bardhan, P. (1989), 'The New Institutional Economics and Development Theory: A Brief Critical Assessment,' *World Development*, **17**, 9.

Barro, R. (1991), 'Economic Growth in a Cross Section of Countries,' *Quarterly Journal of Economics*, **CVI**, 2.

Barry, B. (1978), *Sociologists, Economists and Democracy*, Chicago.

Bauer, B. (1984), *Reality and Rhetoric: Studies in the Economics of Development*, London: Weidenfeld and Nicholson.

Benhabib, J. and B. Jovanovic (1991), 'Externalities and Growth Accounting,' *American Economic Review*, **81**, 1.

Brennan, G. and J.M. Buchanan (1980), *The Power to Tax*, Cambridge.

Fisher, I. (1930), *The Theory of Interest*, New York.

Gray, J. (1984), *Hayek on Liberty*, Oxford: Blackwell.

Harberger, A.C. (1987), 'Neutral Taxation,' in Eatwell et al. (eds), *The New Palgrave*, London: Macmillan.

Hayek, F. (1960), *The Constitution of Liberty*, London: Routledge.

Heckscher, H. (1955), *Mercantilism*, 2 vols, 2nd rev. edn., London: Allen and Unwin.

Henderson, P.D. (1986), *Innocence and Design – The Influence of Economic Ideas on Policy*, Oxford: Blackwell.

Johnson, H.G. (1964), 'Towards a Generalized Capital Accumulation Approach to Economic Development,' in OECD, *The Residual Factor and Economic Growth*, Paris.

Kaldor, N. (1957), 'A Model of Economic Growth,' *Economic Journal*, **67**.

Krueger, A.O. (1977), 'Growth, Distortions and Patterns of Trade Among Many Countries,' *Princeton Studies in International Finance*, no. 40, Princeton, New Jersey.

Lal, D. (1985), *The Poverty of 'Development Economics'*, Cambridge, MA: Harvard University Press.

Lal, D. (1987), 'The Political Economy of Economic Liberalization,' *World Bank Economic Review*, **1**, 2.

Lal, D. (1989), 'The Political Economy of Industrialization in Primary Product Exporting Economies: Some Cautionary Tales,' in N. Islam (ed.), *The Balance Between Industry and Agriculture in Economic Development, vol. 5: Factors Influencing Change*, International Economic Association, London: Macmillan.

Lal, D. (1990), 'Fighting Fiscal Privilege – Towards a Fiscal Constitution,' paper no. 7, London: Social Market Foundation.

Lal, D. and H. Myint (1991), 'The Political Economy of Poverty Equity and Growth,' mimeo, London.

Leamer, E. (1984), *Sources of International Comparative Advantage*, Cambridge, MA: MIT.

Leamer, E. (1987), 'Paths of Development in the Three Factor in Good General Equilibrium Model,' *Journal of Political Economy*, **95**, 5.

Lee, D.R. and R.D. Tollison (1988), 'Optimal Taxation in a Rent Seeking Environment,' in C.K. Rowley et al. (eds), *The Political Economy of Rent-Seeking*, Boston: Kluwer.

Lucas, R.E. (1988), 'On the Mechanics of Economic Development,' *Journal of Monetary Economics*, **94**.

Mill, J.S. (1970), *Principles of Political Economy*, in Donald Winch (ed.), London: Pelican.

Murphy, K.M., A. Shleifer and R. Vishny (1991), 'The Allocation of Talent: Implications for Growth', *Quarterly Journal of Economics*, **CVI**, 2.

Myint, H. (1985), 'Organizational Dualism and Economic Development,' *Asian Development Review*, **3**, 1.

Newberry, D. and N. Stern (eds) (1987), *The Theory of Taxation for Developing Countries*, Oxford.

North, D. (1981), *Structure and Change in Economic History*, New York.
Romer, P. (1986), 'Increasing Returns and Long Run Growth,' *Journal of Political Economy*, **94**.
Romer, P. (1987), 'Crazy Explanations for the Productivity Slowdown,' in S. Fischer (ed.), *NBER Macroeconomic Annual 1987*, Cambridge, MA: MIT.
Romer, P. (1989), 'Capital Accumulation in the Theory of Long Run Growth,' in R.J. Barro (ed.), *Modern Business Cycle Theory*, Cambridge, MA: Harvard University Press.
Schumpeter, J. (1954), *A History of Economic Analysis*, New York: Oxford University Press.
Scott, M. Fg. (1976), 'Investment and Growth', *Oxford Economic Papers*, **28**, 3.
Scott, M. Fg. (1989), *A New View of Economic Growth*, Oxford: Clarendon Press.
Stern, N. (1991), 'The Determinants of Growth', *Economic Journal*, 101 (June).
Williamson, O.E. (1979), 'Transactions Costs Economics: The Governance of Contractual Relations,' *Journal of Law and Economics*, **22**, 2.
Williamson, O.E. (1985), *The Economic Institutions of Capitalism*, NY: Free Press.

European Economic Review 29 (1985) 157–191. North-Holland

GOVERNMENT DEFICITS, THE REAL INTEREST RATE AND LDC DEBT

On Global Crowding Out*

Deepak LAL and Sweder van WIJNBERGEN

World Bank, Washington, DC 20433, USA

Received September 1984, final version received May 1985

The paper uses a three-regions model of global saving–investment balance to present a 'global crowding out' interpretation of present economic trends. The model builds on data which point to a possible shortage of savings; explosive growth of social expenditures, structural public sector deficit in North and South; changes of the age pyramid; real wage rigidity in many industrial countries.

1. Introduction

The two major aspects of the global economy clouding the future prospects of developing countries are the growth of protectionism in industrial countries and the debt crisis. Many hope that the current recovery will be sustained and will resolve these problems. In contrast with this cyclical view, this paper explores other explanations which suggest that more fundamental changes in policies in both developed and developing countries are required.

Development economics has traditionally emphasized the trade linkage between developed and developing countries. However, another emerging and important link between them is the focus of this paper: the integration of world capital markets and the explosion in commercial bank lending in the

*Valerie Kozel provided excellent research assistance, and John Fleming useful comments on a more comprehensive version of this paper which is available as a WDR VII Background Paper in Lal and Wolf (1984); that version also contains an appendix with full documentation of data sources.

The World Bank does not accept responsibility for the views expressed herein which are those of the authors and should not be attributed to the World Bank or to its affiliated organizations. The findings, interpretations, and conclusions are the results of research supported by the Bank; they do not necessarily represent official policy of the Bank. The designations employed, the presentation of material, and any maps used in this document are solely for the convenience of the reader and do not imply the expression of any opinion whatsoever on the part of the World Bank or its affiliates concerning the legal status of any country, territory, city, area, or of its authorities, or concerning the delimitation of its boundaries, or national affiliation.

1970's, stimulated by the recycling of OPEC financial surpluses arising from the two oil price shocks.

The problems of protectionism and debt are in turn linked to certain longer term trends and 'structural' weaknesses of developed and developing countries which have been exposed by the supply shocks of the 1970's. These are the possibility of an emerging global shortage of savings; the explosive growth in social expenditures in most OECD countries; a fiscal problem of prospective structural public sector deficits in both developed and developing countries associated with certain 'structural' features: the aging of the population in developed and its 'greening' in developing countries; the real wage resistance of workers in many industrial countries.

In the first part of the paper we chart these trends and structural weaknesses and their interrelationships; in the second part we present a simple three-region model of global saving–investment balance. In a theoretical analysis of the model we show that deficit financed increases in OECD government expenditure will always lead to a deterioration of the LDC terms of trade. If there is crowding out there will also be an increase in world interest rates. Since LDC's are net borrowers, such an increase inflicts further welfare losses on LDC's, in addition to static welfare losses due to the adverse intratemporal terms-of-trade deterioration. The model was then calibrated with data over the 1970's. The model is largely intended to illustrate our argument and to give some feel for orders of magnitude; confidence intervals around the point predictions are substantial, so precise numerical outcomes should not carry too much weight. The final part summarizes our postulated global interactions.

2. The building blocks

1.1. Trends in OECD real wages, social expenditures and fiscal deficits

The deteriorating economic performance of the global economy and the industrialized countries in particular is well documented [see OECD (1983)]. Two 'structural' aspects of industrialized economies were exposed by the supply shocks of the 1970's: first, the expected real wage growth workers were willing to enforce at the cost of a declining share of profits since the late 1960's; second, the increasing commitments made by governments to various groups to subverse their notions of social justice.

Both features reflected some common assumptions underlying public policy in the post-war decades. A common belief was that, except for minor recessions which could be smoothed by suitable demand management policies, the post-war boom would be unending. This would allow both increases in real wages and social expenditures to be financed without any difficult choices having to be made about the tradeoffs between wages and profits, or consumption and investment [see Crosland (1950) for the classic statement of this view]. Increasingly, since the 1960's, micro-economic interventions (industrial subsidies, regional subsidies, and in the 1970's various forms of protectionism) to maintain workers in particular occupations and locations at income levels above their value marginal product were justified as a legitimate tradeoff between 'economic security' and economic growth. [For a rough quantification of the micro-economic distortions for Europe see Curzon-Price (1982).]

The supply shocks of the 1970's and the universal slowing down of productivity growth in the OECD countries, exposed the unreality of these assumptions and the unviability of the policies they had engendered. The most obvious and best analyzed was the discrepancy between the real wage workers expected and the 'full employment wage' which had been lowered by both the terms-of-trade losses suffered by the OECD countries in the 1970's, as well as their worsened growth prospects due to the productivity slowdown. Sachs (1979, 1983) has shown how slowly the real wage adjusted downwards towards the new 'equilibrium' real wage in different industrial economies — particularly in Europe. The U.S. was an exception, as it succeeded in creating 20 million extra jobs in the 1970's, whereas in Western Europe employment changed by only two million. As labor supply increased markedly with the maturation of the 'baby boom' generation, the result was levels of unemployment unprecedented since the 1930's. The distortion in relative factor prices due to the relative rigidity of real wages, provided producers an incentive to substitute capital for labor [see Scott and Laslett (1978)], whilst the accompanying squeeze on profits attenuated the means to finance investment to create future employment and growth. The rise in commodity prices and the associated structural changes in the economy, moreover, led to a reduction in the 'effective' capital stock, as the expected return on capital employed in oil intensive and other raw material intensive industries declined [see Baily (1981) and Bruno (1982, 1984)].

In these circumstances, conventional demand management policies cannot avoid the transitional unemployment due to a real wage which was higher and only adjusting slowly towards that 'warranted' by the changed circumstances. For the conventional method of reducing such transitional unemployment is premised on the assumption that workers suffer from some money illusion, and therefore by boosting demand and the inflation rate, a lower real wage and unemployment rate can be obtained. However, with the disappearance of money illusion there is no long-run tradeoff and possibly not even a short-run one between inflation and unemployment. The increased labor militancy in Europe in the late 1960's illustrated by the explosion in money wages in the 1964–1970 period, particularly in west European countries [see fig. 1 and Phelps-Brown (1983), Sachs (1979), Soskice (1978)] at a time when productivity was slowing down, can be taken

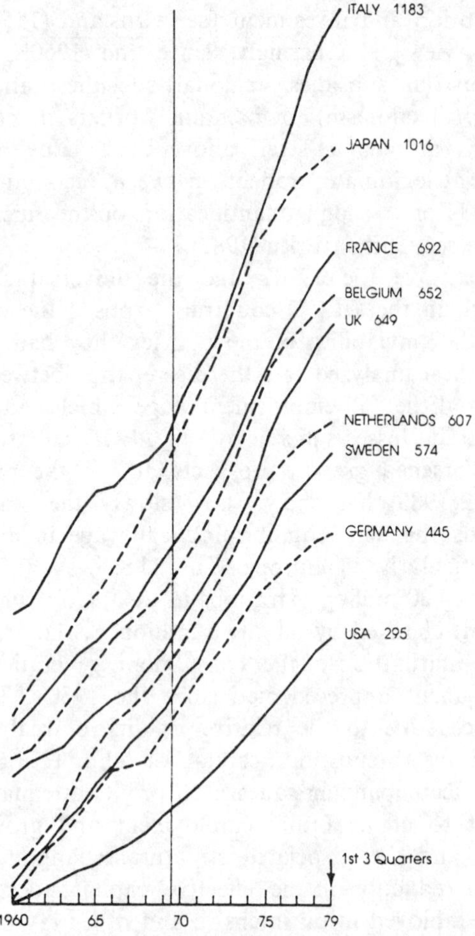

Fig. 1. The origins of trade union power. Rise of hourly rates or earnings, mostly in manufacturing, in nine countries of OECD, 1960–1979, showing change in rate of rise about 1969–1970. [Ratio scale: number at end of each curve gives hourly rates or earnings in 1979 (average of first 3 quarters) as relative to 1960 = 100.] *Source*: Phelps-Brown (1983).

as a sign that, with rising inflation, workers' money illusion had progressively disappeared. The resulting unemployment can then be ascribed to the relative rigidity of real wages rather than a lack of effective demand.

The social commitments of governments posed equally serious problems. Whilst their level and coverage could have been justified on the basis of the growth expectations of the post-World War II golden age,[1] the worsening prospects in the 1970's required some downwards adjustment — even with unchanged social preferences. Instead, until the late 1970's, social ex-

[1]For a comparative analysis of this period over time and space, see Maddison (1982).

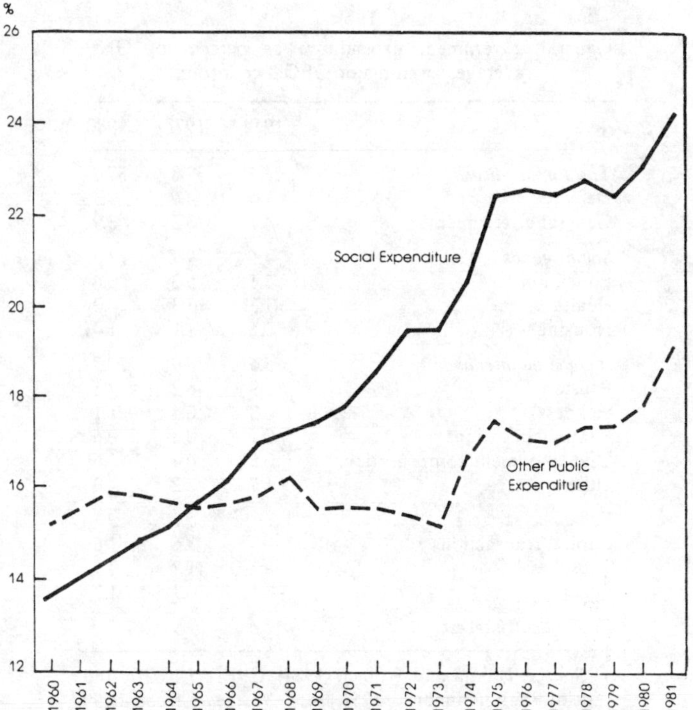

Fig. 2. The growth of social expenditure and other public expenditure: 1960–1981 (averages for the seven major OECD countries). *Source*: Wallich and Hakim (1984) from OECD.

penditures grew rapidly (due to improved levels of benefits) in most OECD countries [see fig. 2 and table 1, and Hakim and Wallich (1984) for a summary of the evidence]. Following the recent project evaluation literature [Little–Mirrlees (1974), Lal (1974, 1980)] a 'critical consumption level' of income can be defined at which a marginal increase in publicly funded income transfers are considered socially as valuable as a marginal change in public revenue. The worsened growth prospects of the 1970's required a downwards adjustment in this critical consumption level. The net effects of both a real wage and critical consumption level higher than warranted by the new circumstances, is a socially suboptimal consumption–savings balance for the economy, requiring a premium on domestic savings.

Instead, this emergence of suboptimal savings also saw the growth of large fiscal deficits in many OECD countries (see fig. 3). The decomposition of these deficits into their cyclical and structural components is controversial, as it requires a judgment on the current (not historical) natural rate of unemployment. However, even in terms of conventional accounting, in the 1980's, the fiscal deficits in some OECD countries (particularly in the U.S.)

Table 1
General government expenditure as percent of GNP; average, seven major OECD countries.[a]

	1954	1973	1980
Total expenditure	28.5	32.8	37.7
Defense	*9.6*	*4.0*	*3.3*
General government	4.7	3.5	3.9
Social goods	*4.9*	*9.7*	*11.1*
Education	3.1	5.3	5.4
Health	1.3	3.3	4.3
Housing	0.5	1.1	1.4
Income maintenance	*5.6*	*10.0*	*12.3*
Pensions	2.9	6.2	7.6
Sickness	0.3	0.4	1.1
Family allocations	0.7	0.8	0.6
Unemployment compensation	0.5	0.4	2.6
Other	1.7	2.2	4.0
Economic services		*6.2*	*3.7*
Capital transactions	—	3.6	1.6
Subsidies	—	1.7	0.9
Other	—	0.9	1.2
Public debt interest	*1.6*	*1.9*	*2.9*

[a]*Source*: Hakim and Wallich (1984), CPE/WP1(82)1, and World Bank Estimates. 1954 from *National Accounts of OECD Countries, 1950–1968*, supplemented as follows: 1954 welfare state expenditures for European countries from J.F. Dewhurst and Associates, *Europe's Needs and Resources* (Twentieth Century Fund, New York) 1961, pp. 313 and 336 for education, p. 383 for medical care, pp. 222 and 235, for housing, p. 391 for pensions, p. 393 for sickness and family payments, p. 386 for unemployment benefits and p. 399 for total transfer payments (including health). Japan 1954 from I. Emi, *Government Fiscal Activity and Economic Growth in Japan, 1868–1960* (Kinokuniya, Tokyo) 1963, pp. 173 and 179, and I. Ohkawa and M. Shinohara, *Patterns of Japanese Economic Development* (Yale University, New Haven, CT) 1979, pp. 372 and 378. USA 1954 from *The National Income and Product Accounts of the United States, 1929–1974*, (U.S. Dept. of Commerce, Washington, DC) pp. 94, 128 and 131.

have an increasing structural component (see fig. 4). It is to the causes and implications of these structural deficits that we now turn.

2.2. *The financing of social expenditures, budget deficits and 'crowding out'*

The implications of the rising budget deficits in OECD countries is best seen by their relationship to the gross domestic savings in the area over time.

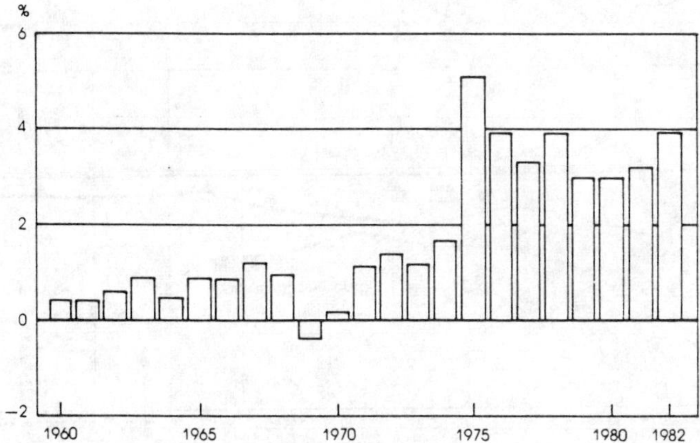

Fig. 3. Seven major OECD countries' budget deficits as % of GDP. *Source*: Hakim and Wallich (1984) from OECD.

In 1970, OECD budget deficits absorbed less than 1% of gross savings; by 1975 this had risen to 44% and by 1983 to nearly 52%. The relationship with respect to the more nebulous notion of net savings was even worse (see fig. 5). The resulting crowding out of private expenditures, particularly investment, that this public draught on available domestic savings represents is the most serious long-term trend in these countries. We explore its implications for the global savings–investment balance, and world interest rates, and thereby the effects on developing countries in the next few sections.

A substitution of public for private uses of available domestic savings in itself poses no problem if the social value of these alternative uses is equated at the margin. There are some grounds, however, for questioning if this is currently the case.

2.2.1. Social expenditures

The increased pressures on budgets is due to increases in expenditure (representing improved levels of benefits as well as extensions in their coverage) in social security (public pensions) and public health provision [see OECD (1984), Hakim and Wallich (1984)]. These expenditures are the equivalent of providing public insurance for expenses incurred on private illness and the possibility of fluctuations in income over the life cycle. They thus provide wealth holders with an asset (whose 'value' is equal to the present expected value of the programmed benefits) which is a substitute for private capital in their portfolios. If these public entitlements were funded through the accumulation of public capital, whose efficiency were no worse than that of private capital, the publicly provided capital asset would purely substitute for a privately provided one in the portfolio of wealth holders. There would be no adverse effects on the overall savings–consumption

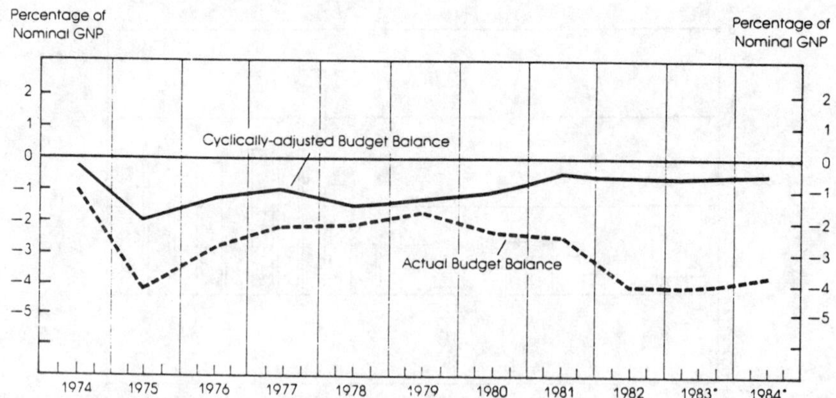

Fig. 4(a). *Source*: OECD (1983) Dec. For definitions and methods of calculations, see Annex Sources and Methods. (*OECD forecasts.)

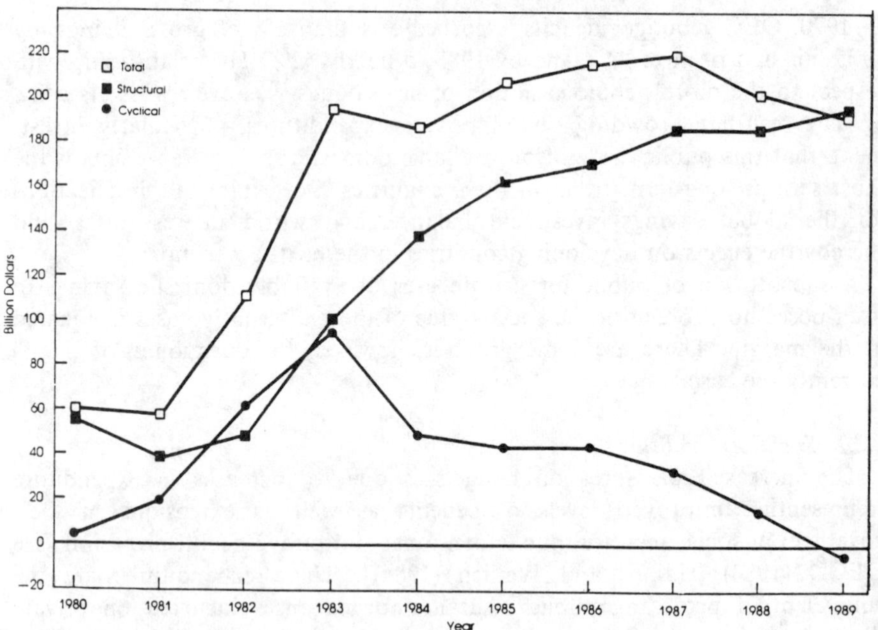

Fig. 4(b). U.S. budget deficit. *Source*: Council of Economic Advisors Report (1984).

balance, the long-run capital stock and intertemporal welfare of the economy.

However, most of these social-insurance-type expenditures in OECD countries are funded through 'pay as you go' schemes, which tax current workers, in order to provide transfers of entitlements to the old and the sick.

The reduction in the privately held capital for these insurance purposes is not then matched by any offsetting capital accumulation by the government. It can be shown [see Johnson (1981) among others] that 'pay as you go' social security systems can substitute for physical capital in private portfolios and thus reduce the long-run equilibrium capital stock, if the size of bequests left by one generation to the next is not subject to economic choice and each generation does not put the same weight on its children's welfare as on its own. If, however, each family is linked to the infinite future because of an altruistic concern for their children, who in turn are concerned about the welfare of their children..., then in effect we have a one consumer 'infinite horizon' model of the choice of the optimal intertemporal time path of consumption. Once this is chosen — given technology and tastes — a government-enforced intertemporal transfer will have no effect on the optimal choices of these infinitely lived consumers (if capital markets are efficient). Private actions will completely offset public ones to yield the same intertemporal outcomes with or without a 'pay as you go' insurance scheme.

However, there may be various reasons why this link between the present and the infinite future maybe snapped: e.g., some consumers may have tastes which do not make it optimal to leave any bequest; some consumers may plan not to have any children; consumers may not care at all about the welfare of their children; there may be capital market imperfections, most importantly due to the difficulty of borrowing against human capital. Then the effect of increased social security wealth on reducing savings and thence the long-run equilibrium capital stock will be reintroduced. Unfortunately the empirical evidence on the effects of social security on savings is inconclusive [see Feldstein (1974), Thompson (1983)] but there would seem to be some support for some reduction in savings resulting from increased social security payments.

2.2.2. Bond financing of fiscal deficits

Besides this 'wealth illusion' effect on savings of recent public expenditure increases financed by taxation on the working population, there is a further reason for concern. Typically, increased expenditures are being funded in many OECD countries (particularly the U.S.A.) through bond financed budget deficits, with further distortionary effects on the savings–consumption balance in OECD countries. For, besides current taxation, there are essentially only two other ways of financing the increased social expenditures — through the seigniorage of printing money, or through bond financing and the implicit future taxes needed to pay the interest on a growing stock of public debt. It has been argued [Barro (1974), Friedman (1978)] that the effects of public spending on the consumption–investment balance in the economy is fully measured by the level of public expenditure. The form of financing, either through explicit taxation or the hidden taxes of inflation

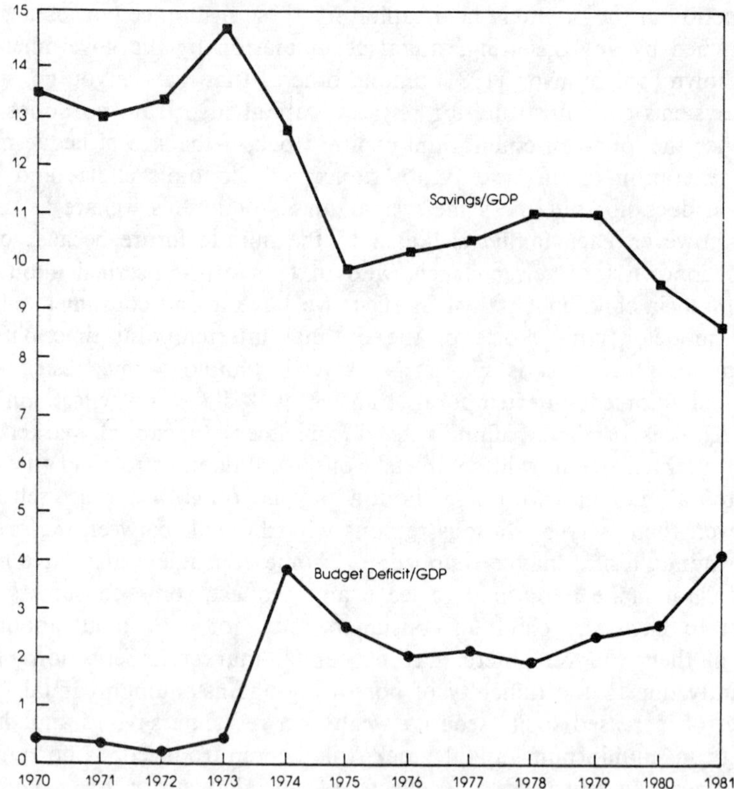

Fig. 5(a). Savings rates and budget deficits as % of GDP; OECD 1970–1981. *Source*: Hakim and Wallich (1984) from OECD National Accounts Statistics, Vol. 1.

(associated with the printing of money) or borrowing from the public (bond financing) is immaterial. This so-called Ricardian equivalence theorem concerning debt neutrality is based on assumptions very similar to those which yield the result that 'pay as you go' social security systems have no effect on the level of savings. This Modigliani–Miller theorem for public finance states that there will be no difference in the effects of tax or bond financing on savings as every wealth holder voluntarily negates the involuntary intergenerational transfer associated with bond financing by reverse changes in intergenerational bequests. As before, if for some reason this private intergenerational link is weak, or else the public suffers from some form of 'debt illusion' and considers government bonds as part of its net wealth, then the expansion of the interest-bearing public debt will lead to a substitution of bonds for real capital in their portfolios, and thence to a decline in aggregate savings and the long-run capital stock. Intertemporal *substitution* effects due to a change in the tax structure from current to future taxation may also

1. Short-Term Interest Rates
91-Day Treasury Bills

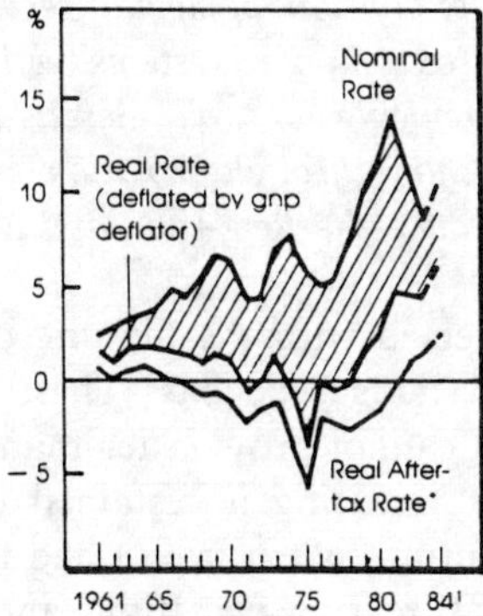

2. Long-Term Interest Rates
20-Year Government Bonds

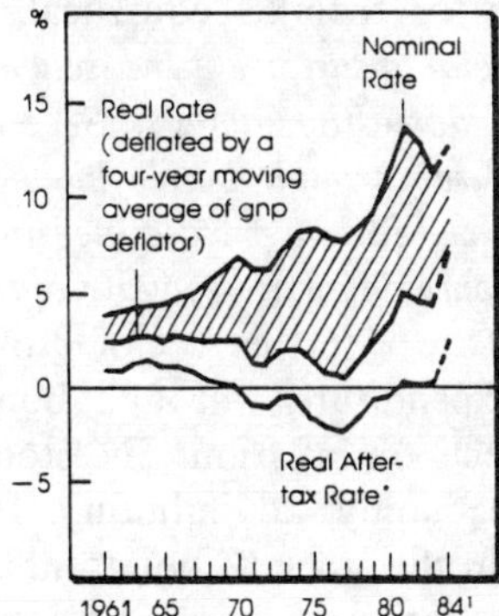

3. Inflation
Annual % Change in
Consumer Prices

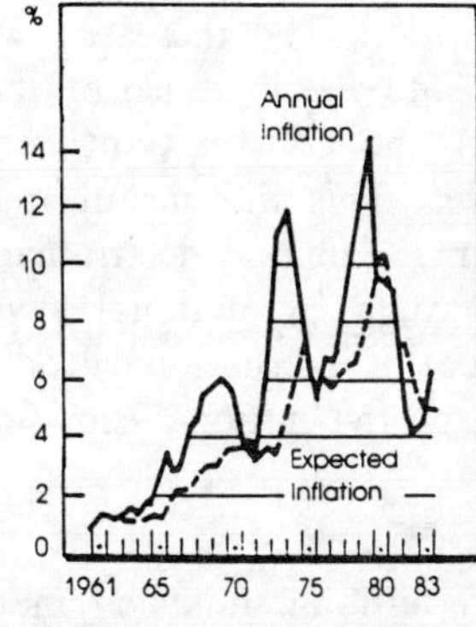

4. Federal Government
Borrowing

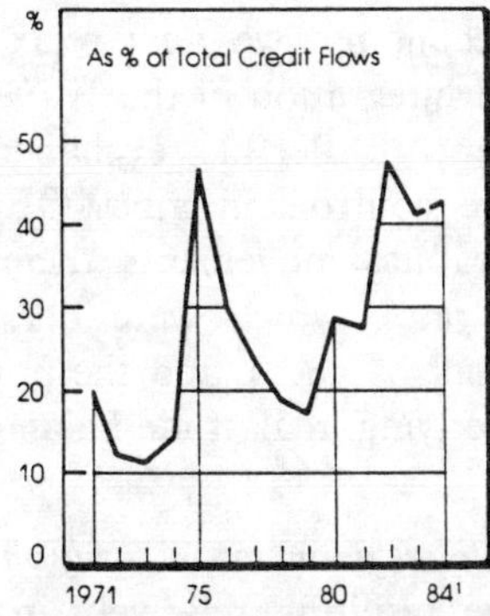

Fig. 5(b). U.S. interest rates, inflation and borrowing. *Source*: Mission Bank; Simon and Coates; Dean Witter Reynolds.
*Assuming a 35% Average Marginal Tax Rate for Bond Buyers.
[1]Forecast.

exert downward influence on private savings via its effect on the tax-inclusive intertemporal terms of trade [van Wijnbergen (1984)]. Although again the econometric evidence is equivocal, Buiter and Tobin's (1980, p. 58) conclusion on surveying it is that 'on the basis of currently available theoretical models and empirical evidence our provisional conclusion is that the case for debt neutrality is not well established'. The most recent empirical test of the hypothesis by Koskela and Viren (n.d.) for nine OECD countries for the period 1964–1979, rejects the debt neutrality hypothesis convincingly, as does our own test in the fifth part of this paper.

Thus, at this stage, we may tentatively accept two links in our chain of reasoning concerning the global economy, whilst noting that the econometric evidence for them is equivocal. *First, the expansion of social security and other social insurance type schemes in 'pay as you go' systems will tend to diminish domestic savings. Secondly, the financing of this increased public expenditure through bond financing rather than through taxation is further likely to crowd out private investment, and reduce the long-run capital stock of the economy below its socially optimal level.*

There are a further set of problems connected with the funding of higher social expenditures through bond financed budget deficits. These concern their effects on inflation. The stock of bonds cannot grow faster than the rest of the economy, ad infinitum. If the public, noticing a sustained excessive growth in the stock of bonds, anticipates a future switch from bond financing to monetization of the deficit, long term inflationary expectations and current inflation will increase [Sargent and Wallace (1981)].

2.3. The global capital market and real interest rates

The discussion up to this point, has implicitly been within the context of a closed economy; we now relax this assumption. The increased worldwide financial integration of the 1970's was aided and accompanied by the general movement to flexible exchange rates and the concomittant removal of exchange controls in most OECD countries. This has meant that in the 1970's capital movements themselves became a major determinant of exchange rates, which were determined as much by national savings and investment balances, and the portfolio choices of international lenders, as by the underlying 'real' trade balances of the respective national economies.

2.3.1. Global financial integration

In the resulting relatively integrated international financial market it is most useful for our purpose to consider a closed world economy, where (to maintain flow equilibrium) the ex ante global savings–investment imbalances are mediated through changes in world interest rates which lead to an ex post equality of global savings and investment. Furthermore, as a useful simplification we can aggregate countries into three 'regional' aggregates in the world economy — the industrialized world (OECD), the oil-exporting countries (OPEC) and the oil-importing developing countries (LDC's).

Historically, most capital flows have been from developed to developing countries. In the 1970's, however, OPEC countries emerged as major suppliers of capital to the world economy, as a result of the rise in the financial surpluses flowing from the two oil price rises in that decade. Whereas until 1974 the major sources of external capital for most developing countries were official capital transfers and direct foreign investment, the recycling of the OPEC surpluses reopened the market for commercial credit to them for the first time after their defaults in the 1930's.

Given the historically low interest rates (whose determinants we discuss below) during the mid 1970's, it was reasonable for many developing countries to finance investment, and even consumption, by foreign borrowing. The accumulated debt, however, became a problem after the second oil price shock and the unexpected tightening of monetary policy in the U.S.A. when real interest rates, instead of remaining at their previous low levels, increased to historically very high levels. This was a major cause of the debt crisis.

In explaining this divergent behavior of real interest rates after the two oil shocks it is important to chart the trends in global savings and investment balances in the 1970's, as well as in the three regions, as there have been important changes in their capital importing and exporting status during the 1970's.

These changing regional balances between savings and investment in turn reflect the effects of particular public policies, primarily fiscal and monetary policies. Table 2, provides a rough indication of regional and global savings during the 1970's.

2.3.2. *Trends and determinants of world interest rates*

What explains the behavior of real interest rates during the 1970's? In a perfectly competitive economy, where all taxes were lump sum and there was no money illusion, the real interest rate on financial assets would equal (i) the cost of capital to the firm and thence the marginal productivity of capital, and (ii) the real return to savers. If the underlying technology (marginal productivity) and tastes (rates of time preference and degrees of risk aversion) remained unchanged, then the nominal interest rate would rise by the rate of inflation leaving the real rate of interest unchanged (Fisher neutrality of inflation on interest rates).

There are, however, various aspects of the interaction of existing income and corporate taxes with inflation which work against the Fisher neutrality hypothesis. Generally, inflation distorts the measurement of profits, interest payments and capital gains. The provision in most income tax codes for the deduction of mortgage interest and other nominal interest payments to derive taxable income introduces a bias towards the expansion of consumer debt and increased demand for housing and against physical capital formation during an inflation. The corporate tax treatment of depreciation, limiting it to the original or 'historic cost' of the firm's capital stock causes the effective tax rate on corporate income to rise with inflation, as the real value of depreciation allowances is reduced. Similarly, firms which use FIFO inventory accounting will be reporting mythical profits with inflation, as they will be deducting the acquisition and not, the replacement cost of inventories.

Table 2
Domestic savings ratios — by region and total — LDC, OECD, OPEC.[a]

	LDC $S_{i\,LDC}$	OECD $S_{i\,OECD}$	OPEC $S_{i\,OPEC}$	Total $S_{i\,Total}$
1950				
1951				
1952		15.0		
1953		15.6		
1954		16.2		
1955		16.7		
1956		17.3		
1957		17.3		
1958		16.4		
1959		16.9		
1960		17.4		
1961		17.7		
1962		17.8		
1963		18.0		
1964	14.4	18.5		
1965	15.4	18.7		
1966	14.9	18.5		
1967	15.4	18.1		
1968	15.8	18.3		
1969	16.7	18.9		
1970	16.6	19.4		
1971	15.9	19.8		
1972	16.8	20.4	45.1	20.2
1973	17.3	21.4	47.8	21.2
1974	15.7	19.8	71.7	20.7
1975	16.5	19.4	56.8	20.0
1976	19.0	18.8	61.7	20.0
1977	18.9	19.2	56.1	20.2
1978	19.0	20.6	47.7	21.0
1979	19.4	20.2	58.5	21.1
1980	19.0	19.5	65.4	20.8
1981		19.4	55.5	

[a]*Source*: Lluch (1984).

[See Feldstein (1983) for these and other arguments.] For all these institutional reasons, the Fisher neutrality hypothesis may not hold.

The historical evidence [surveyed for instance for the U.S. in Summers (1983), for short-term interest rates] does not support Fisher neutrality. But nor does it support the Feldstein position unequivocally. Nominal interest rates have exhibited both greater than and less than unitary response to inflation in different periods.

Wilcox (1983) has attempted to develop and test a model for U.S. short-term rates for the period 1952–1979, in order to explain the low rates in the early 1970's, and mutatis mutandis the higher rates in the late 1970's. He emphasizes the important interactions between the supply shocks flowing from the changing relative prices of primary commodities (particularly energy) and changes in expected rates of inflation during the post-war decades.

The energy shock's main effect was to reduce the net demand for capital, as many studies [e.g., Hudson and Jorgenson (1978)] have found empirically that energy and capital are 'cooperative' in production. This is also borne out by the dramatic fall in the growth rate of investment and its share of total output in industrial countries after relative energy prices rose by about 60% in 1973. Thus, ceteris paribus, the negative supply shocks of the 1970's would have reduced real interest rates.

By contrast, till 1973, the industrial countries were faced with a positive supply shock flowing from a fall in the relative price of primary commodities, mainly energy. Between 1950 and 1970, for instance, the relative price of Saudi crude declined by 55%. This put upward pressure on the real interest rate as the positive supply shock would ceteris paribus raise the net demand for capital.

Against this, the steady and unexpected rise in the inflation rate put downward pressure on real interest rates. The net effect was dominated by the positive effect of the favorable supply shock, and so there was a marginal rise in real interest rates. In the 1970's the negative supply shock reinforced the downward pressure on real interest rates flowing from an unexpected acceleration in the inflation rate. So real interest rates became negative.

To these factors we need to add the shifts in global savings balances that occurred as a counterpart to the oil price rise. The rise in OPEC savings was matched by falls in savings in the other two regions, so that there was no marked deterioration in the overall global savings rate; but as there was a shift in the international distribution of income towards a region with a higher ex ante savings rate, this in itself would ceteris paribus have put downward pressure on real interest rates.

But that was not all, in many industrialized countries particularly the U.K. and U.S., there was an inflationary explosion, which yielded substantial revenue from the inflation tax to cover the public sectors' borrowing requirements. Public debt holders were particularly hit hard by this inflationary tax. In the U.K. the public debt in real terms was reduced by half (public debt to GDP ratio was 95% in 1970 and 58% in 1979), even when nominal debt was rising to cover the actual public sector deficit [see Hakim and Wallich (1984)]. As governments were able to extort the inflation tax from bondholders in the mid 1970's it would appear that the inflation was unanticipated by the capital markets.

Whilst these factors — a decline in the marginal product of capital, and hence demand for investment at a time when global savings did not fall markedly; an unexpected rise in the rate of inflation; the success in recycling the OPEC surpluses to finance the increased public expenditure needs of industrialized and many developing countries — all led to historically low real rates of interest, what explains their subsequent rise?

The supply factors, particularly changes in the real price of energy in the early 1980's and other primary commodities exerted a favorable supply shock in OECD countries, which ceteris paribus could have been expected to raise real interest rates. In addition, the disinflationary policies which most industrial countries had to pursue meant that inflation fell unexpectedly, and this would also ceteris paribus have put upward pressure on real interest rates. But there was a third factor which though speculative, may be of some importance, namely that the inflationary expropriation of bondholders in the 1970's reduced (if it did not completely remove) money illusion in capital markets. Thus from fig. 5b it would appear that until 1980 expected inflation in the U.S. was below the actual, but this pattern has since been reversed. This has meant that subsequently the actual budget deficits (particularly in the U.S. and U.K.) could not be financed by the inflation tax. But this in turn means money would have to remain tight, putting further upward pressure on short-term rates. Meanwhile the loose fiscal policy reflected in large budget deficits would need to be financed through borrowing. The resulting 'crowding out' of private expenditures could also be expected to exert pressure on real interest rates, if for no other reason than that as the share of government debt in private portfolios rises, it will only be held at a lower price (that is higher interest rates). Moreover, taking account of the argument that bond financing of growing public expenditures may worsen expectations of future inflation, lenders fully cured of money illusion may now be including a risk premium to cover the future possibility of another inflationary upsurge, as governments unable to finance further public expenditures in the future (including an increasing interest rate burden on the growing public debt) may be forced to monetize the resulting budget deficits.

2.4. Third world debt, infrastructural investments and fiscal deficits

The final link in our chain of reasoning, concerns the public finances in developing countries, and the role of foreign borrowing in development.

Historically [see Lewis (1978)], the flow of international capital has not *necessarily* been from rich to poor countries, nor from those with high to those with low domestic savings rates. In the 19th century, per capita income was higher in the major borrowing (U.S., Australia, Argentina) than in the lending countries (U.K., France, Germany). The major determinants of foreign borrowing were differences in rates of population growth and the associated urbanization [Lewis (1978, p. 39)].

Urbanization is expensive in terms of capital because of the capital intensity of urban physical and social infrastructure, which requires both more highly priced labor as well as more capital per unit of provision than similar rural infrastructure. Because of its public goods characteristics, this infrastructure is usually publicly provided. The resulting positive link between the growth of public expenditure and urbanization is a well-documented statistical relationship in both current developed and developing countries [see Tait and Heller (1982), Lluch (1984)].

These items of public expenditure in developing countries, unlike the health and social security related ones in developed countries, are complementary to other inputs in the production process. They thus raise the long-run productivity of the economy, as compared with the pure transfer-type effects of developed country social expenditures on the health care and pensions of the 'aged'.

The financing of this expenditure need not pose a problem for the government if domestic savings are sufficient, and can be mobilized through tax revenues. Most developing countries have raised domestic savings rates steadily since the fifties [see Lluch (1984)]. The exception is Africa, where having peaked at about 15% at the end of the 1960's, domestic savings rates have collapsed in the 1970's.

Although taxes have also been raised in many developing countries, these have proved to be insufficient to meet the rise in public expenditure; which has been financed instead by covert taxation usually in the form of the 'inflation tax', particularly in Latin America [see Sjaastad et al. (1984), and Harberger and Edwards (1980)].

The opening up of the commercial loan markets to developing countries in the late 1960's, and the availability of cheap and plentiful commercial credit after the 1973–1974 oil price rise allowed a rising proportion of their growing public expenditure and incipient fiscal deficits (particularly in Latin America) to be financed by commercial borrowing rather than the inflation tax [see Sjaastad et al. (1984)]. With low and even negative rates of interest on the loans, it was not imprudent to borrow to finance even public consumption as the real rates of interest were likely to have been below the country's social rate of time preference, assuming that the decision was based on taking adequate account of risk and future ability to repay the loans. Although there was undoubtedly some waste involved in the public investments financed by foreign borrowing, by and large much of the public investment is likely to have had social rates of return above the real cost of borrowing [see Sachs (1981)].

Problems arose because most of the borrowing was made by countries with weak fiscal systems through commercial bank loans of short maturity and with a floating rate of interest. If the world environment had been stable and real interest rates had remained at their mid 1970's levels, or the government had had complete fiscal control, the uses (on long gestation projects or on consumption) to which the borrowed funds were put could have been justified. If the loans could be rolled over (as they were for a time) at relatively low real interest rates, both public consumption and, of course, investment would have been justified, even if the government's fiscal powers were weak.

The changes in world capital markets in the late 1970's, however, exposed the fiscal weaknesses in the major borrowing countries. The liquidity crisis precipitated by the Mexican government's inability to continue debt service in 1982, was essentially a crisis of confidence in the ability of the *public sector* in many borrowing countries to generate the requisite net resources (through either cutting back public expenditures or raising taxation) to meet the rising cost of public debt service. The resulting rise in the incipient public sector deficits was once again financed by levying the inflation tax [see Sjaastad et al. (1984)]. At the same time attempts were made to cut back public expenditures, usually by cutting back on the infrastructural public investment which in the long run is necessary for the development of their economies.

We thus have an interrelated global economy where the financing of public expenditures in both developed and developing country impinges on the pool of global savings and thus world interest rates. The next part formalizes and integrates this aspect of global interactions with the conventional inter-relationships through the terms of trade between developed and developing countries.[2]

3. A model of global crowding out

3.1. Model description

3.1.1. Model structure and estimation results

We use a simple three-region–three-commodity model with each region completely specialized in the production of its 'own' good. The three regions are OPEC, which only produces oil, and the OECD and LDC's, each of which produce a final good consumed by all others. There is, by assumption, no direct consumption of oil and no use of oil at all in OPEC itself, but LDC's and the OECD use oil as a factor of production.

(*a*) *The OECD.* Consider first the OECD block of the model. With Cobb–Douglas technology we can write output supply (measured by GDP) as a function of the real product wage *WOE*, the real price of oil in terms of OECD goods, *PROIL*, the capital stock *KOE* and the rate of technological

[2]A referee has also pointed out that developing countries were by and large residual clients of the banking system. This has meant that whilst they gained from the supply-induced lending after the first oil shock, they were cut off as soon as the money market became a seller's one again. This marginal position would also help to explain the strength of the 'crowding out' effect on developing countries documented in the next part of this paper.

progress ρ:

$$XOE = CO^{e\rho t} WOE^{C1} PROIL^{C2} KOE^{C3}. \tag{1}$$

Estimation of (1) after taking log differences gives[3]

$$\underset{}{\Delta \log XOE} = -\underset{(0.47)}{0.14}\Delta \log WOE - \underset{(1.28)}{0.03}\Delta \log PROIL + \underset{(0.47)}{0.02}\Delta \log KOE + \underset{(2.42)}{0.038},$$

$$r^2 = 0.301.$$

The derived demand for oil imports, *OILOE*, can be similarly derived and will depend on output and the real price of oil in terms of OECD goods,

$$OILOE = e^{C21} \times XOE^{C22} \times PROIL^{C23}, \tag{2}$$

which, when estimated in loglinear form, gives:

$$\log(OILOE) = \underset{(1.39)}{4.65} + \underset{(2.31)}{0.49} \times \log XOE - \underset{(6.18)}{0.20} \times \log PROIL,$$

$$r^2 = 0.891.$$

Neither equation presents surprises. Output depends negatively on real product wages and the real price of oil and positively on the capital stock; the rate of technological progress is estimated at 3.8%, not an unreasonable number. Real oil imports depends positively on output but negatively on the real price of oil.

Real tax revenues are a function of real output,

$$TAX = -\underset{(2.03)}{213519} + \underset{(12.7)}{0.23} \times XOE, \tag{3}$$

$$r^2 = 0.953.$$

Private consumption depends on the real interest rate and real disposable income. This is the first place where crowding-out issues arise. If the private sector is completely indifferent between different ways of financing the deficit, i.e., if a strong version of the Ricardo equivalence theorem holds, disposable income equals income minus government expenditure, giving rise to the following consumption function:

[3]The figures in brackets are *t* statistics. It should be noted that the insignificant and low value of the log *KOE* parameter reflects the productivity slowdown in the 1970's. As a result, the implicit production function for OECD countries estimated above cannot be used to make projections into the future.

$$PCON = -28717 + 0.85 \times YDNC + 7779 \times RRATE, \quad \text{(4-NCO)}$$
$$\qquad (0.86)\ (11.7) \qquad\qquad (0.77)$$

$$r^2 = 0.961,$$

where *PCON* is real personal consumption, *GCON* and *GINV* are real government consumption and investment respectively, *RRATE* is the real interest rate and NCO stands for No Crowding Out, and disposable income *YDNC* equals GDP plus interest earnings on foreign assets minus government expenditure,

$$YDNC = XOE + RRATE \times FAROE(-1) - GCON - GINV - OIL \times PROIL.$$

If however the private sector does *not* recognize that bond issues give rise to future tax liabilities with a discounted value equal to the value of the issue, *then* a proper measure of disposable income is income minus tax revenues, giving rise to the following private consumption equation:

$$PCON = -433675 + 0.86 \times YDC + 11442 \times RRATE, \quad \text{(4-CO)}$$
$$\qquad (-1.8)\ (17.1) \qquad\qquad (1.7)$$

$$r^2 = 0.981,$$

where CO stands for Crowding Out.

Here disposable income is defined as

$$YDC = XOE + RRATE \times FAROE(-1) - TAX - OIL \times PROIL.$$

This suggests a natural test of whether there is crowding out or not: by including income minus government expenditure (*YDNC*) *and* government expenditure minus tax revenues in the equation, (4-NCO) and (4-CO) become special cases: if the coefficient on the government deficit equals *zero* (4-NCO) is relevant, but if it equals the coefficient of *YDNC*, (4-CO) comes out. In other words if the coefficient is not significantly different from zero, crowding out is not a problem; if it is not significantly different from the coefficient of *YDNC*, crowding out *is* a problem. The results when we ran this regression were

$$PCON = -509700 + 0.85 \times YDNC + 1.72 \times (GCON + GINV - TAX)$$
$$\qquad (2.43)\ (19.7) \qquad\qquad (3.67)$$

$$+ 15938 \times RRATE, \quad (5)$$
$$(2.48)$$

$$r^2 = 0.989.$$

Clearly the coefficient on the deficit is significantly larger than zero but not significantly different from the coefficient of $YDNC$ at normal confidence levels (for example, 5%). This clearly demonstrates that crowding out *is* a problem, *the data do not support the Ricardo equivalence theorem.*

We could finish the OECD block by running an investment equation, and derive the current account as the difference between aggregate savings and investment; instead we choose to go the other way around and use a current account (CA) equation which will, after the appropriate substitutions, give us investment.[4]

In the No Crowding Out case, the CA is independent of the government deficit. We accordingly ran the following equation:

$$\begin{aligned} CAROE = & \underset{(0.67)}{-6916} + \underset{(1.2)}{0.023} \times XOE + \underset{(1.74)}{4998} \times RRATE \\ & \underset{(3.00)}{-158047} \times PROIL, \end{aligned} \tag{6-NC}$$

$$r^2 = 0.666,$$

which shows a positive dependence on the real interest rate and GDP, and a strong negative dependence on the real price of oil (in terms of OECD goods).

The Crowding Out version should depend on the deficit, which gives us an equation like the following:

$$\begin{aligned} CAROE = & \underset{(0.09)}{11128} + \underset{(0.91)}{0.03} \times YDC + \underset{(1.02)}{4056} \times RRATE \\ & \underset{(0.44)}{+0.11}(TAX - GCON - GINV) - \underset{(2.17)}{137188} \times PROIL, \end{aligned} \tag{6-CO}$$

$$r^2 = 0.688.$$

Finally we have to make an assumption on the share of total OECD expenditure falling on OECD goods. We assume that investment uses OECD goods only, while the consumption share will depend on relative prices. Lack of data precluded actual estimation of (7), parameter values in (7) are based

[4]That is, using Walras' law, we have dropped the investment equation and estimated the balance of payments equation instead. This is because we are primarily interested in balance of payments impacts.

on prior beliefs.

$$ADOE = INVOE + 0.95 \times (PRLDC)^{DEOE} \times (PCON + GCON). \tag{7}$$

Investment *INVOE* can be obtained from the savings minus investment equals the current account identity,

$$INVOE = \underbrace{TAX - GCON}_{\text{(government savings)}} + \underbrace{YDC - PCON}_{\text{(private savings)}} - \underbrace{CAROE}_{\text{(current account)}}. \tag{8}$$

(*b*) *OPEC*. The OPEC part of the model is more simplified than the OECD part. In particular we do not distinguish between the government and the private sector, but look at aggregate income, savings and expenditure. OPEC sets the price of oil in terms of OECD goods, *PROIL*, as a policy variable and supplies all oil demanded at that price. Accordingly, the income equals

$$YDOPEC = PROIL \times (OILOE \times OILLDC) + RRATE \times FAROPEC(-1), \tag{9}$$

where *FAROPEC* represent the value of net claims on the rest of the world (in terms of OECD goods).

Net savings and investment behaviour is summarized in a Current Account equation,

$$CAROPEC = \underset{(0.86)}{18128} + \underset{(2.47)}{0.31} \times YDOPEC + \underset{(1.52)}{4513} \times RRATE, \tag{10}$$

$$r^2 = 0.792.$$

Simple accounting then gives us total OPEC expenditure ($YDOPEC - CAROPEC$), all of which is assumed to fall on OECD goods,

$$ADOPEC = YDOPEC - CAROPEC. \tag{11}$$

Finally, the current account equals net foreign asset accumulation,

$$FAROPEC = CAROPEC + FAROPEC(-1). \tag{12}$$

(*c*) *The LDC's*. LDC output is introduced as an exogenous trend, mainly because the lack of good factor price and capital stock data precludes explicit estimation of an aggregate supply curve. The parameters were obtained by running log of real output on a time trend; the usual t statistics do not correspond to any interesting economic hypothesis and are therefore omitted.

$$XLDC = \exp(14.3) \times \exp(0.05 \times \text{time}), \tag{13}$$

$$r^2 = 0.986.$$

The LDC current account equation performs remarkably well:

$$\begin{aligned} CAFLDC = & -\underset{(2.02)}{170559} + \underset{(3.20)}{5606} \times (RRATE - CHCORR) \\ & + \underset{(0.87)}{0.07} \times YDLDC/PRLDC - \underset{(0.74)}{42940} \times PROIL/PRLDC, \end{aligned} \tag{14}$$

$$r^2 = 0.693.$$

CAFLDC is the real CA surplus in terms of LDC goods, *YDLDC/PRLDC* is real LDC income in terms of LDC goods and *PROIL/PRLDC* is the real price of oil in terms of LDC goods. The variable *CHCORR* measures the influence of gradual relative price changes on the real cost of borrowing,

$$CHCORR = (PRLDC - PRLDC(-1)/PRLDC(-1).$$

LDC income (in terms of OECD goods) equals (13) minus real interest payments on foreign debt and minus the value of oil imports,

$$\begin{aligned} YDLDC = & \ XLDC \times PRLDC + RRATE \times FARLDC(-1) \\ & - OILLDC \times PROIL. \end{aligned} \tag{15}$$

LDC expenditure can be obtained by combining (13) and (14); we assume zero price elasticity in LDC demand for OECD goods, which, when combined with (13) and (14), gives us LDC demand for OECD goods,

$$ADLDC = SCLDC \times (YDLDC - CAFLDC \times PRLDC).$$

Oil imports are a linear function of output, time and the real price of oil.

Finally, increases in debt equal the current account deficit (or, as defined here, increases in net foreign assets equal to CA surplus),

$$FARLDC = CARLDC + FARLDC(-1). \tag{16}$$

(*d*) *Closing the model.* The two main endogenous variables are the world rate of interest and the OECD/LDC terms of trade, *RRATE* and *PRLDC*. *PRLDC* is defined as the LDC's final goods terms of trade with respect to the OECD.

The model is closed by requiring OECD goods market clearing,

$$XOE = ADOE + ADOPEC + ADLDC, \tag{17}$$

and by requiring that the world current account equals zero,

$$CAROE + CAROPEC + CAFLDC = 0. \tag{18}$$

Loosely speaking, (17) determines relative prices and (18) ties down the world interest rate.

3.1.2. *A simple diagrammatical analysis of how the model works*

After suitable substitution in the above equations we can reduce the model to two basic equations, with two variables, the real interest rate *RRATE* and the LDC/OECD terms of trade *PRLDC*.

The first equation says that the world current account should equal zero.

$$CA(\underset{(+)}{RRATE}, \underset{(-)}{PRLDC}) = 0. \tag{19}$$

Higher interest rates will lead to an ex ante world current account surplus, but higher LDC/OECD terms of trade will lead to a deficit since it implies a transfer from high to low savers. We depict that relation in a diagram with *RRATE* on the vertical axis and *PRLDC* on the horizontal one (fig. 6).

The curve, labeled CA in fig. 6, slopes upward: higher interest rates would lead to an ex ante CA surplus; a terms of trade improvement for LDC's transfers income to high spenders and pushes the world CA back down.

The second equation sets excess demand for OECD goods equal to zero (see the curve labeled GM in fig. 6),

$$GM(\underset{(-)}{RRATE}, \underset{(+)}{PRLDC}) = 0. \tag{20}$$

Higher rates push down expenditure and so lead to excess supply; higher relative prices for LDC goods will however shift demand to OECD goods and will therefore cure the excess supply. This curve therefore also slopes upwards. Stability analysis based on the assumption that an incipient CA surplus pushes down the interest rate and an excess demand for OECD goods pushes up their relative price indicates that the configuration in fig. 6

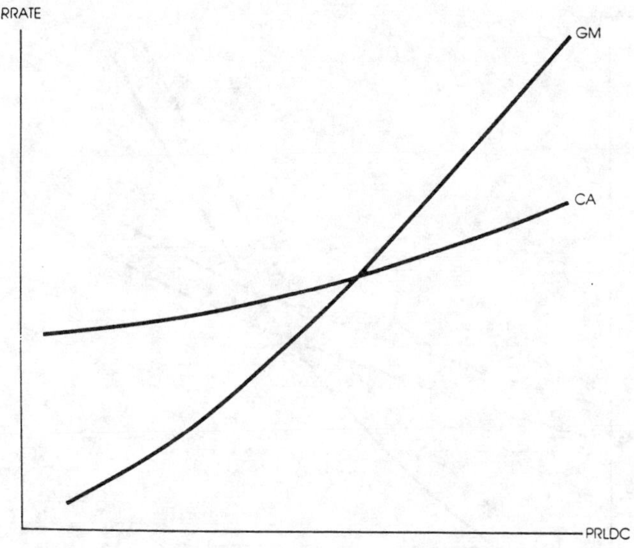

Fig. 6

(GM steeper than CA) is stable; the other case (CA steeper than GM) is not. We therefore confine our attention to the case given in fig. 6.

To get a feel for how the model works we will consider the effects of two 'shocks': an increase in government expenditure *not* financed by taxation or, similarly, a tax cut, and an increase in the real price of oil.

Consider first the deficit-financed increase in government expenditure (cf. fig. 7). An increase in government consumption leads to excess demand for OECD goods and therefore shifts the goods market locus to the left. If there is *no* crowding out, private savings will offset the increased deficit and the CA curve will *not* shift. This leads to an equilibrium with lower interest rates and deteriorated terms of trade for LDC's. *PRLDC* goes down because of incipient excess demand for OECD goods; this transfers income from low net savers (LDC's) to high net savers (OECD) and therefore leads to a fall in interest rates (point *B* in fig. 7).

However, if there *is* crowding out, if private savings are not accommodating the deficit, the world CA will have an incipient deficit which will push up interest rates (CA shifts *up*). This will, if large enough, lead to an equilibrium as at point *C*, where the world interest rate goes up *and* the LDC's terms of trade deteriorate with respect to the OECD. So in the crowding-out scenario, deficit-financed government consumption hits the LDC's twice, via both higher world interest rates and deteriorating final goods terms of trade.

This scenario looks very much like the world situation in the early 1980's.

Consider next an increase in oil prices. Higher oil prices transfer income to OPEC from LDC's and the OECD; OPEC has higher savings propensities

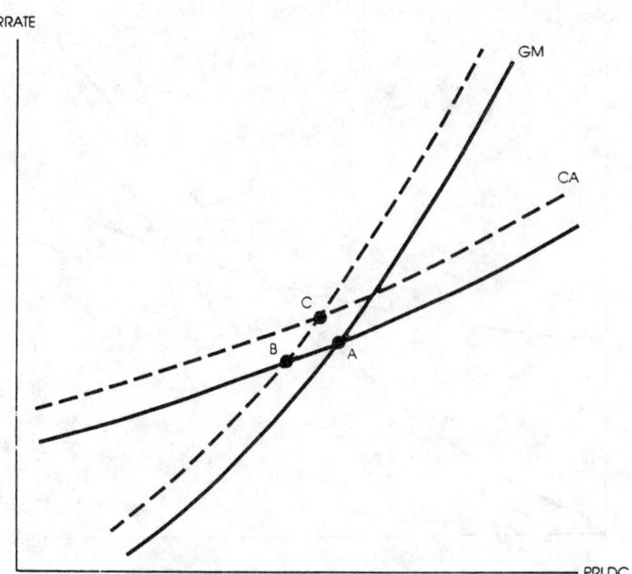

Fig. 7. Effects of deficit-financed increase in government expenditure.

than the other two groups, so there is an incipient world current account surplus: the CA curve shifts down (fig. 8). Supply in the OECD may fall more than demand (although the reverse cannot be excluded), resulting in a leftward shift of GM. If demand falls more than supply, GM shifts to the right.

The first case is given in fig. 8(a), the second in fig. 8(b).

In all cases the interest rate will fall, but the LDC/OECD final goods terms of trade may either improve or deteriorate. The first scenario seems a plausible description of the aftermath of the oil price shocks of 1973–1974.

3.2. *Simulation runs*

The base run of the model tracks the in-sample data remarkably well. (See figs. 9 and 10 which chart the actual and simulated current account surpluses of the three regions and the debt service payments of developing countries.)

We next performed two basic policy experiments with the model. In the first one, we added $400 billion (1980 US$) to aggregate government consumption in 1979 and 1980, under the assumption of *deficit financing*. In the no crowding out scenario not much happens; see figs. 11 and 12.

Private savings increases substantially to offset the increased deficit (between 7% and 8% drop in private consumption in 1978 and 1980) and a small decrease in private investment (between 6 and 7%), to accommodate the increase in government expenditure.

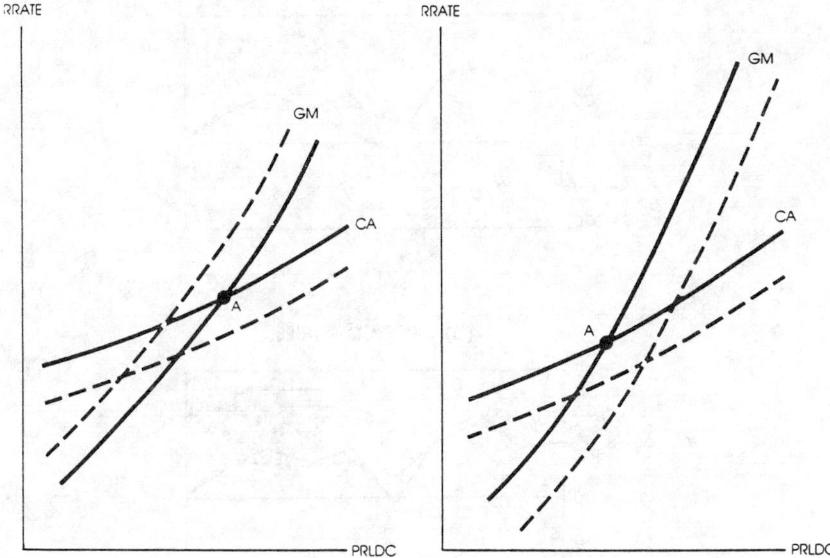

Fig. 8(a). A dominant supply effect of an oil price shock.

Fig. 8(b). Dominant demand effect of an oil price shock.

Accordingly, the CA is not really affected in either of the three countries, and no noticeable change in the interest rate or LDC interest payments on debt result.

The outcome is *very* different in the crowding out scenario however (the version of the model that was supported by our test above). Now private consumption does *not* fall, private saving does *not* accommodate the new deficit and the OECD CA accordingly swings into deficit. To bring the world current account back into equilibrium, there is a 2.9 percentage point increase in the world real interest rate in 1979 and a 2.6 percentage point increase in 1980. This leads to a dramatic fall in private investment, which falls off with a whopping 26.3% in 1979 and 25.8% in 1980. This limits the CA deterioration in the OECD to about US$30 billion in both years. There is a dramatic effect on LDC real interest payments on debt which increase by around US$24 billion in each year.

On top of that comes a small terms of trade deterioration for LDC's of about half a percent.

Similar results obtain in the simulation runs where we cut the marginal tax rate from 0.22 to 0.15 from 1971 onwards. In the no crowding out scenario there is no effect whatsoever on any variable except tax revenues, since the private sector accommodates one-for-one by saving the entire increase in disposable income.

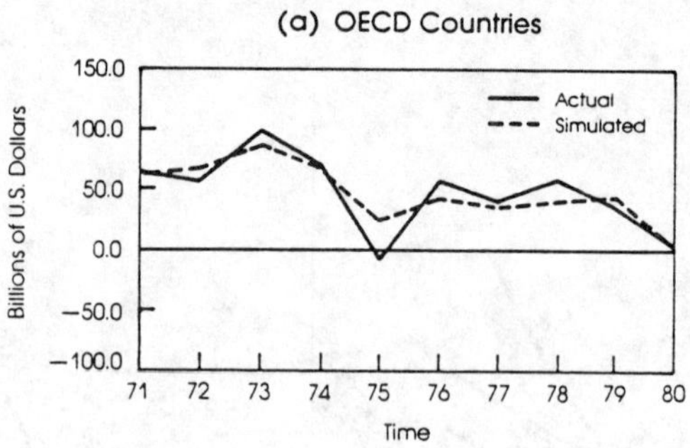

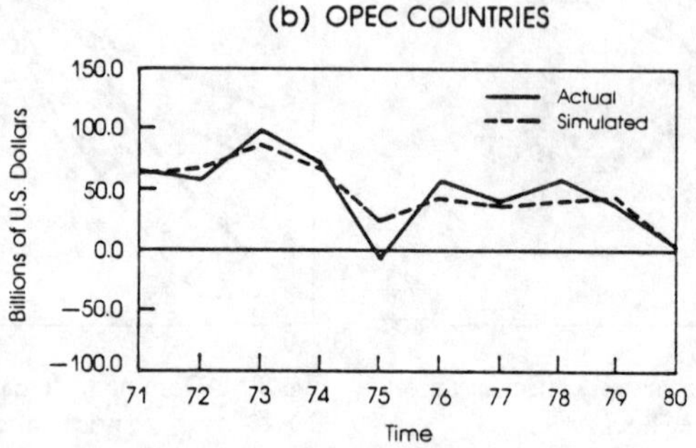

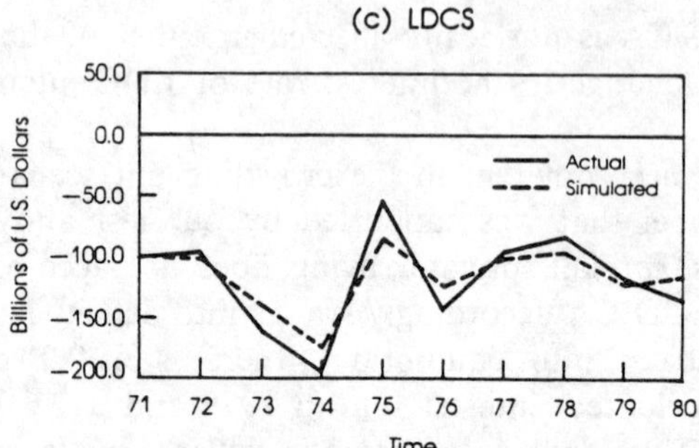

Fig. 9. Current account surpluses.

The results are very different, however, in the crowding out version. Private savings do not go up one-for-one, with the result that the government deficit increases, so that incipient CA deficits and excess demand for OECD goods develop.

The terms of trade deteriorate for LDC's (one percentage point); the real interest rate increases between two and three percentage points throughout the period (fig. 13), leading to around a $20 billion dollar increase in real interest payments for LDC's on debt. The OECD current account deficit

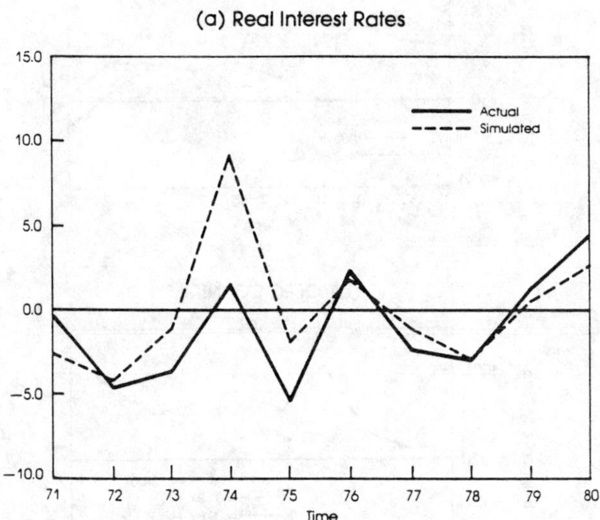
(a) Real Interest Rates
Actual
Simulated
15.0
10.0
5.0
0.0
−5.0
−10.0
71
72
73
74
75
76
77
78
79
80
Time

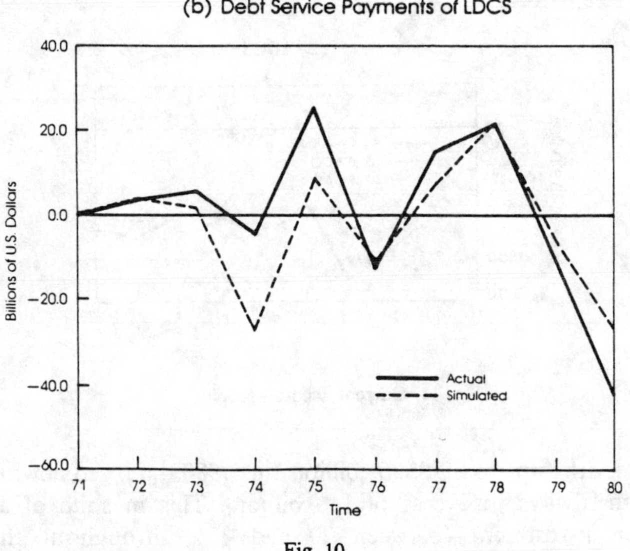
(b) Debt Service Payments of LDCS
Billions of U.S. Dollars
40.0
20.0
0.0
−20.0
−40.0
−60.0
Actual
Simulated
71
72
73
74
75
76
77
78
79
80
Time

Fig. 10

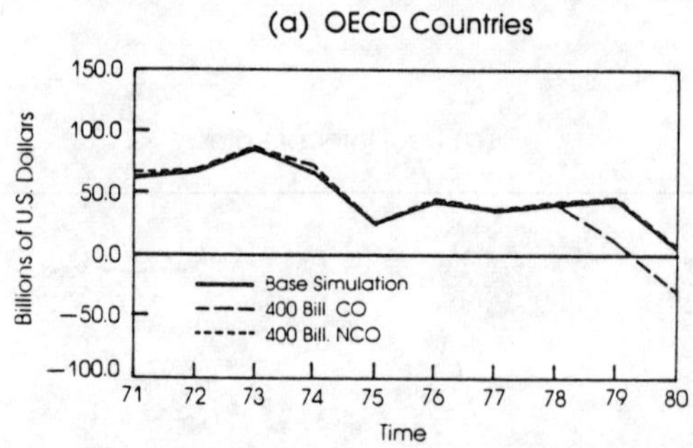

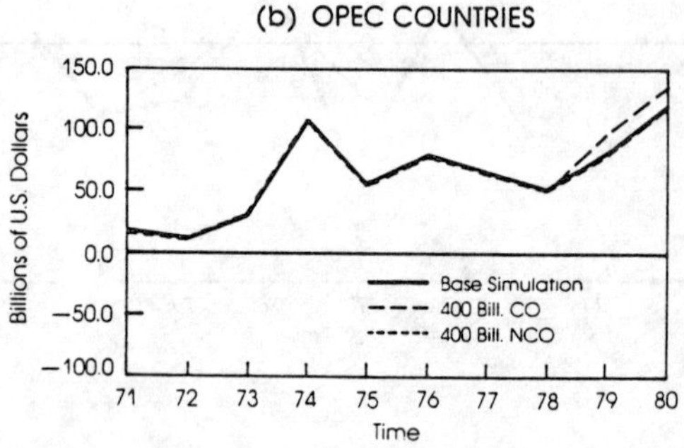

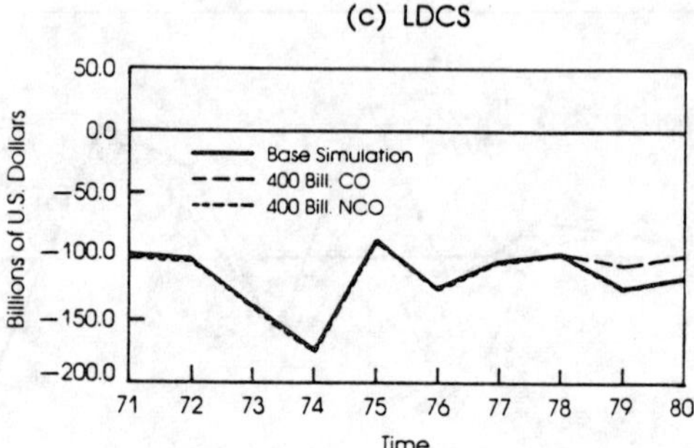

Fig. 11. Current account surpluses.

deteriorates with up to US$36 billion in 1980, and somewhat smaller amounts (but always in excess of $16 billion). This in spite of a dramatic slowdown in investment (between 20 and 30% throughout the decade) leading to a cumulative shortfall in capital accumulation of 30% (the 1980 OECD capital stock is 30% below the base-run value).

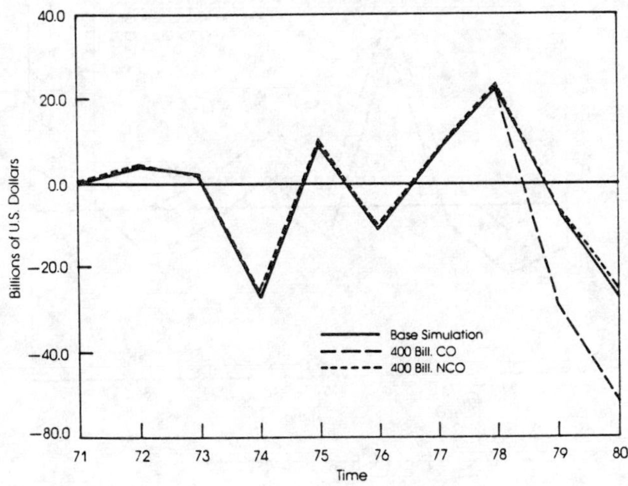

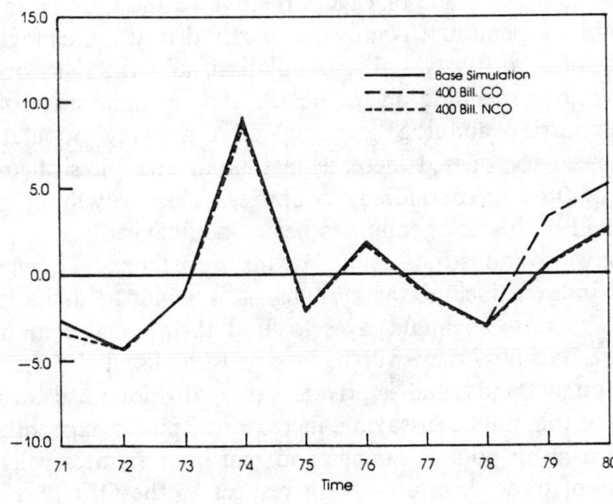

Fig. 12

4. A summary of the global interactions

We thus have arrived at the following interdependent global system, where there is a link the actions and reactions of the public sectors in both developed and developing countries through their effects on world interest

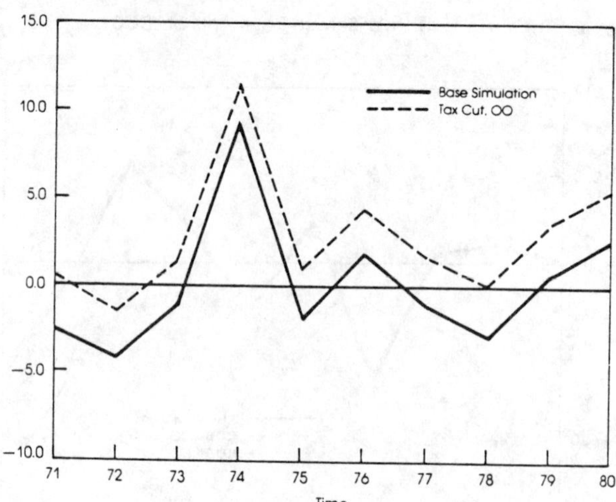

Fig. 13. Real interest rates.

rates and the terms of trade of LDC's relative to the OECD: in both sets of countries public expenditure is growing, partly driven by demographic trends — the aging of a relatively stable population, and the consequent need for increases in public spending on the health and social security of the aged in developed countries; and the 'greening' of a growing population and the consequent need for related increase in human and physical infrastructural public expenditures in developing countries. This growth in global public expenditures in both sets of countries has to be financed.

Increasingly in industrial countries tax resistance — reflected in the adoption of indexed income tax systems — is going to make it difficult for governments to raise adequate taxes to fund their social commitments. This means, ceteris paribus, they will have structural fiscal deficits. If these are financed through bonds, and if private savers do not raise their savings by the amount of this public dissaving, increases in public expenditure will raise the draft on a given pool of savings and real interest rates will rise, and the LDC's terms of trade deteriorate with respect to the OECD. For a country with a large weight in the world economy such as the U.S., the rise in domestic interest rates also leads to an appreciation of its currency as a concomittant of the capital inflow that is induced — some of it from developing countries.

In developing countries, given the inherent weaknesses of their fiscal system and the pressure on the public finances flowing from the need for growing public sector infrastructural expenditures, the rise in world interest rates resulting from the structural public sector deficits in developed countries is likely to worsen the Third World's fiscal crisis. Whilst the concomittant deterioration in their terms of trade with respect to the OECD will worsen their external transfer problem. The opportunity cost of financing infrastructural as well as other investments in developing countries would thus have been raised (via the interest rate linkages of the global market for savings) by the growth of transfer payments in developed countries. In an integrated global market for savings, the growth of 'old age related' social expenditures in developed countries financed through fiscal deficits is thus likely to crowd out, at the margin, the infrastructural developmental expenditures in developing countries required to provide some of the complementary goods necessary to raise the living standards of their poor, young and growing labor forces.

Moreover, a major reason for the big buildup of debt by many Third World countries was the need to finance rising public expenditures, and the associated incipient fiscal deficits. The debt crises arose because the rise in interest rates, and thence the costs of public debt service, exposed the underlying fiscal weaknesses which the earlier buildup of debt by many Third World borrowers had masked. As this rise in interest rates was in part the result of the actual and expected structural fiscal deficits in industrial countries, the current and continuing debt crisis can thus be seen as flowing essentially from a global fiscal crises, that is, a crisis of the public sectors in both developed and developing countries.

References

Baily, M.W., 1981, Productivity and the services of capital and labour, Brookings Papers on Economic Activity, no. 1.

Barro, R.J., 1974, Are government bonds net wealth?, Journal of Political Economy, April.

Berndt, E. and D. Wood, 1979, Engineering and econometric interpretations of energy–capital complementarity, American Economic Review, March.

Bonnell, S., 1981, Real wages and employment in the great depression, Economic Record, Sept.

Bruno, M., 1982, World shocks, macroeconomic response and the productivity puzzle, in: R.C.O. Mathews, ed., 1982.

Bruno, M., 1984, Raw materials, profits and the productivity slowdown, Quarterly Journal of Economics, Feb.

Buiter, W.H. and J. Tobin, 1980, Debt neutrality: A brief review of doctrine and evidence, in: G.M. von Furstenberg, ed., Reprinted as Cowles Foundation paper no. 505.

Crosland, A., 1950, The future of socialism (Jonathan Cape, London).

Curzon-Price, V., 1982, Government intervention as a factor in slower growth in advanced industrial nations, in: R.C.O. Mathews, ed., 1982.

Darby, M., 1975, The financial and tax effects of monetary policy on interest rates, Economic Inquiry, June.

Eisner, R. and P.J. Pieper, 1984, A new view of the federal debt and budget deficits, American Economic Review, March.

Federal Reserve System, 1981, Public policy and capital formation, April.

Feldstein, M., 1974, Social security, induced retirement, and aggregate capital accumulation, Journal of Political Economy, Sept.–Oct.

Feldstein, M., 1983, Inflation, tax rules, and capital formation (NBER, Chicago, IL).

Fisher, I., 1930, The theory of interest (Macmillan, London).

Friedman, M., 1978, The Kemp–Roth free lunch, Newsweek, Aug. 7.

Galli, G. and R. Masera, 1983, Real rates of interest and public sector deficits, An empirical investigation, Société Universitaire Européenne de Recherches Financières colloquium on: Government policies and the working of financial systems in industrial countries, Oct. (Madrid).

Hakim, L. and C. Wallich, 1984, OECD deficits, debt, and savings: Structure and trends 1965–80, WDR VII, Part I, background paper.

Harberger, A.C. and S. Edwards, 1980, International evidence on the source of inflation, Conference on inflation, Dec. (Getulio Vargas Foundation, Rio De Janeiro).

Hudson, E.A. and D.W. Jorgenson, 1978, Energy prices and the U.S. economy, Natural Resource Journal, Oct.

Johnson, L., 1981, Life cycle saving, social security and the long run capital stock, in: Federal reserve system, Public policy and capital formation.

Koskela, E. and M. Viren, National debt neutrality: Some international evidence, Kylos 36, no. 4.

Kravis, I. B., 1970, Trade as a handmaiden of growth — Similarities between the 19th and 20th centuries, Economic Journal, Dec.

Lal, D., 1974, Methods of project appraisal — A review (Johns Hopkins University Press, Baltimore MD).

Lal, D., 1980, Prices for planning — Towards the reform of Indian planning (Heinemann, London).

Lal, D., 1983, The poverty of 'development economics', Hobart Paperback 16 (Institute of Economic Affairs, London).

Lal, D. and M. Wolf, eds., n.d., Stagflation, savings and the state: Perspectives on the global economy, WDR VII background papers. A World Bank research publication (Oxford University Press, New York) forthcoming.

Lewis, W.A., 1980, The slowing down of the engine of growth, American Economic Review, Sept.

Lewis, W.A., 1978, The evolution of the international economic order (Princeton University, Princeton, NJ).

Little, I.M.D. and J.A. Mirrlees, 1974, Project appraisal and planning for developing countries (Heinemann, London).

Lluch, C., 1984, ICORS, savings rates and the determinants of public expenditure in developing countries, i.: D. Lal and M. Wolf, eds., Stagflation, savings and the state: Perspectives on the glocal economy (Oxford University Press, New York) forthcoming.

McCallum, B.T., 1984, Are bond financed deficits inflationary? A Ricardian analysis. Journal of Political Economy, Feb.

Maddison, A., 1982, Phases of capitalist development (Oxford University Press, Oxford).

Makin, J.H., 1983, Real interest, money surprises, anticipated inflation and fiscal deficits, Review of Economics and Statistics, Aug.

Mathews, R.C.O., ed., 1982, Slower growth in the western world (Heinemann, London).

Mundell, R., 1963, Inflation and real interest, Journal of Political Economy, June.

OECD., 1983, Economic Outlook, June and Dec. (OECD, Paris).

OECD., 1984, Social expenditures: Erosion or evolution?, OECD Observer, no. 126, Jan.

Phelps-Brown, H., 1983, The origins of trade union power (Oxford University Press, Oxford).

Ram, Rati, 1982, Dependency rates and aggregate savings: A new international cross-section study, American Economic Review, June.

Ram, Rati, 1984, Dependency rates and savings: reply, American Economic Review, March.

Riedel, J., 1984, Trade as the engine of growth in developing countries, revisited, The Economic Journal, March.

Sachs, J., 1979, Wages profits and macroeconomic adjustment: A comparative study, Brookings Papers on Economic Activity, no. 2.

Sachs, J., 1981, The current account and macroeconomic adjustment in the 1970s, Brookings Papers on Economic Activity, no. 1.

Sachs, J., 1983, Real wages and unemployment in OECD countries, Brookings Papers on Economic Activity, no. 1.

Sargent, T.J. and N. Wallace, 1981, Some unpleasant monetarist arithmetic, Quarterly Review, Fall (Federal Reserve Bank of Minneapolis, Minneapolis, MN).

Scott, M.Fg. and R.A. Laslett, 1978, Can we get back to full employment? (Macmillan, London).

Sjaastad et al., 1984, The debt crisis in Latin America, in: D. Lal and M. Wolf, eds., Stagflation, savings and the state: Perspectives on the global economy (Oxford University Press, New York) forthcoming.

Soskice, David., 1978, Strike waves and wage explosions, 1968–1970: An economic interpretation in C. Crouch and A. Pizzorou, eds., The resurgence of class conflict in Western Europe since 1968, Vol. 2 (Holmes and Meier, London).

Summers, Lawrence H., 1983, The non-adjustment of nominal interest rates: A study of the Fisher Effect, in J. Tobin, ed., 1983.

Tait, A. and P. Heller, 1982, International comparisons of government expenditure, IMF occasional papers 10 (IMF, Washington, DC).

Tobin, J., ed., 1983, Macroeconomics, prices and quantities (Brookings Institution, Washington, DC).

Thompson, L.H., 1983, The social security reform debate, Journal of Economic Literature, Dec.

Van Wijnbergen, S., 1984, On fiscal deficits, the real exchange rate and the real rate of interest, Centre for Economics Policy Research discussion paper no. 21 (London).

Von Furstenberg, G.M., ed., 1979, Social security versus private saving (Ballinger, Cambridge, MA).

Wilcox, J.A., 1983, Why real interest rates were so low in the 1970s, American Economic Review, March.

[16]

World Savings and Growth in Developing Countries

Deepak Lal (1)
University College, London

1. - Introduction

In its recent *World Economic Outlook*, the IMF supports the view that on current demographic trends particularly in Japan and Germany, and assuming unchanged public policies in other countries, there is likely to be an emerging shortage of world savings. This view was first propounded (to the best of my knowledge) in the World Bank's *World Development Report 1984*, with which I was associated, and set out in detail together with the supporting evidence in the background papers prepared for the report and published in Lal and Wolf [17] (2).

As part of the same exercise Sweder van Wijnbergen and I had developed a simple framework of North-South interactions focussing on the global balance between the demand and supply of savings, and which emphasised the interactions of the public sectors in developed and developing countries as major determinants of world interest rates and the terms of trade between the North and South, in an

---

(1) Parts of this paper are based on Ch. 4 of the draft synthesis volume (by LAL D. and MYINT H. of a multi-country comparative study of 21 developing countries financed by the World Bank, of *The Political Economy of Poverty, Equity and Growth*. The author, however, is responsible for the views expressed which must not be ascribed to the World Bank in any form.

(2) This priority is of course not acknowledged by the IMF, or the various other authors who have taken up this same theme more recently!

Advise: the numbers in square brackets refer to the Bibliography in the appendix.

integrated world economy constrained by the overall availability of world savings. This simple model was calibrated with the relevant data for the 1970s and early 1980s and the estimated time path of world interest rates and LDC/OECD terms of trade seemed to track the actual outcomes fairly closely (Lal and van Wijnbergen [16]). The model can be used to provide simple qualitative answers to the question of the likely effects of the increased demands on the pool of world savings flowing from the reconstruction of East European economies. This is an important question concerning the medium run. But we ignore it in this paper, which is concerned more with the long run.

The important long run question concerns the effects on developing country growth rates of the projected decline in the OECD countries savings into the next century. We survey the answers that are provided by conventional theory in Section I before outlining the answers provided by a new growth model due to Scott, in section II. In section III, we provide some rough orders of magnitude of the likely decline in world savings flowing from the ageing of OECD populations and its effects on growth rates in the Scott framework.

1. - The savings rates in developed, developing and OPEC countries in the past are shown in Table I. Most of the decline in the OECD savings rate is accounted for by a fall in public savings. This, as was argued in Lal and Wolf [17] and as is confirmed by various OECD studies (Dean *et* Al. [3], Dean [2]), is due to the expansion of social expenditures on helath and pensions, whose coverage increased dramatically in the 1960s and 1970s. In the early part of the next century, because of the ageing of the population, particularly in Germany and Japan (two of the highest savers currently in OECD countries), demographic pressures are likely to further reduce OECD savings rates.

Future trends in savings rates in developing countries are difficult to discern. First, it should be noted that for many Asian developing countries, savings rates have already reached unprecedentedly high rates. Second, the collapse of savings in Africa in the 1970s, after having risen quite markedly in the previous decade, may be reversed as the basic economic framework (consisting of stable systems of law

TABLE 1

GROSS SAVINGS RATIOS

(*A*)	Non-OPEC LDCS	OECD	OPEC
1966-1970	na (*)	23.3 (**)	na (***)
1971-1980	18.0 (*)	23.5	56.8 (*)
1981-1988	na	20.2	na

DEVELOPING COUNTRIES

(*B*) (***)	All developing countries	Africa	Asia	Europe	ME	W. Hem
1976-1981	26.9	24.1	27.9	25.8	39.1	20.8
1982-1988	22.5	17.7	27.5	25.3	23.1	17.0

(*) From LAL and WOLF [17], Table 7.4.
(**) From DEAN [2], Table 1.
(***) From AGHEVLI, *et* AL. [1], Table 2.

and order, stable money and non-extortionary fiscal regimes) which aids thrift and productivity is re-established. Similarly, once Latin America emerges from its debt-related bust, its savings rates may also recover to their average 1960-1970s levels. Aggregate non-OPEC developing countries savings may, therefore, revert to their average levels in the 1960s and 1970s. At least we shall assume this is so, and examine the likely effects on them of the shrinking in the supply of world savings as a result of the projected demographically led decline in savings in OECD countries early into the next century.

The common sense conclusion would be that this incipient decline in world savings is *ceteris paribus* likely to lower developing country growth rates and hence their future welfare. Surprisingly, conventional theory would deny this conclusion. There are two types of reasons for the counter-intuitive conclusions. The first derives from the so-called habitat view of savings-investment interactions in the world economy due to Feldstein-Horioka [8]. The second follows from the conventional Solow-Swan model of neo-classical equilibrium growth. We deal with both in turn.

The "habitat" view questions the conventional neo-classical view of the determinants of capital flows between countries: namely that in an integrated world economy where capital (but not labour) is mobile, it will flow from regions where rates of return to capital are low to these where they are high until a common rate of return (= world interest rate) is established (3). An empirical prediction of this standard neo-classical model is that national savings and investment rates need not move closely together. Feldstein and Horioka [8] and Feldstein [7], however, provided empirical evidence that, contrary to the neoclassical view, national investment moves closely with national savings. This could be taken to be a sign that world capital markets are very far from being integrated as assumed in the neoclassical view. In which case there would be little impact on investment and hence (on the common sense view) on growth in developing countries from the prospective fall in savings in OECD countries. Each developing country's investment and growth rate would depend upon its own savings propensity and if this did not change, their growth prospects would be unaltered. The subsequent controversy about the degree of international capital mobility which can be deduced from Feldstein-Horioka type regressions is discussed in Dooley, Frankel and Mathieson [6]. For our purpose, however, the conclusions of the recent IMF study by Aghevli *et* Al. ([1], p. 26) are more relevant. They state on the OECD countries: «More recent studies suggest that the close correlation between investment and savings that had prevailed during the 1960s and 1970s began to break down in the early 1980s. This breakdown may be attributed to two coincidental events. One is that the pace of financial reforms was intensified in the industrial countries in the 1980s, particularly in the high savings countries such as Japan and the Federal Republic of Germany. As a result, a substantial source of savings was made available in the international capital markets. At the same time, a widening of budget deficits in a number of low saving countries, particularly the US, created excess demand for savings and attracted foreign savings through higher interest rates».

Whilst for LDCs they found (Table 2) that as a whole there

---

(3) See McDougall [19], Kemp [11], Jones [10]. Also see Lal [14] for a survey of international capital flows and economic development.

TABLE 2

SAVING-INVESTMENT CORRELATIONS
IN DEVELOPING COUNTRIES (*)

	1976-1988	1976-1981	1982-1988
Developing countries	0.68	0.60	0.70
Countries with debt-servicing problems	0.73	0.72	0.74
Countries without debt-servicing problems	0.88	0.84	0.71
High-inflation countries	0.80	0.78	0.76
Low-inflation countries	0.63	0.51	0.65
High-income countries	0.55	0.44	0.61
Low-income countries	0.78	0.69	0.76
Africa	0.74	0.66	0.75
Asia	0.84	0.91	0.57
Europe	0.88	0.80	0.94
Middle East	0.31	0.11	0.44
Western Hemisphere	0.63	0.71	0.65

(*) High-inflation countries: average annual inflation rate of 10 percent or higher in 1982-1988; low-inflation countries: average annual inflation rate of below 10%; high-income countries: average per capita nominal income of US $1,000 or above in 1982-1988; low-income countries: average per capita nominal income of less than US $1,000.

Source: Fund staff estimaters, AGHEVLI *et* AL. [1], Table 4.

remains a close correlation between national savings and investment. Moreover, for the debt problem countries (as would be expected) this correlation strengthened somewhat. However, for countries in Asia and those which avoided a debt crisis, the correlation has weakened substantially since 1982, suggesting that they are increasingly becoming integrated into the world capital market. As the problems of the "debt crisis" countries gets resolved, they too can be expected to be re-integrated into the world capital market. Hence, for both LDCs and OECD countries, the assumption of worldwide capital market integration may not be too farfetched in the future.

This would then restore differential expected rates of return as the major motive for capital flows between countries. A worldwide shortage of savings would imply a rise in world interest rates and hence the labour intensity of production (following from the required rise in the marginal productivity of capital) in both developed and developing countries. But what of the consequences for the growth rates of income and per capita consumption in the South? As is well

GRAPH 1

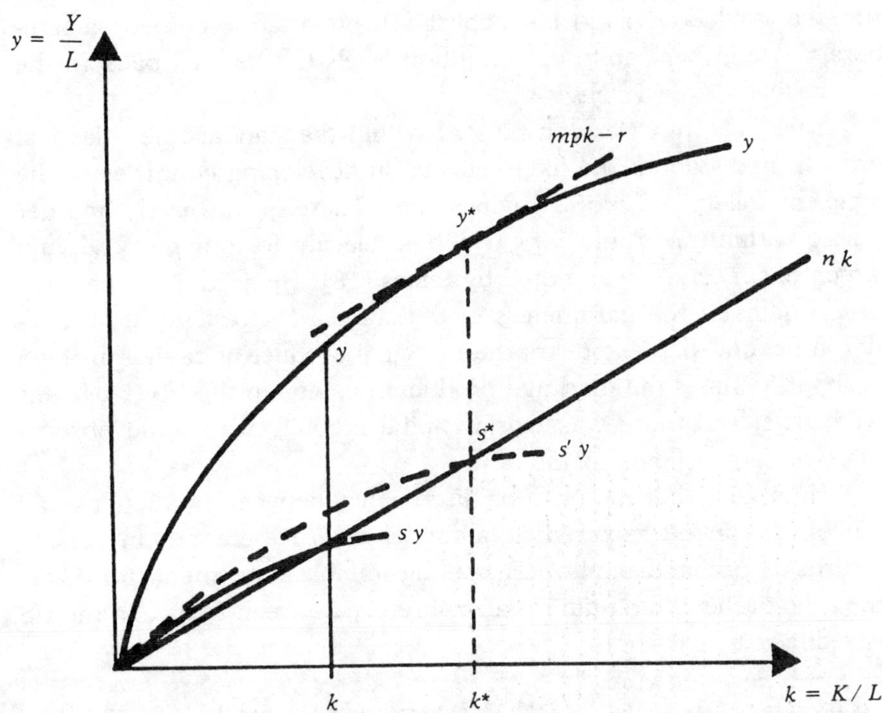

With y as output per capita and k as the capital per capita, this figure shows the standard neo-classical growth model. The natural rate of growth is given exogenously by the rate of technical progress n. With a savings rate s, the economy will converge to a steady state capital labour rate of k, and per capita output of y. If savings were raised to s' (the Golden Rule level), consumption per capita (s^*y^*) would be at a maximum, as the slope of the tangent at y^* (= marginal product of capital) will be the same as the slope of the nk line (the natural rate of growth). Assuming savings higher than s' would clearly be sub-optimal, as it would reduce the steady state per capita consumption level.

known, in the Solow-Swam neo-classical model, this reduction in the world savings rate would have no effect on the steady state growth rate which would continue to be determined by the exogenously given rates of population growth and Harrod neutral technical progress in the respective countries and regions. The new steady state per capita output and consumption would be lower (assuming as is plausible that the previous steady state capital-labour ratio was below the Golden

Rule level (Graph 1) (4). In the transition to the new steady state, the growth rate of capital and output would decline (as the lower steady state capital-labour ratio is established), but there would be a temporary rise in per capita consumption levels till they fell back to the lower steady state levels.

This is as much as can be said within the standard neo-classical growth model about the likely effects on developing countries of the incipient fall in the world savings rate. There is, however, another puzzle within this framework which is relevant for our purpose, and which has recently been noted by Lucas [18]. He argues on the basis of estimates of the parameters of the standard neo-classical production function, that it appears the marginal product of capital in India is about 58 times the marginal product of capital in the US (5). If this were true, and there was world capital mobility we should observe massive capital flows to India.

He argues that the obvious discrepancy between predictions and outcomes can be repaired in a model where there are increasing returns to human capital. After making suitable adjustments for these, the ratio of the differential in rates of return between India and the US is reduced to 1.04 (6).

---

(4) It is well-known (PHELPS [21]) that any savings rate above the Golden Rule level reduces steady per capita consumption and hence cannot be optimal. The Golden Rule of Accumulation is that the marginal product of capital equals the natural rate of growth, or equivalently that the ratio of savings and investment to output equals the rate of profit. Of course, the Golden Rule rate of savings is also likely to be too high on an optimal growth path for well known reasons (DIXIT [5]).

(5) For a standard neo-classical production function $y = Ax^b$, where y is income (output) per worker, x is capital per worker, and b the share of capital in value added, the marginal product of capital in terms of output per worker is:

$$r = b\,A^{1/b}\,y^{(b-1)/b}$$

substituting a value of $b = 0.4$ «an average of US and Indian capital shares», and using SUMMERS and HESTON [24] estimates that US output per worker is roughly 15 times that in India «implies that the marginal product of capital in India must be $(15)^{1.5} = 58$ times the marginal product of capital in the US" (LUCAS [18], p. 92).

(6) Lucas estimates this as follows. With increasing returns (due to externalities) to human capital formation, and denoting y as income per effective worker, x as capital per effective worker, and h as human capital per worker, his production function is $y = Ax^b h^a$ where the term h^a is the external effect of human capital formation. This implies that the marginal productivity of capital (r) is: $r = b\,A^{1/b}\,y^{(b-1)/b}\,h^{a/b}$

He uses KRUEGER [13] estimate of the relative human capital stocks in India and the US. He derives «a ratio of y in the US to y in India of 3». From Dennison (1962) he

But this Lucas (and the other "new growth") method of repairing the Solow-Swan growth model in order to eliminate some of its implausible predictions does not seem too plausible either. Thus Maddison ([20], p. 111) summing up the historical evidence on productivity he has put together for the OECD countries concluded: «It does not seem that the post-war acceleration of productivity growth was matched by an acceleration in the growth of educational capital. Similarly it is clear that the slackening in productivity growth since 1973 is in no way due to a slowing down in the pace of growth of educational capital. Indeed, the evidence available shows more rapid growth in the educational stock in the 1970s than in the 1960s or 1950s».

Also consider the comparison of the diverse historical growth performance of the US and Argentina. As Waelbroeck ([27], p. 2 noted: «Nor is human capital the key to the productivity mystery. The United States and Argentina were equally prosperous at the beginning of the century. Their intellectual achievements were broadly comparable; today, Argentina is a developing country that for scores of years has not been able to take control of its destiny. Yet, the physical capital was not destroyed by wars, nor its human capital depleted by a mass exodus of highly skilled elements of the population; other explanations must be found».

These other explanations of course, as a large amount of empirical research on the divergent outcomes in developing countries have emphasised, must include differences in the efficiency of investment. These are subsumed in the Solow-Swan framework in the exogenously determined black box of technical progress. But this as Scott [22] has recently emphasised in a brilliant book *means:* «orthodox theories of economic growth make its main determinants non-economic» Scott ([22), p. 100) has constructed a new neo-classical growth model in which «the determinants of the volume and efficiency of investment are restored to the centre of attention». We turn to this model, as it provides more plausible and

---

derives an estimate of $a = 0.36$. The ratio of h in the US to India from Krueger is 5. Taking $b = 0.25$, this gives the «rate of return ratio between India and the US of (3) $1.5 \times 5 - 1 = 1.04$» (LUCAS [18], p. 92).

commonsensical answers to the question of the likely effects of a decrease in world savings on the growth performance of developing countries.

2. - Scott's steady state growth model is neo-classical in so far as it assumes profit and utility maximisation. But there are three important departures from the Solow-Swan framework.

First, Scott ([22]- p. 92) argues that: «for all practical purposes, depreciation in a progressive economy should be regarded as essentially a transfer of income from capitalists to workers. The latter benefit from rising wages which result in appreciation which is omitted from the conventional accounts. Were it included, it would offset depreciation on capital assets. It would then be clear that net investment for society as a whole is (approximately) equal to *gross* investment as conventionally measured, and not to gross investment minus depreciation».

Second, Scott argues that there are no diminishing returns to cumulative gross investment (that is the capital stock measured as the sum of all past gross investment), but there could be diminishing returns to the *rate* of investment.

Third, [22(a)] he maintains that there is no need to evoke any independent or exogenous technical progress to explain growth. He argues that: «investment is... by definition... the cost of change, and so will cover all activities associated with growth» (p. 317) and that «growth due to capital and technical progress are both the result of investment» (p. 330) in the sense of «the cost, in terms of consumption forgone, of propelling the economy forward instead of leaving it in a stationary state» (p. 318). «Incurring capital expenditure leads to a rearrangement of the things of this world. It does not lead to there being any more of some substance "capital". There is then simply change which is due to investment, and to population growth. We cannot separate change which is "more capital" from change which is "technical progress". We must abandon the attempt to distinguish between movements along a production function whose arguments are labour, land and all capital, and a shift in that function due to technical progress" (p. 331). Within his proposed framework «the rate of increase of static income is a function of only two variables: total savings and labour force growth. There is no independent technical progress» (p. 331).

Instead of the usual production function, Scott argues that the economy's technology is best depicted by a set of inexhaustible investment opportunities which relate exponential rates of change of output q and employment l per unit of investment expenditure (which is given by the ratio of gross investment (savings) to output s (7).

Scott envisages the investment opportunities available as a cake, which can be depicted by what he calls investment opportunity contour (IOCS's) (of different height) in a diagram which has output per unit of investment q and employment per unit of investment l as its two axes. The height of the contours is the density of projects (Graph 2*a*). «The shape of the cake is shown... by the contours joining points of equal height... The contours increase in height, as we move from the north and west towards the origin. They cross the l-axis to the left of the origin and go off to the north and east. This is because projects which (per unit of investment) do not increase output must save labour, and the more they increase output, the more labour they require (given their frequency). Finally, the contours are concave to the origin because of diminishing returns to labour. For a given frequency of projects, and a given amount of investment, adding further doses of labour increases output by successively smaller amounts» (p. 156-7).

Each IOC corresponds to a particular rate of (gross) investment s. For that rate of investment, one can envisage an equal profits contour (EPC) argues Scott, which is like a knife cutting off the investment opportunities (lying to the north-west of the knife) which yield returns greater, than the expected minimum (or cut off) rate of return for the economy. The latter being determined by rates of time preferences. The slope of the EPC is defined as:

$$\mu = \frac{\Delta q}{\Delta l} = \frac{\lambda}{1 - s} \qquad (1)$$

(7) Term as defined below, if g is the growth rate of output and g_L that of employment, $g = g/s$ and $l = g_L/s$.

GRAPH 2A

INVESTMENT OPPORTUNITY CONTOUR MAP

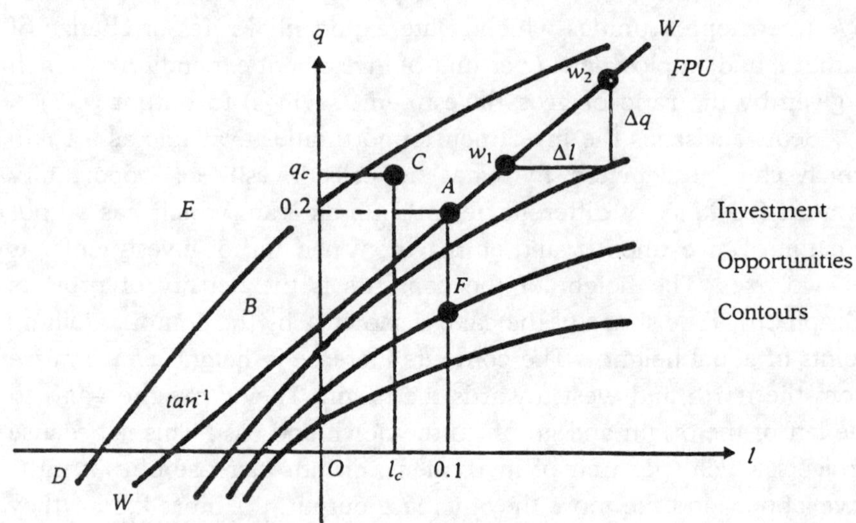

GRAPH 2B

INVESTMENT PROGRAMME CONTOUR MAP

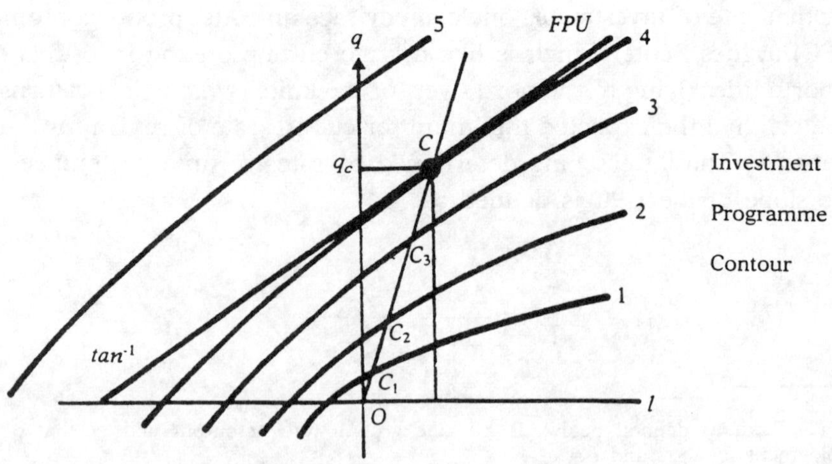

where: μ is output per unit of investment, 1 is employment per unit of investment, λ is the share of wages in output and *s* is the rate of investment.

Scott asssumes that «the cake of investment opportunities is continually remade, and has the same shape in the dimensions relevant to the diagram» when there is steady state growth.

But there are two qualificaticns to this assumption of a constant set of investment opportunities which may be relevant. First, is the possibility of catch up: «What may happen in such cases is that both the favourable stream of new inventions, etc. and the adverse stream of competitive pressures are shut off from a particular country for various reasons. Subsequently, the country is opened up to such influences. Investors in that country then reap the benefits of access to the new inventions, etc. Since competition will not have forced up wage rates, investment opportunities will on balance be enhanced, although the lack of investment in the past will limit this enhancement. As investment proceeds, and the country catches up, wage rates will be bid up and eventually the set of opportunities will become normal» (p. 161).

The second is that the set can shrink or expand. There is no law that requires a constant set. «Some have claimed to be able to detect long waves of invention which should show up as expansions and contractions in the set of opportunities. My own investigation suggests a movement in one direction only — happily that of expansion» (p. 162).

But as a working hypothesis, an inexhaustible constant set of investment opportunities seems plausible. This then lets him derive what he calls an investment program contour (IPC) (Graph 2*b*). This is the locus of the centre of gravity (*C* in Graph 2*a*) as μ (the slope of the IPC) varies for any given rate of investment *s*.

In steady state growth, for a given rate of investment *s*, and ratio of growth of employment *l*, Scott shows that, there will be a unique best point *C* in Graph 2*b*, where the IPC is tangential to the relevant IPC.

The characteristics of investment q_c and q_l will remain constant, and as by definitions:

$$q_c = g/s \quad (2)$$

(3) $$l_c = g_1/s$$

where: g is the growth of output; g_1 is the growth rate of the (quality adjusted) labour force.

The growth rates of output g, of employment g_1 and the rate of investment s, will all be constant, as will the share of wages in output λ, and hence from *(1)* will μ. Scott also assumes that along a ray such as *OC*, the slope of successive IPC's is the same. The distance of any IPC from the origin is then measured by a parameter which he labels *Q*, and which is an index of the efficiency of investment. For any given rate of investment the further away is the relevant IPC from the origin, the greater, *ceteris paribus*, are the returns to investment. The parameter *Q* thus measures two effects. First, the effects of diminishing returns to the rate of investment. As the knife moves towards the origin, inferior and less profitable investments are added to the firm's investment programme. «The speed with which *Q* declines as *s* increases, measures the extent to which returns diminish as the rate of investment is increased». This explains why "big push" investment programmes have been so unsuccessful in most developing countries contrary to some of the models recently coming out of Chicago. The second, «effect measured by *Q* is the expansion or contraction of investment opportunities generally arising from factors outside the model». This includes "catch up". For the same *s* in both countries, *Q* was probably greater in Japan than US after World War II, as the Japanese had far lower output/worker and wage rates and could imitate America fairly easily. This should also apply to the East European economies as they are integrated into the European and world economy.

Scott's model then leads to a simple linear equation to explain growth:

(4) $$g = aQs + g_1$$

By contrast, the standard neo-classical model in which growth depends only upon the exogenous growth of quality adjusted employment and technical progress, the relevant growth equation would be, in Scott's notation:

(5) $$g = a + bg_1$$

Scott then tests his model against the standard neo-classical one on data for 10 countries over a number of sub-periods from the 19th century to 1973. He finds the results are close to the predictions of the model. The investment-output ratio and the growth of quality adjusted labour each explain about half of the growth of output. The term which would capture exogenous technical progress is statistically insignificant and not different from zero.

Moreover, he finds a "catch up" variable (in a disaggregation of *Q)* explains a small but significant portion of growth performance since World War II. Scott also finds that the efficiency of investment increased significantly after the World War II (the value of *Q* increased). It is this changed efficiency of investment which requires explanation (8).

Thus as Scott concludes unlike the Solow-Swan model, which says «no technical change no growth», his model reasserts the importance of the economic aspects of economic growth. «The determinants of the volume and efficiency of investment are restored to the centre of attention, and both have long been the concern of economists. We can, with renewed confidence in their importance, study the behaviour of firms, project appraisal, the working of capital markets, the determinants of saving, systems of taxation, and their impact on savings and the volume and pattern of investment, all of which are very relevant to economic growth in the long run. We do not have to abdicate to scientists and engineers or even to those economists who specialise in the study of technical change. I do not deny for a moment their interest and importance but I do assert the importance of the economic aspects of economic growth».

As part of a multi-country comparative study for the World Bank on poverty and growth, I have applied the Scott test to our sample of 21 developing countries for the period 1950-1985. Given the unreliability of the underlying data and as the assumption of equilibrium growth for all these countries is difficult to justify what surprised me were the results. The Scott equation explained about growth 95% of

---

(8) As McCombie J. in his review of Scott's book (in *The Economic Journal*, March 1990 p. 273 notes: «It is also found that the efficiency of investment increased substantially in the post war period, and this becomes in fact the new residual that requires explanation».

the variance in growth rates as compared with the neo-classical one (of 46%) (all as measured by adjusted R^2). (Lal and Myint [15]).

3. - To put the Scott model to work to see what answer it provides to the question: How will the prospective decline in world savings affect LDC growth prospects, a simplification of Graph 2*b* is useful. We now assume that there are no diminishing returns to the rate of investment. Then there will be only one investment programme contour (IPC) as in Graph 3, «which simply traces the edge of the cake on the plate» (Scott [22], p. 168). If the given rate of savings (investment is *s*, then a shrunken version of IPC can be derived whose co-ordinates are those of the IPC multiplied by *s*. This is the curve *GG'*

GRAPH 3

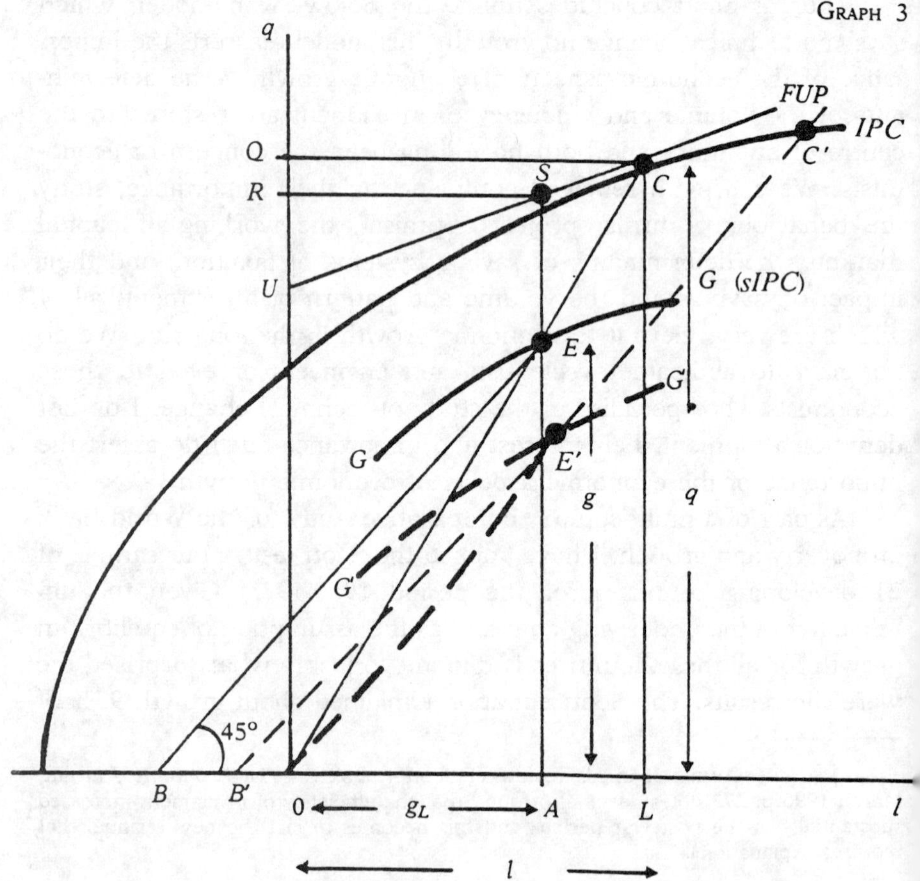

(*sIPC*) in Graph 3 and the point *E* on it has co-ordinates which are *s* times the co-ordinates of *C*. Now, suppose that the exogenously given rate of growth of the labour force is $g_L = OA$. Then the vertical through *A* which intersects the *sIPC* curve at *E*, gives the steady state equilibrium rate of growth of output *g*, whilst the point *C* on the IPC, gives the investment characteristics *q* (output per unit of investment) and *l* (employment per unit of investment) of the steady state investment programme which yields these steady state growth rates.

Now assuming that there is no change in the overall efficiency of the investment programme (so that *Q*, the radius of the IPC, the ray *OC* for instance is unchanged), say the savings/investment rate *s* falls. This will mean that the curve *GG* will shift downward (as $s' < s\ (l)$, the decrease in *s* will lead to a further shrinking of the *sIPC* curve) to *G' G'*. For the unchanged growth rate of the labour force G_L, the new equilibrium point on the *G' G'* curve will lie at *E'*, vertically above *A* and below *E*. The growth rate of output *g* will fall.

The characteristics of the new steady state investment programme are given by the intersection of the ray *OE'* with the unchanged ICC at *C'*. This shows that both *q* and *l* will rise. Moreover, the rate of return to investment (9) in the steady state will also be constant. This rate of return is given by:

$$r = q - \lambda l$$

It is the marginal profit per unit of investment (gross of depreciation) (Scott [22], p. 167 and Ch. 7). The slope of the tangent at *C* gives *u*, whilst the ratio $RQ/QC = \lambda$, and hence the distance *OR* equals *l* (9). Hence the movement from *C* to *C'* implies that *r* will rise. In the steady state, the growth rate of wages g_W must equal the rate of growth of productivity $g - g_L$. Hence if a 45° line is drawn from *E* (on *GG*) to the horizontal axis, the distance $OB = AB - OA = AE - OA = g - g_L = g_W$. With the reduction in the savings (investment) rate, at the new equilibrium point *E'*, on

(9) For as $u = UQ/QC$; $\lambda = u(1 - s)$; and $UR/UQ = US/UC = OE/OC = s$. Thence $(1 - s) = UR/UQ = RQ/UQ$ and hence $\lambda = (UQ/QC)(RQ/UQ) = RQ/QC$ and $r = q - \lambda l = OQ - \lambda\, QC = OQ - RQ = OR$. (See Scott [22], p. 169-70 for details).

$G'G'$, the new "wage line" intersects the horizontal axis as B', and hence g_W falls (as $OB' < OB$).

All these results seem eminently sensible and in line with our commonsensical economic intuition, namely (in summary), the reduction in world savings, and the accompanying rise in real world interest rates, will lower steady state growth rates in the world economy (of both developed and developing countries), raise their rates of profit (real return to investment), increase the labour intensity of output and lower the growth rate of real wages.

Moreover, given Scott's estimated growth equation for the OECD countries, and ours for developing countries, we can provide some rough quantitative assessment of the likely fall in steady state growth rates, assuming that the investment programme contours in both "regions" remain unchanged. First, we need some estimate of the likely decrease in world savings from the demographic changes which will occur in OECD countries. The IMF *World Economic Outlook*, May 1990 («Supplementary Note 3») has estimated that *ceteris paribus* in industrial economies there is «a 1 percentage point decline in private savings rates in the long run in response to a 1 percentage point increase in the dependency ratio». They have also estimated the likely changes in the dependency ratio for the 7 major industrial countries between 1985 and 2025. Using the data on the gross savings rate in these 7 countries between 1981-1987 (given in Dean *et al.* [3], Table 1), and the shares of each country in the total's GDP (in 1980 Kravis dollars in 1983) from Summers and Heston [24], we have estimated the average savings rate of this group of 7 in 1981-1987, and that in 2025, (Table 3). Two estimates are given for the US. The first assumes that there will be no reversal in the low current gross US savings rate of 16.3%, in the near future. The other assumes that this will in the near term revert to its average 1971-1980 value of 19.5% (Dean *et al.* [3]). Table 3 thus shows that *ceteris paribus*, there is likely to be about a 9 percentage point reduction in the savings rate of the Group of 7 due to the ageing of OECD population.

Let us assume this is also roughly the order of magnitude of the reduction in aggregate world savings. What will be the likely reduction in the growth rates of output in the OECD and LDCs within the

TABLE 3

ESTIMATED GROSS SAVINGS RATE IN GROUP OF 7 INDUSTRIAL COUNTRIES
1981-1987 and 2025

Country	(Percentages)			
	Gross savings rate 1981-1987	Share in group 7 real GDP 1987	Change in dependency ratio 1995-2025	Estimated savings rate 2025
(A) (*)	(1)	(2)	(3)	(4)
1) USA	16.3 (19.5) (**)	45.6	7	9.3 (12.5) (**)
2) Japan	31.1	17.4	15	16.1
3) Germany	21.8	10.0	13	8.8
4) France	19.6	8.3	8	11.6
5) UK	17.5	7.5	5	12.5
6) Italy	·15.6	6.5	8	7.6
7) Canada	20.3	4.7	13	7.3

(B) (***)

1. Savings Rate of Group of Seven 1981-1987 = 19.92 (21.38)
2. Savings Rate of Group of Seven 2025 = 10.65 (12.11)

(*) Column (1): From DEAN *et* AL. [3], Table 1; Column (2): derived from data on real GDP per capita and population in 1987, in SUMMERS-HESTON [24], Table 3; Column (3): derived from IMF: *World Economic Outlook*, May 1990, Table 24; Column (4): estimated by subtracting column (3) from column (1).

(**) This is the US gross savings rate for 1971-1980.

(***) These savings rates have been estimated as weighted averages of columns (1) and (4) respectively where weights are those in column (2).

Scott framework. First consider industrial countries. Scott's estimate of his growth equation $g = \mu g_L + aQs$ for the OECD countries yields values of $\mu = 0.9119$ and $aQ = 0.13635$. From the definition of μ (see equation 1) and the estimate of s of about 0.20 derived in Table 3, we get an implicit estimate of the share of wages $\lambda = 0.9119 \times 0.8 = 0.73$. Assuming this remains unchanged (10), then the projected fall of 9 percentage points in the savings ratio in the long run and hence a new long run savings ratio $s^1 = 0.11$ will lead to a new steady state value of $\mu^1 = 0.73/[(1-0.11)] = 0.82$. With no change in the OECD coun-

(10) From the discussion of the Scott model above, we would of course expect λ to fall with the decline in the savings rate. This will further lower the new steady state growth rate by lowering the new steady state value of u.

TABLE 4

ESTIMATED STEADY STATE GROWTH RATES OF OUTPUT IN THE SCOTT FRAMEWORK (*)

(A) OECD Countries	s	g_L	aQ	λ	μ	g
	(1)	(2)	(3)	(4)	(5)	(6)
1970s-1980s	0.200	0.100	0.136	0.73	0.912	0.036
2000 -2025	0.110	0.010	0.136	0.73	0.820	0.015
(B) LDCs						
1970s-1980s	0.203	0.026	0.143	0.60	0.754	0.049
2000 -2025	0.113	0.026	0.143	0.60	0.676	0.034

(*) Column (1): The OECD estimates have been derived as described in the text and Table 1. The 1970s 1980s estimate for LDCs are the average investment rates for the 21 countries in LAL-MYINT [15]. The 2025 figures assume a 9 percentage cut in savings rates; Column (2): The OECD figures are from the LDC figures from LAL-MYINT [15]; Column (3): The OECD figures are the estimates from SCOTT [22] and the LDC figures are from LAL-MYINT [15]; Column (4): Derived from column (5) and (3) for the 1980s data from $\lambda = \mu (1 - s)$; Column (5): The 1970s-1980s estimates are from SCOTT [22] for OECD, LAL-MYINT [15] for LDCs. The 2000-25 figures have been derived from the figures in column (1) and (4), using $\lambda = \mu(1 - s)$; Column (6): This is estimated from columns (1), (2), (3) and (5) by $g = \mu g_L + aQs$.

tries IPC and assuming the same growth of the labour force as in the past (11), this yields the steady state growth rates of output, with current savings rate g and with the projected lower savings rates g^1 shown in Table 4.

A similar exercise based on our estimated growth equation for our 21 developing countries yields the estimates for the growth rates of output at current and projected lower world savings rates of g and g^1 also shown in Table 2. Output growth slows to about 1.5% p.a. in OECD and to 3.4% in developing countries. With population growing at roughly 2.2% p.a. in LDCs and at 0.8% in industrial economies (Table 2 of World Bank: *Social Indicators of Development 1988*), these rates imply very modest per capita growth rates of income in both regions.

For the reasons given in the previous footnotes, our assumption

(11) With the demographic changes being postulated, in fact the growth of labour force will be lower. Thus the new steady state growth rates are likely to be lower than our estimates based on this assumption.

that the share of wages remains unchanged, as does the growth of labour in the OECD countries, is likely to provide an upward bias to these estimates. Furthermore, if the additional social expenditures associated with the ageing of OECD population cannot or are not financed by increased taxation (or fully funded social security systems), there could be structural fiscal deficits in OECD countries (see Lal and Wolf [17] for a fuller discussion). If Ricardian equivalence does not hold, these structural fiscal deficits could further depress future OECD savings rates, and thus lower the new steady state growth rates of both LDCs and industrial countries even further. Against this, the rise in real returns to investment and hence in real world interest rates could increase savings, though the evidence on this remains equivocal (Kotlikoff [12], Deaton [4]).

The picture thus appears fairly gloomy. For many developing countries, however, there is some glimmer of hope. For the estimates we have made based on the growth equations for our 21 developing countries provides an implicit estimate of the "average" rate of return to investment in our sample of countries. But there is a large divergence in relative efficiency in these countries and hence in their rates of return. We were able to calculate average rates of returns for some of our sample countries (for which data on the share of wages was available) in Lal and Myint [15]. These estimates are given in Table 5. This table also shows similar estimates of rates of return for some other countries that I made in the context of shadow pricing exercises in the 1970s. One of these countries was India. These rates of return are also given in Table 5. Finally this table also shows the rates of return to investment that Scott has estimated for various OECD countries in the post-war period.

Two points stand out. First, for many developing countries, growth rates could be increased even if investment rates fall, if the efficiency of investment could be improved. As is now a commonplace, this improvement in efficiency requires a reversal of various irrational dirigiste policies that most developing countries have followed in the past, particularly with regard to foreign trade and foreign investment. The growing realisation that developing countries have to compete for a dimished pool of world savings in an increasingly interdependent world economy, may hopefully strengthen the move-

TABLE 5

RATES OF RETURN TO INVESTMENT (*)

Developing countries	Year	r
	1980-1985	%
1. Thailand		22.2
2. Brazil		21.0
3. Mexico		18.7
4. Turkey		24.0
5. Costa Rica		13.0
6. Colombia		17.8
7. Nigeria		13.1
8. Ghana		− 10.9
9. Uruguay		6.8
10. Egypt		22.7
11. Sri Lanka		18.1
12. Malawi		13.0
13. India	1968	10.0
Developed countries		
UK	1964-1973	18.6
US	1948-1973	15.6
Japan	1961-1973	21.2
Germany	1955-1962	22.0
France	1955-1962	21.3

(*) These rates of return have all been calculated from the formula $r = q - \lambda\, l$ (as explained in the text).

Source: Developing countries 1-12 are from LAL-MYINT [15], Table 4.5. The other countries in the sample of the growth equation but for which data on λ was not available, are Hong Kong, Singapore, Malta, Malaysia, Peru, Jamaica, Mauritius and Madagascar. The estimate for India is from LAL D.: *Prices for Planning*, London Heinemann Educational Books, 1980, Table 1.3. The estimates for the developed countries are from SCOTT [22], Table 7.1.

ment towards the liberalisation of hitherto repressed economic regimes which seems to be a growing worldwide phenomenon. That should help to bolster growth in many countries in the Third World.

Second, Table 5, resolves the purported puzzle for whose resolution Lucas and the other "new growth" theorists seem to have got involved in various contortions within the Solow-Swan neo-classical growth framework. There is no need to bring in increasing returns to human capital etc. to explain why foreign capital (in particular from the US) does not flood into India. The figures in Table 5 speak for themselves!

Beginning with Keynes' paradox of thrift which seemingly overturned one of the classical virtues explaining the wealth of nations, the Solow-Swan model further de-emphasised the role of savings in explaining divergent growth performance. In this paper I have attempted to show how Scott's new growth model can resurrect the importance of savings in explaining relative economic performance and why, as common sense tells us, a decline in thrift is to be deplored. For though as Keynes said "in the long run we are all dead", some of us have children!

BIBLIOGRAPHY

[1] AGHEVLI B. - BOUGHTON J.M. - MONTIEL J.P. - VILLAMERZ D. - WOGLOM G.: «The Role of National Savings in the World Economy», Washington (DC), IMF, *Occasional Papers*, no. 67, March 1990.

[2] DEAN A.: «Changes in International Saving Behaviour, Kiel Institute of World Economics», Paper for conference *Capital Flows in the World Economy*, June 1990.

[3] DEAN A. - DURAND M. - HOELLER P.: «Saving Trends and Behaviour in OECD Countries», Paris, OECD, Department of Economics and Statistics, *Working Paper*, no. 67, June 1989.

[4] DEATON A.: «Savings in Developing Countries: Theory and Review», *Proceedings of the World Bank Annual Conference on Development Economics*, 1989.

[5] DIXIT A.: *The Theory of Equilibrium Growth*, Oxford University Press, 1976.

[6] DOOLEY M. - FRANKEL J.A. - MATHIESON D.J.: «International Capital Mobility: What do Saving-Investment Correlations Tell Us?», IMF, *Staff Papers*, vol. 34, no. 3, September 1987.

[7] FELDSTEIN M.: «Domestic Saving and International Capital Movements in the Long Run and the Short Run», *European Economic Review*, vol. 21, no. 1/2, March-April 1983.

[8] FELDSTEIN M. - HORIOKA C.: «Domestic Saving and International Capital Flows», *Economic Journal*, vol. 90, June 1980.

[9] HAMADA K. - IWATA K.: «On the International Capital Ownership Pattern at the Turn of the Twenty-First Century», *European Economic Review*, vol. 33, no. 5, May 1989.

[10] JONES R.W.: «International Capital Movements and the Theory of Tariffs and Trade», *Quarterly Journal of Economics*, vol. 81, no. 1, February 1967.

[11] KEMP M.C.: «The Gain from International Trade and Investment: a Neo-Heckscher-Ohlin Approach», *American Economic Review*, vol. 56, September 1966.

[12] KOTLIKOFF L.J.: *What Determines Savings?*, Cambridge (Mass.) MIT Press, 1989.

[13] KRUEGER A.O.: «Factor Endowments and Per Capita Income Differences among Countries», *Economic Journal*, vol. 78, September 1968.

[14] LAL D.: «International Capital Flows and Economic Development», in SCOTT M. FG. - LAL D. (eds.): *Public Policy and Economic Development*, Oxford, Clarendon Press, 1990.

[15] LAL D. - MYINT H.: *The Political Economy of Poverty, Equity and Growth. A Comparative Study*, London, University College, Mimeo, February 1990.

[16] LAL D. - VAN WIJNBERGEN S.: «Government Deficits, the Real Interest Rate and LDC Debt: On Global Crowding Out», *European Economic Review*, vol. 29, no. 2, December 1985, reprinted in LAL - WOLF [17].

[17] LAL D. - WOLF M. (ed.): *Stagflation, Savings and the State*, New York, Oxford University Press, 1986.

[18] LUCAS Jr. R.E.: «Why Doesn't Capital Flow From Rich to Poor Countries?», *American Economic Review*, vol. 80, no. 2, May 1990.

[19] MCDOUGALL G.D.A.: «The Benefits and Costs of Private Investment from Abroad: A Theoretical Approach», *Economic Record*, vol. 36, special issue, March 1960; also published in *Bulletin of the Oxford University Institute of Statistics*, vol. 22, no. 3, August 1960.

[20] MADDISON A.: *Phases of Capitalist Development*, Oxford, Oxford University Press, 1982.

[21] PHELPS E.: «The Golden Rule of Accumulation: A Fable for Growthmen», *American Economic Review*, vol. 51, no. 4, September 1961.

[22] SCOTT M. FG: *A New View of Economic Growth*, Oxford, Clarendon Press, 1989.

[22(a)] SCOTT, M. FG: «Investment and Growth», *Oxford Economic Papers*, *28*, 3.

[23] SOLOW R.: «A Contribution to the Theory of Economic Growth», *Quarterly Journal of Economics*, vol. 70, no. 1, February 1956.

[24] SUMMERS R. - HESTON A.: «A New Set of International Comparisons of Real Product and Price Levels: Estimates for 130 Countries, 1950-1985», *Review of Income and Wealth*, March 1988.

[25] SWAN T.: «Economic Growth and Capital Accumulation», *Economic Record*, vol. 32, no. 2, November 1956.

[26] VAN WIJNBERGER S.: «Interdependence Revisited: A Developing Countries Perspective on Macroeconomic Management and Trade Policy in the Industrial World», *Economic Policy*, no. 1, November 1985.

[27] WAELBROECK J.: «1992: Are the Figures Right? Reflections of a Thirty Per Cent Policy Maker», in SIEBERT H. (ed.): *The Completion of the Internal Market*, Tubingen, J.C.B. Mohr, 1990.

PART V

[17]

The Real Exchange Rate, Capital Inflows and Inflation: Sri Lanka 1970–1982

By

Deepak Lal

Contents: I. Introduction. – II. The Real Exchange Rate, Capital Inflows and Internal and External Balance. – III. A Formal Model of Real Exchange Rate Determination. – IV. Estimates of the Required Change in the Real Exchange Rate with Increased Capital Inflows. – V. Estimates of the Contribution of Monetary Expansion and Rise in the Price of Traded Goods on the Price of Non-Traded Goods and the Overall Price Level. – VI. Conclusions. – Appendices.

I. Introduction

With the increased financial integration of developing countries in the world economy, the role of the capital account in the balance of payments and for domestic stabilization policies has assumed importance for many developing countries. In analyzing the efficient absorption of capital inflows movements in the real exchange rate become an important diagnostic tool. To this end the paper delineates the relevance and investigates the determinants of the real exchange rate in Sri Lanka where, since 1977, capital inflows have been a major element in the overall balance of payments.

Table 1 presents some summary statistics for the Sri Lankan economy for 1970–1982. The most important policy change during this period was the liberalization of the economy following the victory of the UNP in the elections of 1976. In particular, import controls were considerably eased, and many quantitative restrictions were replaced by tariffs. Though the pattern of effective protection is still very uneven and biased against exports [see Cuthbertson, Khan, 1981], the trade regime is markedly more liberal than it was before 1977. The new government was also able to mobilize large inflows of foreign aid (Table 1), and in recent years has also borrowed large sums on the commercial Eurocurrency market. In addition, Sri Lankan workers have

---

Remark: This paper has been written whilst working as a consultant to the World Bank. The World Bank does not accept responsibility for the views expressed herein which are those of the author and should not be attributed to the World Bank or to its affiliated organizations. The findings, interpretations, and conclusions are the results of research supported by the Bank; they do not necessarily represent official policy of the Bank. Comments by T. N. Srinivasan and members of seminars at Birbeck College, London and the World Bank and an anonymous referee have helped to improve the paper. Research assistance by P. Srivastara is gratefully acknowledged.

participated in the employment boom in the Middle East following the oil price rises of 1973 and 1978/79. Their remittances also provide a large source of foreign currency inflows to the Sri Lankan economy. Thus these non-trade related foreign currency inflows rose from around 3–5 percent of GDP before 1977, to about 17 percent of GDP in 1981 (Table 1). This makes it essential to integrate the capital account in any analytical framework for analyzing macroeconomic, foreign trade and exchange rate policies in Sri Lanka.

Table 1 – *Summary Statistics for Sri Lanka*

	1970–1977	1971–1981	1977	1978	1979	1980	1981	1982
	Percentage change							
Population		1.7						
GDP, real	2.9		n.a.	8.2	6.3	5.8	5.8	5.0
Cost of living index[a]			n.a.		19.0	37.8	23.7	11.0
Index of real wages			7.0	31.3	5.6	-9.6	-18.6	4.0
	Percentage share in GDP							
Net concessional aid				9.6	8.9	7.8	8.0	n.a.
Net commercial borrowing				-1.4	0.2	5.7	4.9	n.a.
Private remittances				0.8	1.4	3.4	4.5	5.6
Total	2–4		5.5	9.0	10.5	16.9	17.4	20.0
Investment			14.2	20.0	25.8	33.7	27.8	29.6
Public sector deficit			7.7	13.8	13.9	23.1	15.5	19.8
Current account deficit			-3.9	5.5	11.1	19.8	13.3	18.4

[a] Central Bank index.

Source: Central Bank Annual Report, var. years; World Bank data.

Table 1 also shows that this large inflow of foreign currency resources has enabled Sri Lanka to raise its ratio of investment to GDP from 14 percent in 1977 to nearly 30 percent in 1982. This has led to a marked acceleration of the growth rate, which has roughly doubled from its average rate of about 3 percent per annum between 1970–1977, to about 6 percent per annum since. This acceleration of the growth rate has marked all the sectors except for mining and quarrying – particularly impressive being the increase in the growth rate of the agricultural sector. Nor has the quality of growth deteriorated as judged by such indices as changes in real wages, and unemployment rates since 1977.

In addition Table 1 shows various statistics relevant to assessing the macroeconomic balance in the economy. Prima facie, these would appear to show a country in a severe economic crisis with: a public sector deficit which has risen from about 7 percent to 20 percent of GDP between 1977 and

1982; a current account deficit in the balance of payments which has risen from about 5 percent to nearly 20 percent of GDP, and an inflation rate which rose to nearly 40 percent in 1980, and was still 11 percent in 1982; the purchasing power parity real effective exchange rate has risen by more than 20 percent since 1977. Does this mean that the boom, fuelled by foreign capital inflows and lose domestic macroeconomic policies, was unsustainable, and to control inflation and achieve equilibrium in the balance of payments the classical recipe for a macroeconomic crisis - a devaluation and a reduction in the public sector deficit - is required?

To answer this question, we outline a simple geometric extension of the Salter model to a tariff distorted open economy with capital inflows in the next section. This brings out the importance of movements in the real exchange rate - which is distinguished from the PPP real effective exchange rate - as a diagnostic tool in determining the signs of disequilibrium in an economy where large capital inflows need to be absorbed. The following section outlines a simple algebraic version of the model, and applies this to Sri Lanka. The discussion for the most part assumes that current levels of capital inflows are socially desirable and sustainable; an assumption which is cursorily examined in the last part of Section V. The final section summarizes some of the policy conclusions that flow from our analysis.

II. The Real Exchange Rate, Capital Inflows and Internal and External Balance

In most empirical discussions of the real exchange rate (e_r) - defined as the domestic relative price of non-traded (P_N) to traded (P_T^d) goods - the PPP real effective exchange rate (e_p) - defined as the nominal exchange rate (e) adjusted for the difference between the domestic and the foreign price levels (denoted by P_d and P_f, respectively) - has been used as a surrogate [see Harberger, 1982].

Table 2 summarizes the available estimates of e_p and e_r for Sri Lanka. As expected these do not show identical movements over the 1970–1982 period. For, if the "law of one price" does not hold and there are tariffs or quantitative restrictions on traded goods, then the two rates will differ for an economy and moreover with changing tariffs even the movements in the two rates will not be in the same direction (for a formal treatment see Appendix I).

We next demonstrate how and why the real exchange rate e_r, rather than the PPP rate (e_p) is relevant in assessing macroeconomic performance in an open economy with tariffs and non-traded goods.

The Figure depicts an extension of the standard "Australian Model" of an open economy in which there are tariffs and import quotas[1]. The economy

[1] Corden [1977, Ch. 1] provides a lucid exposition of the standard model in which there are no tariffs on tradeables. The extension below to an economy with fixed trade distortions is due to T. N. Srinivasan.

Table 2 – *Exchange Rate Indices*

Year	e	PPP (e_p)	e_r(I)	e_r(II)	e_r(III)
1976			103	120	
1977	110	101	108	105	
1978	100	100	100	100	100
1979	102	121	94.5	96	100
1980	85	117	76	83	84
1981	81	129	76	74	86
1982	87	131	80	94	92
1978–1982 percentage change:			– 20.2	– 5.6	– 8.0
1980–1982 percentage change:			+ 4.5	+ 14.3	+ 10.1

Note: e = Nominal exchange rate; the data are from the IMF (Rs.e = \$1). – e_p = PPP real effective exchange rate; the data are from the IMF ($e_p = P_d \,/\, e \cdot P_f$). – e_r(I) = Real exchange rate derived from the Colombo price index, using the weights 0.88 and 0.12 for imported and exportable goods, on which the index is based to derive the index numbers of traded goods. The index numbers for domestic goods was taken as that for non-traded goods ($e_r = P_N \,/\, P_T^d$). – e_r(II) = Real exchange rate based on the Central Bank's wholesale price index; the weights of imported goods is 0.55 and of exported 0.45. – e_r(III) = Real exchange rate based on the Central Bank's cost of living index (unpublished); the weights for imported goods and exports are 0.68 and 0.32, respectively.

produces three goods, importables (M), exportables (X) and non-traded goods (N). Assuming constant foreign currency prices for importables and exportables and fixed tariff cum subsidy rates, the two tradeable goods can be treated as a composite commodity labelled tradeables (T) where the domestic currency price is determined by the nominal exchange rate (e), the foreign

Extension of the Standard "Australian Model"

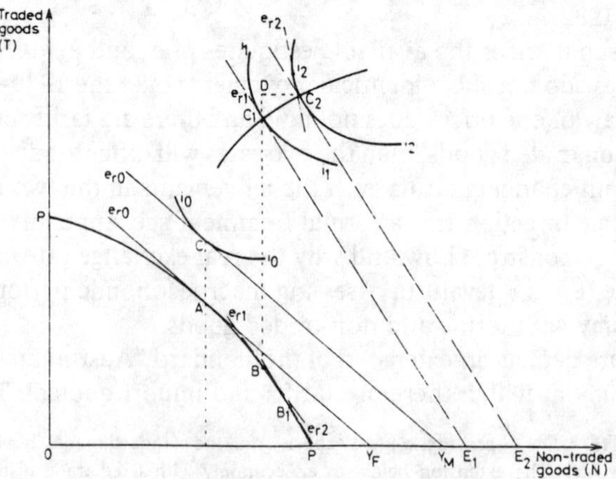

currency price of the composite good (P_f) and the tariff rate (t)[1]. The domestic currency price (P_N) of the non-traded good (which includes potentially tradeable goods converted into non-traded goods by prohibitive tariffs or binding import quotas) is set by domestic demand and supply.

PP in the Figure is the domestic production possibility curve for N and T for given technology and supplies of the two factors of production – capital and labor (for a formal treatment see Appendix II). We assume wage price flexibility, hence full employment in both factor markets[2]. *Without* any inflow of capital, the economy's *initial* equilibrium is, at production point A, and consumption point C. The difference between the value of domestic output (T^s) and domestic expenditure (T^d) of tradeables is the tariff revenue for the fixed tariff rate. The inverse of the common slope of the tangents at A and C is equal to the equilibrium real exchange rate $e_r = P_N/P^d_T$. Domestic output (Y)in terms of non-traded goods at factor cost is measured by $0Y_F$, and at market prices domestic expenditure (E) by $0Y_M$. From the well known national income identity this implies that the balance of trade (B) is zero, that is $B = Y_M - E = 0$. The economy is in internal and external balance at A and C.

Next, suppose the country receives a capital inflow of B_0 (not drawn) which, to abstract from questions of the optimal level of foreign borrowing, is assumed to be a grant. The new production and consumption equilibrium points will be given by B and C_1, respectively. C_1 must lie vertically above B, to equate the demand and supply for the non-traded good. Any emergence of excess demand or supply for the non-traded good will merely lead, ceteris paribus, to the requisite change in the *nominal* (P_N) and hence *relative* price (P_N/P^d_T) of the good.

Moreover, assuming no divergences between domestic consumer and producer prices (another simplifying assumption which does not effect our qualitative conclusions), the slope of the tangents at B (producer price ratio) and at C_1 (consumer price ratio) must be the same. The vertical distance C_1B represents the excess demand for the traded good plus tariff revenue, which gives rise to a trade deficit equal to B_0 valued at *domestic prices*. With the foreign capital inflow of B_0, therefore, the new equilibrium production and consumption points are uniquely determined. Also these points must lie to the right of the initial equilibrium point A (assuming convex indifference curves). Thus, a necessary feature of the new equilibrium is that the real exchange rate (the inverse of the slope of PP) must rise from e_{r0} to e_{r1}, and domestic output of non-traded goods must rise and that of traded goods fall, to allow the transfer of capital[3].

---

[1] P_f is now the foreign currency price of traded goods, and e is the domestic currency value of one unit of foreign currency.

[2] These assumptions are not essential. See Lal [1982a; b] for the working of the model when these assumptions do not hold.

[3] See Lal [1982a; b] for the outcomes when factor supplies are changing.

However, this required rise in the real exchange rate (e_r) can come about with a, *ceteris paribus*, (*i*) appreciation of the nominal exchange rate (fall in e), or (*ii*) a reduction in the level of net trade taxes (lower t), or (*iii*) a rise in the nominal price of non-traded goods (rise in P_N). If either of the first two mechanisms are chosen or induced, the overall price level in the country (P_d) will fall, whilst with the third mechanism the overall price level will rise[1].

Suppose the authorities wrongly consider the trade deficit (BC_1 minus the tariff revenue) at *domestic prices*, which is a necessary counterpart of the capital inflow, to be a problem and attempt to "cure" it through a devaluation (raising e). As the trade deficit *cannot* be eliminated if the capital inflow of B_0 is to be effectively transferred to the home country, the devaluation of the nominal exchange rate to "cure" this deficit will lead to an even greater rise in the nominal price of the non-traded good and the overall price level than under mechanism (*iii*) to bring about the requisite rise in the real exchange rate. Thus directional errors in the movement of the nominal exchange rate could lead to an excessive rise in the domestic price level, even when the latter is under no pressure from expansionary fiscal or monetary policy in the economy.

The effects of an increase in domestic expenditure beyond that justified by the capital inflow, that is an unsustainable monetary or fiscal expansion, can also be depicted in Figure 1. A rise in domestic expenditure above the level given by $0E_1$, say $0E_2$, will lead initially to an additional trade deficit of C_1D and an excess demand for non-tradeables of DC_2. With an unchanged nominal exchange rate (e) and level of net trade taxes (t), the excess demand for non-traded goods will lead to a rise in their price (P_N), and hence a further rise in the real exchange rate (e_r), till the new equilibrium is reached at the production point B_1 and consumption point C_2 – with a higher real exchange rate e_{r2}. There will now be a "secondary" trade deficit of TC_2 (not shown), over and above that of B_0 which is financed by the capital inflow. This secondary trade deficit is clearly unsustainable. To cure it, the real exchange rate will have to fall from e_{r2} to e_{r1}, and domestic expenditure will have to be reduced by E_1E_2. If there is downward inflexibility in the domestic currency price of non-traded goods due say to money (but *not* real) wage rigidity, the required fall in the real exchange rate would necessitate a rise in the domestic currency price of the traded good (P^d_T). This can most easily be brought about by a devaluation (rise in e).

To summarize, if there is no excess expenditure E_1E_2 in the economy, then with rising capital inflows, the real exchange rate *must* rise over time, as will the trade deficit. To seek to cure the trade deficit by a devaluation of the nominal exchange rate (rise in e) would be counterproductive, as the size of this "equilibrium" trade deficit is set by the level of foreign inflows, so that the

[1] See equations in Appendix I.

devaluation would merely require an even greater rise in the price of non-traded goods, to achieve the required rise in the real exchange rate. Under these circumstances a devaluation merely leads to inflation.

In assessing the past macroeconomic performance of Sri Lanka, and whether the economy in 1982 lacked internal and external balance requiring corrective public action depends on the extent to which the trade deficit reflected excess domestic expenditure (E_1E_2) over and above that justified by the actual (and desired) level of foreign capital inflows. The movements in the real exchange rate are an important diagnostic tool in forming this judgement. For the 1982 Sri Lankan situation to be one of macroeconomic disequilibrium it was not sufficient to point to the large current account deficit nor to a rise in the real exchange rate. Firstly, it is necessary to judge whether the movement in the real exchange rate has gone beyond e_{r1} (the inverse of the slope at B) towards e_{r2} (the inverse of the slope at B_1). Secondly, it will be necessary to form a judgement whether expenditure has been allowed to rise by the unsustainable amount E_1E_2. Moreover, if these judgements do point towards an unsustainable secondary trade deficit, it will be necessary to outline the policies required to bring the real exchange rate and domestic expenditure to their equilibrium levels (e_{r1} and $0E_1$, respectively) for the given foreign capital inflows of B_0. Finally, it will be necessary to judge whether the current level of foreign capital inflows are too high, or unsustainable, as that judgement in turn will determine the equilibrium real exchange rate e_{r1}. The next section provides empirical investigations of these issues.

III. A Formal Model of Real Exchange Rate Determination

We can formalize the small open economy macroeconomic model depicted by the Figure, to obtain the determinants of the money price of non-traded goods (P_N), for any given external terms of trade (given P_f) and the level of foreign borrowing (B_0), as follows[1].

The demand (N^d) and supply (N^s) for the non-traded good is given by

$$N^d = a_0 - a_1 (P_N - P_T^d) + a_2Y + a_3B_0 + a_4 (M^s - M^d) \qquad (1)$$

$$N^s = b_0 + b_1 (P_N - w) \qquad (2)$$

$$N^d = N^s \qquad (3)$$

where in addition to our previous notation Y is the domestic output at market prices, w the money wage rate, M^s the supply of money (nominal) and M^d the demand for money (nominal).

[1] The model is a composite of those due to Harberger, and Polak, Argy. To avoid keeping track of tariff revenues, the value of outputs of traded goods is at market prices and not factor cost.

The demand (T^d) and supply (T^s) for traded goods, and the balance of payments, are given by:

$$T^d = a_0 - a_1 (P_T^d - P_N) + (1-a_2) Y + (1-a_3) B_0 + (1-a_4) (M^s - M^d) \quad (4)$$

$$T^s = c_0 + c_1 (P_T^d - P_N) \quad (5)$$

$$B_0 = T^d - T^s \quad (6)$$

Domestic output at market prices is given by:

$$Y = N^s + T^s \quad (7)$$

The money demand function is given by:

$$(M^d/N \cdot P_d) = k (Y/N)^\alpha \quad (8)$$

where N is the population. The money supply process is determined from the following accounting relationship of the consolidated banking system, and a behavioral import function

$$\Delta M^s = \Delta NFA + \Delta D \quad (9)$$

$$\Delta NFA = X - I + B_0 \quad (10)$$

$$I = d_0 + d_1 \cdot (YP_d) \quad (11)$$

where Δ NFA is the change in net foreign assets of the consolidated banking system, ΔD the change in the total domestic credit of the banking system, X the value of exports, assumed to be given exogenously, and I the level of imports.

From (1) to (3), and substituting for Y in (1) from (2), (5) and (7), and rearranging yields an expression for the determinants of P_N as

$$P_N = \text{constant} \quad (12)$$

$$+ \frac{b_1 (1-a_2) - a_2 c_1}{a_1 + b_1 (1 - a_2)} w + \frac{a_1 + a_2 c_1}{a_1 + b_1 (1 - a_2)} P_T^d$$

$$+ \frac{a_3}{a_1 + b_1 (1 - a_2)} B_0 + \frac{a_4}{a_1 + b_1 (1 - a_2)} (M^s - M^d)$$

We use this expression to estimate the required change in the non-traded good price (P_N) for the observed change in foreign borrowing (B_0), and compare that with the actual change in P_N to see whether the non-traded goods price has risen by more than was required for equilibrium (with a constant w and P_T^d, and with $M^s = M^d$). Next, we estimate the required change in P_N for the observed changes in money wages (w), price of tradeables (P_T^d) and any excessive monetary expansion ($M^s > M^d$), to judge whether and to what extent the current real exchange rate in Sri Lanka deviates from the equilibrium rate e_{r1} in the Figure.

In the second of the above exercises it will also be necessary to judge the extent of any excessive monetary expansion ($M^s > M^d$). To do this empirically, consider the following derivations from the monetary sub-model in (8) – (11). The question we ask is: What would have been the required monetary expansion for the observed changes in the level of capital inflows (B_0) and exports (X), so that there was equilibrium in the overall balance of payments, that is for Δ NFA = 0?

First note that from (8), we can derive the standard quantity theory relationship[1]

$$YP_d = v \cdot M \tag{8a}$$

where v, the income velocity of money is given by

$$v = 1/k \cdot y^{\alpha-1} \tag{8b}$$

with $y \equiv Y/N$, per capita income.

Next, from (10) with Δ NFA = 0, we have

$$\Delta X + \Delta B_0 - \Delta I = 0 \tag{10a}$$

substituting for ΔI from (11), for $\Delta(YP_d)$ from (8a), and for ΔM from (9) yields after some manipulation[2], the required expansion in domestic credit $(\Delta D)^{req}$, for an exogenous change in exports and foreign capital inflow ($\Delta X + \Delta B_0$), which leads to ΔNFA = 0, as

$$\Delta D^{req} = (\Delta X + \Delta B_0) \ / \ v \cdot d_1 = [(\Delta X + \Delta B_0)\ (k \cdot y^{\alpha-1})] \ / \ d_1 \tag{13}$$

Comparing the actual expansion in credit from that required for monetary stability for the observed changes in exports and foreign capital inflows as estimated from (13) will provide our estimate of ($M^s - M^d$) in (12).

IV. Estimates of the Required Change in the Real Exchange Rate with Increased Capital Inflows

Normalizing the initial prices (P_N, P^d_T) and the money wage, w, at unity, dP_N, dP^d_T and dw, will represent percentage changes in (12). We first estimate the required change in P_N and the real exchange rate $e_r = P_N/P^d_T$, for the

[1] Defining per capita real money demand $m = (M/NP_d)$ and per capita real income as $y = (Y/N)$, we have from (8) $m = k \cdot y^{\alpha}$. Dividing both sides by y yields: $m/y = k \cdot y^{\alpha-1}$. Noting that $v = y/m$, we have $v = 1/k \cdot y^{\alpha-1}$.

[2] Thus in successive steps: $\Delta X + \Delta B_0 - d_1\Delta Y = 0$; $\Delta X + \Delta B_0 - d_1 v\Delta M = 0$; $\Delta X + \Delta B_0 - d_1 v\ (\Delta NFA + \Delta D) = 0$ as $\Delta NFA = 0$ is our equilibrium condition, the above yields (13).

observed increase in foreign capital inflows dB_0, in Sri Lanka from 1977–1982, assuming that $dw = dP_T^d = d(M^s - M^d) = 0$. From (12), we have

$$\dot{P}_N = [a_3/a_1 + b_1 (1 - a_2)] \, dB \tag{12a}$$

Denoting the elasticity of demand and supply of non-traded goods by η_N and ε_N respectively, we have from (1) and (2) that

$$a_1 = N^d \cdot \eta_N; \; b_1 = N^s \, \varepsilon_N$$

Making use of (3), after substituting for a_1 and b_1 as above, and dividing the numerator and denominator of the RHS of (12a) by real output Y, yields

$$\dot{P}_N = [(a_3 \cdot Y/N)/(\eta_N + \varepsilon_N (1 - a_2))] \, dB/Y \tag{12b}$$

where $N = N^d = N^s$.

Table 3 – *Estimate of* a_3

	1979	1980	1981
Grand total of capital inflows .	7,496	15,316	27,198
(1) Flows with mpm = 1	2,672	4,135	6,198
(2) Flows with mpm = 0.75 . .	3,120	7,909	15,567
(3) Flows with mpm = 0.6 . . .	769	754	1,003
(4) Flows with mpm = 0.5 . . .	935	2,518	4,430
(5) Weighted value	6,722	11,778	20,690
(6) Value of $(1-a_3)$	0,897	0,769	0,761

Note: a_3 = Proportion of foreign inflow spent on non-traded goods. – mpm = Marginal propensity to imports. – (1) = Commodity aid, food aid, IMF Trust Fund, and commercial suppliers credits; as such we assume these inflows directly finance imports. – (2) = Official grants, project aid, and short-term borrowing by the public sector; the Central Bank estimates that the import content of such borrowing is 75 percent. – (3) = Direct investment which we assume has an import content of 60 percent. – (4) = Private remittances which we assume has an mpm = 0.5. – (5) = This weighted value is derived by applying the mpm value to the respective capital flows in each column, and summing. – (6) = This is derived by dividing the weighted value by the total of capital inflows in that year.

Table 3 provides our estimate of the proportion of foreign capital inflows likely to be spent on non-traded goods, viz. $a_3 = 0.24$. If we assume that the weight of non-traded goods in the Colombo consumer price index also equals the marginal propensity to consume non-traded goods, then $a_2 = 0.6$. Assuming that the share of non-traded goods in domestic output is the same as their weight in the wholesale price index, implies that $Y/N = 1/0.5 = 2$.

This leaves estimates for the elasticities of demand and supply of non-traded goods. Harberger [1982] argues that the elasticity of substitution between two large composite commodities like traded and non-traded goods without good substitutes between them is likely to lie between 0.5 and 1.0. The own price elasticity of demand of non-traded goods equals: (1-share in total expenditure) × elasticity of substitution. The share in expenditure of non-traded goods is 0.6 according to the weight in the Colombo price index, and 0.54 according to the Central Bank's cost of living index. This gives a range for η_N of between 0.2 and 0.46.

We have virtually nothing to go on to provide an estimate of the supply elasticity of non-traded goods. Following Harberger's guessestimate for Chile, a range of 0.5 to 1.0 may not also be implausible for Sri Lanka. Substituting these values of the various parameters in (12b) yields a range of estimates for $\dot{P}_N$, as d(B/Y) increases, that is $\dot{P}_N(1)$ and $\dot{P}_N(2)$

$$\dot{P}_N(1) = (0.24 \times 2)/[0.2 + 0.5\ (1-0.6)]\ d(B/Y) = 1.2\ d(B/Y)$$

$$\dot{P}_N(2) = (0.24 \times 2)/[0.46 + 1.0\ (1-0.6)]\ d(B/Y) = 0.56\ d(B/Y)$$

From Table 1 capital inflows averaged between 2 and 4 percent of GDP from 1970–1977. Since then they have steadily risen to about 20 percent of GDP in 1982. This implies that for the 1977–1982 period, we can take d(B/Y) = 0.16. The required change in the equilibrium real exchange rate ($\dot{e}_r$), which for $dP_T^d = 0$ is the same as that in the nominal price of non-traded goods, $\dot{P}_N$, is then within the range

$$\dot{P}_N(1) = 1.2 \times 0.16 = 0.19 \text{ and } \dot{P}_N(2) = 0.56 \times 0.16 = 0.09$$

From Table 2, however, it appears that on all three of our alternative indices the real exchange rate *fell* by 6 to 20 percent between 1978 and 1982. If it is argued that the fall in the real exchange rate after the liberalization was a necessary part of the programme to establish external balance, we can then compare the movements in the real exchange rate (on our three indices) for the period since 1980. This gives a *rise* in the real exchange rate between 1980–1982 ranging between 5 to 14 percent, which is still within the range of the required rise in the rate as a result of the increased capital inflow – that is, within the estimated range of 9–19 percent. Thus, even if we ignore the effects on the real exchange rate flowing from the growth of GDP (which ceteris paribus is likely to require a further rise in e_r) [see Harberger, 1982], the extent movements in the real exchange rate in Sri Lanka since 1978 with the large inflows of foreign capital are unlikely to have placed the economy to the right of the point B in the Figure. *If* the current level of foreign capital inflows is considered socially desirable and sustainable, then there seems to be little evidence that the real exchange rate in Sri Lanka in 1983 was overvalued. If anything, our admittedly crude empirics suggest some slight undervaluation.

V. Estimates of the Contribution of Monetary Expansion and Rise in the Price of Traded Goods on the Price of Non-Traded Goods and the Overall Price Level

We need estimates of the parameters of (13), in order to estimate the equilibrium level of domestic credit expansion consistent with the changes in exports and capital inflows over the 1970–1982 period. Comparing these estimates with the actual credit expansion in each year will provide our estimate of "excessive" credit expansion. These estimates, together with the actual changes in the domestic price level, and traded goods prices will then be used to determine the effects of dP_T^d and d $(M^s - M^d)$ on $\dot{P}_N$ in (12).

Table 4 – *Data for Estimating Money Demand and the Import Function*

Year	ln · m[a]	ln · y[b]	Imports	GDP[c]
			(Rs. 00 million)	
1970	5.54	6.99	23	132
1971	5.59	6.97	22	137
1972	5.67	6.98	22	147
1973	5.54	7.00	26	179
1974	5.39	7.02	47	233
1975	5.33	7.03	53	257
1976	5.54	7.04	54	280
1977	5.67	7.05	63	347
1978	5.80	7.11	156	405
1979	5.96	7.16	226	498
1980	6.05	7.19	339	623
1981	6.07	7.23	361	793
1982	6.18	7.27	419	916

[a] m = Per capita real money. This was estimated by dividing M_2 by the GDP deflator and the annual population. – [b] y = Real per capita income. This was derived by dividing the figures for GDP at constant prices by the annual population. – [c]GDP at current prices.

We first estimated a log linear version of the demand for money equation (8) from the monetary data in Table 4. Denoting per capita real money by $m = (M/NP)$; and per capita real income by $y = (Y/N)$, the estimated equation (for the period 1970–1982) was[1]

[1] In a properly specified demand for money function we should have also included an interest rate and expected inflation rate variable [Fry, 1982], but these refinements are abstracted from in our simple macroeconomic model. Moreover, an examination of the data shows that the movements in real interest rates have been primarily responsible for substitution between the non-interest and interest bearing components of M_2.

$$\text{(R.I)}\quad \log m = -\ 13.4 \underset{(2.32)}{} + \underset{(0.33)}{2.7} \log y \qquad R^2 = 0.88;\ n = 13;\ DW = 2.17;\ P_1 = 0.94;\ P_2 = -\ 0.68$$

(standard errors: 13.4 (2.32); 2.7 (0.33))

with standard errors in parentheses and P = autocorrelation coefficients. This provides the required estimates of v, for each year, required in (13).

Next we estimated d_1, by running an OLS regression for (11), with the data given in Table 4. The estimated equation for the 1970–1982 period was

$$\text{(R.II)}\quad I = -\ \underset{(25.98)}{76.6} + \underset{(0.05)}{0.56}\,(YP_d) \qquad R^2 = 0.93;\ n = 13;\ DW = 1.82;\ P_1 = 0.38$$

Using these estimates of v and d_1, we next estimated ΔD^{req}, and the difference between the actual change in domestic credit ΔD, in Table 5.

Table 5 – *Estimating D^{req} and D^{act}*

Year	ΔK	ΔX	y	x/d_1	ΔD^{req}	D^{act}	x $100^{\Delta D^{req}}$	x $100^{\Delta D^{act}}$
	(1)	(2)	(3)	(4)	(5)	(6)	(7)	(8)
1971	98	−85	1064	0.390	4.92	4481	0.11	7.0
1972	−174	−33	1079	0.397	−80.23	4936	−1.63	9.6
1973	189	447	1101	0.409	255.13	4815	5.30	−2.4
1974	316	1055	1117	0.417	563.13	5828	9.67	19.1
1975	−305	513	1130	0.424	87.20	6233	1.40	6.7
1976	611	794	1142	0.430	599.76	7269	8.25	15.3
1977	−201	1933	1151	0.436	749.28	8796	8.52	19.0
1978	2904	6567	1225	0.472	4555.05	10575	43.07	18.4
1979	2457	2075	1280	0.507	2348.62	15113	15.54	35.7
1980	4827	2321	1332	0.533	3963.76	25636	15.46	52.8
1981	3601	2904	1385	0.565	3854.59	33824	11.40	27.7
1982	3707	927	1431	0.589	2902.75	42412	6.84	22.6

Note: ΔK = Change in foreign capital flows, derived from Central Bank data. – ΔX = Change in exports, derived from Central Bank data. – y = Real per capita income. – $x = (k \cdot y^{\delta-1}) = 1/v$; the estimate $\ln x = -11.28 + 1.4 \ln y$ has been used to determine x. – d_1 = Marginal propensity to import, which has been estimated as 0.56. – ΔD^{req} has been estimated from $\Delta D = (\Delta K + \Delta X) \cdot (x/d_1)$. – ΔD^{req} has been estimated by dividing (5) by (6). – ΔD^{act} = Annual percentage change in (6).

Denoting by $\dot{E} \equiv \Delta\dot{D} - \Delta\dot{D}^{req}$, we finally estimated an inflation equation for the Colombo price index (P_d), and another one for its non-traded goods component (P_N), with $\dot{E}$ representing monetary pressures, and the percentage change in traded goods prices $\dot{P}^d_T$, as the exogenous "cost push" element resulting from changes in the nominal exchange rate e, and in the foreign currency prices of traded goods P_f (see Table 6). The estimated equations were

(R.III) $\dot{P}_d = 2.52 + 0.10\ \dot{E} + 0.50\ \dot{P}^d_T$ $R^2 = 0.92$; $n = 12$
(0.9) (0.04) (0.05) $DW = 1.44$

(R.IV) $\dot{P}_N = 4.96 + 0.04\ \dot{E} + 0.25\ \dot{P}^d_T$ $R^2 = 0.39$; $n = 12$
(1.84) (0.08) (0.11) $DW = 1.51$

Both coefficients are significant in R.III, but only the coefficient of $\dot{P}^d_T$ is significant in R.IV. However, it can be seen from (4) in Appendix I that as the weight of non-traded goods in the overall price index (P_d) is 0.6 [$a = 0.6$ in (4) in Appendix I], and if we denote the estimated coefficients of $\dot{P}_d$ by f_0, f_1 and f_2, respectively, then we can also derive the coefficients of $\dot{P}_N$ from[1]

$$\dot{P}_N\ (f_0/0.6) + (f_1/0.6)\ \dot{E} + [(f_2 - 0.4)/0.6]\ \dot{P}^d_T$$

Given our estimates of f_0, f_1 and f_2 from R.III, the coefficient of $\dot{P}^d_T$ and the constant estimated in R.IV is consistent with the values we would derive by this indirect method, but that of the $\dot{E}$ term is not. If, therefore, we assume that the correct coefficient for $\dot{E}$ in the $\dot{P}_N$ equation is $f_1/0.6$, we will have our best estimate of the elasticity of P_N with respect to excessive domestic credit creation, denoted by $\psi_E = 0.17$; and that with respect to the domestic price of tradeables, denoted by $\psi_{P^d_T} = 0.20$. These are our best estimates for the parameters of the traded goods price change ($\dot{P}^d_T$), and excessive monetary expansion ($M^s > M^d$) terms in (12) above.

Finally, we need an estimate of the coefficient of the money wage (w) term in (12). Noting that $c_i = T^s\ \varepsilon_T$, where ε_T is the supply elasticity of traded goods, and that our estimate of a_2, the marginal propensity to consume non-traded goods, is 0.6 we have

$$\frac{b_1\ (1-a_2) - a_2\ c_1}{a_1 + b_1\ (1-a_2)} = \frac{0.4N^s\ \varepsilon_N - 0.6\ T^s\ \varepsilon_T}{N^d \eta_N + 0.4\ N^s\ \varepsilon_N} = \frac{0.4\ \varepsilon_N - 0.6\ \varepsilon_T}{\eta_N + 0.4\ \varepsilon_N}$$

where we have made use of (3) and (7), and of our estimate that $N^s/Y = 0.5$, and hence that $T^s = N^s$. We had two limiting ranges of estimates for the elasticity of demand η_N and supply ε_N of non-traded goods. Taking the lower of the estimates for $\eta_N = 0.2$, and the higher for $\varepsilon_N = 1.0$, as our best guess of these parameters, we are left with providing a guessestimate of the elasticity of supply of traded goods ε_T. As the majority of Sri Lanka's exports are agricultural and mining, whose supply elasticity is likely to be relatively low in the short run, as compared with the services which are likely to be a major component of non-traded goods, it may not be implausible to assume that $\varepsilon_T = 1/2\ \varepsilon_N = 0.5$. Substituting this value in the above expression yields a value of the elasticity of P_N, with respect to the money wage (w), denoted by $\psi_w = 0.17$.

[1] Thus we have $\dot{P}_d = 0.6\ \dot{P}_N + 0.4\ \dot{P}^d_T$. We have estimated $\dot{P}_d = f_0 + f_1\dot{E} + f_2\dot{P}^d_T$. Substituting for $\dot{P}_d$ in this expression from the first equation yields $\dot{P}_N = (f_0/0.6) + (f_1/0.6)\ \dot{E} + [(f_2 - 0.4)/0.6]\ \dot{P}^d_T$.

Table 6 – *Data for Estimating Determinants of Inflation*

Year	$\dot{P}_{Colombo}$	$\dot{P}_N$	$\dot{P}_T$	$\dot{E}$
1971	2.64	4.11	0.38	6.89
1972	6.08	8.18	3.21	11.23
1973	9.26	3.76	18.14	-7.70
1974	11.61	4.83	20.40	9.43
1975	6.54	7.33	6.37	5.30
1976	1.18	3.12	- 1.67	7.05
1977	1.23	2.58	- 2.07	10.48
1978	11.46	13.15	20.83	- 24.67
1979	10.19	8.58	14.24	20.16
1980	23.22	14.74	36.08	37.34
1981	16.53	16.70	16.72	16.30
1982	10.28	11.73	7.30	15.76

Note: $\dot{P}_{Colombo}$ = Rate of change in the Colombo consumer price index. – $\dot{P}_N$ = Rate of change in the domestic goods component of the Colombo consumer price index. – $\dot{P}_T$ = Percentage change in the import unit value index. – $\dot{E}$ = Percentage excess increase in domestic credit, derived from $\dot{E} = \dot{D}^{act} - \dot{D}^{req}$ from columns 7 and 8 of Table 5.

In summary, our best estimates of the four elasticities in (12) are $\psi_w = 0.17$; $\psi_{P^d_t} = 0.2$; $\psi_{B_0} = 1.2$; $\psi_E = 0.17$.

We then estimated the change in non-traded goods prices $(\dot{P}_N)^{exp}$ which could be expected during the 1978–1982 period, in response to the actual changes in w, P^d_T, B_0, E, during each of these years (see Table 7). These can be compared with the actual changes in $\dot{P}_N$. Taking the period as a whole, it appears from Table 7, that on the basis of our estimating equation (12b)

$$\dot{P}_N^{exp} = 0.17\,\dot{w} + 0.2\,\dot{P}^d_T + 1.2\,(B_0/Y) + 0.17\,\dot{E} = 0.12$$

whereas the actual average annual $\dot{P}_N = 0.13$. This is close enough to provide some confidence in our elasticity estimates in (12b).

Finally, we can decompose the estimated average annual $\dot{P}_N$, to determine the contribution of the four variables w, P^d_T, B_0, E to the rise in prices of non-traded goods. From Table 7, we have the percentage contribution of these variables, on an annual average basis for the 1978–1982 period as follows $\dot{w} = 24$, $\dot{P}^d_T = 31$, $\dot{B}/Y = 34$, $\dot{E} = 11$ percent.

Given the marked increase in the real income growth rate, and accompanying demand for labor, some rise in real (and with ongoing inflation) in money wages is to be expected. Hence we assume that the observed contribution of $\dot{w}$ to $\dot{P}_N$ was unavoidable. There has clearly been some upward pressure on the domestic price level due to excessive monetary expansion above that required to absorb the large capital inflows Sri Lanka has received, but this excess has not been massive, and its contribution to domestic inflation has been fairly modest. By contrast, much of the rise in the

Table 7 – *Determinants of $\dot{P}_N$, 1978–1982*

Year	$\psi_B D(B/Y)$	$\psi_{PT}\dot{P}_T$	$\psi_E\dot{E}$	$\dot{w}$	$\psi_w\dot{w}$	$\dot{P}_N^{exp}$	$\dot{P}_N^{act}$
	(1)	(2)	(3)	(4)	(5)	(6)	(7)
1978 ...	0.082	0.042	- 0.055	0.258	0.0439	0.1129	0.1315
1979 ...	0.038	0.028	0.024	0.346	0.0588	0.1488	0.0858
1980 ...	0.063	0.072	0.047	0.049	0.0083	0.1903	0.1474
1981 ...	0.008	0.033	0.023	0.032	0.0054	0.0694	0.1670
1982 ...	0.019	0.015	0.025	0.167	0.0284	0.0874	0.1173
Average	0.042	0.04	0.01		0.02	0.12	0.13

Note: The expected change in P_N has been estimated for each year by (12b) in the text. The change in money wages ($\dot{w}$) has been estimated from the weighted average of the Central Bank's index of money wages in the private and public sectors, where the weight used is the share of public sector employment in the total labor force which was 20 percent in 1978.

domestic price level is due (on our estimates) to the rise in the domestic price of tradeables, and the need for the non-traded goods price to rise by even more to establish the higher real exchange rate that is required in order to affect the transfer of the large inflows of foreign capital that Sri Lanka has received since 1978. The domestic price of tradeables in turn (see (1) in Appendix I) is determined by exogenous changes in foreign currency prices of traded goods, and the two policy variables, the nominal exchange rate and the level of net tariffs. *Given* the higher level of capital inflows, the apparent symptoms of a "crisis" in Sri Lanka, in the form of marked inflationary pressures, must therefore be primarily placed on inappropriate policies regarding the nominal exchange rate and the level of net tariffs.

The above discussion has been based on assuming that the capital inflows were both socially desirable and sustainable. 46 percent of the inflows were of concessional foreign aid and another 28 percent workers remittances. The bulk of these capital flows were thus virtually costless and should not have been turned down as the social desirability of "free" resources is indubitable. The social desirability of the remaining 26 percent of the flows in the form of commercial borrowing will depend upon the relative cost and returns to this borrowing. In the absence of a proper social cost-benefit analysis this is difficult to judge[1]. The sustainability of the aid and remittance components depends in part upon political factors and hence is beyond our remit.

[1] See Lal [1971] for the criterion for determining the social desirability of the inflows. Based on shadow price estimates we have made elsewhere [Lal, 1979] the breakeven effective real interest rate which would have justified commercial loans with an average maturity of 8 years (the average for Sri Lanka's Eurodollar borrowing) for *(i)* domestic investment (yielding a social return of 12 percent) is 22.5 percent and *(ii)* for consumption is the estimated consumption rate of interest of 3 percent. As Eurodollar rates during 1976–1982 averaged between 1 and 8 percent [see Lal, 1983], it is likely that Sri Lanka's commercial borrowing, too, may not have been socially undesirable.

VI. Conclusions

Our conclusions can be briefly summarized. First, the usual signs of a macroeconomic crisis – a current account deficit, a large public sector deficit, and a high inflation rate – are at best imperfect and at worst highly misleading signals in a country receiving large capital inflows. Nor does appreciation of the PPP effective exchange rate indicate the presence of a crisis when foreign capital inflows. non-traded goods, and a high and changing net level of foreign trade taxes are of importance. Movements in the real exchange rate provide a better diagnostic tool.

Secondly, the appreciation in the real exchange rate in Sri Lanka (till 1982) was probably less than was required for equilibrium with the large increase in foreign capital inflows since 1977.

Thirdly, the adjustment in relative prices of non-traded to traded goods which is required to yield the higher real exchange rate took place in Sri Lanka through a rise in the price of non-traded goods, rather than through a fall in the domestic price of traded goods. Moreover, this rise in non-traded goods prices has been accentuated by the rise in the domestic price of traded goods, due both to a rise in foreign currency prices and the devaluation of the nominal exchange rate. Most of the inflation that Sri Lanka has experienced since 1977 can be accounted for by these two factors.

Fourthly, though there has been some excessive monetary expansion above the levels justified by the large capital inflows, its contribution to inflation has been relatively modest. Nevertheless, it is of importance to devise methods whereby domestic fiscal and monetary policy, whilst reflecting the need for expansion of domestic expenditure above domestic output that is inherent in absorbing capital inflows which are currently running at about 20 percent of GDP, do not add fuel to any inflationary pressures that may result from the inevitable appreciation of the real exchange rate. Though we have provided a rough and ready method for determining the required expansion in total domestic credit for any given change in foreign capital inflows and export earnings, its usefulness as a planning tool, when these exogenous variables can only be imperfectly forecast, is limited. It may be best to keep the size of the public sector deficit down to the level that can be financed through socially desirable foreign borrowing.

Fifthly, as the bulk of the capital inflows since 1977 was in the form of aid and workers remittances, it is unlikely they were socially undesirable. However, for commercial borrowing, it is important to ensure that the social returns to the uses of this borrowing are at least as great as its real cost. As much of this inflow has been and is likely to continue to be into the public sector, it is imperative that well established procedures of social cost-benefit analysis be used to appraise the uses of these funds.

Finally, to prevent any future inflationary pressures that may arise from the inevitable changes in the real exchange rate flowing from increased foreign borrowing, as well as to complete the imperfect adjustment (on our estimates) to the past borrowing, it may be advisable to allow part of the required real exchange rate adjustment to come through a reduction in the domestic price of traded goods, by reducing tariffs and removing quantitative restrictions. Apart from the obvious efficiency gains that would result from the consequent reduction in the level and variance of effective protection in the economy, this would lead to both an appreciation of the real exchange rate (as required to absorb the large capital inflows) and a depreciation of the PPP effective real exchange rate, which is desirable to maintain export competitiveness.

Appendix I

If P_f is the foreign currency price of the traded good, making the small country assumption, the domestic currency price (P_d) for a given nominal exchange rate (e) is

$$P_T^d = e \cdot P_f\,(1 + t) \qquad (1)$$

where (t) is the net effect of domestic import and export taxes and subsidies. The real exchange rate (e_r) is

$$e_r \equiv P_N/P_T^d = P_N/e \cdot P_f\,(1 + t) \qquad (2)$$

whilst the PPP real effective exchange rate is

$$e_p \equiv P_d/e \cdot P_f \qquad (3)$$

The domestic price level (P_d) in (3) is a weighted average of the domestic prices of traded (P_T^d) with a weight (1–a) and of non-traded goods (P_N) with a weight of "a". Hence

$$P_d \equiv a \cdot P_N + (1\text{–}a)\,P_T^d \qquad (4)$$

From (1) to (4) we have

$$e_P = (1 + t)\,[a \cdot e_r + (1\text{–}a)] \qquad (5)$$

The PPP real effective exchange rate will only be equal to the real exchange rate, if the "law of one price" holds, that is, $a = 0$, and if there are no tariffs, that is $t = 0$. Then $e_p = e_r = 1$. Moreover, logarithmic differentiation of (5) with respect to time (n), yields

$$\dot{e}_p = k\dot{e}_r + \dot{\tau} \qquad (6)$$

where $\tau \equiv (1 + t)$; $\dot{x} = (1/x)\,(dx/dn)$; $k \equiv e_r\,[ae_r + (1 - a)]$

Thus, from (2), a rise in tariffs ($\dot{\tau} > 0$) will lower the real exchange rate ceteris paribus ($\dot{e}_r < 0$), but from (6) will lead to a rise in the PPP real effective exchange rate ($\dot{e}_p > 0$).

Appendix II

Thus suppose the domestic output of the three goods is Q_1, Q_2, Q_3, with the first two being traded and Q_3 the non-traded good. P^d is the domestic (tariff inclusive) price of traded good 2 with traded good 1 taken as the numeraire. Then T^s, the domestic supply of the composite traded good is given by

$$T^s = \text{Max}\ (Q_1 + P^d Q_2)$$

s.t. $$F\ [Q_1, Q_2, Q_3; \overline{K}, \overline{L}] = 0$$

where F is the implicit transformation surface, and $\overline{K}$, $\overline{L}$, are the given factor endowments. Clearly T^s is the value of the domestic supply of traded goods at domestic (tariff inclusive) prices given Q_3 (the output of non-traded goods). It is easy to show that at $(Q_1 + P^d Q_2)$ the maximizing value of Q_1 and Q_2

$$P^d = F_2 / F_1$$

As such $$\frac{dT^s}{dQ_3} = \frac{dQ_1}{dQ_3} + P^d \frac{dQ_2}{dQ_3} = \frac{dQ_1}{dQ_3} + \frac{F_2}{F_1} \cdot \frac{dQ_2}{dQ_3}$$

But $$F_1 \frac{dQ_1}{dQ_3} + F_2 \frac{dQ_2}{dQ_3} + F_3 = 0$$

Hence $\dfrac{dT^s}{dQ_3} = -\dfrac{F_3}{F_1}$ = supply price of non-traded goods in terms of the numeraire. On the consumption side, define

$$W\ [T^d, C_3] \equiv \text{Max}\ U\ [C_1, C_2, C_3]$$

s.t. $$C_1 + P^d C_2 = T^d$$

where C_i is the consumption of the ith goods, T^d the consumption expenditure on traded goods at domestic (tariff inclusive) prices, and U the social utility function. It is then easy to show that, when evaluated at the utility maximizing C_1 and C_2

$$W_1 = \frac{\partial W}{\partial T^d} = \frac{\partial U}{\partial C_1} \text{ and } W_3 = \frac{\partial W}{\partial C_3} = \frac{\partial U}{\partial C_3}$$

so that the marginal rate of substitution W_3/W_1 along any W indifference curve gives the demand price of the non-traded good in terms of the numeraire. At the equilibrium, the supply and demand price of the non-traded good are equal and the difference between T^d and T^s (the expenditure on and value of production of traded goods at domestic prices) is the tariff revenue.

References

Corden, Warner M., *Inflation, Exchange Rates and the World Economy.* Oxford 1977.

Cuthbertson, A. G., Muhammad Z. Khan, *Effective Protection to Manufacturing in Sri Lanka.* Colombo 1981.

Fry, Maxwell J., "Analysing Disequilibrium Interest-Rate Systems in Developing Countries". *World Development,* Vol. 10, 1982, pp. 1049–1057.

Harberger, Arnold C., "The Chilean Economy in the 1970s: Crisis, Stabilization, Liberalization, Reform". In: Karl Brunner, Allan Meltzer (Eds.), *Economic Policy in A World of Change.* Amsterdam 1982.pp. 115–152.

Lal, Deepak, "When is Foreign Borrowing Desirable?" *Bulletin of the Oxford University Institute of Economics and Statistics,* Vol. 33, 1971, pp. 197–206.

–, *Estimates of Accounting Prices for Sri Lanka.* London 1979, mimeo.

– [1982a], *The Real Aspects of Stabilization and Structural Adjustment Policies: An Approach.* University College London, Discussion Papers in Economics, No. 32. London, December 1982.

– [1982b], "Stolper-Samuelson-Rybczynski in the Pacific". Forthcoming in: *Journal of Development Economics.*

–, *The Poverty of "Development Economics".* London 1983.

Polak, Jacques J., Victor Argy, "Credit Policy and the Balance of Payments". In: International Monetary Fund (IMF) (Ed.), *The Monetary Approach to the Balance of Payments.* Washington, D.C., 1977, pp. 205–225.

* * *

[18]

Journal of Development Economics 21 (1986) 181–204. North-Holland

STOLPER–SAMUELSON–RYBCZYNSKI IN THE PACIFIC

Real Wages and Real Exchange Rates in the Philippines, 1956–1978*

Deepak LAL

University College London, London WC1E 6BT, UK

The World Bank, Washington, DC 20433, USA

Received December 1982, final version received November 1984

The paper attempts to explain movements of real wages in the Philippines in terms of the standard trade-theoretic Stolper–Samuelson–Rybczynski model. In view of the factor intensities in the Philippines, commodities are aggregated into two composite goods – traded and non-traded – whose relative price – the so-called 'real exchange rate' – is shown to have been an important determinant, with changes in relative factor supplies of less importance in determining real wages. A conventional two-sector model is set out, which distinguishes between the short and long run effects in terms of the 'quasi-fixity' of sector specific capital. A simple regression model is estimated and seems to provide a fairly good explanation of what has hitherto appeared to be a puzzling feature of post-war Philippines economic performance – high growth rates of output and employment, accompanied by declining real wages (in turn being associated with a rising incidence of poverty) in at least two periods.

1. Introduction

This paper attempts to explain post-war movements of real wages in the Philippines in terms of the standard trade-theoretic Stolper–Samuelson–Rybczynski (SSR) model. This may be of interest for three reasons.

First, despite fairly rapid growth in output and employment, there have been at least two periods of marked real wage decline in the Philippines, and

*This paper is based on chapter 3 of Lal (1980), prepared for the World Bank, which, however, should not be identified in any way with our views or analysis. The statistical computations were performed by Ted Black and Pradeep Srivastava. Clifford Wymer provided valuable statistical advice. Comments on earlier versions by Romeo Bautista, Trent Bertrand, J. Borkakoti, Mark Leiserson, Mahar Manghas and members of a seminar at the World Bank and the SSRC's International Economics study group and particularly by an anonymous referee which greatly helped to improve the paper, are gratefully acknowledged. The World Bank does not accept reponsibility for the views expressed herein which are those of the author(s) and should not be attributed to the World Bank or to its affiliated organizations. The findings, interpretations, and conclusions are the results of research supported by the Bank; they do not necessarily represent official policy of the Bank. The designations employed, the presentation of material, and any maps used in this document are solely for the convenience of the reader and do not imply the expression of any opinion whatsoever on the part of the World Bank or its affiliates concerning the legal status of any country, territory, city, area, or of its authorities, or concerning the delimitation of its boundaries, or national affiliation.

an associated increased incidence of poverty. As these cannot be explained in terms of an unsatisfactory overall increase in the demand for labour relative to its supply [see Lal (1980)], various structuralist explanations have been popular [see Khan (1977)]. In our view these too are flawed, as they depend upon various forms of labour market segmentation for which there seems to be virtually no evidence in the Philippines [see Lal (1980, ch. 2)]. Hence our search for an explanation within the standard neo-classical trade-theoretic framework.

Though the SSR theorems are amongst the most thoroughly researched in trade theory, and would seem to be directly relevant to our subject, they have been rarely applied.[1] This may be due to their long run character, as well as the other standard simplifying assumptions on which they are based. Whilst their short run versions in the so-called Ricardo–Viner (RV) model, which assume sector specific capital stocks but mobile labour (in the three-factor two-commodity versions [see Jones (1971), Mayer (1974), Mussa (1974)]) are known to suffer from the so-called neo-classical ambiguity [see Samuelson (1971), Jones (1975)] concerning movements in the short run real wage. These, unlike the long run SSR versions, can no longer be predicted solely from the production structure of the economy and could, moreover, be at variance with the long run predictions. However, as Burgess (1980) has recently shown, once inter-industry flows are introduced into the 'two specific–one mobile factor' model, at least for certain parameter values of the production structure, this neo-classical ambiguity disappears. It is this version of the short run version of SSR that we apply to the Philippines. The dynamics of adjustment to the long run SSR equilibrium, following an exogenous change in relative commodity prices and/or factor supplies, have been studied by Mussa (1978). He shows that in an economy with ongoing capital formation (at increasing marginal cost) and depreciation of existing capital, the qualitative properties of the adjustment path are the same with static or rational expectations.[2] This enables us to sidestep the thorny issue of expectation formation and the adjustment technology in our empirical work, and to determine the time path of real wage movements purely in terms of standard parameters of the production side of the economy, and the exogenous relative price and relative factor supply changes, over time.

Thirdly, as the empirically determined commodity aggregation (dictated by the relative factor intensities of commodities) for the Philippines entails a model that only distinguishes between traded and non-traded goods, the key relative price of these goods is also the so-called 'real exchange rate' of the Australian model of balance of payments adjustment [see Salter (1959), Corden (1977)]. Recently, there has been much concern with the 'social' consequences of various IMF short run stabilisation programmes in develop-

[1]But see Burgess (1976) and Magee (1978).
[2]See section 4 of Mussa (1978).

ing countries [see Nowzad (1981)]. A major component of these programmes are measures to affect the real exchange rate. Hence the analysis and empirics of this paper which explicitly links real wage movements with those in the real exchange rate may also be of interest in the debate on the normative question of the 'optimal' stabilisation scheme for a small open developing country whose exports are natural resource rather than labour intensive.

The paper is in two parts. The first provides the necessary Philippine background, and the particular trade-theoretic model we use to explain Philippines real wage movements between 1956–1978 in the second part.

2. The setting

Tables 1.a–1.b summarise the data on overall trends in the labour force, employment, constant price NNP and various measures of unemployment for the Philippines in the post-war years. Tables 2.a–2.b provide data on the movements in real wages for urban and rural labour. Elsewhere [Lal (1980)] we have studied the available evidence of the functioning of the Philippines' labour markets. The following conclusions from that study and the data in tables 1.a–2.b are relevant for our purposes.

First, job creation has kept up with increases in labour supply, without any dilution in 'quality' as judged by (a) the changes in average hours worked, (b) changes in the numbers (or percentage) of those who want additional work, and (c) changes in the distribution of employment by broad class of worker. Nor is there evidence of any 'discouraged worker' effect flowing from an 'ex ante' labour supply in excess of labour demand [see Lal (1980, ch. 1)].

Secondly, Philippines labour markets function closer to the competitive than the structuralist view which emphasises labour market segmentation, as (i) there is no evidence of trade unions raising organised sector wages above labour's supply price, (ii) there is survey evidence showing considerable inter-cum-intra-generational occupational and geographical mobility [see Castillo (1977), ILO (1974), Abarientos et al. (1972), Castillo (1975)], and (iii) there is also considerable intra-sectoral mobility of labour within the rural sector, with multiple farm and non-farm occupations common amongst rural households, and within the so-called urban informal sector [see Tidalgo and Jurado (1978)]. Nor is there evidence of any obvious barriers to entry into the urban 'formal' or the rural 'plantation' sectors [see Lal (1980, ch. 2)]. Hence, overall increases in labour demand can be expected to be diffused relatively rapidly over the various industrial, occupational and regional labour markets in the Philippines.

Despite this, real wages have declined between 1961–1964 and again from 1969–1974 for most groups in the economy [see Khan (1977), Berry (1978), Lal (1980)].

Table 1.a

Labour force, employment and unemployment, 1956–1978 (in thousands except percent).[a]

	Labour force		Employed		Openly unemployed		Total unemployed			
							Measure 1[b]		Measure 2[c,d]	
Year	Nos. (1)	% change over previous years (2)	Nos. (3)	% change over previous years (4)	Nos. (5)	Percent of labour force (6)	Nos. (7)	Percent of labour force (8)	Nos. (9)	Percent of labour force (10)
1956	9,029		8,009		1,021	11.3	2,013	22.3	1,578	17.5
1957	8,875	−1.7	8,174	2.1	701	7.9	1,879	18.9	1,158	13.0
1958[e]	9,317	5.0	8,555	4.7	762	8.2	1,769	19.0	n.a.	n.a.
1959	9,345	0.8	8,705	1.8	639	6.8	1,075	17.9	n.a.	n.a.
1960[e]	9,521	1.9	8,828	1.4	692	7.3	1,758	18.5	n.a.	n.a.
1961	9,995	5.0	9,245	4.7	750	7.5	1,846	18.5	1,265	12.7
1962[e]	10,479	4.8	9,641	4.3	837	8.0	2,040	19.5	1,380	13.0
1963	10,710	2.2	10,039	4.1	670	6.3	1,980	18.5	1,378	12.9
1964[e]	10,898	1.8	10,253	2.1	641	5.9	1,862	17.1	1,178	10.8
1965	11,127	2.1	10,322	0.7	805	7.2	1,937	16.4	1,460	13.1
1966	11,821	6.2	10,984	6.4	837	7.1	1,966	16.0	1,366	11.6
1967	12,525	6.0	11,526	4.9	999	8.0	2,155	17.2	n.a.	n.a.
1968	12,452	−0.6	11,476	−0.4	976	7.8	2,160	17.3	1,794	14.4
1969[f]	12,605	1.3	11,732	2.2	873	6.9	2,028	16.1	1,370	10.9
1970[f]	12,758	1.2	11,988	2.2	770	6.0	1,893	14.8	n.a.	n.a.
1971	12,911	1.2	12,245	2.1	666	5.2	1,758	13.6	1,037	8.0
1972	13,701	6.1	12,833	4.8	867	6.3	1,996	14.6	1,249	9.1
1973	14,140	3.2	13,450	4.8	690	4.9	1,899	13.4	1,086	7.7
1974 (Aug.)	14,244	0.7	13,666	1.6	578	4.1	1,644[h]	11.5	946	6.6
1975 (Aug.)	15,161	6.4	14,517	6.2	643	4.2	1,896[h]	12.5	1,029	6.8
1976 (Aug.)	16,244	7.1	15,427	6.3	818	5.0	2,221[h]	13.7	1,192	7.3
1977[g] (Oct. 3)	15,200	—	14,470	—	730	4.8	n.a.	n.a.	n.a.	n.a.
1978[g] (Oct. 2)	16,830	10.7	15,753	8.9	1,077	6.4	n.a.	n.a.	n.a.	n.a.

Compound growth rates		
1956–76	3.0%	3.3%
1956–61	2.1%	2.9%
1961–68	3.2%	3.1%
1968–76	3.4%	3.8%

[a]The NCSO labour force surveys were conducted biannually in May and October till 1968, (except for 1958, 1960, 1962 and 1964). A May survey was undertaken in 1969 but none in 1970 when the 'Census of Population and Housing' was conducted. From 1971 a quarterly survey in February, May, August and November was instituted, except that the first quarterly survey in 1971 was in March. The sample design of the survey was changed in 1965 and again in 1971. The employment and labour force data from Tidalgo (1976) shown are averages of the May and October figures from 1956 to 1968, and quarterly averages from 1971 to 1973. 'For the years when only one or no labour force survey undertaken, the average of the preceding and the following year when surveys were undertaken is used instead' [Tidalgo (1976, p. 184)].

[b]The figures till 1973 are from Tidalgo (1976). She states that these are the full time equivalent unemployment of the visibly under-employed defined as below 40 hours and wanting additional work. However, from the November 1973 'Labor Force Survey' (NCSO Bulletin no. 40 T) the total number of workers working under 40 hours and wanting additional work was only 900 thousand, which is *less* than the 1,200 thousand 'fully unemployment' equivalent of these workers reported by Tidalgo in 1973 (column 7). However, there were altogether 858,000 working less than 20 hours and 2,541,000 working less than 39 hours = 3,399 thousand workers (including those not wanting additional work) working less than 40 hours (NCSO Bulletin no. 20, table 12). If it is assumed that the average hours worked was 10 for those under 20, and 30 for those between 20 and 39 hours, we get the full time unemployment equivalent in thousands as: $3/4(858) + 1/4(2{,}541) = 1{,}278$, which is close to Tidalgo's figure. We therefore deduce that Tidalgo's estimates refer to those working less than 40 hours (including those not wanting additional work), and hence are a *rough measure of the surplus labour time* (below a 'full time' employment norm of 40 hours) available in the employed labour force. Our estimates for 1974 onwards therefore are based on this above assumption.

[c]Unemployed (openly) plus the full time equivalent unemployment of the visibly underemployed, defined as those persons working less than 40 hours a week.

[d]These figures have been computed in statistical appendix table A.1, from the NCSO data, for those working less than 40 hours *and* wanting additional work, and they correspond more closely to a notion of *involuntary underemployment*, on the assumption that implicitly those wanting additional work would be willing to work up to 40 hours at their current wages.

[e]Interpolated values by averaging the figures of the previous and the following year with October and May surveys.

[f]Interpolated values by computing the average annual growth rate of 1968–1971.

[g]The labour force definition for these years is different, it is for the population 15 years and older, as compared with 10 years and above for earlier years.

[h]See footnote b above for the basis of computing these figures.

Table 1.b

Employment and output by industry, 1956 till 1977.[a]

	All industry (1)	Agriculture (2)	Industry (3)	Services (4)	Mining & quarrying (5)	Manufacturing (6)	Construction (7)	Electricity, gas and water (8)	Transport (9)	Commerce (10)	Other services (11)
A. Employment											
1956	7,702	4,548	1,217	1,937	31	962	198	26	228	803	906
1957	8,199	4,997	1,275	1,927	27	1,005	228	15	223	785	919
1958	8,329	5,276	1,133	1,920	21	927	161	24	238	743	948
1959	8,575	5,298	1,258	2,019	35	992	210	21	250	811	959
1960	8,539	5,234	1,316	1,999	29	1,036	231	20	271	753	975
1961	9,395	5,618	1,429	2,348	38	1,118	254	19	319	893	1,136
1962	9,680	5,914	1,397	2,374	29	1,084	252	29	337	939	1,094
1963	10,655	6,258	1,702	2,695	33	1,288	343	38	371	1,090	1,234
1964	10,220	6,064	1,401	2,755	31	1,209	341	20	325	1,176	1,053
1965	10,543	6,052	1,570	2,921	28	1,221	299	22	367	1,120	1,428
1966	11,032	6,275	1,707	3,050	28	1,331	323	25	387	1,197	1,465
1967	12,185	5,993	1,821	4,371	52	1,389	347	33	385	1,352	1,633
1968	12,481	7,202	1,838	3,441	46	1,387	378	27	380	1,379	1,684
1969	11,235	6,325	1,720	3,190	51	1,291	349	29	383	1,109	1,696
1970	13,358	6,100	1,876	5,382	51	1,354	438	33	498	838	2,045
1971	12,228	5,966	1,995	4,267	67	1,427	444	57	504	1,579	2,184
1972	12,598	6,794	1,820	3,984	56	1,319	402	43	504	1,497	1,984
1973	13,896	7,592	1,956	4,348	60	1,453	402	41	542	1,551	2,255
1974	13,666	7,547	1,873	4,246	42	1,385	411	35	526	1,547	2,172
1975	14,517	7,768	2,207	4,542	54	1,651	456	46	492	1,623	2,428
1976	15,427	8,126	2,273	5,028	56	1,680	491	46	550	1,864	2,614
1977	14,985	7,046	2,593	5,346	91	1,837	593	72	704	1,851	2,791

B. Real output

1956	23.00	8.20	5.40	9.50	0.31	3.70	1.18	0.15	0.78	5.50	3.20
1957	24.20	8.40	5.80	10.00	0.35	3.90	1.34	0.15	0.82	5.80	3.40
1958	25.20	8.90	5.90	10.40	0.35	4.30	1.16	0.16	0.86	6.00	3.50
1959	26.90	9.40	6.40	11.00	0.39	4.60	1.24	0.17	0.90	6.40	3.70
1960	27.20	9.30	6.40	11.50	0.37	4.70	1.08	0.17	0.95	6.60	3.90
1961	28.50	9.90	6.70	12.00	0.36	4.90	1.22	0.17	1.00	6.90	4.10
1962	29.50	10.30	6.90	12.60	0.36	5.20	1.19	0.17	1.04	7.30	4.30
1963	31.60	11.00	7.50	13.10	0.38	5.50	1.48	0.17	1.10	7.60	4.50
1964	32.60	11.00	7.90	13.80	0.38	5.70	1.65	0.17	1.15	7.80	4.80
1965	34.40	11.80	8.30	14.30	0.40	5.90	1.81	0.19	1.21	8.10	5.00
1966	35.60	12.20	8.70	14.80	0.45	6.30	1.71	0.19	1.27	8.40	5.10
1967	37.50	12.50	9.40	15.60	0.50	6.90	1.82	0.20	1.34	9.00	5.30
1968	39.60	13.40	9.80	16.40	0.60	7.30	1.63	0.23	1.41	9.30	5.60
1969	41.20	13.80	10.30	17.20	0.69	7.60	1.74	0.23	1.48	9.70	6.00
1970	42.60	14.00	10.60	18.10	0.82	8.00	1.54	0.26	1.57	10.10	6.40
1971	44.30	14.40	11.20	18.60	0.99	8.30	1.65	0.29	1.67	10.30	6.60
1972	46.30	15.00	12.10	19.30	1.02	8.80	1.93	0.30	1.76	10.60	6.90
1973	49.90	15.70	13.60	20.60	1.06	10.10	2.08	0.31	1.90	11.20	7.30
1974	51.60	15.90	14.10	21.50	1.04	10.50	2.20	0.32	2.03	11.70	7.90
1975	55.00	16.90	15.20	22.80	1.05	10.70	3.08	0.37	2.15	12.30	8.40
1976	59.80	18.30	17.10	24.40	1.12	11.40	4.15	0.49	2.45	13.20	8.70
1977	63.10	19.20	18.40	25.50	1.26	12.20	4.39	0.52	2.59	13.60	9.30

[a] *Source*: 'Yearbook of Labor Statistics', various years and 'National Income Accounts' data.

Table 2.a

Agricultural real daily wage rate (at 1965 prices, except real wage index base 1972 = 100).

							Author[h]		
							BAECON[i]		
	ILO[a] (pesos)	Berry[b] (pesos)	Hicks–McNicoll[c] (pesos)	Series A[e] (pesos)	Khan[d] Series B[f] (pesos)	Series C[g] (pesos)	Pesos	Index 1972 = 100	NCSU (pesos)
1950	—	—	3.32	—	—	—	—	—	—
1951	—	—	3.16	—	—	—	—	—	—
1952	—	—	3.69	—	—	—	—	—	—
1953	—	—	4.19	—	—	—	—	—	—
1954	—	—	4.42	—	—	—	3.66	145.0	—
1955	—	—	4.45	—	—	—	3.70	146.8	—
1956	—	3.64	3.85	—	—	—	3.59	142.3	—
1957	3.84	3.63	3.87	3.84	3.84	4.78	3.73	147.7	—
1958	3.80	3.59	3.84	3.80	3.80	4.63	3.58	142.0	—
1959	3.85	3.54	3.77	3.85	3.85	4.64	3.70	146.8	—
1960	3.68	3.36	3.69	3.69	3.69	4.40	3.51	139.1	—
1961	3.49	3.26	3.63	6.49	3.49	4.16	3.33	132.0	—
1962	3.41	3.25	3.55	3.41	3.41	4.06	3.40	135.0	—
1963	3.43	2.86	3.61	3.43	3.43	4.03	3.06	121.4	—
1964	3.03	2.78	—	3.03	3.03	3.56	2.85	113.0	—
1965	2.93	—	—	2.93	2.93	3.34	3.09	122.5	—
1966	2.98	—	—	2.98	3.20	3.73	3.23	128.2	—
1967	3.09	—	—	3.09	3.33	4.08	3.16	125.5	—
1968	3.04	—	—	3.04	3.34	4.00	2.81	111.6	—
1969	2.75	—	—	2.75	2.99	3.81	2.86	113.4	6.13
1970	2.44	2.56	—	2.44	2.75	3.43	2.85	113.0	—
1971	2.25	2.44	—	2.25	2.46	3.17	2.46	97.5	4.48
1972	2.17	2.58	—	2.17	2.44	3.04	2.52	100.0	3.71
1973	—	—	—	1.86	—	—	—	—	3.19
1974	—	—	—	1.48	—	—	2.29	90.7	2.01
1975	—	—	—	—	—	—	—	—	1.89
1976	—	—	—	—	—	—	2.95	117.0	1.96
1977	—	—	—	—	—	—	2.96	117.5	—

[a]This series was estimated by the ILO Sharing in Development team, and is reported in Berry (1978). uses data from BAECON wage surveys, or made available directly by BAECON. Deflation was by t consumer price index for areas outside Manila.

[b]Estimated by Berry (1978) from BAECON data.

[c]Hicks and McNicoll (1971), estimates were derived by weighting the money wages for four categories farm workers (ploughmen, planters, harvesters and common labourers) in nine geographical regions, the numbers of workers in each category. It also makes adjustments for payment in kind in the form two meals per day for each worker. The deflator used was the consumer price index for regions outsi Manila (available since 1957) spliced to the Manila price index for domestic consumer goods for the 195 1957 period [see Hicks and McNicoll (1971, p. 91)].

[d]This is reported in Khan (1977).

[e]Series A, is the unweighted average of BAECON wages rates for ploughmen, planters and harveste (for which alone data was available) till 1966, and from 1966 to 1973 onwards also includes t unweighted average of wage rates of cultivators, weeders and sprayers. For 1973 and 1974, the daily ca earnings of salary and wage earners in agriculture for NCSO, 'Survey of Household Bulletin' labor for May series, have been spliced in.

[f]This is also from Khan (1977), and is the unweighted average of BAECON wage data for ploughme harvesters and planters only.

[g]This is also from Khan (1977) and is the wage rate for ploughmen only.

[h]These are our estimates from Lal (1980, table A.10).

[i]These are our estimates of the unweighted average of BAECON wage rates of the same groups as footnote d above, but without any adjustment for payments in kind for meals. As in footnote d above af 1966, the average is across wage rates of cultivators, weeders and sprayers, in addition to ploughme planters and harvesters for all regions. The deflator is the consumer price index for areas outside Man from 1957, to which the Manila consumer price index is spliced for earlier years.

[j]This is our estimate of daily cash earnings from the NCSO labour force surveys.

Table 2.b

Real wage-rate index of skilled and unskilled labourers in Manilla and suburbs: 1956–1978 (establishment data) (1972 = 100).

	Skilled labourers[a]	Unskilled labourers[a]	Common labourers[b] (1972 pesos)	Latheman[b] (1972 pesos)	Foreman (1972 pesos)	Salaried employees	Wage earners
1954	140.1	113.4	11.81	19.39	23.10	118.1	109.5
1955	141.5	117.8	12.27	19.36	23.84	123.5	113.8
1956	138.1	116.6	12.15	18.64	23.90	121.7	112.3
1957	135.7	113.4	11.28	16.80	23.89	122.2	114.2
1958	135.6	110.3	11.49	18.13	23.67	124.6	111.5
1959	139.5	112.2	11.69	18.34	24.48	131.5	117.3
1960	133.4	107.9	11.23	17.53	23.89	133.5	119.3
1961	131.2	108.8	11.34	16.02	24.21	134.4	117.8
1962	125.5	105.9	11.03	14.89	23.05	131.0	113.0
1963	122.3	105.6	11.01	14.47	22.51	128.2	108.1
1964	115.1	98.6	10.28	13.54	21.37	121.0	104.3
1965	115.2	102.7	10.71	13.43	22.13	119.3	107.8
1966	114.9	104.8	10.91	13.49	21.84	119.0	112.8
1967	113.1	103.2	10.75	13.86	20.90	113.8	112.3
1968	119.4	112.1	11.68	13.89	21.89	116.8	110.3
1969	123.3	115.2	11.99	13.92	22.79	119.9	112.7
1970	114.4	111.6	11.63	12.65	20.91	109.7	105.9
1971	105.1	104.1	10.85	11.98	19.29	103.0	99.9
1972	100.0	100.0	10.42	11.26	18.34	100.0	100.0
1973	92.4	90.0	9.38	10.92	17.25	96.6	89.4
1974	75.6	72.8	7.58	9.29	14.61	79.5	73.5
1975	72.7	72.9	7.60	8.82	14.34	82.4	76.1
1976	71.2	72.3	7.53	8.81	14.38	86.7	82.3
1977	72.9	70.4	7.34	8.47	14.01	—	—
1978	76.1	68.4	—	—	—	—	—

[a]Real wage-rate index has been obtained by deflating money wage-rate index by the consumer price index (1972 = 100) in Manila.

[b]Real wages of three classes of labourer are derived by deflating the data in Lal (1980, table A.12) by the Manila consumer price index.

Finally, there is some evidence (mainly from manufacturing) of a falling wage share and output capital ratio and rising capital intensity between 1956–1978 [see Lal (1980)]. Applying Williamson's (1971a) estimate of an elasticity of substitution between capital and labour for Philippines manufacturing of about 0.9 to the aggregate economy this would imply, in growth accounting terms, capital using technical progress strongly biased against labour in the Philippines.[3] But this does not explain the observed real wage movements as the causes of this bias in turn requires explanation and even

[3]As the elasticity is close to unity, with neutral technical progress factor shares would have remained constant. However, sufficiently Hicks or Harrod capital using biased technical progress would yield the stylized facts about the Philippines.

more importantly, why this bias should have been particularly great during the two periods of marked real wage decline.

We, therefore, attempt to explain real wage changes in terms of the aggregative SSR model. The principle we adopt in deriving the aggregate commodities for the model follow from the long run SSR results that ceteris paribus, the real wage would be expected to be inversely (directly) correlated with decreases (increases) in the relative price of the most labour intensive 'commodity' in the economy.

We distinguish three different sectors for the Philippines, those producing (i) importables – manufacturing (which is largely import-substituting), (ii) exportables – the cash crops, mining and other natural resource intensive export activities (manufactured exports being a relatively minor part of this 'sector'), and (iii) non-traded – the rest, which comprise services, non-cash crop agriculture, and the production of various commodities for local/domestic consumption. Data on factor intensities is fragmentary [from Power and Sicat (1971), Hicks and McNicoll (1971), and table 3 below] but it suggests that non-traded commodities are the most labour intensive in the Philippines, and exportables are land and natural resource intensive. Following Kenen (1965) we assume that land and natural resources require *complementary* inputs of capital to be made 'effective', hence both traded goods can be 'lumped together' as being capital intensive relative to the non-traded good. Moreover, in order to allow us to treat traded goods as a Hicksian composite good,[4] we shall assume (though not strictly valid for the Philippines), constant terms of trade, and an unchanging tariff equivalent structure and level of trade restrictions.

2.1. The model

Consider the two-good, two-factor model in which capital (K) is immobile between the two sectors – traded (T) and non-traded (N) – in the short run, but mobile in the long run. Labour (L) is mobile in both the short and long run. Unlike the models of Jones (1971), Mayer (1974), and Mussa (1974), there are intermediate goods flows from both industries, which [unlike Burgess (1980)] also include inputs of each good in its own production. The following equations in Jones' (1965) algebra describe the unit cost and the factor balance conditions of the resulting general-equilibrium model, where Y_N and Y_T are the *gross* outputs of the non-traded and traded goods, p_i is the price of the ith commodity, a_{ij} is the ith input in the production of the jth commodity and w is the common wage rate and r_i the rental rate in the ith

[4]Also note that this aggregation is likely to be a source of measurement error in our empirics of section 3.

industry:

$$a_{ki}r_i + a_{li}w + a_{Ti}p_T + a_{Ni}p_N = p_i, \qquad i = N, T, \tag{1}$$

$$a_{ki}Y_i = K_i, \qquad i = N, T, \tag{2}$$

$$a_{lN}Y_N + a_{lT}Y_T = L. \tag{3}$$

From (2) and (3) we have

$$(a_{lN}/a_{kN})K_N + (a_{lT}/a_{kT})K_T = L. \tag{4}$$

Total differentiation of (1) and (4) and denoting by

$x^* \equiv \mathrm{d}x/x$ percentage changes,

$\theta_{ij} \equiv a_{ij}p_i/p_j$ distributive shares of the inputs i, in industry j,

$\lambda_{ij} \equiv a_{lj}Y_j/L_j$ the share of the labour force in industry j,

and

$\sigma_i \equiv (a^*_{ki} - a^*_{li})/(w^* - r^*)$ the elasticity of substitution of the primary factors in the ith industry, we have

$$\theta_{kj}r^*_j + \theta_{lj}w^* + \theta_{Tj}p^*_T + \theta_{Nj}p^*_N = p^*_j, \qquad j = N, T, \tag{5}$$

$$\lambda_{lN}\sigma_N r^*_N + \lambda_{lT}\sigma_T r^*_T - (\lambda_{lN}\sigma_N + \lambda_{lT}\sigma_T)w^* = L^* - \lambda_{lN}K^*_N - \lambda_{lT}K^*_T. \tag{6}$$

In deriving (6) we have assumed that the production function is separable between primary factors and intermediate inputs, so that the capital labour ratio (a_{kN}/a_{LN}) is a function of only the wage–rental ratio even though intermediate inputs from both sectors are used in production.

Solving (5) and (6) for w^*, and denoting by

$\delta_{iT} \equiv \theta_{iT}/(1 - \theta_{TT} - \theta_{NT})$
$\delta_{iN} \equiv \theta_{iN}/(1 - \theta_{TN} - \theta_{NN})$ the share of factor i, in the value added in the two industries (with $i = K, L$),

$\varepsilon_i \equiv \sigma_i/\delta K_i$ the elasticity of demand for labour in the ith industry,

$v_i \equiv (1 - \theta_{ii} - \theta_{ji})$ the share of value added in gross output in industry i (with $i, j = N, T$),

$\eta_i \equiv \lambda_{li}\varepsilon_i(\lambda_{li}\varepsilon_i + \lambda_{lj}\varepsilon_j)$ the elasticity of the wage rate with respect to commodity price i (with $i, j = \mathrm{N}, \mathrm{T}$), we have

$$w^* = \{[\eta_\mathrm{T}(1-\theta_\mathrm{TT})/v_\mathrm{T}] - [\eta_\mathrm{N}\theta_\mathrm{TN}/v_\mathrm{N}]\}p^*_\mathrm{T} + \{[\eta_\mathrm{N}(1-\theta_\mathrm{NN})/v_\mathrm{N}] - [\eta_\mathrm{T}\theta_\mathrm{NT}/v_\mathrm{T}]\}p^*_\mathrm{N} + (\lambda_{l\mathrm{N}}K^*_\mathrm{N} + \lambda_{l\mathrm{T}}K^*_\mathrm{T} - L^*)/E, \tag{7a}$$

where

$E \equiv (\lambda_{l\mathrm{N}}\varepsilon_\mathrm{N} + \lambda_{l\mathrm{T}}\varepsilon_\mathrm{T})$ the weighted average of the labour demand elasticities, which must be positive.

2.1.1. Relative commodity price changes

The *short run impact* of relative commodity price and factor supply changes on nominal, and thence on real wages can be determined from (7a). First, consider a change in relative commodity prices, with a rise in the price of traded goods, that is with $p^*_\mathrm{T} > 0$, $p^*_\mathrm{N} = 0$. Then,

$$w^* = \{[\lambda_{l\mathrm{T}}\varepsilon_\mathrm{T}(1-\theta_\mathrm{TT})/v_\mathrm{T}] - \lambda_{l\mathrm{N}}\varepsilon_\mathrm{N}\theta_\mathrm{TN}/v_\mathrm{N}\}p^*_\mathrm{T}/E. \tag{7b}$$

This result differs from the standard RV conclusion that the effects on *nominal* wages of a change in traded goods prices is unambiguous, because in our model with non-tradeables using traded inputs, a rise in traded goods prices in effects inflicts an 'oil shock' upon non-tradeables.[5] It raises the rental rate in the traded good sector but lowers it in non-tradeables (as p^*_N is exogenous by assumption), thus inducing substitution toward labour in the former and away from labour in the latter sector. That is why the effects of p^*_T on w^* are ambiguous in (7b) and will depend upon the relative sectoral elasticities of substitution and the cost share of traded inputs in the non-traded good. Table 3 presents estimates of the parameters in (7b) for the Philippines, which suggest that the value of w^* is close to zero. This suggests that the impact effect of a rise (fall) in the relative price of traded goods in the Philippines is a fall (rise) in the real wage rate (W), as $W^* = w^* - p^*_\mathrm{T}$, in terms of either traded or non-traded goods (noting that ex hypothesi any relative price change can be represented by $p^*_\mathrm{N} = 0$ and $p^*_\mathrm{T} \gtrless 0$).

The *long run* equilibrium value of the nominal and real wage change can be determined by removing the sector specific capital assumption of the model summarised by eqs. (1) and (4). With capital mobile between the sectors in the long run, we have the well known SSR result that,

$$w^*_\mathrm{e} = [\alpha_{K\mathrm{T}}p^*_\mathrm{N} - \alpha_{K\mathrm{N}}p^*_\mathrm{T}]/|\alpha|, \tag{8}$$

[5]The same idea has been developed since this paper was first written in a 'structuralist' context by Taylor (1983).

Table 3

A. 1969 two-sector input–output table at net of taxes producer prices[a]

	Traded (T)	Non-traded (N)
Traded	0.347	0.077
Non-traded	0.175	0.283
Total intermediate	0.522	0.360
Wages	0.219	0.398
Rental	0.259	0.242
Value added	0.478	0.640
Total input	1.000	1.000

B. Panel A yields the following values of the production parameters defined in the text:

$\theta_{TT}=0.4,\quad \theta_{TN}=0.1,$
$v_T=0.5,\quad v_N=0.6,$
$\alpha_{LT}=0.4949,\quad \alpha_{LN}=0.6495,$
$\alpha_{KT}=0.5052,\quad \alpha_{KN}=0.3505.$

In Lal (1978), short and long run demand elasticities for labour with respect to the wage rate have been estimated. Using the estimates for large scale manufacturing for traded and traditional services for non-traded goods, gives the following short run elasticities [see Lal (1978, table 53, p. 147)]:

$$\varepsilon_T=0.3,\quad \varepsilon_N=0.5$$

Finally, from the *Philippine Statistical Yearbook, 1978* [NEDA, Manila (1978, p. 46)], 34.1% of total employment was in agriculture, forestry and fishing. From the 1969 input–output table, 7% of the wage bill for this sector was for forestry and fishing. Assuming that employment was also distributed in this proportion yields 2.39% of the labour force in forestry and fishing. Similarly, whilst other manufacturing in the total manufacturing wage bill was 75%, which yields share of other manufacturing in total employment of 12.98%. The total share of traded good employment is thus 2.39 + 12.98 = 15.4%. Hence,

$$\lambda_{LT}=0.15,\quad \lambda_{LN}=0.85.$$

Substituting these values in (7b) yields: $w^*=0\cdot p_T^*$.

[a]*Source*: This table has been derived from the 12-sector transactions table for 1969 for the Philippines given in table 16.1 of the *Philippine Statistical Yearbook 1978* (NEDA, Manila, 1978), as follows. Sectors 1–Agriculture, 2–Fisheries, 5–Food Manuf., 7–Construction, 8–Utilities, 9–Transportation, 10–Trade, 11–Building, Insurance and real estate, and 12–Other services, in the 12-sector table were aggregated as non-traded. The remaining sectors – 3–Forestry and logging, 4–Mining and quarrying, 6–Other manufactures, were treated as traded. The item under depreciation in the original table was treated as part of the rental, and the other item in value added–other value added, which includes both the wage and capital earnings of the self-employed, was broken down into its wage and capital components using the methods detailed in Lal (1978, p. 101).

where

$$|\alpha|=(\alpha_{LN}\alpha_{KT}-\alpha_{KN}\alpha_{LT}),$$

and where we define $\alpha_{ij}=A_{ij}p_i/p_j$, and $\beta_{ij}=A_{ij}X_j/i$, with $i=K,L$, and $j=\text{N},\text{T}$, as the equivalent of the earlier θ's and λ's in terms of the *total* (direct plus indirect) primary factor coefficients, and denote the long run wage change by w_e^*. Given the values of the α's in table 3, which obviously depend only on the factor intensities of the two aggregate commodities, $|\alpha|$ is positive, which means that any relative increase in the price of traded goods, $p_T^*>0$, $p_N^*=0$, $w_e^*<0$, and vice versa for a fall in the relative price of traded goods. Thus the change in the long run equilibrium real wage (W_e) for any change in the relative price of traded goods will be $W_e^*=w_e^*-p_T^*<0$, in terms of either traded or non-traded goods.

Thus, we would expect that the impact effect of a rise (fall) in the relative price of traded goods in the Philippines on the real wage would be further accentuated, and be of the same sign; that is, it would fall (rise) in the long run. It should be noted that we are assuming that in our model P_N is exogenous (an assumption we test *statistically* in the next part), which in turn implies that we have to assume that aggregate demand is being suitably manipulated in the background.

2.1.2. *Changes in factor supplies*

From (7a) the reaction of the nominal wage to a relative rise (fall) in the labour supply, can be readily determined (with $K_N^*=K_T^*=0$, and $L^*\gtrless 0$) as

$$w^*=-L^*/E. \tag{7c}$$

As E is positive, the real wage will initially fall (rise) with a relative rise in labour suppy [as ceteris paribus prices have not changed, the nominal wage change from (7c) will also be an equivalent real wage change], but as is evident from (8), in the long run SSR equilibrium there will be no change in the nominal and hence real wage. Thus during the adjustment process the initial decline (rise) flowing from an expansion (decrease) in relative labour supply will be completely reversed.

2.1.3. *The adjustment process*

It remains to chart the adjustment process between the impact effect and the long run equilibrium resulting from exogenous changes in relative commodity prices and factor supplies. These will depend upon the shifting of capital that will ensue as a result of the divergence in rental rates on the short run sector specific capital stocks. These can be readily derived by solving for r_T^* and r_N^* from (5) and (6).[6] Given a relative rise (fall) in the price of traded goods, $r_T^*>0$, and $r_N^*<0$ ($r_T^*<0, r_N^*>0$). Whilst given a relative rise (fall) in labour supply, both rental rates will rise (fall) but with $r_N^*>r_T^*>0$ ($r_T^*<r_N^*<0$). With depreciation of the existing capital stock and ongoing net investment, replacements and increments to the capital stock will be made in the sector whose relative rental has increased (or fallen least) as a result of the relative commodity price or relative factor supply change. The impact of the nominal wage, and the real wage, (as ex hypothesi during the adjustment process relative prices are constant) will then depend upon the direction and the extent of the shifting of the capital stock, till the rental rates in the two industries are equalised at their long run equilibrium value.[7] To determine the wage changes during the adjustment process (w_a^*) assume (for simplicity) that the capital stock adjustments take place entirely through the replacement in the sector with the higher rental of the depreciated stock in the sector whose rental has fallen. In that case, say as a result of $p_T^*>0$, the increase in the traded good sector's capital stock will be exactly equal to the loss of the non-traded good sector's, that is, during the adjustment process $\mathrm{d}K_T=-\mathrm{d}K_N$. As during the adjustment process prices are constant, $p_j^*=0$. Imposing these conditions on eqs. (5) and (6) and solving for w^* yields the value of the nominal (and because prices are constant, the real) wage during the adjustment process as[8]

$$w_a^*=(L_N/K_N-L_T/K_T)\,\mathrm{d}K_N/LE. \tag{9}$$

As from table 3, $L_N/K_N>L_T/K_T$, nominal and real wages will fall (rise) as capital is shifted from (to) the non-traded sector, as a result of the impact of

[6]Thus, r_T^* and r_N^* are given by

$$r_T^*=\left\{\eta_N\left[\frac{(1-\theta_{TT})}{\theta_{KT}}+\frac{\theta_{LT}\theta_{TN}}{\theta_{KT}v_N}\right]+\eta_T\frac{(1-\theta_{TT})}{v_T}\right\}p_T^*$$
$$-\left\{\eta_N\left[\frac{\theta_{NT}}{\theta_{KT}}+\frac{\theta_{LT}(1-\theta_{TT})}{\theta_{KT}v_N}\right]+\eta_T\frac{\theta_{NT}}{v_T}\right\}P_N^*+\frac{\theta_{LT}}{E\theta_{KT}}[L^*-\lambda_{LN}K_N^*-\lambda_{LT}K_T^*],$$

$$r_N^*=\left\{\eta_N\frac{(1-\theta_{NN})}{v_N}+\eta_T\left[\frac{(1-\theta_{NN})}{\theta_{KN}}+\frac{\theta_{LN}\theta_{NT}}{\theta_{KN}v_T}\right]\right\}P_N^*$$
$$-\left\{\eta_N\frac{\theta_{TN}}{v_N}+\eta_T\left[\frac{\theta_{TN}}{\theta_{KN}}+\frac{\theta_{LN}}{\theta_{KN}}(1-\theta_{TT})\right]\right\}p_T^*+\frac{\theta_{LN}}{E\theta_{KN}}[L^*-\lambda_{LN}K_N^*-\lambda_{LT}K_T^*].$$

[7]The long run equilibrium value of r is given by

$$r^*=[\alpha_{LN}p_T^*-\alpha_{LT}p_N^*]/[\alpha_{KT}-\alpha_{KN}].$$

[8]The relevant equations determining the value of w_a^* are

$$\theta_{Li}w_a^*+\theta_{Ki}r_{ia}^*=0, \qquad i=\mathrm{N,T},$$
$$\sum\lambda_{Li}\sigma_i r_{ia}^*-\sum\lambda_{Li}\sigma_i w_a^*=\left(\frac{\lambda_{LN}}{K_N}-\frac{\lambda_{LT}}{K_T}\right)\mathrm{d}K_N, \qquad i=\mathrm{N,T}.$$

This result has also been derived in another context by Neary (1982).

raising (lowering) the relative rental on traded goods, flowing from the exogenous change in relative commodity prices and/or in relative factor supplies.

3. The regression model

From the results of the previous section it is evident that the time path of real wages for any given exogenous change in relative commodity prices and factor supplies will be determined by eqs. (7a), (8) and (9). Thus consider a simultaneous increase in the relative price of traded goods and of labour relative to capital supply ($p_T^* > 0, p_N^* = 0, L^* > 0, K_T^* = K_N^* = 0$). Then in the first period, the real wage will fall (i) because of the impact effect of the rise in the traded good price [from (7a), and given the likely parameter values in table 3], (ii) because of any readjustment of the capital stock from the non-traded to traded good industries flowing from the rise in the rental on traded good capital relative to non-traded good capital following the rise in the traded good relative price [from (9)], (iii) the impact effect of a relative increase in labour supply from (7a). But this fall in the real wage will be (iv) counterbalanced to the extent that the implicit rise in the rental rate on non-traded goods with a ceteris paribus increase in labour supply, induces a reverse flow of capital from the traded to non-traded good sector in the first period. Over time, the real wage will continue to fall towards its long run equilibrium value due to the rise in the traded good price [from eq. (8)], as the effect (ii) above comes to predominate. But this fall will be tempered by the effects under (iv) above, as the initial decline in the real wage as a result of the relative expansion in labour supply is reversed in the long run.

The speed with which this adjustment process will converge to the new long run equilibrium will depend both upon the nature of expectations and on the costs of adjustment [see Mussa (1978)]. However, for an adjustment process with increasing marginal costs of investment and with ongoing net investment and depreciation, the qualitative properties of the adjustment path will be the same under both static and rational expectations [Mussa (1978, section 4)], namely those summarised under the effects (i)–(iv) above. This implies that the time path of percentage changes in *real* wages (W_t^*) in the Philippines can be represented by the following reduced form equation:

$$W_t^* = a + \sum_{i=t}^{t-z} b_i P_{Ni}^* + \sum_{i=t}^{t-z} c_i P_{T_i}^* + \sum_{j=t}^{t-q} \mathrm{d}_j k_j^* + u_t, \tag{10}$$

where

$P_N^*(P_T^*)$ is the percentage change in the price of traded (non-traded) goods,
k^* is the percentage change in the overall capital–labour endowment,
a represents any time trend,

u is a random error term, and

z, q are the respective lengths of the lags between the impact and equilibrium effects of any exogenous change in relative commodity prices and relative factor supplies, respectively.

We now have a series of powerful independent tests. The SSR theorem is supported if:

(i) the sum of the coefficients on P^*_{N} is positive ($\sum a_i > 0$),
(ii) the sum of the coefficients on P^*_{T} is negative ($\sum b_i < 0$),
(iii) the sum of the two sets of coefficients is not statistically different from zero ($\sum a_i + \sum b_i = 0$), (11)
(iv) the sum of the coefficients of the K/L ratio is approximately zero ($\sum c_i = 0$).

4. The results

Table 4 summarises the data we have used to estimate (10) for the Philippines, and its notes explain the sources. Of the various wage series shown in tables 2.a–2.b, the Central Bank's wage earners series labelled *WE*, and the BAECON's agricultural wage series labelled *WA* are deemed to provide the most reliable available estimates of movements in urban and rural wages, respectively. As our P^* and k^* series are derived series, they are likely to suffer from unknown measurement errors, which should also be kept in mind in what follows.

Before we can proceed to estimate, we need to test the maintained hypothesis underlying the model of section 2 that changes in relative prices are exogenous. We therefore performed a Sims causality test between P^*_{N} and W^*. The F ratios for differing lag lengths for the null hypothesis that W^* *does not cause* P^*_{N} are given in table 5 for our two wage series. It is clear that the null hypothesis is *not* rejected and so we can assume that relative prices are exogenous.

Next we estimated (10). As we have no a priori theory to determine the nature and length of the lags z, q for the Philippines, statistical convenience determined our choice of the use of the Almon polynomial lag on the three independent variables. Next we tested the hypotheses on the coefficients given by (11), using a two-stage procedure. First, we test each of the four components separately. This leads to four null hypotheses,

$\mathrm{H1_0}: \sum b = 0$ against $\mathrm{H1_A}: \sum b > 0$.
$\mathrm{H2_0}: \sum c = 0$ against $\mathrm{H2_A}: \sum c < 0$.
$\mathrm{H3_0}: \sum b + \sum C = 0$ against $\mathrm{H3_A}: \sum b + \sum C \neq 0$.
$\mathrm{H4_0}: \sum d = 0$ against $\mathrm{H4_A}: \sum d \neq 0$.

Table 4

Indices: Prices, real wages and capital–labour ratio.[a]

	d ln *WE* (1)	d ln *WA* (2)	d ln *K/L* (3)	d ln *PT* (4)	d ln *PN* (5)
1957	1.68	3.72	3.23	4.8490128	4.8101266
1958	−2.40	−3.94	6.76	8.1805594	1.6908213
1959	5.07	3.32	5.64	11.5861151	−1.6627078
1960	1.69	−5.39	6.12	0.3624685	4.8309179
1961	−1.27	−5.24	−2.52	4.3567706	4.8387097
1962	−4.16	2.25	2.75	16.5856223	1.9780220
1963	−4.43	−10.62	−2.75	15.0077030	8.6206897
1964	−3.58	−7.17	11.51	−1.6630183	7.1428571
1965	3.30	8.07	4.33	1.9237159	2.5925926
1966	4.53	4.55	2.06	1.0822440	5.7761733
1967	−0.44	−2.13	6.18	4.2052307	2.3890785
1968	−1.80	−11.74	−2.89	8.0648655	1.1666667
1969	2.15	1.60	17.41	−0.3035597	1.8121911
1970	−6.22	−0.35	4.29	26.3493523	21.8446602
1971	−5.83	−14.75	−2.74	9.2802255	18.1938911
1972	0.10	2.53	1.91	4.0193060	12.3595506
1973	−11.20	n.a.	−4.64	25.4900000	19.4000000
1974	−19.58	n.a.	8.55	63.1396924	51.1725293
1975	3.48	3.72	2.18	−4.6159708	5.2077562
1976	7.83	n.a.	2.32	6.6081506	11.4270669
1977	n.a.	0.43	10.82	17.1228468	8.3175803
1978	n.a.	—	—	8.3527462	7.1553229

[a]*Sources:* column (1) is derived from the Central Bank's wage earners series from tables 2a–2b; column (2) is derived from the BAECON agricultural wage series from tables 2a–2b; column (3) is based on table 36 in Lal (1980), where the capital stock figures were derived from the gross investment data in the national income accounts by the use of the perpetual inventory method; column (4) is derived from the Central Bank's wholesale price indices of exportable and importable commodities. The two have been compared, by assigning a weight of 0.34 to the importables and 0.66 to the exportables series as these are the relative proportion of 'manufacturing' and 'agricultural cum quarrying' value added in the sum of value added in manufacturing, agriculture and quarrying; column (5) is derived from the Central Bank's wholesale price indices for locally produced commodities. The figures are for d ln *X*100.

Table 5

Sims causality tests; null hypothesis: d ln *W* *does not* cause d ln *Pn*.

	F ratio	Degrees of freedom
WE series lag 1	0.41	(1, 16)
2	0.58	(2, 13)
3	1.66	(3, 10)
WA series lag 1	0.46	(1, 16)
2	0.33	(2, 13)
3	2.06	(3, 10)

The F-statistics generated by these tests are labeled $F1$, $F2$, $F3$ and $F4$, respectively, in the results presented below. In addition, if $H1_0$ is rejected, we set up the composite null hypothesis

$$H5_0: \sum b + \sum c = 0, \sum d = 0.$$

and again use a two-tailed test. This statistic is labeled $F5$. The results assume greater validity if $H1_0$ is rejected and $H5_0$ cannot be rejected. Note that in the second stage we can equivalently use $H2_0$ instead of $H1_0$.

Since the length of lag, the degree of polynomial and the order of autocorrelation in errors are all unknown a priori, various specifications were tried out. For improving efficiency, the covariance matrix was estimated assuming a Toeplitz structure. The best results for WA are obtained for a lag of two periods on P_N, P_T and K/L when the polynomial and the auto-correlation in errors are both of order one. For WE, the best fit is provided by a second order polynomial, second order autocorrelation in errors, and a lag of three periods on (K/L) and two periods on the other two explanatory variables.

These relatively rapid rates of adjustment are not altogether implausible. It is well known that acreage under different crops adjusts fairly rapidly to relative crop price changes [see Behrman (1968)], and for Philippines manufacturing, Williamson (1971b) found that one to two year lag models provide good statistical fits for the response of relative factor input changes flowing from relative factor price changes.[9]

The regression results are summarised in table 6. The results for the WA series are 'better' than those for the WE series. For both, the first three hypotheses relating to the SSR theorem are powerfully confirmed, as is the

[9]Further support for this relatively rapid rate of adjustment can be provided by the following argument. Suppose that the total capital stock (K) is growing at the rate g, and that the rate of depreciation on both types of capital (K_T, K_N) is d. Then if the initial distribution of the two types of capital stock is $K_T^0/K^0, K_N^0/K^0$, with $K_T^0 + K_N^0 = K^0$, the traded good capital stock, at the new equilibrium following a rise in P_T/P_N, is K_T^t/K^t. Assuming that in the time, t, it takes to reach the new equilibrium, all new additions to the capital stock through *gross* investment are in the traded good sector, it follows that

$$K_T^t/K^t = K_T^0 + \sum_{n=1}^{t} (gK^n + \mathrm{d}K_N^n)/K^0 + \sum_{n=0}^{t} gK^n = 1 - \frac{K_N^0(1-d)^t}{K^0(1+g)^t}.$$

From the national accounts gross investment (GI) to $GNP(Y)$ ratio was roughly 0.2 between 1960–1970. The capital–output (K/Y) ratio for the same period (making use of our estimated capital stock figures) was 1.75. Hence the ratio of $GI/K = 0.2/1.75 = 0.11$. From the national accounts the capital consumption allowance as a proportion of GNP was about 0.07. If this is taken as a measure of depreciation, we have the value of $d = dK/K = (dK/Y)/(K/Y) = 0.07/1.75 = 0.04$, and hence the value of $g = (GI/K) - (dK/K) = 0.11 - 0.04 = 0.07$. We do not have data for the value of K_N^0/K^0 but assume that 0.4 of the capital stock was in the less capital intensive non-traded good in the base period. Suppose that as a result of the rise in the relative price of traded goods, the required equilibrium capital stock in the *traded* good industry has to rise from its base value of 0.6 to 0.7. Then substituting for $K_T^t/K^t = 0.7$, $K_N^0/K^0 = 0.4$, $d = 0.04$, $g = 0.07$ in the above equation and solving for t, we get a value of t between two–three years, for a fairly large shift in capital from the non-traded to traded goods sectors to take place.

Table 6

Regression results.

Case I – WA series

$$W_t = \underset{(-0.57)}{-4.28} + \underset{(2.61)^a}{0.92P_{N_t}} + \underset{(4.51)^a}{1.02P_{N_{t-1}}} + \underset{(5.43)^a}{1.12P_{N_{t-2}}} - \underset{(-2.91)^a}{0.71p_{T_t}} - \underset{(-4.08)^a}{1.01P_{T_{t-1}}} - \underset{(-4.70)^a}{1.31P_{T_{t-2}}} + \underset{(4.75)^a}{0.95(K/L)_t} - \underset{(-0.13)}{0.03(K/L)_{t-1}} - \underset{(-3.21)^a}{1.01(K/L)_{t-2}},$$

$R^2 = 0.9245$, adjusted $R^2 = 0.8489$, RHO (autocorrelation) $= 0.796$, $DW = 1.90$,

$F1 = 99.96$,[b] $F2 = 73.75$,[b] $F3 = 0.012$,[c] $F4 = 0.069$,[c] $F5 = 0.085$.[c]

Case II – WE series

$$W_t = \underset{(-3.83)^a}{-0.11} - \underset{(-2.76)^a}{0.17P_{N_t}} - \underset{(-0.23)}{0.01P_{N_{t-1}}} + \underset{(7.99)^a}{0.59P_{N_{t-2}}} - \underset{(-4.00)^a}{0.20P_{T_t}} - \underset{(1.54)}{0.06P_{T_{t-1}}} - \underset{(-4.45)^a}{0.23P_{T_{t-2}}} + \underset{(7.65)^a}{0.53(K/L)_t} + \underset{(9.06)^a}{0.48(K/L)_{t-1}} + \underset{(6.24)^a}{0.34(K/L)_{t-2}} + \underset{(1.49)}{0.10(K/L)_{t-3}},$$

$R^2 = 0.9949$, adjusted $R^2 = 0.9856$, $RHO1 = \underset{(1.28)}{0.08}$, $RHO2 = \underset{(11.66)^a}{0.73}$, $DW = 3.62$,

$F1 = 49.13$,[b] $F2 = 35.240$,[b] $F3 = 0.83$,[c] $F4 = 85.63$,[b] $F5 = 79.45$.[b]

[a] *t*-statistic, significant at 5% level of significance.

[b] Significant at 5% level of significance.

[c] Insignificant at 5% level of significance.

fourth (on the *d*'s) for the *WA* series, but not the *WE* series. Overall it appears from these results that the SSR model does provide an explanation for the paradoxical real wage movements in the Philippines. Figs. 1 and 2 chart the actual and predicted wage movements for the two wage series.

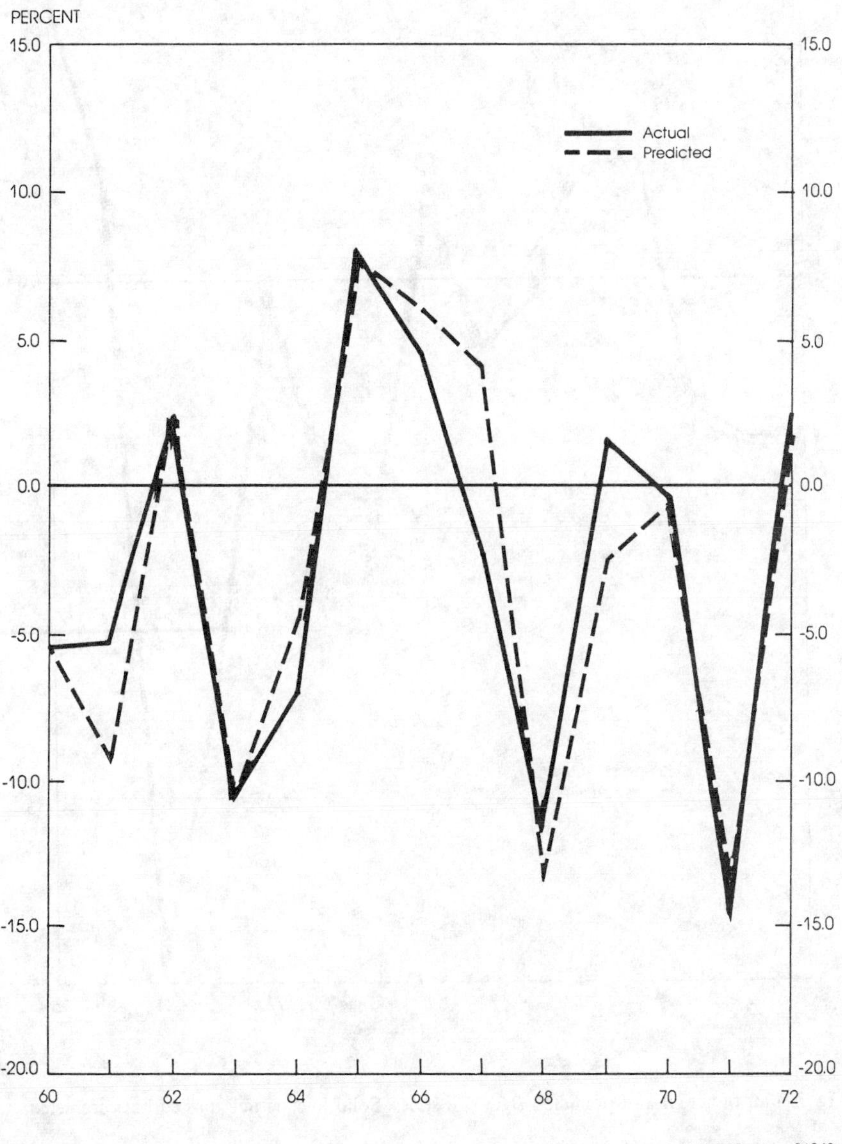

Fig. 1. Plot of actual and predicted *DLNWA* series. Solid line: actual; dashed line: predicted.

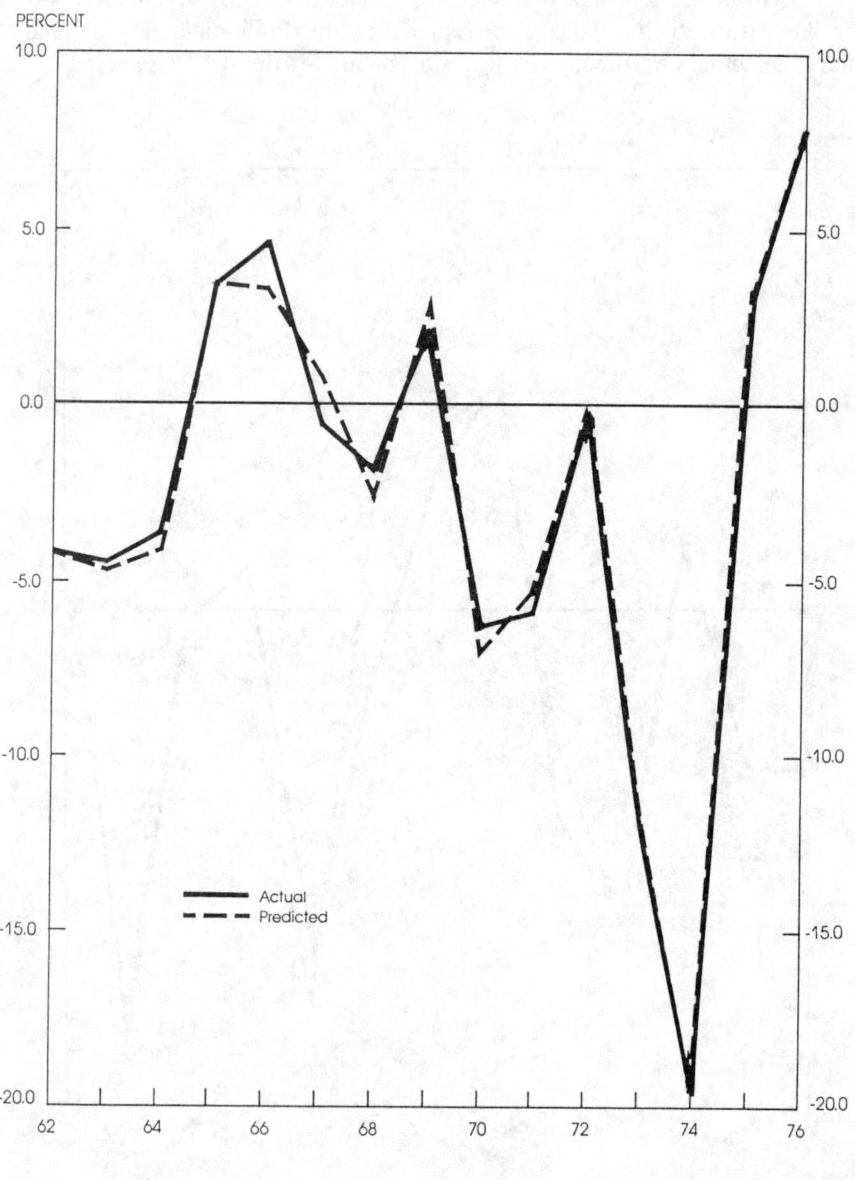

Fig. 2. Plot of actual and predicted *DLNWE* series. Solid line: actual; dashed line: predicted.

5. Conclusions

We conclude therefore that the real wage movements which are a legitimate cause for concern in the Philippines are due to changes in the real exchange rate rather than any malfunctioning of labour markets, or inadequate overall rates of growth of output or employment. The sources of the damaging real exchange rate movements in turn have been due to sub-optimal trade controls and inappropriate monetary and exchange rate policies [see Lal (1983)], but these issues are beyond the scope of this paper.

References

Abarientos, E.P. et al., 1972, Impact of technology and small farmers and their families: An eight-year experience in the Farm Record-Keeping Project 1962–1970 (Department of Agricultural Economics, U.P. College of Agriculture, Los Baños) Aug.

Baldwin, R.E., 1975, Foreign trade regimes and economic development – The Philippines (Columbia University Press, New York, for the NBER).

Behrman, J.R., 1968, Supply response in underdeveloped agriculture (North-Holland, Amsterdam).

Berry, A., 1978, Income and consumption trends in the Philippines, 1950–70, Review of Income and Wealth, Series 24, no. 3.

Burgess, D.F., 1976, Tariffs and income distribution: Some empirical evidence for the United States, Journal of Political Economy, Feb.

Burgess, D.F., 1980, Protection, real wages and the neoclassical ambiguity with interindustry flows, Journal of Political Economy, Aug.

Castillo, G., 1975, All in a grain of rice – A review of Philippines studies on the social and economic implications of the new rice technology (S.E. Asian Regional Centre for Graduate Study and Research in Agriculture, Manila).

Castillo, G., 1977, Beyond Manila – Philippine rural problems in perspective, Mimeo. (University of the Philippines at Los Baños, Los Baños) Dec.

Corden, W.M., 1974, Trade policy and economic welfare (Oxford University Press, Oxford).

Corden, W.M., 1977, Inflation, exchange rates and the world economy (Oxford University Press, Oxford).

Hicks, G.L. and G. McNicoll, 1971, Trade and growth in the Philippines (Cornell University Press, Ithaca, NY).

ILO, 1974, Sharing in development – A programme of employment, equity and growth for the Philippines (ILO, Geneva).

Jones, R.W., 1965, The structure of simple general equilibrium models, Journal of Political Economy, Dec.

Jones, R.W., 1971, A three factor model in theory, trade and history, in: J. Bhagwati et al., eds., Trade, the balance of payments and growth (North-Holland, Amsterdam).

Jones, R.W., 1975, Income distribution and effective protection in a multi-commodity trade model, Journal of Economic Theory, Aug.

Kenen, P.B., 1965, Nature, capital and trade, Journal of Political Economy, Oct.

Khan, A.R., 1977, Growth and inequality in the rural Philippines, in: ILO, Poverty and landlessness in rural Asia (ILO, Geneva).

Lal, D., 1978, Men or machines – A study of labor-capital substitution in road construction in the Philippines (ILO, Geneva).

Lal, D., 1980, Wages and employment in the Philippines, Studies in Employment and Rural Development no. 57 (World Bank, Washington, DC) Nov.

Lal, D., 1983, Real wages and exchange rates in the Philippines, 1956–78, World Bank Staff Working Paper no. 602 (World Bank, Washington, DC).

Magee, S.P., 1978, Three simple tests of the Stolper–Samuelson theorem, in: P. Oppenheimer, ed., Issues in international economics (Oriel, London).

Mayer, W., 1974, Short-run and long-run equilibrium for a small open economy, Journal of Political Economy, Oct.
Mussa, M., 1974, Tariffs and the distribution of income, Journal of Political Economy, Nov./Dec.
Mussa, M., 1978, Dynamic adjustment in the Hecksher–Ohlin–Samuelson model, Journal of Political Economy, Oct.
Neary, P., 1982, Capital mobility, wage stickiness and adjustment assistance, in: J. Bhagwati, ed., Import competition and response (NBER, Chicago, IL).
Nowzad, B., 1981, The IMF and its critics, Princeton Essays in International Finance no. 146.
Power, J.P. and G.P. Sicat, 1971, The Philippines – Industrialization and trade policies (Oxford University Press, Oxford).
Salter, W.E.G., 1959, Internal and external balance: The role of price and expenditure effects, The Economic Record, Aug.
Samuelson, P., 1971, Ohlin was right, Swedish Journal of Economics, Dec.
Taylor, L., 1983, Structuralist macroeconomics (Basic Books, New York).
Tidalgo, R.L., 1975, Wages and wage structure in the Philippines, 1957 to 1969, Ph.D. thesis (University of Wisconsin, Madison, WI).
Tidalgo, R.L., 1976, Labour absorption in the Philippines, 1956–75, The Philippine Economic Journal, no. 30, Vol. XV, nos. 1–2.
Tidalgo, R.L. and G.M. Jurado, 1978, The informal services sector in the greater Manila area, 1976, Philippine Review of Business and Economics, March.
Williamson, J.G., 1971a, Capital accumulation, labor saving and labor absorption once more, Quarterly Journal of Economics, Feb.
Williamson, J.G., 1971b, Relative price changes, adjustment dynamics, and productivity growth: The case of Philippine manufacturing, Economic Development and Cutural Change, July.

[19]

World Development, Vol. 12, No. 10, pp. 1007-1018, 1984
Printed in Great Britain

0305-750X/84 $3.00 + 0.00

Why Poor People Get Rich: Kenya 1960–79

PAUL COLLIER*
Institute of Economics and Statistics, Oxford University

and

DEEPAK LAL
The World Bank, Washington, D.C.

Summary. – This paper challenges the conventional model underlying much thinking on Kenya which has stressed the extant inequality of assets (including human capital) and the presumed weakness of intersectoral links owing to structural rigidities in the system. On the basis of recent survey data, the authors test their hypothesis that the pattern of growth and distribution in the Kenyan smallholder sector is best understood rather as being the outcome of the complex interaction of rural factor market failure and urban labour market participation. The sources of growth may be distinguished as improved resource allocation, capital formation and innovation, so that the transmission mechanisms from factor market malfunctioning and urban employment onto growth and distribution must be via these three components. The arguments which follow question the orthodox views on such phenomena as urban bias, trickle-down growth, the functions of urban–rural remittances, and the need for land reform.

1. SOME TENETS OF ORTHODOXY

The conventional model underlying much thinking on Kenya has stressed the extant inequality of assets (including human capital), and the presumed weakness of intersectoral links owing to structural rigidities in the working of the price mechanism. As a result, growth based on the expansion of the private urban formal sector and capitalist smallholder farming would, it was argued, entail (a) increasing concentration of income and wealth, (b) immiserization of a growing non-formal urban labour force, and (c) increasing proletarianization of the weakest groups in the rural areas. Implicit in this view was the presumption that people and resources flow one way: from the rural to the urban areas. The resulting urban bias was then sought to be corrected by deliberate acts of public policy, aimed both at changing the structure for instance of the existing income and asset distribution, as well as in reducing the one-way rural–urban flows.

Perhaps the best articulated statement of this view is the ILO Report, *Employment, Incomes and Equality.* As reviewed in *World Development*, the report found that 'Kenya is faced with increasingly more serious employment and income distribution problems. . . . Increasing inequalities in incomes . . . have contributed to increasing rates of urban unemployment. Rural residents, . . . under considerable economic pressure in their home areas, are migrating to the towns where wages have been steadily climbing'.[1] Like many other observers of the Kenyan scene, the ILO investigators assumed that people and resources in a supposedly capitalist economy such as Kenya's always flowed from countryside to cities. The investigators also assumed that flows reflected imbalances, 'the imbalance between the growth of the labour force, the urban population, and education and overall growth of the economy, and the imbalance between people's aspirations and expectations of work and the structure of incomes and opportunities available' (ILO, 1972, p. 1). More recently, Kitching, analysing the smallholder sector up to 1970, concluded that 'up to 1970 a considerable majority of smallholders in Kenya were untouched by Kenya's agrarian revolution', while middle-income smallholders were 'a rapidly eroding group' (Kitching, 1980, p. 406).

2. AWKWARD FACTS

Consider the factual basis for these beliefs. Kitching attempts to sustain his views by

*The views expressed in this paper are those of the authors and not necessarily those of the institutions for which they work.

The authors are indebted to a referee for helpful comments.

citing the household income distribution estimated by the ILO Report (ILO, 1972, p. 74) and Kitching (1980, p. 407). However, that estimate was spectacularly refuted by IRS1 1974/5 (Republic of Kenya, 1977). The group of households with income in the range of £120–£200 per annum in 1970 was identified by Kitching as containing 'the remains of the rapidly eroding group of middle-level smallholders'. This group was estimated in the ILO Report as totalling only 240,000 households of whom many were not smallholders. Yet IRS 1 found that among smallholders alone over half a million households had incomes in excess of £120 pa (at 1970 prices). Similarly, the 'considerable majority' untouched by growth, earning less than £60 pa formed not 63% of all Kenyan households as suggested by the ILO Report but around 29%. By choosing 1970 as an end-point for his analysis, Kitching denied himself by far the richest data source then available on smallholder agriculture.

Of course, that a belief about income levels is shown to be seriously erroneous need not imply that a belief about income trends is erroneous. On this question data sources are severely limited. Since, however, the lack of data has not inhibited the thesis of increasing inequality among smallholders, it is worth constructing with some care the one intertemporal comparison of smallholder income distribution and absolute poverty which is permitted by data sources. Trends can be derived only for Central Province, and there only for the period 1963–74, the basis for our estimates being a comparison of two smallholder household budget surveys. During this period Central Province accounted for about a quarter of all Kenyan smallholders. Our comparison is handicapped by the fact that the raw data from the 1963 survey are no longer available so we are restricted to published information.

In their published versions the two surveys are not comparable due to large changes in provincial boundaries and radically different definitions of income. To correct for this the 1974 data was re-analysed on the 1963 boundaries and income definition.[2] An unsatisfactory feature of the published results of the 1963 survey is that in the distribution of income the measure of income is total household income. Clearly, large households need more income than small ones for a common living standard. Being restricted to published data we can only partially correct for this by dividing the mean total household income of each of 16 income groups by the mean number of 'adult equivalents' in that group (where an adult equivalent is either one adult or two children). This is unsatisfactory since the ranking of households by total income will differ from that by income per adult equivalent, so that our identification of 'poor' households is inaccurate.

The best that can be done, however, is to apply precisely the same (unsatisfactory) methodology to both surveys. Budget surveys measure income in the previous year. In the risky conditions of smallholder agriculture this is a poor guide to permanent income which should be better reflected by consumption. Again, no ranking of the 1963 data by consumption is published, but we are able to calculate consumption per adult equivalent for the previously identified income groups.

The results, reported in Table 1, are not easy to interpret. On the criterion of current income, there has been a fairly substantial loss of share of the poorest 40% of the population to the other income groups. The poorest 40% were not immiserized for their real per capita[3] income rose by 9% in 11 years; but this was far short of the 60% increases of other groups. However, this picture of deteriorating distribution is not supported by the data on consumption. Over the period, the poorest 40% of the population maintained their share of consumption whilst the richest 30% lost part of their share to the middle income group. If the data is credible, an explanation for the divergent trends in income and consumption may be that the adoption of innovations has involved smallholders in an objectively greater degree of annual crop risk.[4] This would have the effect of increasing the dispersion of current income more than that of permanent income, so that snapshots of annual income would show a worsening of distribution even if the true distribution, reflected by consumption, was unaltered. On this account the apparent deterioration in income distribution is entirely spurious because the distribution of consumption has not deteriorated.[5] A further indication that the permanent income of poorer smallholders broadly kept pace with the change in the mean is that the real wages of labourers hired on smallholdings in Central Province rose by around 50% over the period.[6] Since many of these labourers were themselves poor smallholders, we expect real wages to change in line with the permanent incomes of poor smallholders which is indeed implied by the consumption data of Table 1.

As Anand has recently demonstrated,

Table 1. *Changes in the distribution of income and consumption in Central Province*, 1963–74

% 'Population'*		% Income‡ 1963	% Income‡ 1974	% Consumption 1963	% Consumption 1974	Transient income § 1963	Transient income § 1974	1974 real income per adult equivalent (1963 = 100)‖ Current income	1974 real income per adult equivalent (1963 = 100)‖ Permanent income
Poorest†	40%	25.2	18.2	32.0	32.9	–6.8	–14.7	109	155
Middle†	30%	24.5	26.2	26.4	32.4	–1.9	–6.2	162	185
Richest†	30%	50.3	55.6	41.5	34.7	+8.8	+20.9	167	126
All	100	100.0	100.0	100.0	100.0	100.0	100.0	151	151

Sources: *Economic Survey of Central Province* 1963/4 (Republic of Kenya, 1968); Kmietowicz and Webley (1977); *IRS* 1 1974/5 (Republic of Kenya, 1977).

*The 'population' is measured in adult equivalent units (see text), *not* households or people.

†The 'population' is ranked by total household income into these three bands.

‡Income is annual receipts from wages, crops (including subsistence), milk sales and own businesses, less all input costs.

§The share of income minus the share of consumption.

‖On the above definition, total household income rose from 1238 to 4139 sh. This is deflated by the low income urban cost of living index re-weighted to correspond to the typical smallholder consumption bundle in 1974, and corrected for the increase in the number of adult equivalents per household.

comparison between budget surveys is liable to be subject to severe biases. However, to the extent that valid comparison can be made and that this generalizes to other regions and date pairs, perhaps the safest conclusion is that no definite statement can be made on the basis of Table 1 as to whether or not the poorest 40% of smallholders experienced a slower growth of income than the average. What seems unambiguous is that the middle income group of smallholders increased its share of permanent income (since it increased its share of both current income and consumption). This directly contradicts Kitching's assertion that middle-income smallholders were a rapidly eroding group.

Trends in poverty are dependent upon the level at which the poverty line is drawn. Adopting that suggested by Thorbecke and Crawford (1978) – 2000 sh pa at 1974 prices, whereas in 1963 50% of the smallholder population of Central Province was in poverty, by 1974 this has been reduced to only 22%. Thus, the comparison of the 1963 Central Province Survey (a source which Kitching uses heavily) with IRS 1 (a source he denied himself), suggests that whatever the nature of the growth process in the smallholder sector, it was remarkably efficacious in alleviating poverty and appears to have strengthened the middle peasantry.

However, even with the benefit of IRS 1 data, the evidence on the change in smallholder income distribution is sufficiently uncertain that a more reliable basis for judgement is to study the processes which determine the pace and distribution of growth of the smallholder economy. Section 3 is devoted to this investigation.

3. THE GROWTH PROCESS IN KENYAN SMALLHOLDER AGRICULTURE

When the focus of study is shifted from unprofitable attempts to quantify changes in aggregate incomes to the processes by which income components are generated, two characteristics of the smallholder economy stand out as liable to be of central importance. First, as we have documented elsewhere (Collier, 1983), smallholder factor markets are severely attenuated. Only around a tenth of labour inputs are supplied through the market, tenancy is almost entirely absent, and access to credit is restricted to a minority of smallholders. Second, there are powerful interactions with the urban labour market through migration and remittances.

Our thesis is that the pattern of growth and distribution in the Kenyan smallholder sector is best understood as being the outcome of the complex interaction of rural factor market failure and urban labour market participation. The sources of growth may be distinguished as improved resource allocation, capital formation and innovation, so that the transmission mechanisms from factor market malfunctioning and urban employment onto growth and distribution must be via these three components. Our thesis starts by abstracting from rural–urban interactions. It is argued that the malfunctioning of rural factor markets has negative implications for both growth and poverty. Rural–urban labour market interactions are then introduced. We argue that these interactions can offset some of the damaging consequences of rural factor market malfunctioning both for growth and for poverty. Hence, given rural factor market malfunctioning, rural–urban interactions are benign.

(a) *Consequences of the malfunctioning of rural factor markets*

Labour allocation within the smallholder sector is severely constrained by the virtual absence of a market in land rental, the curtailment of land sales, the inefficiency of the hired labour contract, and the limited extent of the market for rural credit. The cumulative consequence of these market malfunctions is the failure of the market process to secure an efficient allocation of labour. This has clear, direct effects upon both the level and the distribution of smallholder income. The allocative inefficiency resulting from the inability to equalize the marginal products of factors across farms of different size has been quantified in Collier (1983) as being in excess of 11% of farm output.

The second consequence of allocative inefficiency in rural factor markets is that the distribution of income is different from that which would emerge were efficient transactions feasible. The loss in agricultural output is not shared equally by all households. The groups most affected by the constraints on the market mechanism are those groups with the most atypical land/labour ratios. The effect on income distribution is thus ambiguous, because both the near landless and those with the largest holdings lose.

Whilst the consequences for income distribution are ambiguous, the effect on poverty is unambiguous. The near-landless, poor through their limited land endowments, have their poverty compounded by atypically low returns to labour. Poverty becomes a matter both of inadequate endowments and an atypically low return on those endowments. The near-landless are thus caught between the contractual inefficiencies of factor markets and the low returns at the margin to cultivation of their own holdings. It is because none of the alternatives are attractive that such smallholders decide to use their labour on their own holdings and, hence, why widely differing factor proportions are observed on farms of different sizes.

In addition to allocative inefficiency due to malfunctioning of the land and labour markets, growth is restricted owing to the malfunctioning of the rural credit market. Credit is a rationed commodity largely confined to higher income smallholders. This is borne out in Table 3 below, where loans outstanding are found to be broadly proportionate to current income. Since current and transient income are positively correlated,[7] credit would appear to be elastic with respect to permanent income. The lack of access to credit for most smallholders has consequences for allocative inefficiency, capital formation and innovation. Allocative inefficiency is generated in two ways. First, the inability of most smallholders to borrow, combined with limited liquid assets, constrains consumption closely to current income. In turn this makes a given degree of income risk translate into a greater consumption risk and hence, for a given utility function increases risk-averting behaviour. The failure of the credit market thus raises the equilibrium risk premium. One consequence of a high-risk premium is to generate substantial differences in mean rates of return between risky and less risky activities. Second, the limitations on access to credit create barriers to entry into activities which require substantial investment. The two major non-food agricultural activities both combine high rates of return with large initial investment requirements, namely tree crops and improved livestock (the former because of the high opportunity cost of lost annual crops entailed by long gestation periods). The quantification of activity-specific risks and credit barriers requires more data than is currently available and so no attempt is made to estimate the resulting global output loss.

For a review of the evidence on the existence of credit constraints in smallholder agriculture see Collier (1983). Evidence on risk as a constraint is scanty, for time series data on individual holdings are not available. From the IRS 1, one group of smallholders can, however, be identified as probably having taken atypically high risks, namely that group with negative income for the year observed (1974–75). Some 7% of all smallholder households had negative income, mean cash income being −3799 sh against 2355 sh for all households. Clearly, this group must have had positive permanent income, so that mean transient income was almost certainly more negative for this group than for any other. Not all those with heavily negative transient income have taken a risky stance. Some households who have adopted low-risk strategies will still have been very unlucky. However, definitionally, the proportion of households with low-risk strategies who are very unlucky is very small, while the proportion of households with high-risk strategies who make substantial losses will be large. Hence, it is reasonable to expect that many of the negative income groups of households are among those which took atypically high risks.

If high risk is not a barrier which can only be overcome by the rich, then the taking of such risks will be uncorrelated with permanent income. Further, if risk were not an important barrier to activities the premium on the rate of return to risky activities would probably be small. Conversely, the more severe is the financial barrier to risk taking, the higher will be the premuim on risky activities. Thus, the hypothesis that the financial ability to bear risk constitutes an important entry barrier implies the testable proposition that the permanent cash income of high-risk takers will be substantially above the average, and has the corollary that thereby the risk premium will be high so that differential risk-bearing ability will accentuate differences in permanent income.

The best guide to the permanent cash income of smallholder households is their annual cash consumption expenditure. In considering high risks, and their corollary of large losses, we must however distinguish between *ex ante* and *ex post* permanent income. The household chooses its risk strategy on the basis of *ex ante* expected permanent income. *Ex post*, unlucky households suffer large losses. Consumption can only be sustained by reducing wealth which in turn reduces permanent income. Thus, *ex post* consumption and permanent income are lower than their *ex ante* values on the basis of which risk decisions are taken. The extent to which a loss of wealth reduces permanent income depends upon the rate of return on the assets lost. We will assume that the rate of return on assets is 15%. It will be seen below that this is probably on the low side. The mean wealth loss suffered by negative income households was mean cash consumption, 2732 sh, less mean cash income, −3799 sh, that is a loss of 6531 sh. At 15% this would have lowered permanent cash income by 980 sh pa so that *ex ante* permanent cash income would have been *ex post* cash consumption plus 980 sh, namely 3712 sh.

Recall that if risk was not a barrier, the *ex ante* permanent cash income of high-risk takers should not differ significantly from that of the entire population. In fact, it is higher than any other current income group identified in IRS 1, being some 75% above the mean. That is, stratifying households by current income, that group with the highest *ex ante* permanent income is the group with negative current income. This suggests that the adoption of high-risk strategies is largely confined to the richest smallholders. In turn, this would imply that because entry into risky activities was restricted, the rate of return on risk-taking would be high.

The above argument has been presented in terms of allocative inefficiency: risk and financing of investment constraints constitute barriers to entry in some activities thereby preserving differential returns to factors in those activities. However, implicit in the argument have been consequences for capital formation and innovation, the other components of growth. The argument that entry to some activities requires capital investment so that limited credit restricts access, clearly contains the argument that capital formation is constrained by credit. Similarly, innovation which is both innately risky and commonly embodied in capital investments, is liable to be constrained by high premiums and by access to credit.

The combined effect of cash flow and risk constraints as entry barriers preserving high returns to restricted agricultural activities is to make income from agricultural activities a function of the means of overcoming these barriers. This, of course, has implications for the distribution of the gains from income growth as well as for the rate of income growth. The benefits of growth will accrue to those smallholders with characteristics which enable them to overcome cash flow and risk constraints. Our major thesis is that a prime component of this group are those who participate in the urban economy.

(b) *Urban employment as a substitute for a rural credit market*

While the internal operation of the smallholder economy is subject to the output-reducing factors discussed above, their effects are potentially mitigated by urban–rural market interactions. Those smallholder households with members in urban wage employment are both diversified against agricultural risks and receive a substantial cash inflow. Our thesis is both that risk and credit are important constraints upon agricultural income, and that urban wage employment is an important means of breaking these constraints. We attempt to substantiate this thesis through two approaches. First, using econometric evidence from IRS 1, we estimate a reduced form equation in which agricultural income is explained by non-farm income as well as by direct inputs. Our second approach is to investigate the differences in the characteristics of poor and non-poor smallholder households in three major regions, so as to identify the characteristics which permit constraints on income to be overcome. Income from urban wage employment is only one means of overcoming risk and cash flow constraints in the absence of credit. The generalization of the hypothesis is that liquid wealth and all cash income from non-agricultural activities *ceteris paribus* raise agricultural income. However, urban wage employment is directly or indirectly the dominant source of non-agricultural cash income to smallholder households. Income from regular wage employment (which is predominantly urban) and remittances from relatives (which is almost entirely urban) constitute over three-quarters of all non-agricultural cash income according to IRS 1.

In testing the hypothesis that agricultural income is a function of liquid wealth and other cash income sources we encounter the problem that the major liquid asset, livestock, also enters directly into the livestock production function. For this reason the hypothesis was reformulated on crop income rather than total agricultural income, the independent variables being liquid assets and non-crop cash income, together with a reduced form crop production function on land, family labour, education and purchased inputs. The OLS regression results are presented in Table 2. Both non-crop income and liquid wealth significantly and powerfully contribute to crop income controlling for the direct inputs into production. That is, more productive use is made of given direct inputs either by deploying them in a riskier stance, or by deploying them in higher yield activities which cannot be entered without substantial cash. Doubling the mean level of liquid wealth raises crop output from given inputs by 16%. This represents a rate of return on liquid assets of 11% before allowance is made for

Table 2. *Regression of crop output on liquid assets*‡

Dependent variable: log of crop output

Independent variables:

$\ln L_c$ = log of family labour used on crops
$\ln M_c$ = log of land area devoted to crops
$\ln N_c$ = log of purchased inputs for crops (including hired labour)
E_1 = unity if head of household has at least 1–4 years primary education
E_2 = unity if head of household has at least 5–8 years primary education
E_3 = unity if head of household has at least some secondary education
Y_{nc} = non-crop income
Q = value of liquid assets
A = constant

		S.E.	*F*
$\ln L_c$	0.29*	(0.03)	86.1
$\ln M_c$	0.05†	(0.02)	4.9
$\ln N_c$	0.20*	(0.01)	320.7
E_1	0.18*	(0.07)	6.9
E_2	0.02	(0.10)	0.0
E_3	0.02	(0.17)	0.0
Y_{nc}	0.000018*	(0.00001)	11.9
Q	0.000052*	(0.00001)	104.8
A	3.97		
R^2 = 0.37			
F = 115.5			
N = 1613			

*Variable significantly different from zero at the 1% level (two-tail t-test applied throughout).
†Significant at the 5% level.
‡From Bigsten and Collier (1983). The Cobb–Douglas form was used since experiments with CES established that the elasticity of factor substitution was not significantly different from unity.

their direct yield. Therefore, our earlier assumption of a 15% total return on assets may be an underestimate (in which case the true permanent income of high-risk takers was even higher than our estimate). Doubling the mean level of non-crop income raises crop output by 5% given direct inputs. In fact, as we will demonstrate below, non-crop income also enables the expenditure on purchased inputs to be increased. This results in an understatement of the positive contribution of non-crop income, of which urban wage income and associated remittances is the largest single component.

The principal agricultural decisions which are potentially constrained by risk and cash flow are the use of purchased inputs and the mix of activities. Of these the latter is the more important since it determines many of the input requirements. Kenyan agriculture has been characterized by two crop and livestock innovations in the activity mix which involved high risk and large cash outlays, namely the introduction of tree crops with long gestation periods and large yield and price fluctuations, and hybrid livestock with high mortality rates. We have measured the extent to which smallholders adopt these innovations by a composite index of innovation with weights based upon the values of different innovating investments.[8] We now investigate how important are differences in innovation as a factor contributing to differences in smallholder income, and to what extent such differences in innovation can be explained by differences in non-farm income.

Table 3 shows that poor smallholders have less land, lower inputs (purchased and own produced) per acre, lower non-farm incomes, lower education levels, lower subsistence consumption as well as lower levels of on-farm innovation (as measured by our innovation index) than the smallholder average.[9] Smallholder poverty is not strongly region-specific. In no region do our estimates show less than 20% or more than 50% of smallholders to be poor. Using a Theil index only 4% of the variance in household incomes is explained by inter-regional differences.[10] The major explanations for smallholder poverty, are unlikely, therefore, to be found in regional or ecological differences. Nevertheless, not surprisingly, there are differences in the reasons for smallholder poverty in the different regions. To focus on these we examine the causes of smallholder poverty in greater detail for three regions: *viz.* Central, Nyanza and Western Provinces, which together accounted for 60% of smallholder poverty in 1974.

These three provinces represent different stages of rural development. Thus, Central Province has had a high degree of agricultural innovation (in the form of a switch to cash crops, improved livestock, hybrid maize and a high level of purchased inputs). By contrast, Western Province has had little agricultural innovation, whilst Nyanza is at an intermediate stage.

Table 3 provides some explanations for the higher incidence of poverty amongst smallholders in Western and Nyanza Provinces than in Central Province. Prima facie one would expect that differences in the average incomes of all smallholders in the three regions would be correlated with the differences in the incidence of poverty amongst their smallholders. It can be seen that the mean household income in Nyanza is about 20% less than in Central Province, whilst that in Western Province is nearly half that in Central Province. But, whereas in Western Province both the farm and non-farm components of household incomes are lower than their respective values for Central Province, in Nyanza mean farm income levels of the average smallholder are higher than in Central Province. and the difference in the mean household incomes in the two provinces is explicable entirely in terms of differences in non-farm income. Thus, we would expect that differences in the relative incidence of poverty in the three provinces would be related to the determinants of lower non-farm incomes in Nyanza relative to Central Province, and to both lower farm and non-farm incomes in Western Province. For the latter, from the evidence on the mean inputs of innovation, purchased farm inputs and labour on the average smallholder farm, it appears that all these are lower than those on a smaller average farm size in the other two provinces.

Within each province, Table 3 reveals that the low income households have both low farm and low non-farm incomes. However, comparing lower with higher income households it appears that the relative contributions of land, innovation and inputs to differences in farm incomes is not uniform across regions. In Central Province, which has had substantial exposure to urban employment opportunities in Nairobi, there are large absolute differences between rich and poor households in their level of innovation and in their use of purchased inputs, but only small differences in their use of land. Innovation, and hence smallholder poverty, appear not to be closely related to land size class. As indicated in Section 2, in Central Province the middle-

Table 3. *Smallholder characteristics by selected income groups and province*

Income range (sh pa)	0–999	1000–1999	4000–5999	6000–7999	Mean for all groups
Central Province					
Mean income (sh pa)	489	1514	4823	6778	5082
Farm income (sh pa)	79	269	2602	4144	2961
Land (hs)	2.11	2.35	2.116	2.885	2.67
Purchased farm inputs (sh pa)	395	204	370	747	427
Innovation (index)	750.7	761.9	1762.0	3528.6	2235
Education (percentage of households with)	16	16	31	35	
Non-farm income (sh pa)	410	1245	2221	2634	2121
Regular wage income and remittances (sh pa)	209	548	1250	1420	
Loans outstanding (sh)	207	195	1052	1183	991
Estimated number of households	26,832	36,713	61,109	32,833	
Nyanza Province					
Mean income (sh pa)	673	1511	4683	7082	4327
Farm income (sh pa)	181	904	3109	4789	3205
Land (hs)	1.608	1.637	3.42	5.097	2.67
Purchased farm inputs (sh pa)	55	27	292	40	140
Innovation (index)	170	396	473	720.8	368
Education (percentage of households with)	5	2	20	35	
Non-farm income (sh pa)	492	607	1574	2293	1122
Regular wage income and remittances (sh pa)	150	150	385	1144	
Loans outstanding (sh)	77	46	590	109	247
Estimated number of households	54,068	98,127	48,792	13,845	
Western Province					
Mean income (sh pa)	629	1487	5094	6893	2784
Farm income (sh pa)	222	623	3096	1464	1476
Land (hs)	1.708	3.41	4.507	3.583	3.27
Purchased farm inputs (sh pa)	22	43	214	157	112
Innovation (index)	1.3	20	181.5	70.1	111
Education (percentage of households with)	37	33	55	47	
Non-farm income (sh pa)	407	864	1998	5429	1308
Regular wage income and remittances (sh pa)	168	545	1041	3655	
Loans outstanding (sh)	36	100	618	0	144
Estimated number of households	52,273	99,432	24,194	5495	

Source: IRS 1.
sh pa = shillings a year.

income group of smallholders have matched the real per capita income growth of the richest 30%. That this diffusion of innovation is relatively land size neutral, is also borne out by evidence from a survey of households making sales of milk and tea in two locations in the Central Province in 1965 and 1970 (Cowen, nd). By contrast, in Nyanza and Western Province, which have lacked access to proximate urban employment opportunities, land differences between rich and poor are substantial whilst absolute differences in innovation and use of purchased inputs are far smaller than in Central Province.

The characteristics of smallholder poverty identified above are in terms of the determinants of farm income and the relative contribution of farm income to total household income. Of the determinants of farm income the differences in the size of land-ownership are in a sense structural variables, for which we provide no further explanation and take them as given in what follows. For the two other inputs, innovation and the purchase of farm inputs, we need to explain differences in their values across different smallholder farms.

The importance of non-farm income and/or loans in financing innovation and the purchase of farm inputs is apparent when it is noted that, if the average poor smallholder were to increase his purchased farm inputs to the level of the mean for all smallholders, the financial burden would require a reduction in household consumption of 25% if met out of current income. Table 3 shows that the levels of loans *cum* non-farm income are correlated with the levels of innovation and purchased farm inputs for smallholders in both Central and Western provinces. Furthermore, we would expect that the loan component of the availability of finance for smallholders would be closely correlated with non-farm income, with the level of non-farm income determining both the ability as well as the willingness of smallholders to borrow. The risk of borrowing without an adequate non-farm income is that land offered as collateral might have to be sold.

That this is not an idle fear for smallholders in Kenya, is borne out by the experience of smallholders on the Lugari settlement scheme. On this scheme, smallholders were forced to take out loans to finance both purchases of current inputs as well as the purchases of the freehold of the land. By 1977, 80% of the smallholders had forfeited their land because of loan defaults.

Similarly, lenders in Kenya look to the non-farm income of smallholders as a source of servicing any loans, when extending credit. For example, in a survey of smallholders with loans for farming purposes taken out from the Kenya Commercial Bank, David and Wyeth (1978) found that 70% received income from wage employment. The survey covered Nyanza, Western, Rift, Eastern and Central Provinces. Applying the same coverage and weights to IRS 1 data[11] yields the result that only 9.7% of smallholder household heads received income from wage employment, with only 20.5% undertaking any activity other than operating their own holding. Hence, smallholders taking out loans for farming purposes are heavily biased towards those with above average non-farm incomes.

Further support for this is provided in David and Wyeth, which shows that most farmers taking out loans regarded their salary as more important than their farm incomes. Thus non-farm income is likely to be the most important element in the ability of smallholders to break the financial constraint, which inhibits both innovation as well as purchases of farm inputs (to the requisite level).

This raises the obvious question of what determines variations in non-farm income amongst smallholders. Table 4 shows variations in non-farm income between regions. The share of rural-based non-farm income in total household income is roughly the same in all three regions, and it would be plausible, therefore, to assume that this component of non-farm income was a function of farm income. The variation in non-farm incomes between the regions seem to depend entirely upon variations in the urban-based component of non-farm income.

Table 4. *Sources of non-farm income*

	Central	Nyanza	Western
Mean income (sh pa)	2121	1122	1308
Mean urban-based income (sh pa)	1431	650	1016
Mean rural-based non-farm income (sh pa)	690	472	292
Rural-based non-farm income as percentage of total household income	13.6	10.9	10.5
% smallholder male labour force in urban employment	8.8	5.3	9.7

Source. IRS 1.

Access to urban income is by means of the urban migration and subsequent wage employment of male household members. Urban survey data confirms that wage earners make substantial remittances to rural households. In a survey of Nairobi wage earners conducted in 1971, Johnson and Whitelaw (1974) found that 21% of the urban wage bill was remitted to the rural areas. This establishes one important link, between rural-urban migration and the reverse flow of remittances which form an important part of non-farm rural incomes, *viz.* the urban-based component, which we have seen is an important determinant of differential levels of innovation amongst rural smallholder households.[12]

While remittances from urban wage income may indeed be an important stimulus to smallholder innovation, this process may generate new inequalities. Indeed, Kitching argues that remittances are predominantly sent by the richer urban households to the richer rural households, thereby constituting the most powerful mechanism for social stratification. On this hypothesis the evidence seems unambiguous. The Johnson and Whitelaw survey found the sending of remittances to be strongly income-inelastic: poor urban households remitted a considerably higher proportion of income than richer households (see Table 5). While remittances are sent disproportionately by the urban poor, they might still be disequalizing if their receipt was disproportionately by the rural rich. On this the Johnson and Whitelaw data cannot contribute, but the receipt of remittances was recorded in both of the previously cited rural surveys. The results, reported in Table 5, demonstrate that both in 1963 and in 1974 the receipt of remittances was a highly equalizing component of rural income. Thus, remittances, while contributing powerfully to rural social mobility, do not appear to be a source of stratification.

This evidence on the distribution of remittance receipts is consistent with the process which determines access to urban manual wage employment (the relevant job market for most smallholder households). It has long been known that such migration is educationally selective (see, for example, Rempel, Harris and Todaro, 1968). An excellent case study of this link from education through wage employment to innovation is provided in Momanyi's comparison of two rival sub-clans in South Nyanza (Momanyi, 1976). One had invested in education, and the other had not. The reason for this was that schools take up land and the more powerful sub-clan had used its power to locate the schools on the land of the rival sub-clan. The sub-clan which acquired education was then able to get jobs in the local town (Kisii) and this money was used to purchase improved livestock and to switch into cash crops, especially coffee. All political power still lies with the uneducated sub-clan but their economic fortunes have diverged dramatically from those of the educated sub-clan.

The rapid expansion of education in rural Kenya will have had the effect of more widely diffusing the opportunities of access to wage employment, unless employers have offset educational expansion by raising educational selection criteria (the 'bumping' process). In fact, in the manual wage labour market the bumping process seems not to operate. A good indicator of this is the proportion of male migrants to Nairobi who possessed at most only primary education. Over the period 1964–68, prior to the major impact of educational expansion on the labour market, this proportion was 66%.[13] Despite the subsequent

Table 5. *The distribution of remittances (percentage of income)*

Households by income*	The sending of remittances by urban households	The receipt of remittances by rural households	
		Central Province 1963	Central Province 1974
Low-income households	28	16	24
Middle-income households	21	14	15
Upper-income households	15	5	9
All households	21	10	13

Sources: Johnson and Whitelaw (1983) and as for Table 1.
*Rural households grouped as in Table 1. For urban households, low income is defined as below 350 sh per month and high income as above 900 sh per month.

expansion of primary and especially secondary education, by 1977–79 the proportion was still as high as 49%.[14] Thus, even the most recent data available demonstrates that many smallholders with only primary education had migrated to Nairobi. In itself, this is not inconsistent with a tenet of orthodoxy, namely that migration would fuel unemployment. In fact, the rate of urban male unemployment fell over the same period, from over 10% in 1969 to under 6% by 1978.[15] Those who migrated to cities largely succeeded in finding wage employment. How the urban labour market adjusted so successfully to educational expansion is beyond the scope of the present article (the issue is explored in Collier and Lal, forthcoming). However, that it adjusted in a way which enabled employment opportunities to be spread more widely over the smallholder population is a hopeful counterpoint to fears of the effects of future population growth.

4. CONCLUSION

On the basis of the available evidence assembled and discussed above, many of the implicit assumptions underlying orthodox views should be questioned. The notion that, while allocatively efficient, the Kenyan peasantry suffers from polarizing urban-bias, should be replaced by the proposition that rural–urban interactions have alleviated chronic allocative inefficiency to the particular benefit of the middle peasantry. Growth has in no sense 'trickled down' within Kenyan agriculture. Indeed, the absence of integrated rural factor markets severely inhibits the transmission of income gains within the peasantry. But urban employment opportunities have enabled those with little land to overcome failures in the credit market and thereby achieve substantial increases in income. Hence, arguments for land reform, previously founded on the notion that unequal land ownership was the principal source of inequality, must be reconstructed in terms of efficiency. Just as remittances from urban migration act as a surrogate for a rural credit market, so land reform may be needed not as an antidote for the effects of efficient rural land and labour markets, but as a surrogate.[16]

NOTES

1. *World Development*, Vol. 1, No. 6 (1973), p. 79.

2. Two different definitions of income were used in published results of the 1963 survey. We adopt that of Kmietowicz and Webley (1977) as being the more coherent.

3. Strictly, per adult equivalent.

4. An example would be the greater use of purchased inputs which raise mean yield but do not reduce the climate-related risk of crop failure. Net income has a higher variance as a result.

5. Evidence that the increased risk involved in innovation had by 1974 indeed generated a large component of transient income is presented in Collier and Lal (forthcoming), Chapter 8.

6. See Collier and Lal (forthcoming), Chapter 5(4)(b).

7. Both a priori and from Table 1.

8. A switch in the product mix could be measured by area of land, number of crop units or crop yields. We were constrained by data availability to choose crop units (e.g. trees), but this is in any case probably the most reliably measured survey data of the three possibilities. Crop numbers data was limited to coffee trees, tea trees, cashewnut trees, coconut trees and the number of livestock (measured in 'livestock sampling units' (LSU) which were adjusted for age and type of stock). One major omission among innovatory crops was hybrid maize; however, intensive studies of the adoption of hybrid maize have concluded that the major constraint on further adoption is ecological rather than economic. Coconuts and cashews are non-existent outside Coast Province so we were left with tea and coffee trees. Another omission was pyrethrum (grown in Nyanza and Western). Tea and coffee are common to Nyanza, Central and Western Province. With livestock it was clear that only the possession of improved livestock could be regarded as an innovation. We therefore had the task of building an innovation index as some composite of coffee trees, tea trees and improved livestock. The IRS valued an LSU at 1100 sh. If we get an approximate value of mature coffee and tea trees by estimating their present value at four times their annual income, then a coffee tree would be 115 sh and a tea tree 15 sh so that the weights assigned to the three components of the innovation index were tea tree = 1, coffee tree = 8, LSU = 74.

9. IRS 1 coverage of smallholdings is not complete since large farm areas in which illegal subdivision has taken place are excluded; however, it clearly ranks among the best surveys of African smallholders.

As discussed above, some 7% of households reported negative income during the year. Since these households have high levels of both consumption and assets, negative income is not a sign of poverty. In our subsequent analysis of the poverty group we have excluded the negative income group and also those households whose income is within the band 0–2000 sh pa purely owing to large (transient) livestock losses. Our poverty group is therefore smallholders with incomes between 0 and 2000 sh pa after exclusion of these groups.

10. This is not necessarily an indication that rural poverty is not location specific. Whilst regions are the appropriate units for investigating policy-induced inequalities (being the location-specific budgeting divisions) they are not the best units for the analysis of inequalities due to ecology. However, even when we grouped the IRS 1 data into eight ecological zones, only 10% of the variance in incomes is explained by interzonal differences.

11. Table 6:4 of IRS 1, using teaching, government and urban employment as a proxy for wage employment.

12. Rempel and Lobdell (1978), however, have recently argued that 'the role remittances have played and are likely to play in realization of rural development' is limited. They reach this conclusion, in particular for Kenya, on the basis of survey evidence that, according to the Johnson and Whitelaw survey respondents, the remittances were used for the following particular rural uses: 'school fees – 12 per cent; payment of debts – 2 per cent; maintenance of farms – 4 per cent; and support of family and friends – 96 per cent' (1978, p. 334). From this they conclude that remittances have financed 'increased rural consumption, education and better housing' (p. 336) rather than rural development. But their argument is untenable as it fails to recognize the fungibility of the available resources of the smallholders. Even though (as is well known from the debates on the effects of foreign capital inflows), recipients of remittances claim that most of the remittances were spent on consumption, that does not mean that by increasing overall household incomes, an increase in total productive investment did not also take place. To deny this would imply that investment (future consumption) was an inferior good.

13. From Rempel, Harris and Todaro (1968).

14. Derived from the National Demographic Survey of 1977 and the 1979 Census. The figure is for the age-specific net migration of males aged over 20. See Collier and Lal (forthcoming), Chapter 7.

15. ILO Survey of Nairobi (1969), found 10.3%; *Labour Force Survey* (1977/8) found 5.9%.

16. See Collier (1983a) for a development of this argument.

REFERENCES

Anand, S., *Inequality and Poverty in Malaysia* (New York: 1983).

Bigsten, A. and P. Collier, 'Towards the modelling of smallholder behaviour', mimeo (Oxford: 1983).

Collier, P., 'Contractual constraints upon the processes of labour exchange in rural Kenya', *WEP Working Paper* 59 (Geneva: ILO, 1983a).

Collier, P., 'Malfunctioning of African rural factor markets: theory and a Kenyan example', *Oxford Bulletin of Economics and Statistics*, Vol. 45, No. 2 (1983b).

Collier, P. and D. Lal, *Labour and Poverty in Kenya* (Oxford University Press, forthcoming).

Cowen, M. P., 'Notes on capital, class and household production', mimeo (nd). Department of Economics, Nairobi University.

David, M. and P. Wyeth, 'Kenya commercial bank loans in rural areas: a survey', *IDS Working Paper* 342 (Nairobi: August 1978).

ILO, *Employment, Incomes and Equality* (Geneva: ILO, 1972).

Johnson, G. E. and W. E. Whitelaw, 'Urban–rural income transfers in Kenya: an estimated remittances function', *Economic Development and Cultural Change*, Vol. 22 (1974).

Kenya, Republic of, *Economic Survey of Central Province*, 1963/4 (Nairobi: Central Bureau of Statistics).

Kenya, Republic of, *Integrated Rural Survey, 1, 1974–75* (Nairobi: Central Bureau of Statistics, 1977).

Kenya, Republic of, National Demographic Survey, 1977 (unpublished) (Nairobi: Central Bureau of Statistics).

Kenya, Republic of, *1978 Labour Force Survey* (Nairobi: Central Bureau of Statistics), forthcoming.

Kenya, Republic of, *Kenya Population Census, 1979* (Nairobi: Central Bureau of Statistics), forthcoming.

Kitching, G., *Class and Economic Change in Kenya* (Yale, 1980).

Kmietowicz, T. and P. Webley, 'Statistical analysis of income distribution in the Central Province of Kenya', *East Africa Economic Review*, Vol. 7, No. 2 (1977).

Momanyi, J. O. B., 'Socio-economic change in Gusiiland', B.A. thesis, Department of Sociology, Nairobi University (1976).

Rempel, H., J. Harris and M. Todaro, 'Rural–urban labor migration: a tabulation of responses to the questionnaire used in the migration survey', *IDS Discussion Paper* 92 (Nairobi: 1968).

Rempel, H. and R. A. Lobdell, 'The role of urban-to-rural remittances in rural development', *Journal of Development Studies*, Vol. 14 (1978).

Thorbecke, E. and E. Crawford, *Employment, Income Distribution, Poverty Alleviation and Basic Needs in Kenya* (Geneva: ILO, 1978).

2

The Political Economy of Stabilization in Brazil

Deepak Lal and Sylvia Maxfield

INTRODUCTION

Brazil's GDP grew faster than most developing countries' during the first three decades after World War II, although it has suffered a serious growth collapse since then, as table 2.1 indicates. Throughout the period, inflation has been endemic. As table 2.3 outlines, there have been numerous attempts to end it, but as of this writing only two periods of sustained commitment to stabilization policy. Of the rest, none lasted more than a year and none succeeded in curbing demand or inflation over the medium or long run. The success of the latest effort, Collor's 1990 stabilization plan, is also in doubt. The Brazilian case, in comparison with others in this project, is like Sherlock Holmes' "dog that didn't bark."

Two things are key in explaining the failure of post-World War II stabilization efforts. First, interest groups opposed to stabilization, specifically industry, labor and to some extent coffee growers, were able to exploit politicians' fears of losing their jobs, either to the military or to other politicians, if they continued the policies. Both prior to the 1964 military coup and as gradual political opening occurred after 1975, government leaders aborted stabilization when it generated or threatened to generate considerable support by antistabilization interest groups for heightened military intervention, or for opposition parties as scheduled times for presidential succession approached.

Industry's opposition to stabilization and its sometimes alliance with labor in a progrowth coalition reflects how Brazil's factor endowment shaped industrialists' interests. As a land-abundant, labor- and capital-scarce economy, Brazil enjoyed a comparative advantage in capital-intensive manufacturing. Both labor and capital had an interest in high growth driven by capital-intensive manufacture or heavily protected labor-intensive production, even at the cost of inflation. The international return to capital for capital-intensive manufacture was high. The return to labor

Table 2.1 Comparative performance indicators 1929–87 (annual average compound growth rates)

	1929–50	*1950–80*	*1980–87*	*1950–87*	*1929–87*
			GDP		
Argentina	2.5	3.4	−0.6	2.6	2.6
Brazil	4.6	6.8	2.4	5.9	5.4
Chile	2.6	3.5	0.6	3.0	2.9
Colombia	3.6	5.2	2.8	4.7	4.3
Mexico	4.0	6.4	1.0	5.3	4.8
Peru	1.8	4.9	1.9	4.3	3.4
India	0.7	3.7	4.4	3.8	2.7
Japan	1.1	8.0	3.7	7.1	4.9
Korea	0.7	7.4	8.7	7.6	5.1
Taiwan	1.8	9.1	7.4	8.8	6.2
			GDP Per Capita		
Argentina	0.6	1.7	−2.1	1.0	0.8
Brazil	2.4	3.9	−0.1	3.1	2.9
Chile	0.9	1.5	−1.0	1.0	1.0
Colombia	1.7	2.4	0.9	2.1	2.0
Mexico	1.6	3.1	−1.2	2.3	2.1
Peru	2.0	2.1	−0.7	1.5	2.0
India	−0.5	1.6	2.2	1.7	0.9
Japan	−0.2	6.8	3.0	6.0	3.7
Korea	−1.4	5.2	7.0	5.5	3.0
Taiwan	−0.9	6.2	5.9	6.1	3.5

Source: Appendix 2.1 and Maddison and Associates (1989).

was also high for capital-intensive manufacture because of labor's relative scarcity. In this way factor endowments laid the basis for an industry–labor alliance in favor of rapid growth of capital-intensive manufacturing or internationally protected labor-intensive manufacture.

A second political factor plays a role in explaining the failure of stabilization in Brazil. The financial control institutions of the state, the central bank and finance ministry, were too weak relative to spending authorities to enforce stabilization. Spending/investment-oriented government institutions such as the BNDE (Banco National de Desenvolvimentó Econōmico; the name was later changed to BNDES), the Banco do Brasil, and state-owned enterprises frequently opposed mandates to curb spending. These spending/investment-oriented institutions were often successful in their opposition to spending restraints thanks to specific institutional and legal arrangements which left central monetary authorities weak. Furthermore, the BNDE had powerful pro-spending supporters among its employees, industrialists borrowing from the BNDE, and even military personnel.

The first part of this chapter presents a broad statistical picture of the Brazilian economy since 1950. It sketches the two "big pushes" followed by busts which characterize Brazilian postwar economic history. The second part of the paper outlines the various stabilization failures in more detail, and introduces possible political explanations for them. The third part looks closely at the politics of the failed reform efforts between 1979 and 1984, highlighting the role of industrial opposition to stabilization and the weakness of financial control institutions. The final part uses a Krueger/Leamer three-factor, multicommodity model of an open economy in tying the political explanations to the deeper economic currents flowing from Brazil's changing factor endowments.

1 BRAZILIAN GROWTH AND INFLATION SINCE 1950

Figures 2.1 through 2.5 chart Brazilian GDP growth rates, increases in capital stock, real wages, current account deficits (as a percentage of GDP) and inflation rates from 1950 to 1989. Table 2.2 lists the Presidents of Brazil between 1919 and 1989 and the percentage of the population who voted for them. Table 2.3 lists the various stabilization plans undertaken in the post- war period.

Brazil's postwar economic history can be usefully divided into four phases. The first phase lasted until the military takeover in 1964. It was a period of state-induced industrialization, including the big push in investment under Kubitschek, financed by the forced savings from inflation and rising capital inflows, mainly in the form of direct foreign investment. (Note the big increase in the capital stock between 1956 and 1960 in figure 2.2.) This led to acute inflation by 1963 and a debt crisis (see figure 2.5).

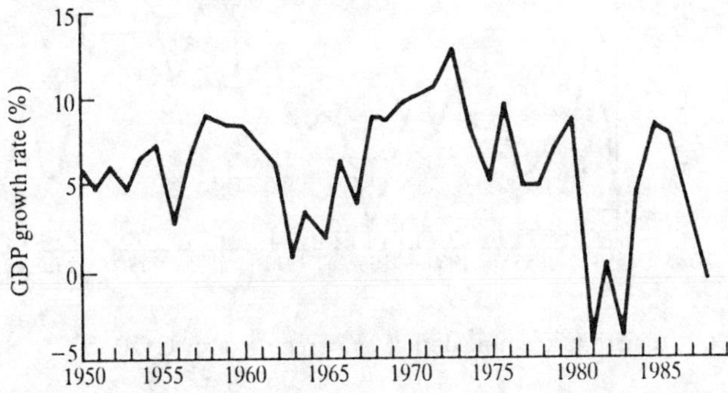

Figure 2.1 Annual growth rates of GDP

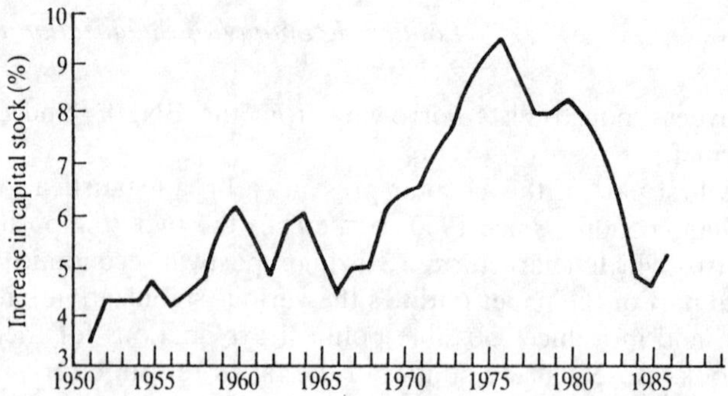

Figure 2.2 Percentage increase in capital stock

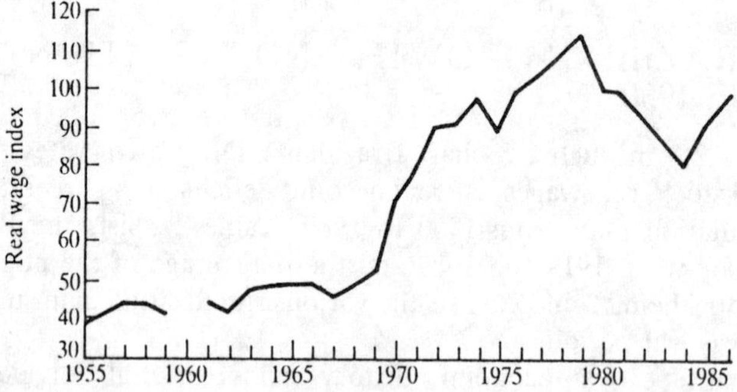

Figure 2.3 Real wage index

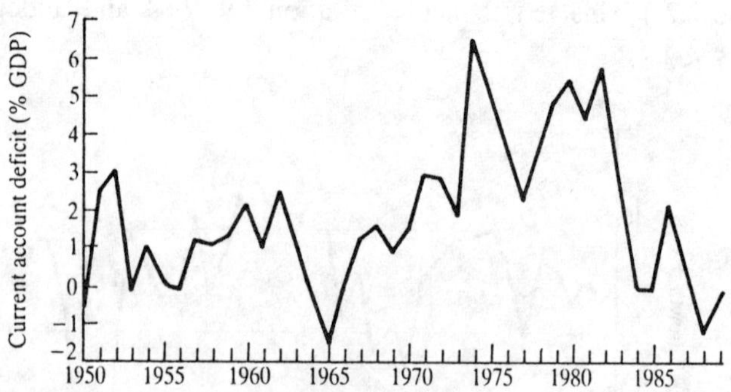

Figure 2.4 Current account deficit as percentage of GDP

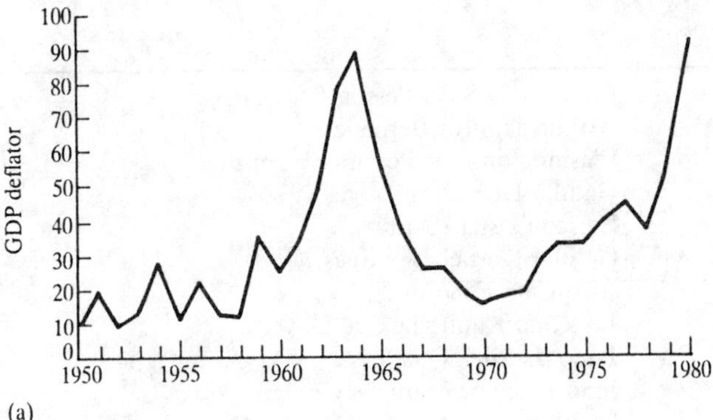

(a)

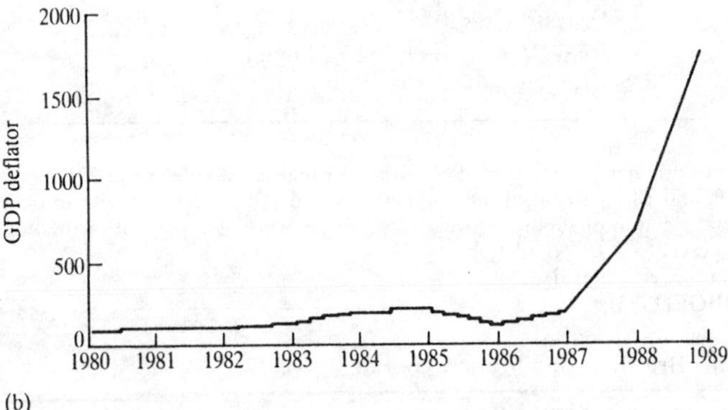

(b)

Figure 2.5 Percentage change in GDP deflator

Inflation yields revenue to the government as long as the rate of inflation is less than the rate of growth of money balances. If real money balances start declining, that means people are escaping the inflation tax, whose yield falls progressively. Table 2.4 provides the series on real money balances. It shows that in 1963 and 1964 there was a concomitant decrease in the yield of the inflation tax. The first sustained postwar stabilization program was launched in 1964.

The second phase of postwar Brazilian economic history is the period of stabilization and liberalization under Bulhões-Campos lasting from 1964 until 1967, which is described in slightly more detail below. The third phase, from 1967 to about 1980, included Brazil's miracle years, as well as another big push under Delfim Netto in the late 1970s. This too, like the Kubitschek big push, was financed at first by cheap foreign loans (this time syndicated bank credit frequently offered at negative real interest rates) and later in the 1970s by inflationary financing.

Table 2.2 Presidents of Brazil 1919–89 and percentage of the population who voted for them

Year		*Vote (%)*
1919–22	Epitacio da Silva Pessoa	1.1
1922–6	Arthur da Silva Bernades	1.6
1926–30	Washington Luis Pereira de Souza	2.2
1930–45	Getulio Dornelles Vargas	0.0
1946–51	Enrico Gaspar Dutra	6.9
1951–4	Getulio Dornelles Vargas	7.2
1954–5	João Café Filho	0.0[a]
1956–61	Juscelino Kubitschek de Oliveira	5.0
1961	Janio da Silva Quadros	7.9[b]
1961–4	João Belchior Marques Goulart	0.0[c]
1964–7	Humberto de Alencar Castelo Branco	0.0
1967–9	Arthur da Costa e Silva	0.0
1969–74	Emilio Garrastazu Medici	0.0
1974–9	Ernesto Geisel	0.0
1979–85	João Baptista de Oliveira Figueiredo	0.0
1985	Jose Sarney	0.0

[a]4.7 percent as vice-president.
[b]In the last "popular" election in 1961, Brazilian registered votes were 22.3 percent of the population and 18.0 percent of the population voted. This compares with the US presidential election of 1960 when registered voters were 59.3 percent of the population and 37.9 percent of the population voted.
[c]6.3 percent as vice-president.
Source: IBGE(1985).

Table 2.3 Brazilian stabilization episodes, 1945–91

Period	*President*	*Common name of plan or key author*
Oct. 1953–May 1954	Vargas	Lafer/Aranha
Aug. 1954–Apr. 1955	Café Filho	Gudin
June 1958–June 1959	Kubitschek	Alkim/Lopes
Mar. 1961–Aug. 1961	Quadros	
Jan. 1963–May 1963	Goulart	Furtado–Dantas Plan
1964–1967	Castello Branco (military government after 1964 coup)	Campos/Bulhões
1974	Geisel	Simonsen
Feb. 1979–Aug. 1979	Figueiredo	Simonsen
1980–1984	Figueiredo/Sarney	Delfim Netto
Feb. 1986–Nov. 1986	Sarney	Cruzado I
Nov. 1986–Feb. 1987	Sarney	Cruzado II
Mid-1987	Sarney	Bresser Plan
Jan. 1989	Sarney	Summer Plan
1990–?	Collor	Collor Plan

Table 2.4 Changes in real money balances (1950–89)[a]

Year	*Real money*
1950	25.80000
1951	−2.400000
1952	5.700000
1953	5.200000
1954	−2.100000
1955	0.200000
1956	−0.600000
1957	19.30000
1958	8.600000
1959	7.099999
1960	12.60000
1961	16.30000
1962	12.90000
1963	−13.40000
1964	−4.900002
1965	17.80000
1966	120.1000
1967	16.50000
1968	16.30000
1969	8.900000
1970	10.70000
1971	12.70000
1972	18.10000
1973	17.40000
1974	−0.500000
1975	9.000000
1976	−4.400002
1977	−7.500000
1978	3.799999
1979	19.60000
1980	−20.30000
1981	−35.10000
1982	−35.60000
1983	−41.39999
1984	−10.00000
1985	111.6000
1986	177.2000
1987	−81.30000
1988	−112.6000
1989	−359.9000

[a]Derived as the change in M1 divided by the GDP deflator.
Source: Appendix 2.1.

This big push also ended with a debt crisis and high inflation – the cure for which was sought in a series of failed heterodox stabilization plans. Once again as in 1963–4, it was not until acute inflation had led to a shrinking of real money balances in 1980–4 that a sustained stabilization effort commenced. Its failure, the lurch to hyperinflation in 1988 and 1989, and a large decrease in real money balances, evident in table 2.4, led to Collor's 1990 stabilization plan.

The timing of the only two sustained stabilization plans in post-World War II Brazil, Bulhões and Campos (1964–7), and Delfim Netto (1980–4), lends credence to a political explanation of stabilization based on state revenue maximization which is implicit in the economic analysis of Lal and Myint.[1] It appears that the state tolerates inflation, if not encouraging it, until the revenues from the inflation tax start declining. While this is a possible explanation of the initiation of stabilization efforts that the government was committed to sustaining, initiation of the numerous failed stabilization efforts corresponds to balance of payments pressure. The failure of stabilization *implementation* in Brazil requires yet a different political explanation. To this we now turn.

2 STABILIZATION FAILURES AND POSSIBLE POLITICAL EXPLANATIONS

Brief history of stabilization episodes

As table 2.3 outlines, Brazil's first post-World War II stabilization effort came under President Getúlio Vargas and lasted from October 1953 to May 1954. It occurred in the context of a $1 billion balance of payments deficit, 21 percent inflation for 1952 (considered a large jump over 1951's 11 percent) and a slowdown in industrial production in early 1953. In June 1953 Vargas's first finance minister, Horacio Lafer, resigned in frustration over the obstacles to formulating and implementing a coherent stabilization plan. The new finance minister, Oswaldo Aranha, had more success. The "Aranha Plan" of October 1953 promised credit restrictions and new multiple exchange controls involving a de facto devaluation. The effort fell apart when Vargas was unable/unwilling to resist pressure for wage increases from civil servants and the military.[2]

Vargas bequeathed a major financial crisis to his successor in 1954, Café Filho. The first of Café Filho's three finance ministers, Eugênio Gudin, previously an Executive Director of the IMF and proponent of orthodox stabilization, pledged in August 1954 to carry out the Aranha Plan. Consulting the IMF and working closely with the head of Brazil's supervisory monetary board (Superintendância da Moeda e Crédito, SUMOC), Octávio Gouvêa de Bulhões, Gudin successfully tightened the money supply. This induced several bank failures and considerable political opposition. Gudin resigned in April 1955 sensing the president's unwillingness to support stabilization. This unwillingness was signaled in part by his negotiations with Jânio Quadros, governor of São Paulo, over easing credit controls hurting São Paulo industrialists. The new finance minister, José Maria Whitaker, whose appointment Quadros had recommended, immediately eased monetary policy.

The next stabilization effort came on the heels of Kubitschek's ambitious big push and the balance of payments trouble and inflationary pressure associated with it. In June 1958 Finance Minister José Maria Alkim resigned amid complaints that he had failed to secure international financing for Brazil or to control inflation. His replacement, Lucas Lopes, and director of the BNDE, Roberto Campos, drafted a two-stage stabilization program announced after the October 1958 congressional elections. There were simultaneous negotiations with the IMF over a standby agreement.[3] The IMF pushed for shock treatment to rapidly reduce inflation and for elimination of multiple exchange controls. The Brazilians preferred a more gradual approach and continuation of exchange controls. Controversy over stabilization widened into a debate over development strategy in general. In June 1959 Kubitschek became the first Latin American president to break off relations with the IMF.[4]

Despite Quadros' earlier lobbying for loose credit on behalf of São Paulo industrialists, during his presidential campaign to succeed Kubitschek in 1960 Quadros made the large federal deficit and need for financial retrenchment a key issue. In March 1961, three months after his inauguration, Quadros announced a new stabilization program, drastically cutting subsidies on consumer imports (wheat and oil), simplifying the multiple exchange rate system, devaluing the cruzeiro de facto, and promising to cut the public sector deficit. Before long, however, Quadros resigned.

The Dantas–Furtado Plan, named after unofficial minister for economic planning, Celso Furtado, and minister of finance, San Tiago Dantas, was a three-year plan with a short-term inflation-fighting component announced in January 1963 by President João Goulart. The plan contained proposals to fight inflation through credit, exchange, federal budget, and wage policies. The IMF nevertheless decided to release new funds only in response to detailed stabilization steps specified after an IMF mission to Brazil. Even before this mission could arrive, salary increases for civil servants and the military became a critical test for the stabilization portion of the Dantas–Furtado Plan. Its failure as an antiinflation program began in May 1963 when Goulart was not willing to resist the military's request for a 70 percent wage hike.

The most sustained stabilization and reform effort in Brazil's post-World War II experience to date came after the military coup of 1964 and lasted until a change in military leadership in 1967. The military government headed by General Castelo Branco brought former SUMOC director Bulhões into government as minister of planning and former BNDE chief under Kubitschek, Roberto Campos, into government as minister of finance. Both had experience in previous Brazilian stabilization attempts. These two designed and implemented a heterodox program of gradual stabilization that relied heavily on fiscal, rather than monetary, measures. It encompassed a program of trade liberalization, introduction of a value-added tax, a gradual reduction of the public sector deficit involving cuts in current but not capital expenditure, creation (at least in principle) of an independent central bank and a policy of indexation in financial markets to boost savings.[5] Foreign exchange rates were simplified, ending subsidies on imported goods such as oil, wheat and newspaper which had been ended and reinstated several times before. A crawling peg was also introduced. Interest rate controls were lifted and policies were implemented to promote capital market growth. After an initial large increase in wages, wage growth was restricted. Inflation was brought under control. In terms of reducing inflation this was a case of successful stabilization, yet even in this case orthodox monetary control measures were avoided.

The next stabilization effort came as inflation began to pick up slightly in the early 1970s, although it remained low by Brazilian standards. The then finance minster, Mário Henrique Simonsen, contracted the money supply in 1974 during the administration of General Geisel. But this modest stabilization effort ended by October in anticipation of November elections.[6] In 1979 Simonsen – who was by then minister of planning for the administration of General Figueiredo – designed a stabilization program including the promise of explicit fiscal transfers to cover subsidized credit, greater government control of state-owned enterprise (SOE) expenditure and gradual reduction of export subsidies. In August 1979 Simonsen was replaced by Antônio Delfim Netto, who immediately embarked on an expansionary path. Balance of payments problems forced Delfim Netto into a stop–go cycle of stabilization beginning in December 1980 and lasting through 1984.

The first civilian administration since 1964, headed by President Sarney, attempted four heterodox stabilizations between 1986 and 1989: the well-known Cruzado Plan I (February–November 1986), Cruzado II (November 1986–February 1987), the mid-1987 Bresser Plan, and the January 1989 Summer Plan. The Cruzado I involved a temporary wage and price freeze after an initial 33 percent wage hike. The Plan included no tax increases or spending cuts and allowed the annual money supply to expand without limits. Cruzado II included more flexible wage and price controls involving price hikes for many state-provided consumer goods such as electricity and for some private consumer goods such as autos. In both Cruzado Plans wage and price freezes ended under industry and labor pressure. When wage and price controls were lifted, inflation returned to its high and growing rate.[7] The Bresser Plan might be considered more orthodox than either of the Cruzado Plans because it allowed prices and the exchange rate to adjust dramatically and called for cooperation with international creditors. Nevertheless one government official involved claims that the plan was rushed out because demand collapsed, "which illustrates how the intention was to expand, not just to stabilize."[8] In any case, Bresser quickly gave up on the plan.

Political explanations

There are five general types of political explanations for macroeconomic policy which might provide insight into the impressive history of failed stabilization in Brazil. These rest on ideology, international pressure, domestic sociopolitical coalitions or interest groups, state institutions, and electoral pressure. In Brazil's case, the first two are partly related to geography. The argument based on ideology suggests that, in part because it is a continental economy, Brazil has developed a strong nationalist and development/growth-oriented ideology prevalent among the elite and state actors. Fishlow cites his failure to take ideology into account as one of two reasons why he underestimated Brazil's future economic problems in his early writing. "I underestimated," he says, "how dominating the *grandeza* theme would prove."[9] In Sikkink's case this argument is associated with a view of the Brazilian state as very strong relative to others in Latin America such as Argentina.[10] Leff cites ideology but connects it with a third category of explanations, those based on the strength of different social and political coalitions. Unlike some less-developed countries, Leff writes, "Brazil's monetary tradition is not one of unquestioned orthodoxy and inexorable opposition to inflation. Rather the prevailing doctrine has been that inflation promotes economic growth; and literally no important actor in Brazilian politics has actually opposed inflation."[11]

The argument about the role of international forces in explaining Brazilian economic policy is also usually made in connection with explanations based on the strength of different domestic social coalitions and their policy preferences. Kaufman notes that much pressure for orthodoxy comes from international financiers and their domestic allies. In Brazil, both public and private sector bankers, frequently natural constituents for international creditors, were politically weak. Domestic opponents of stabilization, in this case industry and labor, were much stronger. Fishlow combines the international and domestic constituency arguments in referring to the 1964–7 stabilization episode. He writes that "by closing down the internal political process and giving virtual carte blanche to Campos and Bulhões, the military government also opted for magnifying the external influence upon domestic economic policy."[12]

Frieden makes one version of the social coalition or domestic constituency argument for the Brazilian case. He argues that Brazil was a case of low class conflict and a strong coalition of "fixed asset holders" – with industrialists at the center – opposed to orthodox economic policy. To the extent that the Brazilian government did turn to orthodox policy this was due to the growing power of the financial sector, "liquid asset holders," and the threat of rising class conflict.[13] Fishlow also mentions his underestimation of the power of industrialists opposed to orthodoxy as one of two reasons explaining his earlier mispredictions about Brazil. The strength of the antirecession constituency, Fishlow suggests, is a corollary to the weakness of the Brazilian state.[14] In the absence of a strong state, policy follows the interests of the strongest domestic constituencies.[15]

Although labor fared relatively poorly under Brazil's inflationary growth policies, until the 1970s at least, it was usually opposed to stabilization, fearing lower nominal and possibly real wages. That industry also opposed stabilization is puzzling to some observers. *Institutional Investor*, a journal of the international financial industry, remarked with apparent incredulity in the early 1980s that "the imperative of continued growth – even at the expense of inflation – is accepted by a surprising number of Brazilian businessmen...."[16] A leading private banker also stressed the extent to which Brazilian industrialists are "biased against tight monetary policy" and recalls a discussion with World Bank economists who remarked on this quizzically after a meeting with leaders of the Federation of Industries of the State of São Paulo (FIESP) in the early 1980s.[17]

Industrialists, including owners and managers of SOEs, private national enterprises, and multinational corporations (MNCs) in basic, consumer durables, and capital goods industries supported Brazil's "inflation-be-damned" economic policy because it benefited them.[18] The key to Brazilian industrialists' interest in growth even at the cost of inflation lies in two important economic conditions, both stemming from the supply side of industrial activity. First, following a three-factor multicommodity model of economic growth, Brazil is a relatively land-rich country with a comparative advantage in capital-intensive industry. The relatively low labor-intensity of production lessened industrialists' concern over inflation-driven rising nominal wages.

Second, Brazilian industry through the 1970s and 1980s was very dependent on bank credit, and to some extent on state subsidized credit, as opposed to internal or equity financing.[19] This made industry highly sensitive to cuts in state or private bank credit and/or rising interest rates. Particularly during periods of tight industrial credit, private bankers were targets of industry criticism. The government often chimed in. One observer writes of Antônio Delfim Netto, agriculture minister and later minister of finance in the General Costa e Silva and Médici governments (1967–74) and minister of planning from 1979 to 1985, "if [he] seemed to have a favorite target for attack, then it was the nation's bankers...."[20]

Although large-scale agricultural exporters, in general, were squeezed by the pre–1964 civilian regime's multiple exchange rate system, coffee exporters were supported and protected by the state to varying extents and through diverse mechanisms from 1906 onward. On several occasions, such as during Kubitschek's stabilization program and after the 1964 reforms, they formed a vocal part of the antistabilization coalition along with labor and industry. This was because stabilization limited the government's freedom to print money to fund surplus coffee purchases under its price guarantee program.[21]

A fourth category of explanations for the failure of stabilization rests on state institutions and the weakness of those necessary for imposing austerity. These explanations focus on the institutional context of economic decision making and policy implementation. In the Brazilian context the argument is that the lack of a central bank able to effectively control the money supply and/or a central monetary authority with control over public sector expenditure are institutional shortcomings which made orthodoxy impossible to implement. For example, until 1986 the Banco do Brazil (the nation's largest commercial bank) had an open-ended rediscounting facility at the Central Bank with a symbolic 1 percent annual interest rate. Furthermore, in the 1970s, roughly 50 percent of all credit came from sources such as the BNDES, the Banco do Brasil and the housing finance system, and was outside the reach of Central Bank policy instruments.[22] State financial control institutions were relatively weak because spending bodies had strong supporting constituencies – among their workers, sometimes the military, and/or other business associates – which the Ministry of Finance and the Central Bank lacked.

In combination with an argument about the strength of domestic constituencies for and against orthodoxy, the state institutions approach amounts to saying that the state and social forces in favor of orthodoxy were relatively weak in Brazil, while those opposed were relatively strong. Elsewhere one of us refers to this situation as one of a relatively weak "bankers' alliance," defined as a loose interest coalition including both public and private sector financiers and their allies.[23] This type of argument, focusing on cleavages which cut across state and society in a manner consistent with an "iron triangles" approach, has the potential to resolve the apparent contradiction between those arguments focused on domestic social forces, which paint the Brazilian state as weak, and those focused on ideology, which depict the Brazilian state as strong. Where there is a weak "bankers' alliance" those state institutions generally in favor of orthodoxy and their potential social constituents, such as bankers, are relatively weak while other coalitions of state and social actors are strong. This argument, combining an emphasis on social constituencies and state institutions and focusing on how they interact, responds neatly to Grindle's call for attention to "what occurs within the state and at the intersection of state and society."[24]

A final set of arguments about the politics of economic policy potentially applicable to the unsuccessful record of orthodoxy in Brazil refers to the often cyclical impact of electoral pressure. According to political business cycle-type arguments, politicians choose economic policies expected to maximize their political power.[25] The more secure their tenure, the more likely politicians will impose orthodoxy that is likely to anger popular sectors whose numbers give them political clout. In authoritarian and semiauthoritarian Brazil we would expect orthodoxy to be undermined whenever the specter of elections arose, or vice versa. Skidmore, for example, suggests that the military government of Castelo Branco could carry out stabilization relying heavily on wage cuts in the 1964 through 1967 period because electoral pressure had been removed.[26] While this may be partially true, cross-national evidence does not clearly support a positive correlation between authoritarian government and successful stabilization.[27] Grindle suggests that even the subtler form of the argument, positing a relationship between insecurity of tenure and adoption of power maximizing policies by government leaders, should be couched in terms of a domestic constituency approach. Government leaders, Grindle writes, "are not undiscriminating in terms of maximizing their capacity [to be reelected]. They have historically and ideologically determined coalition partners and support groups, as well as clearly defined opponents whose support they will not seek, even in the interests of staying in power."[28]

In the next section we turn to evidence from an in-depth examination of Brazil's attempted stabilization between 1979 and 1984 based on interviews and periodical searches, and to a brief comparison of this case with the others outlined above. This evidence lends support to an explanation of Brazil's stabilization failures based primarily on the relative weakness of state monetary institutions involved in initiating and implementing orthodoxy and the strength of social actors opposed to orthodoxy. Political, particularly electoral, and international pressures influence the ability of domestic coalitions for and against orthodoxy to affect policy. There is little evidence in support of the role of ideology as a primary, independent explanation.

4 THE POLITICAL ECONOMY OF THE BRAZILIAN DEVELOPMENT PATH

The political explanation for the repeated failure of Brazilian stabilization plans in terms of institutional weaknesses and interest-based opposition to economic orthodoxy itself raises further questions. The major question which we are finally led to is: What are the deeper economic mainsprings of the interest-based opposition to orthodoxy?

A brief comparison of the polities and economies of Brazil with Argentina and Peru, as they have evolved since the nineteenth century, is instructive. Like Peru (with its large Indian population), Brazil has had a substantial nonwhite population (the descendants of African slaves) which has not been part of the polity. This partly explains why various social indicators relating to health, education and social services in Brazil look very similar to those of Peru. The poorest in both countries are nonwhite and with no "voice" in the political process. Little has been done by the state for their social and economic advancement.[113]

Unlike Peru, however, Brazil is a more resource- and land-abundant country, closer in its factor endowments to Argentina.[114] Like Argentina, Brazil too had a large influx of European immigrants at the turn of the century. This was to meet the rising demand for labor on the booming coffee estates. "Immigration to Sao Paulo alone rose from 13,000 in the 1870s to 609,000 in the 1890s."[115]

However, the patterns of Argentine and Brazilian economic development and growth until the Great Depression were different. This was largely due to differences in geography and climate, which led to specialization in different types of agricultural products. Argentina specialized in temperate-zone agricultural products, Brazil in tropical products, particularly coffee. As Lewis has emphasized, the product wage in producing temperate-zone agricultural products was higher than that for producing tropical products. "The price of tropical products, per man-hour of labor time, was lower than the price of wheat or wool. Tropical farmers produced less food per head than temperate farmers, and therefore received less per head for the alternative commodities which they supplied in international trade."[116] This meant that even with similar factor endowments real wages would have been expected to be higher in Argentina than Brazil. Moreover, Argentina's temperate-zone agricultural exports were increasingly diversified, which reduced "Argentina's exposure to price fluctuations for any one product."[117] This led to sustained growth in Argentina at one of the highest per capita growth rates in the world, until World War I. Brazil, by contrast, specialized in the tropical crop coffee. It rode the coffee cycle, which led to periods of high growth followed by periods of negative growth. The differing estimates surveyed in Reynolds suggest at best a very low average growth of under 1 percent per year in per capita income for Brazil over the 1863–1913 period.

The polities in Argentina and Brazil were similar and evolved along parallel lines. Both countries were under the oligarchic rule of a small elite. As a result of the growth of the export economy and the increasing size of the domestic market, industrialization began by the turn of the century in both countries and led to the slow evolution of an industrial labor force. This process continued more rapidly when both countries eventually "turned inwards" after the collapse of their primary product exports during the Great Depression.

The ensuing expansion in the urban labor force, which increasingly sought a "voice" in the polity, provided an opportunity to political entrepreneurs – Peron in Argentina, Vargas in Brazil – to challenge the old oligarchy by forging a new political coalition including the urban working class. But whereas Peron polarized the Argentine polity with his form of populism, setting rural landed interests against urban labor, Vargas in his populist attack on the old oligarchy stopped short of fomenting class war in Brazil. There was little polarization between the bourgeoisie and labor in Brazil. Thus when the coffee interests diversified into industry, the sharp distributional conflict that Peron fomented in Argentina did not occur in Brazil.[118]

By 1920 there had been very rapid urbanization in Brazil and in the industrial labor force (see tables 2.5 and 2.6). "The volume of industrial production doubled during World War I, and tripled by 1923... Two

Table 2.5 Population growth of the capitals of the major states, 1890 and 1920

State	*1890*	*1920*
Salvador	174,412	283,422
Belo Horizonte	—	55,563
Recife	111,556	238,843
Niteroi	34,269	86,238
Porto Alegre	52,421	179,263
São Paulo	64,935	579,033
Rio de Janeiro (federal capital)	552,651	1,157,873

Source: Burns (1980, p. 313).

Table 2.6 Indicators of industrialization, 1909–40

Year	*Number of industrial establishments*	*Capital invested (1,000 contos)*	*Value of production (1,000 contos)*	*Number of employees*
1907	2,988	665	669	136,000
1920	13,336	1,815	3,200	276,000
1940	70,026	12,000	25,000	1,412,000

Source: Burns (1980, p. 357).

industries, foodstuffs and textiles, accounted for nearly three-quarters of total factory production. By 1920 industrial production [had increased] nearly five-fold since 1907."[119] It was Vargas's political genius to weld these new and growing urban interests into a political multiclass coalition which challenged the political hegemony of the old "landed" oligarchy. "Concentrated in the sensitive and restive urban areas, the proletariat and middle class wielded influence and power disproportionately to their size," writes Burns. "Numerically they never constituted a majority; most Brazilians continued to live in the country side. Except for the small but powerful rural oligarchy, however, they were politically inarticulate."[120]

With the Great Depression, Brazil introduced import controls, with imports falling by about 25 percent between 1929 and 1932. The resulting import substitution that was induced was financed largely from the profits of the "coffee interests" who were politically disenfranchised during the Vargas years.[121] In the postwar period this coalition of essentially urban interest groups was incorporated into a corporatist populist state, which began with the establishment of the *Estado Novo* after Vargas's coup in 1937. This had two major objectives – to deal with the so-called "social question" concerning the urban proletariat and ensuring that industrial profits remained high.

Beginning with the various forms of social legislation developed by Vargas' minister of labor, Lindolfo Collor, in the 1930s, an important objective of the Brazilian state thereafter was "the process of the incorporation or 'cooptation' (cooptação) of the urban, and later rural, working class into a system where conflict was carefully damped down."[122] An essential element in this incorporation of the "dangerous classes" would seem to have been the desire to prevent any decline in real wages which might occur if the demand for labor was not rising rapidly enough to meet the increased supply flowing from population growth which had accelerated from about 2.3 percent in the 1930s and 1940s to 2.8 percent per annum in the 1960s. This can become a fairly acute problem in a land-abundant economy. It is to avoid this politically dangerous outcome that the basic impetus for Brazil's distinctive postwar growth path (outlined in section 1) – with an inflationary cum foreign-financed "big push" followed by a macroeconomic and debt crisis, which once controlled is followed by another "big push" – can be found.

The analytical framework which best brings out these deeper economic impulses is a Krueger–Leamer three-factor multicommodity open economy model. Thus, consider the simple model of a free-trade world depicted by the Leamer endowment triangle in figure 2.6. The three vertices of the Leamer triangle are the origins for the three factors of production – capital, labor, and land. Along the horizontal edge the capital–labor ratio rises as one moves rightward. On the left edge, the land–labor ratio rises as we move towards the land vertex. On any line emanating from one corner of the triangle, the ratio of the other two factors is the same.

Assume all goods are traded and produced with fixed coefficients. There are five manufactured goods produced by labor and capital, of increasing capital intensity whose input vectors are shown as $M_1,\ldots, M_5$ along the "labor-capital" edge of the triangle. There are two agricultural goods: A_1 which is produced only with labor and land and hence lies on the labor–land edge of the triangle, and A_2 which is more land-intensive than A_1 and also uses all three factors of production. For a given set of commodity prices, the endowment triangle can then be divided into seven "regions of diversification" (by connecting the seven input vector points and the three axis coordinates). Countries with factor endowments in the same region of diversification will have the same factor prices and produce the same commodities with vector inputs given by the relevant vertices. Given commodity prices, relative factor intensities determine factor prices in each region.

Now consider two illustrative development paths in this model. The first is that of a typical land- and capital-scarce but labor-abundant country whose endowment point E_A is on, or close to, the "labor–capital" axis. With capital accumulating faster than the growth of the labor force, assume that the country which we label "*labor-abundant*" moves up the ladder of comparative advantage with respect to manufactured goods, with rising capital intensity. Hence on this development path the wage rises and the rentals on capital and land fall.

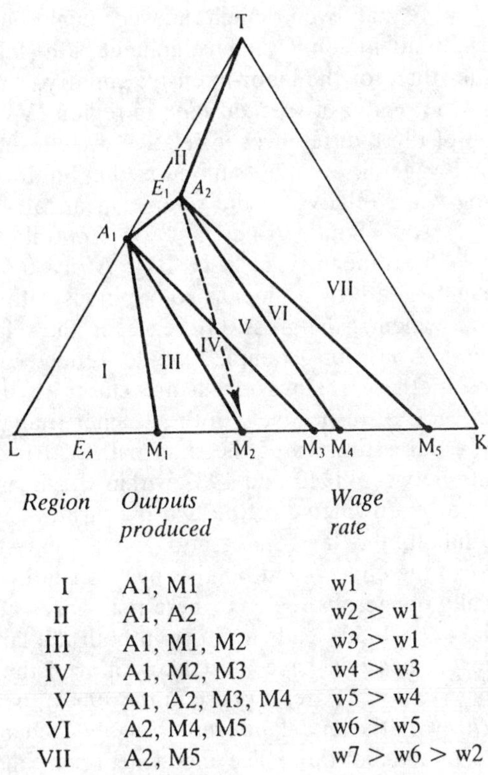

Region	Outputs produced	Wage rate
I	A1, M1	w1
II	A1, A2	w2 > w1
III	A1, M1, M2	w3 > w1
IV	A1, M2, M3	w4 > w3
V	A1, A2, M3, M4	w5 > w4
VI	A2, M4, M5	w6 > w5
VII	A2, M5	w7 > w6 > w2

Figure 2.6 Leamer endowment triangle

The second path is for a *land-abundant*, but labor- and capital-scarce country whose endowment point E_1 lies in the region of diversification II, where it produces both the relatively labor-intensive agricultural good A_1 and the land-cum-capital-intensive good A_2. Consider one possible path of development with both capital and labor growing. Suppose the path of the economy's changing factor endowment is given by the dashed line from E_1. The economy will then move from region I to VII to VI to IV. In this process it will begin to industrialize as soon as it moves into region VI, *but in the most capital-intensive* manufacture. Over time it will move into regions which require *specialization in increasingly more labor-intensive* goods. The factor price consequence of this development path will be a falling wage rate, and from the time the economy moves into region VII, rising rental rates on capital and land. The functional distributional (and *ipso facto* political) implications of the required path of wages on this stylized land-abundant open economy's development path (with a falling wage) would be very different from those of the stylized labor-abundant case (with rising wages) which are also predicted by the standard two-factor models. But note that, even though the wage might be falling in the course of the land-abundant country's development path (for some time), it will still be higher than for the labor-intensive country, until both wage paths converge on the region of *specialization* in region IV.[123]

Some indication of these differences in relative wage levels is provided by average regional wage differentials summarized in Squire (table 16).[124] The manufacturing wage relative to the sample mean of 45 developing countries (1964–72) was: South America 1.27; Central America and Caribbean 1.52; Mediterranean 0.96; Asia 0.44; Africa 0.65.[125] Though these regional categories are by no means coterminous with categories in terms of factor endowments, the gross differences in the relative wage in Latin America and Asia, for example, would reflect the difference between countries in these regions which are closer to the land- and labor-abundant categories, respectively in the Leamer triangle.

Figure 2.7 shows our estimates of the time path of Brazil's changing factor endowments between 1940 and 1987 within the Leamer triangle. The effects on factor endowments of the two big pushes is clear. In the 1940s there is a fall in the land–man ratio and a modest rise in the capital–labor ratio so the endowment point is pushed southward, into the potentially politically dangerous regions where real wages might decline. The first big push of the 1950s leads to a rise in both the land–labor and capital–labor ratios, which will have most likely moved the endowment point into high-wage regions. After a pause in the 1960s, there is another big push in the 1970s with the land–labor ratio roughly unchanged but with a doubling of the capital–labor ratio. The endowment point moves towards the capital vertex, which should have led to rising real wages. The 1980s see the "bust" and a decline in both the capital and land–labor ratios, with their ominous implications for real wages as the endowment path moves southward.

We do not have the requisite information to divide up the triangle into areas of specialization as in figure 2.6, to determine whether the motive behind the two big pushes (in the "deeper" sense of the logic underlying the evolution of the functional distribution of income in the three-factor open economy model) was to avert an otherwise declining wage path (along a counterfactual path of capital–labor ratios). However, if there was such a tendency, the argument underlying figure 2.6 suggests that the polity, besides trying to shift the path toward the capital vertex in the Leamer triangle, would also attempt to enlarge the high-wage areas of specialization artificially through protection.

This last point suggests a way of indirectly inferring whether or not a desire to avoid a potentially politically explosive falling real wage path might underlie the long-run Brazilian cycle of a "big push" with its accompanying dirigiste policies, resulting in macroeconomic instability, which after a hyperinflationary crisis necessitates the standard orthodox cure for past excesses, followed by another big push....

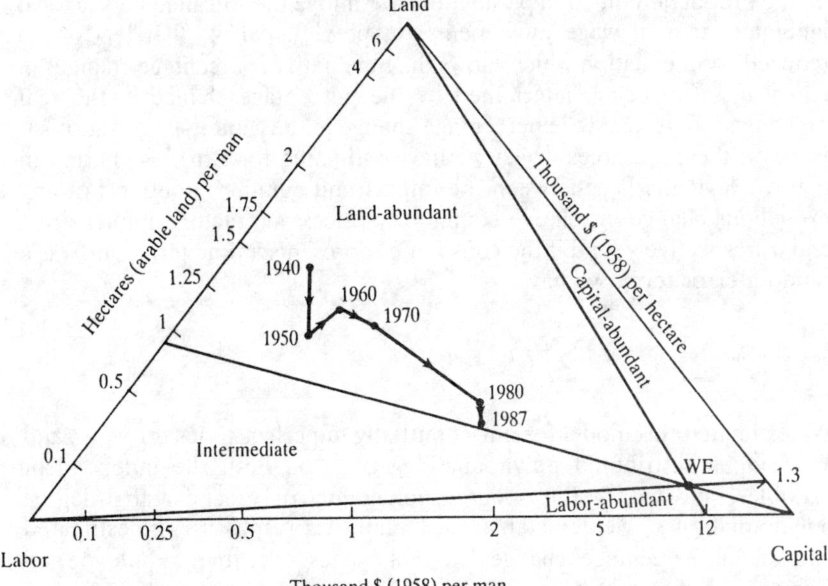

Data:

Year	*Capital/ man*	*Land/ man*
1940	0.42	1.53
1950	0.51	1.21
1960	0.63	1.41
1970	1.04	1.24
1980	2.04	1.23
1987	2.02	1.03
WE	12	0.9

Figure 2.7 Leamer triangle for Brazil; factor endowment path (1940–87). WE = world endowment

If we aggregate the three-factor multicommodity model into the standard two-factor–two-good model (assuming that land requires capital to be made effective) with a composite traded good (which in Brazil would be capital intensive) and a labor-intensive nontraded good, we can derive a relationship between real wage changes and those in the real exchange rate (relative price of nontraded to traded goods) and the capital–labor ratio, within an extended version of the Ricardo–Viner model of trade theory. This relationship is derived formally (including the necessary restrictions on the production function parameters to remove the so-called neoclassical ambiguity in real wage movements) in previous work.[126] It leads to a reduced-form equation which shows the time path of percentage changes in real wages (w) being determined by the percentage change in the real exchange rate (e), and the percentage change in the capital–labor ratio (k). Data on these variables which we have estimated for Brazil is charted in figure 2.8. If the lags between the impact and equilibrium effects of any exogenous change in relative commodity prices and factor supplies are z and q, respectively, and if the constant a represents a time term, and u is a random error term, we have:

$$w_t = a + \sum_{i=t}^{t-z} b_i e_i + \sum_{j=t}^{t-q} c_j k_j + u_t$$

We estimated this model for our admittedly imperfect series for w, e , and k. Using a distributed polynomial lag of 4 on both the independent variables, and with a third-degree polynomial on e, and a first-degree polynomial on k, yielded statistically significant results.[127] The estimated and actual percentage changes in real wages over the sample period 1966–84 are shown in figure 2.8. This provides some confirmation for our hypothesis that Brazil's "big push" cycle is part of the land-abundant country syndrome of avoiding possible real wage declines along its efficient development path.

Further confirmation is provided by the pattern of postwar Brazilian industrialization and its relative efficiency. Bergsman reports that, in the first phase noted above, labor-intensive industries such as textiles (set up initially after the import controls following the Great Depression, and which were further helped during the period of natural protection offered by World War II) had much higher rates of effective protection than intermediate and capital goods industries (see table 2.7).[128] Moreover, he

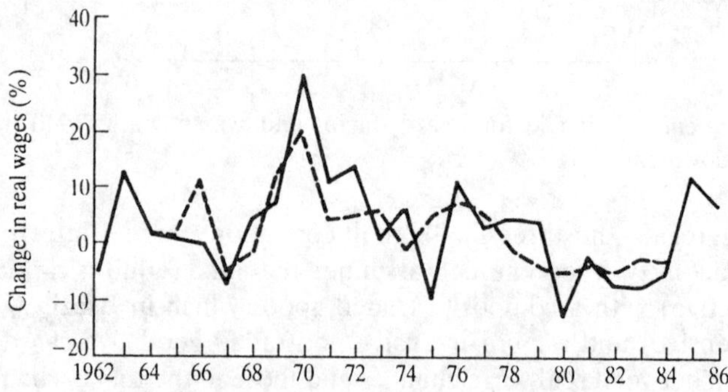

Figure 2.8 Actual (solid line) and fitted (dotted line) percentage change in real wages

Table 2.7 Distortions by industrial sector

Sectors	*Protection*	*Subsidies and other promotion*	*Import substitutiion*
Daddies: consumer nondurables	Very high	Little or none	Had already happened
Infants: consumer durable	Very high	Strong	Virtually complete
Intermediate goods	Low to moderate	Strong	Great
Capital goods	Low	Little	Great

Source: Bergsman (1970, p. 109).

estimates that the production of many of these relatively capital-intensive industries was socially profitable. Secondly, unlike a more labor-abundant country such as India, which followed a very similar industrial strategy, the realized rate of return on investment in Brazil over the 1950–85 period was 21 percent compared with India's 13 percent.[129] This, it would seem, was because within the three-factor framework, Brazil's development (unlike India's) was not, by and large, against its comparative advantage.

As Bergsman concluded, "What are we to make of an LDC which has efficient producers of steel, automobiles and capital goods, but many extremely inefficient textile manufacturers?"[130] The puzzle becomes less acute if we note that a land-abundant country's comparative advantage is likely to lie in capital-intensive industries. Given the difficulties in absorbing the relevant technology and the development of appropriate skills, it will be impossible to realize this comparative advantage "de novo." The development of the "easier" industries like textiles which are labor-intensive would require protection. Once the necessary industrial skills are developed, industrialization could proceed into the capital-intensive sectors in which the country has a comparative advantage. But the earlier "easier" industries would still require heavy protection to survive. The pattern of protection in table 2.7 would thus be in industrialists' interests. They would also naturally benefit from any pump-priming "big push," particularly if the real costs of the foreign financing involved were reduced by what in effect has amounted to debt repudiation! However, without further evidence, on the timing of growth in exports of capital-intensive goods and policy preferences of producers of capital-intensive goods, for example, this effort to resolve Bergsman's puzzle must remain speculative.

If accurate, this framework suggests that Brazil's policy makers have pursued growth at the cost of inflation and eschewed stabilization to prevent the polity being continually at odds with the economy (something which Argentina, for instance, though similar in resource endowments, has not succeeded in achieving). Whether this novel Brazilian tightrope act can continue in the future, unfortunately only time will tell. But if our argument is correct, even if the Collor Plan succeeds, it is more than likely that Brazil will revert to its "bad old ways." Even though the dog may have appeared to bark with the Collor Plan, in this case appearances may be deceptive!

APPENDIX 2.1

Statistical Appendix

Table 2.8 Growth, money and inflation

Year	*GDPGRT*[a]	*M1CHG*[b]	*GDPDEF*[c]	*RLMONY*[d]
1950	6.100000	35.00000	9.20000	25.800000
1951	4.700000	16.00000	18.40000	−2.400000
1952	6.000000	15.00000	9.30000	5.700000
1953	4.800000	19.00000	13.80000	5.200000
1954	6.600000	25.00000	27.10000	−2.100000
1955	7.400000	12.00000	11.80000	0.200000
1956	2.900000	22.00000	22.60000	−0.600000
1957	6.800000	32.00000	12.70000	19.300000
1958	9.100000	21.00000	12.40000	8.600000
1959	8.400000	43.00000	35.90000	7.099999
1960	8.300000	38.00000	25.40000	12.600000
1961	7.500000	51.00000	34.70000	16.300000
1962	6.100000	63.00000	50.10000	12.900000
1963	1.000000	65.00000	78.40000	−13.400000
1964	3.400000	85.00000	89.90000	−4.900002
1965	2.000000	76.00000	58.20000	17.800000
1966	6.300000	158.00000	37.90000	120.100000
1967	4.000000	43.00000	26.50000	16.500000
1968	8.900000	43.00000	26.70000	16.300000
1969	8.700000	29.00000	20.10000	8.900000
1970	9.800000	27.00000	16.30000	10.700000
1971	10.100000	32.00000	19.30000	12.700000
1972	10.800000	38.00000	19.90000	18.100000
1973	12.500000	47.00000	29.60000	17.400000
1974	7.800000	34.00000	34.50000	−0.500000
1975	5.200000	43.00000	34.00000	9.000000
1976	9.400000	37.00000	41.40000	−4.400002
1977	4.700000	38.00000	45.50000	−7.500000
1978	5.000000	42.00000	38.20000	3.799999
1979	7.100000	74.00000	54.40000	19.600000
1980	8.800000	70.00000	90.30000	−20.300000
1981	−4.400000	73.00000	108.10000	−35.100000
1982	0.600000	70.00000	105.60000	−35.600000

Table 2.8 Continued

Year	GDPGRT[a]	M1CHG[b]	GDPDEF[c]	RLMONY[d]
1983	−3.500000	100.0000	141.4000	−41.39999
1984	5.100000	205.0000	215.0000	−10.00000
1985	8.300000	343.0000	231.4000	111.60000
1986	7.600000	321.0000	143.8000	177.20000
1987	3.600000	128.0000	209.3000	−81.30000
1988	−0.300000	572.0000	684.6000	−112.60000
1989	NA	1423.0000	1782.9000	−359.90000

[a]GDPGRT, Annual percentage change in GDP at factor cost; from Maddison and Associates (1989, Table B2).
[b]M1CHG, Percentage change in M1 was obtained up to 1953 from Kahil (1973, p. 275); 1978–86 from IMF; 1986–9 from World Bank and IFS.
[c]GDPDEF, Percentage change in GDP deflation; from Maddison and Associates (1989, Table B2).
[d]RLMONY, M1CHG −GDPDEF

Table 2.9 Balance of payments, wages, real exchange rates and capital labor ratios

Year	FRKGDP[a]	WAGE[b]	REXCHG[c]	CAPLAB[d]
1950	−0.700000	NA	NA	NA
1951	2.500000	NA	NA	100.6000
1952	3.100000	NA	NA	102.0000
1953	−0.100000	NA	NA	103.4000
1954	1.000000	NA	NA	104.9000
1955	0.100000	37.80000	NA	106.8000
1956	−0.100000	40.70000	NA	108.2000
1957	1.200000	43.50000	NA	109.8000
1958	1.100000	44.00000	NA	111.8000
1959	1.400000	41.10000	NA	114.9000
1960	2.100000	NA	111.1000	115.5000
1961	1.100000	43.40000	99.90000	115.0000
1962	2.600000	41.50000	103.6000	114.1000
1963	1.000000	47.40000	121.9000	115.2000
1964	−0.400000	48.40000	102.4000	119.1000
1965	−1.500000	49.00000	100.0000	122.1000
1966	0.100000	49.10000	114.5000	121.2000
1967	1.200000	46.00000	119.2000	124.0000
1968	1.600000	48.30000	115.7000	126.9000
1969	0.900000	52.00000	111.4000	128.2000
1970	1.500000	70.00000	110.6000	132.9000
1971	3.000000	78.10000	105.8000	136.5000
1972	2.900000	89.60000	100.6000	141.0000
1973	2.000000	91.10000	103.6000	146.4000
1974	6.500000	97.40000	113.3000	153.3000
1975	5.200000	89.10000	113.7000	161.4000

Continued overleaf

Table 2.9 Continued

1976	3.900000	100.0000	123.2000	170.4000
1977	2.300000	103.6000	123.3000	178.8000
1978	3.500000	108.5000	118.7000	186.1000
1979	4.900000	113.2000	113.5000	193.8000
1980	5.400000	100.0000	102.9000	202.3000
1981	4.400000	98.5000	117.7000	213.8000
1982	5.700000	91.7000	121.8000	224.5000
1983	3.300000	85.0000	92.8000	233.5000
1984	0.000000	80.4000	90.1000	239.3000
1985	−0.100000	90.5000	NA	244.8000
1986	2.000000	97.0000	NA	251.9000
1987	0.500000	NA	NA	NA
1988	−1.200000	NA	NA	NA
1989	−0.300000	NA	NA	NA

[a]FRKGDP, Current account deficit as a percentage of GDP: 1947–60, Kahil (1973, p. 130); 1960–73, World Bank *World Tables* 1976; 1974–89, (World Bank, 1990).
[b]WAGE, Real wages in manufacturing. Index numbers derived from: 1955–65, Carvalho and Haddad (1981, p. 39); 1966–83, World Bank data (Lal and Myint, 1991); 1984–87, World Bank (1990).
[c]REXCHG, Real exchange rate. Index numbers from Wood (1988).
[d]CAPLAB, derived as shown in notes to Table 2.11.

Table 2.10 Change in capital stock

Year	*KSTINC*[a]	*Year*	*KSTINC*[a]
1950	NA	1970	6.400000
1951	3.500000	1971	6.600000
1952	4.300000	1972	7.200000
1953	4.300000	1973	7.700000
1954	4.300000	1974	8.600000
1955	4.700000	1975	9.200000
1956	4.200000	1976	9.500000
1957	4.400000	1977	8.800000
1958	4.700000	1978	8.000000
1959	5.700000	1979	8.000000
1960	6.200000	1980	8.300000
1961	5.600000	1981	8.000000
1962	4.800000	1982	7.300000
1963	5.800000	1983	6.300000
1964	6.000000	1984	4.800000
1965	5.200000	1985	4.600000
1966	4.500000	1986	5.200000
1967	5.000000	1987	NA
1968	5.000000	1988	NA
1969	6.100000	1989	NA

[a]KSTINC, Percentage increase in capital stock derived from data in table 2.11.

Table 2.11 Derivation of capital–labor ratio

Year	(1) Capital stock (index nos.)	(2) Gross investment	(3) Net investment	(4) KSTINC (%)	(5) LABINC (%)	(6) CAPLAB (index nos)
1950	260.00	12.80	9.20	NA		100.00
1951	269.00	16.20	11.66	3.50	2.90	100.60
1952	281.00	16.70	12.02	4.30		102.00
1953	293.00	17.30	12.46	4.30		103.40
1954	306.00	20.10	14.47	4.30		104.90
1955	321.00	18.70	13.46	4.70		106.80
1956	335.00	20.60	14.83	4.20		108.20
1957	350.00	23.00	16.56	4.40		109.80
1958	367.00	28.80	20.73	4.70		111.80
1959	388.00	33.60	24.19	5.70		114.90
1960	412.00	32.00	23.04	6.20	2.90	115.50
1961	435.00	29.00	20.88	5.60	2.70	115.00
1962	456.00	36.60	26.35	4.80		114.10
1963	482.00	40.40	29.09	5.80		115.20
1964	511.00	36.80	26.50	6.00		119.10
1965	538.00	37.00	26.64	5.20		122.10
1966	615.00	42.60	30.67	4.50		121.20
1967	646.00	45.30	32.62	5.00		124.00
1968	679.00	57.40	41.33	5.00		126.90
1969	720.00	64.20	46.22	6.10		128.20
1970	766.00	69.80	50.26	6.40	2.70	132.90
1971	816.00	81.40	58.61	6.60	3.90	136.50
1972	875.00	93.50	67.32	7.20		141.00
1973	942.00	112.90	81.29	7.70		146.40
1974	1,023.00	131.20	94.46	8.60		153.30
1975	1,117.00	147.70	106.34	9.20		161.40
1976	1,223.00	149.50	107.64	9.50		170.40
1977	1,331.00	148.10	106.60	8.80		178.80
1978	1,438.00	158.80	114.30	8.00		186.10
1979	1,552.00	178.00	128.20	8.00		193.80
1980	1,680.00	187.40	134.90	8.30	3.90	202.30
1981	1,815.00	182.90	131.70	8.00	2.30	213.80
1982	1,947.00	171.30	123.30	7.30		224.50
1983	2,070.00	138.70	99.90	6.30		233.50
1984	2,190.00	141.50	101.90	4.80		239.30
1985	2,272.00	167.10	120.30	4.60		244.80
1986	2,392.00	NA	NA	5.20	2.30	251.90

Notes

The values in this table have been derived as follows:

Maddison (1987, table 6) reports figures supplied by FIBGE (Feb. 1987) for gross increment to capital stock as percentage of 1950 GDP given in column (2), "Gross investment."

Langoni (1974) provides a benchmark estimate of the 1950 ratio of net fixed capital stock to net domestic product (at 1953 market prices) of 2.6. If the index number for real (constant price) GDP in 1950 is 100, this would yield a net fixed capital stock index number of 260 for the 1950 capital stock. This is the first entry in column (1) "Capital stock." The column (2) figures then give us the index numbers for gross capital formation, normalized as is the figure in column (1) on a 1950 GDP index base of 100.

In column (3) we have made a crude adjustment to the figures in column (2) to obtain the relevant index numbers (normalized on a 1950 GDP base of 100) for depreciation. As no figures for depreciation were available for Brazil, we have used the figure for "annual consumption of fixed capital" in India for 1970–82, of 28 percent of gross domestic capital formation, as also applicable to Brazil, as both are large countries with similar industrial structures. This yields the net investment index numbers in column (3).

The post-1950 capital stock series (index numbers normalized on a 1950 GDP base of 100) is then built up by adding each year's net investment figure from column (3) to the previous year's capital stock figure in column (1), on the perpetual inventory method.

In column (4) KSTINC (percentage increase in the capital stock) is obtained as the percentage change between the figures for two years in column (1). Column (6) is derived from columns (4) and (5).

The figures of the annual increase in labor force (LABINC) in column (5) are based on the decadal growth rates implicit in table 11.2(a) of Maddison and Associates (1989).

Table 2.12 Endowment ratios 1940–87

	Percentage increase			*Percentage change*	
(I) *Years*	*capital (K)* *(1)*	*Labor (L)* *(2)*	*Land (N)* *(3)*	*K/L* *(4)*	*N/L* *(5)*
1940–50	41.00	22.00	1.00	19.00	−21.00
1950–60	57.00	33.00	50.00	24.00	17.00
1960–70	95.00	30.00	18.00	65.00	−12.00
1970–80	142.00	46.00	45.00	96.00	−1.00
1980–87	16.00	17.00	1.00	−1.00	−16.00
(II)				*K/L*	*N/L*
1940				0.42	1.53
1950				0.51	1.21
1960				0.63	1.41
1970				1.04	1.24
1980				2.04	1.23
1987				2.02	1.03

Notes

(I) The figures in columns (1) to (3) are derived up to 1980 from table 11.2(a) in Maddison and Associates (1989). The figure in column (1) for 1980–7 is based on the estimate by D. V. Coes and M. Bianconi, cited in World Bank (1990, p. 66). Note that the figures in column (1) differ from those implicit in table 2.11. The decadal figures in this table are more reliable than the crude annual series we have derived in table 2.11. The figure in column (2) for 1980–7 is from the World Bank's *World Development Reports* and in column (3) is assumed to be the same as for 1940–50 base on the judgements contained in the World Bank report cited earlier.

Figures in column (4) are derived from column (1) −column (2); and in column (5) from column (3) − column (2).

(II) We have from Lal and Myint (1991) based on data in Leamer (1984) for the values of the capital–labor and land–labor ratios for 1960. The ratios for the remaining years are derived from columns (4) and (5) in Part (I).

NOTES

Maxfield is indebted to Daniel V. Friedheim for superb and extensive research assistance and to Barry Ames, Thomas Skidmore and the editors of this volume for comments. Lal is grateful to Messrs Roberto Campos and Bresser Pereira in particular for extensive discussions on the themes of this paper. The usual caveats apply.

1 This kind of explanation, developed in the context of economic policies such as taxation, has not been explored in the political science literature on stabilization. On state revenue maximization and tax policy, see Margaret Levi (1989). The economic analysis cited is in Lal (1987) and Lal and Myint (1991).
2 The classic political history of economic policy in Brazil is Skidmore (1967). The more recently published sequel (Skidmore, 1988) is also bound to become a classic.
3 On IMF conditionality in Brazil see Marshall et al. (1983).
4 This set a precedent for Brazil. In the decades of debt renegotiation after the Mexican moratorium of 1982 the Brazilians have more frequently broken off talks with foreign creditors than have other Latin American countries.
5 Indexation later had unintended consequences when it subsequently spread to most of the economy, including to wages. But during this first period of stabilization wage indexation demands by labor leaders were fought off.
6 Fishlow (1989, pp. 88–9).
7 Kaufman (1988) provides a good introduction to the Cruzado Plan history.
8 Interview, Yoshiaki Nakano, August 16, 1990, São Paulo.
9 Fishlow (1989, p. 86).
10 Sikkink (1991).
11 Leff (1968, p. 160).
12 Fishlow (1973).
13 Frieden (1991).
14 Fishlow (1989, pp. 86, 113).
15 The constituent base of government is one of three variables through which politics influences macroeconomic policy choice according to Haggard and Kaufman's broad study of middle-income countries. The other two are state institutions and the tenure security of politicians. The results of the Brazilian case study presented here support their findings (Haggard and Kaufman, 1990).
16 Asheshov and Reich (1980, p. 177).
17 Interview, Olavo Setubal, August 17, 1990, São Paulo.
18 From 1947 to 1962 SOEs and basic capital-intensive industry in general were the main beneficiaries of government economic policy. Kubitschek's Plano de Metas industrialization drive targeted steel, oil, and autos. The majority of lending from the state development bank, the BNDE, between 1952 and 1962, flowed to the steel and electricity sectors. From 1955 to 1961 the government channeled foreign loans to electricity, steel, auto, railroad and

airline, oil, chemical, and metallurgy industries. (Leff, 1968, pp. 40–3). Prior to the mid–1950s, promotion of these basic industries came at the expense of multinationals. However, from 1955 to 1962 MNC investment in basic industries was promoted through favorable exchange regulations, and after the mid–1960s, government policy facilitated MNC domination of consumer durables production.

Domestic capital goods production began to be favored in the late 1960s. In the first capital goods promotion phase both capital and consumer durables producers were winners. The Second National Development Plan, approved in December 1974, made it apparent that continued emphasis on capital goods production was going to cost the consumer durables sector some government support. This fueled the antistate campaign of 1975 led by entrepreneurs from the consumer durables industries and a handful of technocrats. Capital goods producers continued to support the government until the late 1970s when it became apparent that the government could not carry out the pro-capital goods sector policies of the Second National Development Plan. The pathbreaking June 1978 manifesto of business opposition was signed by entrepreneurs from the capital goods sector.

19 There is some debate over the extent of the state credit subsidy. It was at least 2–3 percent below the hypothetical equilibrium market rate.

20 Campbell (1972).

21 The impacts of inflation and stabilization on domestic financiers, and therefore their policy preferences, are less clear than those of labor, industry, or coffee growers. Despite a few periods of high profitability, private financiers' activities and income were restricted, relative to other countries and to their full potential, by the extent of government dominance of credit markets. Before 1964 usury laws severely restricted private financiers' profits. However, they benefited from the 1964 financial reforms, from financial indexing introduced in the mid–1960s, from speculation and arbitrage between subsidized and free portions of the financial market in the 1970s, and, ironically, from credit restrictions in the early 1980s. Whatever their interests, compared with domestic bankers in some other Latin American countries, Brazilian private-sector financiers' economic base and political influence were limited.

Roughly speaking, peasants and traditional small-scale agricultural enterprises and low-technology, small-scale manufacturers have always been losers in Brazil's economic development.

22 Wells (1979).

23 Maxfield (1990).

24 Grindle (1989, p. 46).

25 An excellent example of this type of argument applied to Latin America is Ames (1987).

26 Skidmore (1988, p. 59).

27 Stephan Haggard (1990). Ironically in the Brazilian case, Delfim Netto correlated authoritarian leadership with inflation. "The military is trained to spend," he said. Interview, August 14, 1990, Rio de Janeiro.

28 Grindle (1989, p. 29).

113 In Brazil even though transfer payments have "risen between 1949 and 1973 from 3.1 percent to 8.9 percent of GDP, reflecting the emergence of a modern social insurance system," and the social security system expanded very rapidly in the 1970s, covering 93 percent of the population in 1975 as compared with 27 percent in 1970, Maddison's recent study concluded "overall, it would seem that the tax-transfer system has had a regressive impact" (Reynolds, 1985, p. 98; Mesa-Lago, 1981; Maddison and Associates, 1989).
114 Lal and Myint (1991).
115 Reynolds (1985, p. 93).
116 Lewis (1970).
117 Reynolds (1985, p. 86).
118 This point was made forcefully by Roberto Campos in a personal interview.
119 E. Bradford Burns (1980, p. 356).
120 Burns (1980, p. 414).
121 Burns(1980,p. 423).
122 P. Flynn (1978).
123 It might seem paradoxical that, whilst the *economy's* capital–labor ratio is rising, it is falling in manufacturing. But remember that the rate of growth of labor for the *economy* is not the same as in *manufacturing*. Then, it is possible for the agricultural labor force to grow more slowly (because of fixed land) than for the economy as a whole, thereby allowing and requiring the labor force in the manufacturing sector to grow more rapidly than for the economy as a whole. Thus a rising capital–labor ratio for the economy as a whole can be associated with a falling capital–labor ratio in manufacturing. Of course, there will be some rate of capital growth at which the capital–labor ratio for manufacturing will also be rising along with that for the economy as a whole, and this paradoxical development path would not occur.
124 Squire (1987).
125 The countries included were: Chile, Peru, Brazil, Argentina, Guyana, Ecuador, Trinidad, Nicaragua, Jamaica, Barbados, Panama, Puerto Rico, Dominican Republic, Honduras, Venezuela, El Salvador, Guatemala, Mexico, Columbia, Turkey, Algeria, Cyprus, Egypt, Korea, Taiwan, Sri Lanka, Burma, Vietnam, India, Thailand, Singapore, Philippines, Pakistan, Kenya, Tanzania, Zambia, Uganda, Rhodesia, Ghana, Malawi, Mauritius, Sierra Leone, and Nigeria.
126 Lal (1986).
127 The relevant statistics for the regression from the 1966–84 period are: R^2=0.51, F=2.06, DWS=2.4.
128 Bergsman (1970).
129 Lal (1990).
130 Bergsman (1970, p. 150).

REFERENCES

Ames, Barry 1987: *Poltical Survival: Politicians and Public Policy in Latin America*, Berkeley: University of California Press.

Asheshov, Nicholas and Reich, Cary 1980: "Has Delfim Worked His Last

Miracle?" *Institutional Investor*, August, 175–93.

Bacha, Edmar L. 1983: "Vicissitudes of Recent Stabilization Attempts in Brazil and the IMF Alternative," in John Williamson (ed.), *IMF Conditionality*, Washington, DC: Institute for International Economics.

Bacha, Edmar L. and Malan, Pedro S. 1989: "Brazil's Debt: From the Miracle to the Fund," in Alfred Stepan (ed.), *Democratizing Brazil: Problems of Transition and Consolidation*, Oxford: Oxford University Press, p. 132.

Bergsman, J. 1970: *Brazil*, Oxford: Oxford University Press for OECD.

Boschi, Renato Raul 1978: "National Industrial Elites and the State in Post-1964 Brazil," PhD dissertation, University of Michigan.

Burns, E. Bradford 1980: *A History of Brazil*, 2nd ed., New York: Columbia University Press.

Calabi, Andrea Sandro and Pullen, Pedro 1990: "Finanças Públicas Federais: Aspectos Institucionais, Evolução Recente e Perspectivas," mimeo, July, p. 4.

Campbell, Gordon 1972: *Brazil Struggles for Development*, London: Charles Knight & Co., pp. 108–9.

Cardoso, Fernando H. 1986: "Entrepreneurs and the Transition Process: The Brazilian Case," in Guillermo O'Donnell, Philippe C. Schmitter, and Laurence Whitehead (eds.), *Transitions from Authoritarian Rule*, Baltimore: Johns Hopkins University Press.

Carneiro, Dionisio Dias 1987: "Long-Run Adjustment, the Debt Crisis and the Changing Role of Stabilization Policies in the Recent Brazilian Experience," in Rosemary Thorp and Laurence Whitehead (eds.), *Latin American Debt and the Adjustment Crisis*, Pittsburgh: University of Pittsburgh Press, p. 36.

Carvalho, J. L. and Haddad, C. L. S. 1981: "Foreign Trade Strategies and Employment in Brazil," in A.O. Krueger et al. (eds.), *Trade and Employment in Developing Countries I – Individual Studies*, Chicago: NBER.

Dreifuss, Rene 1986: *1964: A conquista do estado*, Rio de Janeiro: Vozes.

Dye, David and de Souza e Silva, Carlos Eduardo 1978: "A Perspective on the Brazilian State," *Latin American Research Review*, 14(2).

Ellis, Howard S. 1969: "Corrective Inflation in Brazil, 1964–1966," in Howard S. Ellis and Lincoln Gordon (eds.), *The Economy of Brazil*, Los Angeles: University of California Press.

Faria, Hugo Presgrave de A. 1988: "Macroeconomic Policymaking in a Crisis Environment: Brazil's Cruzado Plan and Beyond," in Julian M. Chacel, Pamela S. Falk and David V. Fleischer (eds.), *Brazil's Economic and Political Future*, Boulder, CO: Westview Press, p. 43.

Fishlow, Albert 1973: "Some Reflections on Post-1964 Brazilian Economic Policy," in Alfred Stepan (ed.), *Authoritarian Brazil*, New Haven: Yale University Press, p. 83.

Fishlow, Albert 1989: "A Tale of Two Presidents: The Political Economy of Crisis Management," in Alfred Stepan (ed.), *Democratizing Brazil: Problems of Transition and Consolidation*, Oxford: Oxford University Press.

Flynn, P. 1978: *Brazil – A Political Analysis*, Boulder, CO: Westview Press, p. 100.

Frieden, Jeffrey A. 1991: *Debt, Development, Democracy: Modern Political Economy and Latin America, 1965–1985*, Princeton: Princeton University Press.

Furtado, Celso 1984: *No to Recession and Unemployment*, London: Third World Foundation.

Grindle, Merilee S. 1989: "The New Political Economy: Positive Economics and Negative Politics," Development Discussion Paper No. 311, Cambridge: Harvard Institute for International Development.

Haggard, Stephan 1990: *Pathways from the Periphery*, Ithaca: Cornell University Press, p. 263.

Haggard, Stephan and Kaufman, Robert 1990: "The Political Economy of Inflation and Stabilization in Middle-Income Countries," PRE Working Paper, WPS 444, Washington, DC: Country Economics Department, The World Bank.

IBGE 1985: *Anuario Estatistico 1984*, Rio de Janeiro: IBGE, p. 374.

Joint Brazil–US Economic Development Commission 1954: *The Development of Brazil*, Washington, DC: Institute of Inter-American Affairs, Foreign Operations Administration, p. 42.

Kahil, R. 1973: *Inflation and Economic Development in Brazil 1946–1963*, Oxford: Clarendon Press.

Kaufman, Robert R. 1988: *The Politics of Debt in Argentina, Brazil and Mexico*, Berkeley: University of California Institute of International Studies.

Lafer, Carlos 1975: *O Sistema Politico Brasileiro*, São Paulo: Editora Perspectiva, pp. 113–14.

Lal, Deepak 1986: "Stolper-Samuelson-Rybczynski in the Pacific," *Journal of Development Economics*, 21 (1), 181–204.

Lal, Deepak 1987: "The Political Economy of Economic Liberalization," *World Bank Economic Review*, 1 (2), 273–299.

Lal, Deepak 1990: "World Savings and Growth in Developing Countries," *Revista di Politica Economia*, 53 (12).

Lal, Deepak and Myint, H. 1991: "The Political Economy of Poverty, Equity and Growth," mimeo, London: University College.

Lamounier, Bolivar and Moura, Alkimar, R. 1986: "Economic Policy and Political Opening in Brazil," in Jonathan Hartlyn and Samuel A. Morley (eds.), *Latin American Political Economy: Financial Crisis and Political Change*, Boulder, CO: Westview Press.

Langoni, C. G. 1974: *As Causas do Crescimento Economico do Brasil*, Rio de Janeiro: APEC.

Lara Resende, Andre 1982: "A política brasileira de estabilização: 1963/1968," *Pesquisa e Planejamento Econômico*, 12 (3) (December), 769–70.

Leamer, E. 1984: *Sources of International Comparative Advantage*, Cambridge, Mass.: MIT Press.

Leff, Nathaniel H. 1968: *Economic Policy-Making and Development in Brazil, 1947–1964*, New York: Wiley.

Levi, Margaret 1989: *Of Rule and Revenue*, Berkeley: University of California Press.

Lewis, W. A. 1970: *Tropical Development*, London: Allen and Unwin, p. 42.

Maddison, A. 1987: "Twin Study of Brazil and Mexico – Comparative Graphs and Statistical Tables," mimeo.

Maddison, A. and Associates 1989: *The Political Economy of Poverty, Equity and Growth: Brazil and Mexico*, Oxford: Oxford University Press for the World Bank.

Marshall, Jorge, Mardones S., Mose Luis, and Marshall L., Isabel 1983: "IMF Conditionality: The Experiences of Argentina, Brazil and Chile," in John

Williamson (ed.), *IMF Conditionality*, Washington, DC: Institute for International Economics.

Maxfield, Sylvia 1989: "National Business, Debt-Led Growth, and Political Transition in Latin America," in Barbara Stallings and Robert Kaufman (eds.), *Debt and Democracy in Latin America*, Boulder, CO: Westview Press.

Maxfield, Sylvia 1990: *Governing Capital: International Finance and Mexican Politics*, Ithaca: Cornell University Press.

Mendonça de Barros, José Roberto and Graham, Douglas 1978: "The Brazilian Economic Miracle Revisted," *Latin American Research Review*, 13 (2), 27.

Mesa-Lago, C. 1981: *Employment Policy in Developing Countries*, Oxford: Oxford University Press, p. 86.

Pang, Eul-Soo 1989: "Debt, Adjustment and Democratic Cacophony in Brazil," in Barbara Stallings and Robert Kaufman (eds.), *Debt and Democracy in Latin America*, Boulder CO: Westview Press, p. 130.

Payne, Leigh Ann 1990: "The Political Attitudes and Behavior of Brazilian Industrial Elites," PhD dissertation, Yale University.

Reynolds, L. G. 1985: *Economic Growth in the Third World, 1850–1980*, New Haven: Yale University Press.

Schmitter, Philippe C. 1971: *Interest Conflict and Political Change in Brazil*, Stanford: Stanford University Press.

Schneider, Ben Ross 1987: "Framing the State: Economic Policy and Political Representation in Post-Authoritarian Brazil," in John D. Wirth and Edson de Oliveira Nunes (eds.), *State and Society in Brazil: Continuity and Change*, Boulder, CO: Westview Press, p. 224.

Sikkink, Kathryn 1991: *Ideas and Institutions: Developmentalism in Brazil and Argentina*, Ithaca, NY: Cornell University Press.

Singer, Paul 1989: "Democracy and Inflation, in the Light of the Brazilian Experience," in William Canak (ed.), *Lost Promises: Debt, Austerity and Development in Latin America*, Boulder CO: Westview Press, p. 37.

Skidmore, Thomas E. 1967: *Politics in Brazil 1930–1964*, New York: Oxford University Press.

Skidmore, Thomas E. 1988: *The Politics of Military Rule in Brazil, 1964–1985*, New York: Oxford University Press.

Sola, Lourdes 1988: "The Political Constraints to Heterodox Shock in Brazil: 'Técnicos,' 'Políticos,' and Democracy," paper presented at the American Political Science Association Annual Meeting, Washington, DC, September 1–4, p. 10.

Squire, L. 1987: *Employment Policy in Developing Countries*, Oxford: Oxford University Press.

Wells, John R. 1979: "Brazil and the Post-1973 Crisis in the International Economy," in Rosemary Thorp and Laurence Whitehead (eds.) *Inflation and Stabilization in Latin America*, London: Macmillan, p. 249.

Wood, A. 1988: "Global Trends in Real Exchange Rates 1960 to 1984," *World Bank Discussion Papers*, No. 35, Washington, DC: World Bank.

World Bank 1990: *Economic Stabilisation with Structural Reforms*, Washington, DC: Brazil Department, World Bank.

[21]

ECONOMIC GROWTH IN INDIA

DEEPAK LAL

> Long years ago we made a tryst with destiny, and now the time comes when we shall redeem our pledge, not wholly or in full measure, but very substantially. At the stroke of the midnight hour, when the world sleeps India will awake to life and freedom. A moment comes, which comes but rarely in history, when we step out from the old to the new, when an age ends, and when the soul of a nation long suppressed, finds utterance. It is fitting that at this solemn moment we take the pledge of dedication to the service of India and her people.... The service of India means the service of the millions who suffer. It means the ending of poverty and ignorance and disease and inequality of opportunity. The ambition of the greatest man of our generation has been to wipe every tear from every eye. That may be beyond us, but as long as there are tears and suffering so long our work will not be over (Nehru 1961, p. 13–14).

With these words, Jawaharlal Nehru ushered India to independence on August 15th, 1947, after nearly a century of British rule. Forty years later it is apparent that the world's largest democracy, with a mid-1987 population of 795 million, has far from fulfilled its promise. India's per capita income, for example, is still only about $270.

This paper asks why this should be so. An answer is important not merely because so many of the world's poor are concentrated in the subcontinent, and hence any appreciable dent in world poverty must entail the alleviation of Indian poverty, but because the India of the 1950s seemed to most observers to have the best prospects of fostering modern economic growth in the Third World. It also seemed likely that this could be done within the rough and tumble of democratic politics in a subcontinental polity consisting of a medley of castes, religions, and languages. The lie would then be given to those who believed that only some authoritarian model of development—like those adopted by Stalinist Russia or Maoist China—could foster development.

All the signs were propitious. India had a potentially large domestic market, a relatively diversified natural resource base, fairly large supplies of skilled and semi-skilled labor, no shortage of domestic entrepreneurship, an efficient bureaucracy—the 'steel frame' it had inherited from the British Raj—and a political leadership seemingly committed to development. Moreover, modern industrialization which dated from the 1850s had given India a head start in those activities that promised a relatively easy means of raising the standards of living of the mass of Indians.

For the past forty years there has been slow and steady economic progress, with an average annual rate of growth of NDP of 3.6 percent per annum. With population growing at about 2.2 percent per annum since the 1960s this has meant per capita income increases of about 1.5 percent per annum.[1] This growth rate has been characterized by one writer as "the Hindu rate of growth" and by another as "hastening slowly."

Throughout this time, unlike the experiences of most other Third World countries and despite some vicissitudes, democracy has been maintained in India. This alone would be a notable achievement. In combination with even a slow rate of economic progress it is remarkable. However, compared with India's *potential*, and with the performance of its neighbors in East and South East Asia, its economic performance has been disappointing.

The causes of this relative failure lie almost entirely in the area of policy. A major theme of this paper is the link between certain ideas and the vested interests they have fostered, which has led to the maintenance of policies that are seen by most observers to be inimical to the achievement of equitable growth.

In this paper we first chart the main features of the economic record of the past five decades, and place it in historical context. In a second section we outline the major policy errors that have led to India's relatively poor performance. The third and final section shows how an interlocked system of economic and political interests has emerged as an unintended consequence of the seemingly high-minded policies of planning with controls—controls partially inherited from the British Raj. This system has made it nearly impossible to implement the fundamental changes in policy that are required to end India's continuing economic stagnation.

The Economic Record

Table 1 summarizes the trend growth rates of gross domestic product and per capita income, as well as those of the three sectoral divisions of the economy (broadly comprising agriculture, industry, and services) between 1950 and 1984.

There was some acceleration in the growth rate of aggregate and per capita GDP by about a half percentage point in the last decade compared to the previous period 1950–51 to 1973–74. But this still only implied per capita income growth at 1.74 percent per annum. The primary sector (agriculture) has been growing at about 2.24 percent (a slight rise over its growth rate of 2.13 percent per annum in the previous 20 years), while the secondary sector's (manufacturing) growth rate has declined from about 6 percent (in 1950 to 1973–74) to just over 4 percent in the 1973–74 to 1983–84 period. Much of the recent mild acceleration in the growth rate has been due to a rise of 1.25 percentage points (to nearly 6 percent per annum) in the growth rate of the tertiary (services) sector. This in turn is largely accounted for by the parasitic subsectors of public administration and defense, which have grown at the rate of 7.44 percent per annum in the 35 years since 1950–51.

Not surprisingly, this modest growth performance has had little effect on making any marked dent on the endemic poverty of India's masses. The percentage of India's urban and rural population below a nutritionally based absolute poverty line for different years between 1956–57 and 1978 for which data are available are charted in Figure 1.[2] From this it is apparent that the incidence of both rural and urban poverty has fluctuated since the post

Table 1
Trend Growth Rates

Sl. No.	Period	Trend Growth Rates (% p.a.) of GDP originating in				
		Primary Sector	Secondary Sector	Tertiary Sector	Total GDP	Per Capita GDP
1.	1950–51 to 1973–74	2.13	5.82	4.70	3.53	1.43
2.	1973–74 to 1983–84	2.24	4.15	5.95	3.97	1.74
3.	1961–62 to 1973–74	2.24	4.25	4.26	3.27	1.05
4.	1950–51 to 1983–84	2.18	5.06	4.81	3.55	1.38

Notes: 1. All the GDP estimates are at 1970–71 prices.

2. Trend growth rates have been obtained by fitting a semi-log trend equation so as to get an exponential trend growth rate.

3. Composition of the sectors is as follows:
Primary sector: agriculture, forestry & logging, fishing and mining & quarrying.
Secondary sector: manufacturing, construction, electricity, gas and water supply.
Tertiary sector: transport storage & communication; trade, hotels and restaurants; banking and insurance; real estate and ownership of dwellings and business services; public administration and science, other services.

Source: K. Sundaram, S. Tendulkar, "Growth, trickle down effects and poverty." *Frontline*, May 18–31, 1985, pp. 33–40.

Figure I
Percentage of India's Population Below Poverty Line

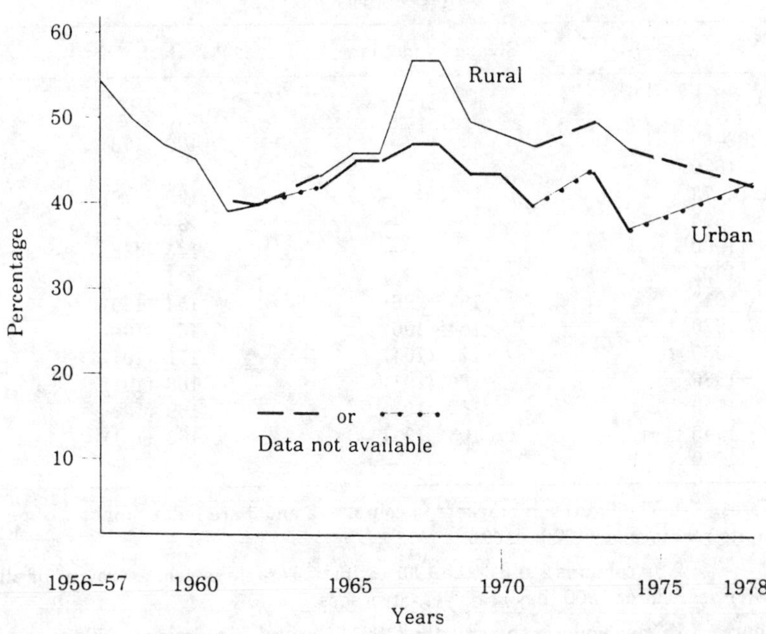

Source: K. Sundaram, S. Tendulkar, "Growth, trickle down effects and poverty," *Frontline*, May 18–31, 1985, pp. 33–40.

Independence decades without any significant statistical trend. Much of India's poverty is rural (see Dandekar and Rath, 1971; Minhas, 1970), and its incidence is inversely related to real agricultural income per head of the rural population—which fluctuates with the weather! (see Ahluwalia, 1978, 1985 and Lal, 1976). The latest figures on the incidence of poverty for 1983–84[3] are 40.4 percent for the rural and 28.1 percent for the urban sector (as compared with 51.2 percent and 38.2 percent in 1977–78).[4] But as 1983–84 was an exceptionally good agricultural year, this decline is probably part of the same trendless fluctuation in the incidence of poverty depicted in Figure 1.

Though there has been an endless debate among Indian economists about whether growth can be expected to "trickle down" to the poor, clearly, with little growth to trickle down, India's post

Table 2 (A)
Trends in Per Capita Income in India
(1946–47 Prices)

Year	Sivasubramonian	Heston
(1)	(2)	(3)
1868–69	—	120 (73)
1870	—	—
1872–73	—	125 (76)
1890	—	134 (82)
1900	—	145 (88)
1902	147 (90)	147 (90)
1910	157 (96)	154 (90)
1920	164 (100)	164 (100)
1930	171 (104)	171 (104)
1935	166 (101)	166 (101)
1940	169 (100)	169 (100)
1945	163 (99)	166 (101)
1950	—	—

Notes: 1. The figures in brackets in columns 2 and 3 are index numbers of per capita real income (1920 = 100).

2. In columns 2 and 3, the 1902 estimates are three-year averages; for all other years after 1900 they are 9 year averages.

Source: Kumar and Krishnamurthy (1981), derived from Heston (1983).

independence economic record cannot tell us whether or not faster growth would have alleviated poverty. However, if we compare India's growth and poverty alleviation experience with that of other countries (for instance the so-called Gang of Four East Asian countries), it is apparent that India's poor growth performance must be held responsible for its failure to make any marked dent on poverty.[5]

To determine the causes of India's relatively poor growth performance, we need to examine its agricultural and industrial growth since Independence in relationship to its performance during the previous near century of British rule.

Table 2 summarizes the best available estimates of the growth rates of net domestic product and of its component sectors, as well as of per capita income between 1868 and 1945. These show that per capita income increased steadily from 1868 to 1930 at an annual compound rate of growth of 0.6 percent per annum and then declined during the inter-war period. The decline in per

Table 2 (B)
Growth of NDP at 1946–47 Prices for Selected Sectors
(Rs. Millions)

Sector	Average 1868–69	Average 1899–1900	Increases Over the Period
(1)	(2)	(3)	(4)
1868–1900			
Agriculture	15486	20952[1]	35.3%
Manufacturing	41	870	2022.0%
Small Scale Manufacturing and Services	8162	9604	17.67%
Government	1708	1997	16.92%
N.D.P.	30293	38576	27.34%

Sector	Average 1900–04/5	Average 1940–46	Increases Over the Period
(1)	(2)	(3)	(4)
1900–1946			
Agriculture	19737	25966	31.0%
Manufacturing	1009	5524	447.5%
Small Scale Industry	4200	4783	13.9%
Government	2139	5375	151.3%
N.D.P.	42244	66422	57.2%

[1]Average of 1897–1900.

Source: Derived from Heston (1983), Table 4.34.

capita income after 1920 was due to the growth of population (which began in the early part of the 20th century), for net domestic product continued growing at 2.6 percent per annum between 1920 and 1930. Nevertheless, the growth in per capita income during the British Raj was extremely modest and much lower than what has been achieved since Independence. It was also modest compared with the growth of per capita income of various other tropical Asian economies like Burma, Thailand, Ceylon, and Malaya during the second half of the 19th and early part of the 20th centuries (see Lewis, 1970, 1978).[6]

As Table 2 indicates, manufacturing industry grew quite rapidly during the pre-Independence period—although from a very low base. But toward the end of the period its rate of growth was declining. By contrast, agriculture grew relatively slowly throughout the period, at the rates of 0.94 percent between 1868 and 1900 and 0.62 percent between 1900 and 1946. The relative historical performance of Indian agriculture and Indian industry since 1868 can be seen by comparing Tables 1 and 2. Agriculture's trend growth rate has accelerated in the post-Independence period, whereas that of industry has remained unchanged at best. It is, therefore, the increase in the agricultural growth rate (and the dubious rise in those for the parasitical public administration and defense sectors) that is responsible for the modest acceleration in the growth rate of India's per capita income after Independence.

What accounts for this rise in the agricultural growth rate, and why has the industrial growth rate not accelerated?

Agricultural Growth. There are two aspects of India's agriculture that need to be emphasized.

First, until fairly recently Indian agriculture has been faced with a shortage of labor.[7] Thus for instance even in 1965–70, total agricultural area per inhabitant in India was 0.33 hectares compared with 0.06 for Japan (Boserup, 1981, p. 171).

Until fairly recently the mild expansion of population that occurred (until about 1921) was accommodated by extending the land frontier, with relatively unchanged technology and cropping patterns. With the more rapid expansion of population after 1920, more intensive methods of cultivation were called for. Ester Boserup has argued that increasing population pressure on land both induces and facilitates the adoption of more intensive forms of agriculture (with a more intensive use of both labor and capital). She maintains that per capita food output is likely to remain constant in subsistence agriculture. Table 3 reveals some interesting stylized facts about the Indian agricultural economy in the periods 1901 to 1940–41 and 1950–51 to 1970–71.

In both periods, there was a rise in the output-to-labor ratio, which accelerated in the second (post-Independence) period. This was due to a more rapid extension of both the net sown area and the double-cropped area, so that the total cropped area increased between 1950 and 1971 in rough proportion to the rural work force. More dramatic, however, was the change in the rate of capital formation in agriculture between the two periods, such that the capital/labor ratio, after being stagnant between 1900 and 1941, rose by about 80 percent between 1950 and 1970. Part of this increased capital formation was of the land-saving variety (mainly in the form of irrigation, which makes multiple cropping possible).[8] But, diminishing returns had already set in with the output/capital ratio declining markedly as more capital was applied to a given land area. Clearly, in this second period, as compared with the first, capital was being used to substitute for land, which was becoming scarce, as is evident from the steady decline in the land/labor ratio over the 70-year period.[9]

That the population growth caused by the exogenous decline in mortality after 1921 was driving these changes is supported by the various crude elasticity estimates we can derive for our aggregates, as is done in panel (C) of Table 3. The elasticity of output with respect to labor supply remained relatively constant over the two periods—a cornerstone of Boserup's hypothesis. But the responses to the differing growth rates of labor supply differed markedly in the two periods. Note that, even though the population explosion started in the 1920s, the population bulge did not reach the rural labor supply until the 1950s. Thus, whereas the rural work force increased by 12.6 percent between 1900 and 1940, it rose by twice that much in the twenty years between 1950 and 1971. Based on Boserup's hypothesis, we would expect that rising population pressures would be most potent in inducing a switch to more intensive methods of agricultural production in the post-Independence period (1950 onward).

This is borne out by the elasticity estimates of panel (C) in Table 3. Thus, as noted above, while the elasticity of output with respect to labor supply remained unaltered, that of land and capital with respect to labor supply increased markedly from the pre-Independence period when labor supply growth was slow to the post-Independence period when it was more rapid. The elasticity of double-cropped land with respect to labor supply rose to unity, both through the increase in new land and in multiple cropping (which, of course, is indirectly the result of the increased capital

Table 3
Some Macro-Aggregates for Indian Agriculture
(1901–1971)

	1901	1940/41	1950/51	1960/61	1970/71	% Change 1901–1940/41	% Change 1950/51 1970/71
A. Aggregates							
1. NDP in Agriculture at Constant 1970/71 prices (Rs 10mil)[a]	5291	6961	10168	13575	16989	31.6	67.1
2. Labor Force in Agriculture (mil)[b]	79.3	89.3	103.6	119.1	129.9	12.6	25.4
3. Capital Stock (Rs 10mil Constant 1970/71 Prices)	na	na	5848	9729	13204	na	125.8
4. Net Sown Area (mil Has)[c]	81.42	83.69	118.75	133.20	140.80	2.8	18.6
5. Total Area Sown (mil Has)[c]	93.56	97.85	131.89	152.77	165.79	4.5	25.7
6. % of Net Sown Area Irrigated[d]	16.9	17.6	17.6	18.5	22.1	4.1	25.6
B. Ratios							
1. Output/Labor (Rs/man)	667.2	779.5	981.5	1139.8	1206.6	16.8	22.9
2. Land/Labor (has/man) (i)	1.03	0.94	1.15	1.12	1.08	–8.7	–6.1
(ii)	1.18	1.10	1.27	1.28	1.28	–6.7	0.8
3. Capital/Labor (Rs/man/Index nos.)	(110)	(110)	564.5 (100)	816.9	1016.5	0.0	80.0
4. Output/Land (Rs/Has) (i)	649.8	831.8	865.25	1019.14	1206.61	28.0	40.9
(ii)	565.5	711.4	770.95	888.59	1024.73	25.8	32.9
5. Output/Capital	na	na	1.74	1.40	1.29	na	–25.0
6. Capital/Land (Rs/Has) (i)	na	na	492.46 443.40	730.40 636.	937.78	na	90.4

Table 3
(Continued)

C. Elasticities	1900–40	1950–70
1. % change in output / % change in labor	2.5	2.6
2. % change in land / % change in labor	(i) 0.22 (ii) 0.36	0.73 1.00
3. % change in capital / % change in labor	(1.00)	4.95
4. % change in output / % change in land	(i) 11.29 (ii) 7.02	3.61 2.61
5. % change in output / % change in capital	(2.5)	0.53
6. % change in capital / % change in land	(i) na (ii) na	6.8 4.9

Notes: na = not available; ( ) approximation; (i) refers to the net sown area land; (ii) refers to total area sown

Source: Lal (1988), Vol. 1, Table 7.4.

formation in land-saving techniques such as irrigation). But the most important factor keeping the elasticity of output with respect to labor constant has been the marked rise in the capital-to-labor supply elasticity. As much of this capital formation is labor intensive, we can assume, following Boserup, that it is more likely that the increased labor supply has induced this increased capital formation rather than the other way around. This is contrary to much of the conventional wisdom, haunted as it is by the shade of Malthus.

The Boserup theory is also supported by two other pieces of evidence. Thus Dandekar (1988, p. 49) has estimated that,

> per capita NDP in agriculture has practically not increased at all in the past 34 years from 1950–51 to 1984–85. In fact, the log linear curve fitted to the entire annual series of per capita NDP in [the] agriculture sector gives the annual growth rate of 0.0074 per cent with R^2=0.0002, which means that, not only there is no growth but that there are only annual fluctuations.

Second, Boserup's explanation of recent aggregate agricultural performance is also supported by examining regional agricultural performance in terms of what I have elsewhere (Lal, 1988) called the Ishikawa Curve. This is a relationship between land productivity and per farm holding of cultivated land.

Ishikawa (1967) hypothesizes that in the traditional subsistence cultivation of rice, this curve is a rectangular hyperbola. So that, roughly speaking, increases in total output keep pace with rural labor supply (which is the force reducing farm size). In Table 4 we present data by state for 1970–71 on the output of foodgrains per hectare, as well as on the average size of *operational* holdings in columns (1) and (2), and for 1981–82 on the foodgrain yield per hectare in column (3), and for 1976–77 for the average size of holding in column (4). It is commonly recognized that the two Western states of Punjab and Haryana—the areas in which there *has* been a "wheat revolution"—have moved out of the traditional low-level subsistence agricultural process. Hence, in Lal (1988) we excluded these states in statistically estimating the Ishikawa curve for the two periods. We also ran a pooled regression for the two periods. Those results are reported in Table 5.

Table 4
Various Statistics of Indian Agriculture by States
(1970–80)

State	Food Grain Output/IIa. 1970–71 (kgs/ha)	Average Size of Operational Holdings (has)	1976–77 Average Size of Holdings (has)	Average Yield Foodgrains/ha (tonne/ha) 1981–82
1. Andhra Pradesh	781	2.51	2.34	1.24
2. Assam	973	1.47	1.37	0.97
3. Bihar	795	1.52	1.11	0.87
4. Gujarat	864	4.11	3.71	1.07
5. Haryana	1235	4.11	3.58	1.39
6. Himachal Pradesh	1156	1.53	1.63	1.24
7. Jammu and Kashmir	1220	0.94	1.07	1.53
8. Kerala	1426	0.70	2.98	0.98
9. Madhya Pradesh	648	4.00	0.49	1.54
10. Maharashtra	433	4.28	3.50	0.72
11. Mysore	830	3.20	3.66	0.74
12. Orissa	883	1.89	1.60	0.91
13. Punjab	1861	2.89	2.74	2.67
14. Rajasthan	686	5.46	4.65	0.55
15. Tamil Nadu	1342	1.45	1.25	1.52
16. Uttar Pradesh	998	1.16	1.05	1.19
17. West Bengal	1224	1.20	0.99	1.07

Source: Lal (1988), Vol. 1, Table 11.5.

Table 5

Statistical Estimates of the Ishikawa Curve

Y — foodgrain output tonnes/hectare
X — average size of operational land holdings (hectares) in each state

(1) 1970–71	Y=0.553 + .66 (1/x) (0.082) (0.119)	R^2 = 0.70 F = 30.33 n = 15
(2) 1981–82	Y=0.783 + .423 (1/x) (0.113) (0.137)	R^2 = 0.42 F = 9.52 n = 15
(3) Pooled	Y=0.676 + .521 (1/x) (0.071) (0.093)	R^2 = 0.53 F = 31.35 n = 30

Note: Figures in brackets are standard errors.

Source: Lal (1988), Vol. 1, Chp. 11.

The statistical fit of the Ishikawa curve is very good for the 1970–71 period, but less so for 1981–82. The latter is to be expected because the available data for the land variable for the 1981–82 regression is for an earlier year, and also is not for operational holdings. The scatter diagram for the pooled regression and the computed Ishikawa curve are shown in Figure 2. From this, it appears that apart from Punjab and Haryana, the other states are still in the Boserup phase, with most of them crawling up the Ishikawa curve as population expands.

Thus, apart from the few Green Revolution States, much of the agricultural growth in India has been induced by population growth.[10] Differences among regions in the performance of agriculture can be explained by ecological conditions, which have until now permitted only a few regions to benefit from the Green Revolution.

These ecological conditions underlie geographical differences in rainfall, the second important factor explaining the recent performance of Indian agriculture. Within the subcontinent, the amount of annual rainfall is extremely variable. Broadly speaking, rainfall increases markedly as one travels eastward (see Map 1). With increasing rainfall the climatic conditions become suitable

Figure 2
The Ishikawa Curve 1970 to 1981–82
(excluding Punjab and Haryana)

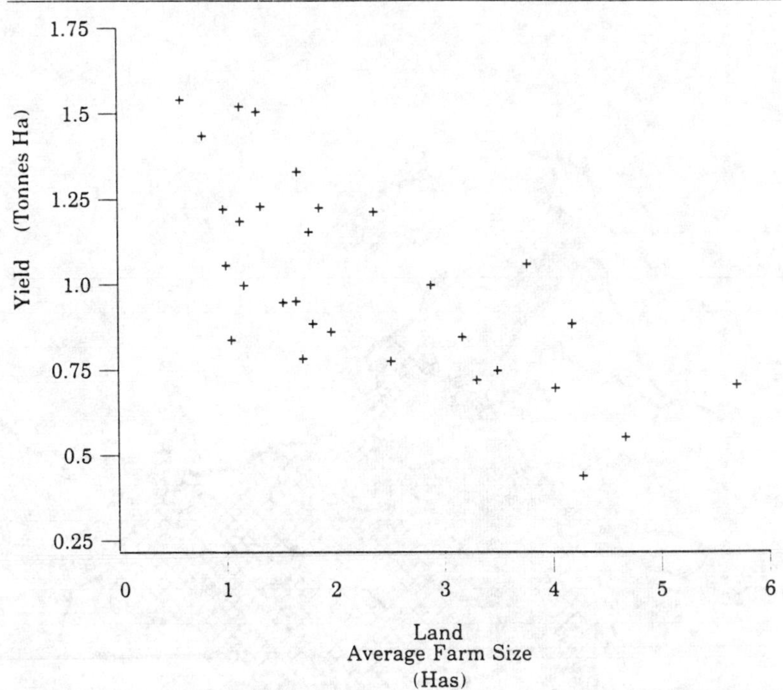

Source: Lal (1988), Vol. 1, Fig. 11.2 (b).

for growing rice, which as the higher-yield foodgrain is the favored crop (see Dharm Narain, 1965, chp. 7). Thus, in the well-watered middle and deltaic regions of the Gangetic plain, rice has been grown for millennia. Moreover, it has been grown under flood or silt-based systems of rice culture[11] yielding about 1.3 metric tons per hectare without much expenditure of capital or labor.

This subsistence rice economy was established in the central and eastern parts of the Gangetic plain in ancient times. It remained unchanged for millennia, and was highly productive by contemporary standards because it allowed a fairly large rural and urban population to be maintained by the agricultural economy.

To move to the next higher stage of rice cultivation in this region requires massive investments in irrigation, drainage, and flood

Map 1
Mean Annual Rainfall and Regions of British India

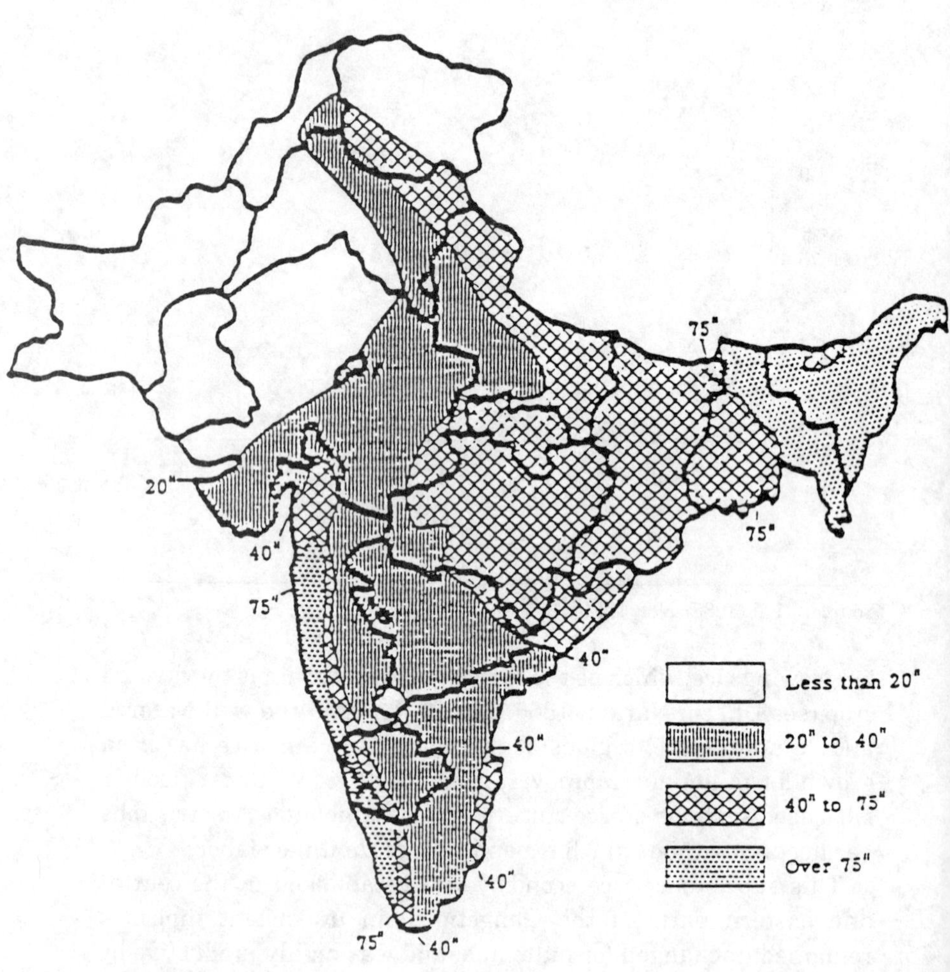

Source: Blyn (1966), Fig. 6.2.

control to achieve a controlled water supply throughout the life cycle of the rice crop. This would raise yields to 2.3 metric tonnes (in terms of paddy/hectare) (see Ishikawa, 1967, p.77).

By contrast, the areas with lower rainfall (mainly in the West and South) can move directly to the more productive forms of rice culture once irrigation from either ground or surface water sources is provided. Thus, the private and social returns to irrigating the low rainfall areas are higher than in the high rainfall Hindu heartland. This has meant that most of the expansion in irrigation and the introduction of new high-yielding varieties of seeds and fertilizers—on which most of the recent agricultural growth has been based—has taken place in the West, in Haryana and Punjab, and in the Southern states of Tamil Nadu and Andhra Pradesh. Paradoxically, the ecologically richest parts of the subcontinent, the central and eastern Gangetic plain and delta—the best watered from natural rainfall and the areas where fertility is periodically renewed by the silt deposited in the flood plain—are likely to be the most difficult to develop agriculturally. For these regions the advent of modern labor intensive industrialization provides an alternative means for raising the demand for labor and thus alleviating their ancient poverty.

Industrialization of India. For historical perspective, it is important to note that India was one of the pioneers of Third World industrialization, having begun the process in the 1860s at a time when laissez-faire and free trade were the cornerstones of economic policies for Britain and its colonies. The rate of growth of Indian industry (10.4 percent per annum) during the latter part of the 19th century (1868–1900) has not been bettered since. Yet the conventional view cites the historical experience of industrialization in India as an example of stunted development during the colonial laissez-faire period, in contrast with the post-Independence promotion of a large and diversified industrial base through a network of the most *dirigiste* industrial policies outside the Communist world. Balogh succinctly expressed this popular view of the effects of 19th century free trade and laissez-faire on the development of Indian industry:

> The destruction of the large and prosperous Indian cotton

> industry by Britain without any compensatory long-run advantage to India simply cannot be explained in these terms: it is altogether different from an event such as the end of the silk industry in Coventry. In the latter case there *was* compensatory expansion. In the former case there was not (p. 11).

Recent research has cast serious doubt on the empirical bases of these historical perceptions fed by influential Marxist and nationalist writings. We cannot go into detail here,[12] but the following points need to be noted. First, there is little doubt that the introduction of cheap Lancashire textiles (between 1812 and 1830) destroyed the Indian export trade in cotton textiles, which according to estimates by Maddison, had amounted to about 1.5 percent of national income in 17th century Moghul India.[13] The decline of India's trade in textiles was inevitable in the face of the technological revolution taking place at that time in the West. There was as a consequence some undoubted destruction of industry-specific factors of production in the traditional (handloom) textile industry. But in the 1850s, with the establishment of modern textile mills using Indian entrepreneurship and capital and imported machinery, manufactured cotton exports from India began to expand. Also, by the late 19th century employment in manufacturing industry (primarily in textiles) increased. With the development of a modern textile industry, Indian products gradually recaptured both the domestic and foreign markets they had lost in the mid-19th century to Lancashire.[14] Thus, there was at most a relative decline in the employment and output of the handicraft sector, as is borne out by the fact that handloom production remains a substantial industry in India. It would be incredible if the current size of the handloom industry (supposedly destroyed in the 1820s) were to be explained as the result of government promotion since Independence in 1947.

The growth of modern industry was not, moreover, confined to cotton textiles during the second half of the 19th century. The first jute mill was set up in 1852, only three years after the first cotton textile mill, and the first steel mill was established by the Tatas in 1911. Other industries, including paper and engineering goods, were also established during the free trade and laissez-faire period. The overall rate of industrial growth was higher in India (4–5 percent per year between 1880 and 1914) than in most other

Table 6

Some Summary Statistics for India

(A) Manufacturing Growth Rates — Value Added (constant prices)	1868 — 1981 percent per annum
1868–1900	10.36
1900–1913	6.00
1919–1939	4.80
1956–1965	6.90
1966–1979	5.50
(B) Rates of Growth of Employment in Manufacturing	percent per annum
1902–1913	4.43
1919–1939	2.29
1959–1965	3.60
1966–1979	3.50
(C) Rates of Growth of Capital Stock in Manufacturing	
1959–1965	13.60
1966–1979	6.80

Sources: (A) Derived from data in Heston (1983) and Sivasubramanian (1977) and post World War II rate of growth from the national accounts.

(B) Pre independence from Sivasubramanian (1977) Post independence from Ahluwalia (1985) Table A.5.2 & 3.

tropical countries, and also exceeded that of Germany (4 percent). As Lidman and Domerese have observed:

> An index of industrial production based on six large-scale manufacturing industries more than doubled from 1896 to 1914. By 1914 the Indian economy had developed the world's fourth largest cotton textile industry and the second largest jute manufacturing industry (p. 320–21).

Nor was India's performance in exporting manufactures to be sniffed at during this first phase of industrialization. By 1913 about 20 percent of Indian exports were of modern manufactured goods. Total exports amounted to 10.7 percent of national income—a share not reached either before or since this free trade

Table 7

Index of Manufacturing Production

(Base 1913 = 100)

Country	Year 1938	Country	Year 1938	Country	Year 1938
South Africa	1,067.1	India	239.7	Roumania	177.9
U.S.S.R.	857.3	Sweden	232.2	Norway	169.2
Japan	552.0	New Zealand	227.4	Canada	161.8
Greece	537.1	Chile	204.2	Latvia	158.0
Finland	300.1	Netherlands	204.1	Germany	149.3
		Denmark	202.1	Czechoslovakia	145.5
		Italy	195.2	Hungary	143.3
		Australia	192.3	U.S.A.	143.0
		World	182.7	Austria	127.0
				U.K.	117.6
				France	114.6
				Poland	105.2
				Belgium	102.1
				Switzerland	82.4
				Spain	58.0

Source: League of Nations, *Industrialization and Foreign Trade*, USA, 1945, Table III, derived in Ray (1979), Table 3, p. 16.

and laissez-faire period. It was India's agricultural export growth rate which was disappointing. While aggregate exports grew at 3 percent per annum between 1883 and 1913, the growth rate of agricultural exports was only 1.4 percent per year. In contrast, Japan's agricultural exports grew at an annual rate of over 4 percent during the same period.

As Table 6 shows, this initial burst of growth was not matched by Indian industry in the 20th century. But even in the 1913–38 period, Indian industrial growth was above the world average (see Table 7). However, unlike the pre-1913 period which was broadly one when free trade and hence "border prices" ruled, the period after the First World War saw the introduction, largely for reasons of fiscal expediency, of a system of discriminating protection. Whereas the market price based growth rates of industrial output (value added) in the free trade period were likely to have reflected genuine improvements in efficiency, much of the later growth was "artificial," at shadow prices, reflecting social costs which were substantially lower than market prices. This growth took place

Table 8
Parameters of Gompertz Curve Fitted to Trends in Various Industrial Sector Variables
($Y = k(a)^{bt}$)

	k	a	b
Industrial Production			
1882–1900	506.13	1.07	1.17
1900–1945	368.67	1.32	1.04
1953–1979	457.09	0.11	0.95
Industrial Employment			
1902–1946	11511.4	0.058	0.986
1953–1976	2200.1	0.001	0.995
Capital Stock in the Non-agricultural Sector			
1948–1967	185.13	25.15	1.02

Note: In interpreting these results,

(i) if $a < 1$ and $b < 1$, the Gompertz curve is increasing at a decreasing rate of growth, with an upper asymptote;

(ii) if $a > 1$ and $b > 1$, the curve is increasing at an increasing rate of growth, with a lower asymptote.

Source: Lal (1988), Vol. 1, Table 11.11.

behind barriers of protection, which gradually grew in scope and intensity after 1913.

Nevertheless, even if we judge performance by crude and inadequate criteria, such as the rate of growth of manufacturing output, employment, and investment, the performance during the pre-1913 free trade period was better than in the protectionist 1919–39 period. Of the industries that were growing in the protectionist period, a proper evaluation of the social return to investment is only available for sugar (see Lal, 1972). This shows that such investment was socially unprofitable.

Comparing the periods 1900–1913 and 1913–39, industrial employment grew twice as fast under free trade as during the protectionist period (see Table 6). Though the investment *rate* did not rise, the increase in the volume of investment, combined with a slower expansion of industrial employment, meant a rise in the capital intensity of industrial production. Moreover, if the whole period of protection (from 1913 until the late 1970s) is considered

Table 9
Total Factor Productivity Growth Estimates
(1959–60 to 1979–80)

	Percent per annum
India	–0.2 to –1.3
Korea	5.7
Turkey	2.0
Yugoslavia	0.8
Japan	3.1

Source: I. J. Ahluwalia (1985), pp. 132–35. The estimates other than India, are Ahluwalia's based on converting Nishimizu and Robinson's (1982) estimates derived from a gross production function to a value-added production function as for India.

then by fitting Gompertz curves to the relevant time series data,[15] it appears from Table 8 that there has been an accelerating trend in the capital employed in industry and a decelerating trend in the labor employed. Since Independence, a decelerating trend has also developed in industrial output. Thus, there has been a rising capital labor ratio (see Table 6) in this labor abundant economy!

Even more telling evidence on the growing relative inefficiency of Indian industry is provided by the estimates of total factor productivity growth (TFPG) in the 1960s and 1970s for India, Korea, Turkey, Yugoslavia, and Japan, summarized in Table 9. It also does not appear that there was any break in this rate of decline in TFPG in India in the mid-1960s, when the Indian industrial sector obviously began to stagnate in terms of output growth. We do not have capital stock data for the earlier periods to ascertain whether the negative rate of factor productivity growth in India is just a post-Independence phenomenon or whether it goes back to the start of the protectionist period in 1913. Our tentative hypothesis is that the latter is likely. Further support for the declining social profitability of industrial investment in India is provided by estimates of social rates of return on Little-Mirrlees lines that we have made elsewhere (Lal, 1980) and summarized in Table 10.

Table 10
Average Social Rates of Return in Indian Manufacturing
(ASI) (1958–68)

Year	SWR = W (%)	SWR = O (%)	SWR = 0.6 W (%)
1958	1.6	36.0	15.4
1960	1.6	39.0	16.6
1961	2.4	37.0	16.2
1962	0.9	29.0	12.1
1963	1.9	29.0	12.7
1964	1.4	26.0	11.2
1968	–6.1	22.6	5.4

Notes: SWR = Shadow Wage Rate; W = Market Wage

Source: Lal (1980), p. 44.

The Policy Framework

It is thus in its failure to industrialize efficiently—despite its head start—that the explanation for the relatively poor post-war performance of the Indian economy must be found. This failure can almost wholly be blamed on the policies pursued since Independence, which at least in two instances—the policy of protecting and maintaining distorted and highly restrictive industrial labor markets—pre-date Independence. They formed part of the general consensus that had emerged among politicians, intellectuals, and businessmen (and, it should be said, economists in the West) at the time of India's independence.

This view had misread the record of the Raj and blamed its twin policies of laissez-faire and free trade (at least during the 19th century) for much of India's continuing poverty. Moreover, in its twilight years, largely on grounds of expediency, the British Raj's commitment to laissez- faire and free trade had been considerably eroded. The Second World War years in particular saw a marked rise in *dirigisme* in the running of the Indian economy. The rationing, price controls, and various other aspects of a bureaucratic command economy, which might have been a necessary expedient during wartime, provided the bureaucracy (which had been partially Indianized) with fresh avenues to assert their power, as well as a faith in *dirigisme*, which was to outlast the circumstances in which it arose. Central planning was the new panacea.

We need not go into the details of the *dirigiste* system of controls that were set up to legislate planned targets (see Lal, 1980). The following points may, however, be noted.

First, based in part on the Stalinist model of development and an extremely pessimistic assumption about Indian export prospects, a heavy industry biased import substitution strategy of industrialization was the centerpiece of Indian planning. *Second*, as agriculture with its myriad producers and spatial dispersion was not easily amenable to the planners desires, it was industry that bore the brunt of the control system that was set up. *Third*, the instruments used to legislate the investment and output targets laid down in the plans (themselves of doubtful provenance) were a complex system of industrial licensing and foreign exchange, price and distributional controls. Independent India is thus best characterized as the Permit Raj. *Fourth*, an expansion of the public sector to man the 'commanding heights' of the economy in producing 'basic goods' and infrastructure became a cornerstone of public policy.

Even by its own terms of reference, Indian planning for the industrial sector has been a dismal failure. There have been large discrepancies between the actual and planned pattern of investments. While no optimality can be adduced to planned targets, it is noteworthy that, as economists would expect, the ultimate pattern of investment and output has been ultimately determined by the relative private profitabilities of different industries. These, in turn, have been affected primarily by the trade control system and the various 'ad hoc' and economically irrational price and distributional controls on a large number of commodities. The ensuing pattern of industrial investment has borne little relationship to that required either for promoting the planned pattern of investment or for equalizing the relative private with the relative social profitability (from a broad economic viewpoint) of industrial investments.

This is best seen in terms of the effects of the trade controls in the form of quantitative restrictions on imports that were instituted after the first serious foreign exchange crisis since its independence that India faced in 1956–58.

After the first serious foreign exchange crisis in 1956–57, a complex system of quota restrictions on imports was instituted. All requests to import were subjected to administrative scrutiny, and even the most petty imported items required a license. Moreover, import licenses were not available for goods that could be produced within India. This led to effective rates of protection that exceeded 200 percent on average, with a high variability of rates around the average. Imports of capital and intermediate goods were allowed while those of consumer goods were banned, with the consequence that, on balance, effective rates of protection of, and hence incentives to invest in, the indigenous consumer goods industries were higher—an outcome at odds with the stated policy of promoting heavy industry! And since the effective rates of exchange were much higher for importers than exporters, there was a strong bias against exports.

The practice of screening requests for imports according to the so-called indigenous availability criterion led to the complete insulation of domestic production from foreign competitive pressures. Coupled with an overall excess of demand in the economy, this meant that producers had little incentive to reduce costs. The rules of thumb used by administrators to allocate imports were based on the principle of fair and historic shares and the installed capacity of producers. The result was a freezing of the relative outputs and market shares of industries and firms. It also led to excess capacity as producers rushed to expand ahead of their requirements, knowing that their licensed capacity determined their import allocation and hence volume of production. Most heinous of all, because the structure of effective protection implied a relative cheapening of capital goods, producers had an incentive to choose relatively more capital-intensive methods of production at the expense of employing more labor. At the same time, the protection afforded to industry as a whole artificially raised the price of manufactured inputs into the agricultural sector relative to the price of its output. This had deleterious effects on agricultural growth.

At various stages during the 1960s and early 1970s these harmful effects of the existing trade control system—particularly on exports—had begun to be acknowledged, even in India. Export incentives, aimed at redressing the bias against exports, were introduced. Not surprisingly, the partial removal of this bias led to a spurt in exports, as economists who were not mesmerized by foreign exchange bottle-necks had always predicted.[17] In many instances, however, the *dirigiste* impulse was not stifled. India matched its highly complex and bureaucratic system of import allocation with an equally complex system of export incentives. The major instrument used was an import entitlement for exporters in the form of import licenses whose premium provided the exporter with a subsidy. The effect was to create a host of new distortions in the export sector.[18] A simple policy of export maximization was pursued; any producer wishing to export found a government willing to grant him an import entitlement whose premium was sufficient to equalize the relatively high domestic costs with the foreign prices of his product. Since the entitlements were usually tied to the import content of exports, these schemes subsidized import-intensive exports rather than those with a high domestic value added. The widespread practice of over-invoicing exports, coupled with different effective exchange rates for exports and imports, meant that a number of goods with a high import content were exported for a price in foreign currency that was below the foreign currency cost of the imports embodied in them! India thus ended up by pursuing import substitution and export promotion without reference to economic costs, guided only by the belief that "India should produce whatever it can and India should export whatever it produces."[19] The inefficiency, waste, and corruption that the Indian trade control system has engendered are incalculable.

These pervasive microeconomic distortions introduced by the Indian planning system were compounded by the inefficient operations of the chosen agent of industrialization in India—the public sector.

The public sector has burgeoned. By 1979, the gross fixed assets of the central public sector (which is defined to include only those enterprises wholly owned by the State, and also excludes the railways and power utilities) exceeded that of the private sector in industry by over 16 percent. In basic industries, the public sector has a near monopoly of domestic production, as it does in power generation, rail and air transport, life and general insurance, and banking. In the 1970s the promotional role of the public sector in developing new basic industries was extended through

Table 11
Relative Profitability of Public Sector
(1974–75)

Industry	Ratio of Value Added to GCE at Market Prices		Ratio of Value Added to GCE at Border Prices	
	Public	Private	Public	Private
Engineering	11.42	23.12	10.57[a]	18.95[a]
Chemicals	6.26	21.26	4.01[a]	10.07[a]

[a]No attempt has been made to calculate gross capital employed (GCE) at border prices. These figures are valid therefore only for intersectoral comparisons.

Source: Jha (1985), Table 2.

nationalization and bailouts for declining and/or sick industries (e.g., some 145 textile mills), many in the consumer goods sector, and in coal mining. Thus, increasingly not only is industrial entry prevented by industrial licensing and the attendant bureaucratic controls, but the exit of the inefficient is also being ruled out through the absorption of sick industries by the public sector.

Judged by conventional accounting criteria the performance of the public sector has been abysmal compared with the private sector. The latter's performance in itself is not particularly noteworthy if we judge it by its social profitability. However, for two industries in which there are both private and public enterprises, Table 11 provides some estimates of their relative private and social (at world prices) profitabilities. The relatively poor public sector performance is manifest.

Even more serious has been the failure of the public sector to provide an adequate flow of services in areas where there is a case for public investment. Despite massive investment in power, Indian industrial development continues to be bedeviled by power shortages, in large part because of a woeful underutilization of existing capacity (see Henderson).

This underutilization of capacity is in turn due to another set of distortions in the functioning of the industrial sector, which is from an economic viewpoint one of the worst legacies of the British Raj. This concerns the system of labor laws enshrining rights for industrial labor which have raised its cost well above its social opportunity cost to Indian industry. This artificial rise in the price of India's most abundant resource, together with the implicit cheapening of capital which has ensued from the foreign trade and other industrial and price controls, have meant that the extant incentives favor the use of capital rather than labor in Indian industry. This is a prime cause for the failure of Indian industry to generate adequate industrial employment growth and poverty alleviation on the scale that many Far Eastern countries have shown so successfully.

Part of the problem leading the Indian textile industry in the early part of the 20th century to seek protection, arose from the 1881 introduction (soon after similar rights had been granted to workers in Britain) of legislation to protect industrial labor from perceived abuses. The first of these factory acts was aptly described as "the result of agitation (in the UK) by ignorant English philanthropists and grasping English manufacturers" (Bhattacharya, p. 171). As usual in such alliances, the selfish English protectionist interest was better served by the legislation than the altruism of the philanthropists. By effectively raising the cost of labor they provided an incentive to producers—an incentive to choose relatively capital intensive techniques in industrial production. As these laws only applied to the large-scale sector, they presented an entry barrier to small-scale producers seeking to expand. They thus began that fragmentation of the industrial sector in India into the industrial caste system that now exists—with special size categories of industries, each with its own specially legislated conditions of employment and controls on output and investment, leading to variously and differentially protected segments of the labor force, as well as of the population of industrial firms.

The rights granted to Indian labor in 1881 hobbled the Indian textile industry in competing for exports, and later the domestic market, with the industry of Japan. Lower Indian wages reflected lower efficiency. Whereas the Japanese textile industry as well as those in most of the Gang of Four were built on using female labor working two shifts a day, "the use of female labor on such a scale was inconceivable in Bombay, nor did the labor laws permit such long working hours" (Ray, p. 67). Indian textile producers demanded protection and got it. The large home market, increasingly protected from imports, provided an easy life and gave little incentive to increase efficiency.

By 1950, in marked contrast to Taiwan, Hong Kong, Singapore, and Korea—the Gang of Four—India

> had built up one of the most comprehensive labor codes to be found in any country at her level of economic development. The standards laid down by the ILO had been accepted and measures were being worked out to attain these standards" (Bhattacharya, p. 186).

No quantification of the adverse effects on the relative industrial performance of India with that of the Gang of Four—with their relatively free industrial labor markets—is possible. But

Table 12
Industrial Disputes in India
(1921–1980)

Year	No. of Stoppages	No. of Workers Involved	Workdays Lost
1921	396	600,351	6,984,426
1925	134	270,423	12,578,129
1930	148	196,301	2,261,731
1935	145	114,217	973,457
1940	322	452,539	7,577,281
1945	820	747,530	4,054,499
1950	814	719,883	12,806,704
1955	1,166	527,767	5,697,848
1960	1,583	986,268	6,536,517
1965	1,835	991,000	6,470,000
1971	2,752	1,615,000	16,546,000
1972	3,243	1,737,000	20,544,000
1973	3,370	2,546,000	20,626,000
1974	2,938	2,855,000	40,262,000
1975	1,943	1,143,000	21,901,000
1976	1,459	737,000	12,746,000
1977	3,117	2,193,000	25,320,000
1978	3,187	1,916,000	28,340,000
1979	3,048	2,874,000	43,854,000
1980	2,856	1,900,000	21,925,000

Source: Karnik (1978), Appendix II, pp.409–410 until 1969, thereafter *Statistical Abstract of India and Basic Statistics Relating to the India Economy.*

Table 13
Characteristics of Sample Firms

Firm Product	Firm Size	Technology	Training by the General	Provided Firm Specific	Pinching of Labor By and From Other Firms	Casual Labor Type Screening of Labor	Use of Existing Workers to Hire Labor	Promotional Ladders	Labor Legislation and Trade Union Pressure Cited as Determinants of Wage Structure	New Neo-classical Type Cost-Minimizing Reasons Given for the wage Structure	Would They Themselves Organize a Trade Union to Ease Supervisory Problems?
1. Shoes	Large	Medium	Yes	Yes	Others pinched	No	No	No	Yes	No	No
2. Oil Mills	Large	High	Yes	Yes	Others pinched	Yes	No	Yes	Yes	Yes	Yes
3. Soap	Small	Low	Yes	No	Others pinched	No	Yes		Yes	No	No
4. Petrochemicals	Large	High	Yes	Yes	Pinched others	No	No	Yes	Yes	Yes	Yes
5. Conglomerate	Large	Medium to High	Yes	Yes	Others pinched	Yes	No	Yes	Yes	Yes	No
6. Printing	Medium	Medium	No	Yes	Pinched others	Yes	Yes	No	Yes	No	No
7. Printing	Small		No	Yes	Others pinched	Yes	Yes	No	Yes	No	No
8. Rubber Plant and Plantation	Large	Medium to Low			Pinched others	Yes	Yes	No	Yes	No	No

Source: Lal (1988), Vol. 2, Table 9.2.

itant steps at liberalizing the system of trade, industrial and price controls have been made.

Recent Attempts at Liberalization. When Rajiv Gandhi succeeded his mother as Prime Minister of India in November 1984, it appeared from his public pronouncements and from some of the actions of his government that he was aware of the need to liberalize the Indian economy if India was to realize its potential. The need was for rapid labor-intensive industrialization— the only means of redressing the ancient poverty of its masses. In 1985 and 1986 the government seemed to have grasped the nettle of liberalization. It eased industrial licensing, allowing industries to choose their product mix and to expand capacity as they saw fit. The aim was to provide internal competition (while still maintaining fairly tight import controls). As the government's *Economic Survey 1985–86* puts it:

> It has become increasingly apparent over the last few years that industrial growth is hampered by unnecessary procedural delays . . . and controls . . . Moreover, uneconomic scales of production coupled with an excessively sheltered industrial environment have fostered monopolistic profits, high costs and products of low quality (p.3).

While removing some of the barriers to entry created by the industrial control system, the government (alarmed by its growing role in saving 'sick' industries) also sought to: "ease exit of unviable units" (*Economic Survey*, ibid, p.34). But here, as the government acknowledged, it was hamstrung by the labor "rights" that had been granted by the Raj and perpetuated by post-Independence governments.

Equally, the intention announced in 1986 to move away from trade controls in the form of quantitative restrictions to tariffs was welcome, as was the intention "to reduce the enormous multiplicity of nominal and effective rates of protection conferred by the customs tariff structure" (ibid, p.63). But the translation of these good intentions into action was at best hesitant and at worst largely window dressing. Thus, while some industries could now import capital goods without having to fulfill the indigenous availability criterion, at the same time there was a shuffling of various items from various lists whose net effective protection effect is at best uncertain.

It was in the area of fiscal policy that the most important measures of liberalization were undertaken by the Rajiv Gandhi government, under its able Finance Minister, V. P. Singh. Direct taxes on both persons and corporations were reduced. Despite the Jeremiahs, direct tax revenue collections *rose* by 24 percent (ibid., p.4). The government has committed itself to pre-announcing its fiscal intentions in a Long Term Fiscal Policy Statement. This envisaged the introduction of a modified value-added (MODVAT) system of indirect taxation, the modification being the multiplicity of VAT rates that is envisaged! Nevertheless, these fiscal measures together with enhanced tax enforcement were aimed at reducing the black economy. At first, the signs were propitious, until the Finance Minister's zeal in tracking down "tax evaders" and "corruption" led him into ordering politically sensitive investigations that cost him his job in early 1987.

By then the Gandhi government was embroiled both in corruption scandals and escalating regional "rebellions." At the same time the embattled Prime Minister was forced to retreat into the wheeling-dealing mode of his mother's regime in order to maintain his hold on power. The result has been that the economic liberalization program is now on hold, and its future appears bleak. This is in no small part due to the regrouping of the ideological and vested interests that have stood to lose from liberalization, and to those who have used the Prime Minister's recent political troubles to launch a movement against his new economic policies. It is these ideas and interests we need to discuss—as we do in the next section—if we are to understand why India adopted policies so inimical for its development, and why it finds changing course so difficult even when many policy makers themselves know and want the changes that are required.

Ideas, Interests, and Dirigisme

To understand the stranglehold of the Permit Raj on the Indian economy, particularly its industrial sector, one must be aware of the ancient, even atavistic attitudes to merchants and commerce which provide the continuing ideological ballast for its continuation. These attitudes, moreover, were given a convenient modern garb by Fabian socialism.

At least since the 6th century B.C., (as we have argued elsewhere, Lal 1988) India has had a substantial and prosperous mercantile class. Yet since its ideological vehicle, the republican anti-casteist sects of Buddhism and Jainism lost out to Brahminical caste polities in the early Christian era, the ideals and values of merchants have never had much appeal to India's rulers. The contempt in which merchants and markets have traditionally been held in Hindu society was given a new garb by the Fabian socialism which so appealed to the newly westernized but traditional literary castes of India.

Not all politicians who were the inheritors of the Raj showed this "aristocratic" contempt of business and commerce. Gandhi, a Vaishya (bania-merchant caste) by birth, certainly did not, but after designating Nehru as his successor he withdrew into the spiritual shadows and, within six months of having achieved Indian Independence, he was dead at the hands of an assassin.

Nehru was a towering personality and an intellectual, but also a Brahmin. He professed to being a socialist, and was much impressed by the *dirigiste* example of the Soviet Union in transforming a backward economy into a world power within the lifetime of a generation. He had imbibed the Fabian radicalism of the inter-war period, and, with so many British intellectuals, was an ardent advocate of planning—which was identified with some variant of the methods of government control instituted in the Soviet Union.

But his was not just a fantasy dreamt up in an intellectual's ivory tower. Many businessmen, who identified their relative success during the last half of the Raj with the gradual erosion of the policies of laissez-faire and free trade, ended up espousing planning as a panacea for India's economic ills. It was nationalist businessmen who produced the early precursors of post-Independence Indian plans, in their so-called Bombay Plan. While Nehru certainly, but the nationalist businessmen more doubtfully, admired the Soviet model, Nehru balked at the suppression of liberty that the Stalinist model of development entailed. He hoped, instead, as a good Fabian socialist, to combine the "order" and "rationality" of central planning with the preservation of individual and democratic rights in India. Moreover, he was, at least in his own mind, a socialist. But it is interesting to see what socialism meant for him. In his *Autobiography*, he writes:

> ... right through history the old Indian ideal did not glorify political and military triumph, and it looked down upon money and the professional money-making class. Honor and wealth did not go together, and honor was meant to go, at least in theory, to the men who served the community with little in the shape of financial reward. Today (the old culture) is fighting silently and desperately against a new and all-powerful opponent—the *bania* (Vaishya) civilization of the capitalist West. It will succumb to the newcomer....But the West also brings an antidote to the evils of this cut-throat civilization—the principles of socialism, of cooperation, and service to the community for the common good. This is not so unlike the old Brahmin ideal of service, but it means the brahmanization—not in the religious sense, of course—of all classes and groups and the abolition of class distinctions.[21]

A more succinct expression of the ancient Hindu caste prejudice against commerce and merchants would be difficult to find. The British, unfortunately, had in their later years and despite the commercial origins of their rule in India, taken over most of the Indian higher-caste attitudes to commerce. The brown sahibs, mostly upper caste Hindus like Nehru, found it congenial to adopt these traditional attitudes. What is more, socialism now provided them with a modern ideological garb in which to clothe these ancient prejudices. Commercial success, as in the past, was to be looked down upon and the ancient Hindu disjunction between commercial power (and, increasingly, political power) and social status, was to continue.

This identification of socialism with both a contempt for commerce and businessmen, and by association that prime symbol of the mercantile mentality—the market—was to color economic policy making in the new independent India. For socialism in India has merely provided the excuse for a vast extension of the essentially feudal and imperial revenue economy, whose foundations were laid in ancient India, and whose parameters successive

some judgments on the effects of the costs of this labor legislation and the attendant growth of trade unionism in India can be formed through Tables 12 and 13. The former shows the number of industrial disputes and mandays lost since the rise of trade unions in 1921 in India. As early as 1928, nearly 32 million mandays were lost through stoppages, a figure nearly as high as that of about 44 million mandays in 1974 and 1979.

Table 13 is based on the results of a series of in-depth interviews I conducted in India in 1980 of about 20 firms covering both large and small-scale industries, and covering the technological spectrum from sophistication (petrochemicals) to simplicity (soap making). Lal (1988) provides details of the interviews, while Table 13 summarizes the responses on some questions concerning the factors that influenced the producers' choices regarding the recruitment and training of labor, as well as the effects of existing labor legislation and trade unionism on their operations. The dominant impression from the interviews was that firms were behaving as cost minimizers, where the major component of labor costs were perceived to be those attached to "troublemakers" and the resulting impediments to the maintenance of labor discipline resulting from the complex iabor legislation granting various legal rights to industrial labor and trade unions. The neoclassical hierarchical labor market reasons (see Lal, 1979 for a review) for promotional ladders and the usefulness of trade unions as a tool for managing labor did, however, seem to be important for the larger and technologically more sophisticated firms. Despite this, it would be fair to say that most industrial producers look upon existing labor laws and legal rights granted to trade unions as major (though unquantifiable) costs in their employment decisions.

These two elements of the economic environment—the current highly complex and differentiated effective protection rates facing Indian industry and the equally complex labor laws it confronts in hiring and firing labor—seem to me to be crucially different in India and the Gang of Four. Taken together with the system of industrial licensing and all the special reservations for industries of different sizes and types, and for different groups of workers, a vast politically determined set of entitlements has been created in Independent India, which defies any economic rationale.

Table 14
Rate of Savings & Capital Formation

	Gross Domestic Savings as % of GDP	Net Domestic Savings	Net Inflow of Foreign Capital as % of NDP	Net Domestic Capital Formation as % of NDP
1961–62	13.1	8.4	2.3	10.7
1970–72	16.8	12.0	1.0	13.0
1978–79	24.7	20.0	0.1	20.1
1980–81	22.6	17.6	1.7	19.3
1985–86	22.8	16.7	1.9	18.6

Source: National Income Statistics.

Savings, Capital Output Ratios, and Macroeconomic Balance

The costs of these politically determined entitlements have until recently been largely manifest in the form of what John Lewis many years ago called a quiet crisis in India. The microeconomic distortions created have led to lower realized returns on the investments made than would have been possible in their absence. Table 14 indicates that there has been an impressive rise in savings (from 13.1 to 22.8 percent for gross and from 8.4 to 16.7 percent for net savings from 1961–1985) and in capital formation (which has been largely financed through domestic sources). The rate of net capital formation has risen from 5.5 percent in 1950–51 to 18.6 percent of domestic product in 1985. In 1950 foreign capital inflow was nil and in 1985 it was about 2 percent of domestic product. In this period the economy's capital-output ratio has risen from about 2.6 in the 1950s to 6.25 in the 1980s (see Dandekar, 1988). It is this declining productivity of investment, due both to an inefficient pattern of investment and serious underutilization of the output capacity that has been created (particularly for major non-traded intermediate inputs produced by the public sector) that largely explains India's lackluster growth performance.

But until recently this productivity crisis due to the policy induced distortions in the working of the price mechanism had not been compounded by loose macroeconomic policies. However, as we have argued elsewhere (Lal, 1987a), one of the surprising dynamic effects of excessive *dirigisme* is a sort of Laffer curve of government interventions, so that after a certain stage, increased government intervention instead of increasing the area of government control diminishes it. The gradual expansion of politically determined entitlements creates specific 'property rights' to current and future income streams for various favored groups in the economy. As these entitlements are implicit or explicit subsidies to these groups, they have to be paid for by implicit or explicit taxation of other groups. This increasing tax burden leads at some stage to generalized tax resistance, avoidance and evasion and the gradual but inevitable growth of the parallel or underground economy. The government's fiscal position worsens, and faced with inelastic or declining revenues but burgeoning expenditure commitments, incipient or actual fiscal deficits become chronic.

India with its tradition of Gladstonian public finance has avoided these chronic macroeconomic imbalances until recently. But the creation of a "rent-seeking" society through the microeconomic distortions introduced by public policy in the last three decades is gradually leading to the fiscal crisis of the State so common in many other developing countries (and some developed ones!). This can be seen first in the marked expansion in the underground or

Table 15

Indian Public Finances

(as percent of GDP Market Prices)

Year	Revenue	Expenditures				PSBR
		Developmental	Non-Developmental	Capital	Total	
1960–61	11.39	5.37	5.51	8.54	19.42	8.42
1970–71	14.43	5.79	8.29	7.90	21.97	7.54
1980–81	20.08	10.89	8.63	11.20	30.73	10.65
1981–82	20.61	11.04	8.83	10.25	30.12	9.51
1982–83	21.04	11.76	9.51	10.26	31.52	10.48
1983–84	20.05	11.73	9.54	9.64	30.91	10.76
1984–85	21.13	12.86	10.33	10.23	33.42	12.30
1985–86	21.19	12.67	11.61	10.01	34.30	12.30

Note: PSBR – Public Sector Borrowing Requirement, has been obtained by adding Dandekar's figures for 'Capital receipts' and 'Deficit Financing' in his Table 10.

Source: Derived from Dandekar (1988), Tables 7, 8, 10.

black economy in India. Notoriously difficult to measure statistically, all observers agree on its growth since the 1950s, and on its current, cancerous hold on all aspects of Indian life. Statistical estimates of its size vary from about 40–45 percent of GDP (see Mohammed and Whalley, 1984) to 18–21 percent of GDP (see Report of the National Institute of Public Finance & Policy, March 1985).

Second, as Table 15 shows vividly, the tax receipts of the government, which nearly doubled between 1960–61 to 1985–86 (when they were about 22 percent of GDP), have been stagnating in the past few years. At the same time the aggregate expenditure of the government has risen from about 19 percent in 1960–61 to over 34 percent of GDP in 1985–86. This rise has been largely due to a rise in non-developmental expenditure, (as the capital expenditure on development has stagnated at about 10 percent of GDP). The imbalance between government expenditure and revenues represents the public sector borrowing requirement (PSBR) of the Indian government.[20]

This PSBR has been growing alarmingly and is estimated to be over 12 percent of GDP in 1985–86, so that the public debt as a percentage of GDP has risen from about 27 percent in 1950–51 to 63 percent in 1985–86. The rising interest burden now accounts for about 15 percent of the revenues of the central and state government. Compared with many other developing countries, however, India's *external* debt to GDP ratio is fairly modest. Thus in 1984–85 external liabilities were only 13 percent of the total net liabilities of the central and state governments, yielding external debt as 7.8 percent of GDP. So there is a lot of ruin of the Latin American type left in the Indian economy!

Thus, summarizing this section, though there are some worrying signs of an incipient fiscal crisis in India, to date the mistakes of Indian policy mainly have been microeconomic. It is in the interlocking effects of a vast network of bureaucratic controls (industrial licensing, foreign trade, and price controls, together with an inefficient public sector) that the causes of the poor industrial performance of India must be sought. Since the mid-1970s the inefficiencies generated by these policy induced distortions have been recognized by many observers and government officials. Hes-

controls.

Moreover, India, unlike most of the Gang of Four, has established import substitution industries in intermediate and capital goods industries. This has made it difficult for India to switch to the type of export promotion policies that Korea adopted when it switched development strategies in the 1960s. Korea successfully offset the biases of the continuing import control system by permitting exporters to work under an essentially free trade regime—allowing them to obtain intermediate inputs at "world prices."

India cannot easily emulate Korea in this, in part because past import substitution policies have created significant industries producing intermediate and capital goods at home, albeit at immense social cost. Thus, when attempts are made to offset the bias against exports, they run afoul of the "indigenous availability" criterion, which protects domestic *producers* of intermediates. These producers have successfully prevented a Korean style export policy from emerging. Their power to block liberalization is strengthened by the fact that (in pursuance of the desire of the Indian planners to put the "commanding heights of the economy" in the public sector) most of these intermediate and capital goods are produced by government enterprises.

Moreover, these public enterprises have provided employment sinecures for those well-connected to the politicians in power. So, apart from the natural resistance that can be expected from the current public sector employees, the politicians are unlikely to give up a source of patronage by liquidating loss-making public enterprises.

In addition, the power to generate rents has allowed incumbent politicians to generate campaign funds for their political party. It has been alleged that the modest liberalization undertaken in the early years of the Rajiv Gandhi regime was possible because an alternative source of campaign funds had been discovered in the form of kickbacks from foreign defense suppliers. The ongoing scandal concerning the Swedish Bofors company has still not resolved this issue, but the link between the creation of politically generated rents and campaign funds is well known.

Apart from those intellectuals who continue to identify socialism with controls, there is an unholy alliance of politicians, businessmen, bureaucrats, and, not least, industrial labor (protected by the barriers to exit of inefficient firms instituted as part of Indian "socialism"). Such an alliance makes it extremely unlikely that a marked movement toward economic liberalization which will hurt their interests is likely in the near future. Equally, without the dismantling of the Permit Raj it is difficult to see how India can raise its industrial growth rate without which any marked alleviation of Indian poverty will be nearly impossible.

NOTES

1. See Dandekar (1988) who fitted a log linear trend to the whole series of NDP estimates from 1950–51 to 1984–85 and estimated the annual growth rate as 3.57 with an R^2=0.993.
2. In the Draft for the Five Year Plan (Vol. 1, p. 6), this is given as RS.40.6 per capita per month at 1972–73 prices for all India.
3. Based on the NSS Consumer Expenditure 38th Round for 1983.
4. See *Seventh Five Year Plan* 1985–90, Vol. 2, p. 4.
5. Thus Korea and Taiwan's per capita GDP grew at the rate of 6.5 percent per annum between 1963–85. The incidence of poverty in Korea in 1977 was 18 percent of the urban and 11 percent of the rural population. The comparable figures for India in 1979 were 40.3 percent urban and 507 percent rural. See World Bank: *Social Indicators of Development 1986*.
6. Thus Lewis estimates that per capita income in these countries was growing at about 1–1.5 percent p.a. between 1880–1913, which was as fast or faster than in Western Europe at the time.
7. In Lal (1988) I argue that the caste system in India evolved in the 5–6th century B.C. as a second best method of tying scarce labor to the land, to allow the relatively labor intensive methods of cultivation (primarily rice) developed in the Indo-Gangetic plain to be utilized.
8. This can be seen by comparing the growth of total crop area (row 5, Table 3A) and the growth of the percentage of the net sown area irrigated (row 6, Table 3A). These are equal in each of the two periods suggesting that multiple cropping (which accounts for the difference between net and total crop area) grew *pari passu* with irrigation.

9. But note that the land/labor ratios in the two periods are not strictly comparable because in the earlier period the acreage figures are for British India, and in the latter for the Indian Union. British India includes areas of post-Independence Pakistan and excludes various native Indian States, whereas the figures for the Indian Union exclude the former but include the latter.
10. There is also little empirical support for the Malthusian fears embodied in Arthur Lewis's notion of surplus labor for Indian agriculture. There is a large and controversial literature on the subject, surveyed in Lal (1988), Vol. 2. The upshot of the rigorous estimates of the supply and demand elasticities for agricultural labor in India by Bardhan (1979, 1984), Rosenzweig (1978, 1984), and by Evenson and Binswanger (1984) is that both the demand and supply of labor in Indian agriculture are fairly inelastic—contrary to the Lewis hypothesis which requires a nearly perfectly elastic supply of labor at some traditional wage. Within Boserup's framework, without some fundamental shift in agricultural technology, we would expect that, as population expanded and the rural economy moved up the Ishikawa curve, these elasticities would remain unchanged. Rightward shifts in the supply curve of labor would be accompanied by rightward shifts in the labor demand curve to maintain a relatively constant rural real wage and hence per capita rural product. Around this long-term trend, however, there would be large short-term shifts (in both directions) in the labor demand curve due to climatic variability, which, given the low wage elasticities of both labor demand and supply, would lead to large short-term movements in real agricultural wages around a nearly constant long-term trend. This in fact seems to have been the pattern of India's historical rural wage trends pieced together in Lal (1987).
11. Ishikawa (ibid., p. 71–73) classifies the rice culture in Asia into four patterns. The *first* is based on the pattern of floods in some of the principal riverine alluvial plains and deltas in Asia. This is the pattern in the Ganges delta. The paddy is sown with the first monsoon rains, it ripens when the floods that follow are at their heights, and is mown after the water has receded. In the

conquerors of India have failed to alter (See Lal, 1988).

Thus, Nehru identified socialism with bureaucratic modes of allocation,[22] with all that it implies in terms of the power and patronage afforded to the ancient Hindu literary classes which formed much of the bureaucracy. But, in this, Nehru was merely echoing the views of his Fabian mentors.

Thus, in *The Discovery of India*, he quotes with approbation a statement of R.H. Tawney's that, "the choice is not between competition and monopoly, but between monopoly which is irresponsible and private and a monopoly which is responsible and public." He then expresses the belief that public monopolies will eventually replace monopolies under his preferred economic system, which he labels "democratically planned collectivism." Under such a system, he notes:

> An equalization of income will not result from all this, but there will be far more equitable sharing and a progressive tendency towards equalization. In any event, the vast differences that exist today will disappear completely, and class distinctions, which are essentially based on differences in income, will begin to fade away (Nehru, 1965, p.555).

That he envisaged this socialist Utopia to be established by the supplanting of the price mechanism, whose essential lubricant is private profit and utility maximization, is evident from the following continuation of the above passage:

> Such a change would mean an upsetting of the present-day acquisitive society based primarily on the profit motive. The profit motive may still continue to some extent but it will not be the dominant urge, nor will it have the same scope as it has today.

We need not go into the details of the *dirigiste* system of controls and planning that was progressively set up.[23] The major point that needs to be made is that the control system was based on the predilections of engineers and not economists. This has continued to plague discussions of economic policy in India, not least those concerning various aspects of labor-market performance, such as unemployment. An engineer is trained to think in terms of essentially a fixed-coefficients world. The problem of trade-offs, and the consequent notion of opportunity costs, which is central to an economist's thinking, is alien to the conventional engineer's thought processes.[24] If coefficients are really fixed, then, of course, prices do not matter and the system of planning without prices, based on quantitative targets to meet fixed "needs" becomes rational. Oddly enough, because this happens, for historical reasons, to be the implicit method underlying the material balance-type planning in the Soviet Union, many socialists, seeking to achieve their Valhalla by imitating the Soviet Union, have just assumed that the world has little substitutability in production and consumption, and hence, the Soviet-type planning methods are economically rational.

By contrast, the Gang of Four—and in particular, Korea—were luckier to have been colonized by the Japanese and to have set up Japan as a model for their development. The famed "rational picking of industrial winners" by the Koreans was little more than an imitation of the early stages of Japanese development. As this coincided with an efficient development path based on their comparative advantage, their *dirigisme* has not (except in the mid-'70s) proved to be dysfunctional. Moreover, the Japanese model with its close alliance between commerce and government, does not lead to that contempt of business so characteristic of India's elite.

These attitudes are not just confined to self-serving politicians who have found in the Indian brand of socialism enormous opportunities for increasing their power and patronage. They carry over to the intellectual community as well. A. Rudra, a distinguished Indian economist, is a good example. He would probably deny most of the assertions made by the "new orthodox" school, yet he hankers after the same panaceas, and objects to the Green Revolution strategy because it promotes the profit motive in agriculture. He writes:

> the task of developing agriculture is being entrusted to the greed and the acquisitive spirit which motivates capitalists. *In traditional Indian agriculture greed was located and condemned in the professional money lender, the speculative trader, etc.* An important discovery of the proponents of the strategy is that the same greed, the same acquisitive spirit, may also be

> found latent in the cultivators; all the components of the strategy are aimed at further encouraging this spirit....This clearly stated aim seems to have been achieved. The 'Holy Grail' which the richer farmers are pursuing is the way of life of the urban middle class; the latter in their turn are craving the comforts of the consumption society of the West (Rudra, 1978, p. 387, emphasis added).

Here is an obvious echo of Nehru's sentiments quoted earlier.

This, then, is the crux of the explanation why so many Indian intellectuals dislike markets and the price mechanism—these depend upon, even if they do not promote, the qualities of greed and acquisitiveness which have always been scorned by the literary and politically powerful castes in India. It is this Brahminical attitude, today imbibed by a large part of the Westernized stratum of Indian society, which is at the root of that seeming *traison de clercs* that apparently has been taking place in India at least over the last two decades.

Their contempt for business, moreover, is joined by a breathtaking ignorance of mercantile activity among the literary castes. This is the result of the endogamous and occupationally segregated caste system. In more socially mobile societies there is always a fair chance that the rulers and their courtiers would have had some mercantile relatives who would have provided them with some knowledge of the nature of trade and commerce, and the importance of risk taking and entrepreneurship in the process of development. The caste system has, however, cocooned the Indian literary castes from any such influences.[25] The danger this represents to the prospects of India's economy was masked till fairly recently, when as a result of the Administrative Revolution (which has greatly extended the hold of the government on the economy), these literary castes have increasingly intervened in spheres outside their traditional purview. Their inbred contempt and ignorance of merchants and markets keep them from recognizing the failures of past interventions and from promoting the evolution of a market economy (albeit controlled through measures which supplement the price mechanism) in India. Unfortunately, such a market evolution is a key factor in determining the future economic prospects of India.

Table 16

Employment in the Public Sector

	1901	1911	1921	1931	1951	1960*	1978*
Total	1,918,916	1,712,958	1,630,365	1,448,336	2,162,117	5,498,000	12,943,000

*These figures refer only to civilian employees, and *are* exclusive of public sector employment in railways and manufacturing.

Source: Lal (1988), Vol. 1, Table 9.2.

There are, however, some hopeful signs that this resulting unworldliness of Indian rulers concerning trade and commerce might be changing. What scribblers cannot achieve, inflation and an excess supply of bureaucrats (see Table 16 for the growth of Indian bureaucracy) might at least engender. For one of the remarkable features of the changes in the relative wage structure in post-Independent India has been the decline in civil service salaries (particularly of those at the top). The corresponding labor market signals have been received by the children of these literary castes who, from casual empircism, seem to be turning toward non-traditional but more lucrative careers in business and politics. As "policy makers" in India become less contemptuous and ignorant about trade and commerce, they may begin to substitute *bania* for *brahmin* ideals and might at last begin to dissolve the intellectual bulwarks of Indian economic stagnation.

One unintended consequence of the Permit Raj, however, was to make it more difficult to shift the prevailing equilibrium of interest groups. This conferred on bureaucrats vast discretionary power over individual production and investment decisions. The bureaucratic control system created rents for the specific allocations of goods required for investment and production. These rents could be allocated to whomever the bureaucrats and politicians favored. Vast resources have been expended on developing 'connections' and attempting to obtain these rents by producers whose efforts would and should otherwise have been directed toward production. The resulting controls on entry and exit in industry meant that a clientistic business class has grown up fearing competition and favoring the continuation of the Permit Raj as much as the Fabian ideologues. There is thus a new powerful group of industrialists who would oppose, as they would be hurt by, any liberalization of

second pattern, followed in the middle reaches of the Ganges, the crop is grown outside the flood season but relies on the utilization of the silt carried by the floods. In the *third* pattern the crop is grown under rainfed conditions or under the system of water fallow. This is the case in the areas adjoining the Western Ghats. The *fourth* pattern is based on both irrigation and flood control to achieve a controlled water supply throughout the life of the crop. This system allows proper manuring and other cultural practices which bring a marked rise in the per hectare yield of rice. This has been the pattern in Tamil Nadu, where for millennia irrigated rice has been grown using water from wells and tanks. Its paddy yields of around 2.7 tons per hectare are comparable to those in Japan during the Meiji era.

12. See D. Kumar (1983) and Lal (1988) for a fuller discussion and references to this literature.
13. Maddison, p. 55.
14. Maddison estimates ". . . in 1868, Indian mills supplied only 8 percent of total cloth consumption; in 1913, 20 percent, in 1936, 62 percent; and in 1945, 76 percent. By the latter date there were no imports of piece goods" (p. 57).
15. See Rudra (1978) for the reasons why this form of curve fitting is desirable, as it enables one to judge whether growth is accelerating, decelerating or constant over the relevant period.
16. This criterion stipulated that any good which could be supplied by a domestic producer could not be imported.
17. Bhagwati and Srinivasan.
18. Lal (1980).
19. Bhagwati and Desai, p. 466.
20. This is the sum of what in Indian public finance terminology are called 'capital receipts' (which are essentially public borrowing from the general public) *and* deficit financing (which is borrowing from the Reserve Bank of India).
21. Nehru (1936), pp. 431–32.
22. See Lal (1985) for a fuller discussion of the validity of identifying 'socialism', as it has been in India, with dirigisme and bureaucratic modes of allocation.
23. These are discussed in Lal (1980), which also discusses the optimal forms of government intervention, given the well-

known limitations of a policy of laissez-fair, and the consequent need to deal with various forms of 'market failure.'

24. Although it should be said that economists, brought up on various fixed-coefficients planning models, have found it easy and natural to slip into this engineering frame of mind, even when they have explicitly been concerned with various economic trade-offs.
25. It may be useful to quote the conclusion of the major historian of the Indian middle classes: "Since India's tradition of caste authoritarianism fitted in well the Imperial scheme of things, Indian bureaucrats, who usually belonged to higher castes, were quick to step into the shoes of the British who left India in 1947. Bureaucracy thus continued to retain its hold over business in India and is increasing its hold with the extension of the state's economic function. This may be beneficial to the educated middle classes, since as officers of Government they step in as controllers of nationalized industries without any personal stake in them. But is is no gain to the country as a whole. The system of state control, in fact, stifles the growth of entrepreneurial elements which India has in the past badly needed to speed up production. Traditionally recruited from the literary classes, with no business acumen, civil servants are most unsuited to accelerate production in Indian conditions" (Mishra, p. 340).

BIBLIOGRAPHY

Ahluwalia, I. J., *Industrial Growth in India* (Delhi: Oxford University Press, 1985.

Ahluwalia, M. S., "Rural Poverty in India: 1956–57 to 1973–74," *Journal of Development Studies*, Vol. 14, no. 3, April 1978.

_________ "Rural Poverty, Agricultural Production and Prices: A Re-examination," in J. W. Mellor and G. M. Desai (eds.), *Agricultural Change and Rural Poverty* (Baltimore: Johns Hopkins University Press, 1985.

Balogh, T., *Unequal Partners*, 2 vols (Oxford: Blackwells, 1967).

Bardhan, P., "Labour Supply Functions in a Poor Agrarian Economy," *American Economic Review*, Vol. 9, no. 1, March 1979.

Bardhan, P., "Determinants of Supply and Demand for Labour in a Poor Agrarian Economy: An Analysis of Household Survey Data from Rural West Bengal," in H. P. Binswanger and M. R. Rosenzweig (eds.), 1984.

Boserup, E., *The Conditions of Agricultural Growth* (London: Allen & Unwin, 1965).

_________ *Population & Technical Change*, (Chicago: University of Chicago Press, 1981).

Bhagwati, J. and P. Desai, *India—Planning for Industrialisation* (London: OECD, Oxford University Press, 1970).

Bhagwati, J. and T. N. Srinirasan, *Foreign Trade Regimes and Economic Development: India* (New York: Columbia University Press, 1975).

Bhattacharya, D., *A Concise History of the Indian Economy, 1750–1950*, 2nd ed. (New Delhi: Prentice-Hall of India, 1979).

Binswanger, H. and M. R. Rosenzweig, *Contractural Arrangements, Employment and Wages in Rural Labour Markets in Asia* (New Haven: Yale University Press, 1984).

Blyn, G., *Agricultural Trends in India 1891–1947* (Philadelphia: University of Pennsylvania Press, 1966).

Dandekar, V. M., "Indian Economy Since Independence," *Economic and Political Weekly*, Vol. 23, nos. 1 & 2, January 1988.

Dandekar, V. M. and N. Rath, *Poverty in India* (Poona: Indian School of Political Economy, 1971).

Evenson, R. E. and H. Binswanger & Rosensweig (eds.)

Henderson, P. D., *The Energy Sector In India* (New Delhi: Oxford University Press, 1974).

Heston, A., "National Income," in D. Kumar (ed.), 1983.

Ishikawa, S., *Economic Development in Asian Perspective* (Tokyo: Kinokuniya, 1967).

Jha, P. S., "The Public Sector in India: an Appraisal," Mimeo, China Division, World Bank, June 1985.

Karnik, V. B., *Indian Trade Unions—A Survey*, 3rd ed., (Bombay: Popular Prakashan, 1968).

Kumar, D., (ed.) *Cambridge Economic History of India*, Vol. 2, (Cambridge: Cambridge University Press, 1983).

Lal, D., "Nationalism, Socialism and Planning," *World Development*, June, 1985.

_________ *Wells and Welfare*, (Paris: OECD Development Centre, 1972).

_________ "Agricultural Growth, Real Wages and the Rural Poor in India," *Economic and Political Weekly*, Vol. 26, June, 1976.

_________ "Theories of Industrial Wage Structures—A Review," *Indian Journal of Industrial Relations*, Vol. 15, no. 2, October 1979, reprinted in *World Bank Reprint Series*, no. 142.

_________ *Prices for Planning* (London: Heineman Educational Books, 1980).

_________ "Trends in Real Wages in Rural India, 1880–1980" in P. Bardhan and T.N. Srinivasan (eds.): *Rural Poverty in South Asia* (Delhi: Oxford University Press, 1987).

_________ "The Political Economy of Economic Liberalization," *World Bank Economic Review*, Vol. 1, No. 2, January 1987.

_________ *The Hindu Equilibrium*, 2 vols, (Oxford: Clarendon Press, 1988).

Lewis, W. A. (ed.), *Tropical Development 1880–1913* (London: Allen & Unwin, 1970).

Lewis. W. A., *Growth and Fluctuations, 1870–1913* (London: Allen & Unwin, 1978).

Lidman, R. and R.J. Domerese, "India" in W.A. Lewis (ed.), 1970.

Maddison, A., *Class Structure and Economic Growth— India and Pakistan Since the Moghuls* (London: Allen & Unwin, 1971).

Mishra, B. B., *The Indian Middle Classes* (London: Oxford University Press, 1960).

J. Mohammed and J. Whalley, "Rent Seeking in India: Its Costs and Policy Significance," *Kyklos*, Vol. 37, no. 3, 1984.

Minhas, B. S., "Rural Poverty, Land Redistribution and Development," *Indian Economic Review*, Vol. 5, no. 1, April 1970.

Narain, D., *The Impact of Price Movements on Areas Under Selected Crops in India 1900–39*, Cambridge, 1965.

Nehru, J., *An Autobiography*, 1st Indian edition, 1962, (New Delhi: Allied Publishers, 1963).

__________ *The Discovery of India*, 6th edition, (Calcutta: Signet Press, 1956).

__________ *India's Foreign Policy* (New Delhi: Publications Division, 1961).

Ray, R. K., *Industrialisation in India* (Delhi: Oxford University Press, 1979).

Rosenzweig, M. R., "Rural Wages, Labour Supply and Land Reform: A Theoretical and Empirical Analysis," *American Economic Review*, Vol. 68, 1978.

__________ "Determinants of Wage Rates and Labour Supply Behaviour in the Rural Sector of a Developing Country," in Binswanger and Rosenzweig (eds.), 1984.

Rudra, A., "Semi Feudalism, Usury Capital, etcetera," *Economic & Political Weekly*, Vol. 9, no. 48, 1974, pgs. 1996–1997.

__________ "Organisation of Agriculture for Rural Development in India," *Cambridge Journal of Economics*, December 1981.

Sivasubramonian, S., "Income from the Secondary Sector in India 1900–47," *Indian Economic and Social History Review*, Vol. 14, no. 4, 1977.

European Economic Review 34 (1990) 1213–1231. North-Holland

THE FABLE OF THE THREE ENVELOPES: THE ANALYTICS AND POLITICAL ECONOMY OF THE REFORM OF CHINESE STATE OWNED ENTERPRISES

Deepak LAL*

University College London, London WC1 6BT, GB

Received May 1988, final version received October 1989

This paper applies the standard theory of trade and welfare to the question of reforming Chinese state-owned industrial enterprises. It shows how a continuation of the unique Chinese system of labour market control by party cadres, accompanied by a liberalisation of commodity and capital markets could reconcile the conflict between political control and economic efficiency which has bedevilled other attempted reforms of Communist economies. Finally, it delineates the ideal sequencing of price reform. removal of industrial planning, foreign trade liberalisation and the reform of the capital market.

1. Introduction

There is a growing movement for the reform of repressed economies[1] in many Communist countries. Its aim is to raise the total factor productivity by improvements in allocative and *X* efficiency through 'the replacement of bureaucratic direction with the impersonal forces of the market' [Perkins (1988, p. 603)]. In many countries, including China, the reform of the agricultural sector has preceded that of industry, whose reform has proved particularly difficult because of the resistance of apparatchiks who stand to lose power and status from any loosening of bureaucratic direction. A central question in the design and success of a programme for the liberalisation of the industrial sector, therefore, concerns the sequencing of its various components so that it is not only economically desirable but politically acceptable.

Whilst the particular circumstances of different communist countries will differ, so will the details of the reform programme. There are nevertheless enough similarities in the economic and political systems of most Communist

*Professor of Political Economy, University College, London. This paper expands on unpublished comments made on the papers in Tidrick and Chen (1987) at a conference to discuss these appers organised jointly by the World Bank and the Chinese Academy of Social Science in Beijing in August 1985. Comments on an earlier draft by Richard Snape, Jean Waelbroek and two anonymous referees are gratefully acknowledged.

[1]A 'repressed' economy is one which for given resource and technological constraints is operating well inside its potential production possibility frontier.

0014-2921/90/$03.50

countries that it may be possible to derive some general principles for their sequencing of a package of industrial reforms. One of the major purposes of this paper is to show how some general prinicples may be derived from the conventional theory of trade and welfare by its application to the problems of reforming state-owned industrial enterprises in China. Additionally I also provide some analysis of the 'political economy' of the resistances that reformers would encounter in the discussion of the proper sequencing of reforms.

The major political resistance in expanding the role of the market in communist economies is likely to arise from the bureaucrats whose power declines with the decease of bureaucratic control of the economy [see Nove (1977), Perkins (1988)]. But what is the power that Communist cadres cherish? It is difficult to believe that it is the power to meddle in the detailed operations of industrial enterprises, per se. It is more likely that the cadres value the power to control people with its accompanying status, prestige, and perquisites, as witnessed by the notorious system of 'nomenklatura' in most Communist systems. If the reforms damage this privileged status of the incumbent bureaucracy, it is difficut to see how party cadres in Communist States can be co-opted into a process of reform which would seem, in effect, to amount to their euthanasia. For this reason, the prospects of any significant reform of most Communist economies under the aegis of their existing bureaucratic elites would appear to be dim.

In China, however, because of its unique system of labour market control and the power it gives the cadres over people, through their control over urban job assignments (see the next section), we suggest that it might be possible to find a unique Chinese path out of this political logjam. This consists of a continuation of the job assignment system in the labour market but with a liberalisation of commodity and capital markets. A second purpose of this paper is therefore to show how this partial liberalisation which is likely to be specific to China, could reconcile the conflict between political control and economic efficiency which has bedeviled other attempted reforms of communist economies.

The paper consists of six parts. The first, section 2, outlines the characteristics of Chinese state-owned industrial enterprises, which provides the stylised facts for our subsequent formal analysis. Section 3 derives the three statics, closed economy, production and possibility frontiers – our 3 envelopes – which are relevant in evaluating different reform packages. Section 4 examines the sequencing of reforms of the commodity market within this static framework. Section 5 drops the assumption of a closed economy and introduces the sequencing of foreign trade liberalisation. Section 6 drops the static assumption and considers the additional reforms (particularly of the capital market) needed for dynamic efficiency. The sixth and final section summarizes our conclusions.

2. Characteristics of Chinese state owned enterprises

Since late 1978 the Chinese have embarked on reforms of their state owned industrial enterprises. In 1981 there were about 84,200 of these enterprises, accounting for about 78 percent of gross industrial output value [Chow (1985, p. 135)]. The aim of the reforms is to improve allocative efficiency through:

> '(1) devotion of greater discretionary authority to enterprises in production and investment activities; (2) use of material incentives (in the form of profit retention schemes for enterprises and bonuses for individual workers) to supplement administrative directives in guiding enterprise decision making; and (3) an expanded role for the market mechanism in resource allocation.'
>
> [Byrd (1983, p. 329)]

Tidrick and Chen (1987) provide a detailed account of the functioning of Chinese state owned enterprises based on a sample of 20 enterprises they studied. Chow (1985) summarizes the working of one large industrial enterprise – the First Lathe Factory of Beijing. Based on these, the following stylised characteristics of these enterprises may be noted.

The first is the large size of these enterprises. One enterprise in the Tidrick–Chen sample, Anshau Iron and Steel Corporation, employs 195,000 workers directly and 180,000 employees in dependent collectives. This would make it larger than the total industrial sectors of many developing countries.[2] Thus, even though there may be increasing returns to scale in some of the *activities* undertaken by the enterprise, it may not be unreasonable to assume that for the *overall* enterprise, constant returns to scale prevail.

The second characteristic (which the reforms are trying to alter) is the dominant role of Communist party cadres in parallel to the factory manager, from top management all the way down to the shop floor [see Chow (1985, p. 137)]. Even though managers have more authority than before under the new reforms, nevertheless as Chow (1985, p. 13) notes: 'The manager is supposed to manage "under the leadership of the party committee"'. This means that in most cases the party cadres still largely remain as the de facto factory managers. A loosening of the control of party cadres and the devolution of authority from party administrators to factory managers, if successful, would cut down the power of the party cadres. This is one serious potential source of opposition to the industrial reform which needs to be borne in mind in assessing whether, as Cheung's (1986) paper asks, 'will China go capitalist?'.

[2]For example in 1980 the *total* industrial labour force in Kenya was only 440.000 [see World Bank: Social indicators 1986 (p. 123)].

The third distinguishing feature of the Chinese state owned enterprises [as emphasised in the papers by Byrd and Tidrick (1987) and Granick (1987)] is the immobility of labour as between enterprises.[3] The power given to local bureaucrats over the lives of most urban Chinese by the job assignment system can be readily envisaged from the following summary of the system for assigning individual workers to particular jobs:

> 'Neither workers nor enterprises have much say in job assignments, and most workers expect to spend their working lives in the enterprise they are assigned to when they leave school. Job swaps to allow families to be together or for other personal reasons are some times allowed, but permission is not assured. Workers have no right to quit their jobs. Residence permits and grain ration coupons have precluded migration to seek employment. And the local labour bureau usually has control over job assignments with an overall quota set by the ministry of Labour.'
>
> [Byrd and Tidrick (1987, p. 68)]

Furthermore, as the fourth feature, Byrd and Tidrick emphasised the 'fixity' of the endowments of 'land' of the enterprises.[4] The fifth feature is that, as in most planned economies, there are limits on the diversification of output from that laid down for the enterprise in the plan.[5]

The third, and fourth features taken together immediately suggest that an interregional variant of the standard theory of international trade which assumes immobility of primary factors but mobility of goods across national (enterprise) boundaries can be usefully employed to provide an analytical framework for discussing issues of economic reform of Chinese state owned enterprises. To bring out the essential features, I shall consider variants of the simplest analytical model, the so-called two-good, three-factor, sector-specific model of interntional trade theory [see Jones (1971)]. These models may be considered to be highly unrealistic in considering a closed and highly repressed economy such as China's. They should be looked upon as fables which simplify reality but thereby allow us some important insights about the world around us. That is the analytical purpose of my fable.

[3]Thus Granick (1987) states that whilst in China unlike the USSR and CEMA the product market seems to be equilibrated through the market mechanism 'the exact opposite, however, pertains to the factor markets for labour in the State indusrial sector'. Whilst Byrd and Tidrick (1987, p. 62) state: 'A worker's welfare is closely tied to the enterprise in which he works. Workers are typically employed in the same enterprise for life and receive housing, medical benefits, and a pension from the enterprise. For the enterprise, labour is virtually a fixed cost because workers cannot be fired. Worker dependence on the enterprise is more like an extreme version of large-scale Japanese firms than the usual worker-firm relationship in a socialist economy.' Futhermore, as Byrd and Tidrick (1987, p. 67) note: 'The control of labour allocation is more far-reaching in China than in Eastern Europe and the Soviet Union because it extends to the assignment of individual workers to particular jobs.'

[4]Byrd and Tidrick (1987, p. 79). Though this seems to be changing.

[5]But see Tidrick (1987) on how the system is much looser than in the CEMA, and many plan targets are subject to bargaining between the enterprises and the planners.

2.1. Political economy

A central question in assessing the likelihood of success of the ongoing reform of the Chinese industrial sector is whether the opposition of the Communist party functionaries who might lose from the reform can be overcome. To minimize this opposition it would be preferable to sequence the liberalisation of the various markets involved – for commodities, capital and labour – in such a way that the 'losses' suffered by bureaucrats do not precede the 'gains' to the general public as producers and consumers that are expected to follow from the reform.

Cheung (1986) has noted that one reason for the undoubted success of the economic reforms in agriculture was that under the new 'responsibility' system the party cadres in agriculture were, in affect, bought out. The 'responsibility system' in agriculture permits households to lease land from the government for a 'rent' of 10 percent of the yield value. Since 1983 these leases – 'responsibility contracts' – can moreover be transferred or sold, and though there are restrictions on the number of workers who can be hired by the 'landlords', these restrictions are hard to enforce. The reason why the former party cadres who were leaders of agricultural production teams have not resisted these agricultural reforms is because the 'often end[ed] up with several responsibility contracts'! [Cheung (1986, p. 66)].

A similar transfer of property rights to the party cadres with power and influence in the pre-reform industrial enterprises is not feasible because of the 'jointness' in most industrial production processes, which makes it difficult to divide up the 'assets' and define exclusive property rights for their use.[6] (See Cheung op cit. for a fuller discussion.) The organizational choices in the industrial sector may therefore seem to lie between maintaining some marginally liberalized version of the existing system where the party cadres in effect still run the factories, or a wholesale eradication of the party cadres 'leadership role' in the factories which would be run solely by their managers. The latter choice of course, whilst aiding to efficiency, would undercut the power and influence of the party cadres, many of whom according to Chow [1985, p. 137) 'do not have the required educational background or administrative experience to play a leadership role', and hence are unlikely to emerge as managers in their own right in a fully meritocratic enterprise system.

However, for China there may be a third way – at least for some time (a generation perhaps?). This would keep the influence of the party cadres largely intact by preserving the job assignment system and their control over individuals, but leaving all other economic decisions to managers guided by the signals from liberalised markets in commodities and capital. Thereby China may be able to find its own unique road to socialism, maintaining

[6]See section 6 below.

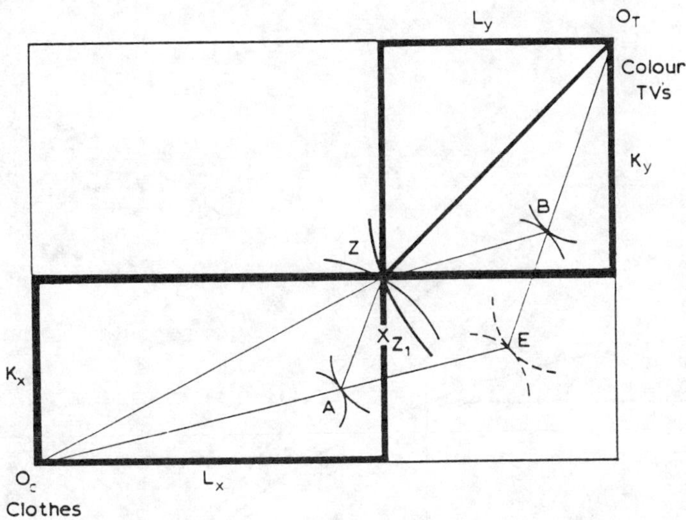

Fig. 1

relatively equal income-sharing within enterprises, and the political control over individuals sought by Communist parties, with most of the efficiency gains of a market economy.

The following sections, thus, seek to provide an analytical framework for thinking about a sequencing of industrial reforms, which accepts the continuation of two important and unique institutional features of the Chinese economic system – the system of job assignment and of 'sharing from a common pot'. I do not discuss nor seek to evaluate the morality of the system of job assignment, and the undoubted grave infringement of human rights entailed from a Western ethical viewpoint, though these have to set against the possible gains in economic security, which are emphasised by many advocates of so-called 'positive' liberty. [See Berlin (1958), Lal (1981)]. To that extent this is an essay in positive rather than normative economics.

3. The three envelopes

Consider an 'economy' composed of two 'industries' producing clothes and televisions, respectively, each with given and fixed stocks of capital and labour represented by point Z in fig. 1. The underlying production functions are assumed to have constant returns to scale. Television production is assumed to be relatively 'capital' intensive compared to clothes. The two firms are completely specialized in producing one or the other output. They are not allowed to diversify outputs.

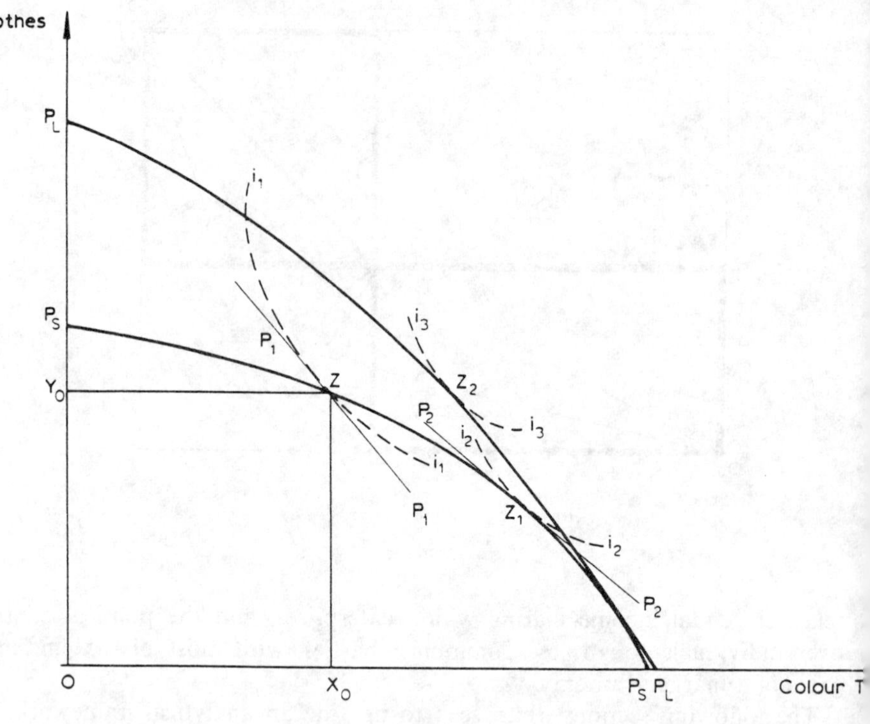

Fig. 2

Relative factor prices need not be equal in the two industries as can be readily seen in fig. 1. The resulting fixed outputs of the two goods is also given by the point Z in fig. 2. The assumption that neither capital nor labour can be shifted between the two 'industries' yields the rectangular production possibility curve X_0ZY_0. This is our *first* envelope. It depicts an economy whose production decisions in both sectors are insensitive to either relative price changes or alterations in aggregate demand, which merely determines where along their fixed K/L rays in fig. 1 production takes place and/or the size of inventories that are built up.

Given the assumption that for political reasons labour mobility *cannot* be introduced, it would appear, at first sight, that the solution is to move capital between enterprises. Thus, assume that whilst labour remains specific and immobile between the two 'industries', capital – in the form of malleable capital goods – is allowed to be shifted between the two industries.

In fact, the 'capital' stock will be embodied in specific machines and the industry-specific skills – human capital – of the fixed labour force in each industry. Its shifting between the enterprises could come about either through trading in 'machines' or through the process of depreciation. Whilst for human capital, the enterprise-specific stock can be altered over time through training. Thus, in the long run the assumption of allowing capital mobility through malleable capital may not be too unrealistic.

Second, assume that the planners whilst insisting on the specialization by each industry in producing a particular good specified by the plan, however, allow enterprises to vary the quantities of the specific products that it produces.

Finally, assume that as a result of price reforms (to be discussed in the next section) the market determined relative prices facing producers and consumers are the same.

Starting from the rigid allocation at point Z, producers will then be able to shift malleable capital goods between the two industries in response to altering relative rates of return. Thus, we now have an exact analogue to the two goods, two specific, one-mobile factor model of Jones and others.

The two enterprise economy's possibility frontier (PPF) will now be given by P_sP_s, in fig. 2, which obviously will lie outside the immobile labour-cum-capital PPF, X_0ZY_0. This is our *second* envelope. Say, the new equilbrium with market-determined relative prices and outputs of the two commodities, with mobility of capital but *not* of labour, is at Z_1. The resulting movement from Z to Z_1 in fig. 2 is shown in fig. 1 as a movement form Z to Z_1 in terms of allocation of factors and changes in relative returns in the two industries. These obviously depend upon the relative factor intensities of the two 'entities' and the relative price change in moving from Z to Z_1. As drawn in fig. 2, the relative price and relative and absolute quantities of (televisions) rises compared with (cloth) and as televisions are relatively capital-intensive, the wage rate in television production will rise relative to that in clothing, as the production point shifts to Z_1 in fig. 1. Thus inevitably, allowing capital mobility will imply accepting increases in inequalities of labour incomes between enterprises. But, as the second envelope lies outside the first, the efficiency of the economy would be greater.

However, there is another way to achieve even higher efficiency, whilst maintaining immobility of *both* labour and capital. This yields our *third* envelope. To derive it, we maintain the assumption (as in deriving the first envelope) that both capital and labour are immobile; there are constant returns to scale and television production is more capital intensive than clothes. As in deriving the second envelope we assume that as a result of price reforms producer and consumer prices are equal and alter in line with changing excess demand for the two goods. But we now relax the assumption (made in deriving both the first and second envelopes) that enterprises are forced to specialize in producing one or the other good. We now assume that *enterprises can choose their output mix*; that is, though still maintaining capital and labour immobility, the planners allow enterprises to diversify output by producing whatever they like of the two goods so that they are no longer completely specialized in one product.

With the removal of diversification restrictions on the enterprises assume that both enterprises produce the two goods and face common commodity prices. The latter will determine the common factor proportions and relative factor prices in the two industries (clothes and TV) in both enterprises (X and Y). Say these are given (in fig. 1) as points $A(B)$ in the $X(Y)$ enterprise – with the factor proportions in clothes and television production being the same (the common slope of rays O_CA and ZB (clothes) and ZA and O_TB (televisions)).

The *aggregate* output of the two commodities produced by the two enterprises will be given by the point E, the intersection of the extended rays O_CA (clothes) and O_TB (televisions). For from elementary geometry, $AZ=EB$ and $ZB=AE$. Thus for the given commodity price ratio, even with labour and capital immobile, the economy's aggregate production will be *as if* there was full labour and capital mobility, so that it is operating on the contract curve of the economy-wide Edgeworth–Bowley box.

This must be true of each and every commodity price ratio. Thus given that both enterprises produce both goods, face the same relative commodity prices for their outputs and have access to the same technology, neither the labour immobility arising from job assignment nor capital immobility will prevent the economy from attaining its full efficiency production possibility frontier. Thus the economy's production possibility curve will be given by P_LP_L in fig. 2. This is our *third* envelope.

Note that in deriving this envelope we have made all the assumptions necessary for the factor price equalization theorem to hold.[7] Hence, there will in principle also be equalization of factor prices in the two enterprises. Though, in practice, as obviously the assumptions of the theorem are unlikely to hold, this equalization is unlikely.

Equally unrealistic is our implicit assumption that, once enterprises are allowed to choose their output mix, and the domestic commodity (but *not* capital and labour) markets are freed, there is in effect perfect competition in goods markets. But as the recent developments in trade theory incorporating imperfect competition show [see Helpman and Krugman (1985)] the basic insights about the efficiency gains from inter-regional trade incorporated in the outermost envelope P_LP_L, in fig. 2, would still endure.

[7]These assumptions are perfect competition: linear homogenous production functions; identical production functions in different countries: diminishing marginal productivity of factors; absence of complete specialisation; absence of factor intensity reversals; perfectly inelastic factor supply curves for each country; and absence of tariffs and transport costs. [See P. Samuelson (1948)].

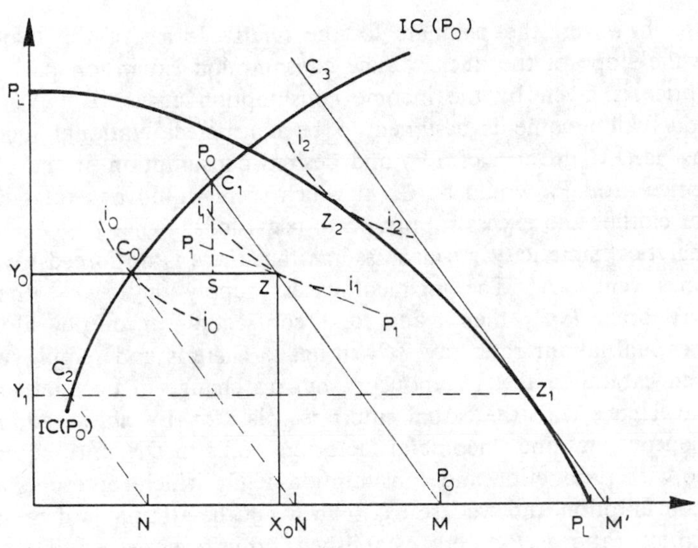

Fig. 3

4. Sequencing reforms in a closed economy

The *first* important conclusion about the sequencing of reforms emerges directly from our derivation of these three envelopes. At least for *static* efficiency, inter-enterprise capital mobility is not important. The most important reform is to remove diversification restrictions by allowing enterprises to choose their output mix, which, even with *labour and capital immobile*, will allow the economy to operate on its fully efficient frontier – our third envelope $P_L P_L$ in fig. 2.

In deriving our second and third envelopes we had assumed that producer prices were market determined. To explain what this means, we need to introduce the consumer side of our model economy, to determine the nature and role of price reforms and their effects on economic welfare.

In fig. 3 we reproduce our first and third envelopes $Y_0 Z X_0$ and $P_L P_L$ (which are both based on assuming that the given enterprise specific capital and labour endowments are immobile).

Before reform, the economy is at Z on the first envelope $X_0 Z Y_0$, with inflexible supplies of the two goods. Given consumers tastes, represented by a set of indifference curves, $i_1 i_1$ is the highest attainable indifference curve (as it passes through Z). If the relative prices set by the planners corresponded to the slope of $i_1 i_1$ at Z, then there would be full equilibrium in this economy. Alternatively, if the two outputs were allowed to be traded freely on a market, the same price ratio of P_1 would be established.

Suppose, however, the planners fix the relative price of the two goods given by the slope of the line P_0. The consumption expansion path at this relative price is given by the income consumption curve IC (P_0). In this static model all income is assumed to be consumed. National income at factor cost is OM in term of TVs and desired consumption at the planners relative price ratio P_0 would be C_1 at which there would be excess demand of C_1S for clothes and excess supply ZS of televisions.

For analytical simplicity we also assume that there is no forced savings or change in inventories.[8] The incipient excess supply of TVs at the given commodity price P_0P_0 then leads to a contraction of output along the constant capital/labour ratio ray ZO_T in fig. 1. There is underemployment of labour and capital in the TV industry, but no change in its relative factor price ratio. Hence with the actual enterprise plan for TV *not* scheduling full capacity output, national income at factor cost falls to ON until equilibrium is reached with production and consumption at C_0, which represents a lower level of consumption and welfare i_0i_0 than would be attainable if the market clearing price ratio P_1P_1 were established.[9] thus even with all the other constraints (on factor allocation and output targets) taken as binding, it is obvious that price reforms, leading to the establishment of the market clearing price ratio P_1P_1, is clearly welfare improving.

If price reforms are combined with the removal of restrictions on diversifying output, the consumption and production point will be Z_2 on the outermost envelope P_LP_L in fig. 3.

What should be the sequencing of price reform and the removal of restrictions on the diversification of output? To answer this question consider fig. 3. Without price reform the prices facing producers and consumers are the pre-reform planners prices P_0. At these prices, following the removal of mandatory planning, producers operating on the third envelope P_LP_L will be producing at Z_1 where the marginal rate of transformation equals the relative price ratio P_0P_0. At the domestic factor incomes corresponding to this production point of OM', desired consumption is at C_3 and is clearly

[8]In practice, the wage bill in pre-reform China was tightly controlled by the central planners and this cash income was sought to be kept broadly in line with the increase in consumer goods sold at fixed consumer prices. Frustrated consumption demand was exhibited in the form of involuntary increases in savings deposits and the building up of inventories of goods for which there was excess supply. We do not discuss the important macro-economic implications of these shortages and slacks, which requires an intertemporal analytical framework. But see Kornai (1982).

[9]It should be noted, however, that if forced savings and unwanted inventory increases are the mode of adjustment, then in fig. 3, C_0Z would be an involuntary increase in savings deposits with an equivalent increase in unwanted inventories of TVs. Given the marginal utility of the forced savings, the welfare contour for the consumer would then cut the C_0Z line to the right of C_0. The qualitative judgements we make about alternative sequencing would thus not alter, but the geometry would be more messy with this more realistic form of adjustment.

infeasible. As before, we assume that the excess supply of TVs leads to a reduction in their output and a corresponding decline in factor incomes till production and consumption are at C_2, where the income consumption curve cuts the Y_1Z_1 line. Clearly (as drawn) welfare is lower at C_2 than at C_0 (the consumption and production point without the removal of mandatory planning). However, if the P_LP_L production possibility curve dropped sufficiently steeply to the south-east of Z_2, it is conceivable for C_2 to be above C_0. thus, in principle, price reform could either precede or follow the liberalisation of production assignments. However, as the gains from production liberalisation without price reform are likely to be negligible and, most likely, negative there is a presumption that price reform should not *follow* production liberalisation. Similarly, if price reform precedes production liberalisation, though there will necessarily be gains, they will be limited (the consumption point moving from C_0 to Z). The economy would have undertaken the costly and complicated process of recalculating appropriate prices (for point Z), but, without production liberalisation, would not have reaped any efficiency gains. Hence it would seem that price reform and the liberalisation of production assignments should be undertaken *simultaneously*.

What form should this price reform take? It has usually been assumed that market clearing prices should be established by raising the prices of goods in excess demand. In principle, however, as a *relative* price change is required, the requisite reform could equally effectively involve *reductions* in the prices of goods in excess supply. If, however, the cross price elasticity of the goods in excess demand are low (e.g., food for poor people) some rise in the prices of goods in excess demand may be unavoidable. The political dangers of such price rises are obvious, but they may be of less concern in China if, as we have assumed, the 'system of eating from a common pot' is maintained. This continuance of the provision of communal food and housing (two of the basic necessities) as part of the job assignment and social security system in enterprises could mitigate some of the popular resistance to price reform in China which has undermined reform efforts in other Soviet style economies (most notoriously in Poland recently).

There is, however, a need to guard against another danger in price reform which our simple analytical model can help to pinpoint. In fig. 3, consider the pre-reform economy given by the consumption and production point C_0 on the first envelope. As price reform is instituted the output of TVs (in our model) will increase and pari passu factor incomes. Suppose, as part of the system of mandatory planning, the planners misjudge the required increase in factor incomes, and increase them by more than NM. Unavoidable inflationary pressure will then arise, and the resulting *general* rise in prices could through the popular resistance it generates undermine the required *relative* price reform.[10] As the examples of many developing countries attest, macro-economic stability is a sine qua non of effective liberalisations [see Krueger (1978), Choksi and Papageorgiou (1987), Lal (1987)]. But issues concerning macro-economic balance are beyond the scope of this paper.[11]

5. Sequencing reforms in an open economy

So far we have been assuming a closed economy. Dropping this assumption has two important implications. First, it allows the implementation of an important method (the Little–Mirrlees shadow pricing procedure) for calculating the 'efficiency' producer prices during the price reform. Second, we need to see how the controlled foreign trade regime should be liberalised, and what the sequencing (if any) of this trade liberalisation should be with respect to the price reform and liberalisation of production planning discussed in the previous section.

Consider the question of calculating the 'new' relative producer prices during the price reform. We have seen that it is highly unlikely that it will be desirable for price reform to *follow* the liberalisation of production assignments (which yields the third envelope $P_L P_L$, reproduced in fig. 4). But once producers can choose their production mix, at what prices should they maximize 'profits'?

To answer this question, suppose that, in fig. 4, pre-reform, with the economy on the first of our envelopes $Y_0 Z X_0$ the two goods in our fable were both tradeable. But imports of clothes (assumed to be the importable) were subject to tight import controls, whereby imports are rationed to their available foreign exchange equivalent value of $C_1 X_1$ derived from exports of $X_1 Z$ of TVs at the world relative prices (terms of trade) the country faces of $P_W P_W$. Assume that as a result of price reforms domestic consumer prices are market clearing. Consumption will then be at C_1 with the domestic price ratio $P_D P_D$. The government now removes mandatory planning so that the relevant production possibility curve is $P_L P_L$ (of fig. 2) in fig. 4. Next, suppose it also instructs the enterprises to price their inputs and outputs (for determining the profitability of the enterprise – on which more below) at 'world prices', the so-called Little–Mirrlees shadow prices [see Little and Mirrlees (1974), Lal (1974, 1980)].[12] The production point of the economy

[10]There is some evidence of such macro-economic overheating following the first of China's attempts to reform prices [see Perkins (1988), Wu and Reynolds (1988)].

[11]But, see Perkins (1988) and Wu and Reynolds (1988) for the importance of combining price reform with that of fiscal and financial systems to prevent excess aggregate demand from arising.

[12]These would have to be centrally determined by well known methods and given to the enterprises. See Lal (1980) for estimates for India.

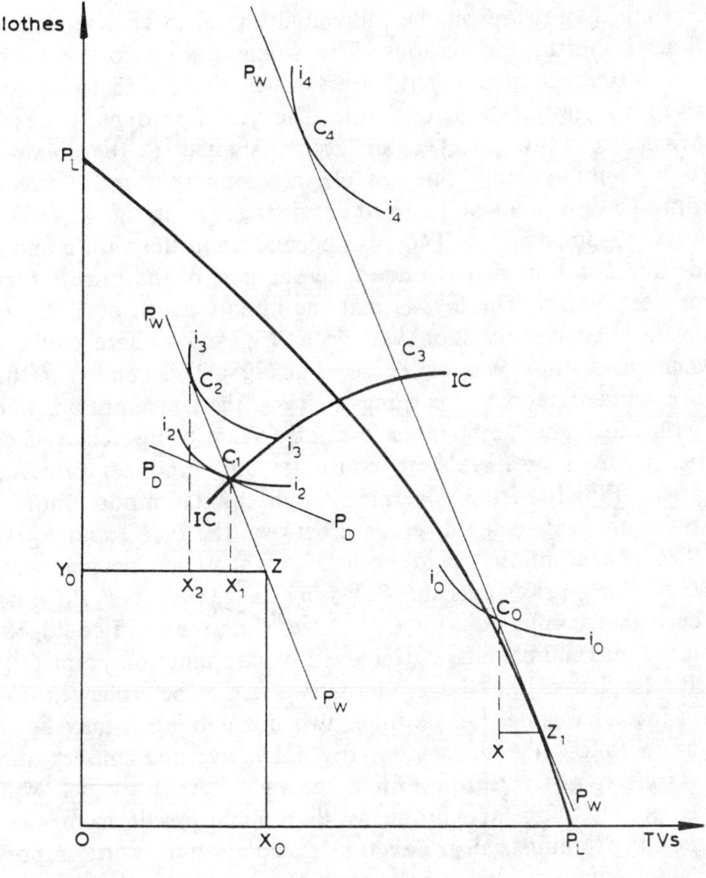

Fig. 4

will then move to Z_1, where the terms of trade line $P_W P_W$ is tangential to the $P_L P_L$ production possibility frontier.

This use of world prices as reference prices for production decisions will ensure productive efficiency, even if domestic consumer prices remain 'distorted' (given by the slope of $P_D P_D$). The consumption point will then lie on the intersection of the income consumption curve IC (for the given consumer price ratio $P_D P_D$) and the 'world price' based producer price ratio $P_W P_W$ (tangential to $P_L P_L$). This will unambiguously raise welfare. This use of world prices as reference producer prices also cuts out the tedious and time consuming process whereby producers would otherwise have to calculate what prices should be (say on the basis of input–output based calculation, or through an iterative mimicking of the Walrasian procedure). Apart from the well-known technical difficulties in conducting such an exercise, there would also be political pressure on the individual 'firms' to change their numbers for various opportunistic reasons. The whole price reform process could thence be incomplete after several years which could lead to a conservative backlash to restore the status quo ante. The use of producer prices based on Little–Mirrlees shadow prices, as an accompaniment to the liberalisation of production planning would, thus, enable the economy to move directly to the efficient production point on its third envelope ($P_L P_L$ in fig. 4).

What of consumer prices? They will depend upon the nature and extent of the trade liberalisation that is undertaken as part of the price reform. There are three possibilities. The first is that the import quota of $X_1C_1(=XC_0)$ is maintained. Then consumption will be at C_0, and welfare could be lower than when production was at Z [see Lal (1980)]. Secondly, if the import quota is expanded as export earnings increase the consumption point would be C_4 with the highest attainable level of welfare being achieved as (in the limit) free trade is attained with consumer and producer prices equalling world prices. Finally, if the government replaces the import quota of C_1X_1 by a tariff equivalent to the divergence between the $P_W P_W$ and $P_D P_D$ lines in fig. 4, then consumption would be at C_3 (where the income consumption curve IC at $P_D P_D$ prices cuts the $P_w P_W$ line tangential to $P_L P_L$), and welfare would be higher compared with C_1.[13] Over time the tariff could be reduced to attain the maximum welfare level given by consumption point C_4.[14]

Clearly, the first of the above alternatives has to be eschewed, as it could lead to a loss of welfare. Of the other two possibilities, it may be politically expedient to follow the third alternative of converting import quotas into explicit tariffs for two reasons. First, the tariff revenue which will emerge would ease any budgetary problems that might result from the internal liberalisation of industrial production. Second and more important the replacement of import quotas by a tariff system would obviate the need for import controllers, and the discretionary allocation of imports to users. The latter as attested by the example of numerous developing countries leads to rent seeking [see Krueger (1974)]. As the party cadres are likely to be the main beneficiaries of this form of corruption, maintaining import quotas administered by them would make the eventual removal of import regulations politically very difficult. It would be better, therefore, to prevent the rise of import quota 'rent-seeking' party cadres by moving to a tariff based system of trade management at an early stage of the economic reforms.

This suggests the following sequencing of welfare-improving reforms of the

[13]If the government liberalized foreign trade without removing mandatory planning then the economy's consumption point would be C_2, imports are C_2X_2 and unless the potential export surplus of X_2X_1 is actually exported, there will be an equivalent balance of payments deficit [see Srinivasan (1987)].

[14]See Corden (1974) and Lal (1980, technical appendix 6), for the reasons why this would be welfare improving.

Chinese industrial sector (assuming as we have throughout this paper that land and labour are immobile and also in this section that capital is too). At the start, as in fig. 3, domestic market clearing prices (P_1P_1) should be established. Simultaneously, mandatory production planning should be eliminated, allowing enterprises to diversify output, with the managers being instructed to maximize profits at *LM* 'border prices'. They will then be operating on the third of our envelopes. Third, the import quotas should be replaced by explicit tariffs which are roughly equivalent to the existing tariff equivalents of the quotas. Finally and gradually, the tariffs should first be unified and then the uniform tariff reduced towards zero, so that both consumer and producer prices are the same and equal to 'border prices'. At this final stage as market and 'shadow' prices would be the same, the enterprises would not need to be provided with 'shadow' prices at which profits would be maximized as they would be able to achieve production efficiency at market prices.

6. Dynamic aspects

Finally, we examine some dynamic issues relevant to the reform of Chinese industrial enterprises. In the absence of factor price equalisation, and with the growth in the stocks of capital and labour over time, considerations of dynamic efficiency require that *incremental* capital is allocated to enterprises with relatively higher expected rates of return. A genuine capital market, with investment funds provided at market clearing interest rates to enterprises is necessary. At the same time there needs to be provisions for the exit of unprofitable firms through some form of bankruptcy, and an end to the State subsidisation of loss-making enterprises. Related to this are questions concerning incentives for managers of enterprises to improve productive efficiency. These interrelated problems of achieving and maintaining dynamic efficiency can be subdivided into two general problems. The first is the form and sequencing of capital market liberalisation. The second, the means of introducing and enforcing a 'hard budget constraint' instead of the current 'soft budget constraint' [see Kornai (1979)] on enterprises. We examine each in turn.

One possibility for liberalizing the capital market is to give the workers, managers and cadres, shares in the existing enterprise – equal to its current capital value.[15] These shares are then allowed to be traded on a newly established national stock market. Owners of shares in their own enterprises

[15]There will be serious problems in determining this true value without the introduction of market clearing prices for the produced inputs and outputs of the enterprise. Hence this stage of the reform should follow the price reforms discussed earlier. Dong Fureng (1987) discusses this question of the ownership of Chinese enterprises. For contrasting Chinese views on the desirability of creating a stock market in China see Reynolds (1987).

could then trade them, and/or the dividends they receive, for shares in other enterprises. The pattern of investment in different enterprises and hence the disposition of the economy's savings would be determined as in a decentralised market system. Moreover, given the continuing political allocation of fresh entrants to the labour force to jobs in different enterprises, the capital intensive bias which is introduced in similar profit sharing schemes (e.g., the worker-management enterprises in Yugoslavia) would not arise. For the supply of labour and hence of the number of 'shares' in each enterprise's equity would be determined exogenously. Existing 'workers' could not maximize average product per worker by limiting employment as in a labour managed economy, and hence there would be none of the perverse effects on output and employment discussed in the literature on labour managed firms [see Meade (1972), Ward (1953), Vanek (1970)].

This liberalisation of the domestic capital market, in effect allows 'foreign' – inter-enterprise – portfolio investment. It should take place *after* the reforms of the domestic price structure outlined in the previous section, as capital flows into a price-distorted economy can be immiserizing [see Brecher and Diaz-Alejandro (1977)].

The second problem of introducing and enforcing a hard budget constraint is more problematic. The introduction of true market allocation of investment and credit, along with provisions for the bankruptcy of loss-making firms, would in principle provide a hard budget constraint. But its enforcement would require the depoliticisation of enterprise's managerial decision making. There are two hurdles.

The first are the party cadres in enterprises, who might not be satisfied with merely controlling the labour market through job assignments, and may still wish to meddle with managerial decision making. One way of overcoming this problem would be to mimic the agrarian reforms, by offering the cadres a 'share' in the profits of the enterprise. Besides 'buying them' out, such shares would also provide an incentive to the cadres to forbear interference in the efficient management of these enterprises.

The second problem concerns the question of 'who hires, fires and promotes managers'. We take it that the pecuniary rewards of managers will be linked directly to the profitability of their enterprises. But, even with a hard budget constraint, managers may pay special attention to the interests of the planning bureaucracy if they hope some day to be amongst its members [Perkins (1988, p. 618)]. It has been suggested that independent boards of enterprises should select managers [see Reynolds (1987)]. But how will the independence of the boards, be assured and maintained? Though these organisational questions are beyond the scope of this paper, one possible way of overcoming these 'political' obstacles might be to have two completely separate and independent sets of career choices open to ambitious individuals. One for party cadres, with a position in the party hierarchy providing the main source of utility. The other, for managers of enterprises, who would not be allowed to become party cadres, and vice versa, and who would derive utility from their profit related discounted income streams.

7. Conclusions

Our conclusions can be brief. A continuation of the job assignment system could be an important means of gaining the acquiescence of party cadres to the liberalisation of other factor and commodity markets. The associated job security and meeting of basic needs through the continuance of the policy of 'eating from a common pot' would protect workers against some of the distributional consequences of the reforms. The political opposition to economic reforms found in many other socialist economies may thereby be overcome in China. Moreover, analogous to the Hecksher–Ohlin theorems concerning the gains from international trade (with land and labour immobile) China could still achieve most of the efficiency gains of a market economy through the liberalisation of capital and commodity markets.

The first two steps, in moving down this unique Chinese road to socialism, we have argued, are the establishment of market clearing prices even within the existing organization of Chinese state owned enterprises, and the (possibly) simultaneous removal of mandatory planning. The latter would allow enterprises to diversify their output. Their managers should be instructed to maximize accounting profits at Little–Mirrlees 'border prices'. The third step would be to replace existing import quotas by 'guess-estimates' of the equivalent tariffs. These tariffs should then be unified, and the common tariff reduced. Any balance of payments problems that emerge being managed by appropriate changes in the exchange rate and overall macroeconomic policy. Finally the workers, managers and cadres should be given equity in their enterprises which can be traded on a national stock exchange – which should be established. Though there would still be the inevitable inefficiencies that might remain in terms of the incentive effects on workers of the job assignment system, they could be looked upon as the political cost of obtaining the efficiency gains from the other measures of liberalisation we have discussed.

References

Berlin, I., 1958, Two concepts of liberty (Clarendon Press, Oxford).

Brecher, R. and C. Diaz-Alejandro, 1977, Tariffs, foreign capital and immiserizing growth, Journal of International Economics 7.

Byrd, W. and G. Tidrick, 1987, Factor allocation and enterprise incentives, in: G. Tidrick and J. Chen, eds., op cit.

Cheung, Steven, 1986, Will China go capitalist? 2nd edition, Hobart paper no. 94 (Institute of Economic Affairs, London).

Choski, A. and D. Papageorgiou, ed., 1987, Economic liberalisation in developing countries (Blackwells, Oxford).
Chow, Gregory C., 1985, The Chinese economy (Harper and Row, New York).
Corden, W.M., 1974, Trade policy and economic welfare, Oxford.
Fureng, Dong, 1987, Increasing the vitality of enterprises, in: G. Tidrick and J. Chen, eds., op cit.
Granick, D., 1987, The industrial environment in China and the CMEA countries, in: G. Tidrick and J. Chen, eds., op cit.
Helplman, E. and P. Krugman, 1985, Market structure and foreign trade (MIT Press, Cambridge, MA).
Jones, R., 1971, A three factor model in theory, trade and history, in: J. Bhagwati et al., Trade, the balance of payments and growth (North Holland, Amsterdam).
Kornai, J., 1979, Resource-constraint versus demand-constrained systems, Econometrica, July.
Kornai, J., 1982, Growth, shortage and efficiency (Blackwells, Oxford).
Krueger, A.O., 1978, Liberalisation attempts and consequences (NBER, Ballinger, Cambridge, MA).
Lal, D., 1974, Methods of project analysis: A review (Johns Hopkins, Baltimore).
Lal, D., 1980, Prices for planning, Heinemann Educational Books.
Lal, D., 1981, Resurrection of the pauper-labour argument, Thames Essays no. 28 (Trade Policy Research Centre, London).
Lal, D., 1987, The political economy of economic liberalisation, World Bank Economic Review 1, no. 2, Jan.
Little, I.M.D. and J.A. Mirrlees, 1974, Project appraisal and planning for developing countries, Heinemann Educational Books.
Meade, J., 1972, The theory of labour – managed firms and of profit-sharing, Economic Journal, Special issue, March, Suppl.
Nove, A., 1977, The Soviet economic system (Allen & Unwin, London).
Perkins, D.H., 1988, Reforming China's economic system, Journal of Economic Literature, June.
Reynolds, B.J., ed., Journal of Comparative Economics special issue: Chinese Economic Reform: How Far, How Fast? 11, no. 3, Sept.
Samuelson, P., 1948, International trade and equalisation of factor prices, Economic Journal.
Sen, A.K., 1975, Technology, employment and development (Oxford University Press, New York).
Srinivasan, T.N., 1987, Economic liberalisation in China and India: Issues and an analytical framework, Journal of Comparative Economics.
Tidrick, G. and Jiyuan Chen, eds., 1987, China's industrial reform (Oxford University Press, New York).
Tidrick, G., 1987, Planning and supply, in: Tidrick and Chen, eds., op cit.
Vanek, J., 1970, The general theory of labour managed market economies (Cornell).
Ward, B., 1953, the firm in Illyria: Market syndicalism, American Economic Review, Sept.
Wu, J. and B.L. Reynolds, 1988, Choosing a strategy for China's economic reform, American Economic Review, May.

Name Index

Economists of the Twentieth Century

Monetarism and Macroeconomic Policy
Thomas Mayer

Studies in Fiscal Federalism
Wallace E. Oates

The World Economy in Perspective
Essays in International Trade and European Integration
Herbert Giersch

Towards a New Economics
Critical Essays on Ecology, Distribution and Other Themes
Kenneth E. Boulding

Studies in Positive and Normative Economics
Martin J. Bailey

The Collected Essays of Richard E. Quandt (2 volumes)
Richard E. Quandt

International Trade Theory and Policy
Selected Essays of W. Max Corden
W. Max Corden

Organization and Technology in Capitalist Development
William Lazonick

Studies in Human Capital
Collected Essays of Jacob Mincer, Volume 1
Jacob Mincer

Studies in Labor Supply
Collected Essays of Jacob Mincer, Volume 2
Jacob Mincer

Macroeconomics and Economic Policy
The Selected Essays of Assar Lindbeck, Volume I
Assar Lindbeck

The Welfare State
The Selected Essays of Assar Lindbeck, Volume II
Assar Lindbeck

Classical Economics, Public Expenditure and Growth
Walter Eltis

Money, Interest Rates and Inflation
Frederic S. Mishkin

The Public Choice Approach to Politics
Dennis C. Mueller

The Liberal Economic Order
Volume I Essays on International Economics
Volume II Money, Cycles and Related Themes
Gottfried Haberler
Edited by Anthony Y.C. Koo

Economic Growth and Business Cycles
Prices and the Process of Cyclical Development
Paolo Sylos Labini

International Adjustment, Money and Trade
Theory and Measurement for Economic Policy, Volume I
Herbert G. Grubel

International Capital and Service Flows
Theory and Measurement for Economic Policy, Volume II
Herbert G. Grubel

Unintended Effects of Government Policies
Theory and Measurement for Economic Policy, Volume III
Herbert G. Grubel

The Economics of Competitive Enterprise
Selected Essays of P.W.S. Andrews
Edited by Frederic S. Lee and Peter E. Earl

The Repressed Economy
Causes, Consequences, Reform
Deepak Lal

Economic Theory and Market Socialism
Selected Essays of Oskar Lange
Edited by Tadeusz Kowalik

Trade, Development and Political Economy
Selected Essays of Ronald Findlay
Ronald Findlay

General Equilibrium Theory
The Collected Essays of Takashi Negishi, Volume I
Takashi Negishi

The History of Economics
The Collected Essays of Takashi Negishi, Volume II
Takashi Negishi

Studies in Econometric Theory
The Collected Essays of Takeshi Amemiya
Takeshi Amemiya